Visual C++ .NET
Developer's Guide

John Paul Mueller

McGraw-Hill/Osborne

New York Chicago San Francisco
Lisbon London Madrid Mexico City
Milan New Delhi San Juan
Seoul Singapore Sydney Toronto

i

McGraw-Hill/Osborne
2600 Tenth Street
Berkeley, California 94710
U.S.A.

To arrange bulk purchase discounts for sales promotions, premiums, or fund-raisers, please contact **McGraw-Hill**/Osborne at the above address. For information on translations or book distributors outside the U.S.A., please see the International Contact Information page immediately following the index of this book.

Visual C++ .NET Developer's Guide

1234567890 CUS CUS 01987654321

Book p/n 0-07-213262-0 and CD p/n 0-07-213282-5
parts of
ISBN 0-07-213281-7

Publisher	Brandon A. Nordin
Vice President & Associate Publisher	Scott Rogers
Acquisitions Editor	Ann Sellers
Project Editor	Katie Conley
Acquisitions Coordinator	Tim Madrid
Technical Editor	Bill Burris
Copy Editor	Carl Wikander
Proofreader	Carol Burbo
Indexer	Irv Hershman
Computer Designers	Tara A. Davis, Lauren McCarthy
Illustrators	Michael Mueller, Greg Scott, Lyssa Wald
Cover Illustration	Eliot Bergman
Cover Series Design	Greg Scott

This book was composed with Corel VENTURA™ Publisher.

This book is dedicated to Micah Schlobohm. I appreciate her kindness, thoughtfulness, and desire to help. She's the kind of friend that more people should have, but unfortunately don't.

About the Author

John Mueller is a freelance author and technical editor. He has writing in his blood, having produced 53 books and over 200 articles to date. The topics range from networking to artificial intelligence, and from database management to heads down programming. Some of his current books include a SOAP developer guide, a small business and home office networking guide, and a Windows 2000 Performance, Tuning, and Optimization book. His technical editing skills have helped over 25 authors refine the content of their manuscripts. John has provided technical editing services to both *Data Based Advisor* and *Coast Compute* magazines. He's also contributed articles to magazines like *SQL Server Professional*, *Visual C++ Developer*, and *Visual Basic Developer*. He is currently the editor of the .NET electronic newsletter for Pinnacle Publishing.

When John isn't working at the computer, you can find him in his workshop. He's an avid woodworker and candle maker. On any given afternoon, you can find him working at a lathe or putting the finishing touches on a bookcase. One of his newest craft projects is making glycerin soap, which comes in handy for gift baskets. You can reach John on the Internet at JMueller@mwt.net. John is also setting up a Web site at: http://www.mwt.net/~jmueller/; feel free to look and make suggestions on how he can improve it. One of his current projects is creating book FAQ sheets that should help you find the book information you need much faster.

Contents

Part II   Visual C++ .NET and Database Management

Part III   **Visual C++ and Online Computing**

Part IV   Visual C++ .NET and Microsoft.NET

Acknowledgments

Thanks to my wife, Rebecca, for working with me to get this book completed. I really don't know what I would have done without her help in researching and compiling some of the information that appears in this book (especially the Glossary). She also did a fine job of proofreading my rough draft and page proofing the final result.

Bill Burris deserves thanks for his technical edit of this book. He greatly added to the accuracy and depth of the material you see here. I really appreciate the time he devoted to checking my code for accuracy. Bill also supplied some of the URLs you see in the book and other helpful tips and hints.

Matt Wagner, my agent, deserves credit for helping me get the contract in the first place and taking care of all the details that most authors don't really consider. I always appreciate his help. It's good to know that someone wants to help.

Finally, I would like to thank Ann Sellers, Timothy Madrid, Katie Conley, Carl Wikander, and the rest of the production staff at McGraw-Hill/Osborne for their assistance in bringing this book to print. I especially appreciate Ann's patience when things didn't go exceptionally well. Tim provided me with many thought-provoking messages and was always willing to talk with me when I needed help.

Introduction

Unless you've been hiding in a cave in a remote part of the earth, Microsoft has inundated you with news of .NET by now. Microsoft's marketing machine is working overtime, as usual, to ensure you don't miss their latest and greatest product. If you listen to the Microsoft hype, it seems that they expect everyone to drop billions (trillions?) of lines of code and adopt .NET tomorrow. What the hype doesn't mention is that adopting .NET completely means starting from scratch.

The real world is a different place than the fantasyland of Microsoft hype. In the real world, developers have to maintain existing code at the lowest possible cost and still produce new applications in record time. The task seems impossible when you have two completely different technologies to develop these applications. On the one hand, you have the realm of MFC and the Win32 API. On the other hand, you have the new .NET Framework. Which do you choose for a given task?

Answering the question of which technology to use is one of the biggest problems this book will tackle. We'll discuss how to use the old, the new, and, most importantly, the mixed environments of Visual C++ .NET. Knowing when .NET can actually help you create an application faster is the key to managing application development in an environment where you have two different architectures to consider.

Microsoft's .NET Framework is an exciting new technology for a developer looking for every productivity enhancement available. My purpose in writing this book is to help you balance the usefulness of this new technology against the need to maintain existing code. By the time you complete this book, you'll not only know how to work with .NET to create some relatively complex applications, but you'll better understand when .NET is a good choice for application development.

What's in This Book

Visual C++ .NET Developer's Guide contains a mix of theory and programming examples, with a heavy emphasis on the programming examples. You'll find a mix of Win32, MFC, ATL, and .NET code within the book. In some cases, I'll show you how to mix an existing technology with a new one—Visual C++ .NET is definitely a transitional language, one that will help you move from Win32 application development to .NET. Here's a brief overview of the six parts of this book.

Part I—Visual C++ in General

This part of the book introduces you to some of the new features in Visual C++ .NET. We'll also discuss some basic programming principles. You'll learn how to create various types of applications. Most of the code in this part is unmanaged. However, this part includes some managed code examples that show how you'd create the same result as an unmanaged counterpart using the .NET Framework.

You'll also learn some advanced coding processes in this part of the book. We'll discuss threads in Chapter 3, and I'll show you how to create two types of threads. The graphics programming examples in Chapter 4 include both static graphics and animated graphics using GIFs. Chapter 5 will help you understand the intricacies of Active Directory, while Chapter 6 shows how to create components using both ATL and MFC.

Part II—Visual C++ .NET and Database Management

Database management is an essential part of every business today. Chapter 7 of this part tells you about the various technologies and indicates when you can best use them to your advantage. We also look at how to create and use DSNs.

Chapter 8 is the unmanaged coding example for this part. You'll learn how to use OLE-DB to create a basic database application that includes a form view, printing, and search routines. This section of the book also tells you how to get around certain problems with the Visual C++ .NET environment. For example, Visual C++ .NET doesn't ship with all of the controls found in Visual Studio 6. Some of your applications might require these controls, so I show how to install them. Unfortunately, some controls won't work even if you do install them, and I show you how to get around some of these problem areas.

Chapter 9 is the managed coding example for this part. We discuss ODBC .NET in this chapter. Unfortunately, ODBC .NET wasn't ready in time for the book, so you won't see a coding example. We'll create a managed example using ADO .NET that includes use of the new DataGrid control (among others). This section also shows how to create a print routine and other database application basics.

Part III — Visual C++ and Online Computing

Distributed applications are becoming more prominent as businesses move to the Internet in an effort to remain connected with partners, employees, and customers. This part of the book shows you how to work with SOAP and discusses Web Services in general. You'll also learn how to work with alternative devices such as PDAs. Chapter 10 contains a simple ASP.NET example that helps you understand the benefits of this technology. Chapter 11 shows you how to create both ISAPI Filters and ISAPI Extensions as well as a SOAP application that relies on the Microsoft SOAP Toolkit. Most of the examples in this part of the book rely on unmanaged programming techniques.

Part IV — Visual C++ .NET and Microsoft.NET

Most of the examples in this part of the book rely on managed programming techniques. You'll learn how to create various types of managed applications that rely exclusively on the .NET Framework. Chapter 12 is unique because it compares Visual C++ .NET to C# and even provides an example in both languages for comparison purposes. This is also the chapter to read if you want to learn how to move your applications to .NET. Chapter 13 is your key for learning about the new attributed programming techniques provided with Visual C++ .NET. Attributes greatly reduce the coding burden for the developer. Examples in this chapter use both managed and unmanaged coding techniques. Chapter 14 shows you how to work with managed components. You'll also create a custom attribute and use reflection to read its contents from the compiled application.

Part V — The Developer View of Visual C++ .NET

This part of the book contains a mix of topics that didn't fit well anywhere else, but are extremely important for the developer. Chapter 15 discusses the inner workings of Security within Windows 2000 and Windows XP. Security is an important topic in a world where crackers make it their business to test your applications for holes in every way possible. Chapter 16 shows how to create administration tools for your applications. Most complex applications require some type of configuration and "tweaking" as part of the installation and maintenance cycle. Using the Microsoft Management Console (MMC) to maintain your application makes sense because it reduces the user interface design burden for the developer and reduces the amount of code required to create the management program. Chapter 17 shows you how to create various types of help files. Microsoft is always moving on to some new form of help, but sometimes you need to use the older forms of the help file as well. This chapter shows how to create both. Finally, Chapter 18 shows how to package your application once you finish building it.

Part VI — Appendixes and Glossary

This last part of the book contains two appendixes and a glossary. Appendix A tells you how to get the best deal for your next component purchase. It also helps you find some "must have" components for your next application. Appendix B is an online resource guide that helps you locate additional information about Visual C++ .NET. Sometimes it's good to know where to find additional help. Finally, the Glossary contains a complete list of every esoteric term and acronym used in the book.

What You'll Need

There are some assumptions that I've made while writing the application programming examples in this book. You need at least two machines: a workstation and a server. This two-machine setup is the only way that you'll see Visual C++ .NET in action and truly know it works as anticipated. In addition, your development workstation and server must meet the minimum .NET requirements (and hopefully provide more than the minimum). You might experience problems with the database and other large examples when running a minimal machine configuration.

During the writing of this book, I used a Windows 2000 and Windows XP workstation. There's no guarantee that any of the code in the book will work with Windows 9x; although, most of it will. The server was loaded with Windows 2000 Server with the latest patches and service packs installed. You'll need a Pocket PC compatible PDA to work with the SOAP example in Chapter 10. You must install the latest service packs for all products before the examples will work properly. .NET is a new technology and relies on the latest versions of many DLLs and the .NET Framework.

NOTE

Many of the concepts you'll learn in this book won't appear in your online documentation. Some of it is so new that it appears only on selected Web sites. You'll find either a tip or a note alerting you to the location of such information throughout the book. In addition, Microsoft made some material available only through selected channels, like an MSDN subscription. Other pieces of information are simply undocumented, and you won't find them anywhere except within a newsgroup when someone finds the feature accidentally.

I tested all of the examples in this book with Visual C++ .NET Enterprise Architect Edition. Microsoft made a considerable number of changes to Visual C++ .NET, so none of the examples will load in previous versions of the product, even if the code will compile. None of these examples are guaranteed to work with any other programming language products, and none of them will work with the educational versions Visual Studio.

Some of the example programs rely on a database manager. I used Microsoft Access for all of the examples in this book for the sake of simplicity. The source code CD contains copies of all of the databases used in this book.

Conventions Used in This Book

In this section we'll cover usage conventions. This book uses the following conventions:

[<Filename>]	When you see square brackets around a value, switch, or command, it means that this is an optional component. You don't have to include it as part of the command line or dialog field unless you want the additional functionality that the value, switch, or command provides.
<Filename>	A variable name between angle brackets is a value that you need to replace with something else. The variable name you'll see usually provides a clue as to what kind of information you need to supply. In this case, you'll need to provide a filename. Never type the angle brackets when you type the value.
ALL CAPS	There are three places you'll see ALL CAPS: commands, filenames, and case-sensitive registry entries. Normally, you'll type a command at the DOS prompt, within a PIF file field, or within the Run dialog field. If you see ALL CAPS somewhere else, it's safe to assume that the item is a case-sensitive registry entry or some other value like a filename.
File | Open	Menus and the selections on them appear with a vertical bar. "File | Open" means "Access the File menu and choose Open."
italic	There are three places you see italic text: new words, multi-value entries, and undefined values. You'll always see a value in italic whenever the actual value of something is unknown. The book also uses italic where more than one value might be correct. For example, you might see FILE*xxxx*0 in text. This means that the value could be anywhere between FILE0000 and FILE9999.

monospace	It's important to differentiate the text that you'll use in a macro or type at the command line from the text that explains it. This book uses monospace type to make this differentiation. Every time you see monospace text, you'll know that the information you see will appear in a macro, within a system file like CONFIG.SYS or AUTOEXEC.BAT, or as something you'll type at the command line. You'll even see the switches used with Windows commands in this text. There is another time you'll see monospace text. Every code listing uses monospaced code to make the text easier to read. Using monospaced text also makes it easier to add things like indentation to the coding example.
URLs	URLs will normally appear highlighted so that you can see them with greater ease. The URLs in this book provide sources of additional information designed to make your development experience better. URLs often provide sources of interesting information as well.

Icons

This book contains many icons that help you identify certain types of information. The following paragraphs describe the purpose of each icon.

NOTE

Notes tell you about interesting facts that don't necessarily affect your ability to use the other information in the book. I use note boxes to give you bits of information that I've picked up while using Visual C++, Windows 9x, Windows 2000, or Windows XP.

TIP

Everyone likes tips, because they tell you new ways of doing things that you might not have thought about before. Tip boxes also provide an alternative way of doing something that you might like better than the conventional (first) approach I provided.

CAUTION

This means watch out! Cautions almost always tell you about some kind of system or data damage that'll occur if you perform certain actions (or fail to perform others). Make sure you understand a caution thoroughly before you follow any instructions that come after it.

BROWSER ALERT

The Internet contains a wealth of information, but finding it can be difficult, to say the least. Web Links help you find new sources of information on the Internet that you can use to improve your programming or learn new techniques. You'll also find newsgroup Web Links that tell where you can find other people to talk with about Visual C++. Finally, Web Links will help you find utility programs that'll make programming faster and easier than before.

What Happened to Hungarian Notation?

At one time, Hungarian notation was an essential for developers because the IDEs provided with early compilers didn't tell you much about the variables, methods, and other programming constructs in your application. Today, IDEs commonly provide detailed information about the constructs in your application and even help you to make good decisions about formatting your code. Hungarian notation has become a verbose method of writing code that addresses a problem that doesn't exist anymore.

For the most part, this book doesn't use Hungarian notation. The variable names you see describe the purpose of the variable, rather than the variable type. You might see a bit of Hungarian notation floating around in places where I felt it would help, but these uses are minimal.

PART

I

Visual C++ In General

OBJECTIVES

► Learn about the new features of Visual C++ .NET

► Obtain an overview of the development tools

► Create a workstation and server setup

► Learn to build various types of desktop applications

► Discover how threads can help you create more efficient applications

► Build applications that use standard graphic files

► Build applications that use animation techniques

► Learn how to work with Active Directory

► Create ActiveX controls using two different techniques

Getting Started

Many developers see Visual C++ as the old shoe of the programming trade—it feels comfortable and they know it well. This language represents time-tested programming technology. In addition, it's a robust language capable of creating any type of application. It does excel at certain types of development, as we'll see as the chapter progresses. Of course, even good technology has to keep pace with current development needs, and it has to provide an environment that developers continue to feel comfortable using. In this chapter, we'll talk about how Visual C++ .NET (Version 7.0) meets those objectives. If you already know the capabilities of Visual C++ .NET by heart, you can skip to the workstation and server requirements at the end of the chapter.

This first chapter is an introduction to the product and to the development platform that I'll use for the examples in the book. The first section—"What's New in this Version?"—will tell you about the exciting new features that Visual C++ .NET has to offer. It's important to remember that Microsoft designed Visual C++ to work in a LAN environment. Visual C++ was never designed to work in the distributed environment of the Internet, so many of the changes you'll see in this version address that issue. You'll also find there are changes that affect group productivity. For example, this version uses a common IDE with the rest of Visual Studio .NET.

The second section of the chapter, "Downloads You Should Know About," will tell you about the various add-ons that you may need while working with the examples in this book. It also talks about important service packs and other pieces of software that you may want to consider installing before you install Visual C++ .NET. Finally, a few of these downloads provide required technical information. You won't necessarily need them to use this book, but you'll want to have them when you start developing projects of you own.

TIP

Make sure you check out the resources in Appendix A and Appendix B. These appendices will provide you with a list of products to look at and places to go for additional information. I'll also sprinkle Web site and newsgroup information throughout the rest of the book as appropriate.

The third section of the chapter, "Tools You Should Know About," will discuss the set of tools provided with Visual C++. These tools provide useful additions to the development environment that help you test your application. We'll use many of these tools as we look at the output of sample applications in the book, so it's important to know how the tools are used. Even if you decide not to test the sample applications in the book, you'll need to know about these tools to test your own applications.

The final two sections of the chapter, "Creating a Workstation Setup" and "Creating a Server Setup," will tell you how I set my system up before working on the examples for this book. Knowing how to set up a good test environment is essential. Using a two-machine setup is also critical in today's distributed development environment. I also want you to know what I'm using for development purposes, so that you'll better understand how the examples in this book related to the hardware used for testing.

What's New in this Version?

Visual C++ has been a staple of the Windows programmer's toolkit for quite some time now. Yes, other languages allow developers to prototype and develop applications faster, but nothing can replace Visual C++ for such low-level development tasks as creating components. In addition, applications where execution speed is important always benefit from the use of Visual C++ as a development language. For most programmers, Visual C++ is the language of choice where development speed isn't as much of a concern as are access to low-level operating system features and application execution speed.

As Windows has matured, so have the capabilities of Visual C++. In fact, Microsoft marketing claims aside, Visual C++ is Microsoft's language of choice for many tasks including operating system and application development. One of the reasons that Microsoft uses Visual C++ so heavily is the flexibility it provides. For example, developers have a choice between the Microsoft Foundation Classes (MFC) and Active Template Library (ATL) when creating components. You'll also find that attributed programming (described in the sections that follow) removes many of the barriers a programmer once experienced when creating components. The .NET Framework-managed environment provides yet another component development option. It's the ability to perform any given task in more than one way that makes Visual C++ such a flexible solution, but this flexibility also results in a higher learning curve and longer development times.

Some of the flexibility in Visual C++ is the result of compromise. For example, Microsoft originally developed two methods to create components because some developers view MFC as an error-prone method of creating them. MFC does allow relatively quick component development. ATL arrived on the scene to provide developers with an alternative method to create components that execute quickly and have a small memory footprint. The tradeoff with ATL is the complex development environment and longer development times.

Because of the compromises Microsoft has had to make with Visual C++ along the way, some developers question the role of Visual C++ in future development efforts, while others cling to outdated methodologies in an effort to reduce development time. For all of the faults that people find in Visual C++, however, developers still use it to create new products because they know all of the ins and outs of this development language. Few developers deny the power of Visual C++ as a programming tool, and so most know they need it in their toolkits. In short, Visual C++ has become the old shoe of the programming world. It's a little ragged around the edges, but that's ignored because it's a comfortable product to use.

The following sections provide an overview of important new features for Visual C++ .NET. We'll discuss many of these features in more detail as the book progresses. The main purpose for these sections is to acquaint you with what I consider the big changes for Visual C++ .NET. These are the reasons that you'd want to upgrade to Visual C++ .NET, at least for specific types of projects.

New Development Environment

One of the problems with previous versions of Visual C++ concerned the integrated development environment (IDE) it provided. People argue about the viability of the old IDE; but in my opinion, the old IDE worked just fine. The real problem is that it's completely different from the IDE used by other Visual Studio products. This makes life difficult for developers who use more than one language on a regular basis and for development teams where coordination between members is important. A consistent IDE isn't necessarily better, but it is more efficient from a productivity standpoint.

Visual Studio.NET IDE Layout

Visual C++ .NET will use the same IDE as the rest of Visual Studio.NET. While the use of a new IDE is going to add to the learning curve of Visual C++ in the short term, it should enhance productivity in the end. Figure 1-1 shows the standard Visual Studio.NET IDE with a Visual C++ application loaded. Note that I've identified the various functional areas of the IDE—we'll use these names as the book progresses.

The default setup contains five functional window areas. This includes the four standard panes shown in Figure 1-1, plus two additional hidden windows. The hidden windows appear when you place the mouse cursor over the Toolbox or Solution Server Explorer tabs on the left side of the display. Each of the four visible window areas uses tabs to allow access to individual pieces of information. For example, every file you open in the editor area will open one of several editors. Likewise, there are tabs that allow you to choose between the Properties window or the Dynamic Help window in the lower-right corner of the display. Using tabs keeps the display relatively clear, while providing full access to all of the IDE features.

Server Explorer and Toolbox Tabs
(windows hidden)

Editor windows (code and text shown)

Solution Explorer

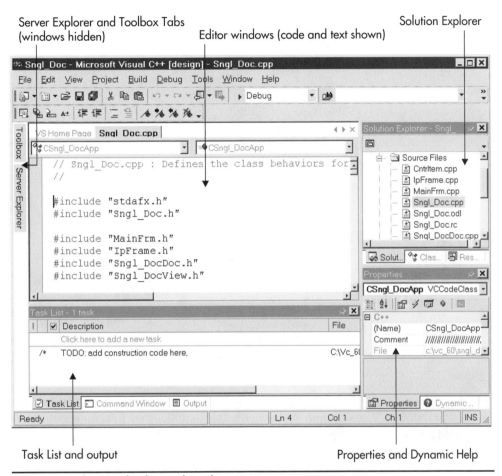

Figure 1-1   *The standard Visual Studio.NET IDE*

Task List and output

Properties and Dynamic Help

Visual C++ users are already familiar with the editor windows—they haven't changed much in appearance since the last version of Visual C++. Likewise, the Resource View and Class View tabs should look familiar. The Solution Explorer tab is simply an updated form of the FileView tab of previous versions of Visual C++. While these views are all familiar, they do include added functionality that helps a developer increase productivity. We'll explore these productivity enhancements throughout this chapter and the rest of the book as we work on examples together.

The Toolbox window is both familiar and new. Here's what it looks like:

As you can see, the Toolbox window looks much like the Toolbox provided for the previous version of Visual Studio. You can use this new Toolbox to keep various tools separated by use. For example, the illustration shows the Dialog Editor tools. There are also General and Clipboard Ring separators in this illustration.

Another window is the Server Explorer, which is new to Visual Studio as a whole. The following shows what it looks like.

The Server Explorer allows you to locate and manage services on local or remote machines. One of the main purposes of this feature is to allow developers to locate databases with greater ease and use them within applications. You can even perform tasks like checking the contents of the Event Viewer (a feature I find works even better than the Event Viewer provided with Windows 2000, because the events are categorized by type within the logs). You'll also find support for Visual Studio-specific items such as Crystal Reports. We'll use this feature often within the book, so I won't describe it in detail now.

Starting the IDE from the Command Line

You may find that you don't like the standard setup for the Visual Studio.NET IDE. Of course, the IDE does provide all of the usual customizations that you've come to expect from Microsoft products. For example, you can modify the toolbars or the colors used to display program elements. However, you can make changes that are even more drastic to the IDE using command line switches. Here's the Visual Studio.NET command line:

```
DevEnv [<Solution File> | <Project File> | <Code File>] [<Switches>]
```

Microsoft designed DevEnv to work with large enterprise applications. As a result, you'll find a new term called the *solution file*. A solution file has a .SLN extension and contains all of the information required to construct an enterprise-level application environment. A solution consists of one or more projects. Each project defines the requirements for a single application element, such as a component. As with previous versions of Visual C++, a solution can contain just one project that may execute by itself outside of the normal enterprise environment. Finally, you can also work with individual code files. As usual, if you type **DevEnv /?** at the command line, you'll see a list of available switches. Table 1-1 shows the command line switches and their meanings.

Switch	Description
/?	Displays help for the DevEnv program. This includes usage instructions and a list of command line switches. It doesn't include full information on how to use the switch. For example, it doesn't say which switches you need to use together or the arguments you must supply with the switch.
/build	Builds a solution; has the same effect as using the Build | Build command within the IDE. You must provide a solution filename and a configuration name. The valid configuration names depend on the type of project. For example, you might use "Debug" as the configuration name. You may optionally use the /project and /projconfig switches with this switch.
/clean	Removes the intermediary and output directories. You must provide a solution filename and a configuration name. The valid configuration names depend on the type of project. For example, you might use "Debug" as the configuration name. You may optionally use the /project and /projconfig switches with this switch.
/command	Executes a command after the Visual Studio IDE starts. These commands must fall within the range of predefined IDE commands or custom macros you've created.

Table 1-1 *DevEnv Command Line Switches*

Switch	Description
/debugexe	Launches the debugger, loads an executable, and applies optional switches to modify executable behavior. You must provide the name of an executable to debug. The Visual Studio IDE ignores any switches provided after this switch and applies them to the executable you want to debug.
/deploy	Deploys an application after a rebuild. You must provide a solution filename and a configuration name. The valid configuration names depend on the type of project. For example, you might use "Debug" as the configuration name. You may optionally use the /project and /projconfig switches with this switch.
/fn	Use the specified font within the Visual Studio IDE.
/fs	Use the specified font size within the Visual Studio IDE. The font size is specified in points.
/LCID or /l	Loads resource strings in the specified locale within the Visual Studio IDE. You must provide a valid locale identifier number. For example, specifying 1033 would load the English language resource strings.
/mdi	Use the multiple document interface (MDI). This is similar to the interface used by Visual C++ 6 (with obvious differences). For example, the layout of the display still reflects the new Visual Studio.NET view of the world. You'll also get all of the enhancements that Visual Studio.NET provides.
/mditabs	Use tabbed MDI. This is the default interface used by Visual Studio when you set it up.
/nologo	Starts the Visual Studio IDE without displaying the copyright splash screen.
/noVSIP	Disables the Visual Studio Integration Program (VSIP) developer's license key for VSIP testing. VSIP allows developers to add new capabilities to Visual Studio like new project types, a customized editor, or advanced debugging capabilities.
/out	Specifies an output file for errors during a command line compile. You must provide the name of an output file. Visual Studio will automatically clear the file if it exists, so that you see only the errors from the current build.
/project	Builds a project instead of a solution. You must provide a solution filename, project name, and a configuration name. The valid configuration names depend on the type of project. For example, you might use "Debug" as the configuration name. You may optionally use the /build, /rebuild, /deploy, and /clean switches with this switch, but must select one of them to perform a task. This switch also works with the /projectconfig switch.

Table 1-1   *DevEnv Command Line Switches* (continued)

Switch	Description
/projectconfig	Specifies the project configuration for the project specified by the /project switch. You must provide a solution filename, project name, project configuration, and a configuration name. The valid configuration and project configuration names depend on the type of project. For example, you might use "Debug" as the configuration or project configuration name. You may optionally use the /build, /rebuild, /deploy, and /clean switches with this switch, but must select one of them to perform a task.
/rebuild	Performs a combination of the /clean and /build switch tasks. You must provide a solution filename and a configuration name. The valid configuration names depend on the type of project. For example, you might use "Debug" as the configuration name. You may optionally use the /project and /projconfig switches with this switch.
/resetskippkgs	Allows the IDE to load VsPackages that were previously marked as having failures.
/run or /r	Compiles and runs the specified solution or project configuration. You must specify a solution or project name. The IDE will display any error or change message boxes before it terminates the application.
/runexit	Compiles and runs the specified solution or project configuration. You must specify a solution or project name. The IDE terminates the application without displaying any message boxes or allowing you to save changes.
/safemode	Loads only the default environment and services. This allows you to maximize the stability of the development environment.
/sdi	Use the single document interface (SDI). This is similar to the interface used by Visual Basic 6 (with obvious differences).

Table 1-1   *DevEnv Command Line Switches* (continued)

One of the popular alternative IDE displays is the Single Document Interface (SDI) display. Normally, Visual Studio .NET assumes you want to use the Multiple Document Interface with tabs (/mditabs) display. You can access the SDI display by adding the /sdi switch. Figure 1-2 shows the same application shown before (Figure 1-1), this time loaded into the SDI IDE display. Notice that you can enlarge any of the windows to consume the entire display area. While this makes it easier to concentrate on a particular area (such as when you're coding), some developers feel it makes the IDE less accessible during the design process. Of course, the choice of display is a personal matter, and you'll need to decide which you like best.

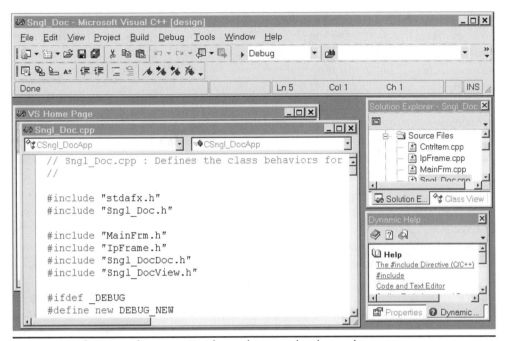

Figure 1-2   *The SDI style IDE is popular with many developers because it presents a simple appearance.*

Enhanced Debugging

Previous versions of Visual C++ relied on an entirely different IDE than the one used for Visual Studio.NET. Therefore, one obvious debugging change is the environment you'll use to trace through your applications. Visual C++ .NET combines the flavor of both Visual C++ 6.0 and Visual Basic 6.0. It allows you to use a single debugging environment for all of the languages within your application. Of course, this debugging environment includes support for all new features of Visual C++, including managed extensions. The use of an integrated debugging environment means that debugging is less time-consuming and more convenient.

You'll find that the debugger is also more robust. One of the more interesting features is the ability to attach the debugger to a running application on a local or a remote machine. This feature allows you to perform tasks like checking a user's application while it's still in an error state. Instead of trying to re-create an error condition, you can attach the debugger to the existing application and see the problem in a real world situation. Figure 1-3 shows the Processes dialog box you use to attach it to another process. You access it using the Debug | Processes command. Notice that the dialog displays all of the current processes for the workstation listed in the Machine field. You can choose a new machine and even select the protocol used to communicate with it.

The ability to attach to a running application also comes into play with multiple-application debugging. You can set this feature up by starting multiple applications within the IDE or by attaching to existing applications. This feature is going to be very useful in a distributed application environment, because it allows you to see how an application reacts when multiple versions are running. For example, you could use this feature to verify that the database locking mechanism for an application works before you even place the application components on a test server.

The new version of the debugger also allows you to perform more checks on your application. For example, you can perform runtime error checks. These checks help you look for problems such as stack pointer errors, local array overruns, stack corruption, uninitialized local variables, and data loss due to type casts. You'll also find that the new checks help you find buffer overrun problems—a difficult error to locate when it occurs during a call to another DLL.

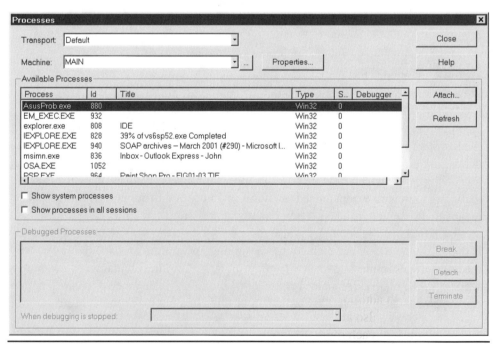

Figure 1-3 *The Processes dialog box allows you to attach the debugger to an application that's already running on a local or remote machine.*

HTML Editing Environment

Visual Studio 6 included a language element called Visual InterDev. This product was supposed to make it easier to create Web sites. However, many developers complained that the tool relied too heavily on FrontPage and that it didn't provide enough in the way of generic editing features. One of the first things that many developers will notice about Visual Studio.NET is that Visual InterDev is missing—at least as a separate language.

Visual InterDev is part of Visual Studio, and you can access the full power it provides from within Visual C++. (You won't see Visual InterDev mentioned because Microsoft has fully integrated it with the rest of Visual Studio as part of their Web-based application development emphasis.) What this means is that you, as a Visual C++ developer, will be able to include Web elements within your application with greater ease than ever before. In fact, Microsoft provides the following items for you to use within your applications.

- ► HTML Page
- ► ASP Page
- ► ATL Web Service
- ► MC++ Web Service
- ► HTML Frameset Page
- ► XML File
- ► Stylesheet

Many of these items will convert to other items that you may need for a particular application. For example, the XML File item is useful for various other file types, such as those used by the Simple Object Access Protocol (SOAP). I used it to create a Web Service Description Language (WSDL) file recently as well as an XML Data Reduced (XDR) file. Both of these file types have uses within SOAP applications.

Task List

One of the new additions for Visual C++ .NET is the Task List. No longer will you have to scout around for the little reminders left by wizards when you create an application. In addition, you'll be able to leave yourself "to do" notes and find them later. This is also an excellent addition for team projects—project members can leave notes for each other, and the team leader can make assignments directly in the source code.

Dynamic Help

Developers are under ever-increasing pressure to deliver applications quickly. Meanwhile, development environments become more complex, forcing the developer to spend more time learning new techniques. In short, a developer today has to know where to find specific information in the shortest time possible. That's one of the reasons that Dynamic Help is so exciting. It automatically displays help information based on the current cursor position. Click a method within your application and you'll automatically see the appropriate help displayed in the Dynamic Help window.

How good is Dynamic Help? Dynamic Help is better than anything else that I've seen in a development environment so far. An experienced developer will find that help automatically becomes available about 90 percent of the time. So, although you can't throw out your Microsoft Developer Network (MSDN) subscription, you'll spend a lot less time looking for the information you need. Obviously, this feature will help novice programmers more than those with a lot of experience, but I think that everyone will benefit from this new feature.

Command Window

Some people really hate using the mouse. They want to use the keyboard—end of discussion. Until now, most of us have had to put up with the mouse because it provides functionality that you can't otherwise obtain within the IDE. The Command Window feature changes all of this. Now you can type in a command, press ENTER, and watch its execution just as if you had used mouse clicks to perform the task. For example, typing **Open MyProg.CPP** in the Command Windows and pressing ENTER will open that file—just as if you had used the File | Open command with the mouse.

After trying this feature for a while, I can honestly say that it increases productivity. The caveat is that using commands won't replace the mouse in all situations. Sure, you can type commands to perform every task, but the mouse is more efficient in some situations. On the other hand, the Command Window is definitely more efficient in other situations. Even though I'll use the standard menu commands throughout the book, you can be sure that I'm using the Command Window to perform certain tasks, such as opening files, while writing this book. The Command Window fills a gap in IDE functionality.

Programmable IDE

There's little doubt that the new Visual Studio IDE is flexible. You can do everything from customizing the toolbars to changing the entire look of the IDE using command line switches. It's hard to imagine that you could make the IDE any better than it is right now. Every developer can have an IDE that matches their programming style and usage needs.

Visual C++ has supported the use of macros for several versions now. However, in this version you'll find that macro support has increased. You have full control over every aspect of the programming environment and can even create extensions to that environment using a simple macro command. This added functionality makes it possible to create an IDE that Microsoft didn't envision—one that includes tools that you or your company develops.

However, the true programmability of the Visual Studio.NET IDE becomes apparent when you look in the Extensibility Projects folder of the New Projects dialog box. There you'll find two new entries. The first allows you to create shared add-ins, while the second allows you to create Visual Studio.NET Add-Ins. I can foresee a brisk business in third party add-ons for Visual Studio.NET developing. Eventually, you may find that the IDE you get from Microsoft doesn't resemble the one you use for creating applications at all.

Attributed Programming

Visual C++ .NET is going to be an entirely new programming environment in a lot of ways. Everyone is going to get some new features to play with and find new ways to create applications faster. One of the more exciting changes for ATL programmers is the addition of *attributed programming*. Attributes tell the compiler what you'd like to do with your code in a given circumstance, which greatly reduces the amount of descriptive code you have to create. For example, you may want to create an event source, so you'd use the event_source attribute to do it. The compiler automatically generates all of the required "boiler plate" code for you based on the event source description you provide in your code as part of the normal development process. In some cases, you'll be able to get rid of those IDL files that you've had to maintain all of these years.

NOTE

Attributed programming is a complex topic that will require substantial coverage to understand. I'm giving you the 50,000-foot level view of attributed programming in this chapter. We'll talk more about attributed programming in Chapter 13.

So, why is this feature so important? Imagine writing the components you always have in the past, but with as little as 25 percent of the code you use today. Less code means fewer potential errors and a shorter development time. Programmers from all walks are finding they have a hard time meeting delivery dates, given shortened deadlines and increasing application complexity. Any technology that promises to reduce development time using a tool that you're already familiar with is a welcome relief. Attributed programming promises to reduce development time by an order of magnitude.

Managed Environment

Visual C++ .NET will actually support two completely different application execution environments: managed and unmanaged. A *managed environment* is one where a framework, in this case the .NET Framework, manages the application. The framework controls everything from how the application creates objects to the way it allocates memory. An application talks to the framework, which determines if it can fulfill the request, and then the framework talks to the Windows API to complete the request. The addition of the .NET Framework allows better interoperability between languages, reduces errors due to common programming problems like memory management, and provides the means for creating better distributed applications.

Visual C++ .NET will default to using an unmanaged environment, but a developer can choose to use the managed environment in order to gain access to features of the .NET Framework. The developer needs to make a choice between functionality (the .NET Framework) and flexibility (direct Windows API access). A developer also has the option of mixing managed and unmanaged modules in a single application, so your investment in older code remains intact.

Unlike the unmanaged environment, which produces a machine language file, the compiler creates something known as an Intermediate Language (IL) file when it creates a managed application. The IL file still has an EXE or DLL extension, just as it did in the past. However, the contents of this file will differ because it contains tokens instead of the more familiar machine code. You can't run a managed application on just any machine—the machine must have the .NET Framework installed in order to read the IL file. The Common Language Runtime (CLR) compiles the tokenized file specifically for the machine you want to run it on, which has certain advantages and still allows the application to execute quickly.

The whole topic of managed code is relatively complex. You'll see your first example of managed code in Chapter 2, when we create a simple component using this technique. Chapter 12 will discuss the relative merits of using managed code for your next project, while Chapter 13 will tell you how to implement managed code using a variety of attributes. The issue of managed versus unmanaged code is already creating a lot of controversy. With the amount of change that managed code brings on the one hand and the increased productivity and potential performance benefits it provides on the other, the controversy promises to continue for many years to come.

.NET Framework

As Visual C++ .NET developers working in the managed environment, you also gain access to the .NET Framework, which relies on namespaces that encapsulate (contain) functionality normally found in libraries. The use of dot syntax to access specific types of functions means you no longer have to memorize the Win32 API guide to remain productive as a developer. The IDE can help you locate the function you need because Microsoft has organized those functions in a hierarchical fashion according to type.

The .NET Framework is also a *philosophy*—a view on the world of distributed application development. People often compare Java to Microsoft products like Visual C++ and C#. When viewed from a .NET Framework perspective, Java is an answer to development problems that says the operating system is unimportant as long as you use Java. In other words, you're restricted to a single language that can operate across platforms. The .NET Framework is a development answer that says the language is unimportant as long as you use the .NET Framework. In other words, the .NET Framework makes it possible for a developer to accomplish the same goals using any supported language (and there are plans to support a wealth of languages). Of course, the ability to achieve programming goals doesn't necessarily mean that accomplishing those goals will be easy. I still believe that every developer should have several tools in his or her programming toolbox.

Currently, the .NET Framework is an answer to Windows-specific development problems. However, there are also plans to make the .NET Framework platform independent, which means applications you write today may someday execute on other platforms without change. The secret is in the IL that we discussed in the "Managed Environment" section.

While this book is about Visual C++ .NET, it's important to see the bigger picture when considering the .NET Framework. Besides Visual C++, Visual Basic, C#, and potentially other Microsoft languages, you'll find that the .NET Framework will support some of the other language favorites in your developer toolbox. The following list provides URLs for just some of the language offerings I was able to find. Of course, the list is incomplete as of this writing, but still impressive.

- ▶ COBOL: **http://www.adtools.com/info/whitepaper/net.html**
- ▶ Eiffel: **http://www.eiffel.com/doc/manuals/technology/eiffelsharp/ white_paper.html**
- ▶ Mondrian: **http://www.mondrian-script.org/**
- ▶ Haskell: **http://haskell.cs.yale.edu/ghc/**

▶ Mercury: **http://haskell.cs.yale.edu/ghc/**

▶ ML and SML: **http://research.microsoft.com/Projects/SML.NET/index.htm**

▶ Oberon (Lightning Oberon): **http://www.oberon.ethz.ch/lightning/**

▶ Perl and Python: **http://www.activestate.com/Products/NET/**

▶ SmallTalk: **http://www.qks.com/** or **http://www.cs.mu.oz.au/research/ mercury/information/dotnet/mercury_and_dotnet.html**

This represents the tip of the iceberg. If the developer community accepts the .NET Framework as readily as Microsoft expects, other language vendors will get into the act. For example, there are rumors that Rational Software will eventually introduce a version of Java for the .NET Framework (**http://www.rational.com/ index.jsp**). Companies like Rational may wait until they see the level of commitment to the .NET Framework before they actually create a product. The point is that learning about the .NET Framework will yield productivity benefits well beyond Visual C++ .NET. Greater productivity and a reduced learning curve are the two reasons that the .NET Framework is such an important addition to Visual C++ .NET.

We'll talk a lot more about the .NET Framework as the book progresses. Every managed code Visual C++ .NET programming example in the book will show you something about the .NET Framework. The first of these examples is a simple console application in Chapter 2, and the book will contain many such examples. In addition, Chapters 12 through 14 will provide you with an in-depth look at this technology.

ADO.NET

Microsoft named this technology incorrectly and it's going to cause an untold number of developers problems. Active Data Objects (ADO) is a database technology that rides on top of Object Linking and Embedding for Databases (OLE-DB). It allows you to create a connection between the client and server with a minimum of fuss and with fewer configuration requirements on the client. Overall, ADO is a great technology that makes database development a lot easier.

You may think that ADO.NET is going to be a superset of ADO, but it isn't. ADO.NET provides functionality in addition to ADO. In other words, you'll continue using ADO for some applications and add ADO.NET to others. When you think about ADO.NET, think about distributed applications. ADO.NET will do for distributed applications what ADO did for LAN-and WAN-based applications.

One of the most promising features of ADO.NET is the idea of a disconnected recordset. You can work with this recordset just as you would any other. The only difference is that it doesn't require a connection to the server. Given the fact that many users now need to access a database in disconnected mode, the use of ADO.NET should help many developers jump remote access application hurdles they never could in the past. We'll talk more about this technology in Chapters 7 through 9.

C# Language

There's a new language in town named C# and it ships as part of Visual Studio.NET. You've probably heard a lot about this language from the trade press already. Some say that C# is merely Microsoft's attempt to create a better Java. In some respects, C# does have Java qualities, but I wouldn't consider it a direct replacement, because the intended uses for the two languages are so different. Needless to say, C# has generated controversy. Since this is a Visual C++ book, I'm not going to try to convince you one way or the other about the merits of using C# as your development language of choice. However, given the amount of hype surrounding this language, we'll take a detailed look at it in Chapter 12 as part of the .NET architecture discussion.

Researching C# on the various Internet newsgroups did bring some interesting facts to light. Many of the developers who've tried C# are favorably impressed. In capability and complexity, it occupies a middle ground between Visual C++ and Visual Basic. C# supports only managed code, so you won't be able to replace Visual C++ with C# in the near future. However, C# does provide valuable features and makes a valuable asset for the Visual C++ developer. Given the new level of integration between languages in Visual Studio.NET, you may find that C# is the tool of choice for at least some of your new application development needs.

ATL Server

This is a new set of libraries for Visual C++ .NET that are designed to allow developers to create server side applications such as Web services with relative ease. The ATL Server library is associated with the new ATL Server, ATL Server Web Service, and Managed C++ Web Service projects. You can use these projects to create a variety of Web clients, services, and applications. These applications will support cryptography, Simple Mail Transfer Protocol (SMTP), and message queuing, so that you can create both synchronous and asynchronous applications with data security. We'll talk more about the ATL Server and Web Services in general in Chapter 12.

Web Services

Distributed application development is a major concern for many developers today. It's no longer good enough if an application runs fine on a local server—it also has to perform across the Internet with customers and partners as well. With this in mind, Microsoft has added Web Services to Visual Studio.NET. This is essentially a set of programming libraries, templates, and projects that help you expose component functionality across and Internet or intranet connection using a combination of HTTP and SOAP. We'll talk more about Web Services in Chapter 12.

NOTE

It's important to remember that SOAP is associated with a lot of other standard-supported technologies, such as WSDL, and that SOAP can transfer data across more than just one protocol. While Visual Studio.NET currently relies on HTTP for a transport protocol, you'll probably see support for other transport protocols such as SMTP in the future. In fact, some SOAP toolkits already provide "other protocol" support right out of the box. For the purposes of this book, however, we'll concentrate on using SOAP with the HTTP protocol.

Web Forms and Win Forms

Web Forms and Win Forms are two sides of the same coin. Both allow you to create a user interface in less time than you may have required in the past. The use of forms technology isn't new, but it is new to Visual Studio.NET.

You'll normally use Web Forms with Internet or Web-based applications. They provide a Web page-like interface that the user can use from within a browser (assuming that the browser provides the required support). On the other hand, you'll normally use Win Forms with desktop applications. They provide the same interface that users have come to accept with most desktop applications such as word processors.

More important than the user interface technology is the power base for each of these interfaces. When using Web Forms, you'll rely on ASP.NET and a server side connection for most of the processing power. Win Forms rely on the local workstation for most interface processing needs. In short, you need to consider where data gets processed as part of your choice between Win Forms and Web Forms. We'll talk about these issues and more as the book progresses.

Enterprise Templates and Policy Definitions

Team development is always difficult because we're all human and think differently from each other. A method for accomplishing a task that seems intuitive and easy to one person may seem difficult and even dangerous to someone else. It doesn't help that there's always more than one way to correctly program any application and get the same results. If you look at input and results alone, then you may find later that the code in between is a nest of snakes ready to strike at anyone in your organization foolish enough to attempt modification. In short, you need to ensure that everyone is using approximately the same coding techniques and adheres to certain policies when creating code.

Technology is changing so fast that no one can keep up with everything. As a result, organizations usually assign developers to focus on one or two technologies within their area of expertise. These developers then publish what they have found out in the form of a white paper or other documentation. The problem is that no one has time to read all of those white papers because they're busy researching other technologies in their area of expertise.

Enterprise templates can help a great deal by packaging the methods that you want programmers on your team to use. Once your organization decides to use a new technology, placing it in an enterprise template ensures that every developer will have access to the technology and begin to use it in new projects. Using enterprise templates greatly reduces the learning curve for other developers who need to use a new technology but haven't necessarily had time to read everything about it. Not only that, the enterprise template will provide guidance to these other developers on the usage of the new technology within applications.

While enterprise templates provide guidance and reduce application development complexity, policy definition files ensure that team members actually use the new techniques in their code. A policy definition file provides a means of validating code automatically to ensure that it meets certain programming criteria. In addition, you can use policies to limit team member access to certain types of IDE features. For example, if you don't want team members to use a particular control within applications, you can turn off access to that control in the toolbox. A policy can also automatically set properties. For example, you may want to set the name of a dialog box the same every time a developer uses it. A policy would automatically set this property for you and ensure consistency between application modules.

As you can see, templates and policies can make team development easier and more consistent. We'll talk more about this issue in Chapter 12.

Downloads You Should Know About

You may be reading this right after you've installed Visual Studio.NET on your machine for the first time. The thought that you'd need anything else, at this point, seems ludicrous. Of course, programming is never as easy as it should be. You'll find that you need to download additional products even for a new Visual Studio.NET installation. Microsoft usually offers these products separately, so that it can update them faster to meet industry trends. In addition, some of these products work with more than one version of Visual Studio—keeping them in separate packages allows all Visual Studio developers to use them, no matter which version of Visual Studio they use.

Throughout the book, you'll find that we spend a lot of time talking about the Windows Platform software development kit (SDK). The Platform SDK is a collection of add-ons that address general programming needs like the Windows 32 API, various services (base, component, data access, graphics and multimedia, management, and so on), and security. The most current version of the Platform SDK at the time of this writing is the October 2000 version, which is what I'll use. However, Microsoft updates the Platform SDK on a regular basis, so you'll need to check for new versions regularly. You'll find current Platform SDK information at **http://msdn.microsoft.com/ downloads/default.asp?URL=/code/topic.asp?URL=/msdn-files/028/000/123/ topic.xml**. Incidentally, you'll get a copy of the Platform SDK with a Microsoft Developer Network (MSDN) subscription, which saves you the time of downloading it online. You can find out more about getting an MSDN subscription at **http://msdn.microsoft.com/subscriptions/prodinfo/overview.asp**.

NOTE

I'll refer to the October 2000 version of the Platform SDK as simply the Platform SDK throughout this book. Make sure that you get the newest possible version of the Platform SDK before you begin working with the examples in this book. Some of the Platform SDK features that I talk about in the book are subject to change, so you may not see every feature that I mention, and some of the features may have changed from the time of this writing.

Visual Studio.NET will likely provide full support for SOAP when it arrives on your desktop. However, SOAP is a moving target for a number of reasons. For one thing, many of the technologies it relies on are still in the hands of committees who are trying to create a specification before standardization. With this in mind, you'll probably want to install a copy of the Microsoft SOAP Toolkit on your workstation if you intend to work with any of the SOAP examples in the book. You can find this toolkit at **http://msdn.microsoft.com/webservices/**. Note that this Web site also includes a wealth of other links that you'll want to check out when it comes to distributed application development.

I'm going to be using two special tools as the book progresses. These tools work well for me, but you may find that you like something else. The first tool, tcpTrace, allows you to see the HTTP message that contains the SOAP message for a distributed application. You can find this tool at **http://www.pocketsoap.com/tcptrace/**. The second tool, XML Spy, allows you to view the content of XML formatted files, including the Web Service Description Language (WSDL) files required by Microsoft's SOAP implementation. I'll use this tool to help you understand how SOAP uses various files to reduce the complexity of distributed application development. You can find XML Spy at **http://www.xmlspy.com/**.

Tools You Should Know About

Visual Studio and the Platform SDK both provide a wealth of tools that make development easier (or at least doable). This section will provide a brief overview of the tools that you'll likely need for most of the book. I'll also include sections in other chapters that provide information about tools for specific types of projects. For example, the database tools appear in the database section of the book.

Visual Studio versus Platform SDK Tools

Developers often find they have more tools than they need after installing both the Platform SDK and Visual Studio. It doesn't help that Microsoft has a habit of renaming utilities as they release new versions. Sometimes the utilities have changed, sometimes they haven't. In some cases, even a small change in marketing orientation will cause a change in the name of a utility. For example, OLE View has gone through more than a few name changes in the past few years. It seems that it has a different name with every release of Visual Studio or the Platform SDK. In short, you may think a tool is gone, only to find it under a different name later. For this reason, it's a good idea to check out every tool in both Visual Studio and the Platform SDK, just to make sure you know which tools are present.

The Platform SDK ships with a full toolbox of utilities that you can use to craft applications. In most cases, you should use the Platform SDK tools instead of the tools provided with Visual Studio, because the Platform SDK tools could have features that make development under Windows 2000 easier. In addition, the Platform SDK often ships with development tools that you won't find at all within Visual Studio. Finally, since Microsoft updates the Platform SDK on a regular basis, using the tools in the most current Platform SDK version ensures that you'll avoid at least some of the bugs that developers found in previous versions.

CPU Stress

The CPU Stress utility does just what its name implies—it places a load on a CPU to see just how well it works in a given situation. The program creates from one to four threads and specific priority levels. You can also choose how busy that thread should be during the testing process. Here's the initial CPU Stress display.

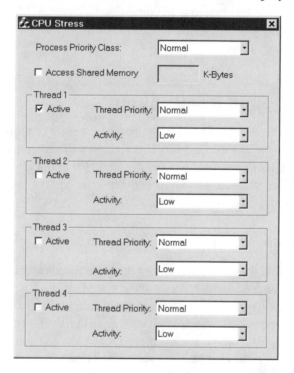

Other than setting the number of threads, the thread and process priority, and the level of activity, you don't have to do anything with the CPU Stress utility. This program is already doing the work you need it to do as soon as you start it. You can use this utility to measure the ability of your application to work with other applications on a single system. It also comes in handy for placing a load on your system so that you can simulate the performance characteristics of a less capable system.

Depends

Have you ever sent out an application and found out later that the person using it didn't have all the files needed to install it? Most of us have done that at one time or another. In at least some cases, the problem is accidental because the application relies on some unknown DLL. It seems as if every file in Windows relies on every other file in some way—trying to untie this knot is something even Houdini would have a problem doing.

Depends will show you the dependencies of your application. It tells you which files your application needs to run. Not only that, but it traces out the dependency hierarchy of all the support files in the dependency tree. Using this utility makes it easier for you to put application packages together that contain everything the user will need the first time.

There are several versions of Depends. The version that you get with Visual Studio.NET should match the current Platform SDK version. However, it's important to use the latest version because Microsoft keeps adding features to this product. I've divided Depends coverage into two parts: 1.x features and 2.x features. This will allow those of you who are already familiar with older versions of Depends to skip right to the new features.

Depends 1.x Features

Dependency Walker (or Depends, as it's listed on the Microsoft Visual Studio 6.0 Tools menu) helps you prevent the problem of the missing file. It lists every file that an application, DLL, or other executable files depends on to execute. You can use the output of this application to create a list of required files for your application. Loading a file for examination is as easy as using the File | Open command to open the executable file that you want to examine. Figure 1-4 shows an example of the output generated for the SayHello.EXE file. This is a typical example of a minimal MFC-based Visual C++ application. In fact, you can't get much more minimal than the example program in this case. The point, of course, is that even a very small and simple application may require more support files than you think.

TIP

It's interesting to note that Dependency Walker doesn't include any kind of print functionality. Fortunately, you can highlight a list of items you want to print, click Copy (or press CTRL-C) to copy them to the clipboard. Use the Paste function in your favorite word processor to create a document you can print for future reference.

As you can see, this application provides you with a lot of information about the dependencies of your file. In the upper-left corner is a hierarchical view of dependencies, starting with the executable file that you want to check. The hierarchy shows the files that each preceding file requires to run. So, while the application itself relies on MFC70.DLL (along with other files), the support DLL relies on input from a host of other files.

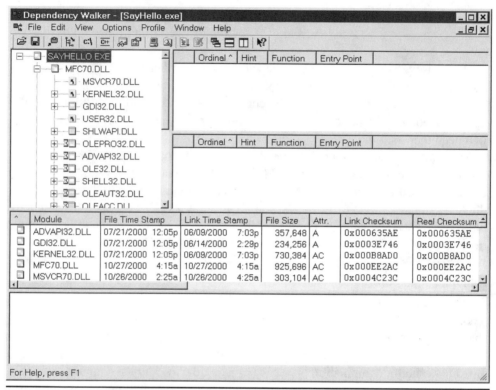

Figure 1-4   *Dependency Walker can help you determine what external files your component needs to operate.*

To the right of the hierarchical view are two lists. The upper list tells you which functions the parent executable imports from the current file. The lower list tells you which functions the highlighted executable exports for other executables to use. The sample application doesn't export any functions because it's an end-product. You'll typically see a blank export list for applications. Figure 1-5 shows a typical list of imported and exported functions for a DLL.

At the very bottom, you'll see an alphabetical list of all of the files along with pertinent information like the executable file's version number and whether you used a debug version of that file while creating and testing your application. This list comes in handy when debugging an application. It allows you to check for problems that might occur when using an older version of DLL or to detect potential corruption in a support file. You'll also find it handy when you want to check that final release build before you release it for public use. Many applications have tested poorly because they still had "hidden" debug code in them.

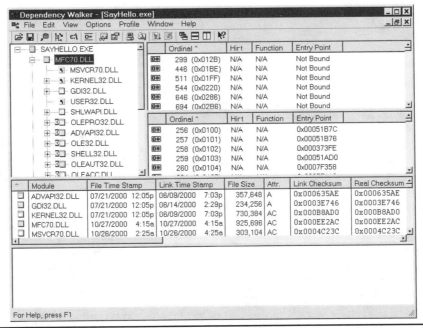

Figure 1-5   *DLLs normally import and always export functions that applications and other DLLs use.*

Depends 2.x Features

It's time to look at some of the new features that Depends 2.x provides. One of the more interesting features is the ability to profile your application. In this case, profiling doesn't have anything to do with performance; we're talking about tracing every call that your application makes. To start the profiling process, choose the Profile | Start Profiling command. You'll see a Profile Module dialog box like the one shown in Figure 1-6.

There are actually two sections to this dialog box. The first section allows you to provide a command line argument for the application and change the application's starting path. In most cases, you won't need to change either entry. You can also choose whether Depends clears the Log window before it begins the profiling process. The Simulate ShellExecute option determines how the application is started. Normally, you'll keep this checked to ensure that the application path information is provided to the application when it starts. The only exception is when you're troubleshooting problems related to the application path. If you uncheck this option, then Depends will start the application using the CreateProcess() API call rather than using ShellExecute().

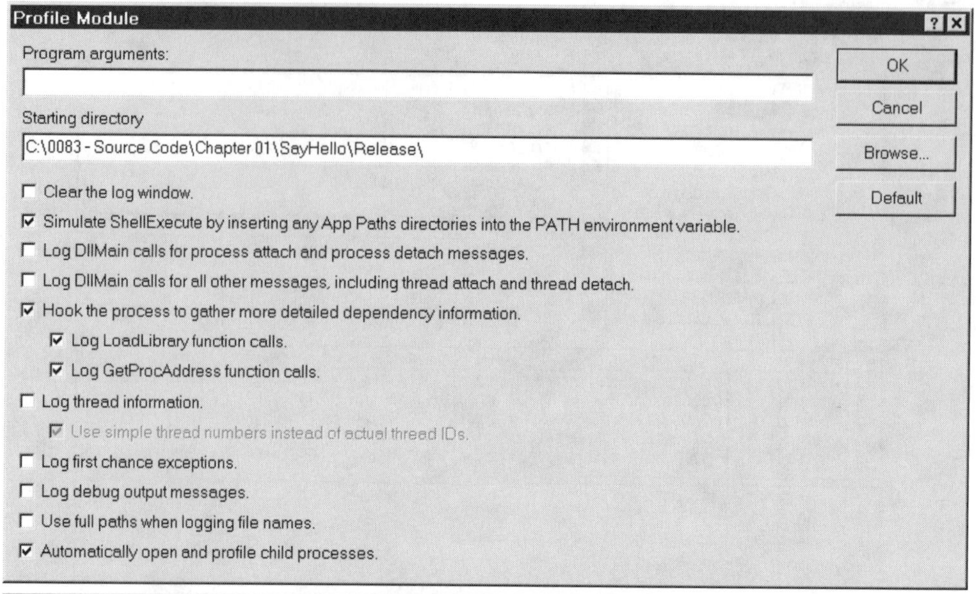

Figure 1-6 *The Profile Module dialog box allows you to add a command line argument and adjust the kinds of information that Depends will track.*

The second section contains a list of items that you want to monitor. For example, you might be interested only in profiling the libraries that your application loads and when it loads them. In this case, you'd select the Log LoadLibrary function calls option. The number of entries in the Log window can build very quickly, so it helps to decide what you really need to monitor at the outset, rather than wading through a lot of useless information that you don't really want. Figure 1-6 shows the default information that Depends will collect about your application. This setup is useful in determining how an application uses the various libraries that it requires to operate. It's interesting to note that you can even use Depends to monitor Debug output messages that you've placed within an application, making it a handy tool for monitoring application activity outside of a programming language's IDE.

Once you've decided how to start the application and what you want to monitor, click OK. Depends will load the application and start displaying profile information. Figure 1-7 shows the Log window entries for the SayHello.EXE application we looked at earlier. As you can see, there's a lot of activity that occurs even starting an application.

Even though you can't see it in the screen shot, Depends has noted two problem calls made by the application during startup. These calls are highlighted in red in the Log window. In addition, the affected modules are highlighted in red in both the

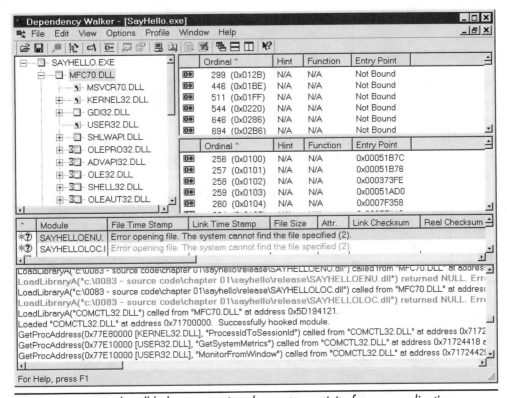

Figure 1-7   *Depends will help you monitor the startup activity for any application you create.*

module list and the hierarchical display. What this means to you, as a developer, is that Depends has gone from being a simple analysis aid to an application that can help you diagnose application problems. In this case, the two errant calls aren't part of the application code; they're caused by the Visual Basic runtime. Microsoft will likely fix these problems when it updates Visual Studio for Windows 2000.

Depends returns control of the application to you as soon as the application finishes loading. You can work with the application just as you normally would and monitor the results in the Log window. When you finish working with an application, you can stop the logging process using the Depends Profile | Stop Profiling command.

There are quite a few other new features provided with Depends, but the ability to profile your application is probably the highlight of the list. One of the new capabilities allows you to save a Dependency Walker Image (DWI) file. This option creates a file on disk that allows you to restore your setup as needed. Microsoft didn't include the

DWI file feature in previous versions of Depends because the application environment provided fewer options. However, the latest version of Depends would prove time consuming to configure without this feature.

The View menu contains three options that you really need to know about. The first is a System Information command that displays a dialog similar to the one shown in Figure 1-8. This short summary provides a quick view of your current system configuration, which could be important if you want to stress the application under a set of specific conditions like low memory. There are also options to display the full paths for all files and to undecorate those really weird function names that you'll normally find within C++-generated DLLs.

One final feature that improves the usability of Depends is the ability to search for specific information. For example, you can highlight a module of interest and use View menu options to search for other occurrences of the same module within the hierarchical view. This allows you to better see where specific modules are used and by whom. Another search feature, this one found on the Edit menu, allows you to search the Log window for words, just as you would with a text editor. You could use this feature to help find errors (the logs do get very long very fast) or to find instances where a specific module is used for tasks like application initialization.

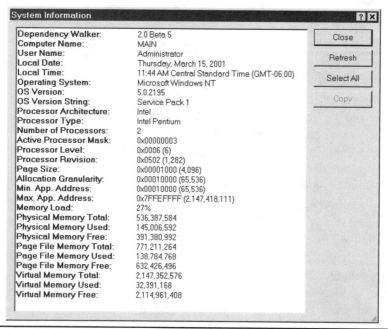

Figure 1-8   *The System Information dialog box gives you a quick overview of your system.*

Process Viewer

The Process Viewer utility (shown as PView on the Platform SDK Tools menu) allows you to see what processes are currently running on your machine, what threads they've spawned, and the priority of those threads. You can also use this utility to kill a process that isn't working as intended using the Kill Process button. Figure 1-9 shows what the Process Viewer utility looks like in action. Notice that I've started a copy of the SayHello test application that we used earlier in the chapter for demonstration purposes.

TIP

The Process Viewer automatically updates its display at a given interval (depending on current processor load). You can force an update of the display by pressing F5 or by using the Process | Refresh command.

The upper window contains a list of all of the processes currently running on the machine. It includes information about each process, like the process ID number, the number of threads that it owns, the base priority of the process (used for multitasking), whether it is a 16-bit or 32-bit process, and the full path to the process.

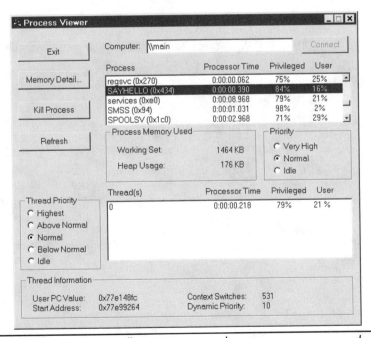

Figure 1-9   *The Process Viewer allows you to see what processes are currently executing on your machine.*

Highlighting a process displays thread information for it in the lower window. In this case, we see the one thread owned by SayHello.EXE. Thread information includes the thread ID, the ID of the process that owns the thread (useful when you have threads starting other threads), and the priority of the thread (normally the same or lower than the base priority for the process as a whole).

There's one additional Process Viewer feature that you may want to look at. Click Memory Detail and you'll see the Memory Details dialog box, shown in Figure 1-10. As you can see, this dialog box contains very detailed information about precisely how a process is using memory. This dialog will tell you how much memory the application uses privately, how the memory is mapped into various functional areas, and how much virtual memory the process is using.

The User Address Space field of the Memory Details dialog box contains the name of the address space that you're view7ing. The Total Commit value means that you're looking at the memory used by the entire process. If you click the arrow next to the combo box, you'll see a list of all of the DLLs and EXEs used by this application. Select one of these entries and you'll see the memory used just by that piece of the application. For example, the executable portion of the file uses a mere 4-KB in this case. Since most of these DLLs are shared, the application is most likely using only the 4-KB for the executable and the 32-KB for the runtime file.

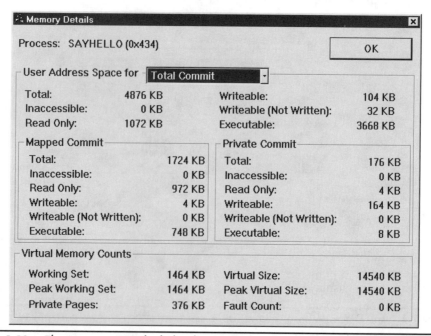

Figure 1-10   *The Memory Details dialog box provides extremely detailed information about how a particular process is using memory.*

You can use the Memory Details dialog box to troubleshoot applications with subtle memory problems by looking at the values in two of the fields. First, look for a number in the Inaccessible field. Any value other than 0 in this field tells you that the process has some type of memory problem. The second item is the Total memory field. Compare this entry for the Total Commit entry to the Total memory field value for other address spaces. If you see that one DLL is using a substantial amount of memory and the others some small amount of memory, you need to ask why this one DLL is acting in that way. In many cases, you'll find nothing wrong, but there are a few situations when a buggy DLL will keep grabbing memory until it begins to impinge on the resources available to other applications.

ROT Viewer

The IROTView utility (it appears as ROT Viewer in both the Platform SDK and the Visual Studio Tools menus) allows you to view OLE's running object table (ROT). So, what does this buy you? Well, if you're testing the OLE capabilities of your application, you can use this ability to see how well your application interfaces with other objects. For example, what happens if you open a compound document object? Does your application actually make the connection? Figure 1-11 shows what the IROTView utility looks like with several objects loaded.

The upper window gives you a complete list of the currently running objects. The GUIDs are running applications that can act as containers for other objects. Figure 1-11 shows two applications: Word and Paintshop Pro. Above each GUID is a list of the documents that the application is running. Every time an application receives focus, this list gets updated. You can also perform a manual update using the Update! menu option.

The lower window gives you more information about the highlighted object. The following list tells you what each field contains.

NOTE

A moniker *is a name for some kind of a resource. For example,* C:\MyStuff\MyDoc.Doc *is a moniker for a document file that appears in the MyStuff folder on the C drive of your machine. Monikers can include all kinds of resource types. For example:* **http://www.microsoft.com/** *is the moniker for Microsoft's Web site. You can even reference objects by their moniker by using the class ID (ClsId). For example, a moniker for Microsoft Word 97 is {000209FF-0000-0000-C000-000000000046}.*

- ▶ **Name:** The display name of the moniker. For example, in the case of a file, you'd see the complete path for the file. Applications normally use their class ID.

- ▶ **Reduced:** The reduced name of the moniker. Normally, this is the same value as the Name field.

► **Inverse:** The anti-moniker for this object. You add this value to the end of the moniker to destroy it. In most cases, this value is set to: "\..".

► **Enumerated:** A list of the items in this moniker. If this isn't a composite moniker (as is the case in most situations), then the field displays "N/A."

► **Hash Value:** The 32-bit hash value associated with the moniker.

► **Running:** Displays TRUE to show that the application is running or FALSE so show that it's halted. The entry for the application will always disappear when the application is terminated, so FALSE always indicates a halted, but active, application.

► **Last Change:** This is the last time that the moniker's data was updated.

► **Type:** The type of moniker displayed. Standard values include Generic Composite Moniker, File Moniker, Anti-Moniker, Item Moniker, Pointer Moniker, and Not a System Moniker.

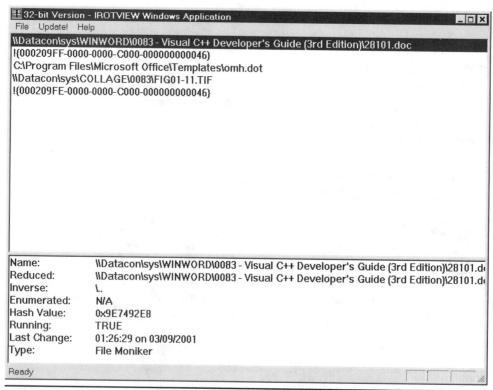

Figure 1-11 *The main purpose of the IROTView utility is to keep track of the OLE running object table.*

ShellWalk

ShellWalk is a handy utility for finding bugs in namespace implementations. You can use it to walk through the namespace hierarchy and look for problems in applications that you create. The testing includes checks related to folder, item, PIDL (identifier list pointer), and COM, which means that ShellWalk will find most namespace-related problems. All data logging occurs through the LOR logging utility.

There are two ways to use ShellWalk. You can use the command line method or directly interact with the application interface. The command line parameters include \tp, which makes a single pass through the namespace hierarchy, and \stress, which allows the utility to pass through the namespace hierarchy infinitely. In most cases, you'll want to use the \tp command line switch to make a single pass through the namespace hierarchy and log and problems that the ShellWalk utility finds.

Figure 1-12 shows what the ShellWalk utility looks like. As you can see, the left pane contains a hierarchical view of the namespace. The right pane contains the results

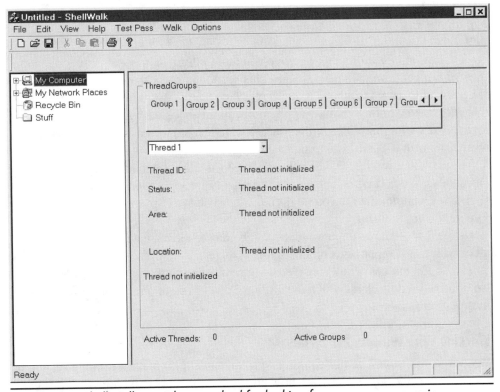

Figure 1-12   *ShellWalk provides a method for looking for namespace errors in applications you create.*

for any tests that you run. Unlike the command line, the user interface allows you to select multithreaded as well as single-threaded testing. There are also settings for the breadth and depth of testing. The testing depth affects just how deep in the hierarchy that ShellWalk will look for errors. There are several test types. The Walk menu options allow you to walk the namespace starting at a specific point in the hierarchy, while the Test Pass menu options will test the entire hierarchy. Note that you can't perform a leak test without a checked build of Windows 2000.

Before you can use ShellWalk for the first time, you need to make some configuration changes. There are two INI files in the ShellWalk directory. The first is MTShellWalk.INI. This file contains the location of the LOR logging DLLs. You need to change the two entries in this file to point to the ShellWalk directory on your hard drive, which is going to be C:\Program Files\Microsoft Platform SDK\ Bin\ShellWalk for the Platform SDK in most cases. The second is LorLogging.INI, which contains the logging settings. You'll need to set the log filename and logging path entries at a minimum. The other entries control which logs the LOR logging utility will generate.

Spy++

Spy++ is a complex utility that can give you more information about your application than you might have thought possible. This section is going to give you a very brief overview of this utility. What I'll do is point out some of the more interesting features that will make working with the applications in this book easier. Make sure you take time to work with this utility further once you've learned the basics. We'll also spend more time with it as the book progresses.

The first thing you'll see when you start Spy++ is a list of windows. A window can be any number of object types, but the most familiar is the application window. Figure 1-13 shows an example of what you might see when you start Spy++ with the SayHello sample application running.

Notice Spy++ shows three windows that belong to the main application window— all of which are components on the dialog box. In this case, the OK, Cancel, and the Say Hello test buttons are all considered windows. The buttons are all objects derived from the CWindow class, which means that Spy++ is right on track displaying the information as it has.

Working With Window Properties

Windows are a central part of working with Spy++. They represent the method you'll normally use to begin deciphering how an application works and how well it runs.

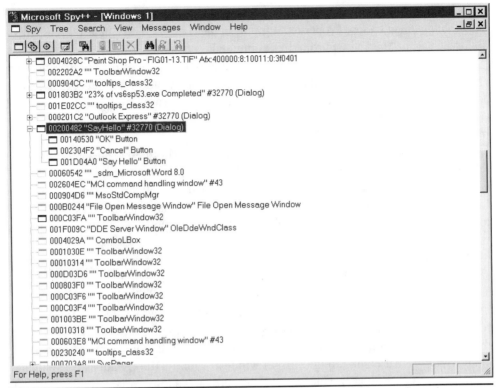

Figure 1-13   *Spy++ allows you to take your application apart and see it from the Windows perspective.*

It makes sense, then, that you can access every aspect of an application, its child windows, processes, and threads through the Window Properties dialog box shown here:

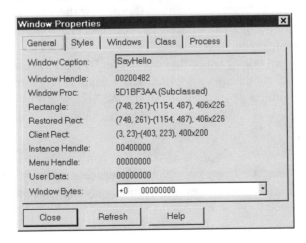

Accessing this dialog box is easy: All you need to do is right-click the window you want to view, then choose Properties from the context menu. You can also access this dialog box using the View | Properties command.

The General tab of the Window Properties dialog box tells you about the window as a whole. It includes the window's display name, the window's handle, the virtual address of the window's procedure, the size of the rectangle used to display the window (both present and restored sizes), and various other pieces of general application information.

The Styles tab contains a list of the window style constants used to create the window. For example, you'll commonly find WS_VISIBLE as one of the items in the list, unless you're dealing with an invisible window. This same tab contains extended styles for the window, like WS_EX_APPWINDOW. These constants should be familiar to someone with C/C++ programming experience, since you need them to display windows in most cases.

The Windows tab contains five entries. You can move between windows at the same level by clicking the links in the Next Window and Previous Window fields. The Parent Window field will contain a link if this is a child window or (None) if this is a main window. If the window contains child windows (like the components for the SayHello.EXE program), you'll see an entry in the First Child field. Clicking this link will take you down one level in the hierarchy so that you can examine any child windows that belong to the current window. Finally, the Owner Window field will contain a link if another window owns the current window—except for the Desktop, in which case the field displays a value of (None).

The Class tab tells you about the class used to create the window. For example, the main window for the SayHello.EXE program uses the #32770 (Dialog) class, while the components are all listed as being part of component-specific classes like the Button class used for the Say Hello test button. You'll also find class-specific information, such as class style codes, number of data bytes used by this class instance, a window instance handle, number of bytes used by the window, and window details like the name of any associated menus.

The Process tab provides a list of process IDs and thread IDs associated with the current window. Clicking the links associated with each field will display the properties dialog associated with the process or thread ID. We'll look at this properties dialog in more detail in the Viewing Processes section that follows.

Viewing Messages

Windows runs on messages. Every activity that the user engages in generates a message of some sort. It's important to monitor those messages and see how your application reacts. For example, if you expect a certain message to get generated when the user clicks a button, you can monitor the message stream to see if it really does get sent.

There are a number of ways to display the Messages window for a window that you're debugging. You could right-click on the window and choose Messages from the context menu. However, in this particular case, the best way to start the message monitoring process is to use the Spy | Messages command. Using this command will display the Message Options dialog box shown here:

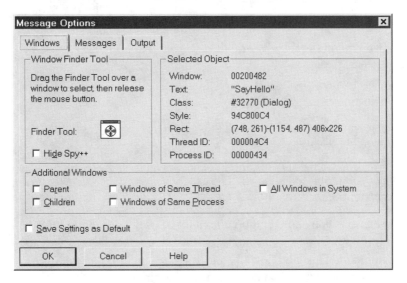

NOTE

You don't get the Message Options dialog box when you use the context menu method of displaying the Messages window.

Notice the Selected Object frame on the right side of the dialog box. This frame provides you with information about the object that you've selected. This additional information enables you to determine if this is the window that you want to monitor. The Finder Tool on the left side of the dialog box is interesting as well. Drag this tool to any displayed window, then release the mouse button, and the information on the right side will change to match the data for that window. (The windows will get highlighted as you drag the mouse cursor over them so that you can see which one is being selected.) The Windows tab also allows you to choose additional windows. For example, you may want to monitor the child windows as well as the parent window for a specific kind of message.

There are 849 different messages that Spy++ can track for the average window. The Messages tab shown here gives you some idea of just how extensive the message coverage is.

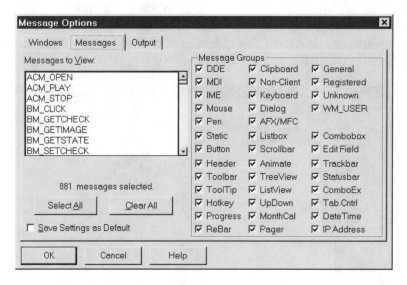

Needless to say, you could end up with a lot of useless tracking information if you don't trim this number down to a more reasonable number. That's why the Messages tab is so important. This tab allows you to choose which messages Spy++ tracks in the Messages window. You can choose messages singularly or in groups. A Select All button allows you to choose all of the messages, while a Clear All button allows you to clear the current selections. Make sure you tune these settings before you display the Messages window, or your chances of getting the input you need will be very small indeed.

It's also important to determine how you want information displayed in the Messages window. In most cases, the default options on the Output tab will work just fine. Spy++ assumes that you want to display only decoded information and only on screen. However, there are options for displaying raw message information. You can also choose to send the output to a file as well as to the screen.

Once you have the options set for your Messages window, you can click OK and Spy++ will display it for you. Figure 1-14 shows an example of what a Messages window would look like if you choose to monitor a subset of button and mouse events. As you can see, just selecting these two message groups generates a lot of message traffic.

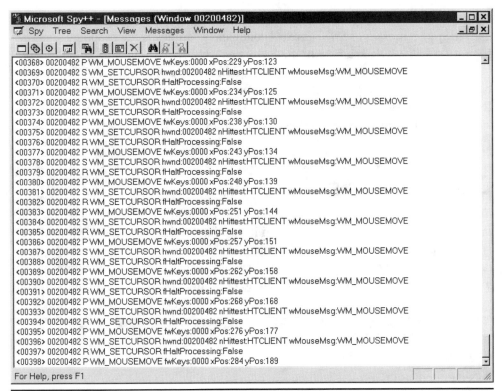

Figure 1-14 *The Messages window will display the messages that you choose to monitor for an application.*

In this case, I clicked the Say Hello button several times and moved the mouse around on screen. Notice that the log entries contain the handle of the window where the action occurred, the action performed (mouse button up or down, mouse move, or set cursor), and the position where the action occurred. Obviously, this is a simple test case, but it's also easy to see that monitoring messages can provide you with very important debugging clues for your application.

Viewing Processes and Threads

Every application you create will have at least one process and one thread. Consider a process as the overall application identifier, while a thread consists of a particular set of actions taking place within that process. In a multithreaded application, each thread of execution is performing a single task that affects the application (the process) as a whole.

Spy++ allows you to monitor both processes and threads. All you need to do is use the Spy | Processes or Spy | Threads command to display the appropriate window. Figure 1-15 shows an example of the Processes window.

It's interesting to note that the Processes window also contains a list of any threads owned by the process in a hierarchical format. For this reason, you'll normally want to use the Processes window over the Thread window. You get more information in an easier-to-use format with the Processes window.

Creating a Workstation Setup

To get anywhere with this book you need a development workstation on which you install Windows 2000 (or Windows XP if it's available when you read this), write your code, and perform any desktop-level testing. Avoid using your regular workstation for development for two reasons. First, there's no guarantee that an application is going to work the first time, and you don't want to crash the machine that contains all your

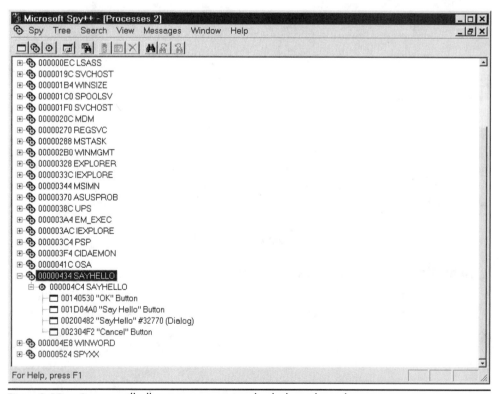

Figure 1-15   *Spy++ will allow you to monitor both threads and processes.*

data. Second, you want to create the cleanest possible environment so that you know for sure that any bugs are the result of application errors, not compatibility problems.

The version of Windows 2000 you install depends on personal taste and the number of machines that you plan to use. You definitely want to install one of the server versions of Windows 2000 if you plan to use only one machine as both a development workstation and a server. However, the programming examples work better and demonstrate more if you use two machines. (I'll always assume that you have two machines: one with Windows 2000 Professional installed for development purposes and one with Windows 2000 Server installed for the server.) If you're using two machines, you can set up the development workstation using Windows 2000 Professional. You may want to use this operating system rather than the server version so that you can get a better idea of how things will actually look from the user's perspective. The server versions include many features that the user won't see, and these features might taint the results of any tests you perform.

CAUTION

Developing applications for production purposes on a single-machine setup will result in applications that are unreliable and not fully tested. Most applications today run in a distributed environment, so a multiple-machine setup for developers is a requirement. For example, there isn't any way to develop COM+ applications and completely test them without a two-machine setup. In addition, you want to ensure that you have some flexibility in the methods used to connect the two machines. At the very least, you want a private network setup where you can disconnect the development workstation from the server without disturbing other people working on the network. A telephone connection (or a simulation) is also valuable for testing disconnected applications fully. Make absolutely certain you set up a good development environment before you begin your first production application or you'll definitely get unreliable results.

For a development workstation that you're going to use exclusively for development and not for testing purposes, make sure you get a fast processor, a lot of RAM, and even more hard drive space. My test workstation includes 512MB of RAM, dual 450MHz Pentium II processors, and a 9GB hard drive. This setup worked well for my needs in creating code for this book—you'll obviously need to increase your hard drive space as you add more features and create complex applications. I initially tested every application on my development machine, then on the server, and finally on a test workstation. The test workstation is a 166MHz Pentium machine with 64MB of RAM and a 4GB hard drive. The test workstation you use should reflect the standard-issue machine for the environment in which the application will perform. In all cases, I'm using Windows 2000 as my operating system. I used the server version of the product where appropriate.

I installed the minimum number of user-level features on my machine. You'll need to install all of the features required for your application. For example, if you want to work with Queued Components, then you'll need to install Microsoft Message Queue (MSMQ) support on your workstation. The example sections in this book will note any special user-level features you may have to install to make the examples work. It's important to consider this requirement when setting up your test workstation for your own projects.

Install Visual C++ next. I performed a full install of all features. This book will concentrate on Visual C++ 7 (.NET). However, at least some of the examples will work with older versions of Visual C++ as well. In some cases, you'll need to make modifications to the example code in order for the example to work with older versions of Visual C++. You must install Visual Studio Service Pack 3 (as a minimum) to get Visual C++ 6 to work with Windows 2000. Service Pack 5 (or the most current service pack as you read this) is available at **http://msdn.microsoft.com/vstudio/ sp/vs6sp5/default.asp**.

Creating a Server Setup

You must have a Windows 2000 Server setup in order to work with many of the examples in this book. I wrote the examples using the standard server product on a dual-processor 450MHz Pentium processor machine with 512MB of RAM, although you could probably get by with a single 450MHz processor machine with 256MB of RAM installed. I recommend a minimum of 9GB of hard drive space, although more is certainly better considering how much space you'll need for the various programming language additions.

The test server will require access to a number of Windows-specific components if you want the examples in the book to work. The following list summarizes the components that I installed while writing this book:

▶ Internet Information Server (IIS) (complete)

▶ Management and Monitoring Tools (all)

▶ Message Queuing Services

▶ Microsoft Indexing Service

▶ Networking Services (all)

▶ Terminal Services (optional, but good to have)

After your test server is up and running, you'll need some additional programs in order to work with some of the examples in the book. The number of features that you install depends on which examples you want to work with. Obviously, you need a database manager to work with the database examples. I based the following application list on the assumption that you want to work with all of the examples.

► Microsoft Front Page Server Extensions

► Microsoft Posting Acceptor 2.0

► Microsoft Visual Studio Enterprise Edition (Server Components)

► Microsoft Visual Studio Analyzer Server (part of Visual Studio)

► Remote Machine Debugging (only if you want to debug your server from a remote location)

► SQL Server Debugging (part of Visual Studio)

► Visual SourceSafe Server (part of Visual Studio)

► VSEE APE Server (part of Visual Studio)

Building Desktop Applications

IN THIS CHAPTER:

Writing an Informational Console Application

Writing a Utility Dialog-Based Application

Writing a Text-Editing, Single-Document Application

With all of the current emphasis on Internet and distributed development, some people might think that desktop development is outdated. After all, according to current theory there isn't anywhere else to go on the desktop. Unfortunately, such shortsighted viewpoints miss the realities of business application development; not every application requires the capabilities provided by the distributed application environment. For example, you need a desktop application, not a distributed application, to monitor the status of your hardware. While there may be a need to provide an agent on the local machine so a network administrator can monitor the system from a remote location, local monitoring occurs using a standard desktop application.

BROWSER ALERT

*Any serious Visual C++ programmer will spend some time on the Internet learning about new programming techniques. Microsoft hosts a variety of Visual C++ newsgroups, some of which are quite specific. The most general newsgroup is **microsoft.public.vc.language**. If you want to learn what's going on with ActiveX technology, you might want to look at **microsoft.public.vc. activextemplatelib**. A good place to look for database specifics is **microsoft.public.vc.database**. One of the most active newsgroups is **microsoft.public.vc.mfc**, which is devoted to working with the Microsoft Foundation Classes (MFC). However, there are two other MFC-related newsgroups: **microsoft.public.vc.mfc.docview** and **microsoft.public.vc.mfc.macintosh**. Finally, don't forget to check out the general windows programming groups located under the **microsoft. public.win32.programmer** folder (there's a whole list of programmer-related newsgroups, so you'll need to choose the ones that best suit your needs). For those of you looking for managed code-specific newsgroups, try **microsoft.public.dotnet.languages.vc** and **microsoft.public.framework.interop**. The first helps you discuss important Visual C++ language change topics, while the second enables you to discuss interoperability questions.*

It's easy to imagine that you'll always work on new projects, but the reality is that companies have a wealth of applications right now and have invested heavily in them. Many developers will need to update existing applications. In some cases, it's a lot less expensive to tweak an existing application than start over from scratch with the latest technology. Updates will always be a part of developer activity, so it's important to know how to work with desktop applications. In short, no matter what type of development you're doing today, eventually you'll need to work with the desktop.

Desktop applications can take a variety of sizes and shapes. Each of these desktop application versions fulfills a specific task within the grand scheme of application development within your organization. Visual C++.NET is quite capable of creating any application you can imagine. However, there are five application types that exemplify applications as a whole, and they're what we'll concentrate on first.

▶ *Console applications* represent those situations where you really need to maintain some type of compatibility with legacy systems or where you don't need a full-fledged interface for the user to work with. We'll look at two console applications. The first provides a simple information display that requires no user interaction. The second will perform simple script processing, similar to the processing you might perform during an installation or update.

▶ *Dialog-based applications* normally act as utilities or an application that's too small to require a complete menuing system. This is also the most popular application type for testing small routines before you incorporate them into a larger application. Consequently, dialog-based applications represent the desktop application class you'll get to know best. We'll look at two types of dialog-based applications: utility and configuration.

▶ *Single-document applications* are representative of simple applications that work with their own data, like note takers or small database front ends. These applications also require a menuing system of some type. Even large applications can use the Single Document Interface (SDI) model. The important consideration is that a SDI application displays just one document at a time. We'll look at two SDI applications in this chapter. The first allows you to work with a single document type, while the second will work with more than one document type using more than one view.

▶ *Multiple-document applications* normally include larger applications like word processors and spreadsheets. When you think about it, they represent that fringe area of C++ programming where you need to weigh the flexibility of C++ against the development speed offered by RAD programming environments like Visual Basic. A Multiple Document Interface (MDI) application can display more than one document at a time. This means that application development is much harder. We'll look at one example of an MDI application in this chapter.

▶ *HTML-based applications* work with data of some type (like single-document or multiple-document applications) but with an Internet twist. Instead of a standard editor, your user will see what amounts to a Web browser front end. We'll look at one example of an HTML-based application that uses an SDI format. You can also create MDI versions of HTML-based applications.

NOTE

Remember that we're talking about applications in this chapter. Visual C++ is capable of creating all kinds of different code. You can use it to create DLLs, ActiveX controls, ISAPI extensions, device drivers, background-executing programs like screen savers, and even extensions to Visual C++ itself. We're only talking about general applications in this chapter, but we'll cover many of these other possibilities as the book progresses.

Visual C++ also creates two flavors of applications in this release: managed and unmanaged. An unmanaged application is one that uses the same processes and techniques that you've always used. It's the one that you'll spend the least amount of time learning. The managed application relies on the .NET Framework to perform certain tasks such as memory management. This new technology will compile to an intermediate language (IL) module instead of a native EXE, which means you'll need to have the .NET Framework installed on all client machines as well. We'll begin a discussion of managed code in this chapter, with more to follow as the book progresses.

BROWSER ALERT

*You may not think about the font you use to work on your machine, but using monospaced fonts all day can lead to eyestrain, bugs (as when, for example, you confuse an l and a 1), and other problems. Microsoft's choice of Courier New as its monospaced font hasn't been well received by many users. Fortunately, there are alternatives, some of which are free. Paul Neubauer's Web site at: **http://home.bsu.edu/prn/monofont/** discusses how to use monospaced fonts on a typical Windows system and what replacement fonts are available should you decide you really don't like Courier. This Web site even includes reviews of the various fonts so that you can make a good choice the first time around.*

Writing an Informational Console Application

A console application, as previously stated, enables you to move the business logic of your application from DOS to Windows. You also may be able to move some (or even most) of the display logic, but you'll likely want to dress it up with features that MFC can provide. In essence, a console application can look just like your old DOS application with a few added features. You need to completely test the application once you get it coded to make sure any features you move from DOS to Windows still work as anticipated.

Let's look at a simple example of what you can do with a console application. In this case, we're not looking at functionality as much as at what you can do overall. The first step, of course, is to create the program shell. The following procedure will take you through the steps required to get that part of the job done.

1. Open Visual C++ if you haven't done so already.

2. Use the File | New command to display a New Project dialog, like the one shown here. Notice that I've already chosen the Visual C++ Projects tab and highlighted the project type that we'll use in this example.

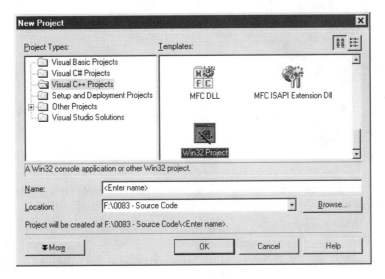

3. Once you choose Win32 Project, type a name for your program in the Project Name field. The sample program uses the name Console. You may need to change the contents of the Location field as well. Just click the browse button next to the field and you'll see a Choose Directory dialog, where you can choose a destination directory for your application.

4. Click on OK. You'll see the Win32 Console Application Wizard dialog. Select Application Settings and you'll see the display shown next. Notice that you have a choice of several application types to get you started. Microsoft originally

introduced this feature in Visual C++ 6.0. Before that time, Visual C++ would have created an empty project for you. Visual C++ .NET enhances the appearance of the wizard and adds a few new options. For example, you can add either ATL or MFC support to your console application.

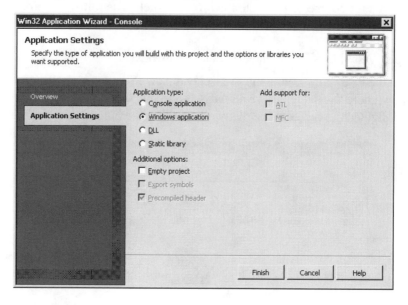

5. Select the Console Application option. Note that you can select other application types, such as a Windows application.

6. Check the Empty Project option. Notice that when you select the Empty Project option, the wizard automatically disables the MFC and ATL options. Click Finish. The Win32 Console Application Wizard will create the example for you.

NOTE

For those of you who are used to the Visual C++ 6.0 way of doing things, you'll notice that you don't see a summary dialog anymore. The new interface makes this feature unnecessary because you can see the entire project at a glance. However, as we progress through the chapter, you'll see that the summary dialog would still be a welcome feature.

You need to perform one more step before this project will be ready to go. It needs to use MFC classes. While you could have added this support as part of the wizard setup, converting DOS applications to Windows use requires less code rewriting if you go this route. Highlight Console in Solution Explorer. The object you select in this window determines the results you obtain when using certain commands. Use the View | Property Pages command to display the Console Property Pages dialog shown here:

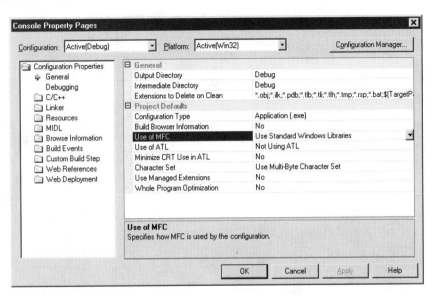

Notice that Visual C++ .NET centralizes the settings for your application into a series of hierarchical folders in the same dialog box. Choose the General folder of the dialog. Choose the Use MFC in a Shared DLL option in the Use of MFC field. Click OK to complete the action.

Now it's time to add some code to our example. The first thing you'll need to do is add a file to the project. Let's look at the process for doing that.

1. Use the File | New | File command to open the New File dialog. Choose the Visual C++ folder. You'll see a whole list of file types, including Resource Template File and various graphics files like Icon File.

2. Highlight the C++ File option, and then click Open. You'll see a blank C++ source file. We need a C++ source file because we'll be adding classes to the sample code.

3. Click Save. Select the correct directory for your source code files. Type **Console** in the File Name field. (Visual C++ will automatically add the correct extension for you.)

4. Click Save. This will add the file to our project directory. If you were using Visual C++ 6, this is where you'd stop. However, when working with Visual C++ .NET, you need to go one step further.

5.   Right-click Source Files in Solution Explorer and choose Add | Existing Item from the context menu. You'll see an Add Existing Item dialog box.

6.   Highlight Console.CPP, and then click Open. The file is now part of your project.

Now that you have an empty file to use, it's time to add the code. Listing 2-1 contains the C++ source for our example. Notice that it includes straight C code mixed with the C++ code. I did that on purpose so that you could better see how things work in this environment.

Listing 2-1

```
#include <afxcoll.h>      // Provides access to MFC functions.

class CDrawBox : public CObject
{
public:

    // Draws the box.
    void DoDraw(char* string);
};

void CDrawBox::DoDraw(char* cValue)
{
    size_t          iCount;     // Loop counter.
    size_t          iSpaces;    // Amount of spaces to add for string.

    // Draw the top of the box.
    fprintf(stdout, "\311");
    for (iCount = 1; iCount <= 78; iCount++)
    {
        fprintf(stdout, "\315");
    }
    fprintf(stdout, "\273");

    // Figure out the center of the string, then display it
    // with the box sides.
    iSpaces = (80 - strlen(cValue)) / 2;
    fprintf(stdout, "\272");
    for (iCount = 1; iCount <= iSpaces; iCount++)
    {
        fprintf(stdout, " ");
    }
    fprintf(stdout, "%s", cValue);

    // Compensate for odd sized strings, then complete the side.
    if ((strlen(cValue) % 2) == 1)
    {
        iSpaces--;
    }
```

```
    for (iCount = 1; iCount <= iSpaces; iCount++)
    {
        fprintf(stdout, " ");
    }
    fprintf(stdout, "\272");

    // Draw the bottom of the box.
    fprintf(stdout, "\310");
    for (iCount = 1; iCount <= 78; iCount++)
    {
        fprintf(stdout, "\315");
    }
    fprintf(stdout, "\274\n");
}


int main(int argc, char** argv)
{
    char*       cName;         // Name of person typed at command line.
    char*       cLocale;    // Program execution location.
    CTime       oMyTime;    // A time object.
    CString       cDate;        // String used to hold time and date.
    CDrawBox    oMyDraw;    // Special text display.

    // See if we have enough command line arguments.
    if (argc != 2)
    {
        fprintf(stderr, "Type the program name followed by your name.\n");
        return 1;
    }

    // Get the command line arguments.
    cLocale = argv[0];
    cName = argv[1];

    // Get the current time and put it in a string.
    oMyTime = CTime::GetCurrentTime();
    cDate = oMyTime.Format( "%A, %B %d, %Y" );

    // Display everything we've collected.
    fprintf(stdout, "Hello %s\n\n", cName);
    fprintf(stdout, "Program is executing from:\n%s\n\n", cLocale);
    fprintf(stdout, "The date is: %s\n", cDate);

    // Use our class to draw a box around some text.
    oMyDraw.DoDraw("It's a box!");

    return 0;
}
```

TIP

Some people are confused about how Visual C++ interprets the "" and <> symbols for the #include and #using directives. If you use the quotes form, Visual C++ searches, in order, the current directory, the paths included with the /I compiler switch, and finally the paths included with the INCLUDE environment variable. If you use the angle bracket form, then Visual C++ searches only the paths included with the /I compiler switch and the paths included with the INCLUDE environment variable. Use the angle bracket form when you know the file is part of the Visual C++ library to speed compilation. The quotes form slows compilation slightly because Visual C++ has to search the local directory first.

As you can see, I'm showing you four essential techniques in this example. The first thing you'll notice is that the code checks for the proper number of command line arguments. If they aren't there, it displays an error message to the *stderr* device and then exits with an error code. You can detect this error code from a DOS batch command, but it doesn't affect Windows at all. Once the code establishes that there are enough command line arguments, it places them in a couple of variables for display later.

Until this point, you could have been looking at any DOS application. Notice that the second thing the code does is get the current time. It uses an MFC call to get the job done. So how do you gain access to MFC functions from within a console application? As you'll see, I included AFXCOLL.H at the beginning of the code. This file contains all of the defines and class definitions that you'll need to implement a limited number of MFC calls within your console application.

Don't get the idea that you can use MFC calls indiscriminately, though. For example, you can't create a CDialog object and then actually expect to use it. Even if you do manage to get the code to compile, you'll end up with a runtime error or the application will ignore the dialog code altogether.

TIP

A good rule of thumb when deciding which MFC classes to use is to see if the class works with graphical elements. If it does, there's no chance of you using it within a console application. In addition, you'll find that certain system calls are out of reach and that you'll have to exercise care when it comes to security and disk access. If in doubt, stick with the calls listed in AFXCOLL.H (and any associated header files like AFX.H) to the exclusion of everything else. You can safely use all of the calls within AFXCOLL.H in any console application.

Now that we have some data to display, the code sends it to the *stdout* device. That's the third technique I wanted to show you. In most cases, stdout will be the display, but you can easily send it elsewhere if so desired. The point is that you use the same formatting as before. For that matter, you could simply use an **fprint**() function call in place of the more elaborate **fprintf**() function call shown in the code.

There's one remaining call in our **main**() function. We send data to a class called CDrawBox, the fourth technique I wanted to show you. All that this class does is center the text within a text box (using the upper ASCII character set). I designed the box for an 80-character screen, but you can easily change it to accommodate other screen sizes. You've probably seen many DOS applications that do the same thing. The idea here is that we've derived a new class from the MFC CObject class, then used that class within a console application. Likewise, nothing stops you from performing similar tricks with the programs you've created. As I said before, the temptation to add bells and whistles to a DOS application as you move it to Windows certainly is strong. Whether or not an update makes sense depends on how much time you've got for the move and the relative value of the update when viewed within the context of the total application.

Our console application is all ready to go. However, like many of the DOS applications you've written, this one requires a batch file for testing purposes. Listing 2-2 shows the source for the batch file we'll use in this case. All it does is call the program, test for an error value, and then echo a message if the application registered an error.

Listing 2-2

```
@ECHO OFF
CONSOLE
IF ERRORLEVEL==1 ECHO IT'S BAD
CONSOLE JOHN
IF ERRORLEVEL==1 ECHO IT'S BAD
@ECHO ON
```

I gave my batch file a name of TestConsole.BAT, but any filename will do. Figure 2-1 shows the output from this example.

OK, so this example doesn't do enough to impress anyone. The point is that it's a simple example you can use for experimentation. For instance, you might try rewriting the example to accept a screen size as input, or use a different coding technique. The following sections explore this same example using a few other coding techniques you might want to try.

Using Straight Code

Our previous example is a little complex for the job it has to perform. You could write it as straight code without using a class. You could convert the **DoDraw**() method into a function with relative ease. The \Chapter 02\Console2 directory of the CD-ROM has

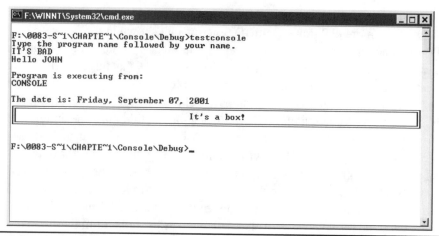

Figure 2-1   *A simple example of a console application in action*

an example of this form of the application. You might expect a reduction of size in the final application, but the reduction is small in this case. However, in a larger application, you'd likely see a relatively larger reduction in size when using straight code.

The use of classes also presents a small performance penalty. Again, the difference is so small that you'd never notice it in this case. Larger applications require classes for organizational purposes, code reuse, and all of the other reasons we use classes. In short, there's little reason to use straight code to enhance performance unless you're writing a real-time application.

One of the biggest reasons to use straight code in this situation is readability. Even if you present the **DoDraw()** method as a function, the code requires less space. The presentation is easier to see. Of course, the reason that classes have become popular is that using straight code tends to lead to situations where the code becomes incomprehensible. The point is that you can use straight code for simple examples and actually gain some amount of readability in the bargain.

Using Structs in Place of Classes

Visual C++ .NET can also handle this example using a *struct*. You'll find this version of the code in the \Chapter 02\Console3 directory of the CD-ROM. Some developers forget that you can use structs to hold code in addition to data. If you look at the example, **DoDraw()** is a member of the CDrawBox struct. The advantage of using a struct, in this case, is that it provides all of the organizational benefits of a class, but without many of the size and performance penalties.

Structs also provide advantages you won't easily find in a class. For one thing, you can pass them around as you would any variable. You can allocate them singly or place them in an array. In short, there are ways you can use structs that classes can't match. Of course, classes still provide the ultimate in code handling.

Using Managed Code

So far, we've looked at a series of methods for creating this simple example using traditional unmanaged Visual C++. However, you might want to try creating this application using managed code. This is a perfect way to see if there really are any differences from a development perspective. Of course, this means using a different project type. You'll want to select a Managed C++ Empty Project in this case. I gave the example project a name of Console4, but you could give it any name you want. One of the first things you'll notice about this project is that you won't see a wizard of any kind. Visual C++ .NET simply creates an empty project for you.

You'll perform the same tasks as you would for the other projects. Begin by right-clicking Source Files in the Solution Explorer, then choosing Add | Add New Item from the context menu. You'll see an Add New Item dialog box where you can choose the C++ File entry. I also gave the C++ file a name of Console4. Right click the Console4 project in Solution Explorer, then choose Properties. Select the Use MFC in a Shared DLL option in the Use of MFC field, then click OK. You're ready to add some code. This example still uses the code in Listing 2-1; you don't have to change it at all. When you build the project and run it, you'll notice a little delay as the .NET Framework compiles the IL code within the application. However, you won't notice any difference during subsequent runs. Except for a significant decrease in application size, you won't notice anything else about the managed application.

The first time you'll see a real difference between the managed and unmanaged versions is when you open the ILDASM.EXE program found in the \Program Files\ Microsoft.NET\FrameworkSDK\Bin directory on your hard drive. You'll use the Intermediate Language Disassembler from time to time to learn more about your code. Figure 2-2 shows what the Console4 example looks like when you load it. Note that if you try to load any of the other examples, ILDASM will tell you that it can't read them. Only the managed example will load.

You may have read about how a managed application is put together, but this utility shows you graphically how things work. Notice that the entire assembly begins with

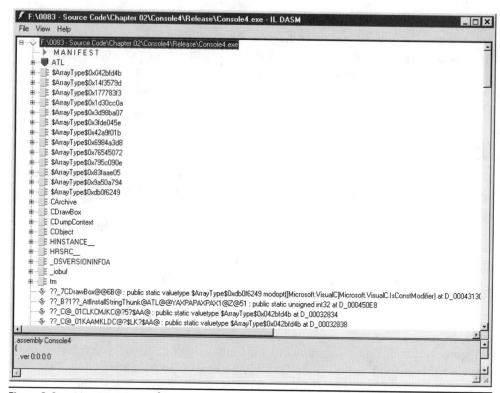

Figure 2-2   *Use ILDASM to learn more about managed code in Visual C++ .NET.*

a manifest. Double-click the manifest and you'll see the contents of the assembly, as shown in Figure 2-3. As you can see, the manifest contains a complete list of all of the assemblies for the example application and the contents of each assembly—at least, the contents as they pertain to the application.

The File | Dump command sends the data you see on screen to a file on disk for further analysis. The IL file contains everything that Visual Studio .NET (no this isn't C++ code anymore) needs to re-create the application. In fact, you can theoretically modify the IL and assemble it into an application again.

The application tokens shown in Figure 2-2 are messy because we've used native calls. The ILDASM utility can interpret the manifest and assembly information of any managed code application. However, when using Visual C++, you can mix managed and unmanaged code in the same module. By placing the code from Listing 2-1 into the managed application, all we did was move unmanaged code into a new container.

```
/ MANIFEST                                                              _ □ X
.assembly extern mscorlib
{
  .publickeytoken = (B7 7A 5C 56 19 34 E0 89 )                 // .z\V.4..
  .hash = (09 BB BC 09 EF 6D 9B F4 F2 CC 1B 55 76 A7 02 91      // .....m.....Uv...
           22 88 EF 77 )                                        // "..w
  .ver 1:0:2411:0
}
.assembly extern Microsoft.VisualC
{
  .publickeytoken = (B0 3F 5F 7F 11 D5 0A 3A )                 // .?_....:
  .hash = (4A D5 1A 11 0A 17 D0 E3 6D 69 68 80 D7 CB DD 8D      // J.......mih.....
           BA 79 FA D0 )                                        // .y..
  .ver 7:0:9254:59748
}
.assembly Console4
{
  .permissionset reqmin = (3C 00 50 00 65 00 72 00 6D 00 69 00 73 00 73 00   // <.P.e.r.m.i.s.s.
                           69 00 6F 00 6E 00 53 00 65 00 74 00 20 00 63 00   // i.o.n.S.e.t. .c.
                           6C 00 61 00 73 00 73 00 3D 00 22 00 53 00 79 00   // l.a.s.s.=.".S.y.
                           73 00 74 00 65 00 6D 00 2E 00 53 00 65 00 63 00   // s.t.e.m...S.e.c.
                           75 00 72 00 69 00 74 00 79 00 2E 00 50 00 65 00   // u.r.i.t.y...P.e.
                           72 00 6D 00 69 00 73 00 73 00 69 00 6F 00 6E 00   // r.m.i.s.s.i.o.n.
                           53 00 65 00 74 00 22 00 0D 00 0A 00 20 00 20 00   // S.e.t.".....  .
                           20 00 20 00 20 00 20 00 20 00 20 00 20 00 20 00   //   . . . . . .
                           20 00 20 00 20 00 20 00 20 00 76 00 65 00 72 00   //    . . . .v.e.r.
                           73 00 69 00 6F 00 6E 00 3D 00 22 00 31 00 22 00   // s.i.o.n.=.".1.".
                           3E 00 0D 00 0A 00 20 00 20 00 20 00 3C 00 49 00   // >.....  . .<.I.
                           50 00 65 00 72 00 6D 00 69 00 73 00 73 00 69 00   // P.e.r.m.i.s.s.i.
                           6F 00 6E 00 20 00 63 00 6C 00 61 00 73 00 73 00   // o.n. .c.l.a.s.s.
                           3D 00 22 00 53 00 79 00 73 00 74 00 65 00 6D 00   // =.".S.y.s.t.e.m.
                           2E 00 53 00 65 00 63 00 75 00 72 00 69 00 74 00   // ..S.e.c.u.r.i.t.
                           79 00 2E 00 50 00 65 00 72 00 6D 00 69 00 73 00   // y...P.e.r.m.i.s.
                           73 00 69 00 6F 00 6E 00 2E 00 53 00 65 00 63 00   // s.i.o.n...S.e.
                           63 00 75 00 72 00 69 00 74 00 79 00 50 00 65 00   // c.u.r.i.t.y.P.e.
                           72 00 6D 00 69 00 73 00 73 00 69 00 6F 00 6E 00   // r.m.i.s.s.i.o.n.
                           2C 00 20 00 6D 00 73 00 63 00 6F 00 72 00 6C 00   // ,. .m.s.c.o.r.l.
                           69 00 62 00 2C 00 20 00 56 00 65 00 72 00 73 00   // i.b.,. .V.e.r.s.
```

Figure 2-3   *The manifest tells you about the content of your application.*

Listing 2-3 shows the Console application in a somewhat managed form. Note that you can also find this application in the Chapter 02\Console5 directory of the CD.

Listing 2-3

```cpp
#include <afxcoll.h>     // Provides access to MFC functions.

#using <mscorlib.dll>    // Provides access to the .NET Framework.

using namespace System; // Uses the System namespace.

class CDrawBox : public CObject
{
public:
```

```
    // Draws the box.
    void DoDraw(char* string);
};

void CDrawBox::DoDraw(char* cValue)
{
    size_t    iCount;  // Loop counter.
    size_t    iSpaces; // Amount of spaces to add for string.
    CString   myString;

    // Draw the top of the box.
    Console::Write(S"\x2554");
    for (iCount = 1; iCount <= 78; iCount++)
    {
        Console::Write(S"\x2550");
    }
    Console::Write(S"\x2557");

    // Figure out the center of the string, then display it
    // with the box sides.
    iSpaces = (80 - strlen(cValue)) / 2;
    Console::Write(S"\x2551");
    for (iCount = 1; iCount <= iSpaces; iCount++)
    {
        Console::Write(" ");
    }
    Console::Write(cValue);

    // Compensate for odd sized strings, then complete the side.
    if ((strlen(cValue) % 2) == 1)
    {
        iSpaces--;
    }
    for (iCount = 1; iCount <= iSpaces; iCount++)
    {
        Console::Write(" ");
    }
    Console::Write(S"\x2551");

    // Draw the bottom of the box.
    Console::Write(S"\x255A");
    for (iCount = 1; iCount <= 78; iCount++)
    {
        Console::Write(S"\x2550");
    }
    Console::Write(S"\x255D\n");
}
```

```
int main(int argc, char** argv)
{
    CString   cName;      // Name of person typed at command line.
    CString   cLocale;    // Program execution location.
    CTime     oMyTime;    // A time object.
    CString   cDate;      // String used to hold time and date.
    CDrawBox  oMyDraw;    // Special text display.

    // See if we have enough command line arguments.
    if (argc != 2)
    {
        Console::WriteLine("Type the program name followed by your name.\n");
        return 1;
    }

    // Get the command line arguments.
    cLocale = argv[0];
    cName = argv[1];

    // Get the current time and put it in a string.
    oMyTime = CTime::GetCurrentTime();
    cDate = oMyTime.Format( "%A, %B %d, %Y" );

    // Display everything we've collected.
    Console::WriteLine("Hello " + cName);
    Console::WriteLine("\nProgram is executing from:\n" + cLocale);
    Console::WriteLine("\nThe Date is: " + cDate);

    // Use our class to draw a box around some text.
    oMyDraw.DoDraw("It's a box!");

    return 0;
}
```

As mentioned, Listing 2.3 is a start on a managed example. In this case, we've brought in the .NET Framework core library and used it to write the output with the **System::Console::WriteLine()** method. Because the **WriteLine()** method uses Unicode characters, we have to perform special formatting when using certain characters, such as the box drawing characters. In this case, you must also declare the entry as a string, and not a character, by using the "S" in front of the string, like this: Console::Write(S"\x2554"). Visual C++ doesn't support the \u escape sequence for Unicode characters, so you must use a hexadecimal Unicode character number instead. Note the "using namespace System" entry at the beginning of the code. This enables you to write the code without entering System at every line.

Understanding Which Method Is Best

Developers often look for the "best" method to accomplish a task. The problem is that the definition of best is often elusive. A method that works well for one person may be completely incomprehensible to someone else. The definition of best varies by person.

Is there a best method for this example? My personal preference is the straight coding method because the example is small and simple. However, experimenting with the other techniques proved educational. For example, the struct method brings with it an elegance that I might not be able to achieve using other techniques. It's a good choice in situations where you want the organization of a class without the work.

Obviously, the managed method is the new kid on the block, and most developers are anxious to use it with something. Managed code has a place in my toolkit, as it should in yours. For the most part, I see myself using managed code for new projects or projects that require complete overhauls. Managed code requires the .NET Framework, so it's necessarily limited to the corporate environment until .NET becomes as well established as Microsoft's other libraries.

Writing a Utility Dialog-Based Application

You'll most commonly use dialog-based applications for smaller tasks, such as utility programs, system monitors, or even a wizard. In most cases, you'll design these utilities to keep complexity at a minimum. In fact, it's safe to assume that a dialog-based application should always use a minimum of controls.

We're going to look at another simple example. However, in this case, our application is going to use a combination of ActiveX controls and built-in functionality to keep the amount of coding you actually have to do to a minimum. The following procedure will help you get an empty structure together, which we'll fill with code later.

1. Open Visual C++ (if you haven't done so already).

2. Click New Project on the Start page (or use the File | New | Project command) to display the New Project dialog box.

3. Highlight the MFC Application icon in the Visual C++ Projects folder.

4. Type a name for your application in the Project Name field. The sample application uses the name "Dialog," but you could easily use any name you like. Make sure you change the Location field if necessary (click the browse button next to the Location field).

5. Click on OK. You'll see an MFC Application Wizard dialog box. Click the Application Type entry and you'll see a dialog box similar to the one shown here. This dialog box enables you to select an application type, project style, and the use of MFC. Notice that the dialog example now sports an HTML interface option, which means your dialog examples can use Web pages as a means of displaying data and controls.

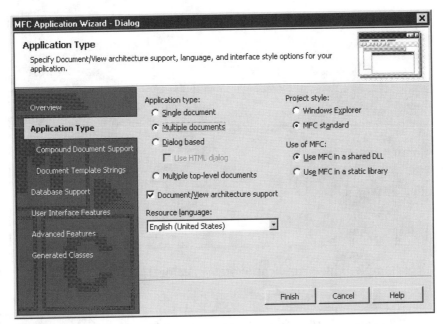

TIP

Statically linking MFC to your application has the benefit of reducing the number of files you have to distribute with your application. In fact, you'll only need to give someone the executable if you want to. It may also improve the chances that your application will run on every machine it's installed on, since your application will always have access to the same version of MFC that you used to design it. The downside to static linking is that your application will be a lot bigger and waste a lot more memory when loaded. In addition, you'll need to relink your application any time you want to add a new feature to it, which can become quite a nuisance after a while.

6. Choose the Dialog Based option. Select User Interface Features. You'll see a dialog box similar to the one shown next. This dialog box helps you choose features for your application, such as an About dialog box and a system menu. You can also use the Dialog Title field to change the title bar entry for the

dialog- based application. Notice that you must now choose the Thick Frame option to obtain a dialog-based application with resizing capability.

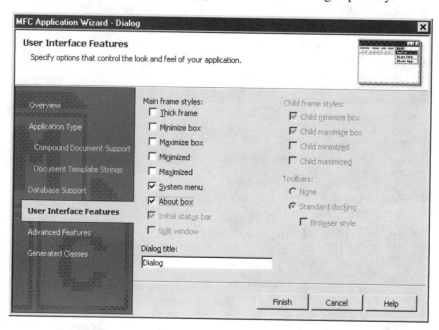

7. Type **Sample Dialog Application** in the Dialog Title field.

TIP

It's helpful to look at the other entries on the other tabs. For example, the Advanced Features tab contains options such as ActiveX controls and automation. This is also the place you select context sensitive help for the application. You'll also find a new feature called Common Control Manifest. You must check this option if you want to use the new common controls provided with Windows XP. However, you can save memory, increase performance, and reduce application complexity by clearing this option when not needed. The Generated Classes tab tells you the names of the files that Visual C++ creates when you finish the application. Older versions of the dialog-based application always used the same base class. However, now that Visual C++ .NET supports HTML dialogs, you'll find that you can choose between two base classes for your dialog-based applications (one standard and the other HTML-based).

8. Click Finish. Visual C++ will generate the required code for you. Notice that Visual C++ automatically displays the dialog resource for you. In addition, you'll see the Toolbox open so all you need to do is begin adding controls to the dialog box. Microsoft is trying to emphasize the "design first, code later" approach in its products by using this technique.

Now it's time to get your dialog box designed. Figure 2-4 shows how I put my dialog together. I used the new Month Calendar Control entry found in the Toolbox. The current dialog box size is 200×300. I made the Calendar control itself 140×230 in size so that the numbers would be easy to see. Notice that the Calendar control immediately displays the current date, even though the application isn't active right now. That's because the ActiveX control has to activate itself when you place it on the dialog. Although the application isn't active, the ActiveX control is. This is an important troubleshooting tip when working with ActiveX controls. If you place a control on the dialog and it just sits there, you may not have it installed correctly. Obviously, you'll want to check any documentation to make sure the control is acting as expected.

The dialog box also contains a simple Edit Control. The Edit Control is 36×230 in size. You'll also want to set the Multiline property to True, the Read Only property to True, and the ID to IDC_RESULT. These property changes will make the control easier to work with later.

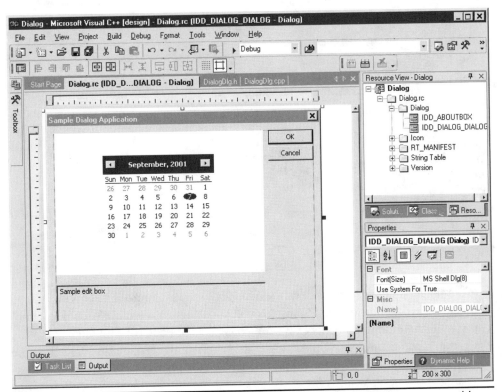

Figure 2-4   *The sample dialog-based application begins to take shape once you add the controls.*

TIP

You'll always see the current control size in the second box of the status bar on the right side of the screen. Directly to the left of this box is another box containing the selected control's position in relation to the upper-right corner of the display area. You can use the contents of these two status bar boxes to accurately size and position the control on your dialog box.

If you compiled and ran the application, at this point you'd find that it was only semifunctional. The calendar would allow you to choose new dates, and you could click on the OK button and see the dialog disappear. Other than that, the program wouldn't do much.

Before we can attach any code to the Month Calendar Control, we have to create a member variable for it. Doing so is relatively easy. CTRL-double-click on the Calendar control and you'll see an Add Member Variable Wizard like this one:

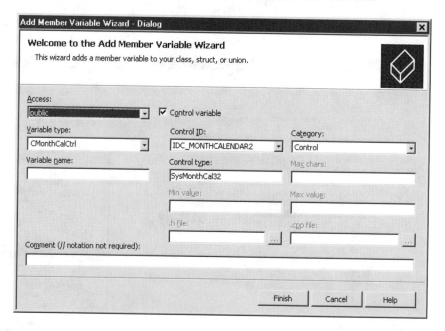

Note that you can also right-click the Month Calendar Control and choose Add Variable from the context menu to display the Add Member Variable Wizard. As you can see, the Add Member Variable Wizard enables you to control a lot more than just the variable name and type. This dialog box also contains settings for controlling the variable scope and some data entry options, such as the minimum and maximum values the variable can hold. Visual C++ will only enable the entries that apply to this control, so you'll notice that Visual C++ disabled many of them in this case. The one field that Visual C++ will never disable is Comment, which allows you to document your new memory variable. Since this is our first Month Calendar Control, type **m_Calendar1** in the Variable Name field. Type **A month selection calendar control variable.** in the Comment field. Click Finish to create the variable. Visual C++ will open the DialogDlg.H and DialogDlg.CPP files so you can see the results of the changes.

We also need to add a member variable for the Edit Control. Select the Dialog.RC tab, right-click the Edit Control, and choose Add Variable from the context menu. Type **m_Result** in the Variable Name field and **Contains the results of the user selection.** in the Comment field. Click Finish to create the variable. You now have the input and the output required for the application to run.

Detecting a user change to the control is the next thing we need to do. Select the Dialog.RC tab so you can see the dialog design area again. Right-click on the Calendar control and you'll see a context menu. Choose Add Event Handler from that menu and you'll see an Event Handler Wizard dialog like this one:

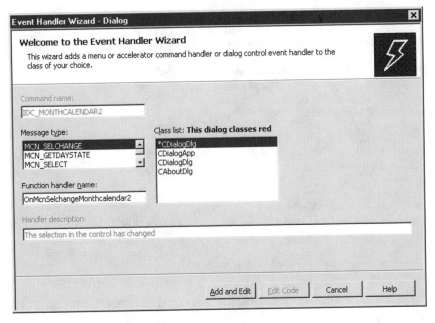

As you can see, the wizard uses a Class List field to control the content of the Message Type field. A choice in the Message Type field will change the entries in the Function Handler Name and Handler Description fields. In fact, you can't modify the content of the Handler Description field in this case. The Command Name field always contains the name of the control that you originally selected from the design area.

The Event Handler Wizard dialog contains a complete list of all the events that your control can monitor. The programmer set these events up during the design phase of the control. In this case, we'll want to monitor the MCN_SELCHANGE event. This event monitors user selections in the calendar. If you wanted to wait until the user actually made a choice, you'd use the MCN_SELECT event instead. You'll find that other calendar events monitor features such as a change in system theme.

Highlight the MCN_SELCHANGE event entry, then click on the Add and Edit button. Visual C++ will create a blank function. Now all you need to do is add some code to make it work. Listing 2-4 shows the code you'll need to make this control functional.

Listing 2-4

```
void CDialogDlg::OnMcnSelchangeMonthcalendar2(NMHDR *pNMHDR, LRESULT *pResult)
{
    CString  cSelectedDate; // Date selected by user.
    CString  cDay;          // Selected day.
    CString  cYear;         // Selected year.
    CTime    cSelDate;      // The selected date from the calendar.

    LPNMSELCHANGE pSelChange = reinterpret_cast<LPNMSELCHANGE>(pNMHDR);

    //Get the date from the calendar control.
    m_Calendar1.GetCurSel(cSelDate);

    // Get day from calendar control.
    itoa(cSelDate.GetDay(), cDay.GetBuffer(2), 10);
    cDay.ReleaseBuffer(-1);
    cSelectedDate = cDay;

    // Get month from calendar control.
    switch (cSelDate.GetMonth())
    {
    case 1:
       cSelectedDate = cSelectedDate + " January ";
       break;
    case 2:
       cSelectedDate = cSelectedDate + " February ";
       break;
    case 3:
       cSelectedDate = cSelectedDate + " March ";
       break;
    case 4:
       cSelectedDate = cSelectedDate + " April ";
       break;
    case 5:
       cSelectedDate = cSelectedDate + " May ";
       break;
```

```
case 6:
    cSelectedDate = cSelectedDate + " June ";
    break;
case 7:
    cSelectedDate = cSelectedDate + " July ";
    break;
case 8:
    cSelectedDate = cSelectedDate + " August ";
    break;
case 9:
    cSelectedDate = cSelectedDate + " September ";
    break;
case 10:
    cSelectedDate = cSelectedDate + " October ";
    break;
case 11:
    cSelectedDate = cSelectedDate + " November ";
    break;
case 12:
    cSelectedDate = cSelectedDate + " December ";
}

// Get the year.
itoa(cSelDate.GetYear(), cYear.GetBuffer(4), 10);
cYear.ReleaseBuffer(-1);
cSelectedDate = cSelectedDate + cYear;

// Display the date.
m_Result.SetWindowText("You clicked on: " + cSelectedDate);

*pResult = 0;
}
```

At this point, you can run the application and it'll actually do something. Try building and running the application. Double-click on any date and you'll see a message in the IDC_RESULT similar to the one shown in Figure 2-5. Essentially, it displays the date you selected from the Calendar control in an easy-to-read format. While this may not seem very useful now, you could easily expand this utility program in several ways. For example, you could have a little notepad pop up every time you double-clicked on a date. That way you could enter notes for each day as needed. Needless to say, you won't replace your contact manager with this utility anytime soon, but it does work very well for short notes. Utilities such as this are especially helpful on a laptop where space is limited and you don't want a large application using up your battery.

The Calendar control does provide quite a bit of added functionality—most of which we won't look at in this chapter. One thing that would be handy to have is a button for resetting the date back to today's date after you've wandered about during

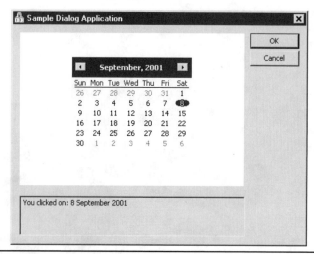

Figure 2-5   *The Sample Dialog Application displays a dialog telling you the date you selected.*

a telephone conversation. Adding such a button is easy. Just place it under the Cancel button that already appears on the dialog box. The Reset Date button has an ID of IDC_RESET_DATE and a caption of Reset Date. The dialog will look best if you position the control at 243, 39 and make it 50×14 in size.

Now that we have a button, let's add some code to it. Right-click on the button and choose Add Event Handler from the context menu. You'll see an Event Handler Wizard dialog box. Select the BN_CLICKED event, then click on Add and Edit. You'll see a blank procedure. Listing 2-5 provides the code you'll need to make the procedure work.

Listing 2-5

```
void CDialogDlg::OnBnClickedResetDate()
{
   CTime oCurrent;    // Current date and time.

   // Reset selected calendar date to today.
   m_Calendar1.SetCurSel(oCurrent.GetCurrentTime());
}
```

Now, whenever you click on the Reset Date button, the Calendar control will return you to the current month and year. While this code isn't very complicated, it shows you one way that you can add functionality to a dialog-based application without making it too unwieldy to use. Of course, even a few of these buttons could get quite cumbersome after a while.

Writing a Text-Editing, Single-Document Application

Every version of Microsoft's Wizards for Visual C++ has gotten a little better, so it shouldn't surprise you that you can get very close to producing a working application using one. However, there are a few things that a less-than-watchful eye might miss when setting up an application in the first place.

This section will look at a single-documentation application—which you could probably use for a small text editor or other lightweight, general-purpose document editor. In this case, we'll create a rich text editor that really doesn't do much more right now than allow you to edit text. Later in the book we'll add functionality to this program and make it something a little more worthwhile.

Creating the Basic Application

Begin this project by selecting New Project on the Start page to display the New Project dialog. Choose the MFC Application project type. Type a name in the Project Name field. The sample application uses Sngl_Doc as an application name, but you can use anything you like. Click OK and you'll see the MFC Application Wizard dialog. Select Application Type. Choose the Single Document option.

Some applications need to act as containers for data generated by other applications. For example, your word processor might need to hold the graphics created by your CAD application. Visual C++ .NET handles this in the same way as previous versions— by using a container selection option. Click Compound Document Support. You'll see a dialog box similar to the one shown here:

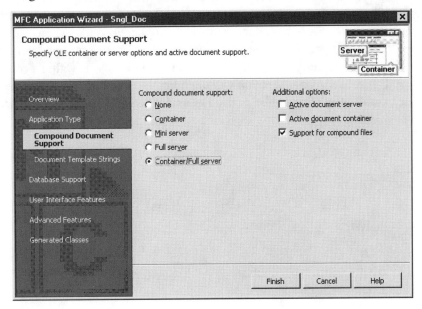

This dialog determines the level of OLE support you'll add to your application. The more support you add, the larger your application will be. The basic level of support is to act as a container. A container can act as a client and store linked and embedded objects. The next level of support, mini-server, enables you to create compound documents. A mini server can't work as a stand-alone. In addition, it can work only with embedded documents. A full server does have the full OLE capability to work as a server, but it can't act as a container. An application that provides server capabilities would work much like Microsoft Paint. You can embed or link a Microsoft Paint document into your application, but Microsoft Paint can't hold objects created by other applications. Finally, the Both Container and Server option gives your application a full array of local OLE support. You can use it as both a server and a client. However, this kind of application won't work with an Internet browser—it's not designed as an ActiveX Document server.

TIP

This is a good time to point out that choosing a single-document application type has enabled more of the tabs for the MFC Application Wizard. For example, you can add database support to your application. We'll spend quite a bit of time looking at this topic in Part 2 of the book, so I won't cover it here.

Notice that there are three check boxes to the right of the Compound Document Support options. If you check the first box, Visual C++ will add support to make your application an ActiveX Document Server. An Active Document Server has the ability to create and manage ActiveX documents. The second check box, Active Document Container, allows your application to contain ActiveX documents within its frame. In essence, you'll be able to host documents from applications like Microsoft Word or Excel. Visual C++ enables the Support for Compound Files option by default. Selecting this option forces your application to load all of the objects within a compound document. This means your application will run faster, but it will also use more memory. Select the Container/Full Server, the Active Document Server, and the Active Document Container options.

NOTE

Visual C++ 6.0 had this problem: if you selected any of the compound document support options, it would remove certain base classes from view. For example, you couldn't select the CRichEditView class. Visual Studio .NET appears to have fixed this problem, at least as of the time of writing. If you find that you can't select the base class you need in the Generated Classes tab, then deselect the container options and try again.

When you select the Active Document Server option, the MFC Application Wizard will tell you that you need to create a file extension for your application. You'll do this by creating template strings that define your application document. Click the Document Template String tab and you'll see a dialog box like the one shown here:

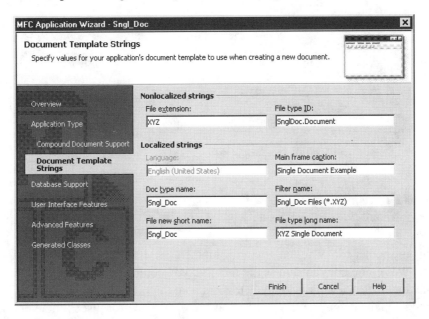

Set up your Advanced Options dialog as shown in the illustration. What you'll end up with is an application that uses the XYZ file extension. The title bar for your application will read "Single Document Example." Every time you see a File Open or File Save dialog, the filter field will read "XYZ Single Document Files (*.xyz)." Finally, when you display the properties dialog for a document you create with this application, it'll inform you that this is an "XYZ Single Document" type of document.

There's a final step in creating this application. We need to decide what type of display to create. You'll do that by adjusting the application classes. Click Generated Classes and you'll see a dialog box that looks similar to this one:

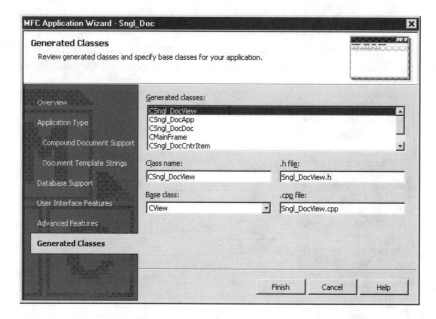

This is another tricky application development area. If you didn't take a good look at what was going on, you'd miss the fact that you could use any base class you like for the document view class. Why is that such an important consideration? If you were to keep the default setting, you'd have to write code for just about every action your application performed on the document. That's probably fine if you're creating an entirely new kind of document, but most programs just don't do that. What you really want to do is make an application that acts sort of like another application but offers features that application lacks. In our case, we're creating a text editor, so it doesn't make sense to use CView (the default base class). Using the CEditView or CRichEditView class as a base class will save us a lot of work, because the application will already know how to act as a simple word processor right out of the package. You won't even have to add any code to get this functionality.

To show you just how this works, choose the CRichEditView base class for the CSngl_DocView class in our application. Click on Finish to complete your setup. Visual C++ will create the application for you.

Now build the application and start it. You'll find that you can type text and save it in an XYZ document. This application will read other text and RTF documents with the proper code additions. You can easily expand the application in other ways as well. For example, since it relies on the rich edit control, you can add text formatting and colors. The OLE capabilities that we've added mean that you'll be able to insert graphics as needed. In fact, what you've really ended up with is something that has a lot of potential after very little work.

In case you haven't noticed by now, this particular sample didn't require one ounce of coding on your part. The result was good and quite unexpected for a C programmer. Figure 2-6 shows the results for this application so far, but count on seeing this application again as the chapter progresses.

Working with Resources

Resources are a central part of working with applications. What's a resource? It's easiest to think of a resource as anything you can "bolt onto" the application to make it work better, look nice, or perform some additional task. For example, icons, cursors,

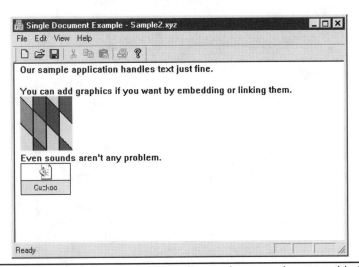

Figure 2-6   *Our sample application works well considering we haven't added any code to it.*

and bitmaps are all examples of resources. The application consumes these resources in order to improve the appearance of the application as a whole.

Of course, graphics are the resource that everyone can *see* as a resource. However, your application can consume other types of resources. For example, menus, string tables, and applications themselves are all forms of consumable resources. Your application uses all of these resources to add functionality that the user will see as a feature.

Now that you have a better idea of what resources are, let's spend some time talking about them. The following sections provide a brief overview of resources. Because we'll use resources throughout the book, this brief overview only acquaints you with the resources and shows how you'd use them. You'll find detailed information as the book progresses.

Where Did OpenAs Go?

The Visual Studio IDE normally makes good decisions on how to open the files we want to edit. For example, when you open a RC file, the IDE knows that you'll probably want to use a GUI environment to modify the objects the file contains. However, there are times when you need to open RC files in a text editor to see the code the IDE automatically generates for you (and, in some cases, tweak it). Some of you may have noticed that the Open dialog box no longer contains the Open as field shown in this Visual C++ 6.0 IDE here.

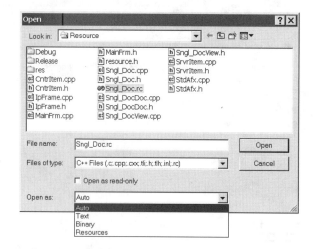

Visual Studio .NET still allows you to open a file using any of a number of editors. It actually gives you more options from which to choose. The difference is in the way you access the editors. Look for the small down arrow next to the Open button when you display the Open Files dialog box. Click this arrow and you'll see a drop-down list box with two options. Choose Open With... and you'll see an Open With dialog box, like the one shown here:

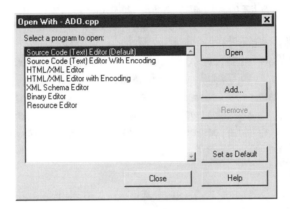

Notice that you get several new entries with Visual Studio .NET, including two HTML/XML editor options. This new method of opening a file using an alternative editor gives you greater flexibility than ever before. The only problem is that the feature is somewhat hidden from view. Just remember to look for the down arrow next to the Open button. In fact, you may want to start observing all of the buttons within the Visual Studio .NET IDE more closely.

Application Icons

Every MFC application program you create with Visual C++ will have a default application icon. In fact, the icon will always have the same name: IDR_MAINFRAME. You'll find that this icon not only defines how the program icon looks within Explorer (or any other application that displays program icons), but it also affects the internal representation of your program as well. For example, the About box normally displays this icon as part of its presentation of application information to the user. All of the MFC applications you create will also have the same icon to start with.

A second default icon appears when you decide to create a document with your application, as we did in the Sngl_Doc example earlier in the chapter. In that case, you'll see an IDR for each of the document types you've created. In our example, it's IDR_Sngl_DocTYPE. They all use the same icon to start with, though. Unlike the application icon, it's almost mandatory to customize your document icons if your application supports more than one document type.

NOTE

Visual C++ .NET has added a lot of capacity to the icons you use for presenting your application to other people. The default icon you see when you open an icon resource is only the tip of the iceberg. Right-click within the icon area and choose Current Icon Types. You'll see a list of the icons that Visual C++ defined for the application. The main icon sizes are 16×16, 32×32, and 48×48. Windows 2000 won't use the 48×48 size, but this size does appear in Windows XP. Color depths include 16, 256, and 16-bit color. In short, you need to modify nine icons to make the typical application ready for use under any Windows operating system. Fortunately, you can always remove icons you don't want to define from the file by right-clicking in the icon window and choosing Delete Image Type from the context menu. This will remove the currently displayed icon.

Besides the ability to draw, you need to know a little about the tools at your disposal if you want to create effective icons. All the tools you'll require appear at the top of the IDE window on the Image Editor toolbar. They include a set of standard drawing tools.

You'll also find a Color toolbar on the left side of the display. Double-click any color and you'll see an Adjust Colors dialog box that enables you to change the color palette used for your icon. The Color toolbar also contains two special colors you need to know about. They're easy to find since they use a monitor symbol in place of a color square.

The upper monitor creates a clear area. In other words, you'll see whatever appears below the area on the desktop or wherever else you place the program icon. The lower monitor creates an area that uses the same color as the user's window foreground color selection. In other words, as you change the window color, the color of this area in your icon will change as well. You'll see the current foreground and background color to the left of the two monitors. The foreground color appears in the upper square, while the background color appears in the lower square.

Let's look at a sample of what you can do with these two icons. Figure 2-7 shows sample icons I drew for my version of the program. They may not be very artistic compared to other icons you've seen—a definite argument for having an artist on your staff—but they're better than the default icons you get with Visual C++. Obviously, you can customize your icons any way you want. Try using a variety of colors.

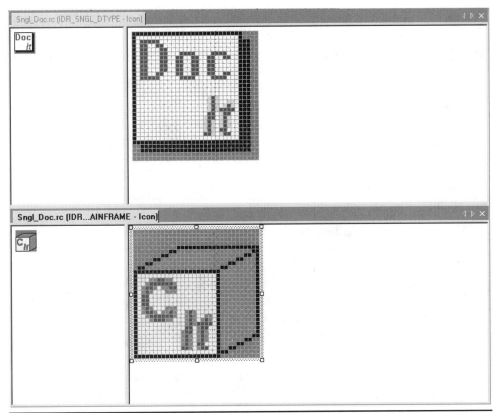

Figure 2-7   *These icons identify your application and associated data files to anyone who uses them.*

Make sure you experiment with the two custom colors that I mentioned, since they're especially important when creating icons. (Many programmers create strange looking icons that don't really fit in with the rest of the icons on your desktop because they don't know how to use the two special colors effectively.)

CAUTION

Never assume that you can use any icon (or other graphic for that matter) you find on the Internet in a program you plan to sell or give to other people. Always assume that these resources are good for inspiration and not much else until you've gotten permission in writing from the originator to use them in any other way. Copyright infringement is a serious offense and somewhat easy to commit given the open environment that the Internet provides. The best rule of thumb is to either create your own icons or license them for commercial use from a reliable source.

Notice that I used the clear color on both icons and that I've given them a 3-D look. Again, it's not that they're very artistic, but they do give the user a specific feel for my program. Obviously, the clear coloring shows up differently inside the editor than when the user sees (or actually fails to see) it. Make sure you compile your program again after you've changed the icon, or it won't show up in Explorer. Running the program is a good idea too, since Visual C++ does make registry entries for you when you run the program the first time. Finally, make sure you use the View | Refresh command within Explorer. Otherwise, you'll see the old icons that Explorer stored previously.

BROWSER ALERT

If you need some inspiration for creating icons, the Internet has many useful sites you should check out. One of the better sites is **http://crab.rutgers.edu/icons_new/icons.html.** *Although this site contains mostly GIF icons, the 3,000 examples it provides should give you more than a few ideas. Most of these icons deal with popular topics like The Simpsons. Fortunately, the designer indexed the icons so you don't have to dig through all 3,000 at one time. You can also find a good number of topic-specific sites. For example,* **http://www.geocities.com/Area51/8604/xfiles.htm** *contains a set of X-Files-specific icons (in ICO format).*

Version Information

You might skip the version information resource automatically provided by Visual C++ without really thinking about it. At one time, this information was pretty much hidden from everyone but programmers who knew how to retrieve it. The problem is that, with the Explorer interface provided by Windows 9X and Windows NT/2000/XP, you can't afford to skip the version information anymore. All you need to do now to display the version information provided by an application is right-click the program icon in Explorer and then choose Properties from the context menu. Select the Version tab of the Properties dialog and here's what you'll see:

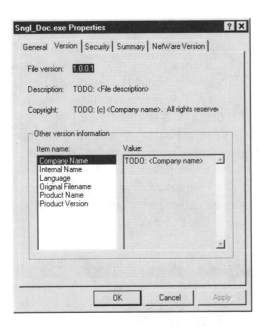

As you can see, the default version information is a lot less than informative. If you leave it in place, users won't know even what company they're dealing with. Since more and more users are becoming aware of what the Properties dialog has to offer, it's becoming more important for programmers to put the right kind of information in here.

TIP

Filling out the version information for your application doesn't have to be a one-way street. You can use this information to fill out other areas of your application as well, which means that you'll only have to change the information in one place to keep it current. We'll look at how you can use this technique for the About box in this section of the chapter, but you'll likely want to use it in other places as well.

Let's take a look at the version information for our sample application. You'll always find the default information under the Version folder in Resource View. The default resource name is VS_VERSION_INFO. Figure 2-8 shows what the default version information looks like. The entries above the heavy line normally reflect your application settings. You usually won't need to modify them. It's the entries below the heavy line that begin with Block Header that are of interest.

You can modify any of the text entries by double-clicking them. Visual C++ will open an edit box that you can use to change the information. At a minimum, you'll want to update the CompanyName, LegalCopyright, and ProductName fields. I normally add some information to the Comments field as well. For example, it's handy to know whom to contact regarding an application or other executable, so I usually add my name and e-mail address. Exactly what you add to this area depends on company policy,

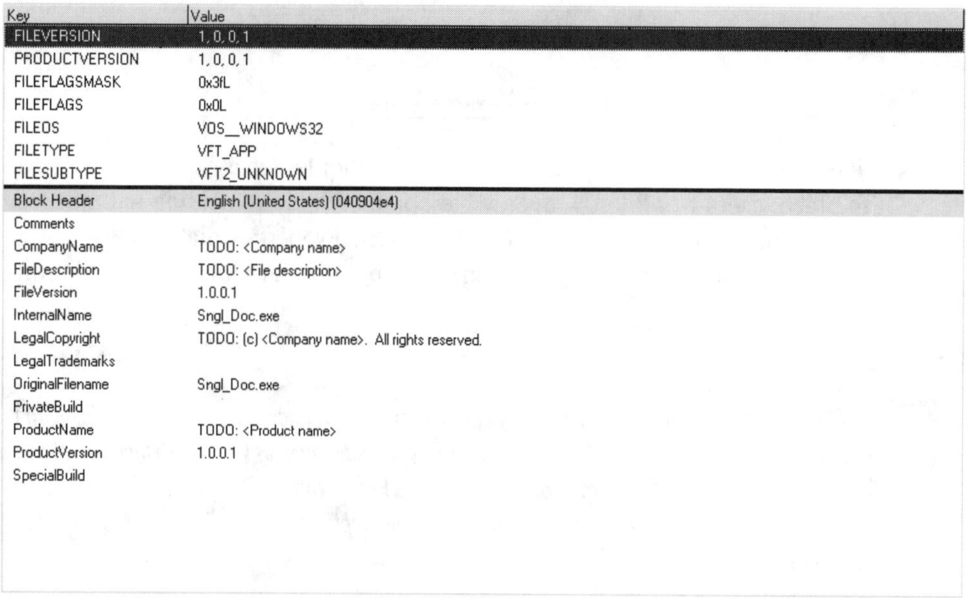

Key	Value
FILEVERSION	1, 0, 0, 1
PRODUCTVERSION	1, 0, 0, 1
FILEFLAGSMASK	0x3fL
FILEFLAGS	0x0L
FILEOS	VOS__WINDOWS32
FILETYPE	VFT_APP
FILESUBTYPE	VFT2_UNKNOWN
Block Header	English (United States) (040904e4)
Comments	
CompanyName	TODO: <Company name>
FileDescription	TODO: <File description>
FileVersion	1.0.0.1
InternalName	Sngl_Doc.exe
LegalCopyright	TODO: (c) <Company name>. All rights reserved.
LegalTrademarks	
OriginalFilename	Sngl_Doc.exe
PrivateBuild	
ProductName	TODO: <Product name>
ProductVersion	1.0.0.1
SpecialBuild	

Figure 2-8   *Modify the default version information to match the actual information for your company and product.*

legal needs, and personal preference. Here's what my modified version information looks like when viewed in the Properties dialog:

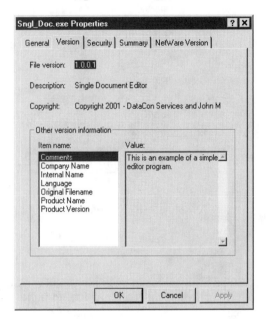

Working with Accelerators and Menus

Menus and accelerators go hand in hand. The two resource types are designed to work together to make it easy for the user to get tasks done. You all know what a menu is— it's the physical representation of a hierarchical command structure. An accelerator provides the shortcuts in that structure to speed up certain operations. For example, to create a new file, you can normally use the File | New command or the accelerator CTRL-N. Either method produces the same results.

Visual C++ stores menus and accelerators as two different resources. Figure 2-9 shows the main menu and associated accelerator for our sample application. It's interesting to note that both resources use the same name, IDR_MAINFRAME. You'll want to remember this fact because the resource name links the two resources (menu and accelerator) together.

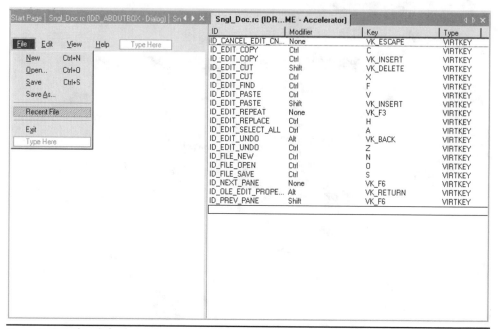

Figure 2-9   *The default menu provides the standard functions that you'd expect. An accelerator resource is linked to its associated menu through the name you assign it.*

Let's look at how menus and accelerators work together. Adding a new entry to an existing accelerator resource is easy.

1. Right-click in the Accelerator window, then select New Accelerator from the context menu. Visual C++ will create a new accelerator entry for you.

2. Double-click the ID field. Choose an ID from the drop-down list box. Menu IDs normally use a combination of the menu levels you need to pass in order to get to the desired menu entry prefaced by ID. For example, if you want to create an accelerator for the View | Toolbar command (as I did for the example), you'd choose ID_VIEW_TOOLBAR in the ID field. You'll want to associate a speed key with the accelerator entry.

3. Double-click the Modifier field and choose a modifier for your control key. Double-click the Key field and type or select a speed key for the accelerator. You can also choose between an ASCII and a virtual keystroke (VirtKey). For the purposes of this example, I used CTRL-T, so I selected CTRL in the Modifier field and "T" in the Key field.

If you compiled and ran the program right now, the accelerator you just added would work without a hitch. In fact, you may want to do just that. However, the user wouldn't have any idea there there's an accelerator available for executing a menu command quickly. To add the accelerator keystroke to a menu, you need to modify the current menu.

Adding new text to a menu command is easy. Open the View menu, then click on the Toolbar entry. The Properties pane will automatically fill with the properties for this menu entry. What we need to do is change the Caption field to consider the new accelerator. You can use all of the C and Windows formatting characters that you could normally use for text. Changing the Caption field to read "&Toolbar\tCtrl-T" tells Windows that you want to see the word "Toolbar," with the "T" underlined, then a space, and finally CTRL-T to tell the user what accelerator key to use for this menu command.

So, what do you do if you want to add new menu entries? Just select a blank spot on either the menu bar or an existing menu and start typing. For this example, we'll add a Format entry to the menu bar with one option, Font. (Remember to type **&Format** and **&Font** so that the first letter of each entry will be underlined.) Once you have the new menu items added, grab the Format entry and move it to the left of the Help menu. Your menu should look like this:

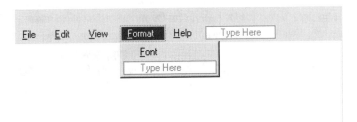

Now we need to add some code to make this new menu entry functional. Make sure your Font menu ID is set to ID_FORMAT_FONT or it might not work. Right-click the Font entry, and then choose Add Event Handler. You'll see an Event Handler Wizard dialog box. Select COMMAND from the Message Type list. Click Add an Edit. Listing 2-6 shows the code required to add font characteristics to our program. Only a rich text editing screen (CRichEdit control) will have this ability in native form, although you could add it to a CEdit control as well.

Listing 2-6

```
void CMainFrame::OnFormatFont()
{
    CFontDialog     oDialog;     //Create a font dialog.
```

```
    //Display the Font common dialog box.
    oDialog.DoModal();
}
```

As you can see, adding the ability to work with fonts in our example is almost too easy. If you compile the example now, you'll be able to change the default font or select text and change the font that way. Here's an example of the ways in which you can change fonts now that we've added this capability to the sample program:

TIP

You don't have to work all that hard to display most of the menus you need for an application. All you really need to do is use the right IDs for the various menu options and associated buttons on the toolbars. Unfortunately, many of these special IDs aren't documented right now. For example, if you want to implement a font dialog without doing any programming, make sure that the ID for the menu item is ID_FORMAT_FONT. Likewise, use the same ID for any toolbar button you add to the application. You can find all of the special IDs, documented or not, in the AFXRES.H file located in the MFC\INCLUDE folder.

Working with Toolbars

If accelerators are the keyboard method for speeding up program access, then toolbars are the mouse counterpart. You'll find that toolbars have become less of an accessory and more of an essential part of the user interface. However, toolbars can quickly become too cumbersome to use if you crowd them with a host of buttons that may or may not fit the user's needs. One of the ways around this problem is to create multiple toolbars and then allow the user to decide which ones they need.

Working with toolbars is just about as easy as working with menus and accelerators. In this case, though, you have to create some linkage between the toolbar and its associated menu command. The default toolbar, IDR_MAINFRAME, includes some of the more common buttons, like the ones needed to open files or create new ones.

Let's begin this example by creating a new toolbar—one designed to allow the user to format text. Right-click on the Toolbar folder in Resource View, then select Insert Toolbar from the context menu. Visual C++ will automatically create a new toolbar for you. However, the name it gives (IDR_TOOLBAR1) isn't very descriptive. Click the IDR_TOOLBAR1 entry so you can change the properties in the Properties pane.

Type **IDR_FORMAT** in the ID field. (Don't worry about changing the File Name field; it changes automatically when you change the ID field.) Press ENTER to make the change permanent.

Now we need to add some buttons to this toolbar. The buttons will allow the user to perform a variety of tasks without resorting to using the keyboard or moving through the menu system. Here's the sample toolbar we'll use for this example (the buttons represent underline, strikethrough, bold, italic, and font dialog):

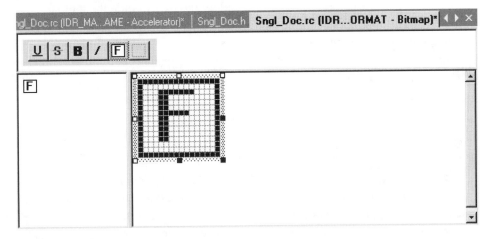

Adding the buttons to the toolbar won't do very much. All you really have is a bitmap of what you want to do in the future. Click the Underline button so you can see its properties in the Properties pane. Modify the ID field to read ID_UNDERLINE and the Prompt field to read "Underline." Change all of the other buttons in a similar way—ID_STRIKETHROUGH (Strikethrough), ID_BOLD (Bold), ID_ITALIC (Italic), and ID_FORMAT_FONT (Font Dialog). Make sure you type all of the IDs carefully or you'll have problems making the buttons work later. The reason I'm using ID_ FORMAT_FONT for the last button is to reduce the amount of coding you'll need to create. Using this ID means that you don't have to add one line of code to make this button functional. Visual C++ will automatically take care of this button for you through MFC.

It's time to associate the toolbar with the rest of the application. You need to create a message map as a starting point. Listing 2-7 shows the entries you'll need to make in MainFrm.CPP.

Listing 2-7

```
BEGIN_MESSAGE_MAP(CMainFrame, CFrameWnd)
    ON_WM_CREATE()
    ON_COMMAND(ID_BOLD, OnBold)
    ON_COMMAND(ID_ITALIC, OnItalic)
    ON_COMMAND(ID_STRIKETHROUGH, OnStrikethrough)
    ON_COMMAND(ID_UNDERLINE, OnUnderline)
    ON_COMMAND(ID_VIEW_FORMATTOOLBAR, OnViewFormattoolbar)
END_MESSAGE_MAP()
```

As you can see, every entry associates a button with a function that we'll eventually add to the application. Also, notice the ID_VIEW_FORMATTOOLBAR entry. We'll use this entry near the end of this section to allow the user to hide the toolbar.

You'll also need to declare all of the functions we'll use in the MainFrm.H file. Listing 2-8 shows these entries.

Listing 2-8

```
    void OnBold(void);
    void OnItalic(void);
    void OnStrikethrough(void);
    void OnUnderline(void);
    void OnViewFormattoolbar(void);
```

We can add code to the program now to make the buttons functional. Click on any of the member function names (like OnUnderline), then click the Edit Code button. Visual C++ will display the code editing area. You'll see the function shells that we've just created. Listing 2-9 shows the code you'll need to add.

Listing 2-9

```
void CMainFrame::OnBold()
{
    CRichEditView*    poView;          // Create a variable to hold our view.

    // Get the active view from the current window. Typecast it as a
    // CRichEditView rather than a CView, the standard return value.
    poView = (CRichEditView*) GetActiveView();

    // Change the font settings as needed.
    poView->OnCharEffect(CFM_BOLD, CFE_BOLD);
}
```

```
void CMainFrame::OnItalic()
{
    CRichEditView*    poView;         // Create a variable to hold our view.
    CHARFORMAT        cfFont;         // Create a structure for the font data.

    // Get the active view from the current window. Typecast it as a
    // CRichEditView rather than a CView, the standard return value.
    poView = (CRichEditView*) GetActiveView();

    // Get the current font settings, then change them to Italic.
    cfFont = poView->GetCharFormatSelection();
    cfFont.dwMask |= CFM_ITALIC;
    cfFont.dwEffects |= CFE_ITALIC;

    // Change the font settings as needed.
    poView->SetCharFormat(cfFont);
}

void CMainFrame::OnStrikethrough()
{
    CRichEditView*    poView;         // Create a variable to hold our view.

    // Get the active view from the current window. Typecast it as a
    // CRichEditView rather than a CView, the standard return value.
    poView = (CRichEditView*) GetActiveView();

    // Change the font settings as needed.
    poView->OnCharEffect(CFM_STRIKEOUT, CFE_STRIKEOUT);
}

void CMainFrame::OnUnderline()
{
    CRichEditView*    poView;         // Create a variable to hold our view.

    // Get the active view from the current window. Typecast it as a
    // CRichEditView rather than a CView, the standard return value.
    poView = (CRichEditView*) GetActiveView();

    // Change the font settings as needed.
    poView->OnCharEffect(CFM_UNDERLINE, CFE_UNDERLINE);
}
```

As you can see from the source code, there are two distinct methods for changing
the font attributes you see for a selected group of characters. The first is the easier
of the two. All you need to do is get the active view—the part of the window that
contains the text that the user is editing. Once you have the view, you can use a
special function named **OnCharEffect()** to change the font attributes. To make
this function actually work, you'll need to provide the same font attributes for

both arguments. (The CHARFORMAT documentation contains a complete list of attributes and associated defines.)

The second method requires a little more work, but it's also more flexible. In this case, you still have to get a copy of the active view. However, this time you use it to fill a CHARFORMAT structure with the current font characteristics. This structure includes everything you need to know, like the font name and color, along with font attributes like bold and italic. Once you get the CHARFORMAT structure filled, just change the members you want to change on-screen and then use the **SetCharFormat()** function to make the actual change.

In most cases, you'll want to use the first method I showed you for changing font attributes like bold and italic. It's a lot less code and you don't have to fiddle with a structure to get the job done. However, it's nice to know that the CHARFORMAT structure is available in case you need it to make more extensive changes on-screen.

We have a toolbar and some code to make it work. Our sample program is still lacking one important feature. If you run it right now, you won't even see the toolbar. The final step is to add a menu item and some code to make using the toolbar easy. Let's begin with the menu item. All I did was add a new menu item to the View menu using the same procedure we talked about for the Format menu. In the Menu Item Properties dialog, I used ID_VIEW_FORMATTOOLBAR as an ID, &Format Toolbar as a caption, and "Show or hide the format toolbar\nToggle Format ToolBar" as a prompt. You'll also want to check the Checked check box since we'll display the toolbar as a default.

There are three places you need to add code for the toolbar. The first bit of code appears in the MAINFRM.H file. You need to add a new variable in the Protected section, right under the initial toolbar variable. The new variable code looks like this:

```
CToolBar m_wndToolBar2;
```

The next bit of code appears in the MAINFRAME.CPP file (see Listing 2-10). This is the code that sets the toolbar characteristics and makes it visible when you start the program. Notice that there are some special coding considerations for making the toolbar dockable (so that you can move it from place to place within the application).

Listing 2-10

```
int CMainFrame::OnCreate(LPCREATESTRUCT lpCreateStruct)
{
    if (CFrameWnd::OnCreate(lpCreateStruct) == -1)
        return -1;

    if (!m_wndToolBar.CreateEx(this,
                          TBSTYLE_FLAT,
                          WS_CHILD | WS_VISIBLE | CBRS_TOP
```

```
                          | CBRS_GRIPPER | CBRS_TOOLTIPS |
                          CBRS_FLYBY | CBRS_SIZE_DYNAMIC) ||
        !m_wndToolBar.LoadToolBar(IDR_MAINFRAME))
    {
        TRACE0("Failed to create toolbar\n");
        return -1;       // fail to create
    }

if (!m_wndToolBar2.CreateEx(this,
                            TBSTYLE_FLAT,
                            WS_CHILD | WS_VISIBLE | CBRS_TOP
                            | CBRS_GRIPPER | CBRS_TOOLTIPS |
                            CBRS_FLYBY | CBRS_SIZE_DYNAMIC) ||
    !m_wndToolBar2.LoadToolBar(IDR_FORMAT))
  {
      TRACE0("Failed to create toolbar\n");
      return -1;       // fail to create
  }

    if (!m_wndStatusBar.Create(this) ||
        !m_wndStatusBar.SetIndicators(indicators,
          sizeof(indicators)/sizeof(UINT)))
    {
        TRACE0("Failed to create status bar\n");
        return -1;       // fail to create
    }

    // TODO: Delete these three lines if you don't want the toolbar to be dockable
    m_wndToolBar.EnableDocking(CBRS_ALIGN_ANY);
    m_wndToolBar2.EnableDocking(CBRS_ALIGN_ANY);
    EnableDocking(CBRS_ALIGN_ANY);
    DockControlBar(&m_wndToolBar);
DockControlBar(&m_wndToolBar2);

    return 0;
}
```

There are three main areas where you need to work with the toolbar code. The first creates the toolbar and then loads the IDR_FORMAT toolbar into it. If this procedure fails, you'll get a "fail to create" message before the application even starts. The second area defines the toolbar style. I used the default settings, which allow the user to resize and move the toolbar around. Tool tips will also appear when the mouse is rested over a button. The final section of code enables toolbar docking, defines where the user can dock the toolbar, and actually docks the toolbar we've created. At this point, your toolbar is visible; the user can move it around and can remove it from sight using the Close box.

Getting the menu command (View | Format Toolbar) to work is easy. Listing 2-11 shows the code you'll need to get this part of the program to work.

Listing 2-11

```
void CMainFrame::OnViewFormattoolbar()
{
    CMenu*     poMenu;            // Create a pointer to the current menu.

    poMenu = GetMenu();     // Get the menu.

    // Determine if the View | Format Toolbar option is checked. If it
    // is, then hide the format toolbar and uncheck the option. Otherwise,
    // display the toolbar and check the menu item.

    if (poMenu->GetMenuState(ID_VIEW_FORMATTOOLBAR, MF_CHECKED))
    {
        ShowControlBar(&m_wndToolBar2, FALSE, FALSE);
        poMenu->CheckMenuItem(ID_VIEW_FORMATTOOLBAR, MF_UNCHECKED);
    }
    else
    {
        ShowControlBar(&m_wndToolBar2, TRUE, FALSE);
        poMenu->CheckMenuItem(ID_VIEW_FORMATTOOLBAR, MF_CHECKED);
    }
}
```

As you can see, we begin by getting a copy of the CWnd class menu object. Once we have the menu object, it's easy to figure out if the Format Toolbar option is currently checked. If the option is checked, the toolbar is visible. You'll use the **ShowControlBar()** function with the second and third parameters set to false to make the toolbar invisible. The **CheckMenuItem()** function allows you to remove the check mark from the View | Format Toolbar menu option. Conversely, you use the opposite procedure to make the toolbar visible and check the menu option again.

Go ahead and compile the application one more time so you can check out the various features we've just added. Make sure you try out all of the formatting options and the ability to dock and hide toolbars. Obviously, this application isn't as complex as some of the programs you'll see out there right now, but it does make good use of resources.

Working with Threads

Developers are constantly looking for ways of using machine resources more efficiently without spending more time developing applications. One way to do this is to write an application to perform more than one task as a time. Windows provides this ability using threads. A *thread* is essentially a single subject of execution within an application (also known as a single path of execution). In other words, a single application can do more than one task at a time. For example, it could print and spell check a document in the background while the user is typing in the foreground.

NOTE

You actually need to be aware of two entities when talking about threads. The term thread describes one set of contiguous instructions for performing a single task. A process, on the other hand, describes the application as a whole. Every executing application has at least one thread and one process. There's never more than one process for an application, but Win32 applications can always produce more than one thread. The distinction between processes and threads will become more clear as the chapter progresses.

Threads don't perform any kind of magic. They won't make the user's machine any faster, and the processor still can't perform more than one task at a time. In other words, threads don't allow a machine to perform more than one task simultaneously unless that machine has the resources (that is, multiple processors) to perform multiple tasks simultaneously.

What threads do allow is an application to use machine resources more efficiently. They also provide better response times for the user by performing some application housekeeping tasks in the background. For example, a document can print in the background while the user works in the foreground because the user isn't likely to require full use of the processor all of the time. Making use of idle time while the user thinks allows the machine to work more efficiently. Since the processor only services a particular task during idle time, the user regains use of the machine immediately after requesting that the application perform the task.

This chapter provides you with a wealth of information about how threads work and how you can use them in your applications to make things run more efficiently. It's important to understand how threads get used in various types of project types as well as to be aware of the kinds of threads you have at your disposal when using Visual C++ and MFC. (There isn't any actual distinction between threads from a pure Win32 perspective.)

We'll also explore safety considerations when using threads. For example, critical sections ensure that two calling processes don't try to use the same portion of code at the same time. However, even if you have your code properly written to ensure thread safety, the developer of the libraries that you use may not have had the same considerations in mind. This chapter also explores the things you need to consider to ensure thread safety when working with local libraries.

Finally, we'll spend time working through two example programs. The first program shows you how to use threads within an application. The second program will deal with using threads within libraries. Obviously, part of this example is to show the library in action, so that you can actually see the effect of using threads in this environment.

Thread Uses

Theoretically, you can use threads in any Visual C++ application, including something as small as an ActiveX component. Using threads in the managed environment is similar to the unmanaged environment in that you have the same thread types to consider and the underlying process is the same. In short, threads are a nearly universal solution to some types of problems.

Threads don't necessarily need to be large or complex to make an application more efficient and responsive to user needs. In fact, you can use threads to perform small maintenance tasks in the background at regular intervals—tasks that you may not want to interrupt your main application to do. A thread can also replace timer-related tasks in some cases. In other words, threads aren't limited to performing any particular task.

However, you do need to consider some issues before you start using threads for every small task that your application may need to perform. It's important to use threads correctly in order to avoid some common problems that developers seem to face with them. The following list provides you with some guidelines on what you should think about before using threads.

▶ **Debugging**   The biggest consideration from a developer perspective is that threads greatly increase the difficulty of debugging an application. A thread can actually hide bugs or, at least, make them more difficult to find, since you have to watch more than one thread of execution at a time.

▶ **Development**   Most developers are used to thinking about application programming in a linear fashion. In other words, given a specific event, the application will perform a series of steps to handle it. Using a multiple-thread approach forces the programmer to think about application processes in parallel, rather than in a linear fashion.

▶ **True efficiency**   While it's true that placing some tasks into background threads can make use of idle time in the application, there are situations when there isn't any idle time to exploit. In this situation, you'll find that the application is actually less efficient than before because there's a certain amount of overhead and housekeeping associated with using multiple threads. In other words, use threads only in situations when you anticipate there will be some amount of idle time to exploit.

▶ **Reliability**   Multiple threads of execution don't necessarily make an application failure prone, but there are more failure points to consider. Any time you add more failure points to anything, it becomes less reliable. There's a greater probability that the application will break simply because there are more things that can go wrong with it.

▶ **Unexpected side effects**   No matter how carefully you craft a multithreaded application, there are going to be side effects that you have to deal with, especially if the threads in the application interact. Even if you make your application thread safe and use critical sections, there's a chance that two threads will try to access the same variable at the same time in an unanticipated way. Not only do these unexpected side effects increase development and debugging time, they make it more likely that a user will come across a problem that you can't duplicate with your setup. In other words, multithreaded applications will more than likely increase application support costs.

Now that you have a good overview of the way in which you can use threads in general, let's look at some specific multithreaded usage types. The following sections will explore the three most common ways that you'll see multiple threads in use: applications, DLLs, and system services. Each of these areas represents a major application type. We'll explore two of these multithreaded usage examples, applications and DLLs, later in the chapter.

NOTE

Of the three major uses for threading, you can use the managed techniques only for applications. While you can create managed DLLs using Visual C++, they lack the global perspective of native executable files—you can use them only with managed applications. If you plan to put effort into a DLL that requires a thread, it's best to use unmanaged programming techniques so you can use the DLL with a wider variety of applications. One of the strengths of Visual C++ is that it enables you to create both native (unmanaged) and managed DLLs. Under no circumstances, should you attempt to create a service using managed code.

Applications

We've already explored this topic to some extent. Applications can benefit from multiple threads of execution in a number of ways. In fact, some of those ways will seem quite natural from a programming perspective because the tasks in question can be broken away from the main thread of execution quite easily. The following list will give you some ideas on how you can use multiple threads with applications:

▶ **Printing**   This major task can always benefit from multiple threads in any application. Queuing a print job takes time, which means that the user is sitting and staring at the screen, doing nothing at all. In fact, some print jobs take enough time that the user would give up trying to use the computer at all and do something else while waiting. Printing in the background in a separate thread is always an efficient way to handle this task.

TIP

There are probably a few things you should consider not adding to background threads, simply because it's not feasible to do so. The one rule of thumb you should use is whether the user will need to interact directly with the thread. In many cases, you should handle anything that requires direct interaction on a constant basis as part of the main thread. On the other hand, anything the user can set once, then allow the computer to complete is a good candidate for a separate thread. Make sure the application will realize an efficiency gain and the user increased responsiveness any time you create a thread. A thread that causes the entire machine to slow is somewhat counterproductive, and you should consider running the task as quickly as possible to reduce system down time.

▶ **As the user types**   There are many tasks that fall into the "as the user types" category, but the two most common are spelling and grammar checks. Many applications offer the ability to check the user's spelling and grammar as they type, which reduces the need to check the whole document later. Of course, there are a lot of less common tasks that fall into this category as well. For example, you could check the validity of an equation as the user types it or make sure that a database entry is correct. For that matter, you could even suggest (as some applications do) a completed entry for the user based on past input.

▶ **Repetition**   Repagination and other repetitive tasks can always occur as background threads. There isn't any need to take up the foreground task's time with things like updating the application clock. Most repetitive, continuous tasks can be relegated to a background thread.

▶ **Data saves**   Most applications now include an automatic save feature simply because many users are very poor at saving data themselves. It's not hard to figure out why—the user is engrossed in getting their document completed and simply forget to perform the data save. An automatic data saving feature can allow the user to complete a document without worrying about power failures or other computer glitches that can cause data to disappear.

▶ **Updates**   As users rely more and more on remote computing, their ability to get updates in the field gets more important. Updates, in this case, aren't necessarily limited to data. For example, a user might check in with the company each morning for updated pricing schedules. A system administrator could make use of this habit by also including a background thread that downloads any system updates the user may require. In other words, the user would receive both a data update and an application update at the same time. Of course, automatic data updates are a nice feature as well. The application could update pricing tables or other forms of application-specific information in the background at regular intervals, provided the machine has the capability of creating a remote connection to the company.

TIP

You can combine multiple threads and system updates in other ways. For example, you might want to include a virus checking thread that runs in the background and checks all of the incoming data before it actually is placed on the client machine. Another use of background threads is to run diagnostics in the background as the user works to ensure their machine is fully functional. An alarm would tell the user that their machine requires service and that they should save any data before it's too late. As you can see, there are a lot of ways that you can use threads to protect users, their data, and the client machine from damage.

▶ **Calculations**   Math operations are notorious for consuming vast amounts of processor cycles. In some cases, you have to accept the heavy penalty of a calculation because the user requires an answer immediately. However, there are other situations when the application could complete the calculation just as easily in the background as a separate thread. In fact, many spreadsheet and graphics applications use this technique now to make foreground features more responsive to user input.

DLLs

Dynamic link libraries (DLLs) have been around since Microsoft first introduced Windows. In fact, DLLs are actually the successors of the libraries used by DOS applications. For the most part, DLLs allow for the same uses of threads as applications do. The main difference is that you'd want to place common thread types in DLLs—threads that perform work that you may need to do in more than one application. However, developers do place some thread categories in DLLs, simply because they're major components of an application that the developer may not want to recompile every time the application is updated.

▶ Spelling and grammar checkers

▶ Print routines

▶ Non-automated data formatting

▶ Data processing routines

▶ Report builders

You could potentially add other items, but this list should provide you with enough ideas to get started. The reason that these items could appear in a DLL is that the developer normally creates and debugs them separately from the main part of the application. It pays to keep these elements in a DLL to reduce debugging time for the main application and to reduce application compile time.

System Services

For the most part, users never interact with system services. System services sit in the background and perform tasks such as enabling the hardware to operate or creating network connections. Consequently, there are some specialized uses for threads within a system service. The following list will provide you with a few ideas.

▶ **Service priority upgrade**   Some system services execute as low-priority background tasks. You normally don't want them to consume valuable processor cycles unless the machine is idle or there's some type of priority task to perform. When you use a service in the second capacity, high-priority threads come into play. Rather than change the priority of the entire service, you can simply launch a single thread to perform the high-priority task.

▶ **Discovery**   Most system services are low-level applications that need to discover a great deal about the system to ensure that it's working properly. This discovery phase can occur once during service initialization in some cases, but, in other cases it's an ongoing process. Consider the network driver that has to keep track of the current system configuration, including the status of remote resources. A good use of threads, in this case, would be to allow the service to perform multiple levels of discovery at the same time, without reducing its availability to the system as a whole.

▶ **Multiple copies of the same task**   Some services, such as the Indexing Service, perform a single task. However, they might need to perform this single task on multiple data streams or objects. In the case of the Indexing Service, each thread handles a separate catalog, ensuring each catalog receives the same amount of processing power. It's important to handle some tasks like this to ensure that each data stream is handled in a timely manner.

Thread Types

From a Windows perspective, you have threads and the processes that contain them and nothing else. However, from an MFC perspective, there are actually two kinds of threads: UI and worker. Both are threads that can perform a single sequence of execution within the application. The difference comes in the way that you implement and use these two kinds of threads. The following sections talk about these two thread types and show how they're used.

TIP

*You can use the Win32 **CreateThread()** function to create a thread that doesn't rely on MFC. The advantage of doing so is that you eliminate some overhead normally encountered using the MFC libraries. In addition, this method conserves memory. The downside, of course, is that you can't use any of the capabilities that MFC provides. In most cases, you'll find that **CreateThread()** works best for worker threads that perform simple repetitive tasks.*

Worker Threads

Worker threads are normally used for background tasks that require no or minimal user interaction. They're implemented as a function that returns a UINT result and accepts one argument of the LPVOID data type, as shown here:

```
UNINT MyThread (LPVOID pParam)
{
    return 0;
}
```

A worker thread normally returns a value of 0, which indicates that it successfully completed whatever task it was designed to perform. You can return other values to indicate either errors or usage counts. However, the calling application has to be designed to retrieve the exit value using the **GetExitCodeThread**() function.

Another way to end a worker thread and generate an exit code is to use the **AfxEndThread**() function. Using this function will stop thread execution and perform any required cleanup before exiting to the calling application. The calling application would still need to use the **GetExitCodeThread**() function to retrieve the exit value provided to the **AfxEndThread**() function. The exact meaning of any exit codes is up to you, so the calling application will need to be designed to work with a specific thread function before it will know what an exit code means.

The pParam argument can contain any number of 32-bit values. However, passing a pointer to a data structure has several benefits that you may want to consider. For one thing, using a structure allows you to pass more than one argument to the thread. In many cases, a single argument won't be enough to provide the thread with everything needed to perform useful work, so a structure is the only way to get around the single input argument requirement. In addition, using a structure allows the worker thread to pass information back to the caller. All that the worker thread would need to do is modify the contents of a structure member during the course of execution. Note that some developers also pass the "this" pointer because it provides full access to the calling object. This has the advantage of providing full object access, so you don't have to create a complex structure. However, using this technique also means you can't hide data members as easily.

UI Threads

As the name suggests, UI threads are usually created to provide some type of user interface functionality within an application. You'll derive the UI thread from the CWinThread class instead of using a function, as with the worker thread. Obviously, this means that implementing a UI thread is more complex than using a worker thread, but you also get more flexibility.

NOTE

*Terminating a UI thread is much the same as terminating a worker thread. However, a UI thread requires a little special handling if you want the caller to retrieve the exit code for the thread. First, you need to set the m_bAutoDelete data member to FALSE, which prevents the CWinThread object from deleting itself. Second, you'll need to manually delete the thread and release any memory that it uses. As an alternative, you can always duplicate the CWinThread handle that you receive during thread creation using the **DuplicateHandle()** method. In this case, you'll want to create the thread in the suspended state, duplicate the handle, then start the thread using the **ResumeThread()** method.*

MFC provides only one CWinThread class method that you must override when creating a new UI thread, although there are several others that developers commonly override as well. The **InitInstance()** method is the one method that you must override because it's the first one called after the thread is created. The **InitInstance()** method should contain all of the code required to initialize your thread. Obviously, this means displaying a main dialog for the thread, if necessary.

The **ExitInstance()** method will normally get overridden only if you need to perform some thread cleanup or post processing. The only place that you can call this method is from the **Run()** method (should you decide to override it as well). **ExitInstance()** performs the default tasks of deleting the CWinThread object, if m_bAutoDelete is TRUE. It's always the last method called before the thread terminates.

Of the other methods available to you, the only ones that you may need to override are **OnIdle()**, **Run()**, **PreTranslateMessage()**, and **ProcessWndProcException()**. The **OnIdle()** method handles any idle time processing for the thread. For example, **OnIdle()** would get called if the application displayed a dialog box and the user wasn't doing anything with it. **Run()** controls the flow of activity within the thread—this includes the message pump. **PreTranslateMessage()** filters messages before they're sent to either **TranslateMessage()** or **DispatchMessage()**. Finally, the **ProcessWndProcException()** method handles any unhandled exceptions thrown by the thread's message and command handlers. However, you'd normally want to handle these exceptions within the handler, rather than wait until it reaches this point of the thread.

Understanding Critical Sections

A *critical section* is a piece of code that application threads can access only one thread at one time. If two applications require access to the same critical section, the first to make the request will obtain access. The second application will wait until the first application completes its task. In short, critical sections create bottlenecks in your code and can affect performance if you're not careful.

Some forms of critical sections ensure that the thread completes a code sequence without interruption. For example, you wouldn't want to begin a save to a database and have another thread of execution interrupt that save. The first application must complete the save before starting a second thread in order to ensure data integrity. MFC doesn't provide special calls to perform magic in this case; you must develop the thread in such a way that it saves the data safely. In short, the critical section helps ensure database integrity.

You may want to create a critical section for many different reasons, the most important of which is application data integrity. An application changes the contents of variables and the status of objects to meet the needs of a particular user. If another user suddenly decides to execute the same code, the lack of a critical section to protect the variable and object content would ruin the application for both parties.

There are two ways to create a critical section for use with threads: a variable of type CRITICAL_SECTION or a CCriticalSection object. Of the two, the CCriticalSection object is the easiest and least error prone to use. All you need to do is create a CCriticalSection object, then use the **Lock()** and **Unlock()** methods as needed to either restrict or allow access to a section of code. Here's an example of what a typical critical section sequence might look like.

```
CCriticalSection    oMySection;    // Critical section object.

// Lock the critical section.
if (!oMySection.Lock())
   AfxMessageBox("Failed to lock critical section", MB_OK);

// Do some critical work here.

// Unlock the critical section.
if (!oMySection.Unlock())
   AfxMessageBox("Failed to unload critical section.", MB_OK);
```

Using the CCriticalSection object is easy. It returns a BOOL value that signifies success or failure. You'll normally need to handle a failure to either lock or unlock the critical section in some way. In this case, I used a simple dialog. A production application would likely use some kind of loop to try to lock the critical section multiple times. Note that you can supply a numeric value for the **Lock()** method that tells how long to wait for the critical section to get unlocked before a failure result gets returned. Make sure you set this value to a reasonable amount so that the user doesn't think the application is frozen.

Thread Safety

One of the benefits of using libraries is code reuse. Once a developer writes and tests the code, he or she can place it in a library and forget about it. The functionality you'll need will be available without a lot of additional work. All you need to do is access the DLL. Windows uses this technique for all of the APIs that it supports.

Unfortunately, the functionality of libraries can be a two-edged sword. One of the biggest problems when using libraries with threads is that the library isn't thread-safe. In other words, if two threads attempt to access the same object or function at the same time, there could be a collision, resulting in a frozen application, lost data, or other unanticipated results.

Fortunately, you can protect your libraries in a number of ways. One way is to use critical sections as needed to ensure that a sequence of events takes place without interruption. A second way is to allocate variables and objects on the stack. Finally, it's extremely important to reduce the risk of collisions by not allowing more than one thread to access the same variable—use techniques that ensure each thread will have its own set of variables to use.

Even Microsoft's libraries aren't totally thread-safe. For the most part, any MFC object is thread-safe at the class level but not at the object level. In other words, two threads could access different objects derived from the same class, but not the same object. If you have a single CString object that two different threads need to access, then you need to write code that ensures that each object will have separate access to the CString object. In addition, the first thread will need to completely finish any work with the CString object before you allow access by the second thread.

If you want to use MFC at all within a thread, you must create that thread using one of the two techniques we discussed earlier. These are the only two methods that ensure you can access the MFC libraries safely. The reason you must use these recommended techniques is that they tell the MFC libraries to initialize internal variables that allow for multithreaded access of the routines.

Writing a Desktop Application with Threads

As mentioned in the previous paragraphs, there are many ways to use threads in an application, and MFC provides two different kinds of threads from which to choose. This example is going to look at both kinds of threads in a very simple scenario. We'll use dialog boxes just to make the whole interface of the project that much easier.

The first part of the example will use a UI thread. You'll normally call on this kind of thread when you need to create multiple windows to display information for the user. For example, you might use this kind of thread setup when writing a network diagnostic program. A single window could display all of the statistics for one problem point on the network. The network administrator could then look at the windows one at a time and prioritize the most severe ones for immediate repair.

The second part of the example will look at a worker thread. The UI thread will actually call the worker thread as part of the initialization process. You'll normally use worker threads to perform non-user interface tasks in the background. In this

case, our worker thread won't really do all that much. All that it'll do is wait five
seconds and terminate.

Defining the Main Dialog

Now that you have an idea of where this project is going, let's create the main dialog
for it. This will include creating the application itself. The following procedure will
help you get the project set up.

1. Create a new MFC Application project named Threads. You'll see the
    MFC Application Wizard dialog.

2. Select the Application Type tab. Choose the Dialog based option.

3. Select the User Interface Features tab. Type **Thread Demonstration** in
    the Dialog Title field. Clear the About Box option.

4. Click Finish. Visual C++ will create the new project for you, then display
    the main application dialog.

5. Remove the Static Text control and add a Button control below the OK and
    Cancel buttons.

6. Change the button ID property to IDC_ADD_THREAD and the Caption
    property to Add Thread. Your dialog should look like the one shown here:

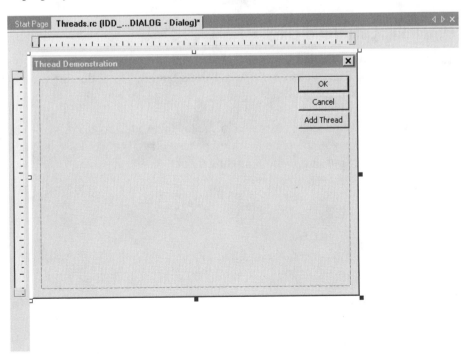

7. Right-click the IDC_ADD_THREAD button and choose Add Event Handler from the context menu. You'll see the Event Handler Wizard.

8. Select the BN_CLICKED option in the Message Type field, then click Add and Edit. Visual C++ will add a new procedure for the button to the application.

At this point, the main application dialog is ready to go. All we need to do is add some code to make the Add Thread button functional. Listing 3-1 shows the code you'll need to add.

Listing 3-1

```
void CThreadsDlg::OnAddThread()
{
    // Begin a new UI thread.
    CWinThread     *pThread = AfxBeginThread(
        RUNTIME_CLASS ( CUIThread ) );
}
```

As you can see, this code is extremely simple. All we do is create a new thread based on the CUIThread class. Unfortunately, there's no CUIThread class associated with our application now. That's the next step—creating a new class to hold our thread.

Creating the CUIThread Class

The first kind of thread we'll create is a UI thread. What this thread will do is display a dialog box when the user clicks on the Add Thread button. The following procedure will show you how to create the class.

1. Use the Project | Add Class command to display the Add Class dialog shown here. This dialog helps you to create any kind of new class, but we'll use it to create a new thread for our application, as shown next.

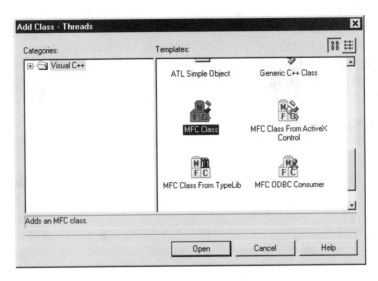

2. Select the MFC Class option, as shown in the illustration, and click Open. You'll see the MFC Class Wizard shown next. This dialog box enables you to create any class supported by MFC. Of course, Visual C++ supports myriad other class types.

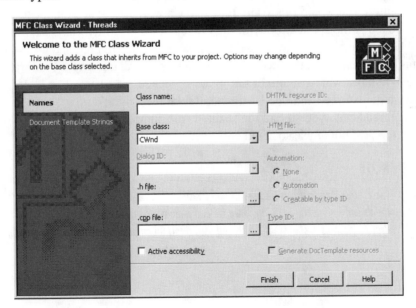

3. Type **CUIThread** in the Class Name field. (Visual C++ will automatically name the files for the new class UIThread—you can change this default filename by clicking Change.) The value you provide in the Name field determines the class name throughout the application. It's traditional to preface all class names with a C, although there's no rule that you absolutely have to add the C.

4. Choose CWinThread in the Base Class field. The base class determines the initial characteristics of the class. Some classes, like CDialog, require you to provide a Dialog ID as well, but we don't need one in this case.

5. Click Finish. Visual C++ will add the CUIThread class to the application.

Even though we've added the CUIThread thread class to the application, the CThreadsDlg class—where we added the **OnAddThread**() method in the previous section—still can't see it. We need to add an include statement at the beginning of the ThreadsDlg.CPP, like the one shown here:

```
// Add our thread header.
#include "UIThread.h"
```

At this point, you could compile and run the application. If you clicked the Add Thread button, you wouldn't see anything happen with the application itself. However, if you looked at the application with the Process Viewer utility that's supplied with Visual C++, you'd see one additional thread for each time you pressed the Add Thread button. (If you don't see the Process Viewer, you can install it from the Platform SDK.) Figure 3-1 shows what you might see if you'd clicked Add Thread once. In this case, we have a main thread and one UI thread. (Obviously, there's no dialog associated with the thread class yet, so looking at the results in Microsoft Spy++ will show only the new threads, not any associated controls.)

NOTE

*The Process Viewer shows that the thread doesn't consume any time in Figure 3-1. That's because the thread isn't doing anything. Once we add a dialog to the thread's **InitInstance()** method, the Process Viewer will show that the thread uses a certain amount of Privileged and User time.*

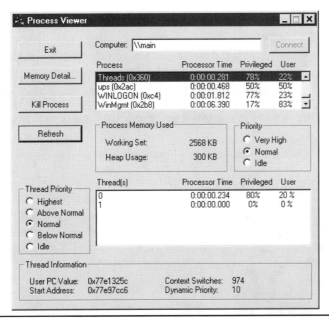

Figure 3-1   *The Process Viewer showing the Threads application ready to create new threads.*

Adding a Thread Dialog

A UI thread always contains some type of user interface element. There are many ways to create this element, but by far the simplest is to use a standard resource. Therefore, the first thing we'll do in this section is design a new dialog that the CUIThread class can display, using the following procedure:

1. Right-click the Dialog folder on the Resource View tab of the Workspace window, then choose Insert Dialog from the context menu. You'll see a new dialog added to the application.

2. Change the ID of the dialog to IDD_NEW_THREAD_DIALOG. The dialog is now ready for display, but the CUIThread class needs a dialog class for access purposes. (We won't do a lot with this dialog because it's there for display purposes only.)

3. Right-click the new dialog and choose Add Class from the context menu. You'll see an MFC Class Wizard dialog like the one shown here. Notice that the wizard automatically enters some class values for you. For example, Visual C++ has already chosen the CDHtmlDialog class for you in the Base Class field. However, we'll want to use the straight CDialog class for this example.

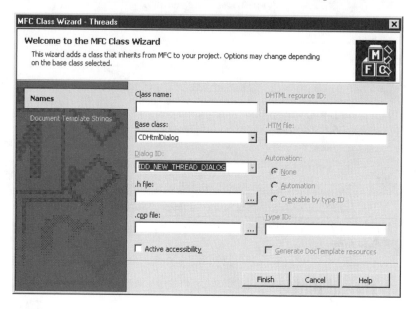

NOTE

In most cases, you'll create a new class for a dialog. About the only time you'd choose to add a dialog to an existing class is if that class natively supports dialogs and doesn't have one assigned to it. For example, if you had previously created a CDialog class derivative and hadn't assigned a dialog to it, you could use this method to do so.

4. Select CDialog in the Base Class field. Type **CNewThreadDlg** in the Name field, then click Finish. (Normally, you'd also need to make a choice about adding automation support to the dialog, but it's not required in this case.) Visual C++ will add the new class for you.

It's time to add the new dialog to the CUIThread class. The first thing we'll need to do is add two entries to the UIThread.H file. Then, you'll need to create a variable the class can use to access the dialog. Both of these additions appear in bold type in Listing 3-2.

Listing 3-2

```
// Include support for the New Thread Dialog
#include "NewThreadDlg.H"

#pragma once

// CUIThread

class CUIThread : public CWinThread
{
    DECLARE_DYNCREATE(CUIThread)

protected:
    // protected constructor used by dynamic creation
    CUIThread();
    virtual ~CUIThread();

public:
    virtual BOOL InitInstance();
    virtual int ExitInstance();

// New Thread Dialog access
CNewThreadDlg     dlgNewThread;

protected:
    DECLARE_MESSAGE_MAP()
};
```

The **InitInstance()** method is what controls the starting point for each new thread that the application will create. We'll simply place the dialog display code in there. Listing 3-3 shows the code you'll need to use in this case.

Listing 3-3

```
BOOL CUIThread::InitInstance()
{
    // Display the thread dialog.
    m_pMainWnd = &dlgNewThread;
    dlgNewThread.DoModal();

    // Returning TRUE will destroy the thread.
    return TRUE;
}
```

All that this code does is assign the dialog as the main window for the thread. This is a very important thing to do, because otherwise you'll only be able to create a single new thread. (Displaying the dialog modally without assigning it as the main window prevents you from going back to the initial dialog and clicking Add Thread.) Once you assign the dialog as the main window for the thread, the code displays it modally. When the user clicks OK, the dialog call returns and the thread returns TRUE. This act destroys the thread.

Creating a Worker Thread

At this point, you could compile the application and see the effects of a UI thread. Of course, the thread dialog isn't doing anything at this point. That's where the worker thread we'll create in this section comes into play. We'll perform two tasks required to create a worker thread that sleeps for five seconds and then ends.

This section will also look at some thread synchronization issues. For example, you'll learn about the importance of waiting for any worker threads to end before terminating a main thread (in this case, the UI thread we created in the previous section). In this case, we'll modify the functionality of the OK button to ensure that the worker thread has actually ended before we close the dialog. This ensures that the dialog doesn't create any memory leaks.

TIP

*The **Sleep()** method shown in this section can be used to replace a timer when working with threads. The thread will sleep for a certain amount of time, wake itself up, then perform whatever work it needs to do before going back to sleep.*

The first thing we'll need to do is create the thread. I've chosen to create the thread as part of the process of creating the dialog, which means we'll have to change the default functionality of the **OnInitDialog**() method. Since our application doesn't include the handler for the **CNewThreadDialog::OnInitDialog**() method, we'll need to add it. To do this, select the CNewThreadDlg entry in Class View. Click Overrides in the Properties dialog, then add a handler for the OnInitDialog message. Here's what the Properties dialog will look like.

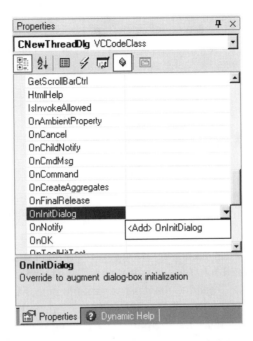

Click <Add> OnInitDialog to create the new method definition. Listing 3-4 shows the code you'll need to add for this example.

Listing 3-4

```
BOOL CNewThreadDlg::OnInitDialog()
{
    // Perform the default action.
    CDialog::OnInitDialog();

    // Create a worker thread.
    pThread = AfxBeginThread(SleepABit,
        NULL,
        THREAD_PRIORITY_BELOW_NORMAL,
        0,
        0,
        NULL);

    return TRUE;  // return TRUE unless you set the focus to a control
                  // EXCEPTION: OCX Property Pages should return FALSE

}
```

The default action and return code are both provided by the MFC ClassWizard for you, so the only thing you need to add is the **AfxBeginThread()** function. You'll need to define the pThread variable in the public section of the NewThreadDlg.H header file as shown here.

```
CWinThread    *pThread;    // New thread pointer.
```

There are six arguments you pass to **AfxBeginThread()**. The following list describes each argument and what you'd use it for.

▶ **Function name**   The first argument is the name of the worker thread function, which can't be a member of the current class. (We'll see how this works in a moment.)

▶ **Function parameter**   The second argument is a parameter that you can pass to the worker thread function. It's of type LPVOID, so you'll need to typecast it within the worker thread to the desired variable type. Many thread writers use this parameter to pass a BOOL that tells the worker thread to terminate. However, you can use the parameter for any purpose and could even pass multiple parameters in the form of a structure.

▶ **Thread priority**   This is the default thread priority. It's actually a relative measure of the thread's priority when compared to the parent, not an absolute priority level. The example code shows the worker thread starting at a priority level one point below the parent thread. A value of THREAD_PRIORITY_ NORMAL would start the thread at the same priority as the parent.

▶ **Stack size**   Providing a value of 0 means that you want to use the default stack size, which is 1 MB maximum in most cases. Windows doesn't actually allocate 1 MB of stack space, it allocates only what the application actually needs. The only time you'd want to specify a stack size is if you wanted to ensure that recursive code or other code elements didn't overflow the stack. Obviously, you'd also need to provide a value here in those rare situations when a thread might need more than 1 MB of stack space.

▶ **Creation flags**   At present, there are only two creation flags. A value of 0 tells Windows to start the thread immediately. You can also supply a value of CREATE_SUSPENDED, which means that you'd have to resume the thread before it would run the first time. The **Suspend()** method will allow you to stop a thread after it's created, while the **Resume()** method will start it, so you still have control over the thread later using the thread object pointer. This is one of the reasons we saved the thread object pointer as a public variable.

▶ **Security**   Providing a NULL value for this argument starts the thread with the same security attributes as the parent thread. You'd need to provide a pointer to a SECURITY_ATTRIBUTES structure if you wanted to change any of the thread's security levels. We'll look at the SECURITY_ATTRIBUTES structure in Chapters 21 and 22 of the book.

Now that we have a thread, we'll need to do some synchronization to ensure the UI thread doesn't try to end before the worker thread does. That means adding some code to the **OnOK()** method of the CNewThreadDlg class. To add the new method, right-click the OK button of the IDD_NEW_THREAD_DIALOG dialog and choose Add Event Handler. Select BN_CLICKED in the Message Type field and click Add and Edit. Listing 3-5 contains the code you'll need to add for the **OnOK()** method.

Listing 3-5

```
void CNewThreadDlg::OnOk()
{
    // Wait until the thread has terminated.
    WaitForSingleObject(pThread->m_hThread, INFINITE);

    // Perform the default OnOK() processing.
    CDialog::OnOK();
}
```

The **WaitForSingleObject()** function allows us to detect when the thread has finished executing. The INFINITE argument tells Windows that we'll wait forever for the worker thread to end. There's a potential problem with using this particular argument. Unless you're absolutely certain that the thread will actually end, the application could appear to freeze if the thread doesn't end for some reason. In many cases, it's actually better to provide a value in milliseconds for the second argument. If the thread doesn't finish executing a given amount of time, you can always add code that allows your application to detect the problem, display an error message for the user, and end gracefully.

Calling **CDialog::OnOK()** allows the parent class to complete any handling for the event. It's important to ensure that the event gets handled. Obviously, unless you have some special processing to perform, it's easier to allow the parent class to handle the default processing needs.

It's finally time to add the worker thread code. You'll need to add a function declaration before the class definition in NewThreadDlg.H like the one shown here:

```
// Add a declaration for our worker thread.
UINT SleepABit(LPVOID pParam);
```

NOTE

Make absolutely certain that you add the worker thread function declaration before the class declaration or the example won't compile properly. The worker thread function isn't part of the CNewThreadDlg class and therefore won't appear in the ClassView tab of the Workspace window. In addition, a worker thread must always follow the format shown in the declaration. It must return a UINT and accept a LPVOID parameter value, even if the parameter isn't used within the worker thread function.

The **SleepABit()** function itself is relatively simple. You'll add this function to the NewThreadDlg.CPP file. Listing 3-6 shows the source code for this function.

Listing 3-6

```
UINT SleepABit(LPVOID pParam)
{
    // Sleep for 5 seconds.
    Sleep(5000);

    // End the thread
    return 0;
}
```

As you can see, the source for the worker thread is extremely simple. All we do is tell the thread to sleep for 5,000 milliseconds, then end.

Testing the Threads Application

Compile the Threads application so that you can see how the various threads work together. There are several ways that you can view this example. First, start the application, click Add Thread, then immediately click OK on the resulting Dialog dialog. The dialog won't actually disappear for five seconds. What you're seeing is the result of the combination of the **Sleep()** and **WaitForSingleObject()** functions. The worker thread sleeps for five seconds after it gets created. Since the worker thread is created as part of creating the UI thread, there isn't any way to close the dialog for five seconds after you start it.

Let's look at this from a different perspective. Open the Process Viewer. Find the Threads application in the Process list, click Add Thread on the Threads Application, then Refresh on the Process Viewer. You'll see three threads as shown in Figure 3-2. The first thread is the main application thread, which will stay even after you close any created thread dialogs. The second is the UI thread, which will remain until you click OK on the Dialog dialog. Finally, the third thread is the worker thread—it'll cease

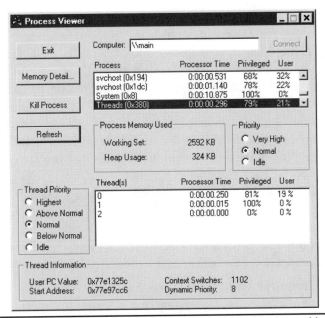

Figure 3-2   *The Process Viewer shows which threads are executing and how much processor time they're using.*

to exist in five seconds. Wait five seconds, click Refresh, and you'll see that the worker thread has indeed disappeared from the thread list.

NOTE

Notice that the worker thread shown in Figure 3-2 isn't using any processor time because it's in sleep mode. In addition, if you click on the worker thread entry, you'll see that the Thread Priority field changes to Below Normal and that the actual worker thread priority is at least one below the main thread priority.

Writing a Local DLL with Threads

DLLs have always been one of the mainstays of the Windows programmer. The reasons for using them are easy to understand. A DLL allows you to place commonly used code within an easy to access module that you don't need to recompile every time you create a new version of your application. In addition, DLLs allow you to modularize your application, making it easier to troubleshoot (especially since you'll have already debugged the code within the DLL). Using DLLs can also be very memory efficient.

The DLL loads only when and if you actually need it (provided you code your application correctly), making the initial memory footprint for an application smaller.

It's no surprise that some developers want to combine the good features of threads with DLLs. Placing your common thread code within a DLL makes sense for the same reasons that you'd use this technique with any application code. In addition, there isn't any reason why a DLL can't use internal threads as well. DLLs create these threads for the sole purpose of making the DLL more efficient and responsive.

There are a few caveats when using threads within DLLs. The following list will provide you with some of the more common problems that you'll experience.

▶ **Thread safety** When you place a thread within an application, you're fairly certain about the application that will access it and how that access will occur. Any number of applications could access a thread within a DLL, and you need to take that into account. Thread safety becomes more critical, in this case, to ensure that data access is checked and critical areas are protected.

▶ **Exporting requirements** You'll find that worker threads are much easier to place within a DLL simply because they're easier to export. In many cases, exporting complex UI thread objects proves more difficult and error prone.

▶ **Development/debugging time** The problems that you'll experience writing and debugging code for an application are only exacerbated when working with DLLs. You have to take not only parallel processing into account, but the DLL as well. In other words, you may want to consider developing the thread code within the application environment first, then moving it to a DLL if needed. Debugging the thread code first will make it easier to determine where a problem lies when you create the DLL.

Now that we have a few preliminaries out of the way, let's look at an example of a worker thread that we can call from a DLL. The thread function will reside within a DLL. As with the previous example, the thread itself will be very simple so that you can better see the mechanics of using the thread itself. The following sections will help you create the example program.

Creating the DLLThread DLL

Our application will actually consist of two projects. The first is a DLL that will hold the worker thread. The following procedure will get you started.

1. Create a new MFC DLL project named DLLThread. Make certain that you create a DLL project, not an EXE project. Visual C++ will display the MFC DLL Wizard dialog.

2. Click Application Settings. You'll see the dialog shown here. As you can see, the MFC DLL Wizard allows you to choose from three different DLL types. The first two options produce DLLs that any application can call. The second type links the required MFC functions statically, which increases the size of the DLL in memory, but ensures that the required MFC support is bundled with the DLL. The third DLL option produces an MFC extension. Only MFC applications can call this type of DLL, making it an unlikely choice for general application development.

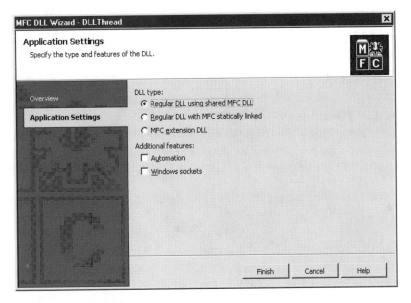

3. Choose the Regular DLL using the shared MFC DLL option, then click Finish. Visual C++ will create the DLL shell for you.

Adding the worker thread to the DLL is relatively easy. Listing 3-7 shows the code you'll need to add for this example.

Listing 3-7

```
__declspec(dllexport) UINT DoDialog(LPVOID pParam)
{
```

```
// Required pre-processing.
AFX_MANAGE_STATE(AfxGetStaticModuleState());

// Display a confirmation message.
AfxMessageBox("Thread Started", MB_OK);

// End the thread
return 0;
}
```

Notice that the general calling syntax for this worker thread is the same as before. The big difference is the addition of __declspec(dllexport) to the beginning of the call. This extra code tells the compiler that we want to export the **DoDialog()** function for use outside of the DLL (we'll see the effect of this extra code in a moment).

TIP

The __declspec() function is a Microsoft-specific extension to Visual C++, which makes the code unportable to other environments. You can get around this problem by using the more common DEF file technique for exporting the function. However, this means maintaining extra code, which the __declspec() function takes care of for you automatically. The only other reason to use a DEF file is if you need to control the ordinal order of the exported functions. Using __declspec() means that you have to reference a DLL function by name rather than ordinal number.

Let's look at the **DoDialog()** function. The first call is to the AFX_MANAGE_ STATE() macro, which performs a context switch from the main application to the DLL. This macro ensures that Windows looks for resources within your DLL rather than in the main application. You have to include this macro if you plan to use any MFC calls or local resources like icons or bitmaps in most functions. There are, however, exceptions to the rule. For example, Windows automatically performs a context switch when you call the **InitInstance()** method of a class.

The remaining code is quite simple. The **DoDialog()** function displays a standard message box. After the user closes the message box, the function returns a 0, which terminates the thread.

Compile the DLL. Open the DLLThread.DLL file you'll find in the project Debug or Release folder using Dependency Walker. You should see a mangled form of DoDialog in the exported functions list. Right-click the Exported Functions pane and choose Undecorate C++ Functions from the context menu. Your display should look similar to the one shown in Figure 3-3. If you don't see the exported function, be sure to check your code for errors.

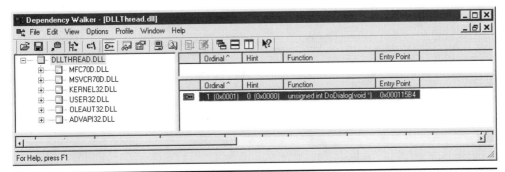

Figure 3-3   *The Quick View utility shows a list of exported function names for your DLL.*

Creating the DLLTest Application

It's time to create an application that can use the DLL that we just created. We'll use a dialog-based application that looks very similar to the one that we created earlier in the chapter.

1. Create a new MFC Application project with the name DLLTest.
   You'll see the MFC Application Wizard dialog.

2. Select the Application Type tab. Choose the Dialog based option.

3. Select the User Interface Features tab. Type **DLL Thread Demonstration**
   in the Dialog Title field. Clear the About Box option.

4. Click Finish. Visual C++ will create the new project for you, then display
   the main application dialog in the Design window.

5. Remove the Static Text control and add a Button control.

6. Change the button ID to IDC_ADD_THREAD and the Caption to Add Thread.

7. Right-click IDC_ADD_THREAD and choose Add Event Handler from the
   context menu. Select BN_CLICKED in the Message Type field and click Add
   and Edit. Visual C++ will add a new procedure for the button to the application.

NOTE

Before we can add any code for the new procedure, we also need to make changes to the project settings so that Visual C++ will know where to access the DLLThread.LIB file. This file contains the information required to use the DLLThread DLL that we created in the previous section.

8. Use the Project | Properties command to display the DLLTest Property Pages dialog.

9. Choose the Linker | Input tab of the DLLTest Property Pages dialog. You should see a list of link settings like the ones shown here.

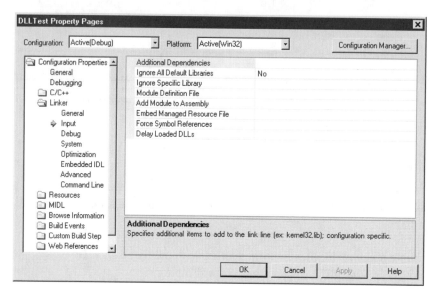

10. Type **DLLThread.LIB** in the Additional Dependencies field; you may need to change this entry depending on where the DLLThread.LIB file is located on your machine.

11. Choose the Linker | General tab of the DLLTest Property Pages dialog. Select the location of the DLLThread\Debug or DLLThread\Release directory on your machine in the Additional Library Directories field.

12. Click OK. Visual C++ will change the project settings to include a location for the DLLThread.LIB file.

We'll need to make some changes to the DLLTest.H file as well. The first will add an import entry for the **DoDialog()** function. The second is a CWinThread object pointer, like the one we used in the previous example. Both of these changes are shown in bold type in Listing 3-8.

Listing 3-8

```
// DLLTestDlg.h : header file
//

#pragma once
```

```
// Import the DoDialog() function.
__declspec(dllimport) UINT DoDialog(LPVOID pParam);


// CDLLTestDlg dialog
class CDLLTestDlg : public CDialog
{
// Construction
public:
    CDLLTestDlg(CWnd* pParent = NULL);    // standard constructor

// Dialog Data
    enum { IDD = IDD_DLLTEST_DIALOG };

    protected:
    virtual void DoDataExchange(CDataExchange* pDX);    // DDX/DDV support


// Implementation
protected:
    HICON m_hIcon;

    // Generated message map functions
    virtual BOOL OnInitDialog();
    afx_msg void OnPaint();
    afx_msg HCURSOR OnQueryDragIcon();
    DECLARE_MESSAGE_MAP()
public:
    afx_msg void OnBnClickedAddThread();
CWinThread    *pThread;    // New thread pointer.
};
```

At this point, the main application dialog is ready to go. All we need to do is add some code to make the Add Thread button functional. Listing 3-9 shows the code you'll need to add.

Listing 3-9

```
    void CDLLTestDlg::OnBnClickedAddThread()
    {
        // Create a worker thread.
        pThread = AfxBeginThread(DoDialog,
            NULL,
            THREAD_PRIORITY_NORMAL,
            0,
            0,
            NULL);
    }
```

As you can see, all that this code does is create a thread using the imported
DoDialog() function. In sum, calling the DLL version of the worker thread isn't
all that different from using a worker thread within the application itself.

NOTE

*You must copy the DLLThread.DLL file into the DLLTest application folder before you attempt to
run the application. Otherwise, Windows will complain that it can't find the DLL file.*

If you ran that application, at this point you'd see many of the same things we did
for the previous example. The process viewer would show a new thread every time
you click the Add Thread button. Using a DLL does require a little more memory—
as you'll see when using Process Viewer. Looking at the application with Spy++ will
show the main thread and associated window, along with any worker threads that you
create. However, since we're creating a message box within the worker thread this time,
you'll also see a dialog associated with each worker thread.

Working with Graphics

IN THIS CHAPTER:

Visual C++ Graphics Support

Writing a Graphics Desktop Application

Animation Techniques Using GIF Files

W indows is a graphical environment. Therefore, it's little wonder that most Windows desktop applications have some type of graphics support within them. In the "Working with Resources" section of Chapter 2, we discussed graphics as a resource. For example, most applications sport an icon that identifies them in Explorer and within the Start menu. In addition, applications that work with data generally support one or more icons for each file extension they support. Resources are fine when working with some types of graphics such as icons.

You'll run into situations where you need to support other kinds of graphic images or the image you need to support isn't known at design time. For example, if you want to display a PCX image on the hard drive, it's unlikely that you'll place it within the application as a resource. In this situation, you'll access the graphic externally, which means loading it into memory from the hard drive and displaying it on screen.

Visual C++ provides graphics support at several levels. For example, you can load images from a data stream (such as an Internet connection) or your can load them from the hard drive. Visual C++ .NET also includes two distinct methods for working with graphics: managed and unmanaged. The unmanaged method relies on the same Win32 calls you've always used in the past. This is the method you should use when you need to create a native executable file for platforms that don't (or won't) support the .NET Framework. The managed method relies on new classes in the .NET Framework. You'll find that these classes have a lot to offer, but also have some pitfalls. We'll discuss the pros and cons of using both graphics techniques.

Visual C++ Graphics Support

Visual C++ provides a lot in the way of graphics support. In fact, given the way Microsoft has structured Visual Studio .NET, Visual C++ might have more to offer than any other language you could use. We'll discuss just what Visual C++ has to offer in the sections that follow. You'll learn about the expanded graphics support that you'll find in Visual C++ .NET. This first section also tells you what you have to pay in order to receive these additional benefits. It's important to understand the tradeoffs of using any programming language.

The second section discusses the Image Editor utility. You need to know about this utility in order to get the most out of Visual Studio. The IDE does support some types of resources natively, such as icons. However, if you're reading this section of the book, you need something more than what the Visual Studio .NET IDE can provide. Image Editor is a simple, yet effective tool for creating drawings. Of course, if you need something more robust or want to create animations, you'll need a third party product. We'll discuss such products in the "Animation Techniques Using GIF Files" section of the chapter.

The remaining three sections that follow help you understand graphics programming support for Visual C++ developers. We'll discuss the Windows API for those of you writing unmanaged applications in the third section. This section won't discuss every nuance of every API call, but does provide you with a good overview. The fourth and fifth sections discuss the two .NET Framework namespaces you need to know about for managed programming under Visual Studio .NET. Again, we'll discuss the two namespaces from an overview perspective, rather than delve into every nuance. (You'll see many details while working through the coding examples in the chapter.)

Expanded Graphics Support

Visual C++ is a low-level language. Consequently, some people have never viewed Visual C++ as the optimum choice for end user graphics programming, but they do view it as an optimal choice for many types of graphics manipulation. Visual C++ provides the low-level bit manipulation that many graphics routines require, and it provides the speed necessary to allow processor hungry graphics routines to run quickly on a typical workstation. The sticking point has always been the amount of code required to create the Visual C++ application. Some languages, such as Visual Basic (and now C#), provide the means to write graphics display routines quickly.

Visual C++ .NET changes the programming picture somewhat and makes it much easier to work with graphics. If your only goal is to display graphics and you can target a machine that supports the .NET Framework, you can use the same techniques as everyone else to display graphics. The code is relatively simple and even debugging it is painless. In fact, using .NET makes working with certain types of graphics applications almost trivial.

Microsoft carefully considered the working environment for most developers when creating the .NET Framework. The .NET Framework isn't a one-for-one replacement of the Windows API, especially when it comes to writing graphics applications. While the .NET Framework does make writing graphics applications easy, it also lacks the depth of support that you'll find in the Windows API. For example, all graphics handling in the .NET Framework is two-dimensional. If you want three-dimensional support, you need to use Windows API calls and provide access to DirectX. In short, the emphasis of the .NET Framework is business applications that can rely on two-dimensional presentation.

You'll find that Visual Studio .NET places a greater emphasis on the Internet, even greater than Visual Studio 6 did. One of the results of this emphasis is support for a greater number of graphics file types. Two of the most important additions are support for Joint Photographic Experts Group (JPEG or JPG) and Portable Network

Graphics (PNG) file formats. You'll also find better support for older graphics formats such as Graphics Interchange Format (GIF). Of course, you only get this support when working with the .NET Framework. The Windows API still limits you to the graphics formats of the past, such as bitmap (BMP), cursor (CUR), and icon (ICO).

NOTE

At the time of this writing, Visual Studio .NET support of a non-native graphics format such as GIF and JPG is less than perfect. The IDE loads the image as a custom resource and refuses to display it as anything but hexadecimal data. While this limitation doesn't keep you from using the image in your application, it does mean you can't see the image in the IDE. If you plan to work with non-native types, you must use a third party editor to create the image.

One of the more important features for all users of Visual Studio .NET are the enhanced drawing features found in the IDE. Figure 4-1 shows a typical example of an icon for Visual Studio .NET. Notice that this icon is in 256 colors. You can also choose higher and lower color depths (up to 32-bit color). Visual Studio .NET supports 16×16, 32×32, and the new 48×48 pixel icons. You also have the option to create the usual cursors and bitmaps. We discussed these capabilities as part of the "Working with Resources" section in Chapter 2.

The term *bitmap* is more generic in Visual Studio .NET than in previous versions of the product. You can now use BMP, Device Independent Bitmap (DIB), GIF, JPG, JPE, and JPEG files as bitmaps, which makes Visual Studio .NET far more flexible. The only problem with the bitmap support is that it supports only single image files. You can't place an animated GIF within your application. We'll discuss a technique for getting around the animated graphic problem in the "Animation Techniques Using GIF Files" section of the chapter.

Using Image Editor

Given the advanced drawing features found in Visual Studio .NET, you might wonder why anyone would require an external editor. Image Editor is a tool of convenience. It enables you to create new graphics without starting the Visual Studio .NET IDE. (The memory footprint difference between the two products is substantial.) In addition, the graphics you create with Image Editor will work with every version of Visual Studio and Windows. You'll use Image Editor when you want to ensure your application provides maximum compatibility using a common image capability approach.

The Image Editor is a typical drawing tool. You could equate it to something like Paint, since it has about the same capabilities from a drawing perspective. However, the similarity with other tools ends with drawing capabilities. Image Editor helps you to create new icon (ICO), cursor (CUR), and bitmap (BMP) files. All versions of Windows support these native graphic file types.

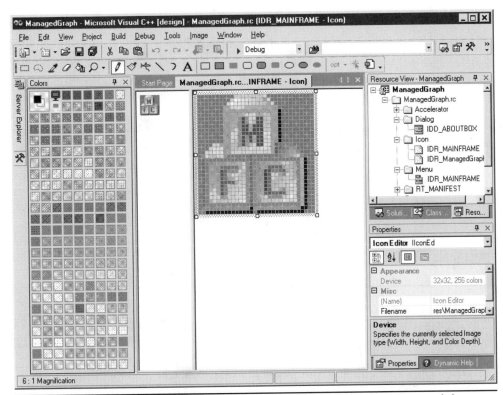

Figure 4-1   *The Visual Studio .NET IDE provides better graphics drawing capabilities than previous versions.*

NOTE

*Visual Studio .NET includes Image Editor at the time of this writing. However, given that Visual Studio .NET does include substantially better graphics support, Microsoft may choose to drop this tool from the list of supported tools. You'll still find Image Editor in the Platform SDK. In fact, the Platform SDK contains many image management tools that you won't find in Visual Studio .NET. If you plan to use many graphics in your applications, it pays to install a copy of the Platform SDK and associated tools on your system. However, make sure you get the most recent Platform SDK from **http://www.microsoft.com/msdownload/platformsdk/ sdkupdate/** to ensure you gain maximum compatibility with Visual Studio .NET.*

Figure 4-2 shows the Image Editor with an icon loaded. While the tools won't vary with the kind of resource you create, the size and the format of the image will. The display you see may vary from the one shown here depending on what type of resource you decide to create.

Image Editor allows you to create three different kinds of resources: cursor, bitmap, and icon. Selecting the File | New command will display the Resource Type

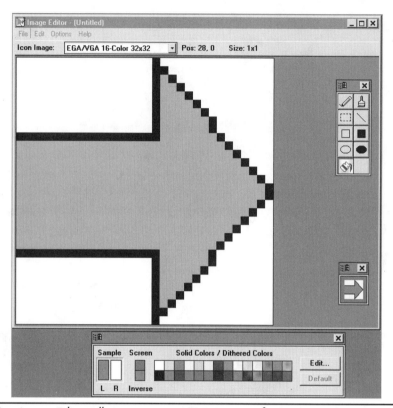

Figure 4-2 *Image Editor allows you to create a variety of resources using common drawing tools.*

dialog box, shown here, which allows you to choose the type of resource you want to create.

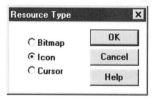

Once you select a resource type, you may see a second dialog box that allows you to choose the size and (optionally) color depth of the resource you'll create. Choose the settings you want to use for the resource, then click OK on the second dialog box to create the initial resource.

Using the Standard Win32 API Calls

Developers have struggled with the Win32 API since Windows NT first appeared on the scene. While it's relatively easy to perform some tasks, such as getting the current machine state, working with graphics has always been notoriously difficult. Part of the difficulty stems from the requirement to share the one screen resource with multiple applications. However, inconsistent API calling conventions also play a role in making the Win32 API difficult to use.

Visual Studio .NET developers have two canvases they can use when working with the Win32 API . The first is the display device context (DC); essentially a piece of virtual paper you use to create output. The DC acts as output media, which the system displays on screen as soon as possible. The second canvas is relatively new. You can also draw on some controls. For example, we'll discuss the use of a CStatic control as a bitmap drawing framework in this chapter. At a low level, the system is still using the DC, but the use of a control hides this fact from the developer. Consequently, most developers find that using the control approach requires less work while producing the same results. (We'll see other benefits for using the control approach as the chapter progresses.)

The Win32 API provides a wealth of functions for working with graphics. MFC provides wrappers to make working with the functions easier, but you gain essentially the same list of functions when using MFC. In both cases, you can view the functions as falling into four categories:

- ▶ Canvas management
- ▶ Pre-rendered graphics display
- ▶ Drawing
- ▶ Miscellaneous

An example of the canvas management calls is **GetDC**(). You must gain access to the DC before you can draw on it. The DC is associated with a window, with the desktop being the top-most window that you can access. Windows automatically clips anything you place in the DC to the bounds of the associated window. Therefore, if you select a dialog box as your canvas, you can draw only within the bounds of the dialog box. When working with a DC, you must use the **ReleaseDC**() function when you finish drawing. Windows provides a limited number of DCs, so failure to release a DC can have serious consequences.

Microsoft has tried to reduce the complexity of using a DC by introducing the CPaintDC, CClientDC, CMetafileDC, and CWindowDC classes. These classes enable you to use a DC without worrying as much about pointers. In addition, using these classes reduces the amount of code you need to produce by taking care of some issues for you automatically. For example, you don't need to release the DC manually. We'll see how the CClientDC class works in the sections that follow.

The easiest method to work with pre-rendered graphics (those that you add as resources to your application or read from another source such as the hard drive) is to use a CStatic or other suitable control. Otherwise, you have to read the various elements of the graphic file into memory individually, which can become an exercise in frustration. Along with the commands for reading bitmaps, icons, and cursors, the Win32 API (and by extension, MFC) provides calls for stretching or performing bit manipulations on a bitmap as a whole. However, you must perform these manipulations using the CBitmap object before you draw the object on screen using the CStatic object.

The Win32 API also includes a wealth of drawing primitives that you can use to render line art on screen. The native functions work only with two-dimensional drawings, however, so you'll need to use DirectX for full three-dimensional support. You do obtain functions for drawing the following primitives:

- ▶ Line
- ▶ Hollow rectangle
- ▶ Solid rectangle
- ▶ Rectangle with rounded corners
- ▶ Arc
- ▶ Chord
- ▶ Pie wedge
- ▶ Circle/ellipse

I'll demonstrate all of these primitives in the coding sections that follow. Most of them require some knowledge of the math principles they're based on. For example, when working with a circle, you need to know what type of bounding square to create in order to achieve a specific type of circle (or ellipse). Besides the **DrawXXXX()** functions used to actually create the drawings, you also need to know how to use brushes and pens. Every time you want to create a different affect, you need a new brush or pen. The CBrush and CPen classes make the process of creating brush or pen relatively painless.

A Quick Overview of the System.Windows.Forms Namespace

The easiest way to think of the System.Windows.Forms namespace is as a replacement for the diverse set of commands traditionally used to "draw" a dialog box or other window on screen. Any managed application that requires a window (graphical interface) requires this namespace. Consequently, you'll add this namespace to your managed applications more often than any other namespace. We'll discuss this namespace with some regularity in the book, and the following list provides an overview of the types of classes and methods that it provides:

▶ **Forms**   One of the main contributions of this namespace is forms of various types. In fact, you'll inherit from the Form class in many of the examples in this book and in real world applications that you create.

▶ **Controls**   This namespace contains all of the familiar controls, including Button, ComboBox, Label, ListView, PropertyGrid, TextBox, and Toolbar. Note that you no longer need to place a "C" in front of everything. Using the .NET Framework means using the same standard names as all Visual Studio .NET languages.

▶ **Components**   Some, but not all, of the components used for general form design appear in this namespace. You'll find ContextMenu, ErrorProvider, Help, HelpProvider, Menu, MenuItem, and ToolTip components for starters. You'll learn how to use some of the components later in the chapter.

▶ **Common Dialog Boxes**   Instead of doing anything odd to access dialog boxes within your application, you'll have access to classes with easy to understand names and relatively consistent configuration methods. For example, you'll use the OpenFileDialog class for creating a standard Open dialog box. You'll also find FontDialog, PageSetupDialog, PrintDialog, PrintPreviewDialog, and SaveFileDialog classes.

▶ **Message Boxes**   The final significant entry is the MessageBox class. Many developers will find this one oddity in the mix. Instead of merely calling MessageBox as you did in the past, you must now use **MessageBox::Show()**. It's a small change, but one that serves to confuse, rather than help. **Message::Show()** is one example of the price that you as a developer will pay for object orientation—no more global functions.

A Quick Overview of the System.Drawing Namespace

The System.Drawing namespace contains all of the classes for displaying any type of graphic information on screen. The technique for using this namespace is completely different from anything you may have learned with Win32. For the most part, the classes are easy to understand. The best part of all is that you won't have to work a DC any longer.

We'll discuss this namespace as part of the source code in the sections that follow. The namespace contains everything you'd expect. You'll find classes for creating pens and brushes, working with bitmaps, and rendering images on screen. The first big change you'll notice is that the namespace provides enumerations of common values so you don't need to "remember" them as you develop the application. For example, if you want to create a black brush, you'll specify the Color::Black value instead of an RGB value.

The drawing commands are also easier to use than the ones found in the Win32 API. All of the drawing commands begin by defining a pen for drawing the image and a rectangle with bounding coordinates for the graphic. When working with primitives such as the arc, you'll define a starting location using an angular measurement in degrees. The end point is defined as an angular measurement from the starting point.

The bottom line is that the System.Drawing namespace provides most (but not all) of the functionality of the Win32 API with little of the inconsistency. There's one feature provided by this namespace that you won't find in the Win32 API (this will be discussed in the "Animation Techniques Using GIF Files" section of the chapter). While the GDI+ functionality provided by the System.Drawing namespace is phenomenal compared to the Win32 API, the one thing lacking is support for three-dimensional drawing. There are several likely reasons for the lack of three-dimensional drawing support. First, developers working in game programming aren't likely to show interest in managed code any time soon. Second, while the scientific community could make good use of three-dimensional drawing support, many of these developers rely on UNIX or Linux. Finally, Microsoft's focus is on the business user—a developer who can make use of two-dimensional graphics and doesn't really need the capabilities provided by three-dimensional drawing.

Writing a Graphics Desktop Application

As mentioned during the introduction, Visual C++ is unique in the Visual Studio .NET language setup because it handles managed and unmanaged code with equal ease. In addition, you can produce native EXE applications with the same ease that you can produce applications that rely on the .NET framework.

The two sections that follow present basic graphics applications. The unmanaged code example shows how to perform basic tasks such as load bitmaps, cursors, and icons. We'll also discuss how to perform basic drawing tasks, such as using drawing primitives. The managed code example will likewise show how to work with the .NET Framework to load bitmaps, cursors, and icons. You'll also learn about drawing primitives from a .NET perspective. By comparing the two sections, you can learn about the capabilities of Windows drawing in the managed and unmanaged environments—at least where these capabilities overlap. (Remember that you'll still use unmanaged code to access features such as DirectX.)

Using Unmanaged Code

As mentioned in this introduction, this example shows you how to load and unload basic graphics and use the drawing primitives. The unmanaged code example uses the MFC Application project. I gave my project a name of UnmanagedGraph, but any name will work. You'll want to use the Dialog Based application type (found on the Application Type tab). Give the dialog a title of Unmanaged Graphic Example on the User Interface Features tab. Once you make these changes, click Finish to create the project.

At this point, you'll see the blank dialog box. Add three buttons to it. Give the first button an ID of IDC_ICONS and a Caption of Icons. The second button will have an ID of IDC_GRAPHICS and a Caption of Graphics. The third button will have an ID of IDC_DRAWING and a Caption of Drawing.

Working with Icons

We need to add a handler for loading the standard icons into the display area. Right-click IDC_ICONS and choose Add Event Handler from the context menu. When you see the Event Handler Wizard, select BN_CLICKED in the Message Type field, and then click Add and Edit. You'll see an **OnBnClickedIcons**() function added to the application. Listing 4-1 shows the code you'll add for this function.

Listing 4-1

```
void CUnmanagedGraphDlg::OnBnClickedIcons()
{
   HICON    hIcon;    // An icon handle.
   CRect    oRect;    // Text display area.

   // Initialize oRect
   oRect.bottom = 36;
   oRect.top = 4;
   oRect.left = 40;
   oRect.right = 256;
```

```
// Get the device context for the current window.
pdc = this->GetDC();

// Load and display the icons.
hIcon = LoadIcon(NULL, IDI_APPLICATION);
DrawIcon(pdc->m_hDC, 4, 4, hIcon);
DrawText(pdc->m_hDC, "Application", 11, LPRECT(oRect), DT_VCENTER);

// Release the device context.
this->ReleaseDC(pdc);
}
```

Listing 4-1 shows you the essentials of working with icons using a standard DC strategy. In fact, this is the same method developers have used for every version of the Win32 API. The code on the CD-ROM is a bit longer than the code shown in the listing. You'll see all of the icons listed in the source code. The steps you need to perform are always the same when rendering an icon or cursor on screen.

1. Create a DC for the device that you want to use.

2. Load the icon or cursor that you want to display.

3. Draw the icon on screen using the DC.

4. Release the DC.

This example shows how to use the standard Windows icons. You can also load icons into your project. If you plan to use anything other than a BMP, ICO, or CUR file, you'll need to click Import. Visual C++ .NET supports a variety of other file types, but lists them as custom resources. To add a new icon, right-click anywhere in the Resource View tab and choose Add | Add Resource from the context menu. You'll see an Add Resource dialog box shown next, where you can choose from any of the standard resources.

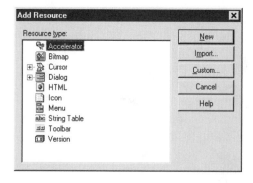

Notice that the example code in Listing 4-1 also contains a **DrawText()** function call. This call enabled you to see the name of each icon resource on each screen. Notice that the **DrawText()** call also includes a handle to the DC, a bounding rectangle for the text, and one or more constants that determine how Windows draws the text. In this case, we're using DT_VCENTER to display the text centered on screen. A bug in the current product implementation prevents the text from displaying correctly, but Microsoft might fix this problem by the time you read this chapter.

As mentioned earlier, you do have alternatives for creating a DC. Listing 4-2 shows the effect of using the CClientDC class. (Note that I added this as an Icons 2 button to the example, and you can see the associated information on the source code CD.) You'll notice that this code is shorter than the code in Listing 4-1. While the basic techniques are the same, the CClientDC class performs some of the work for you. In addition, the class eases your workload by incorporating the necessary draw commands as part of the class. Rather than use a pointer, you can call **DrawIcon()** or **DrawText()** as a method within the CClientDC class.

Listing 4-2

```
void CUnmanagedGraphDlg::OnBnClickedIcons2()
{
    HICON     hIcon;    // An icon handle.
    CRect     oRect;    // Text display area.

    // Initialize oRect
    oRect.bottom = 36;
    oRect.top = 4;
    oRect.left = 40;
    oRect.right = 256;

    // Create the client DC.
    CClientDC    pdc(this);

    // Load and display the icons.
    hIcon = LoadIcon(NULL, IDI_APPLICATION);
    pdc.DrawIcon(4, 4, hIcon);
    pdc.DrawText("Application", 11, LPRECT(oRect), DT_VCENTER);
}
```

The **OnBnClickedIcons2()** also shows you how to use a custom icon within your application. (You'll find the RedIcon.ICO file in the Chapter 04 folder of the source code CD.) The essential difference lies in the way you load the icon. Here's the new icon loading code that you'll find in the source code CD file.

```
hIcon = LoadIcon(AfxGetInstanceHandle(), MAKEINTRESOURCE(IDI_RED_ARROW));
```

The finished Icons button produces a list of standard icons. You'll use these icons within message boxes and for other uses in Windows. Following is the output of the full code found on the source code CD.

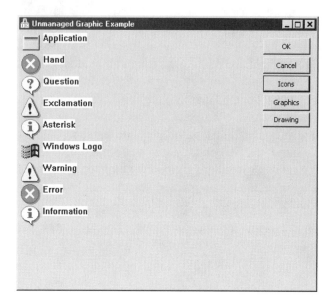

Working with Bitmaps

Bitmaps are a bit trickier than other types of graphics you'll work with. They require special handling because you're not drawing the bitmap on screen in the same way as you would a graphics primitive. In addition, bitmaps use many non-standard file formats. This section of the chapter relies on the ColorBlk2.BMP file found in the Chapter 04 folder of the source code CD. Of course, you can use any other bitmap that you'd like.

As part of the preparation for this section, you'll need to load a bitmap into a control created in the display area. You'll add the bitmap to the project using the same Add Resource dialog box that we discussed in the previous section. After you add the bitmap to your project, add an event handler for the Graphics button. Right-click IDC_ GRAPHICS and choose Add Event Handler from the context menu. When you see the Event Handler Wizard, select BN_CLICKED in the Message Type field, then click Add and Edit. You'll see a **OnBnClickedGraphics()** function added to the application. Listing 4-3 shows the code you'll add for this function.

Listing 4-3

```
void CUnmanagedGraphDlg::OnBnClickedGraphics()
{
    CRect     rect; // Client bounding area.

    // Load the bitmap.
    if (bmp.m_hObject == 0)
        bmp.LoadBitmap(IDB_BITMAP1);

    // Get the client area.
    this->GetClientRect(LPRECT(rect));
    rect.right = rect.right - 90;

    // Create a static control to display the graphic,
    // then display the image.
    if (disp.m_hWnd == 0)
        disp.Create(_T("Sample"),
                    WS_CHILD | WS_VISIBLE | SS_BITMAP | SS_CENTERIMAGE,
                    rect,
                    this);
    disp.SetBitmap(HBITMAP(bmp));
}
```

If you're thinking this code is considerably shorter than other code you might have seen for displaying a bitmap using Visual C++, the magic is in the CStatic object, disp. As you can see from the code, you need to load the bitmap from the resource file. Notice that, not as with the icon file in the previous section, we don't need to do anything special in this case. The bitmap loads without conversion. The BMP loading technique represents one of the inconsistencies that tend to drive developers crazy, because you never really know if the problem is in your code or some quirk in the Win32 API.

Creating the CStatic object is easy. All you need to do is supply window text (you'll never see it when working with a bitmap), some display options where you want to display the CStatic object, and the parent window. The only optional display option shown above is SS_CENTERIMAGE. You must provide SS_BITMAP so the CStatic object knows what to do with the bitmap when you load it. While the WS_VISIBLE option is theoretically optional, there isn't much point to keeping the bitmap hidden if you plan to load it immediately.

Displaying the bitmap is easy. Just call the **SetBitmap()** method of the disp object after you create it. Notice the conversion to an HBITMAP in the code. The **Setbitmap()**

method doesn't provide an override for CBitmap objects. Here's what the output of this code looks like:

Working with Graphics Primitives

The final area of consideration is creating some code that shows basic drawing functionality. Right click IDC_DRAWING and choose Add Event Handler from the context menu. When you see the Event Handler Wizard, select BN_CLICKED in the Message Type field, and then click Add and Edit. You'll see a **OnBnClickedDrawing()** function added to the application. Listing 4-4 shows the code you'll add for this function.

Listing 4-4

```
void CUnmanagedGraphDlg::OnBnClickedDrawing()
{
    CRect     rect;     // Text display area.

    // Get the client area.
    this->GetClientRect(LPRECT(rect));
    rect.right = rect.right - 90;

    // Get the device context for the current window.
    pdc = this->GetDC();

    // Initialize the brushes and pens.
    if (oBackBrush.m_hObject == 0)
```

```
  {
    oBackBrush.CreateSolidBrush(RGB(0, 0, 255));
    oForeBrush.CreateSolidBrush(RGB(255, 0, 0));
    oPen.CreatePen(PS_SOLID, 5, RGB(0, 255, 0));
  }

  // Set some default colors.
  pdc->SelectObject(&oForeBrush);
  pdc->SelectObject(&oPen);

  // Fill the drawing area with one color.
  pdc->FillRect(rect, &oBackBrush);

  // Move to the starting point, then draw a line.
  pdc->MoveTo(10, 10);
  pdc->LineTo(100,100);

  // Draw a solid rectangle.
  pdc->Rectangle(40, 200, 90, 120);

  // Draw a hollow rectangle. The only brush width is 1.
  pdc->FrameRect(CRect(200, 25, 320, 250), &oForeBrush);

  // Draw a rectangle with rounded corners.
  pdc->RoundRect(150, 80, 265, 320, 25, 25);

  // Draw an arc.
  pdc->Arc(0, 0, 150, 150, 200, 200, 0, 0);

  // Draw a chord.
  pdc->Chord(200, 200, 350, 350, 0, 500, 300, 0);

  // Draw a pie wedge.
  pdc->Pie(120, 120, 240, 240, 120, 0, 0, 240);

  // Draw a circle.
  pdc->Ellipse(0, 240, 150, 390);

  // Release the device context.
  this->ReleaseDC(pdc);
}
```

The first thing you should notice is that this code follows the same path as the icon-loading example earlier in the chapter. However, you'll find that this example has a few interesting additions. First, notice that you must create at least a pen or a brush before you can draw anything on screen. The pen and brush describe how the application should draw the image on screen. Windows will use a pen for features such as the outer line for a rectangle. It uses the foreground brush to color the inside of a solid object. By mixing pen and brush colors and effects, you can achieve just about any effect on your drawing.

Most of the drawing primitives are straightforward. All you need to do is call the drawing primitive with the appropriate input (which normally begins with a bounding box). Drawing a line is a two-step process. You must position the caret at the starting position using the **MoveTo()** function and then draw the line using the **DrawTo()** method. Here's what the output of this part of the example looks like:

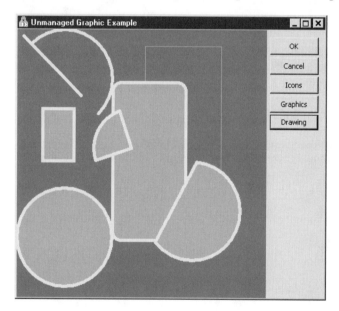

Using Managed Code

It's time to look at an example of some managed code. You'll find that Visual C++ .NET does make drawing a little easier than the previous example. At least you'll find a few less inconsistencies when creating your application.

NOTE

This application produces output similar to the output produced by the UnmanagedGraph example in the previous section. As a result, this section won't show the output of the application and will concentrate on the code instead.

The wizards Microsoft provides to create managed applications are nearly invisible, which means you don't get all the nice extras provided by an MFC application. To begin this project, create a Managed C++ application. The example has a name of ManagedGraph, but you can use any name you like. You'll notice that Visual C++ creates the new application for you immediately after you click OK in the New Project dialog box.

What you have right now is the barest of console applications—not what we're looking for in this section of the chapter. You can modify the application to work with you by adding the code shown in bold below to the ManagedGraph.CPP file. It's essential that you add the code now or you'll experience problems with some of the tasks we'll perform as the section progresses.

```
#include "stdafx.h"

#using <mscorlib.dll>
#include <tchar.h>

using namespace System;

// Libraries used to support application.
#using <System.DLL>
#using <System.Drawing.DLL>
#using <System.Windows.Forms.DLL>

// Add some namespaces.
using namespace System::Windows::Forms;
using namespace System::Drawing;
```

The application still doesn't provide anything more than console capability, but you have access to far more. Adding the namespaces enables Visual C++ to locate elements of the .NET Framework beyond those found in the System namespace. The following sections show how to build a managed code application that performs some basic graphics tasks.

Modifying the _tmain() Method

As previously mentioned, the wizard assumes that everyone wants to create a console application. This means you have a **Console::Write**() call in the **_tmain**() function, and that's about it. The **_tmain**() function does play a large role in console applications. However, for windowed applications, it merely serves as a means to start the application. Listing 4-5 shows the **_tmain**() code we'll use for this example.

Lisitng 4-5

```
// This is the entry point for this application
int _tmain(void)
```

```
{
    ManagedGraph*  mainForm;    // Create a copy of the main form.

    // Initialize the main form.
    mainForm = new ManagedGraph();

    // Start the application.
    Application::Run(mainForm);

    return 0;
}
```

As you can see, the **_tmain**() function creates an instance of the ManagedGraph class (we'll create this class in the next section) and uses it to start the application. The **Application::Run**() method starts the application and enables it to continue running. The two main methods for stopping the application once you start it are to call **Application::Exit**() or close the main form. The only reason that closing the main form works is that the application returns from the **Application::Run**() call and there's nothing more to process. We'll use this particular form of **_tmain**() for many of the examples in the book. However, Chapters 12, 13, and 14 will expand on this part of the application development process somewhat.

Creating the ManagedGraph Class

Every windowed application you create will contain a minimum of one class. This class will contain the code for the main form of your application. It doesn't matter what type of application you want to create. (Creating dialog-based applications is the easiest route to start with.). Listing 4-6 contains the main form class for this example.

Listing 4-6

```
// Create a managed class for handing the display.
__gc class ManagedGraph :
    public Form
{
public:

    ManagedGraph(void)
    {
        // Initialize the form appearance.
        Text = "Managed Graphic Example";
        ClientSize = Size::Size(478, 384);

        // Create a menu system.
        MainMenu* menu = new MainMenu();
```

```
        // File menu.
        MenuItem* FileItem = menu->MenuItems->Add("F&ile");
        FileItem->MenuItems->Add("E&xit",
                                new EventHandler(this, OnFileExit));

        // Display menu.
        MenuItem* DisplayItem = menu->MenuItems->Add("D&isplay");
        DisplayItem->MenuItems->Add("N&othing",
                                    new EventHandler(this, OnDisplayNothing));
        DisplayItem->MenuItems->Add("I&cons",
                                    new EventHandler(this, OnDisplayIcon));
        DisplayItem->MenuItems->Add("Gr&aphics (Normal)",
                                    new EventHandler(this, OnDisplayGraphics));
        DisplayItem->MenuItems->Add("Graphics (S&ized to Fit)",
                                    new EventHandler(this, OnDisplayGraphics2));
        DisplayItem->MenuItems->Add("&Drawing",
                                    new EventHandler(this, OnDisplayDrawing));

        Menu = menu;
    }

    virtual ~ManagedGraph(void)
    {
    }

protected:
    // Override OnPaint to allow graphics display.
    void OnPaint(PaintEventArgs* e);

private:
    // Declare all of the menu selections.
    void OnFileExit(Object* sender, EventArgs* e);
    void OnDisplayNothing(Object* sender, EventArgs* e);
    void OnDisplayIcon(Object* sender, EventArgs* e);
    void OnDisplayGraphics(Object* sender, EventArgs* e);
    void OnDisplayGraphics2(Object* sender, EventArgs* e);
    void OnDisplayDrawing(Object* sender, EventArgs* e);

    // A variable for tracking the current drawing type.
    int _DrawSelect;
};

// Begin function descriptions for managed class.

void ManagedGraph::OnFileExit(Object* sender, EventArgs* e)
{
    // Exit the application.
```

```
      Close();
}

void ManagedGraph::OnDisplayNothing(Object* sender, EventArgs* e)
{
   // Set the drawing selection and refresh the screen.
   _DrawSelect = 0;
   Refresh();
}

void ManagedGraph::OnDisplayIcon(Object* sender, EventArgs* e)
{
   // Set the drawing selection and refresh the screen.
   _DrawSelect = 1;
   Refresh();
}

void ManagedGraph::OnDisplayGraphics(Object* sender, EventArgs* e)
{
   // Set the drawing selection and refresh the screen.
   _DrawSelect = 2;
   Refresh();
}

void ManagedGraph::OnDisplayGraphics2(Object* sender, EventArgs* e)
{
   // Set the drawing selection and refresh the screen.
   _DrawSelect = 3;
   Refresh();
}

void ManagedGraph::OnDisplayDrawing(Object* sender, EventArgs* e)
{
   // Set the drawing selection and refresh the screen.
   _DrawSelect = 4;
   Refresh();
}
```

The main form class derives from Form. You'll find that most of your forms derive from this class. Notice that the class definition begins with __gc. This attribute tells Visual C++ .NET that this is a garbage-collected (managed) class. You must add this attribute to all managed classes within your application. Otherwise, Visual C++ assumes they're unmanaged, and the application won't compile.

The constructor, **ManagedGraph()**, contains the basics for any dialog-based application. The code initializes the form appearance by changing the title bar caption and resizing the form as needed for the application. It's at this point that you should spot the first inconsistency between the unmanaged and the managed worlds. Notice the dimensions of the client rectangle in this example. When you run the application, you'll see that it's the same size as the 320×250 form in the unmanaged code example. You'll find that the managed code size is correct and directly correlates to what you'll see on screen. On the other hand, many developers find dialog box sizing in the unmanaged environment frustrating at best.

The next section of code in the constructor creates a menu, and then assigns it to the Menu property of the form. You create the top-level menu items using the MainMenu class. The **Add()** method enables you to add new entries. For some reason, the "&" doesn't work as anticipated at the time of this writing, but it should work by the time you read this. You'll create submenu entries by creating a MenuItem object. You must have one MenuItem object for each main menu entry. Note that you also use the **Add()** method to add the entries. However, you'll notice that the submenu entries also include **an EventHandler()** entry that associates the menu item with an event handler in your code.

The class block ends with declarations of event handlers and global variables. Every menu event handler uses the same format. The menu event handler must accept a pointer to the sender and an event object. Notice that we also override the **OnPaint()** method. When you override a method, you'll face constraints placed on the method by the base class. In this case, you must make **OnPaint()** protected—you can't hide it from view. The **OnPaint()** method only accepts a pointer as input to an event object that also provides access to the DC (although we'll never access the DC directly).

Each one of the Display menu event handlers performs the same task. First, it selects a drawing mode that matches the menu entry. Second, the method calls **Refresh()** to ensure the user sees the new content.

Overriding OnPaint()

The **OnPaint()** method deserves special consideration because you'll use it in many of your applications to ensure the data the user sees always remains current. This is especially important for drawing applications if you want the user to see the data after a redraw. Listing 4-7 shows the code we'll use for this example. The code is shortened, in this case, because many elements are repetitive. You can find the full source code on the source code CD. Notice the use of the switch statement to control the display of data according to the user selection.

Listing 4-7

```
void ManagedGraph::OnPaint(PaintEventArgs* e)
{
    // Create a font, set of brushes, and a pen.
```

```
Drawing::Font* oFont = new Drawing::Font("Arial", 12);
SolidBrush*     oBrush = new SolidBrush(Color::Black);
Pen*            oPen = new Pen(Color::LightGreen, 5);
SolidBrush*     oForeBrush = new SolidBrush(Color::Red);
SolidBrush*     oBackBrush = new SolidBrush(Color::Blue);
Pen*            oBrushPen = new Pen(Color::Red, 2);

// Create a pointer to the graphics routines.
Graphics* g = e->Graphics;

// Create some drawing primitives.
Drawing::Icon* oIcon = SystemIcons::get_Application();
Bitmap* oBitmap = new Bitmap("ColorBlk2.bmp");

// Select the proper drawing mode.
switch (_DrawSelect)
{
case 1:
   // Draw the standard icons.
   g->DrawIcon(oIcon, 4, 4);
   g->DrawString("Application", oFont, oBrush, PointF(40, 4));
   oIcon = SystemIcons::get_Hand();
   g->DrawIcon(oIcon, 4, 38);
   g->DrawString("Hand", oFont, oBrush, PointF(40, 38));
   break;

case 2:
   // Draw a graphic normal size.
   g->DrawImage(oBitmap, 4, 4, oBitmap->Width, oBitmap->Height);
   break;

case 3:
   // Draw a graphic that fills the client rectangle.
   g->DrawImage(oBitmap, ClientRectangle);
   break;

case 4:
   // Fill the client area with a single color.
   g->FillRectangle(oBackBrush, ClientRectangle);
```

```
    // Create a drawing using graphics primitives.
    g->DrawLine(oPen, 10, 10, 100, 100);
    g->FillRectangle(oForeBrush, 40, 120, 50, 80);
    g->DrawRectangle(oPen, 40, 120, 50, 80);
    g->DrawRectangle(oBrushPen, 200, 25, 120, 225);
    g->DrawArc(oPen, 0, 0, 150, 150, 225, 180);
    g->FillPie(oForeBrush, 120, 120, 120, 120, 165, 90);
    g->DrawPie(oPen, 120, 120, 120, 120, 165, 90);
    g->FillEllipse(oForeBrush, 0, 240, 150, 150);
    g->DrawEllipse(oPen, 0, 240, 150, 150);
    break;
  }
}
```

The **OnPaint**() method begins by creating the fonts, pens, and brushes used for the rest of the method. Notice that creating a new drawing tool is easier than using the Win32 API. Instead of having to remember weird constants or filling out extensive data structures, you create the drawing elements using simple, human-readable terms. This first section also creates the drawing primitives used to present information on screen and a pointer to the graphics routines.

It's faster to draw the standard icons using managed code than using the Win32 API. For one thing, you use less code. It takes only three lines of code to draw a single entry. Positioning the icons is easier. Notice that we don't discuss a DC in any of the calls. The **DrawString**() method also provides better control over the output text. You have a choice of font and brush (color used to draw the text). Positioning is also easier because you don't have to define a drawing rectangle.

Drawing a bitmap on screen is similarly easy. The example code includes two methods for drawing the bitmap. The first technique draws the bitmap fully sized. The second technique stretches the bitmap to fit within the client rectangle.

The final drawing task is to use drawing primitives. It's the one area you'll find that the .NET Framework fails to produce the desired functionality. For example, you won't find any equivalents for the **FrameRect**() and **RoundRect**() API calls. The **Chord**() API call is also missing. You can simulate these features using other namespace features, but you'll require a lot more code to do so because you'll have to define a path for the application to follow. Also, notice that the drawing primitives don't automatically fill the area inside the graphic. You must use a **FillXXX**() call to perform this task. This means that creating a filled ellipse requires two calls in place of one.

Animation Techniques Using GIF Files

Many applications today use simple animation to get a point across to the user. For example, Windows Explorer uses animations to show a file moving from one location to another. One of many ways to create animations it to use a GIF file. GIF files have been around for quite some time. You see them all the time on the Internet. All of those little animations you see on Web sites are very likely GIF files. A GIF file works by placing multiple images in a single file. Commands separate the images. Each command tells the displaying application how to present the next frame of the animation and how long to present it.

BROWSER ALERT

*You can see animated GIFs in action on many Internet sites. One of the more interesting places to look is **http://www.wanderers2.com/rose/animate.html**. The site offers an index of sites you can visit to see various kinds of animated GIFs. Looking at a variety of sites will help you understand what works and what doesn't. You can also download an animated GIF Wizard, make your own animated GIF online, and learn all about how to make animated GIFs.*

Visual Studio doesn't support GIF files as an IDE add-on. If you try to add an animated GIF to your project, you'll receive an error message saying the GIF is damaged or simply incorrect. Even if you can view the GIF inside Internet Explorer, Visual Studio .NET will steadfastly refuse to load it. This section of the chapter shows how to get around the problems that Visual Studio .NET presents when it comes to GIF files.

The following sections divide the task of working with GIFs into two parts. The first part is to create the animation using a GIF editor. Because Visual Studio .NET doesn't provide such a tool, we'll use the GIF Construction Set from Alchemy Mindworks. The second part will show how to display the animated GIF on screen. In this case, we'll use unmanaged code. However, you can achieve similar effects using managed code.

Creating the Animated GIF

If the previous section didn't show you enough techniques to make your Web site sparkle, there are a host of other ideas you can use. A favorite idea of webmasters the world over is the use of animated GIFs. All that an animated GIF does is pack several pictures into one file. The browser plays these pictures back one at a time—allowing you to create the illusion of continuous animation. You can also use special effects to create a slide show using a GIF. The only problem with this approach is the download time—a slide show tends to put quite a strain on the user's download capability.

NOTE

*This section will show you how to create a GIF using the GIF Construction Set from Alchemy Mind Works. You can download it from several places. The best place is straight from the vendor at **http://www.mindworkshop.com/alchemy/gifcon.html**. You can also download it from the animated GIF viewing site mentioned earlier in the chapter: **http://www.wanderers2.com/rose/animate.html**.*

We'll use the GIF Construction Set in this example for two reasons. First, since it's shareware, all of you can download it from the Internet and follow along with the examples. Second, it's a great program, and most people find that it works just fine for creating animated GIFs. You'll notice the lack of an actual drawing program with this program, but Windows already supplies that in the form of Paintbrush or MS Paint.

NOTE

This chapter uses the 2.0a version of the GIF Construction Set. The procedures and methods don't work with the 1.0q version of the product.

You'll also need a graphics conversion utility if your drawing program doesn't support the GIF file format directly (neither Paintbrush nor MS Paint do). Both Graphics Workshop from Alchemy Mind Works and Paint Shop Pro by JASC, Inc. are excellent graphics conversion programs. Both vendors provide shareware versions of their product. You can find Alchemy Mind Works at the Internet site provided in the previous note. The JASC product appears on various BBS and CompuServe forums (they may also have an Internet site by the time you read this).

Start the GIF Construction Set program. Use the File | Open command to view the contents of the \Chapter 04\Animated Graphic directory of the source code CD. Notice that the directory has several GIF files in it already. Time0.GIF is a base file—a blank used to create the animation effect. You can save a substantial amount of time by creating such a blank whenever you create an animation. In fact, cartoonists use this very technique. They draw the common elements of an animation once on separate sheets, and then combine them to create the animation. Only unique items are drawn one at a time. Time1.GIF through Time12.GIF are the actual animation files—think of each one as an animation cell.

Let's create an animated GIF using these "cel" files. The following procedure isn't meant to lock you into a particular regimen, but it does show one way to use the GIF Construction Set to create an animated GIF.

1. Use the File | New command to create a new GIF. You'll see a blank GIF dialog. GIF Construction Set always assumes a standard display size of 640×480 pixels. We'll need to change that value.

2. Double-click on the Header entry. You'll see the Edit Header dialog shown here. It allows you to change characteristics associated with the GIF—for example, its size. Notice the Loop option on this dialog. If you keep this value set to 0, the GIF will continue looping indefinitely. This is a great idea, in most cases, but you might want to set this value to something else to save system resources when needed.

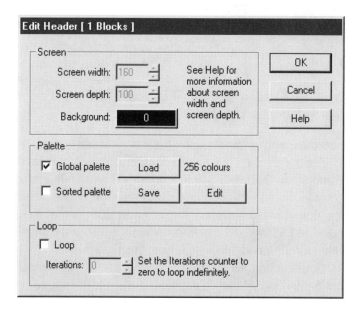

3. Set any header options. The example sets the number of loops to 10 for testing purposes, but you can set this value as you see fit. Click on OK to make the change permanent.

4. Click on the + button and select Image from the drop-down list (or use the Block | Merge command). This allows you to add an image to the GIF. You'll see a standard File | Open dialog.

5. Double-click on the first file you want to use in the animation. In this case, you'd double-click Time1.GIF. You'll see the Palette dialog shown here. The palette for this graphic doesn't match the standard palette used by GIF Construction Set. Note older versions of the GIF Construction set provided more options.

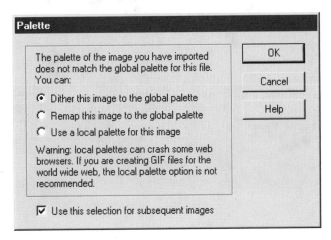

6. Select the "Dither this image to the global palette" setting for compatibility reasons. Click on OK to complete the process. GIF Construction Set will insert a new graphic into the GIF.

7. Click on the + button and select Image from the drop-down list. You'll see the same File | Open dialog as before.

8. Select the next image in the series and click OK. Click OK again if GIF Construction Set asks you about the palette setting. GIF Construction Set will automatically insert the image in the next position of the animation sequence.

9. Repeat steps 7 and 8 for the remaining GIFs in this animation (Time2.GIF, Time3.GIF, and so on). Now we have to insert some controls to make this image work properly.

10. Double-click Block 3 (the second image). You'll see an Edit Image dialog like the one shown here. Notice that this dialog tells you about the image. You can also use this dialog to add control blocks between image elements. Control blocks allow you to modify the behavior of the animated GIF. For example, you can use a control block to set the time between pictures. Many browsers expect a control block between every image in your animated GIF, so you must add a control block starting with the second image.

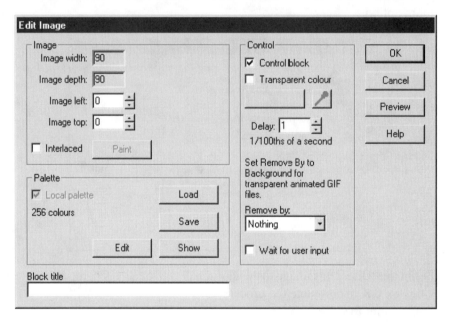

11. Check the Control Block option. Set the Delay field to 1. Click OK to add the control block. You won't see any difference in the main window.

12. Click on the next Image entry.

13. Repeat steps 11 and 12 for each of the images. You'll end up with a series of images, as shown next. (Make sure you add a Control object to the last image, since the animated GIF will automatically loop back to the first image.)

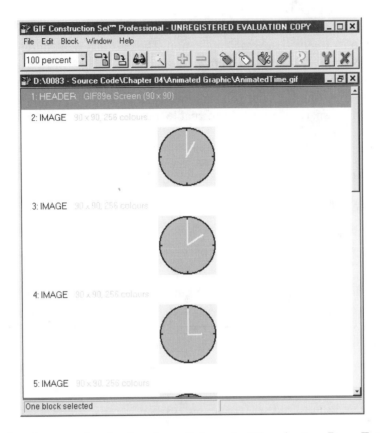

14. To view the completed animation, click on the View button. Press Esc to exit the viewing area.

15. The only thing left to do is save your animated GIF file. Use the File | Save As command to do that. You could use any filename, but for the purposes of this example, save the file as AnimatedTime.GIF.

Designing the Animation Application

In the previous sections, I mentioned that the .NET Framework provides only two-dimensional drawing capabilities. However, it does provide one easy to use feature that you'll find very appealing; the ability to show animated files on screen. This section shows how you'll use the animated GIF created in the previous section by animating it on a standard desktop application. The part that will amaze you is just how easy it is to present the animation.

To begin this example, create a new Managed C++ Application. The example uses a name of "Animated," but you can use any name desired. You'll need to add the drawing namespaces shown here to enable the application to access the .NET Framework functionality.

```
// Libraries used to support application.
#using <System.DLL>
#using <System.Drawing.DLL>
#using <System.Windows.Forms.DLL>

// Add some namespaces.
using namespace System::Windows::Forms;
using namespace System::Drawing;
```

The **_tmain**() function will require the same modifications as in our previous example. Only the name of the class will change. Listing 4-8 shows the code we'll use. We'll look at other ways of working with **_tmain**() in Part IV, but this technique works well enough for the examples now.

Listing 4-8

```
// This is the entry point for this application
int _tmain(void)
{
   Animated*   mainForm;    // Create a copy of the main form.

   // Initialize the main form.
   mainForm = new Animated();

   // Start the application.
   Application::Run(mainForm);

   return 0;
}
```

All we need now is a class to do the work of animating the GIF. The Animated class appears in Listing 4-9.

Listing 4-9

```
// Create a managed class for animating the GIF file.
__gc class Animated :
   public Form
```

```cpp
{
public:

   Animated(void)
   {
      // Initialize the form appearance.
      Text = "GIF Animation Example";
      ClientSize = Size::Size(478, 384);

      // Create a menu system.
      MainMenu* menu = new MainMenu();

      // File menu.
      MenuItem* FileItem = menu->MenuItems->Add("&File");
      FileItem->MenuItems->Add("E&xit",
                              new EventHandler(this, OnFileExit));

      // Animate menu.
      MenuItem* AnimateItem = menu->MenuItems->Add("&Animate");
      AnimateItem->MenuItems->Add("Sta&rt",
                                 new EventHandler(this, OnAnimateStart));
      AnimateItem->MenuItems->Add("Sto&p",
                                 new EventHandler(this, OnAnimateStop));

      Menu = menu;

      // Initialize the bitmap.
      oBitmap = new Bitmap("AnimatedTime.gif");
   }

   virtual ~Animated(void)
   {
   }

protected:
   // Override OnPaint to allow graphics display.
   void OnPaint(PaintEventArgs* e);

private:
   // Declare all of the menu selections.
   void OnFileExit(Object* sender, EventArgs* e);
   void OnAnimateStart(Object* sender, EventArgs* e);
   void OnAnimateStop(Object* sender, EventArgs* e);

   // Declare an event handler for the animation.
   void NextFrame(Object* sender, EventArgs* e);
```

```cpp
   // Declare local variables.
   int     _DrawSelect;    // Drawing mode.
   bool    _Animated;      // Animation active.
   Bitmap* oBitmap;        // GIF bitmap.
};


// Begin function descriptions for managed class.

void Animated::OnFileExit(Object* sender, EventArgs* e)
{
   // Exit the application.
   Close();
}


void Animated::OnAnimateStart(Object* sender, EventArgs* e)
{
   // Initialize the animating the first time the user selects it.
   if (!_Animated)
   {
      ImageAnimator::Animate(oBitmap,
                             new EventHandler(this, NextFrame));
      _Animated = true;
   }

   // Select a drawing mode.
   _DrawSelect = 1;
}

void Animated::OnAnimateStop(Object* sender, EventArgs* e)
{
   // Select a drawing mode that stops the animation.
   _DrawSelect = 2;
}

void Animated::NextFrame(Object* sender, EventArgs* e)
{
   // Force OnPaint() to redraw the animation.
   Invalidate();
}

void Animated::OnPaint(PaintEventArgs* e)
{
   // Create a pointer to the graphics routines.
   Graphics* g = e->Graphics;

   switch (_DrawSelect)
   {
```

```
case 1:
   // Animate the GIF file.
   ImageAnimator::UpdateFrames();
   g->DrawImage(oBitmap, 4, 4, oBitmap->Width, oBitmap->Height);
   break;


case 2:
   // Draw a graphic normally.
   g->DrawImage(oBitmap, 4, 4, oBitmap->Width, oBitmap->Height);
   break;
   }
}
```

The example code begins in the same way as the previous example. The constructor defines some dialog box elements, including a menu system. The final constructor step is to create the animated GIF bitmap. Notice that you can use the same Bitmap class for any of the file types that Visual Studio .NET supports. The class also declares event handlers for each menu entry and overrides the **OnPaint()** method. We need a special event handler for this example to handle the animation.

The **OnAnimateStart()** method begins by checking the animation status. This example assumes that once the animation starts, it won't stop until the user closes the application. A full-fledged application might start and stop the animation as needed to avoid flickering. This method also selects a drawing mode.

The **OnAnimateStop()** method has a single purpose. It sets the drawing mode to a non-animated setting.

Animation relies on timed presentation of the frames within the animated file. For this reason, we need a special event handler in the form of **NextFrame()** to force the display of the next frame of the animation. The example doesn't require special timing because the control blocks within the animated GIF control execution time between frame elements. The only call that **NextFrame()** requires is one to force **OnPaint()** to do something.

OnPaint() uses the same switching mechanism as the previous example to determine what to draw on screen. The two cases are essentially the same; they draw the bitmap on screen. It's important to note the call to **ImageAnimator::UpdateFrames()**. This is the bit of code that performs the animation magic. It selects the next frame within the animated GIF file. **DrawImage()** normally assumes you want to draw the first frame in the file. This call tells **DrawImage()** to use another frame—the next frame in line. You'll find that when you run the application, you can stop the graphic at any point along the animation route. In other words, clicking stop doesn't mean returning to the first frame—the application will continue to display the currently selected frame.

CHAPTER 5

Working with Active Directory

For anyone who's worked with Windows for a long time, Active Directory represents yet another step in a progression of data storage techniques. The path begins in Windows 3.x, where developers mainly used INI files to store application data. Windows NT introduced the concept of the registry. Windows 2000 introduced Active Directory. All of these technologies have two things in common. First, they store more data than their predecessors. Second, they cure perceived problems with the preceding storage technique.

The INI file is the least centralized method of storing data, while Active Directory represents the most centralized method. INI files stored setting and other application-specific information. The registry stretched data storage to include multiple applications, users, and machine configuration. However, the registry stores information only for a single machine, which means network administrators still have to rush from machine to machine to find what they need. Active Directory stores even more information and does it in a centralized server location for all of the machines on the network. If you're working in an enterprise environment, this is where Windows should have been at the outset.

Active Directory is an extremely complex topic because it covers so much ground. This chapter provides you with an overview of the topic and shows you a few coding techniques, but it doesn't tell you everything you'll ever need to know about Active Directory. However, you shouldn't build Active Directory into an insurmountable mountain either. From a strictly technological perspective, Active Directory is simply a large hierarchical database with some built-in redundancy and extensibility. If you know how to work with databases, you already have the knowledge to begin working with Active Directory.

We'll also discuss the most important part of working with Active Directory, the *interfaces*. The Active Directory Service Interface (ADSI) provides you with a standardized means for working with this rather complex database. The two common methods for working with ADSI are through a set of COM interfaces or by the .NET Framework. We'll discuss both methods of using ADSI in this chapter. The example program will use the COM interface approach.

NOTE

This chapter assumes that you've already installed Active Directory. Windows 2000 Server automatically installs this support when you promote the server to a domain controller. At the time of this writing, it looks like Microsoft's new servers will use this same technique. You can install the Active Directory tools on a local drive by right-clicking the AdminPak.MSI file found in the server's \WINNT\System32 folder and choosing Install from the context menu. The tools will install properly on any Windows 2000 machine. If you have Windows XP, you might need to check the Microsoft Web site for the proper administration tools. Some users reported problems using the Windows 2000 Server tools on a Windows XP machine. In all cases, you can also manage Active Directory from the server console.

What Is Active Directory?

You can look at Active Directory in many ways, most of which are overly complex. The simple way to look at Active Directory is as a massive database designed to make network management easier for everyone. However, you may not realize just how massive this database is. Everyone expects that Active Directory will hold the usual network information, such as user and group security setups. In addition, after looking at Novell's Novell Directory Services (NDS) offering, you'd expect Active Directory to help you manage network resources like disk drives and printers.

What we'll look at in this section of the chapter are a few of the things that you might not expect Active Directory to do. We'll also look at a few potential pitfalls you should consider when working with any network management system like Active Directory.

NOTE

Active Directory requires a server. Windows XP isn't a server platform; it's used for the desktop alone and therefore doesn't provide Active Directory support. Because the new name for Microsoft's server product changes daily, I'll use the term Windows Server throughout the chapter to reference any Windows 2000 or newer server product.

An Overview of the Interface

Microsoft has put a lot of effort into creating a new management tool look for Windows 2000 in the form of Microsoft Management Console (MMC) and a series of snap-ins (add-on modules). Windows XP follows in this tradition and there's no reason to expect Microsoft's latest server product to do otherwise. In short, MMC is a *container application* for specialized components. If you get the idea that MMC is some form of COM technology, you'd be right. A snap-in is really nothing more than a component that uses MMC as a container. In fact, we'll discuss this issue in Chapter 16 as we build an MMC snap-in. You need to use a few of the Active Directory snap-ins to work with the example in this chapter, so it's a good idea to review them now.

Figure 5-1 shows a typical Active Directory Users and Computers console. Any predefined selection of MMC snap-ins is a console. You can also create custom consoles for your own use—something we'll discuss in Chapter 16. As you can see from the figure, the Active Directory Users and Computers console provides access to computer and uses resource information on your network. All of this information appears within Active Directory database entries on the server.

Let's spend a few minutes talking about the various components of the display shown in Figure 5-1. At the top of the tree is the Active Directory root. Below this is the single domain in this tree, DataCon.domain. If there were multiple domains, then there would

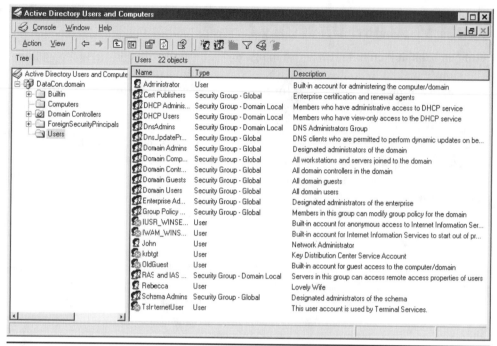

Figure 5-1 Use the Active Directory snap-in to view the entire network at a glance, although you can't manage some network details directly.

be multiple entries at this level of the tree. Don't confuse the domain controller with the domain as a whole. A domain can have more than one domain controller, and these controllers would appear in the Domain Controllers folder. The Builtin folder contains all of the built-in groups for the domain. The Computers folder holds a list of all the computers that have logged into the domain. Active Directory manages these first three folders—Builtin, Computers, and Domain Controllers—automatically. Normally, you won't need to add new entries, but you'll have to configure the ones that Active Directory adds for you.

The name of the last folder, Users, is misleading because it can contain a lot more than just users. This folder can actually contain computers, contacts, groups, printers, users, and shared folders—as a minimum. An administrator can create other classes of objects to add into this folder, and you can design components to work with these classes. For the most part, you'll spend the most time in this folder unless you create additional folders of your own. Active Directory allows you to add new entries at every level of the database including the domain level. At the domain level you can add computers, contacts, groups, organizational units, printers, users, and shared folders.

However, unless you want a messy, hard to follow directory, you'll usually limit the entries at the domain level to organizational units.

TIP

The workstation you use must have a domain connection to work with Active Directory. One of the best ways to check whether your computer has logged into the domain and exchanged the proper information is to look in the Computers folder. The client machine will appear in this folder automatically after a successful logon and the client and server have exchanged information. This information exchange is essential for many kinds of COM related activities.

Developers often need to check the status of their development machines. For example, you may want to ensure that the operating system is up-to-date. A developer can use Active Directory to check on the status of any accessible machine from a remote location. Open either the Computers or Domain Controllers folder and then double-click on a computer icon. You'll see a Properties dialog that enables you to check machine statistics, such as the fully qualified domain name of the computer and the version of the operating system installed.

There are times when you need better access to the machine than the computer Properties dialog will provide. For example, you may need to know the hardware configuration of the machine or the status of the drivers. This information is also available from Active Directory. All you need to do is right-click the computer of interest and choose Manage from the context menu. You'll see the Computer Management console for that machine. The console groups the entries by System Tools (hardware), Storage (the content and organization of the hard drives), and Server Applications and Services (a list of services including COM+ and MSMQ).

One of the most important MMC consoles for this chapter is Component Services. Figure 5-2 shows a typical example of this console. As you can see, this console provides detailed information about your COM+ applications. You can view all of the features of an application, its associated components, and even the details of those components. We'll discuss this utility in detail as the chapter progresses. For now, all you need to know is that the Component Services console is an essential part of most distributed application development efforts today.

By this time, you should have a better idea of why Active Directory, even the interface portion, is important for you as a programmer. Given the right tools, you can manage most testing scenarios and troubleshoot most application failures without even leaving your desk. In addition, Active Directory gives you access to real-world data, something that was difficult to collect in the past. Users tend to behave differently when you watch them directly. This difference in behavior affects the results you get when running tests and ultimately results in applications with less than perfect

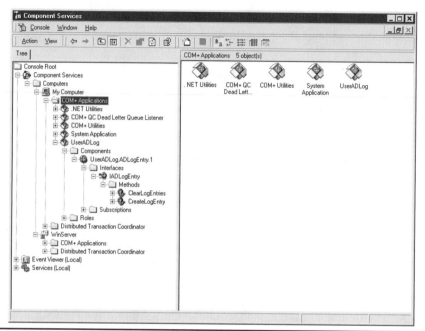

Figure 5-2   *Component Services provides important management functionality for Active Directory development.*

performance characteristics. While I'm not advocating a "big brother" approach to application testing, getting real-world data is an important part of working in today's complex application programming environment.

Why Use Active Directory?

Active Directory has a lot to offer both the network administrator and developer alike. One of the most important considerations is that it provides complete information security. Not only will Active Directory allow you to set the security for individual objects, it will also allow you to set security on object properties as well. This level of functionality means that you can create an extremely detailed security policy that gives users access to what they need. In addition, you can block rights at the object level or at the property level, which means that giving someone access to an object no longer means that they necessarily get full access. Finally, you can delegate the authority to manage security on an object or even a property level.

Policy-based administration is another feature that Active Directory provides. Policies are an implementation of role-based security. Active Directory objects always have a context that defines how a particular user is using the object and expresses the user's rights to the object. All of this information is stored in the Active Directory database, making it easy for an Administrator to create policies that dictate the rights for entire groups of users. The combination of context, role-based security, and groups means that an administrator can manage security using a few groups of users, rather than manage individual users, and still be sure that individual users are getting the access they require.

As a developer, you're already well aware of the extensibility that Active Directory provides. However, what you may not know is that the administrator can extend Active Directory by adding new object classes or new attributes to existing classes. For example, you may want to add the number of sick leave and vacation days an employee has to their entry in Active Directory. A component that you build could keep this value updated so that the employee and management could track this information without relying on another resource. Instead of a simple contact list, you might create special kinds of contacts so that you could keep outside consultants separate from large customers that the company relies on for income.

Scalability is another feature that makes Active Directory a good choice. Active Directory enables you to include multiple domains in a single database. Each domain could contain more than one domain controller. You can organize the entire setup into a contiguous namespace that Microsoft calls a *directory tree*. If your organization is so large that a single tree would be impossible to manage, you can combine directory trees into a non-contiguous namespace called a *forest*. The ability to scale a single Active Directory database over the largest organization means that when you search for a specific domain within your application, you'll find it as long as you have a connection and the server is online.

As previously stated, DNS and Active Directory are *coupled*. What this means to you as a programmer is that the domain controller and other servers could use the same name no matter how they're accessed. A user who normally accesses a server from their desktop computer within the company wouldn't need to make any adjustment when accessing that same server using an Internet connection (assuming that you've properly registered your domain name). In addition, the components you create can access the server in the same way using any connection type.

Active Directory can use two standard directory access protocols for access purposes. The most common method is the Lightweight Directory Access Protocol (LDAP). You can find out more about this access method at **http://www.faqs.org/rfcs/ rfc2251.html**. A secondary access method is Name Service Provider Interface (NSPI). This is a Microsoft standard used with Microsoft Exchange version 4.0 and above. Many third party products work with Microsoft Exchange; so from a Microsoft-specific programming perspective, this second access method is just as important as LDAP. However, you'll probably use LDAP when working with multiple directory types.

The last benefit of using Active Directory is the ability to query the database using any of a number of methods. From a user perspective, you can find any object on the network using Search, My Network Places, or Active Directory Users and Computers. We'll see in the next chapter that querying the database within your application is just as easy and flexible. Finding what you need isn't a problem with Active Directory.

Active Directory Programming Pitfalls

It would be frivolous to say that Active Directory will take care of every need you've ever had and will have. That just isn't realistic, despite what Microsoft's marketing arm would have you believe. A network management system like Active Directory can be a hindrance in more than a few ways. The following list provides you with a few ideas.

▶ **Domain versus Workgroup**   Active Directory assumes that the domain is everything and that workgroups, as such, really don't exist. Obviously, any company with more than a few employees will have workgroups, because this is the easiest way to work in many situations. Logging into the workgroup rather than the domain, though, can have unexpected results. For example, you can't set up services like MSMQ without a domain connection—at least not as an independent client.

▶ **Server Loading**   Moving from Windows NT to newer Windows Server versions can create performance problems. Unfortunately, many administrators will blame the new suite of components you've developed to take advantage of Windows Server features. However, a more likely culprit is the polling and data processing that Active Directory requires. All of that information takes processing cycles and system resources to collect.

▶ **Interface Complexity**   Microsoft's new MMC snap-ins may be one of the better ways to manage Active Directory, but the learning curve for this utility is astronomical, and the complexity of Active Directory doesn't help. It seems as if there's a specialized snap-in for every situation. For the most part, you'll find that writing applications that take advantage of everything Active Directory has to offer greatly increases the administrative learning curve unless you can work within the confines of the current interface.

▶ **Storage**   Active Directory stores everything you can imagine and probably a few things that you don't even know exist. As a result, disk storage needs for Windows Server have greatly increased for the same setup you had for Windows NT. This means you'll have to exercise care when expanding the database schema or face the consequences of large disk usage increases.

▶ **Programmer Learning Curve** Active Directory relies on COM/COM+ components. Many developers are just learning COM, and a few may be working with their first applications. The problem is that Active Directory uses some of Microsoft's most advanced technologies, making the learning curve for developers steep.

As you can see, there are many limitations when using Active Directory, and many developers categorize them in one of two ways. Most of the limitations are due to new resource requirements or the complexity of the Active Directory interface. It's important to keep these limitations in mind as you design projects that require Active Directory. The most important limitation now is the newness of the technology compared to other directory services on the market. Novell required several years after their initial release of NDS to make their product completely functional and at least moderately reliable.

BROWSER ALERT

*Microsoft provides places where you can get help from peers and Microsoft support personnel. Microsoft newsgroups include: **microsoft.public.active.directory.interfaces**, **microsoft.public.exchange2000.active.directory.integration**, **microsoft.public.platformsdk.active.directory**, and **microosft.public.win2000.active_directory**.*

Understanding the Active Directory Service Interface (ADSI)

Active Directory provides many features that make it easier to manage large networks and safeguard the information they contain. While the MMC snap-ins that Microsoft provides as part of Windows 2000 perform adequately for standard classes that come with Active Directory, customized classes may require more in the way of management capability. Consequently, it's important that Active Directory also comes with a set of services that you can access through an application program. ADSI helps you to interact with Active Directory using a single set of well-defined interfaces.

Microsoft designed ADSI to be easy and flexible to use. ADSI provides few interfaces, and they're all relatively easy to understand—this means your learning curve won't be as steep as for other products currently on the market. Two completely different groups use ADSI as a means for automating directory services tasks. Network administrators fall into one group. Because ADSI relies on COM, a network administrator could access the features that it provides with relative ease from a scripting language. Obviously, developers fall into the other group. Microsoft is hoping that developers will create Active Directory-enabled applications using the lower-level ADSI features.

BROWSER ALERT

Active Directory has garnered a lot of interest from non-Microsoft sources that can help you decipher what Active Directory can mean for your organization. One of the better places to look for information about the Active Directory Server Interface (ADSI) is the 15 Seconds Web site at: **http://www.15seconds.com/focus/ADSI.htm**. *This site contains articles, links to other sites, a few examples, and a list of Microsoft Knowledge Base articles for ADSI specific topics. If you want to learn about Microsoft's view of ADSI, then check out the Active Directory Services Interfaces Overview site at* **http://www.microsoft.com/windows2000/techinfo/ howitworks/activedirectory/adsilinks.asp**.

Now that I've introduced you to ADSI, let's take a more detailed look. The following sections will help you understand what ADSI can provide in the way of programming support. We'll look at the actual mechanics of using ADSI in the next chapter.

Working with a Common API

ADSI has some advantages besides working with Active Directory, if you take the Microsoft approach to performing tasks. Most organizations have more than one directory service structure in place. The three most common directory services are those used by the network, e-mail program, and groupware. If all of the directory service products in your organization conform to either the LDAP or NSPI standards, then you could use ADSI to manage them all. Of course, ADSI won't work in some situations because the product vendor didn't know about ADSI during development and didn't provide the required interface elements.

NOTE

ADSI actually contains two levels of API support. The first level provides support for Active Directory structures that can support automation. The COM components that provide access to these structures are accessible from just about any language, as long as the language supports automation. This includes support for Java, Visual Basic, VBScript, JavaScript, and ASP. Administrators also obtain this level of support through a standard MMC snap-in. The second level of support is for structures that can't support automation. To gain access to this second level of support, you must use a programming language like Visual C++.

So, how does Microsoft hope to get these third party directory services to work with ADSI? Most of the core logic depends on LDAP or NSPI, which are common standards for directory access. All a third party vendor really needs to do is write an ADSI provider that allows directory services access through the components that Microsoft provides. That's why access to any directory service is theoretical at this point—Microsoft has to convince third parties to supply the required provider so you can gain access to these other directory services using one interface.

If Microsoft does successfully write ADSI providers themselves or convince third party vendors to perform the task, then you'll gain an important benefit. Any application designed to work with ADSI will also work with any directory service. In short, you could write a single application that would allow you to manage groupware, e-mail, and the network. What this means for developers is that you'll spend a lot less time writing the same application multiple times because the directory services API is different for each product that your company uses.

Creating New Objects

Active Directory doesn't limit you to the objects that Microsoft provides for ADSI. You can write new objects that extend the tasks that ADSI can perform. In some respects, this means you can write your own customized programming platform. Of course, accessing the directory database won't be a problem because ADSI supports OLE-DB.

ADSI also divides the kinds of objects that you can create into two categories. *Container objects* can act as objects. However, in most cases, they hold other objects and help you interact with those objects in a consistent manner. *Leaf objects* are stand-alone components designed to perform a single task.

Working with Namespaces

Every object on a network has to have a unique identification. Depending on the directory service, this identification method might look similar to the method you use to access a file on your hard drive. However, most namespaces use the X.500 standard for naming, which consists of object type definitions, followed by the object type value. Here's an example:

```
CN=John;OU=Editorial;O=NewMagPub
```

In this example, John is the object that we want to work with. CN stands for the context name. John is located within an organizational unit known as Editorial, which is part of an organization called NewMagPub. As you can see, this method of accessing a particular object on the network is very easy to understand and use.

ADSI doesn't support every namespace, but it does support four of the most common namespaces: Active Directory services (ADs://), LDAP (LDAP://), Windows NT/2000 (WinNT://), and Novell Directory Services (NDS://). Notice that this namespace convention looks like an URL. You'll find the namespace ends up looking like an URL because of the DNS support that Active Directory provides. In fact, this is one of the reasons that Microsoft makes it so easy to find the fully qualified DNS name for the resources on your network.

Working with the Active Directory

Active Directory is a complex part of Windows Server. You must consider database elements, interaction with other directory services, management issues, and even a new set of programming features implemented by the COM components that make up ADSI. This section discusses the programming considerations for Active Directory. The fact that we're managing a large distributed database changes the entire picture for the programmer. You need to consider programming requirements that other kinds of applications don't even touch. For example, how do you create a connection to an object that may reside in another city or country? Because Active Directory replicates all of the data for the entire database on each domain controller access is faster, but replication can work against you when it comes to recording changes in the schema or object attributes.

One of the most important tools for working with Active Directory is the ADSI Viewer. This utility enables you to find data elements within the database. In addition, many developers use it to obtain the correct syntax for accessing database elements within an application.

We'll discuss three important programming considerations in this chapter. The following list tells you about each concern:

▶ **Security**   Security is always a concern, especially when you're talking about the configuration data for a large organization.

▶ **Binding**   Microsoft calls the process of gaining access to Active Directory objects *binding*. You're creating a connection to the object to manipulate the data that it contains.

▶ **Managing Users and Groups**   One of the main tasks that you'll likely perform when working with directory objects is modifying the attributes of groups and users. Even if your application doesn't modify users or groups, you'll interact with them to determine user or group rights and potentially change those rights.

ADSI Viewer

The Active Directory Services Interface (ADSI) Viewer enables you to see the schema for Active Directory. The schema controls the structure of the database. Knowing the schema helps you to work with Active Directory, change its contents, and even add new schema elements. In order to control the kinds of data stored for the applications you create, you must know the Active Directory schema. Otherwise, you could damage the database (given sufficient rights) or at least prevent your application from working correctly.

NOTE

You'll find the AdsVw application in the \Program Files\Microsoft Visual Studio .NET\Common7\ Tools\Bin folder. This folder contains many of the other utilities we use throughout the book.

When you first start ADSI Viewer, you'll see a New dialog box that allows you to choose between browsing the current objects in the database or making a specific query. You'll use the browse mode when performing research on the Active Directory schema structure. The query approach provides precise information fast when you already know what you need to find.

In most cases, you'll begin your work with Active Directory by browsing through it. This means you'll select Object Viewer at the New dialog box. Once you do that, you'll see a New Object dialog box like the one shown here.

This figure shows a sample ADs Path entry. You'll need to supply Active Directory path information, which usually means typing **LDAP://** followed by the name of your server (WinServer in my case). If you're using Windows 2000 to access Active Directory, you'll want to clear the Use OpenObject option.

Once you've filled in the required information in the New Object dialog box, click OK. If you've entered all of the right information and have the proper rights to access Active Directory, then you'll see a dialog box like the one shown in Figure 5-3. (Note that I've expanded the hierarchical display in this figure.)

This is where you'll begin learning about Active Directory. On the left side of the display is the hierarchical database structure. Each of these elements is an Active Directory object. Clicking the plus signs next to each object will show the layers of objects beneath. Highlighting an object displays detailed information about it in the right pane. For example, in Figure 5-3 you're seeing the details about the domain object for the server. The heading for this display includes object class information and help file location and shows whether the object is a container used to hold other objects.

Below the header are the properties for the object. You can choose one of the properties from the Properties list box and see its value in the Property Value field. Active Directory is extensible, which means that you can add new properties to an existing object, change an existing property, or delete properties that you no longer

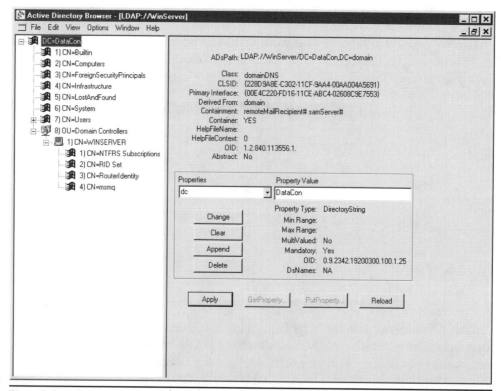

Figure 5-3   Opening a new object browser allows you to see the Active Directory schema for your server.

need. If you want to add a new property, all you need to do is type its name in the Properties list box and assign it a value in the Property Value field, then click Append. This doesn't make the change final, however; you still need to click Apply at the bottom of the dialog box. Deleting a property is equally easy. Just select it in the Properties list box, then click Delete. Clicking Apply will make the change final.

Leaf properties often have additional features that you can change. For example, the user object shown in Figure 5-4 helps you to change the user password and determine user group affiliation. When working with a computer object, you can determine the computer status and even shut it down if you'd like.

Security

Like the rest of Windows Server, Active Directory relies on a system of access tokens and security descriptors to ensure the security of each object on the machine. Gaining access to Windows Server doesn't necessarily mean that you have automatic access to all of Active Directory. During the process of binding, the requesting object provides

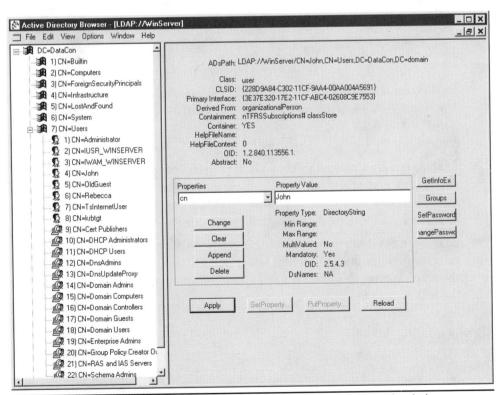

Figure 5-4   *Some containers and leaf objects provide special buttons that help you to perform tasks associated with that object.*

an access token that describes the object rights to the system. If the requesting object has sufficient rights, Windows Server creates a connection between the requesting object and Active Directory. From that point on, the requesting object has access, but nothing else. Every time the requesting object asks Active Directory to perform a task, Windows Server compares the access token to the Active Directory object security descriptor. This process goes on continually to ensure that the requesting object always acts within the confines of its rights.

So, what happens with child objects? The parent controls the rights inherited by a child object. Depending on how security is set up, a requesting object may have more or less access to child objects than to the parent. In fact, if the requesting object doesn't require access to the child object, the parent may not grant any rights to use it at all.

There's also a matter of delegation. Active Directory assumes that only a select few administrators have complete access to the objects in the directory. However, delegating control allows workgroup managers and others to work with select portions of the directory database. You can add delegation as part of the setup for your application, or you can ask the administrator to add this later. Delegation can occur at any level of the directory tree, except at the directory level.

Let's look at the security interfaces in a little more detail. The following list shows the three security related interfaces and describes their purpose.

▶ **IADsAccessControlEntry**   Allows the calling application to gain access to individual ACEs within an object. The interface methods allow access to the access mask, ACE type, flags, object type, inherited object type, and trustee information.

▶ **IADsAccessControlList**   Allows access to one of the ACLs that contain the ACEs used to access an object. The interface methods allow you to work with the ACL revision number, determine the number of ACEs that it contains, add or remove ACEs, copy the ACL, and enumerate the ACL contents.

▶ **IADsSecurityDescriptor**   Provides access to the security descriptor for a directory service object. There are interface methods that allow you to access the revision number and owner and group information and to work with both the SACL and DACL.

Binding

At the simplest level, *binding* is a process of finding an Active Directory object, requesting permission to access it, and then connecting to it. Once you have a reference to an object, you have access to any information, methods, or attributes the object provides. Any application you create will have to solve two problems. The first is finding the object. If you don't know where the object is, then you can't ask for access to it. The second is gaining access to the object once you've found it. ADSI provides two functions and one interface you can use to perform this work, as listed below.

- ▶ ADsGetObject()
- ▶ ADsOpenObject()
- ▶ IADsOpenDSObject::OpenDSObject()

Of these three, the two methods are the preferred way to access a directory services object if you're using Visual C++ because they require less code and fewer processing cycles. The **ADsGetObject()** method is the one that you'll use if you want to access the object using the name and password of the person currently logged into the system. If you need to access the object using an alternate name and password, then you'll want to use the **ADsOpenObject()** method because it takes additional arguments that enable you to specify a name and password. You'll also use **ADsOpenObject()** if you want to encrypt the data moving between your application and the directory services object or if you want to specifically bypass authentication so that you can access the object using the Everyone or Guest accounts. In all cases, you'll receive an indirect pointer to the requested object interface once the method succeeds.

You'll need to specify the name of the object that you want to access in some way. Active Directory currently allows you to use one of two methods shown here:

```
GC://<Host Name>/<Object Name>
LDAP://<Host Name>/<Object Name>
```

Except for the access method, both of these examples are the same. You'll need to specify the name of the host for the object, which would include the fully qualified DNS name for the container, along with the name of the object that you want to access within that container. The host name is optional, in many cases, but including it is a good idea if you want to ensure fast access. The object name can include a distinguished name, canonical name, an object GUID, or a SID. The use of GC allows you to access the object using entries in the global catalog, while LDAP allows you to access the object using that protocol. Of the two, GC normally provides the fastest access, but LDAP is the most flexible when it comes to multiple directory service scenarios.

Managing Users and Groups

Users and groups form the two most common kinds of objects that you'll find in any directory service. After all, the whole purpose of creating a network is to allow its users to share both resources and data. Using groups allows the network administrator to manage large groups of users with relative ease. Groups allow the network administrator to make one change that will affect many users, rather than many changes that will affect a single user. As a result of the emphasis on users and groups in Active Directory, you'll find that this particular category has received special attention from Microsoft.

Let's talk about the interfaces that Active Directory provides to work with users and groups. The following list shows the five interfaces that you'll commonly work with to view, add, delete, or modify both user and group information.

▶ **IADs**   Provides access to object properties and methods. You can also use this method to determine the object name, class, GUID, Active Directory path, parent, and schema.

▶ **IADsPropertyList**   Allows you to read, modify, and update property values within an object.

▶ **IADsUser**   Allows you to read, modify, and update an end user account. You can also use this interface to obtain user statistics, such as the last time the user logged on, the number of bad login attempts, personal information like home address, and work information like the user's manager. In short, this interface works with the unique properties of the User object.

▶ **IADsGroup**   Allows you to read, modify, and update a group account. There are methods for adding objects to and removing objects from the group, along with a method for testing group membership.

▶ **IADsMembers**   Supports group membership for individual accounts. This interface includes methods for counting the group members, obtaining a new group enumeration, and viewing or setting filters applied to the group membership.

▶ **IDirectoryObject**   Provides nonautomation clients (like Visual C++) access to either User or Group objects. Using this interface not only provides better performance for nonautomation clients, but it also means that you need to know more about the attributes associated with individual objects.

Notice there are only two interfaces that are specific to users and groups. All standard objects within Active Directory have interfaces that fall into the persistent object category (we'll discuss other categories of interfaces in the Working with the ADSI API section of the chapter). You'll use the rest of these interfaces for other purposes within Active Directory.

Working with the ADSI API

ADSI is the API that enables you to work with Active Directory and helps you add the new features that Active Directory provides to your applications. Like many other parts of Windows Server, ADSI relies heavily on COM components.

BROWSER ALERT

It's interesting to note that only Windows Server products come with Active Directory as part of the package. Microsoft provides Active Directory support for Windows 9x, along with a setup for older versions of Windows NT. You can find links for all four levels of support at http://www.microsoft.com/NTServer/nts/downloads/other/ADSI25/. This site also includes a link for the Active Directory Services Interfaces SDK. If you want full ADSI information, check the Active Directory Service Interfaces Web site at http://www.microsoft.com/windows2000/techinfo/howitworks/ activedirectory/adinterface.asp.

At this point in the chapter, we've discussed many common interfaces and discussed how you can use them to work with Active Directory. However, ADSI provides a lot more in the way of interfaces than what we've covered so far. Table 5-1 contains a list of additional interfaces that we either haven't discussed or haven't covered fully. You'll want to spend some additional time learning about these interfaces as you work with Active Directory using ADSI.

NOTE

Table 5-1 doesn't contain a complete list of ADSI interfaces. Some of these interfaces are in other areas of the chapter, so they don't appear again here. In addition, this table doesn't include any of the NDS specific interfaces. The table does include the more common interfaces.

Interface	Description	Purpose
Core:		
IADs	Defines the basic features, properties and methods of any ADSI object.	Helps you to learn about the features common to every object such as its name, parent, class, GUID, path, and schema. Special methods enable you to work with either single-value or multiple-value properties.
IADsContainer	Enables an ADSI container to create, delete, enumerate, and manage ADSI objects.	Allows you to learn more about objects held within an ADSI container. You can count objects, create filters to exclude objects from an enumeration or count, enumerate objects, move objects to another location, or create copy that you can modify.
IADsNamespaces	Allows you to work with namespace objects.	Contains two methods for working with namespaces. The first obtains the namespace container name, while the second modifies the namespace container name to a new value. The new namespace container name becomes the default namespace container for the user.
Data Type:		
IADsLargeInteger	Allows you to work with large (64-bit) integers.	Permits use of 64-bit integers within Active Directory. Because many compilers can't handle 64-bit integers, there are two sets of methods. The first set deals with the lower 32 bits, while the second set deals with the upper 32 bits.
Dynamic Object:		
IADsComputerOperations	Manages computer operations across the network.	Contains two methods. The first helps determine the status of any computer. The second helps you shut a computer down from a remote location.
IADsFileServiceOperations	Manages file services across the network.	Enables you to work with the open and active file services sessions for the domain. The two methods include one that works with resources and another that deals with sessions.
IADsPrintJobOperations	Provides access to print jobs executing on the domain.	Obtains the status of print jobs. In addition, there are methods for pausing, reordering, and resuming print jobs.
IADsPrintQueueOperations	Provides access to print queues within the domain.	Obtains the status of the print jobs residing within the queue. There are also methods for pausing, resuming, and purging print jobs.

Table 5-1 *Active Directory Automation Interfaces*

Interface	Description	Purpose
IADsResource	Works with open file service resources.	Permits viewing of open file service resource attributes, including user, user path, resource path, and the resource lock count. A file service resource is open when the user accesses it and creates a connection to it.
IADsServiceOperations	Works with system services, active or not.	Stops, starts, pauses, or continues system services on the domain. In addition, you can determine the system service status and set the system service password.
IADsSession	Works with active file service sessions.	Permits viewing of user statistics for the active file service sessions. A session is active when a user creates a connection to the file system and opens one or more files. The user statistics include user name, user path, computer name, computer path, the amount of connection time for the session, and the amount of time that the connection has been idle.
Extension:		
IADsExtension	Implements an application extension model.	Adds application-specific behaviors into existing ADSI objects. An application extension uses aggregation to modify the behavior of the existing object.
Persistent Object:		
IADsCollection	Manages an arbitrary collection of objects.	Provides methods for adding, removing, retrieving, and enumerating objects within the array. Collections are specialized arrays that can hold any type of directory services object.
IADsComputer	Allows access to any computer type.	Obtains common information about workstations, servers, or other computer types on the network.
IADsDomain	Represents a domain and helps manage accounts on the domain.	Permits account security management. You can determine password length, the age at which passwords are changed, the maximum number of bad logins allowed, lockout parameters, and other password attributes.
IADsFileService	Represents the file service and user access management.	Modifies the file service description and the number of users allowed to use the file service at the same time.
IADsFileShare	Allows you to modify the attributes of any file share on the network.	Provides the methods to determine the user count for a file share. In addition, you can both view and set the file share description, host computer path, shared directory path, and maximum user count.

Table 5-1   *Active Directory Automation Interfaces* (continued)

Interface	Description	Purpose
IADsLocality	Represents the domain's geographical location.	Views or sets the locality description, region name, postal code, or "see also" (note) information.
IADsO	Represents an Organization object within the domain.	Views or sets the organization description, locality, postal address, telephone number, fax number, and "see also" information.
IADsOU	Represents an Organizational Unit object within the domain.	Views or sets the organization description, locality, postal address, telephone number, fax number, "see also" information, and business category.
IADsPrintJob	Defines individual print jobs within the print queue.	Provides management methods for active print jobs. Methods enable you to view the host print queue location, user name, user path, time submitted, total pages, and size. In addition, you can view or set the description, priority, start time, until time, notification value, and notification path.
IADsPrintQueue	Represents a print job destination on the network.	Manages printer options. You can view or change the printer path, model, data type, print processor, description, location, start time, until time, default job priority, queue priority for processing data on the printer, banner page, print devices, and network addresses.
Property Cache:		
IADsPropertyEntry	Manages attribute values as defined within the schema.	Manipulates an individual entry within a property list. The methods in this interface help you view or modify the name, data type, control code, or value of individual attribute values.
IADsPropertyList	Contains one or more property entries associated with an object attribute.	Manages the value entries associated with an object attribute. You can list the entries, obtain a total number of all entries, get or put entries, reset the values within an individual entry or purge the entire list.

Table 5-1 *Active Directory Automation Interfaces* (continued)

Interface	Description	Purpose
Schema:		
IADsClass	Manages object descriptions within the schema.	Provides interfaces for describing Active Directory object creation, including the class identifier (CLSID), object identifier (OID), mandatory and optional properties, and help file data.
IADsProperty	Manages object attributes within the schema.	Determines how Active Directory manages and creates a property. The methods in this interface include the OID, syntax object path, minimum and maximum ranges, multivalued properties, and any additional required property qualifiers.
IADsSyntax	Manages automation data types that describe schema object property values.	Provides a single method that returns the automation value for a property. These are the virtual types like VT_BOOL (for a BOOL value) used in other parts of Visual C++ to describe the type of a variable or constant.
Utility:		
IADsDeleteOps	Deletes an object from the underlying directory structure.	Contains a single method that an object can call to delete itself from the directory structure once it's no longer needed.
IADsObjectOptions	Allows you to manage provider-specific options for working with ADSI.	Contains two methods for viewing and modifying ADSI provider options. There are four standard options: server name, referrals, page size, and security mask. Individual providers may support other options.
IADsPathName	Parses Windows and X.500 paths within ADSI.	Enables you to work with paths provided by application programs, users, other directory services, and other objects.

Table 5-1   *Active Directory Automation Interfaces* (continued)

Working with the System.DirectoryService Namespace

The System.DirectoryServices namespace is simply a managed version of the interface we've discussed to this point. It enables you to access Active Directory using managed—rather than unmanaged—techniques. The namespace includes class counterparts for the interfaces we've discussed so far (and will continue to discuss as the chapter progresses). The main focus of the classes provided in the System.DirectoryService namespace is implementation of the **IADsOpenDSObject** interface. Once you have an open connection to Active Directory, you can begin to manipulate the data it contains. The following list contains a description of the major classes found in the System.DirectoryService namespace.

- ▶ **DirectoryEntries**   Provides access to the child entries for an Active Directory entry. Essential tasks include adding, removing, and finding the child entries. You'll use the DirectoryEntry class to modify the child entries.

- ▶ **DirectoryEntry**   Provides access to a single Active Directory entry, including the root object. You can also use this class to access some of the information found in schema entries. Essential tasks include modifying name and path, identifying children and parent, modifying properties, and obtaining the native object. When working with the native object, you must cast it to an IADs COM object.

- ▶ **DirectorySearcher**   Enables you to search Active Directory for specific entries. You can search for one or all matching entries, cache the entries locally, filter and sort the search results, and set the search environment. For example, you can set timeouts for both client and server.

- ▶ **DirectoryServicesPermission**   Sets the code access permissions (security) for Active Directory. The **Assert()** method enables you to validate that the calling code can access the requested resource. You can also copy, deny, and demand permissions as well as perform other tasks.

- ▶ **DirectoryServicesPermissionAttribute**   Permits a declarative System.DirectoryServices permission check. You can either match a permission to a specific permission or create a new permission.

- ▶ **DirectoryServicesPermissionEntry**   Sets the smallest unit of code access security permission provided by System.DirectoryServices.

- ▶ **DirectoryServicesPermissionEntryCollection**   Creates a strongly typed collection of DirectoryServicesPermissionEntry objects. You can perform all of the usual collection tasks, including counting the number of items and working with a specific item. Other methods enable you to add, remove, insert, or copy permissions.

- ▶ **PropertyCollection**   Enables you to examine the properties for a single DirectoryEntry object. You can count the number of properties, obtain a list of property values, obtain a list of property names, or extract the value of a single property.

▶ **PropertyValueCollection**   Enables you to examine the property values for a single DirectoryEntry object. You can count the number of values, set a specific property value, or set the values for the entire collection. Methods help you perform all of the usual collection tasks, including counting the number of items and working with a specific item. Other methods enable you to add, remove, insert, or copy permissions.

▶ **ResultPropertyCollection**   Enables you to examine the properties for a SearchResult object. You can count the number of properties, obtain a list of property values, obtain a list of property names, or extract the value of a single property.

▶ **ResultPropertyValueCollection**   Enables you to examine the property values for a SearchResult object. You can count the number of items in the collection and work with specific items. Methods enable you to perform specific tasks such as copying the collection to an array or determining if the collection contains a specific property.

▶ **SchemaNameCollection**   Contains a list of schema names that you can use with the SchemaFilter property of the DirectoryEntry object. You can count the number of items in the collection and work with specific items. Methods help you perform all of the usual collection tasks, including counting the number of items and working with a specific item. Other methods enable you to add, remove, insert, or copy permissions.

▶ **SearchResult**   Contains the results of using a DirectorySearcher object to look for specific Active Directory entries. The SearchResult object contains an entire Active Directory node, beginning with the location of the first object found.

▶ **SearchResultCollection**   Contains a collection of SearchResult objects. You can obtain a count of the of the SearchResult objects, obtain a handle to the **IDirectorySearch::ExecuteSearch** interface, work with a specific item, or obtain a list of properties used for the search. Methods enable you to perform specific tasks, such as copying the collection to an array or determining if the collection contains a specific SearchResult object.

▶ **SortOption**   Determines how Windows XP sorts the results of a search. You can specify both the search direction and search property.

As you can see, you can perform most tasks using managed code. In the few cases where you need to perform a task using the COM interfaces, you can obtain a copy of the object using built-in method calls (see DirectoryEntry as an example). Of course, several issues besides ease of access remain. One of the most important issues is thread safety—an important consideration in a distributed application. Generally, you'll find that public static class members are thread-safe, while instance members aren't. This limitation means you must use class members carefully and take steps to ensure method calls occur in a thread-safe manner.

Writing a COM+ Application that Relies on Active Directory

This section provides you with one example of how to use Active Directory to track users on the road. We're going to create an application that allows a user to "punch the clock" while on the road.

On the server, we'll create a component that runs all of the time looking for requests from users on the road. When a user activates the application, the component will store the time values within Active Directory. In this way, a manager can keep track of how much time employees on the road are spending performing certain tasks that require a login to the system. This type of application has many uses; I've chosen to implement a simpler example of something that could provide a lot of value to a company. The following sections will help you design, build, and test both a client side application and a server side component.

Creating the Component

The first thing we need to do to create this application is design a component that will receive input from the client application on the user's machine. This component will interact with Active Directory by looking for the user's name and then placing text in the user's "info" or Note entry. The user's Note entry appears on the Telephones tab of the User Properties dialog box.

In the following sections, we'll create a component shell, add two methods to it, and then some code to perform the required interactions. We'll need two different methods for this example. The first will add new login entries, while the second will clear all of the entries after the network administrator has viewed them or the user has arrived home.

Creating the Component Shell

Begin by creating an ATL Project. I've given the example project a name of UserADLog, but you can use any name you'd like. The following procedure will help you create the component shell required for this example.

1. Create the new ATL Project. Select Application Settings. You'll see the Application Settings dialog box shown here.

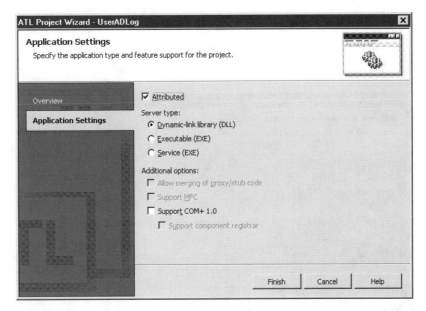

2. Clear the Attributed options. (We'll discuss how to use attributed programming techniques in Chapter 13.) This example shows how to work with Active Directory directly, and attributed programming will hide some details. In addition, you can't merge proxy and stub code or use MFC when working with attributes.

3. Check the "Allow merging of proxy/stub code" and "Support MFC" options. Since this is going to be a COM+ application, we'll use the Dynamic Link Library (DLL) server type.

4. Check Support COM+ 1.0. Visual Studio .NET will support COM+ 1.5, but this support will appear only on Windows XP. Most of the applications this book targets will need to run on both Windows 2000 and Windows XP, so we'll use COM+ 1.0 throughout.

5. Click Finish. Visual C++ will create the new component shell for you. At this point, we'll need to add a new ATL object that will contain the code that the client application will call later.

6. Right-click the UserADLog folder found on the Class View tab, then choose Add | Add Class from the context menu. You'll see the Add Class dialog box.

7. Highlight the Simple Object option, then click Open. You'll see the ATL Simple Object Wizard dialog box shown here.

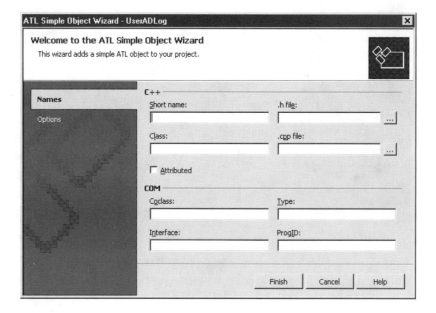

8. Type **ADLogEntry** in the Short Name field. Visual C++ will automatically fill in the other field values for you.

9. Click the Options tab. Check No for Aggregation and then click OK. Visual C++ will create the new class for you.

10. Right-click the IADLogEntry folder entry on the Class View tab, then choose Add | Add Method from the context menu. You'll see the Add Method Wizard dialog box shown here:

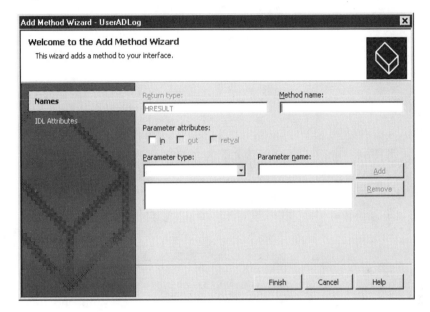

11. Type **CreateLogEntry** in the Method Name field. Select BSTR in the Parameter Type field and type **strUserName** in the Parameter Name field. Select In for Parameter Attributes. Click Add. This is all you need to define the first method we'll use.

12. Click Finish. Visual C++ will add the method to the interface.

13. Repeat steps 10 through 12 for the ClearLogEntries method.

14. Highlight the UserADLog entry in Solution Explorer. Use the Project | Properties command to display the UserADLog Property Pages dialog box and select Linker | Input page, shown here:

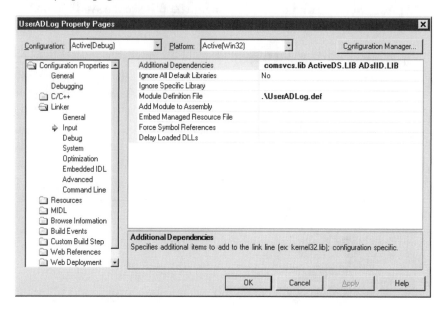

15. Add the ActiveDS.LIB and ADsIID.LIB entries shown in the screenshot. The component won't link without these two libraries. While the Microsoft documentation tells you about the first one, it doesn't tell you to add the ADsIID.LIB entry. At this point, the component shell is ready to go. All we need are the two methods to demonstrate one aspect of Active Directory.

Adding Some Code

It's time to add some code to the component. Listing 5-1 shows a typical example of an Active Directory access component. The **CreateLogEntry()** method adds to the Notes field of the Active Directory entry for the user, while the **ClearLogEntries()** method removes all entries from the Notes field.

Listing 5-1

```
STDMETHODIMP CADLogEntry::CreateLogEntry(BSTR strUserName)
{
    // Default code.
    AFX_MANAGE_STATE(AfxGetStaticModuleState());
```

```
IADsUser *pUser;      // Pointer to user object.
CString  UserName;    // Name input.
CString  LDAPConn;    // LDAP connection to server.
CString  OutString;   // Output string.
HRESULT  hr;          // Operation result.
VARIANT  Output;      // Variant output.
CTime    CurrTime;    // Current time.

// Initialize COM.
CoInitialize(NULL);
USES_CONVERSION;

// Create a connection to the server.
UserName = strUserName;
LDAPConn = "LDAP://WinServer/CN=" +
           UserName +
           ",CN=Users,DC=DataCon,DC=domain";
hr = ADsGetObject(T2W(LDAPConn.GetBuffer(256)),
                  IID_IADsUser,
                  (void**)&pUser);
LDAPConn.ReleaseBuffer(-1);

// If the connection failed, exit.
if (FAILED(hr))
   AfxMessageBox("Failed to create connection.");
else
{
   // Get the user object.
   hr = pUser->GetInfo();
   if (FAILED(hr))
   {
      AfxMessageBox("Failed to get user object.");
      CoUninitialize();
      return hr;
   }

   // Get the current user information.
   pUser->Get(T2BSTR("info"), &Output);
   if (Output.vt == VT_BSTR)
      OutString = Output.bstrVal;

   // Create a user login string.
   CurrTime = CTime::GetCurrentTime();
```

```
            OutString = OutString +
                    "User Logged In: " +
                    CurrTime.Format("%d %b %Y") +
                    " at " +
                    CurrTime.Format("%H:%M:%S") +
                    "\r\n";
        Output.bstrVal = OutString.AllocSysString();
        Output.vt = VT_BSTR;

        // Output the value to the user record.
        hr = pUser->Put(T2BSTR("info"), Output);
        if (FAILED(hr))
        {
           AfxMessageBox("Failed to output user data.");
           CoUninitialize();
           return hr;
        }

        // Make the information permanent.
        hr = pUser->SetInfo();
        if (FAILED(hr))
        {
           AfxMessageBox("Failed to enter data in Active Directory.");
           CoUninitialize();
           return hr;
        }

        // Free the string we allocated.
        SysFreeString(Output.bstrVal);
    }

    CoUninitialize();

    return S_OK;
}

STDMETHODIMP CADLogEntry::ClearLogEntries(BSTR strUserName)
{
    AFX_MANAGE_STATE(AfxGetStaticModuleState());

    IADsUser *pUser;      // Pointer to user object.
    CString  UserName;    // Name input.
    CString  LDAPConn;    // LDAP connection to server.
```

```
CString  OutString;  // Output string.
HRESULT  hr;         // Operation result.
VARIANT  Output;     // Variant output.

// Initialize COM.
CoInitialize(NULL);
USES_CONVERSION;

// Create a connection to the server.
UserName = strUserName;
LDAPConn = "LDAP://WinServer/CN=" +
           UserName +
           ",CN=Users,DC=DataCon,DC=domain";
hr = ADsGetObject(T2W(LDAPConn.GetBuffer(256)),
                  IID_IADsUser,
                  (void**)&pUser);
LDAPConn.ReleaseBuffer(-1);

// If the connection failed, exit.
if (FAILED(hr))
   AfxMessageBox("Failed to create connection.");
else
{
   // Get the user object.
   hr = pUser->GetInfo();
   if (FAILED(hr))
   {
      AfxMessageBox("Failed to get user object.");
      CoUninitialize();
      return hr;
   }

   // Clear the user login information.
   Output.bstrVal = SysAllocString(T2BSTR(""));
   Output.vt = VT_BSTR;

   // Output the value to the user record.
   hr = pUser->Put(T2BSTR("info"), Output);
   if (FAILED(hr))
   {
      AfxMessageBox("Failed to output user data.");
      CoUninitialize();
      return hr;
```

```
        }

        // Make the information permanent.
        hr = pUser->SetInfo();
        if (FAILED(hr))
        {
            AfxMessageBox("Failed to enter data in Active Directory.");
            CoUninitialize();
            return hr;
        }

        // Free the string we allocated.
        SysFreeString(Output.bstrVal);
    }

    CoUninitialize();

    return S_OK;
}
```

NOTE

The source code contains an LDAPConn string entry. This entry is specific to every server setup, so you'll need to change this string for your particular server setup. This means changing both the server name and context.

As you can see from the code, both methods perform essentially the same task; they just make a different kind of entry. Because of the similarities, we'll discuss both method implementations at the same time.

The Active Directory Services Interface (ADSI) allows you to work with Active Directory using a standard set of interfaces. We're using one of those interfaces in this example. Both methods create an Active Directory user object that we'll use to access the Notes field of the Telephones tab of the User Properties dialog box. One of the more difficult tasks is building an LDAP string that we can use access a particular resource, but using the ADSI Viewer makes that task a lot easier. See the "ADSI Viewer" section of the chapter for details.

NOTE

*The source code in Listing 5-1 is sprinkled heavily with **AfxMessageBox()** calls. A standard server side component should never display information this way, because there's no guarantee that anyone will monitor the server console. Using the Event Log is the recommended procedure. The example uses the message boxes as a convenience only.*

You'll instantiate pUser by using the **ADsGetObject()** method. The **ADsGetObject()** method requires an object reference in the form of a string, which is where the LDAP string comes into play. It also requires that you provide the name of the required interface, IID_IADsUser, and a pointer to the IADsUser variable. However, instantiating pUser isn't enough to fill it with information we can use. The code also calls on the **GetInfo()** method, which populates the variable with specific user data.

Now that we have an object and some data to work with, it's time to do something with the "info" context, which is actually the Notes field in disguise. **The CreateLogEntry()** method has to obtain the current log information so it can add a new entry to it. This means calling the **Get()** method and requesting the info field. Notice that the code checks the Output.vt parameter to ensure it contains a value. The default of a "no" value won't return a VT_BSTR value in this field. If you attempt to set OutString to a "no" value (essentially a bad pointer), you'll receive an error and the component will terminate.

Both methods place data in the info field. In one case, we'll add a new login entry to the existing contents of the Notes field; in the other we'll truncate the contents of the Notes field. Placing the new information in Active Directory is a two-step process. First, we use the **Put()** method to transfer the data to Active Directory. Second, we use the **SetInfo()** method to make the change permanent. Unless you follow both steps, the data change won't be reflected in Active Directory.

Creating the output value presents two traps that you need to consider whenever you work in the COM+ environment. The first is that you need to set both the data and the data type for a VARIANT. Notice that the code uses Output.bstrVal to hold the output data and sets Output.vt to VT_BSTR so it reflects the variant data type properly. The second problem is one of memory. You must allocate a system string (the code shows two techniques—one for each method) and then free the system string using **SysFreeString()**.

You'll also need to add support for Active Directory to the component. All you need is the following line of code. Place the entry at the top of the ADLogEntry.CPP file that holds the code for the two methods.

```
// Add Active Directory support.
#include <ActiveDS.h>
```

Installing the Component

The component is ready to use. Before you can install it on the server, you'll need to compile it. Place the compiled component on the server. You don't need to register it, but the component does need to appear in an easily remembered location. Many developers simply create a special directory for all of their components. When working with COM+, you install the component within an application. The following steps show how to create the application.

1. Open Component Services. Right-click the COM+ Applications folder and then choose New | Application from the context menu. You'll see the Welcome to the COM Application Install Wizard dialog box.

2. Click Next. You'll see the Install or Create a New Application dialog box. You can choose to install pre-built applications or create a new application.

3. Click Create an Empty Application. You'll see a Create Empty Application dialog box that requests an application name and type. A library application activates in the client's process, while a server application always activates in a separate process.

4. Type a name for the application in the "Enter a name for the new application" field. The example uses UserADLog for an application name.

5. Check Server application and then click Next. You'll see the Set Application Identity dialog box. Normally, the default user security works fine for the application. However, this is one situation when you may want to enter a specific username and password. Because the client won't be available for security queries, the user can't compensate for incorrect password entries and the like. Unfortunately, the question of whether to use full security or a known good identity is a hard one to answer, and you should view the question with your particular application in mind. In some cases, the security problems incurred using a known good identity just aren't worth the risks, so it's better to have the component answer the client request based upon the user's actual security.

6. Click Next. You'll see a final COM AppWizard dialog box.

7. Click Finish. Windows 2000 will create the new COM+ application for you.

At this point, we have an application, but we still need to add a component to the application. The next series of steps will help you install the component we created in this chapter within the UserADLog application:

1. Right-click the Components folder under the UserADLog application in Component Services and then choose New | Component from the context menu. You'll see the Welcome to the COM Component Install Wizard dialog box.

2. Click Next. You'll see the Import or Install a Component dialog box. This dialog box enables you to install a new component, import a component that's already registered on the server, or install a new event class.

3. Click "Install new components"—since we're adding a new component to this application. You'll see a Select Files to Install dialog box.

4. Locate UserADLog.DLL file, highlight it, then click Open. You'll see an Install New Components dialog box similar to the one shown here. This dialog box should contain the name of the components you've defined for the module. In this case, we only have one named ADLogEntry.

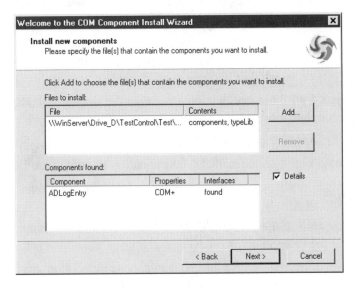

5. Click Next. You'll see a final COM Component Install Wizard dialog box.

6. Click Finish. Windows 2000 will add the new component to the UserADLog application for you.

Exporting the COM+ Application

The COM+ component now resides on the server, and a client could access it through the COM+ application. However, COM relies on a proxy and stub to make communication between the client and server seamless. Unlike DCOM, where you have to use different calls to access a remote component, COM+ applications use the same call. Using this technique means you must create a local proxy for the client.

This proxy will take the place of the component on the server from the local machine's perspective. Creating a proxy is relatively easy; the following steps will show you how.

1. Right-click UserADLog in Component Services, then choose Export from the context menu. You'll see a Welcome to the COM Application Export Wizard dialog box.

2. Click Next. You'll see an Application Export Information dialog box. This is where you'll choose the name and type of export application created. We need a proxy application, in this case, so that the installation routine will direct UserADLog requests to the server, not to the local machine.

3. Click Browse. You'll see an Export Application to File dialog box. Choose a location for the installation program. The wizard automatically gives the application an MSI extension. The example uses an installation program name of UserADLog Install, but you can use any name you wish.

4. Click Save. You'll see the location entered in the Application Export Information dialog box.

5. Choose the Application Proxy option.

6. Click Next. You'll see a final COM Application Export Wizard dialog box.

7. Click Finish. At this point, the wizard has created the application; all you need to do is install it on the client machine.

8. Locate the UserADLog Install.MSI file from the client machine. You'll need to install the proxy application on every machine.

9. Right-click UserADLog Install.MSI, then choose Install from the context menu. An installation dialog will appear for a few moments, then go away. At this point, you have access to the server side component through the proxy application.

If you open Component Services on the client machine at this point, you'll see that there's a new application named UserADLog. However, this application isn't the full-fledged application found on the server—it's an application proxy. Open the UserADLog Properties dialog box and you'll notice that you can't change any of the application options. This application precisely replicates the server application.

Creating the Test Application

It's time to test the component. You'll want to create an MFC Application. Use a dialog-based application to keep things simple. The example has a name of UserADLogTest. The test application is relatively simple. All we need to do is instantiate the object, call the selected method, and view the results. The dialog box will contain two pushbuttons (IDC_MAKE_ENTRY and IDC_CLEAR_ENTRIES) to test the two methods and a text box (IDC_USER_NAME) where you can enter the username.

Create event handlers for both of the pushbuttons. Create a member variable for the text box. The example uses a name of m_UserName. You'll need to add references to the component in the source code. The first reference appears as follows in the UserADLogTestDlg.cpp file.

```
// Add support for the UserADLog component.
#include "..\UserADLog\UserADLog.h"
```

The second reference appears in the UserADLogTestDlg.h file. Use the following code.

```
// Include UserADLog component support.
#include "..\UserADLog\UserADLog_i.c"
```

Now that you have the references in place, let's look at the test code. Both buttons perform the same task. The only difference is the method they call within the component. Listing 5-2 shows the source code for **OnBnClickedClearEntries()**.

Listing 5-2

```
void CUserADLogTestDlg::OnBnClickedClearEntries()
{
    IADLogEntry *pLog;      // UserADLog instance.
    HRESULT     hr;         // Result of calls.
    CString     UserName;   // Active Directory user name.

    // Initialize the COM environment.
    CoInitialize(NULL);
    USES_CONVERSION;

    // Instantiate the component.
    hr = CoCreateInstance(CLSID_ADLogEntry,
                          NULL,
                          CLSCTX_ALL,
                          IID_IADLogEntry,
                          (void**)&pLog);
    if (FAILED(hr))
        AfxMessageBox("Component Creation Failed!");
    else
    {
```

```
        // Get the user name from the dialog box.
        m_UserName.GetWindowText(UserName.GetBuffer(40), 40);
        UserName.ReleaseBuffer(-1);

        // Clear the user log entries.
        hr = pLog->ClearLogEntries(T2BSTR(UserName));
    }

    // Uninitialize the COM environment.
    CoUninitialize();
}
```

As you can see, the code begins by creating an instance of the component. If the component creation is successful, the code converts the username input from the dialog box and calls the appropriate component method. Normally, the code would also tell the user that the call was successful or make some entry in a local log so the user would know when to check in next.

Testing the Application

After you compile the test application, it's time to test it out. Open a copy of the Component Services snap-in so you can monitor the application. Make sure you have both the local machine and the server open. Start the application. Enter your name or the name of a test user in the username field. Click Make Entry. Watch the icon for the UserADLog entry on the local machine and you'll see the ball rotate within the box for a moment or two until the client hands the request off to the server. Note that the client side activity may occur so quickly that you won't see the icon animation. The icon on the server will also animate, but for a much longer period. The icon animation shows the application in action. The client rotates for only a few moments, because it places the application in direct contact with the server.

Open the Active Directory entry for the affected user. Click the Telephones tab. You should see one or more entries in the Notes field, as shown here.

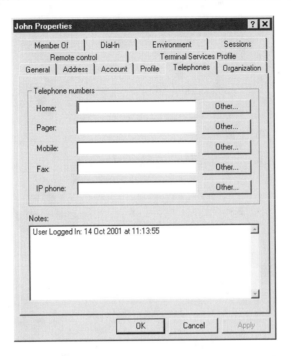

Close the user record. Click Clear Entries in the test application. Open the user record, click Telephones, and you should see that the Notes field is blank. While this example demonstrates only one of many Active Directory entries, the principles for modifying any entry are the same. It's important to remember that Active Directory is simply a large centralized database. Of course, a user's individual rights determine which parts of Active Directory they can access. User rights also determine what tasks the user can perform.

CHAPTER

6

Creating Components

IN THIS CHAPTER:

ActiveX Controls

Component Testing Aids and Techniques

Creating components with Visual C++ has never been a problem—there are more than a few ways to accomplish this task. Deciding which method to use when creating components has presented problems because there are tradeoffs to consider no matter what technique you choose. Use Active Template Library (ATL) to create a component and you'll find that complexity and coding time both increase. On the other hand, using Microsoft Foundation Classes (MFC) means dealing with code bloat and versioning problems. Visual C++ .NET retains these older methods of creating components, but I think you'll find that the new methods it introduces are superior in a number of ways. That's what this chapter is all about—choices. We'll look at the choices you have with Visual C++ .NET—at how you can leverage those choices to create new components fast.

This chapter also discusses how to test your components after you create them. We'll begin with the techniques you'll use to register and unregister your controls. The test section also shows how to use ActiveX Control Test Container and the OLE/COM Object Viewer utilities. Knowing how to use these utilities can save you time and effort spent diagnosing problems with your components. More importantly, these utilities can point out subtle differences between component implementations that cause one component to behave differently from another.

ActiveX Controls

This section of the chapter tells you about ActiveX control development. Visual C++ supports several types of ActiveX control development. The two main types are MFC and ATL controls. We'll begin with a discussion of the differences between MFC and ATL. This section answers the question of why you would use one development environment over another. It pays to know how to use both because they do fulfill different development requirements.

NOTE

This chapter won't show you how to use attributed programming techniques; we'll discuss attributed programming in Chapter 13. You'll find that attributed programming can make a big difference in the time required to develop new components, but it might not be the right choice for upgrading existing projects.

After we discuss the differences between the two control types, it will be time to see them in action. The next three sections show how to create and test the same control using the MFC and ATL coding techniques. The first time we'll create the control using MFC; the second time we'll use ATL. Both controls perform the same task, but you'll see significant differences in the development environment. A third section will show you how the control works within a standard application.

MFC Versus ATL Based Controls

One of the ways that Visual C++ shows its robust development environment compared to other programming languages is the inclusion of two technologies to create ActiveX controls: MFC or ATL. (You also have the choice of using standard or attributed coding as well as creating managed or unmanaged controls.) Unfortunately, this flexibility can cause some problems that other developers don't have to face. For one thing, how do you determine which type of control to create? Some developers have rendered the question moot by using the same technology for all their controls, but following this route means that you haven't really explored and used Visual C++ to its full potential.

There really isn't any way to say definitively that one method of creating a control is better in a given situation. What you really need to do is define what you expect the control to do, what you're willing to invest to get that functionality, and your level of expertise. Obviously, there are situations when one control creation method is preferred over another, as the two methods do have distinctly different advantages and disadvantages. To give you some idea of what you need to consider when looking at an ATL ActiveX control versus one created using MFC, read through the following list. What you'll find are ideas that can help you make a decision on which route is best for you.

▶ **Development speed**   Using the MFC ActiveX Control Wizard is the fastest method to create a control. The Wizard takes care of most of the interface details so that what you end up with is a skeleton that's ready for some control logic. In fact, it usually takes the developers twice as long to use the ATL method for creating a control. Obviously, your results will vary depending on factors like control complexity and your programming experience.

▶ **Control size**   If you want to create the smallest possible ActiveX control, then go the ATL route. ATL gives you full control over every aspect of the control and makes it feasible for you to hand-tune every control element without getting bogged down in MFC-specific code. Not only are MFC-based controls larger, but clients may also have to download the MFC libraries before they can use the control, which is a significant amount of code.

▶ **Learning curve**   ATL controls are much harder to create than MFC controls, simply because you have to consider more things like interfaces. In most cases, it pays to create your first couple of controls using the MFC ActiveX Control Wizard so that you can learn the ropes of creating the control logic.

▶ **Compatibility**   By definition, MFC-based ActiveX controls require clients to have the MFC libraries installed on their machine. However, there are more than a few versions of those libraries floating around, and they aren't all compatible. What happens when users download your control and the associated libraries, then can't use an important application because the new libraries are incompatible with their application? Since the MFC libraries are stored in the SYSTEM directory, a client machine can have only one version. That's where the compatibility problems come into play.

▶ **Ease of use**   The MFC ActiveX Control Wizard tends to throw everything but the kitchen sink into a control, because it assumes nothing about your ability to write control code. What this means is that you end up with a wealth of interfaces you may not need or use. All of this wasted functionality bloats the size of the control and makes it harder to use.

▶ **Ease of code modification**   Creating an MFC-based control is very easy the first time around. Since the Wizard adds much of the code for you, application development goes quickly. However, what happens when you decide to update that control? Now you have source files that may contain a good deal of code that wasn't written by a staff programmer and that may require additional time to research and understand.

▶ **Component services**   ATL presents one of the better ways to develop components that reside on the server and perform a specific service for a client. You'll find component services used for COM+, MTS, and Queued Components. Many companies are making the move to component services today. However, given the number of legacy applications, this move will continue for quite some time to come.

▶ **Future programming needs**   Microsoft is betting that .NET will take off immediately and that everyone will instantly move their applications to it. The reality is that most companies will begin *experimenting* with .NET in the near future and won't begin *moving* applications to it for several years. As a developer, you need to prepare for future application programming needs as well as keeping abreast of today's technology. Managed components present one view of programming in the future.

MFC ActiveX Control Example

I can't think of a single application on my machine that doesn't rely on a pushbutton or two. In fact, the pushbutton is one of the very few Windows controls that you could say every application has. Even an application that displays information in a simple dialog usually relies on an OK button to close the dialog. Suffice it to say then that the pushbutton is the one control on your machine that has to work well. The control has to provide all of the features you need, and it's the one that programmers change the most.

With this much emphasis on the utility of one control by programmers, it didn't take me too long to figure out which control to show you how to modify in this section of the chapter. I also wanted to add a unique feature—something that everyone will need eventually. That's why I chose an on/off button as the basis for the control in this chapter.

NOTE

The example on the source code CD has modified forms of the About Box, control icon, version information, string table, and control bitmap. One especially important change is to modify the IDS_PBUTTON1 string to read "On/Off Pushbutton Control (MFC)." We've already discussed these issues as part of the "Working with Resources" section of Chapter 2. See the resource file in the \Chapter 06\PButton1 folder of the source code CD for ideas on how you can change the resources for your own controls.

Writing the Code

It's time to look at a simple coding example. Let's begin with a new C++ project. However, unlike other projects you may have created, you'll want to start with the MFC ActiveX Control project to create your workspace. The MFC ActiveX Control Wizard provides you with a framework that you can build on to create the final version of this example. This example uses PButton1 for a project name. You'll see the MFC ActiveX Control Wizard dialog after you create the application. The Application Settings tab enables you to add a runtime license and automatically generate help files. The Control Names tab contains a complete list of the filenames and registry name entries for the control. Generally, you can leave these tabs alone for a simple control. However, you'll want to select the Control Settings tab shown next.

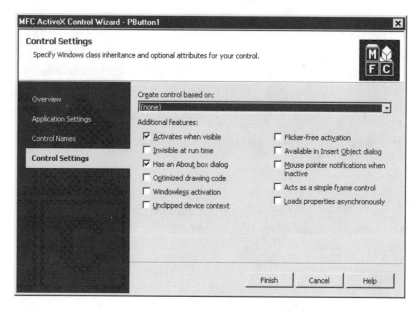

Select the BUTTON class on the Control Settings tab to create the example in this chapter. Otherwise, look through the list of available classes to determine what you want to use as a basis for your control. Notice that Visual C++ allows you to create your own basic class. Click on Finish to create the project.

Some of the options on the Control Settings tab can have unforeseen consequences when used in the wrong environment. For example, Visual Basic requires controls that create a window; otherwise you can't interact with them. The Windowless Activation option does provide a performance boost for your control, but at the cost of compatibility. The Optimized drawing code option also enhances performance, but can cause flicker in some situations. The Unclipped device context option not only enables you to create irregularly shaped controls, but also allows your control to draw outside its window, making it possible to trash the screen. The Flicker-free activation option does eliminate most causes of flicker, a plus for graphics controls, but your control will take a performance hit when using this option. The other Control Settings tab options enable your control to perform special tasks, such as appearing within a compound document.

Adding Properties and Events

Let's get down to the business of creating an ActiveX control. The first thing you'll
want to do is make some of the button control properties and events visible to someone
using the ActiveX control. For example, it might be nice to be able to detect when
the user clicked the button. You'll definitely want to be able to change default
properties, such as the caption displayed on the button front. There aren't very many
properties visible when you first create a button. To make these various elements
visible, you'll need to use the Add Property Wizard. You can access the Add
Property Wizard by right-clicking _DPButton1 (found in the PButton1Lib folder
in Class View) and choosing Add Property from the context menu.

We'll use two different kinds of properties in this example—Microsoft provides
access to a lot more. The first type is a stock property. You'll find that things like
the Caption property that we all take for granted aren't visible when you first create
an ActiveX control. A *stock property* is one that the parent class supports by default.
Visual C++ enables you to select stock properties using the Property Name field in
the Add Property Wizard dialog, as shown here.

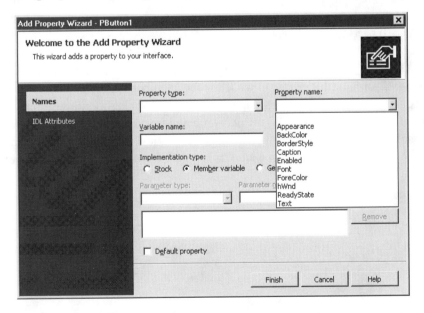

The second type is a custom property. A *custom property* is one that you've added
to a particular class when you subclass it. One of them is the OnOff property that

we'll use to create an OnOff control. We'll look at the process for doing this later in this chapter. The following table shows all the properties that we'll create in this example and tells you if they're custom or stock implementations.

Property	Type
Caption	Stock
Enabled	Stock
Front	Stock
ModalResult	Custom
OnOff	Custom
StdButtonType	Custom

To add a stock property, select its name from the Property Name field of the Add Property Wizard, verify that you have the Stock implementation type selected, then click Finish. Create all of the stock properties for this example program now.

We'll also need three custom properties: ModalResult, OnOff, and StdButtonType. To create these properties, type the names I've just mentioned into the Property Name field. You'll need to select a data type in the Property Type field as well. In this case, the ModalResult and StdButtonType properties are the LONG type, while OnOff is a VARIANT_BOOL. You have a choice between a member variable or get/set implementation. For this example, we'll use the Member Variable option. Add all of the custom properties to the example.

We also need to add a **Click**() event. Fortunately, you can add a stock Click handler to the control. Right-click CPButton1Ctrl in Class View and choose Add | Add Event from the context menu. You'll see an Add Event Wizard like the one shown next:

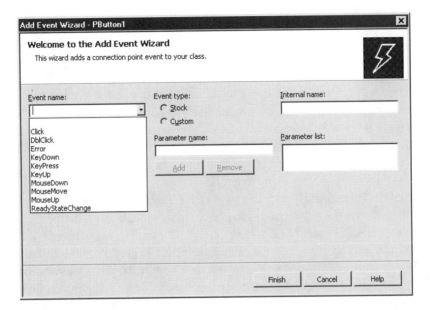

Notice that you can select a number of stock events in the Event Name field. Choose Click from the list and click Finish. That's all you need to do to add a stock event.

Defining the Property Pages

Now it's time to add some functionality to the default property page. You access it by double-clicking IDD_PROPPAGE_PBUTTON1 in the Dialog folder of Resource View. Developers use the property page for a variety of purposes—most of them configuration oriented.

There are two standard sizes of the property page supported by Visual C++. The small size, which is the default for an ActiveX control, is 250×62. This is going to be too small for our purposes, so we'll need to resize it to the large property page size of 250×110. Make sure you use one size or the other when creating a control. Nothing bad will happen if you don't use a standard size, but users get warning messages saying that you didn't use a standard-sized property page.

What we'll do now is add a method for defining standard button types to the page, as shown in Figure 6-1. These are radio buttons. You'll need ten of them. (Don't worry about how to configure them just now; I'll tell you how in the paragraphs that follow.) Each radio button should have a different ID so that you can detect which one the user clicks (see the ID field on the General page of the Radio Button Properties dialog).

You'll need to make a few subtle changes to your radio buttons before they look like the ones in Figure 6-1. First, select True for the Push-like property of each button. You'll also need to place the radio buttons into a group so that the current selection gets deselected when you choose a new button. To place the radio buttons in a group set the Group and the Tabstop properties to True on the first radio button (IDC_RADIO1). Set only the Tabstop property to True for all of the other radio buttons, or you'll end up with ten groups of one button instead of one group of ten buttons. Visual C++ starts with the first button it sees that has the Group checkbox selected as the starting point for the group. The group continues with each radio button in tab order until Visual C++ sees the next one with the Group checkbox selected.

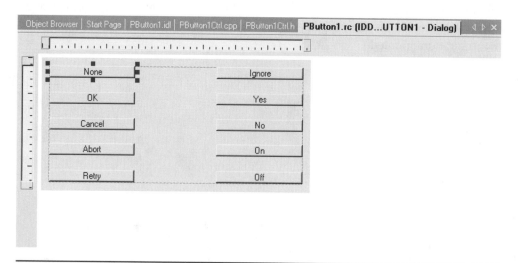

Figure 6-1   *The Property Page dialog allows the user to create standard button types in addition to the on/off button.*

We have to do one more thing with the radio buttons in this dialog. To create an OLE connection between the radio buttons and the ActiveX control, you have to assign their output to an OLE property. Begin by creating a public integer value named m_StdButtonType in the PButton1PropPage.h file. You'll also need to add the code (in bold) shown in Listing 6-1 to the PButton1PropPage.cpp file.

Listing 6-1

```
void CPButton1PropPage::DoDataExchange(CDataExchange* pDX)
{
DDP_Radio(pDX, IDC_RADIO1, m_StdButtonType, _T("StdButtonType") );
DDX_Radio(pDX, IDC_RADIO1, m_StdButtonType);
DDP_PostProcessing(pDX);
}
```

The **DDP_Radio()** call synchronizes the content of the IDC_RADIO1 group with the StdButtonType property. The **DDX_Radio()** call manages transfer of int data from the radio button group to the m_StdButtonType variable.

One of the stock properties we added was the Font property. MFC automatically manages many of the stock properties for you. However, in the case of the Font property, you do need to perform a little extra work. Look in the PButton1Ctrl.cpp file and you'll see a list of property page identifiers. This list normally contains just one item, the default property page. To add font support to your control, you'll also need to add the stock Font property page, as shown in Listing 6-2.

Listing 6-2

```
BEGIN_PROPPAGEIDS(CPButton1Ctrl, 2)
    PROPPAGEID(CPButton1PropPage::guid)
    PROPPAGEID(CLSID_CFontPropPage)
END_PROPPAGEIDS(CPButton1Ctrl)
```

As you can see, the addition consists of adding a stock property page identifier using the **PROPPAGEID()** macro. Notice that you also have to change the number of property pages from "1" to "2" in the **BEGIN_PROPPAGEIDS()** macro.

Adding Some Control Code

All of the code we've added so far helped set the control up for use. Now it's time to add code that enables the control to perform useful work. The first thing we want to do is add some code so our control can exchange data with the client. For example, when you see a properties dialog for a control, you normally want to see the current values of those properties. Likewise, when you change a property value, you want to be sure that the actual control state will change. Listing 6-3 shows the code you'll need to add.

Listing 6-3

```
void CPButton1Ctrl::DoPropExchange(CPropExchange* pPX)
{
    ExchangeVersion(pPX, MAKELONG(_wVerMinor, _wVerMajor));
    COleControl::DoPropExchange(pPX);

    // Make all of our properties persistent.
    PX_Bool(pPX, "OnOff", m_OnOff, FALSE);
    PX_Long(pPX, "ModalResult", m_ModalResult, mrNone);
    PX_Long(pPX, "StdButtonType", m_StdButtonType, None);
}
```

One of the problems with the **PX_Bool()** function is that it doesn't work with the VARIANT_BOOL type that the IDE forces you to use for properties. You'll find that developers use a number of methods to deal with this problem. For example, you could write a new form of the **PX_Bool()** function that will accept the VARIANT_BOOL type. Some developers also use

```
PX_Short(pPX, "OnOff", m_OnOff, VARIANT_FALSE);
```

to make the property persistent, but this method proves unreliable in testing. However, the easiest way of dealing with the problem is to change the VARIANT_BOOL type into a BOOL in the PButton1Ctrl.h file. Don't change the entry in the IDL. This technique works fine in our example and in most other situations.

Now let's say that you want the button to display a specific caption when the user inserts it onto a Web page or other layout. You can change the caption property in the **OnReset()** function. Listing 6-4 shows the code you'll need to change. Notice that we use the COleControl class functions to make the required change. The **SetText()** function allows us to change the caption of the button. Every time the user inserts this control, the caption of "Button" will appear.

Listing 6-4

```
void CPButton1Ctrl::OnResetState()
{
    // Resets defaults found in DoPropExchange
```

```
COleControl::OnResetState();

//Modify the control appearance.
COleControl::SetText("Button");
}
```

Now that we have a method for exchanging information and we've set the control up the way we want it to look, it's time to implement the three custom properties that we created. Every time you create a custom property, you'll need to define some code to make that property do something. Otherwise, it'll just sit there and do nothing at all. Listing 6-5 shows the code you'll need to add to implement the ModalResult, OnOff, and StdButtonType properties. Note that I've removed some of the repeated code that you'll find on the source code CD. I'll explain the inner workings of this code in the next section. For right now, all you need to know is that it implements the properties we created.

Listing 6-5

```
void CPButton1Ctrl::OnModalResultChanged(void)
{
    AFX_MANAGE_STATE(AfxGetStaticModuleState());

    //Set the modified flag.
    SetModifiedFlag();
}

void CPButton1Ctrl::OnStdButtonTypeChanged(void)
{
    AFX_MANAGE_STATE(AfxGetStaticModuleState());

    // Change the modal result and button
    // caption to match the user selection.
    switch (m_StdButtonType)
    {
    case 0:
        m_ModalResult = mrNone;
        COleControl::SetText("Button");
        break;
//
// Cases 1 through 8 on source code CD.
//
    case 9:
        m_ModalResult = mrOff;
```

```
        COleControl::SetText("Off");
    }


    // Set the OnOff property to false
    // since the user selected another type.
    m_OnOff = FALSE;

    //Set the modified flag.
    SetModifiedFlag();
}


void CPButton1Ctrl::OnOnOffChanged(void)
{
    AFX_MANAGE_STATE(AfxGetStaticModuleState());

    // If the programmer set the OnOff property true,
    // take appropriate action.
    if (m_OnOff)
    {
        COleControl::SetText("On");      //Change the caption.
        m_SetOn = TRUE;                  //Set an internal caption flag.
        m_ModalResult = mrOn;            //Set the modal result value.
    }
    else
    {
        COleControl::SetText("Button");  //Restore default caption.
        m_SetOn = FALSE;                 //Turn our caption flag off.
        m_ModalResult = mrNone;          //Use the default modal result.
    }

    //Set the modified flag.
    SetModifiedFlag();
}
```

At this point, the user can change properties. However, what happens when a user clicks the button? If he or she is using one of the standard button types, the OnOff control will return a modal result value. However, the OnOff control also has a special behavior. If you set the OnOff property to True, the button should switch between on and off as the user clicks it. We need to add some special event code to handle this situation. Click the Overrides button in the Properties window and you'll see a list of events you can override. Click the down arrow in the field next to the OnClick entry and choose <Add> OnClick from the list. Visual C++ will add a new method for you.

Now it's time to add some code to the **OnClick()** function. Click the Edit Code button, and Visual C++ will take you to the new function. Listing 6-6 shows the code you'll need to add.

Listing 6-6

```
void CPButton1Ctrl::OnClick(USHORT iButton)
{
    // See if the OnOff flag is set.  If so, change
    // the caption and internal caption flag.  The effect
    // you should see from this code is a toggling of the
    // caption text.
    if (m_OnOff)
    {
        if (m_SetOn)
        {
            COleControl::SetText("Off");
            m_SetOn = FALSE;
            m_ModalResult = mrOff;
        }
        else
        {
            COleControl::SetText("On");
            m_SetOn = TRUE;
            m_ModalResult = mrOn;
        }
    }

    // Call the default OnClick processing.
    COleControl::OnClick(iButton);
}
```

Using a VARIANT_BOOL type for the OnOff property enables the user to see a nice drop-down list box containing True and False. Wouldn't it be nice if you could also provide a drop-down list box for ModalResult and StdButtonType? To make this feature work, you need to add the two enumerations shown in Listing 6-7. Add them to both the beginning of the IDL file (right beneath the #include statements) and to the Public area of the class definition in the PButton1Ctrl.h file.

Listing 6-7

```
// Define the valid ModalResult property values.
typedef enum ModalType
{
    mrNone = -1L,
    mrOK = 1L,
    mrCancel = 2L,
    mrAbort = 3L,
    mrRetry = 4L,
    mrIgnore = 5L,
    mrYes = 6L,
    mrNo = 7L,
    mrOn = 8L,
    mrOff = 9L,
}MODALTYPE;

// Define the valid StdButtonType property values.
typedef enum StdButton
{
    None = 0L,
    OK = 1L,
    Cancel = 2L,
    Abort = 3L,
    Retry = 4L,
    Ignore = 5L,
    Yes = 6L,
    No = 7L,
    On = 8L,
    Off = 9L,
}STDBUTTON;
```

Adding the enumerations helps, but you also need to change the two properties in the IDL file. Note that the type of the properties remains long. All we've done is assign an enumeration to the property so that it provides help to the user. Here are the small, but important, changes you need to make to the two properties to enable the drop-down list boxes.

```
[id(1), helpstring("property ModalResult")] ModalType ModalResult;
[id(2), helpstring("property StdButtonType")] StdButton StdButtonType;
```

The final coding item is a special variable. You'll notice in the code that I keep referring to an m_SetOn member variable, but this variable isn't part of the class right now. All you need to do is add it as a type BOOL to the Protected area of the PButton1Ctrl.h file.

Breaking the Code into Pieces

Let's start taking this code apart. The first function that you modified is **DoPropExchange()**. This function performs only one service in this example— it enables you to make your custom properties persistent. Essentially, the PX_ series of function calls stores the value of a particular property from one session to the next. There's one function call for each variable type that you define. Each one of them accepts four variables like this:

```
PX_Bool(pPX, "OnOff", m_onOff, FALSE);
```

The first variable is a pointer to a property exchange structure. Visual C++ defines this structure for you automatically—all you need to do is use it. The second parameter contains the external name of the property, the one that the user will see in the Properties window. The third parameter is the internal name for the property. That's the one you'll use throughout the program to define the property. Finally, we have to define a default value for the property.

The next function you have to modify is **OnResetState()**. This function provides some of the aesthetic details that users will see when they add the component to a form. In this case, we'll give the component a default caption. The important thing to remember is that the **OnResetState()** function allows you to perform any setup required to use your control.

Two of the three modified functions in the message-handlers section of the code require some kind of change. The **ModalResultChanged()** function doesn't require any modification, so I won't talk about it here. The property associated with the **ModalResultChanged()** function, ModalResult, gets changed by the other two functions. The **OnOffChanged()** function is the first one we'll look at. What we need to do is set an internal caption flag and the initial caption. If the programmer sets the OnOff property to True, we'll set the control up as an on/off switch button by setting its caption to On. We also provide a different modal result value when the pushbutton is used as an on/off switch. Notice that the m_onOff internal property variable tracks the status of the flag. The m_SetOn internal property tracks the current condition of the OnOff control (On or Off). Since the button is initially On, we set the m_SetOn flag to True.

Now it's time to look at the processing required for the property page feature of this ActiveX control. The **OnStdButtonTypeChanged**() function is nothing more than a simple case statement. It changes the button's Caption and ModalResult properties as needed to create various default button types. Notice that we also have to turn off the OnOff pushbutton processing if the user selects a default button type.

The **OnClick**() message-handling function is active during runtime. There are two levels of processing. First, the code determines if the programmer defined this button as an on/off switch. If so, it changes the internal state variable (m_SetOn) and the button caption. The function switches the button state between on and off. Once the code finishes the internal processing, it calls the default OnClick processing routine. Failure to call this default routine will cause the ActiveX control to skip any code specific to the programming environment that you attach to button events. For example, if you were to use this control in a Visual C++ application, Visual C++ would ignore any code attached to the exposed events.

ATL ActiveX Control Example

This section of the chapter is going to look at the ATL version of the component that we just created using MFC in the previous section. You'll find that many of the procedures for creating a component using ATL are completely different from what we did in the previous section, because ATL assumes a lot less about what you'll need.

Just to make it easier for you to compare the creation process for ATL and MFC components, we'll follow approximately the same sequence of construction steps; it's just that the way you need to perform the steps will be different. The following sections will show you how to create a duplicate of the OnOff pushbutton control that we've just created using MFC.

NOTE

The ATL version of the control uses approximately the same resources as the MFC version of the control. However, implementing the resources requires more code than an MFC control because nothing is automatic in an ATL control. For example, you have to write all of the code required to display an About Box. See the source code found in the \Chapter 06\PButton1 folder of the source code CD for details.

Creating the ATL Version Program Shell

As with the MFC example, the first thing we need to do is create a program shell for our ActiveX control. However, in this case, we'll need to perform additional preparatory work, because ATL doesn't assume anything at all about the control you want to create. For example, the program shell won't include any objects, which means that you'll need to add everything manually. The following sections will show you how to create an ATL program shell that approximates the MFC shell we created in the previous section.

Creating an ATL Program Shell   The first task is to create an ATL program shell. Begin by creating a new ATL Project using the options in the New Project dialog box. The example uses a name of PButton2. The following procedure shows you how to complete the shell.

1. Select the Application Settings tab of the ATL Project Wizard. We'll need to use the DLL format for this control—even though an ActiveX control normally uses an ActiveX control extension, it's really a DLL. In addition, we'll want to combine the proxy and stub code so that the resulting file consumes just one DLL instead of two.

2. Clear the Attributed option. (We'll discuss attributed programming techniques in Chapter 13.)

3. Check the Allow merging of proxy/stub code option. Choosing this option will allow Visual C++ to create a single control file.

4. Click Finish. Visual C++ will create the empty ATL project shell for you.

Adding an Object to the Program Shell   All of the extra work you have to do to create an ATL shell pays off in one respect: design flexibility. When you create an ActiveX component shell using MFC, there's a single field on one of the wizard dialogs that allows you to choose how many objects the component will contain. If you change your mind later on, you have to go through a lot of extra work to add another object— and forget about removing an object without a lot of hair pulling. ATL makes life easier by allowing you to add objects when you decide that you need them. Removing an object may be a little harder, but it's not nearly as difficult as when you use MFC. The following procedure shows you how to add an ATL ActiveX object to the program shell we created in the previous section.

1. Right-click the PButton2 folder on the Class View tab, then choose Add | Add Class from the context menu. You'll see the Add Class dialog.

2. Highlight the ATL Control icon, then click Open. You'll see the ATL Control Wizard. The Names tab is where you assign a name to your control. This tab also contains the names of the files used to support the control.

3. Type **PButton2Ctrl** in the Short Name field. Visual C++ will automatically add default entries to the remaining fields for you. However, the name in the Type field isn't very descriptive, and that's what will get displayed in the various control selection dialogs.

4. Type **On/Off Pushbutton Control (ATL)** in the Type field. Changing this entry will make it easier for someone to find the control in a list and reduce the chance that someone will choose it by mistake.

5. Click the Options tab and you'll see a list of control options. This is where you'll choose the characteristics of the object. In most cases, these settings are fine. However, since we want to support events, we'll need to add connection points support to the control.

6. Check the Support Connection Points option. This will allow us to add events to the control later.

TIP

You can reduce the size of the resulting control by setting Aggregation to No. However, this means that the control can't be used as a basis for creating other controls. If you choose the Only option, then this control could only be used as a basis for creating other controls — not by itself.

7. Click the Appearance tab. This tab contains a variety of configuration options for the control, like which general control to use as a base. This tab also includes drawing options, like whether the control always needs to appear within a window. It's important to know what kinds of features the environment that the control will appear in supports.

8. Check the Acts Like Button and Windowed Only options, then choose Button in the "Add control based on list" box. The Acts Like Button option allows the control to become a default control in a dialog box. The "Add control based on" list box determines what general control to use as a basis for creating this control. Notice that Visual C++ .NET doesn't select the Windowed Only option for you, which forces the pushbutton to appear in a Window (allowing it full access to mouse and other user interface events). If you plan to use the control with older versions of some Microsoft products, such as Visual Basic, you must check the Windowed Only option.

9. Click the Stock Properties tab. You'll see a list of stock properties that ATL supports. This is where you'll determine what stock properties the wizard adds to your control, although you could always add them later. In this case, we'll add the same stock properties that we added for the MFC version of the control: Caption, Enabled, and Font.

10. Highlight the Caption, Enabled, and Font properties in turn, then click the > (right arrow) button. The wizard will add the stock properties to the Supported list on the right side of the dialog.

11. Click Finish. Visual C++ will create the new control for you.

Adding a Property Page to the Program Shell   At this point, we have an object to work with, but no property page to change the object properties with when working in environments that don't support a Property Window. This section will show you how to add a custom property page to the project. You'll need to use this manual procedure for any property page you want to add.

1. Right click the PButton2 folder on the Class View tab, then choose Add | Add Class from the context menu. You'll see the Add Class dialog.

2. Highlight the ATL Property Page icon, then click Open. You'll see the ATL Property Page Wizard. The Names tab is where you assign a name to your control. This tab also contains the names of the files used to support the property page.

3. Type **PButton2PropPage** in the Short Name field. Visual C++ will automatically enter values for the rest of the fields for you. In this case, the default entries will work fine (although you could change the Type field if you wanted something more descriptive for the property page).

4. Click the Strings tab. This dialog contains the strings that give the property page a title and tell the client where to find the property page's help file. In this case, we'll give the property page the same title as its MFC counterpart and won't assign a help file to it. The Doc String field provides balloon help for the property page, but it isn't used by most programming languages.

5. Type **On/Off Button Settings** in the Title field and Set the Standard Button Type for the On/Off Pushbutton Control in the Doc String field.

6. Clear the Helpfile field.

7. Click Finish. Visual C++ will create the required files and resources for the property page object. This includes creating a dialog that you can use to add controls to the property page.

Adding Properties and Events to the ATL Version

We added all of the stock properties to the control as part of the creation process, so we won't need to do that again. However, we still need to add the ModalResult,

OnOff, and StdButtonType custom properties. The following procedure shows you how.

1. Right-click the IPButton2Ctrl interface on the Class View tab, then choose Add | Add Property from the context menu. You'll see the Add Property Wizard. This dialog enables you to define a property name, its return value, and any arguments required for using it.

2. Choose LONG in the Property Type field. Type **ModalResult** in the Property Name field. At this point, we have the property defined, but notice that the property description shown in the Implementation field is less than helpful.

3. Click Attributes. This tab helps you change property attributes like the help string associated with the property. We need to set some attributes for this property so that the client will fully understand how to interact with it.

4. Type **Control Return Value** in the helpstring field.

5. Click Finish. Visual C++ will add the requested property to your IDL file.

6. Repeat steps 1 through 5 to add the OnOff and StdButtonType properties. Make sure you add an appropriate helpstring value, like Sets OnOff Mode When True or Selects the Type of Button Created. You'll also want to change the property type as appropriate (VARIANT_BOOL for OnOff and LONG for StdButtonType).

It's time to add the **OnClick()** event. ATL handles events through a different interface than the one used for properties and methods. You'll need to work with the _IPButton2CtrlEvents (found in the PButton2Lib folder) interface in this case. Adding an event is essentially the same as adding a method, except you can use something other than an HRESULT return value when working with events. The following procedure will show you how.

1. Right-click the _IPButton2CtrlEvents interface folder on the Class View tab, then choose Add | Add Method from the context menu. You'll see an Add Method Wizard dialog.

2. Type **Click** in the Method Name field, and then select "void" in the Return Type field. Because there aren't any parameters for the Click event, we don't add anything else in this case.

3. Click Finish. Visual C++ will add the event method to your application.

At this point, we need to implement the event interface that we've created within the CPButton2Ctrl object. Simply right-click the CPButton2Ctrl folder within the

Class View tab and choose Add | Add Connection Point from the context menu. You'll see an Implement Connection Point Wizard dialog. Select the interface that you want to implement (there should be only one in this case) by highlighting it and clicking the right arrow (you should see the _IPButton2CtrlEvents interface appear in the Implement Connection Points list), then click Finish. What you'll see added is a new proxy class named CProxy_IPButton2CtrlEvents<class T> with a single method named **Fire_Click()** in Class View, which allows you to output Click events to the client. You can also use this technique to implement interfaces other than the custom interface created specifically for the control.

Writing the ATL Version Code

This section will show you how to add the code required to make the ATL version of our OnOff Pushbutton Control functional. You'll notice quite a few similarities between this code and the code used for the MFC version. However, it's the differences that are the most important. ATL requires making changes in the way you handle some of the method coding. There are also additional requirements for making things like the About dialog functional that you didn't need to worry about with the MFC version. (You'll find the About Box code on the source code CD.) The following sections describe each of the major code segments for this version of the control.

Creating Persistent Properties   Making properties persistent when working with ATL is totally different from what you did with MFC. In fact, you'll make the required entries in the Pbutton2Ctrl.H file instead of the CPP file. Listing 6-8 shows the code you'll need to add in bold.

Listing 6-8

```
PROP_ENTRY("Caption", DISPID_CAPTION, CLSID_NULL)
PROP_ENTRY("Enabled", DISPID_ENABLED, CLSID_NULL)
PROP_ENTRY("Font", DISPID_FONT, CLSID_StockFontPage)
// Add the custom properties.
PROP_ENTRY("ModalResult", DISPID_MODALRESULT, CLSID_NULL)
PROP_ENTRY("OnOff", DISPID_ONOFF, CLSID_NULL)
PROP_ENTRY("StdButtonType", DISPID_STDBUTTONTYPE, CLSID_NULL)
```

These entries are relatively easy to understand. The **PROP_ENTRY()** macro takes three arguments. The first is the text name of the property as it'll appear in a Properties Window. The second is the dispatch identifier of the property. The third entry specifies a special dialog, if any, used to configure the property. Notice that the Font entry contains an entry of this sort—the stock font property page. If the property doesn't require any special configuration, then you need to supply the CLSID_NULL value as shown.

You may be wondering where the dispatch identifiers shown in Listing 6-8 came from. I defined them in the Pbutton2.IDL file, as shown in Listing 6-9 in bold. There isn't any requirement to create these entries, but doing so will make your code a lot easier to understand. If you don't create the DISPID values, then you'll need to use the numbers that ATL originally supplied (which means you'll need to keep some kind of reference for those numbers handy). You can also replace the ID values for the custom properties with their custom DISPID value counterparts for consistency.

Listing 6-9

```
interface IPButton2Ctrl : IDispatch{
    // Create some defines for the various dispatch IDs.
    const int DISPID_MODALRESULT    = 1L;
    const int DISPID_ONOFF          = 2L;
    const int DISPID_STDBUTTONTYPE  = 3L;
```

Defining Get/Put Methods for the Properties   Unlike the MFC version of our control, the ATL version uses Put, instead of Set methods to change the current value of a property. Fortunately, this is a difference in naming only, not a real difference in how ATL implements the method. However, you need to be careful when porting your code from one environment to the other because of these differences. You'll begin by defining the same series of member variables that we defined for the MFC version of the control, as shown Listing 6-10.

Listing 6-10

```
// Member variables for maintaining property state.
long            m_ModalResult;
VARIANT_BOOL    m_OnOff;
long            m_StdButtonType;
```

Once you have some variables to use, you can add the code required to make the Get/Put methods work, as shown in Listing 6-11. While the methodology of this code should look familiar, you should also see some definite differences between this code and the MFC version.

Listing 6-11

```
STDMETHODIMP CPButton2Ctrl::get_ModalResult(LONG* pVal)
{
   // Return the stored value.
   *pVal = m_ModalResult;

   // Return a non-error message
   return S_OK;
}

STDMETHODIMP CPButton2Ctrl::put_ModalResult(LONG newVal)
{
   // Set the ModalResult value.
   m_ModalResult = newVal;

   // Register the update
   SetDirty(true);
   FireViewChange();

   // Return a non-error message
   return S_OK;
}

STDMETHODIMP CPButton2Ctrl::get_OnOff(VARIANT_BOOL* pVal)
{
   // Return the stored value.
   *pVal = m_OnOff;

   // Return a non-error message
   return S_OK;
}

STDMETHODIMP CPButton2Ctrl::put_OnOff(VARIANT_BOOL newVal)
{
   // Set the ModalResult value.
   m_OnOff = newVal;
```

```
    // If the programmer set the OnOff property true,
    // take appropriate action.
    if (m_OnOff)
    {
       m_bstrCaption = T2BSTR("On"); //Change the caption.
       m_SetOn = TRUE;                //Set an internal caption flag.
       m_ModalResult = mrOn;          //Set the modal result value.
    }
    else
    {
       m_bstrCaption = T2BSTR("Button");//Restore default caption.
       m_SetOn = FALSE;               //Turn our caption flag off.
       m_ModalResult = mrNone;        //Use the default modal result.
    }

    // Register the update
    SetDirty(true);
    FireViewChange();

    // Return a non-error message
    return S_OK;
}


STDMETHODIMP CPButton2Ctrl::get_StdButtonType(LONG* pVal)
{
    // Return the stored value.
    *pVal = m_StdButtonType;

    // Return a non-error message
    return S_OK;
}


STDMETHODIMP CPButton2Ctrl::put_StdButtonType(LONG newVal)
{
    // Set the ModalResult value.
    m_StdButtonType = newVal;

    // Skip if the OnOff option is true.
    if (m_OnOff)
       return S_OK;

    // Change the modal result and button
    // caption to match the user selection.
```

```
   switch (m_StdButtonType)
   {
   case 0:
      m_ModalResult = mrNone;
      m_bstrCaption = T2BSTR("Button");
      break;
//
// Cases 1 through 8 on source code CD.
//
   case 9:
      m_ModalResult = mrOff;
      m_bstrCaption = T2BSTR("Off");
   }

   // Register the update
   SetDirty(true);
   FireViewChange();

   // Return a non-error message
   return S_OK;
}
```

As you can see, the basic idea of setting and getting control properties is the same when using ATL; it's the actual implementation that varies. In this case, we're working with BSTR values. You don't have access to the COleControl class as you did in the MFC example. These changes account for a large part of the differences in the code shown in Listing 6-11.

Notice that there are a couple of additions to the MFC code. For one thing, you need to use the **SetDirty()** method to tell the control to update its property values. In addition, you'll want to use **FireViewChange()** method to ensure the control gets repainted to show any modifications to its appearance.

Defining the OnClick() Event   The **OnClick()** event requires some special monitoring when working with ATL. You need to monitor the user's mouse clicks and keystrokes to determine when to fire a click event. What this means is that two new Windows message handlers need to be added to our code; one monitors the left mouse button, while the other monitors the ENTER key. The following steps show how to add the two message handlers.

  1. Click the Messages button in the Properties window. You'll see a list of messages you can override.

2. Highlight the WM_LBUTTONDOWN message. Select <Add> OnLButtonDown from the drop-down list box. This will add a new handler for a left mouse button down event.

3. Highlight the WM_KEYDOWN. Select <Add> OnKeyDown from the drop-down list box. Visual C++ will add the new message handler and take you directly to the new functions.

Now that we have some new functions to work with, let's look at the code required to make them work. Listing 6-12 shows the code for the WM_LBUTTONDOWN and WM_KEYDOWN message handlers. Normally, you require only these two handlers for a pushbutton.

Listing 6-12

```
LRESULT CPButton2Ctrl::OnLButtonDown(UINT uMsg,
                                     WPARAM wParam,
                                     LPARAM lParam,
                                     BOOL& bHandled)
{
   // Perform the normal button processing.
   m_ctlButton.DefWindowProc(uMsg, wParam, lParam);

   // See if the OnOff flag is set.  If so, change
   // the caption and internal caption flag.
   if (m_OnOff)
   {
      if (m_SetOn)
      {
         m_bstrCaption = T2BSTR("Off");
         m_SetOn = FALSE;
         m_ModalResult = mrOff;
         m_ctlButton.SetWindowText(_T("Off"));
      }
      else
      {
         m_bstrCaption = T2BSTR("On");
         m_SetOn = TRUE;
         m_ModalResult = mrOn;
         m_ctlButton.SetWindowText(_T("On"));
      }
   }

   // Perform the default action.
   Fire_Click();
```

```
        return 0;
}


LRESULT CPButton2Ctrl::OnKeyDown(UINT uMsg,
                                 WPARAM wParam,
                                 LPARAM lParam,
                                 BOOL& bHandled)
{
    // Perform the normal button processing.
    m_ctlButton.DefWindowProc(uMsg, wParam, lParam);

    // Determine the current key code.  If the key code is
    // the Enter key, then change the button status; otherwise,
    // exit.
    if (!(wParam == 13))
        return 0;

    // See if the OnOff flag is set.  If so, change
    // the caption and internal caption flag.
    if (m_OnOff)
    {
        if (m_SetOn)
        {
            m_bstrCaption = T2BSTR("Off");
            m_SetOn = FALSE;
            m_ModalResult = mrOff;
            m_ctlButton.SetWindowText(_T("Off"));
        }
        else
        {
            m_bstrCaption = T2BSTR("On");
            m_SetOn = TRUE;
            m_ModalResult = mrOn;
            m_ctlButton.SetWindowText(_T("On"));
        }
    }

    // Perform the default action.
    Fire_Click();

    return 0;
}
```

Both of these methods do the same thing—they allow the control to detect
user input. The **OnKeyDown()** method begins by performing one check that the
OnLButtonDown() method doesn't need to perform. It uses the wParam input to
detect which key the user pressed. The **OnKeyDown()** method will react only to the

ENTER key. Both methods allow the default procedure to perform whatever tasks it needs to do first by calling the **DefWindowProc()** method of the m_ctlButton object (this object is created automatically for you by the ATL wizard and allows the control to handle standard button events). The button changing process works the same as the MFC version of the control. Even though the method used to fire a click is different, this process works the same as the MFC version of the control as well.

Adding Some Initialization Code   Initialization for the ATL version of our control is much more complicated than the MFC version. For one thing, ATL assumes nothing about the initial state of the variables and, unlike MFC, there isn't any way to define an initial state as part of the process of making the properties persistent. Obviously, we need another initialization alternative, which is to add the **InitNew()** method to the control. The programming environment calls the **InitNew()** method to initialize the control's properties if you're creating a new control. Listing 6-13 shows the source code for the **InitNew()** method.

Listing 6-13

```
STDMETHODIMP CPButton2Ctrl::InitNew()
{
  CComPtr<IFont>  p;     // The ambient (default) font pointer.
  CComPtr<IFont>  pFont; // A copy of the font for local use.

  // Tell Visual C++ that we'll be converting BSTR values.
  USES_CONVERSION;

  // Get the default font, create a copy of it, then initialize
  // our Font property with it.  if(!m_pFont)
    if(SUCCEEDED(GetAmbientFont(&p)) && p)
      if(SUCCEEDED(p->Clone(&pFont)) && pFont)
        pFont->QueryInterface(IID_IFontDisp, (void**)&m_pFont);

  // Initialize the rest of the properties.
  m_bEnabled = true;
  m_bstrCaption = T2BSTR("Button");
  m_ModalResult = -1;
  m_OnOff = FALSE;
  m_StdButtonType = 0;

  // Set the initial control size.
  m_sizeExtent.cx = 2100;
```

```
    m_sizeExtent.cy = 580;

    // Register the update
    SetDirty(true);
    FireViewChange();

    // Set the initialization variable so that we don't
    // initialize the control twice.
    m_bInitialized = true;

    // Return a non-error result.
    return S_OK;
}
```

Let's talk about the **InitNew()** method first. This is the method that the programming environment calls when creating a new control. The first bit of code checks to ensure the Font property is defined. If not, the method assigns the current system font to the control. Initializing the other properties is as easy as assigning them a value. You'll want to be sure that all of the defaults you assign work together. All ATL controls start out as a moderately large square, which isn't a very good shape for a pushbutton. The next bit of code assigns a more believable size to the control that roughly equates to the size of a standard Visual C++ pushbutton. Once all of the initialization is complete, you must use the **SetDirty()** method to ensure the control values get changed and the **FireViewChange()** method to ensure the changes also get reflected in the control's appearance. Finally, the **InitNew()** method tells the control that it's initialized by setting m_bInitialized to true, then returns a non-error result to the control.

Another potential problem is the appearance of the control itself. You may not see the control you'd expected to see when you place it in the IDE. Part of the problem is that ATL makes no assumptions about how you want to create the control—it creates the most basic form available without considering any special features of a subclassed control. With that in mind, you need to change the control's **OnCreate()** method as shown in Listing 6-14 to take better advantage of the inherent features that control has to offer.

Listing 6-14

```
LRESULT OnCreate(UINT /*uMsg*/, WPARAM /*wParam*/, LPARAM /*lParam*/, BOOL& /*bHandled*/)
{
    // Determine how big to make the control.
```

```
// Tell Visual C++ that we'll be converting BSTR values.
USES_CONVERSION;
// Determine how big to make the control.
RECT rc;
GetWindowRect(&rc);
rc.right -= rc.left;
rc.bottom -= rc.top;
rc.top = rc.left = 0;

// Make sure you modify the default Create() method syntax
// to create the kind of button that you want.
m_ctlButton.Create(m_hWnd, rc,
    OLE2T(m_bstrCaption),
    BS_PUSHBUTTON | WS_VISIBLE | WS_CHILD | WS_TABSTOP);
// Return a non-error result.
return 0;
}
```

For the most part you'll find that ATL creates a simple box for you to look at, and it's up to you to do something with it. In this case, we add a caption to the pushbutton and give it some of the standard pushbutton flags. The flags you add will depend on the type of control you're creating. In some cases, the default ATL settings will work just fine; but in most cases, you'll need to make some minor changes. Obviously, the control has to support the flags you choose.

Visual C++ users will see a problem almost instantly after they compile the control code and try to use it within a Visual C++ application. What you'll get for a default presentation in the IDE is a blank white box. Fortunately, the control appears as normal when you compile and run the application. The problem is that Visual C++ doesn't InPlaceActivate the control. As a result, the **OnPaint()** method never gets called to paint the control on screen, and the ATL implementation for **OnDraw()** doesn't do anything. Listing 6-15 shows one way to get around this problem by implementing the **OnDraw()** method yourself.

Listing 6-15

```
HRESULT CPButton2Ctrl::OnDraw(ATL_DRAWINFO &di)
{
    // Control's bounding rectangle.
    RECT& rc = *(RECT*)di.prcBounds;

    // If the control isn't InPlaceActive, then we
    // need to draw it.  Otherwise, the control gets
    // drawn as part of a call to OnPaint().
```

```
if (!m_bInPlaceActive)
{
  // Tell Visual C++ that we'll be converting BSTR values.
  USES_CONVERSION;
  // Make the control display a simple rectangle with text.
  Rectangle(di.hdcDraw,
    rc.left,
    rc.top,
    rc.right,
    rc.bottom);
  DrawText(di.hdcDraw,
    OLE2T(m_bstrCaption),
    -1, &rc, DT_SINGLELINE | DT_CENTER | DT_VCENTER);
}

  return S_OK;
}
```

I chose to create a very simple presentation, in this case, because the drawing code isn't very important. All the user really needs is a box to show the extent of the control and the caption text. Creating an image that looks like a button would be nice, but not required.

There's one absolute necessity. Notice that the code checks the InPlaceActivate status of the control before it draws anything. You must perform this step or the user will see a flawed button appearance when the application is running.

NOTE

At this point, you'd add a property page to the control similar to the one for the MFC version of the control. In addition, you'd want the ModalResult and StdButtonType properties to use drop-down list boxes similar to those found for the MFC version of the control. You'll find both of these additions on the source code CD.

Testing the Control

After you create a new ActiveX control, you have to test it to make sure it works as anticipated. I'm going to use Visual C++ throughout the following sections. You could use any programming environment that supports ActiveX controls. For example, you might want to test the OnOff control with Visual Basic to see how it works with another language. The important consideration isn't the language you use for testing but that you test the control fully with some programming language that includes full debugging support. You want to make sure that the control you've created actually works as anticipated in the safest possible environment designed to do so. Since many Internet tools are in the testing stage, you may find that a control that seems like it should work doesn't. Being able to eliminate the control itself by testing it in a known environment is one step toward troubleshooting the problem.

Performing the ActiveX control test doesn't have to be a long, drawn-out affair. All you really need to do is create a project using your standard programming environment, then add the ActiveX control you've created. Make sure all of the properties work as expected. Take time to check out the property page thoroughly as well.

Start by creating a new project in your favorite programming environment. For the purposes of this example, you could easily test the control by creating a dialog-based application in Visual C++. The MFC AppWizard takes care of most of the work for you. (We look at the process for creating a dialog-based application using Visual C++ in Chapter 2.) I gave my project the name PButton1Test (the source code CD also includes a PButton2Test for testing the ATL version of the control).

After you have a new project in place, create a form (if needed) and add the ActiveX control to it. Visual C++ automatically registers ActiveX controls for you, so the control we created in the previous sections should appear in the list of controls available to you. Most programming environments also provide a way to view all of the properties associated with a control at one time. Verify the properties work as expected. If you expect to see a drop-down list box for a property, then it should appear when you click on the property and should contain the values you set for it.

You'll probably want to add some test code to the program as well. That way you can check the effects of various control events. For example, the On/Off pushbutton in our example provides a variety of modal result values depending on how you set the button properties. Setting the OnOff property to True creates a special switch button. The ModalResult property switches between two values. However, you could just as easily select one of the standard button values from the Property window.

Add a member variable for the control to the test application by right-clicking the control and choosing Add Variable from the context menu. The member variable enables you to access the control within the test code. The example uses a member variable name of m_OnOffButton. You'll also need to add an event handler for the Click event. Listing 6-16 shows the C++ test code for this example. Notice the use of the **GetModalResult**() wrapper class function that Visual C++ automatically creates for the control.

Listing 6-16

```
void CPButton1TestDlg::OnClickOcxexmplctrl1()
{
    //Get the current ModalResult value.
    long liModalResult;
    liModalResult = m_OnOffButton.GetModalResult();

    //Determine which modal result was returned and display a message.
    switch (liModalResult)
    {
    case -1:
        MessageBox("None button pressed", "State of Control", MB_OK);
        break;
    case 1:
        MessageBox("OK button pressed", "State of Control", MB_OK);
        break;
//
// Cases 1 through 8 on source code CD.
//
    case 9:
        MessageBox("Button is Off", "State of Control", MB_OK);
        break;
    }
}
```

Now that you have a simple form with your control attached to it, try testing it. The example program will display a simple dialog box with the ActiveX control on it. Click the control and you'll see another dialog telling you the state of the button.

Component Testing Aids and Techniques

So far, we've discussed the mechanics of creating a control using two different techniques. However, working with controls also requires knowledge of the tools at your disposal for working with controls and properly testing them. The following sections will tell you about some useful tools that you should add to your arsenal.

Unregistering Your Control

In your SYSTEM (or SYSTEM32) folder you'll find a little program called RegSvr32. It's the program responsible for adding entries for your ActiveX control to the registry. The same program can unregister your control using a little known command line switch, -U. So, if you wanted to unregister the control we created in this, you'd type **REGSVR32 -U PBUTTON1.OCX** at the command line. If you're successful, you'll see a dialog like the one that follows.

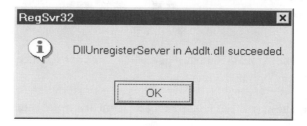

Some people find that they don't like using the command prompt to register and unregister their components using RegSvr32. You'll find an alternative method in the Xteq COM Register Extension at **http://www.xteq.com/downloads/index.html#comr**. This utility adds two new menu entries to your system, as shown next.

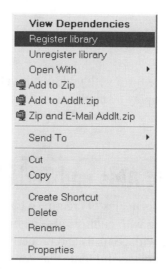

All you need to do is right-click the component and choose "Unregister library" to unregister it. Likewise, choosing "Register library" will add it to the registry. You get the same RegSvr32 messages as you normally would. The only difference is that you don't have to go to the command line to perform the task.

ActiveX Control Test Container

Component technology has freed many programmers from the need to perform some types of repetitive tasks. For example, the addition of standard dialog box support to Windows, like the File Open dialog box, has reduced the need for everyone to create their own version of this very standard application feature. Command buttons, labels, and text controls have all had their share in reducing the programmer's workload as well. Consider what it would take to write a modern application using only the C code that programmers of the past had to use and you can see why component technology is so important.

Because of the faith that many programmers place in the ActiveX controls they use, it's important to test components fully. That's when the ActiveX Control Test Container (TSTCON32.EXE) comes into play. This utility helps you to test the features of your ActiveX control in a special environment designed to help you locate flaws quickly. Figure 6-2 shows what the ActiveX Control Test Container looks like with the PButton1 component loaded.

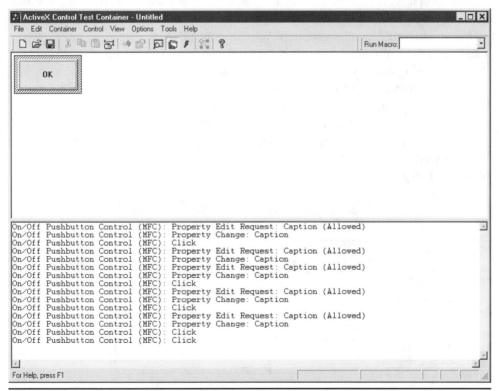

Figure 6-2 *The ActiveX Control Test Container allows you to check the operation of components that you create.*

NOTE

To load an ActiveX control in the test container, use the Edit | Insert New Control command. You'll see an Insert Control dialog box that lists all of the registered components on the local machine. You can also insert an ActiveX control into the current test container from a stream or from storage using the appropriate Edit menu command.

The following sections explore a few of the more important tasks you can perform with ActiveX Control Test Container. You'll likely need to perform one or more of these tasks as the book progresses. For example, when using an ActiveX control in a multi-language environment, you'll normally want to test it using this utility. At a minimum, you'll want to check to see that you can access the methods and properties that the component provides.

Checking Methods and Properties

There have been a number of situations when I thought I had defined a property or method properly, only to have it fail to appear when needed in the final application. In some cases, the failure isn't anything in my code, but a difference in the way the two programming languages support ActiveX controls. Unfortunately, unless you can isolate the component and test it in an independent test environment, you'll have trouble figuring out precisely what the problem is.

ActiveX Control Text Container checks the availability of both methods' properties. In addition, you can change these features of your ActiveX control to see if they work as intended. Let's look at properties first. The normal method used to change the properties is through a property page. Simply click on the Properties button (or use the Edit | Properties command) to display a component's Property dialog. Here's what the Property dialog for PButton1 looks like:

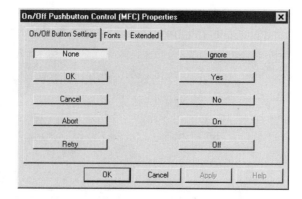

There might be times when you won't want to place a property on the component's Properties dialog box. Perhaps the property affects something that the application designer won't normally change, or it might be something that would only change during runtime, instead of at design time. Even if the properties for a component you design aren't listed in their entirety on property pages, you can still access them by looking through the list of methods supported by your component. You'll find that ActiveX Control Test Container creates a get and set method for every property your component supports. However, for the most part it's still easier to access properties (at least those created for design-time use) through a property page.

Let's talk about methods for a moment. All you need to do to look at the methods your component supports using the Control | Invoke Methods command (you can also click the Invoke Methods button on the toolbar). In addition to the get and set methods for various properties, you'll find all of the other methods that your component supports in the Invoke Methods dialog box shown following:

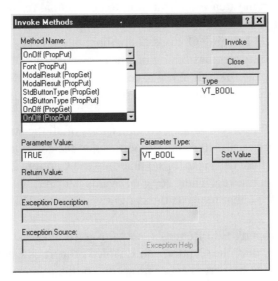

Tracking Events

Events are the basis of many ActiveX control activities. The ActiveX Control Test Container has two windows. The upper window displays the components you've loaded for testing, while the bottom window displays any output from the component. Output occurs (in this case and most others) because some event has fired. Some events are derived from custom programming, others occur as part of normal component operation. For example, you'll normally see a Click event generated when the user clicks a button.

ActiveX Control Test Container provides two levels of event logging. The first level is at the container level. To set these logging options, use the Options | Logging… command to display the Logging Options dialog box. The Logging Options dialog box allows you to choose where the logging output appears. As mentioned earlier, the default setting sends any log entries to the Output window. You can also choose to stop logging all events from all components that you currently have loaded or to place the log entries in a file. The "Log to debugger window" option is supposed to send the log entries to the debug window of your favorite programming language product, but support for this feature is flaky at best. You'll find that this option works best with the latest versions of Visual C++ and only marginally well with Visual Basic.

The second level of logging is at the component level. Normally, ActiveX Control Test Container logs all component events, but that can lead to overload and make the detection of a specific event more difficult. It's important to select a specific set of events to monitor, in most cases, if you want to get optimal results. You must select the component that you want to work with before using the Control | Logging command to display the Control Logging Options dialog box.

The Control Logging Options dialog box has three tabs. Each tab controls a major event-logging type. The first tab, Events, contains a list of all of the events that you component can fire. For example, when a user clicks the component, it normally fires an event.

The second tab, Property Changes, contains a list of all the standard property changes, but not necessarily all of the properties that the component provides. In the case of the PButton1 control, you'll find that only the Caption, Enabled, and Font property changes get tracked. These logging events get fired only if an actual change takes place, not if the client requests the current value or the ability to change the property.

The third tab, Property Edit Requests, contains a list of property edit requests. In this case, you'll find only the Caption and Enabled properties listed, since the Font property uses a special property page. The special property page handles the request event for a font change. A request event gets fired whenever the client requests the ability to edit the property, which generates the logging event. In other words, a request event log entry will appear even if no actual change takes place.

The Property Edit Requests tab allows you to do something that the other logging options don't allow. The Always, Prompt, and Never options allow you to tell ActiveX Control Test Container what to do with edit requests. In most cases, you'll want to allow the component to accept changes normally. However, there are some situations when you may want the component to prompt you before it grants permission or to deny permission so that the property value remains constant during testing. Whichever option you choose, the edit request event will still get logged so that you can maintain a record of component activity.

TIP

You can load more than one ActiveX control at a time to see how two or more components interact. For example, you might have a visible component that relies on input from an invisible component like a timer. This capability is especially important when working with data-related components like those used to set the database and table source.

Testing Persistence

Persistence is the ability of an ActiveX control to retain its values from one session to the next. In most cases, you want your component to retain any property values that the user sets. Read only properties, on the other hand, may change from session to session and therefore don't require persistence. It doesn't matter whether a property is persistent or not—you still have to ensure that it reacts as intended.

ActiveX Control Test Container provides three levels of persistence testing: property bag, stream, and storage. Generally, it's a good idea to test your component in all three environments to make sure that the persistence it provides actually works. Two of the testing methods, stream and storage, require you to save the component to disk, then read it back into the test container. The third method, property bag, provides instant feedback.

OLE/COM Object Viewer

Every OLE object you create, whether it's an application or an ActiveX control, relies on interfaces of some sort. Even language extensions, like ActiveX Scripting, rely on interfaces. An interface is a method for bundling functions in a way that's independent of a programming language. Interfaces are one of the basics of OLE. In addition to the custom interfaces you'll create for your object, every object also supports standard interfaces, like IUnknown.

Visual Studio provides a handy utility, named OLE/COM Object Viewer, that you can use to see these interfaces in more detail (Microsoft shortened the name to OLE View in recent versions of Visual Studio). We'll use this utility several times in the book, so you may want to install it if you haven't done so already.

It's important to understand how the OLE/COM Object Viewer can help you during the development process. Say you want to find out about the interfaces provided by a component like the PButton1 control that we talked about earlier in the chapter. The OLE/COM Object Viewer could help you find out about those interfaces and the associated entries in the registry. You could use this information to debug problems with the way that a component (or other COM object like a document server) registers itself. Obviously, this information also comes in handy in developing a better view of how the component is put together.

Open the OLE/COM Object Viewer. You'll see a set of folders that encompass the various types of objects, similar to the one shown in Figure 6-3. Notice that these statically defined classes are rather broad. There's a very good chance that a component or other type of COM server could appear within more than one folder, depending on which interfaces it implements.

Open the Controls folder and then open the On/Off Pushbutton Control (MFC) folder. You'll see a list of interfaces that MFC implemented for you as you built the component, as shown in Figure 6-4. Notice that the component entry contains information about the registry, implementation details like the location of files and

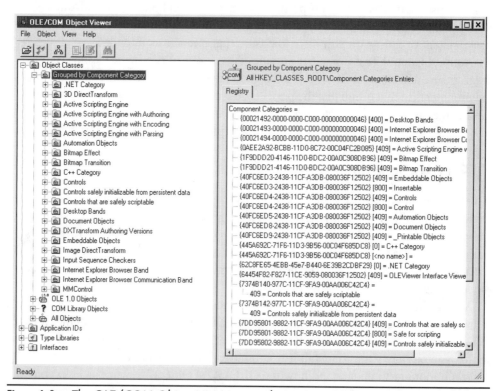

Figure 6-3   *The OLE/COM Object Viewer sorts the various COM servers into easily understood categories.*

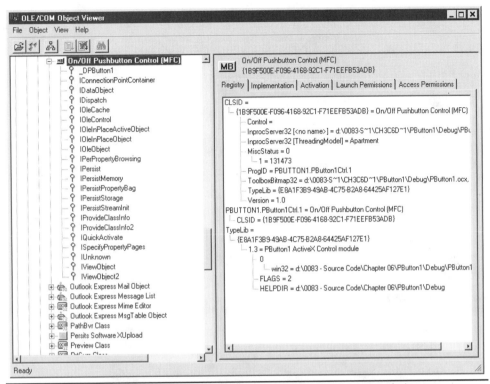

Figure 6-4   *The OLE/COM Object Viewer shows a hierarchical view of objects, starting with the object type, then the name, and then the interfaces the object supports.*

threading model, activation details like the remote activation site (when required), launch permissions (who can run the application), and access permissions (who can look at the component's settings). All of these settings have default values.

PART

II

Visual C++ .NET and Database Management

OBJECTIVES

► Learn about various database technologies including ODBC, ODBC .NET, OLE-DB, ADO, and ADO.NET

► Work with data source names (DSNs) of various types

► Obtain an overview of database development tools

► Create an unmanaged database application using OLE-DB

► Discover techniques for troubleshooting errant LAN database applications

► Learn how to create database applications that perform well on a LAN

► Create a managed database application using ODBC .NET

► Create a managed database application using ADO.NET

Visual C++ Database Technologies

Businesses run on data. This is a simple truth that many enterprise developers discover soon after their introduction to their first company. No matter how many other gizmos you want to introduce into the business environment, the main event will remain database management. If anything, database management becomes more important as a company grows and begins to cultivate partnerships with other companies.

Because database management is so important, technologies for managing data proliferate at an astounding rate. Every time the developer thinks that the latest technology will stick around for a few months, another new technology appears on the scene to take its place. In short, not only is database management a mission critical business requirement, it's also a moving target, which makes writing code difficult, to say the least.

This chapter discusses the latest database technologies provided with Visual Studio .NET. Of course, the big news is ADO.NET. However, many developers aren't ready to move to ADO.NET yet because it fulfills a specific purpose, so you'll still see applications written for both ActiveX Data Object (ADO) and Object Linking and Embedding for Databases (OLE-DB). In fact, despite what you may have heard from early Microsoft documentation, Open Database Connectivity (ODBC) is still alive and well. We'll discuss a new form of this aging, but well entrenched technology, ODBC .NET.

BROWSER ALERT

You don't have to go it alone when it comes to working with Visual C++ and databases. Database-specific newsgroups like microsoft.public.access can help you with the mechanics of creating a database in the first place. However, these newsgroups provide general information that won't be all that useful when it comes to actually writing an application. The newsgroups you want to look at for Visual C++-specific issues are microsoft.public.vc.database and microsoft.public.vc.mfcdatabase. If you decide to use ODBC to access your database, you may want to look at the microsoft.public.odbc.sdk newsgroup, which talks about a lot more than just the SDK. Programmers interested in the latest technology will want to check out the microsoft.public.ado newsgroup, which talks about ADO, or the microsoft.public.oledb (Object Linking and Embedding Database) newsgroup, which talks about the technology underlying ADO. There's an ADO subgroup at microsoft.public.ado.rds that talks about remote data access.

We'll also discuss some handy database tools you should know about. We'll use these tools as the book progresses. For the most part, you'll find that these tools make life a little easier, but they don't take all of the work out of creating a database management system or performing the endless hours of rework afterward.

ADO and OLE-DB—Rungs on the Same Ladder

One of the more confusing things about working with ADO is that it's not the lowest rung on the ladder. OLE-DB is the basis for anything you do with ADO; it provides the basis for communication with the database. ADO is simply a nice wrapper around the services that OLE-DB provides. In fact, you can even bypass ADO and go right to OLE-DB if you want to. However, using ADO will help you to develop applications much faster. The following sections will help you understand both OLE-DB and ADO.

Understanding OLE-DB

So, what is OLE-DB? As the name implies, it uses OLE (or more specifically, the component object model—COM) to provide a set of interfaces for data access. Just as with any other COM object, you can query, create, and destroy an OLE-DB object. The source of an OLE-DB object is a provider. The Visual C++ package provides a variety of OLE-DB providers, and more will likely arrive as vendors upgrade their database products. The nice thing about OLE-DB is that the same provider works with any Visual Studio product: Visual C++, Visual Basic, and C#.

OLE-DB also relies on events, just as any COM object would. These events tell you when an update of a table is required to show new entries made by other users or when the table you've requested is ready for viewing. You'll also see events used to signal various database errors and other activities that require polling right now.

Microsoft defines four major categories of OLE-DB user. It's important to understand how you fit into the grand scheme of things. The following list breaks the various groups down and tells how they contribute toward the use of OLE-DB as a whole.

- ▶ **Data provider**   Someone who uses the OLE-DB SDK (software development kit) to create an OLE-DB provider. The provider uses interfaces to interact with the database and events to signal special occurrences.

- ▶ **Data consumer**   An application, system driver, or user that requires access to the information contained in a database.

- ▶ **Data service provider**   A developer who creates stand-alone utilities (services) that enhance the user's or administrator's ability to use or manage the contents of a database. For example, a developer could create a query engine that allows the user to make natural language requests for information in the database. A service works with the OLE-DB provider and becomes an integral part of it.

► **Business component developer** A developer who creates application modules or components that reduce the amount of coding required to create a database application. A component could be something as generic as a grid control that allows you to display a subset of the records in the database at a glance or something specific to the type of database being accessed.

Microsoft designed OLE-DB as an upgrade to ODBC. The fact is that many people still use ODBC because they perceive it as easier to use than OLE-DB or ADO. The pervasiveness of this view finally led Microsoft to create ODBC .NET for those developers who refuse to make the change. In addition, more database vendors provide ODBC access, although this is changing now. So, how does OLE-DB differ from ODBC? Table 7-1 shows the major differences between the two products. We'll discuss how these differences affect your usage decisions later in this chapter.

Element	OLE-DB	ODBC	Description
Access type	Component	Direct	OLE-DB provides interfaces that interact with the data; user access to the data is through components designed to interact with OLE-DB.
Data access specialization	Any tabular data	SQL	Microsoft designed ODBC to use SQL as the basis for data transactions. In some cases, that means the programmer has to make concessions to force the data to fit into the SQL standard.
Driver access method	Component	Native	As mentioned earlier, all access to an OLE-DB provider is through COM interfaces using components of various types. ODBC normally requires direct programming of some type and relies heavily on the level of SQL compatibility enforced by the database vendor.
Programming model	COM	C	OLE-DB relies on COM to provide the programmer with access to the provider. This means that OLE-DB is language independent, while ODBC is language specific.

Table 7-1 *OLE-DB to ODBC Technology Comparison*

Element	OLE-DB	ODBC	Description
Technology standard	COM	SQL	OLE-DB adheres to Microsoft's COM standard, which means that it's much more vendor and platform specific than the SQL technology standard used by ODBC.

Table 7-1   *OLE-DB to ODBC Technology Comparison* (continued)

Don't get the idea that OLE-DB and ODBC are two completely separate technologies meant to replace each other. Microsoft offers an ODBC OLE-DB provider that enables you to access all of the functionality that ODBC provides through OLE-DB or ADO. In other words, the two technologies complement each other and don't represent complete replacements for each other. Can you replace ODBC with ADO or OLE-DB? Yes, but you won't get the very best performance from your applications if you do. The whole idea of OLE-DB is to broaden the range of database types that you can access with your Visual C++ applications. Obviously, if you do need to access both ODBC and tabular data with a single application, OLE-DB provides one of the better solutions for doing so.

Understanding ADO

Now that you've gotten a little better handle on OLE-DB, where does ADO fit in? As previously mentioned, ADO provides an easy method for accessing the functionality of an OLE-DB provider. In other words, ADO helps you to create applications quickly and allows Visual C++ to take care of some of the details that you'd normally have to consider when using OLE-DB directly.

ADO represents a new way to provide database access through the combination of databound ActiveX controls and an ADODC (ADO Data Control). The ADODC acts as a data source that identifies the information storage location and defines the requirements for accessing that data. ADODC requires six pieces of information: OLE DB provider name (like SQL Server), DSN (the data source name as specified in the ODBC applet of the Control Panel), username, password, record source (usually a SQL query), and connection string. You'll use ActiveX controls to display the contents of the data source.

ADO provides several advantages over previous database access methods. The following list will describe them for you.

▶ **Independently created objects**   You no longer have to thread your way through a hierarchy of objects. This feature permits you to create only the objects you need, reducing memory requirements and enhancing application speed.

▶ **Batch updating**   Instead of sending one change to the server, you can collect them in local memory and send all of them to the server at once. This feature results in improved application performance (because the update can be performed in the background) and reduced network load.

▶ **Stored procedures**   These procedures reside on the server as part of the database manager. You'll use them to perform specific tasks on the dataset. ADO uses stored procedures with in/out parameters and a return value.

▶ **Multiple cursor types**   Essentially, cursors point to the data you're currently working with. You can use both client side and server side cursors.

▶ **Returned row limits**   You get only the amount of data you actually need to meet a user request.

▶ **Multiple recordset objects**   Helps you to work with multiple recordsets returned by stored procedures or batch processing.

▶ **Free threaded objects**   Enhances Web server performance.

There are two databinding models used for ActiveX controls. The first, simple databinding, allows an ActiveX control like a text box to display a single field of a single record. The second, complex databinding, allows an ActiveX control like a grid to display multiple fields and records at the same time. Complex databinding also requires the ActiveX control to manage which records and fields the control displays, something that the ADODC normally takes care of for simple databinding. Visual C++ comes with several ActiveX controls that support ADO, including these controls:

▶ DataGrid

▶ DataCombo

▶ DataList

▶ Hierarchical Flex Grid

▶ Date and Time Picker

Like OLE-DB, Microsoft-based ADO on COM. ADO provides a dual interface: a program ID of ADODB for local operations and a program ID of ADOR for remote operations. The ADO library itself is free threaded, even though the registry shows it as using the apartment threaded model. The thread safety of ADO depends on the OLE-DB provider that you use. In other words, if you're using Microsoft's ODBC OLE-DB provider you won't have any problems. If you're using a third party OLE-DB provider, you'll want to check the vendor documentation before assuming that ADO is thread safe (a requirement for using ADO over an Internet or intranet connection).

You'll use seven different objects to work with ADO. Table 7-2 lists these objects and describes how you'll use them. Most of these object types are replicated in the other technologies that Microsoft has introduced, although the level of ADO object functionality is much greater than that offered by previous technologies. We'll talk more about the ADO classes in the overview section of this chapter.

NOTE

ADO represents some objects by interfaces rather than actual classes. Table 7-2 also tells you about object associations, which helps you understand how to derive the objects not directly represented by Visual C++ classes.

Object	Class	Description
Command	CADOCommand	A command object performs a task using a connection or recordset object. Even though you can execute commands as part of the connection or recordset objects, the command object is much more flexible and allows you to define output parameters.
Connection	CADOConnection	Defines the connection with the OLE-DB provider. You can use this object to perform tasks like beginning, committing, and rolling back transactions. There are also methods for opening or closing the connection and for executing commands.
Error		ADO creates an error object as part of the connection object. It provides additional information about errors raised by the OLE-DB provider. A single error object can contain information about more than one error. Each object is associated with a specific event like committing a transaction.

Table 7-2   *ADO Object Overview*

Object	Class	Description
Field		A field object contains a single column of data contained in a recordset object. In other words, a field could be looked at as a single column in a table and contains one type of data for all of the records associated with a recordset.
Parameter	CADOParameter	Defines a single parameter for a command object. A parameter modifies the result of a stored procedure or query. Parameter objects can provide input, output, or both.
Property		Some OLE-DB providers will need to extend the standard ADO object. Property objects represent one way to perform this task. A property object contains attribute, name, type, and value information.
Recordset	CADORecordset	Contains the result of a query and a cursor for choosing individual elements within the returned table. Visual C++ gives you the option of creating both a connection and a recordset using a single recordset object or of using an existing connection object to support multiple recordset objects.

Table 7-2   *ADO Object Overview* (continued)

ADO.NET the New Microsoft Vision for Database Management

ADO.NET is a new technology that Microsoft originally named ADO+ (among other names). The ADO+ moniker is actually more appropriate for the version of ADO.NET that appears in Visual Studio because this version of the product is essentially an add-on for distributed computing environments. Most developers have found that they need to continue using ADO for LAN development or in scenarios where an application requires good two-way communication. The reason ADO.NET is such a good addition for the distributed computing environment is that it relies on disconnected datasets and client side cursors—two requirements for applications used on the road. Using loosely coupled access also reduces the resource load on a server, making more resources available for all users.

One of the secrets of ADO.NET is the use of eXtensible Markup Language (XML) as the data transfer media. The use of plain ASCII text by XML enables the data to pass through firewalls unhindered. Binary data transfers often encounter problems with firewalls because the use of binary data hinders the efforts of virus checkers. Firewalls also close data ports that older data transfer methods require. The problem with ports is that administrators normally keep as many ports closed as possible to help reduce the chance of cracker intrusions. XML uses port 80, the same port commonly used for HTML data transfers. Binary data transfer problems became one of the reasons that developers asked for something better than the Distributed Component Object Model (DCOM) and also the reason they need something better than ADO or OLE-DB for database management.

Before you can access any data, you need a provider that works with the Database Management System (DBMS) in question. ADO.NET fully supports all of the providers that ADO supports. In addition, you gain access to the providers in the .NET Framework. However, don't get the idea that having two sources for providers increases your opportunities to connect to other servers. Most of the drivers provided with the .NET Framework at the time of this writing are for big name DBMS, such as Oracle, or Microsoft's own products, such as SQL Server. In fact, you'll find that the two main namespaces are System.Data.SqlClient and System.Data.OleDB. You must have SQL Server 7.0 or later to use the System.Data.SqlClient namespace. Note that the OLE-DB driver for ODBC (MSDASQL) doesn't work—you must download the separate ODBC .NET provider discussed in the next section.

As with the other data access technologies discussed so far, you use objects to work with data under ADO.NET. It's important to remember the purpose of ADO.NET as you look through the list of objects. These objects focus on the needs of distributed applications—you'll still use ADO or OLE-DB for LAN or WAN applications. The following list describes the four objects and tells how you use them.

▶ **Connection**   Every data communication requires a connection to a data source. A DBMS manages the data source, and you must establish communication with the DBMS before you can access the data. The connection process includes setting aside resources for the data exchange and security issues such as user verification.

▶ **Command**   The act of accessing data or making some other request of the DBMS after you establish contact with it is a command. Many developers know something about structured query language (SQL) commands, because SQL is the default standard for most DBMS communications. When you work with ADO.NET, you can either process the results of a command directly or place the results in a DataReader.

► **DataReader**   The DataReader is a special type of object that provides read-only access to the results of a command. You can read the data in a forward-only direction, and your application must rely on client side cursors. The purpose of the DataReader is to provide client side access to data in a disconnected scenario. In short, the client doesn't require access to the server to access the information.

► **DataAdapter**   You'll use the DataAdapter to populate a dataset. It also updates the data source as users make changes to the dataset. The DataAdapter enables you to update information on the remote server, but requires special handling and a live connection to the server. You'd use this object to upload new information a user creates while working in disconnected mode.

ODBC .NET: Microsoft Breathes Life into an Existing Technology

ODBC is the technology that Microsoft was originally going to leave out of Visual Studio .NET. After all, the reasoning was that everyone should have moved onto something newer and better. However, not everyone has moved to OLE-DB or ADO, not to mention their .NET counterparts. After profuse screaming on the part of a multitude of beta testers, Microsoft finally relented and provided us with ODBC .NET.

NOTE

*The only problem is that you won't see ODBC .NET in the Visual Studio .NET package. Because ODBC .NET got a late start, you won't actually see it for a few months after the release of Visual Studio .NET. However, you can find it at **http://msdn.microsoft.com/downloads/ sample.asp?url=/MSDN-FILES/027/001/668/msdncompositedoc.xml.** You can also learn about the latest ODBC .NET developments on the **microsoft.public.dotnet.framework.odbcnet** newsgroup.*

After you install the ODBC.NET provider, you'll find a new namespace on your system: System.Data.Odbc. The new namespace uses the same four objects as ADO.NET, so you have access to a Connection, Command, DataReader, and

DataAdapter object. Working with the namespace is similar to working with the two ADO.NET namespaces. However, you have the same options that you would with any ODBC implementation. For example, you can use Data Source Names (DSNs) to create a connection to a data source.

Windows supports three basic types of DSNs: User, System, and File. The User and System DSN are essentially the same. However, the User DSN affects only the current user, while the System DSN affects everyone who logs onto the current machine. The File DSN is a text representation of a DSN. You can open a File DSN in a program like Notepad and see how it's put together. The following sections show you how to create the three DSN types and log the ODBC activities on your system.

CAUTION

You'll normally need to create an entry on the User DSN tab for single-user databases and on the System DSN tab for machine databases. Under no circumstances create an entry on both the User DSN and System DSN tabs that uses the same name. What will normally happen is that you'll attempt to access the database remotely and get really strange and inconsistent error messages from your server. In fact, the ODBC applet is one of the first places you should look if you get strange error messages during remote database access.

Working with User and System DSNs

Designing a database is the first step of any database application. You need to know how you'll store and access data for your application. After you have a database designed, you need to create an ODBC DSN for it. That's what we'll look at in this section. The following procedure shows one technique for getting a data source configured.

1. Double-click the 32-bit ODBC applet in the Control Panel. (Some versions of Windows use a simple ODBC applet if there are no 16-bit drivers installed on the current system. Windows 2000 and Windows XP place the Data Sources (ODBC) applet in the Administrative Tools folder.) You'll see the ODBC Data Source Administrator dialog.

2. Click the Add button. You'll see a Create New Data Source dialog like the one shown here:

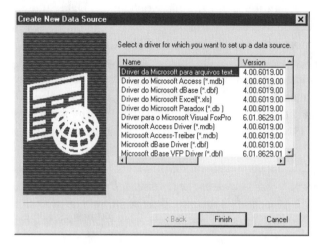

TIP

You can ensure that you're using the most current ODBC drivers available by checking the Drivers and the About tab of the ODBC Data Source Administrator dialog. These tabs contain the version numbers of the various ODBC DLLs, the name of the vendor who created them, and the name of the file as it appears in the SYSTEM folder. In most cases, you'll be able to use the version number as a method for verifying that your ODBC driver is up-to-date.

3. Choose one of the data sources. For this exercise, I chose an Access data source. Click Finish and you'll see some type of configuration dialog like the ODBC Microsoft Access Setup dialog shown here:

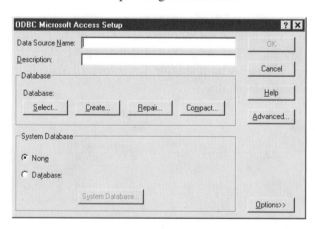

NOTE

If you select a data source different from the one I've chosen in this example, the steps required to configure it will differ from the ones shown here—each ODBC driver requires a different type of configuration.

4. Type a data source name in the Data Source Name field. Make sure you choose something descriptive but not overly long. I chose Address Database because I'll eventually create a link to a simple Address database.

5. Type a description in the Description field. You'll want to make this entry a bit longer than the previous one since it describes the purpose of your database. On the other hand, you don't want to write a novel the size of *War and Peace*. For this exercise, I typed the following: *This database contains a contact management list.*

6. Click the Select button. You'll see a Select Database dialog where you can choose an existing database. The example uses the MyData.MDB database found in the \Chapter 07 folder of the source code CD. The ODBC driver will automatically choose the correct file extension for you.

TIP

You don't have to design your database before you create a DSN for it. Notice that the Access ODBC driver also includes a button to create a new database. Most, but not all, ODBC drivers provide this feature. Clicking this button will start the database manager application and allow you to design the database. It's interesting that the Access ODBC driver also provides options to compress or repair the database from this dialog.

7. Choose a system database option. In most cases, you'll choose None unless you specifically created a system database for your application.

8. Click the Advanced button and you'll see a Set Advanced Options dialog. You won't need to modify many of the entries. However, it usually pays to add the guest user name to the Login Name field and the guest password to the Password

field. This enables a guest to access your database without really knowing anything about the access at all—not even the name the guest used to log in.

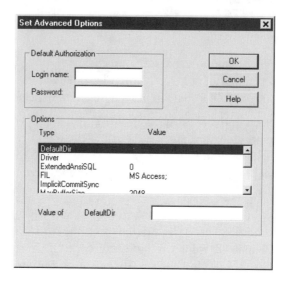

TIP

You may want to look through the list of advanced options provided by your ODBC driver for potential areas of optimization. For example, the Access ODBC driver allows you to change the number of threads that the DBMS uses. The default setting of 3 usually provides good performance, but you may find that more threads in a complex application will speed foreground tasks. Using too many threads does have the overall effect of slowing your application down, since Windows uses some processor cycles to manage the thread overhead.

9. Click OK once you've set any advanced options that you need.

10. Click OK again to close the ODBC Microsoft Access Setup dialog. You should see your new entry added to the ODBC Data Source Administrator dialog. If you need to change the settings for the database later, simply highlight it and click Configure. Getting rid of the database is equally easy. Just highlight the DSN and click Remove.

Working with File DSNs

You may have noticed a problem with the example in the previous section. It works fine if you want to configure every machine on your network individually, which probably isn't your idea of a good time. There's another way to store the information needed to create a data source: the file DSN. That's what we'll look at in this section. The following procedure will give you a general idea of how to set up a file DSN.

1. Double-click the 32-bit ODBC applet in the Control Panel. You'll see the ODBC Data Source Administrator dialog. Select the File DSN tab. The first thing you'll need to do is choose a place to store the DSN information. The example uses the \Chapter 07 folder on the source code CD.

2. Click the Look In drop-down list box. You'll see a list of directories and drives for the current machine. You can use any storage location for the DSN. I normally choose the database storage directory on the network. Using UNC (universal naming convention) directory paths means that everyone will access the DSN file using the same path. Note that you'll need to click Set Directory to change the default directory to the one you select using the Look In drop-down list box.

TIP

The Up One Level button (next to the Look In drop-down list box) works just the way it does in Explorer. You can use this button to go up one directory at a time. Eventually, you'll end up at My Computer and see a listing of all the drives on your machine.

3. Click Add. You'll see a Create New Data Source dialog.

4. Choose one of the ODBC drivers in the list, then click Next. For this example, I again chose Access. You'll see the next page of the Create New Data Source dialog. This is where you'll choose a name and storage location for your data source. Click Browse and you'll see a "File Open" type dialog box where you can choose a storage location. Type a filename and the ODBC wizard will automatically add DSN as the extension. I chose SAMPLE.DSN as the name for the DSN file in this example.

5. Click Next and you'll see a summary dialog like the one shown here. It tells you the parameters for the DSN you're going to create.

6. Click Finish. At this point, you'll see a modified version of the ODBC Microsoft Access Setup dialog. You won't be able to add information in the Data Source Name or Description fields as we did in the previous section. However, everything else will work the same way as before.

7. Make sure you enter the name of a database by clicking the Select button and then choosing the database you want to use. (You can also click Create if you want to create a new database.)

8. Click OK when you complete the configuration process. You'll see a new DSN file entry in the ODBC Data Source Administrator dialog.

Unlike the previous DSN that we created, this one actually creates a file that you can view and edit with a text editor. Figure 7-1 shows what my file looks like. Notice that it follows a standard INI file format. You can see the [ODBC] heading at the top. All of the settings I chose follow. This file will allow me to choose a data source from Visual C++, yet it's very easy to transfer from machine to machine. I could even change the locations as required during the installation process—this is a real plus when you don't know what kind of setup the user will have.

Logging ODBC Transactions

It's always nice to have a log of whatever you're doing when it comes time to debug an application. The ODBC Data Source Administrator dialog offers this capability as well. You can choose to track the various transactions you make to a database through ODBC. Of course, these logs can get rather large, but you won't be using them all the time.

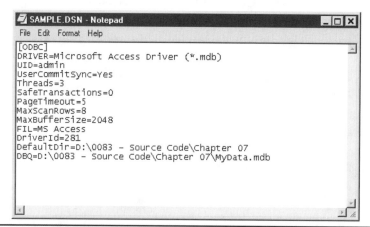

Figure 7-1   *The SAMPLE.DSN file contains all of the settings required to use my database from within Visual C++.*

All you need to do to start logging transactions is open the ODBC Data Source Administrator dialog by double-clicking the 32-bit ODBC applet in the Control Panel. Choose the Tracing tab. You'll see a dialog like the one shown next:

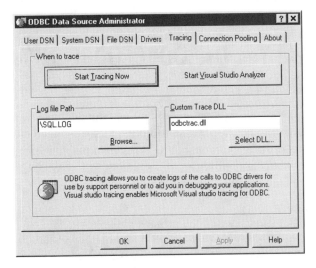

NOTE

You might see variations in the content of the Tracing tab based on the version of Windows that you use and the Visual Studio features you install. The version shown is for Windows 2000 with Visual Studio Analyzer installed. In some cases, you'll see three radio buttons that determine when you'll trace the ODBC calls. The default setting is Don't Trace. You'd select All the Time if you were going to work on debugging a single application. The One-Time Only traces the ODBC calls during the next connection—tracing gets turned off as soon as the connection is broken. This is a good selection to choose when a user calls in with a specific problem. You can monitor the connection during one session and then use that information to help you create a plan for getting rid of the bug.

The trace won't start automatically. You'll need to click on the Start Tracing Now button. The pushbutton caption will change to Stop Tracing Now as soon as tracing starts. Click on the button again to turn tracing off.

The only other setting that you'll need to worry about is the Log File Path. ODBC normally places the transaction information in the SQL.LOG file in your root directory. However, you may want to place the logging information on a network drive or use a location hidden from the user. The default location normally works fine during the debugging process.

NOTE

Unless you want to create your own logging DLL, don't change the setting in the Custom Trace DLL field. The DLL listed here, ODBCTRAC.DLL, is responsible for maintaining the transaction log.

When Should You Use ODBC, ODBC .NET, OLE-DB, ADO, or ADO.NET?

It's never easy to figure out which database connection technology to use, especially when the usage environment changes constantly. You may need a common utility to handle more than one database type; part of your data may appear on a local hard drive, part on a network, and still other parts on a mainframe. Even the products that a client normally installs on his or her machine may make the choice more difficult. For example, the level of ODBC support you can expect might rely on which version of Microsoft Office is installed, since this product does provide ODBC support. You'll also find that ADO classes offer more objects and methods than ODBC classes do. ADO may offer some features you absolutely have to have in your program—for example, you'll find that both OLE-DB and ADO support DFX_Currency, which has no counterpart in ODBC—but you'll pay a penalty in speed to get them.

There are a few general rules of thumb you can use for making the choice between OLE-DB and ODBC. Since ADO is actually a wrapper for OLE-DB, these same rules apply to it. You'll find the .NET choices make good sense as extensions to existing technology. The following list provides some guidelines you can use to help decide between the various database technologies.

▶ **Non-OLE environment** If you're trying to access a database that already supports ODBC and that database is on a server that doesn't support OLE, then ODBC is your best choice.

▶ **Non-SQL environment** Microsoft designed ODBC to excel at working with SQL. However, many vendors provide ODBC drivers now, making ODBC the best compatibility choice. If your vendor does supply an OLE-DB provider, OLE-DB might be the better choice, especially for new coding projects.

▶ **OLE environment** The choice between OLE-DB and ODBC may be a toss-up when looking at a server that supports OLE. Normally, it's a good idea to use ODBC if you have an ODBC driver available; otherwise, OLE-DB may be your only choice.

▶ **Interoperability required**   If you need interoperable database components, OLE-DB is your only choice. OLE-DB provides a broad range of low-level methods that enable a developer to create robust applications that don't rely on DSNs and offer maximum flexibility.

▶ **Distributed application environment**   If you need to service users on the road, you have two good choices. Use ADO.NET if you're working with new code and want to gain the maximum benefit from new .NET Framework features. On the other hand, use ODBC .NET if you need to update older code or require maximum compatibility with existing databases.

▶ **Extended application environment**   Many companies today find themselves with a fully developed database application that works fine on a LAN, but fails when working with partners over an Internet connection. Because the Internet has become such a big part of business-to-business communication, you need to use matching technologies to extend the existing application. For example, you'd use ODBC .NET with an application that already uses ODBC.

Other issues tend to compound the problem, or, at least, remove a handy rule that you can use to differentiate the two technologies. For example, ADO and ODBC have many of the same features in common. One of these is that Visual C++ allows you to access either technology directly. This means you'll always have full access to every feature that both ADO and ODBC can provide. (Yes, this really is a plus, but it's also a minus because the lack of differentiation makes it difficult to make a decision based on feature set alone.)

Some of these technological similarities actually help you move your application from ODBC to ADO, or vice versa, if you make a wrong decision. Both technologies rely on database objects to manage the underlying DBMS, while recordset objects contain the results of queries made against the DBMS. In addition, both ODBC and ADO use database and recordset objects with similar members. Even though you'll need to make some changes to class and member names, you'll find that the code for both ODBC and ADO programming is remarkably similar.

There's one place where you absolutely can't use ADO. If you need 16-bit data access, ADO is out. You'll have to use ODBC whether you want to or not. However, very few people are even working with 16-bit databases anymore. Most of your new projects will use 32-bit interfaces, which means you'll have a choice. Since old projects already have a data access method embedded in the code, you really won't need to make a decision there either.

One area where ODBC falls short is that you can't follow transactions as precisely as you can with ADO. When using ADO you get workspace-level support for transactions. ODBC only offers transaction support at the database level, which means that you could be tracking transactions from several different workspaces at once. (This lack of functionality makes debugging very difficult, and it could cause other kinds of problems as well.)

Database Tools You Should Know About

Developing database applications means working with several machines, checking the operation of components from remote locations, and dealing with a level of complexity that can turn the developer's hair white. It pays to know about every tool that Microsoft provides to make the job of creating database applications easier. This section of the chapter discusses the tools that many developers find useful. These tools will likely appear in the Enterprise Architect version of Visual Studio .NET. They also appear in the Platform SDK, and you can download them separately from several places on the Internet.

BROWSER ALERT

*There are a number of places to download the Platform SDK. However, one of the easiest places to get it is the Microsoft Platform SDK site at **http://www.microsoft.com/msdownload/ platformsdk/sdkupdate/**. This site allows you to download just the Setup program first. After you make choices as to which Platform SDK elements you want to install, the Setup program will download them from the Internet for you. You can also order the Platform SDK on CD from this site. Those of you who want the entire SDK will need to go to Microsoft's FTP site, which is currently **ftp://ftp.microsoft.com/developr/PlatformSDK/**. Be prepared for a very long wait if you choose more than just a few Platform SDK elements and you have a dial-up connection. A full download will take approximately 36 hours with a 56 Kbps dial-up connection. You can also get the Platform SDK with an MSDN subscription, which is probably the easiest method if you don't have a high-speed Internet connection.*

Local Test Manager

Local Test Manager allows a developer to perform conformance testing on a database provider using any of a number of languages. A database provider creates a buffer between the DBMS and the client application. For example, when you use OLE-DB, a database provider translates the calls between your client application and the DBMS on the server. The DBMS sees your generic OLE-DB API calls as specific commands to perform various types of work. The Local Test Manager only checks database provider conformance—it won't perform tests like stress analysis or performance monitoring; you'll need other utilities to perform that kind of testing.

Normally, you'd need to create your own test suite DLL for Local Test Manager. However, the version of Local Test Manager that comes with the Platform SDK also includes a sample test suite DLL that you can use. You'll need to load this test suite the first time you start Local Test Manager using the Tests | Tests | Add command. You'll see an Add Test Module dialog box (essentially the same as a File Open dialog box). Find the QuickTest.DLL (could be listed as QuikTest.DLL) file in the Platform SDK's Bin or the \Program Files\Microsoft Visual Studio.NET\Common7\ Tools\Bin directory, then click Open. You'll see Quicktest added to the Default Suite entry, as shown in Figure 7-2.

You can expand the Quicktest entry to see what kinds of tests it will run. The tests are grouped into categories, then into individual tests. The test entries include an interface name and method within that interface, as shown in Figure 7-2. What this mean is that selecting a test will check the specified method within a given interface. For the purposes of this example, I've chosen to run the TCDataSource group of tests.

Selecting a group of tests is only the first step in the process. You'll also need to select a data source. Click the Create a New Alias button and you'll see an Alias for MSDASQL dialog box like the one shown next:

To perform a simple test, all you need to do is choose a provider and create an initialization string. Click Data Link and you'll see the Data Link Properties dialog box. The first step is to select a provider from the list on the Provider tab. Notice that one of the entries will allow you to test the provider for Active Directory. I'll be using the Microsoft OLE DB Provider for SQL Server provider for this example.

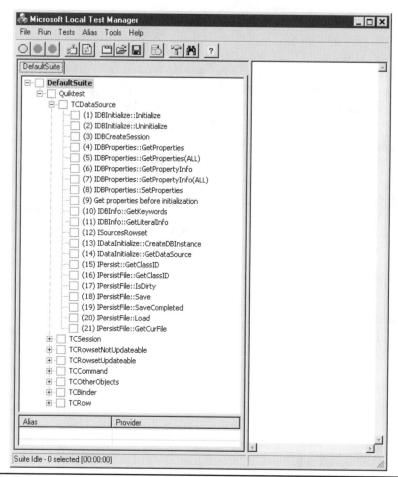

Figure 7-2   *You'll need to select a suite of tests to run against the database provider.*

Click Next and you'll see a list of connection items for the provider. To create a basic SQL Server connection, you'll need to choose a server, supply some type of username and password (or use Windows 2000 integrated security), and select a database from the list of databases available on the server. I chose to use the Northwind sample database that comes with SQL Server for demonstration purposes, but you could use any database desired. Click Test Connection to ensure you actually have a connection to the server, then click OK. Be sure you select the correct provider in the Alias for MSDASQL dialog box. In this case, I'll use the SQLOLEDB provider. Click OK to close the Alias for MSDASQL dialog box.

At this point, you can run a test on the provider of your choice. Make sure you check both a provider to test and a series of tests to run. Click the Execute Selected Tests button. If the test is successful, all of the checked items will turn green. You'll also see a report similar to the one shown in Figure 7-3.

ODBC Test

You'll use Open Database Connectivity (ODBC) Test to check the compatibility and functionality of the ODBC drivers and ODBC Driver Manager on a machine. The

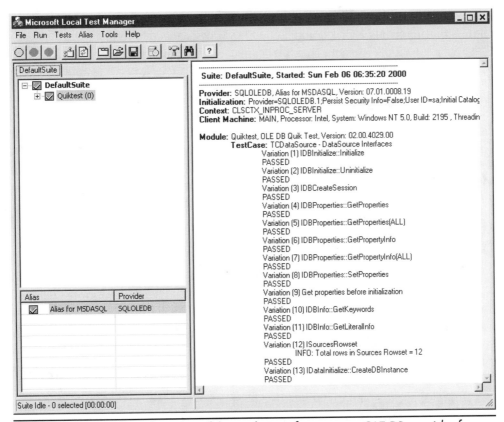

Figure 7-3   *Output from the successful completion of tests on an OLE-DB provider for SQL Server.*

OdbcTE32 utility appears in the \Program Files\Microsoft Visual Studio .NET\ Common7\Tools\Bin directory. This utility checks network connections, DBMS configuration, and other factors as much as it tests the capability of the driver itself. So, for example, you could check the driver's ability to make a connection to a particular server and obtain data from the DBMS installed on it. There are four different areas of testing or test configuration that you can perform using this utility, as listed below.

▶ **Functions**   A single ODBC command. This level of testing is good when you want to check the compatibility of the driver. It allows you to check for the availability of individual features.

▶ **Function Tools**   One or more commands work together to complete a given database task. For example, a full connect will test all of the commands required to create a connection to a particular data source. This level of testing allows you to check the ability of all of the database elements to work together to produce a predefined result.

NOTE

ODBC Test allows you to perform tests using ODBC 2.x or ODBC 3.0 commands. You can adjust the ODBC Test menus so that they reflect the kind of testing you want to perform using the options on the ODBC Menu Version tab of the User Options dialog box. Use the Tools | Options command to display the User Options dialog box.

▶ **Tools**   Configuration options within ODBC Test. These options allow you to change application parameters, like the level of error reporting to use, or determine whether ODBC Test automatically disables menu options that a particular driver doesn't support.

▶ **Auto Tests**   As with the Local Test Manager utility discussed earlier, you can create a DLL for ODBC Test that will allow automated testing of the ODBC drivers and ODBC Driver Manager on a machine.

Getting started with ODBC Test is relatively easy. All you need to do is click the Full Connect button on the toolbar or use the Conn | Full Connect command to display the Full Connect dialog box shown next.

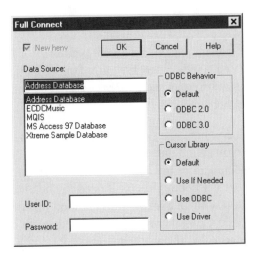

You can highlight one of the existing data sources, or leave the Data Source field blank, then click OK. If the Data Source field is blank, you'll be required to create a new Data Source Name (DSN) using the standard ODBC connection techniques (we'll discuss these techniques later as part of the programming sections of the book). You'll see a display similar to the one shown next once ODBC Test successfully creates a connection:

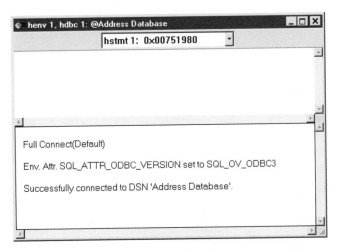

Once you have a connection in place, you can begin working with the database driver. This includes using all of the predefined commands in the various ODBC Test menus, as well as entering SQL statements in the upper half of the result window.

TIP

The Platform SDK provides both ANSI and Unicode forms for the ODBC Test utility. Make sure you use the right utility for the type of work that you're doing. ANSI and Unicode support usually appear in separate drivers, which means that any testing you perform for one driver won't necessarily reflect the capabilities in the other.

In most cases, you'll combine a set of SQL statements and menu commands. For example, I opened the Northwind database for this example, then executed a simple SQL statement that selected all of the columns from the Employees table. (Just typing the SQL statement isn't enough; you'll need to click the Execute button, which appears as a button with an exclamation mark on the toolbar.) After this, I used the Results | Describe Col All command to display a list of the columns from the Employees table. Figure 7-4 shows the result.

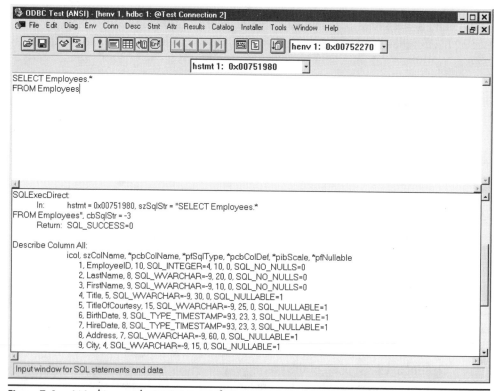

Figure 7-4 *Working with ODBC Test often means combining SQL statements with menu commands to achieve a specific result.*

As you can see, ODBC Test could double as an SQL statement tester in addition to a utility that's designed to check driver compatibility. Since Visual Basic has extensive database resources built in; you won't normally need to use this utility while working with Visual Basic directly. However, it could come in handy for other purposes.

The last step of every testing session is to clear all of your database connections. The reason for doing this is simple. If you don't clear the connections before you exit the program, there's a chance that Windows or SQL Server won't release some resources. As a result, continued testing could result in a large memory leak or other system problems. Just use the Conn | Full Disconnect command to disconnect from a database session. The connection window will disappear, indicating that ODBC Test has cleared the connection.

Rowset Viewer

The Rowset Viewer is yet another utility that allows you to work with a remote database from your local workstation. However, in this case, it's more like a mini-design utility than anything else we've looked at so far. In fact, you'll find that this utility provides you with just about everything needed for any kind of database design work that you need to perform.

Using Rowset Viewer begins just like the other utilities that we've discussed so far. You need to create a connection to the data source. However, there's a multitude of connection types available for Rowset Viewer. For example, you can choose to enumerate the provider root to determine which providers are available. The resulting table will provide you with the GUIDs of the various providers installed on the current machine, along with other information you can use to research the capabilities of a particular setup better. You can also work with the root binder and with service components. However, we're going to look at data links in this section, just as we have in other sections of the chapter so far.

To create a data link connection, you'll begin with the File | Data Links command. This command will display a Data Link Properties dialog box. As before, you can select the provider you want, then fill out the required connection information. I'll be using the Microsoft OLE DB Provider for SQL Server in this section of the chapter and the Northwind database as before. If the connection succeeds, then you'll see a command window where you can enter SQL statements and perform other tests on your database. In most cases, an SQL statement will generate a rowset that you can use for working with the data in the selected table. Figure 7-5 shows an example of the Employees table in this utility.

At this point, you may be wondering what makes this utility so important. The Rowset Viewer will allow you to add or remove data from the table, but that's not

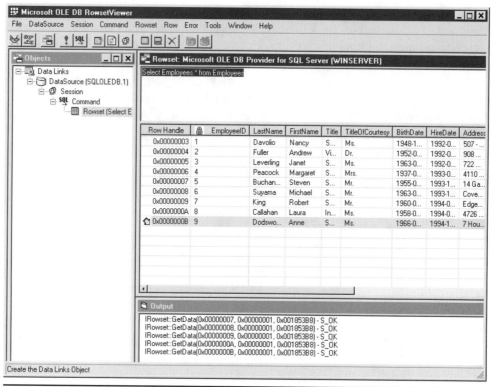

Figure 7-5 Rowset Viewer allows you to manipulate the data in tables, or entire databases if you want.

where the real power of this utility lies. Click the Get Schema Rowset button on the toolbar and you'll generate a list of every table in the database. You can add new tables to the database using this table as a starting point. In fact, you can generate a rowset for any database element and use the resulting rowset to manage that element. Double-click any row in a rowset and you'll see a details table that allows you to change the data in that row. Just click Set Data to make any changes permanent.

We haven't even begun to look at the menu options. The Data Source, Session, Command, Rowset, and Row menus across the top of the utility contain a list of interfaces associated with that part of the database connection hierarchy. The interfaces will get enabled when you've highlighted an object that they pertain to. Under each interface option is a list of methods associated with that interface. You can use these methods to interact with the database, tables, rows, and associated data. What this means is that you can test out coding ideas in real time using this utility. Since you know the interface and associated method, you can transfer what you learn right to the application code. The result of any command you issue using the menus will appear in the Output window, along with any errors generated by the use of the methods.

Table Copy

Have you ever wanted to test a new procedure, but didn't want to do it on an existing table? Table Copy allows you to create a precise copy of a table (or any subset that you might need for testing purposes). Using a copy of the table allows you to test a new procedure using live data, but without the hazards of damaging that data in some way. You'll find the Table Copy utility in the \Program Files\Microsoft Visual Studio .NET\Common7\Tools\Bin directory.

As with every other utility in this section, you'll begin using Table Copy by creating a connection to the data source. Once you've established a connection, you can create a copy of any of the tables within the selected database. The following procedure shows you how.

1. Highlight a table within the database. The rows for that table will appear in the right pane of the Table Copy utility, as shown next.

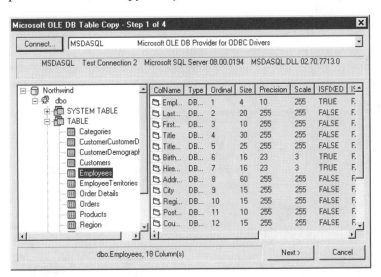

2. Highlight the columns that you want to copy to a new table. Table Copy doesn't force you to make a precise replica of the original table, which is handy when you need to test a procedure on only a subset of the data.

3. Click Next. You'll see a list of indexes associated with the current table. Notice that Table Copy differentiates between primary keys and foreign keys. It also tells you about any index settings that you need to know about in order to make a decision.

4. Select one or more of the indexes to add to the copy of the table.

5. Click Next. Table Copy will ask you to provide a destination for the new table. You'll need to create another connection if you want to copy the table to another database. Otherwise, you'll need to supply a new table name for the copy.

TIP

Table Copy doesn't restrict connections to other kinds of databases. In other words, you could theoretically use Table Copy to move tables from one DBMS to another. Obviously, there are situations when this won't work because the two databases have incompatible data formats, and you'll experience some level of data loss during the transfer. It pays to check for incompatibilities before you use this utility, but Table Copy does offer one solution to a problem that plagues many developers.

6. Select another connection. Change the target table name if necessary. Make sure you provide either a unique connection or a unique table name, as a minimum, or the data transfer will fail.

7. Click Next. You'll see an options dialog box like the one shown next. This dialog is where you'll choose the options that Table Copy will employ to make the transfer. For example, you can choose to include all data rows or just some of the rows (enough data to perform the test).

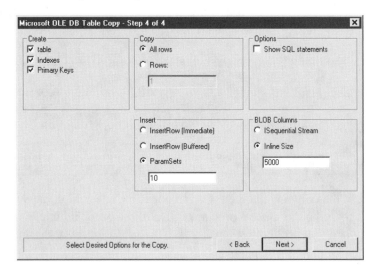

8. Select options as needed to complete the table copying process.

9. Click Next. You'll see a final output dialog box that shows how the data from the source table will get mapped into the target table. Normally, this table will show an exact copy when you use the same DBMS for both source and target table. However, you'll want to check it carefully when the source and target DBMS aren't the same. Since DBMS rarely provides the same level of data type support, you may find that some data is compromised due to data translation.

10. Click Finish if you're happy with the target data and format. Otherwise, click Cancel. If you select Finish, then Table Copy will create the new table for you.

An Overview of Visual C++ Classes

Any discussion of creating database applications in C++ will eventually get to the classes you need to know about in order to actually do something. Each class performs a very specific task, so it's important to know which class to use and where to use it. The overall goal of all the classes is to get specific data from the server and display it on your screen or output it to your printer.

The first class you need to know about is CDatabase (ODBC) or CADOConnection (ADO). The objects you create with these classes allow you to gain access to the data within the database. You'll either create a pointer to a particular record or download an entire query; the database object creates the connection that you'll need. What kind of data access you get depends on whether you've created a form view (one-record display of all the data) or a record view (a grid of all records matching a specific criteria).

NOTE

It helps to think of a database object as a pipe that will bring data from the data well to your computer.

Once you've got a connection to your database, you'll need some kind of container to hold the information it contains. That's where the CRecordset (ODBC) and CADORecordset (ADO) classes come into play. A *recordset* holds the data that you'll eventually display onscreen. It helps to think of a recordset as a container for holding the data in your database. There are three kinds of recordsets:

▶   **Table**   A table-type recordset represents the data in one table of a database. You can do anything to this single table, including add, remove, or edit records.

▶ **Dynaset**   You'll use a dynaset-type recordset when you need to use a query to extract information from one or more tables in a database. As in a table-type recordset, you can add, remove, or edit records in a dynaset-type recordset.

▶ **Snapshot**   This is a static copy of the data contained in one or more tables in a database. As in a dynaset, you'll use a query to extract the information. Unlike in the dynaset, you can't modify the contents of the records. However, you can use a snapshot-type recordset to find data or generate reports.

You may have noticed that I mentioned the term "query" when talking about recordsets. A *query* is simply a question. All you're doing with a query is asking the database to provide you with a set of records that meet specific criteria. When using ODBC, you'll rely on CRecordset class data members to change the query for the records that you want to see. ADO is a little different. You can use the CADOCommand class to create special queries or the CADOConnection to perform standard queries. CADOCommand is a lot more flexible than CADOConnection. You can use it to perform a wide variety of tasks with the database. For example, you can use it to manipulate the structure of the database or perform other administrative tasks.

The final set of classes we'll look at in this chapter are for actually viewing the data once you have it. The CRecordView (ODBC) and CADORecordView (ADO) classes allow you to actually see the data you've collected. Essentially, all this class does is move the data from the recordset object to controls on your dialog or window. You'll also use it to monitor when you've reached the beginning or end of the recordset.

Building Unmanaged Database Applications

IN THIS CHAPTER:

Database applications come in a variety of sizes and types suited to meet specific business and personal needs. For example, I've created small database applications to manage my contacts and to keep track of how I spend my time during the day. These applications are simple and perform a single task well. Inventory management and other development projects I've worked on are much larger and more complex. In short, database management projects encompass the broadest range of any application you might develop.

Chapter 7 provided you with a very brief overview of the database technologies included with Visual C++ .NET and discussed the tradeoffs of using each database technology in an application. This chapter will use those technologies to demonstrate how you can create various database projects using Visual C++. Each of the examples in this chapter relies on a different technology to perform its work.

Application Compatibility: Moving from Visual Studio 6.0

Many of the small utilities and other programs that I worked with in Visual Studio 6.0 moved to Visual Studio .NET without too many problems. Unfortunately, I can't say the same of the database applications I created with Visual Studio 6.0. Moving these older applications to a clean machine with Visual Studio .NET meant a lot of additional work. It also seems like Microsoft went out of its way to ensure you'd pay a big price to use Visual C++ .NET with your old database applications. The following sections provide you with some tips on fixing common problems with older database applications.

Application Can't Find the Provider

The first thing I noticed is most database applications compiled with Visual Studio 6.0 won't even start. Microsoft has updated the providers in Visual Studio .NET, which means a clean machine won't have your old Visual Studio 6.0 provider installed. If you see a missing provider message when you start the compiled application, determine whether you want to use a new provider (the feature and bug fix solution) or install the old provider (the compatibility and quick fix solution).

Project Doesn't Open Correctly

Another problem will occur when you open the project for the first time. You'll want to convert it to Visual Studio .NET format—that's the automatic step. However, the first time you try to open a form with Visual Studio 6.0 controls, you'll see an error message stating the controls are no longer installed on your machine. That's right, Visual Studio .NET lacks direct support for the controls found in the previous version of the product. To restore support, you need to follow these steps:

1. Copy the controls from your Visual Studio 6.0 disk. You can perform this automatically by starting Setup and choosing only the ActiveX option. However, the best way to ensure you get only the controls you want and maximum compatibility is to copy the controls manually, then register them on your machine. Use the REGSVR32 <Name of OCX> command to register the controls. Don't copy the DBGRID32.OCX file to the System32 folder or register it.

2. Locate the \Extras\VB6 Controls folder on your Visual Studio .NET distribution CD (Disk 4 for the Enterprise Architect version). In this folder, you'll find DBGRID32.OCX, README.TXT, and VB6CONTROLS.REG.

3. Review README.TXT for any important information.

4. Copy DBGRID32.OCX to your System32 folder. Register the new OCX using REGSVR32 DBGRID32.OCX. Make sure you don't register the old version.

5. Double-click the VB6CONTROLS.REG to enter the licenses in your registry.

At this point, you should have full access to the components in your Visual Studio 6.0 application. However, if you try to compile your application at this point, it will likely fail. Microsoft made some changes to the MFC classes that cause just enough problems to make life interesting. One of the most common changes is the move of CRecordset from a MFC class to an ATL template. You'll need to convert the CRecordset entries in your application header file to a template form like this: virtual **CRowset<>* OnGetRowset()**. The corresponding **OnGetRowset()** code also changes to look like this:

```
CRowset<>* CADO1View::OnGetRowset()
{
    return m_pSet->GetRowsetBase();
}
```

After the application compiles, you'll likely find that it still won't run properly. Visual Studio .NET includes more code checking than Visual Studio 6.0 did. Consequently, you'll find that the application will generate more ASSERT error messages than ever before. The additional ASSERT error messages are actually a good feature of Visual Studio .NET because they help you locate marginal code that may have generated intermittent or difficult to find errors in the past.

Working with Grids

Working with a grid view in Visual C++ .NET is problematic under any condition. Put aside any thoughts you might have had about using the Microsoft DataGrid Control and ADO Data Control from previous versions of Visual Studio. Microsoft doesn't even include them as part of the Visual Studio .NET package. With a little trickery, you can install the controls from Visual Studio 6.0 and add them to your project (see the "Project Doesn't Open Correctly" section for instructions). However, these two controls won't work with Visual Studio .NET in most conditions, and neither will any of your old projects that rely on these controls. In short, you need to redesign your existing applications to use a new technique.

The source code CD contains an example in the \Chapter 08\NoGrid folder that demonstrates the problems with data grid controls. The example will make it easier to diagnose problems in your own code. When you first start this application, everything will look fine. The grid will contain the data from the Food.MDB database on the source code CD. However, you'll notice that the upper-left corner of the grid is blank, as shown here:

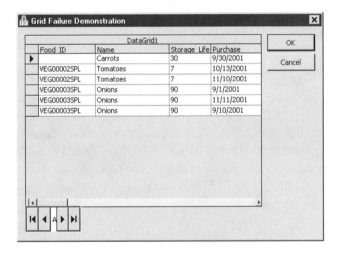

Any attempt to move the cell pointer will result in an error message. In addition, when you close the database, you'll receive another error message. Finally, in some situations, the problem is severe enough to cause damage to your database. Following is the message that you'll see when the application attempts to write a NULL value to the database.

Don't try to debug the application at this point, unless you're working with scrap data you don't care about losing. Generally, the application won't work no matter how much effort you put into it. The underlying problem is that Microsoft has changed certain data types and didn't design the older controls to work with these new data types.

The only grid at your disposal is the DBGrid Control. Unfortunately, Microsoft designed this control to work with Visual Basic, and using it within Visual C++ is difficult, to say the least (it *is* possible with a lot of coding). The end result is that you can't create a pure unmanaged database application in Visual C++ that uses a grid view without a lot of effort. Hopefully, Microsoft will receive enough requests to warrant fixing this hideous problem, but in the meantime, your best option for complex unmanaged database applications that require a grid view is to keep them in Visual Studio 6.0.

Writing an OLE-DB Application

OLE-DB is one of the latest in a long string of database technologies that Microsoft introduced over the years. For Visual C++ developers, OLE-DB is the latest product to use for unmanaged applications. We discussed the theory behind this technology in Chapter 7; Chapter 9 will show you how to create managed code using ODBC .NET and ADO.NET. This chapter shows you how to create an unmanaged application using OLE-DB that includes a form view and printing. As mentioned in the "Working with Grids" section, you'll experience significant problems working with grids in an unmanaged environment in Visual Studio .NET.

We'll also discuss some of the issues regarding OLE-DB in this chapter. For example, unlike ODBC, you don't use the DDX_FieldXxx functions to provide data exchange between the controls on the form and your database—we'll use the DDX_Xxx functions to move data between the database and controls instead. These differences between ODBC, DAO (Data Access Objects), and OLE-DB are important if you plan to move from one technology to another in order to improve the flexibility or performance of your applications.

BROWSER ALERT

You may find that you want some additional training once you get done reading this chapter. There are a lot of places on the Internet that provide training for using Visual C++ with OLE-DB, OLE-DB, DAO, and ODBC. For example, you'll find that Universal Software Solutions at **http://www.unisoftinc.com/courses/** *provides in-depth courses on using Visual C++, relational databases, and newer Microsoft object technologies like DCOM and COM+. Another good source is DevelopMentor at* **http://www.develop.com/**. *DevelopMentor offers a variety of courses on both object technology and Visual C++ (including various forms of database access). This company used to offer some DAO-specific classes but have since dropped them.*

Creating the OLE-DB Project

This section of the chapter shows how to create the OLE-DB Project shell. Setting up a database application is only slightly more complex than creating other application types. However, you do need to perform a few special tasks to get a good start on your application. The following steps show you how.

1. Create a new MFC application named OLE-DB. You'll see the MFC Application Wizard dialog.

2. Select the Application Type tab. Choose the Single Document option.

3. Select the Database Support tab. You'll see a dialog box similar to the one shown here (the screenshot shows the Database View Without File Support option selected—normally the tab has the None option selected).

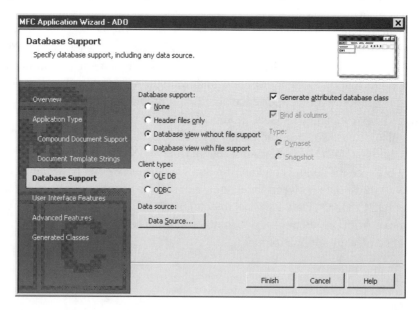

4. Choose Database View Without File Support from the list of options. Now we need to choose a data source for our application. Remember that OLE-DB uses a provider in place of the mechanism used by ODBC; therefore, we have no need for a DSN.

5. Click Data Source. You'll see the Provider tab of the Data Link Properties dialog. We'll use this dialog to choose the data source and determine how we'll access it. Since we're using an Access database for this example, we'll work with the Microsoft Jet 4.0 OLE DB Provider (working with the other OLE-DB providers is about the same). You'll go through the same steps listed here, but the entries that you'll be required to make on the various tabs will vary by provider. For example, SQL Server will require you to enter a server name along with other connection criteria, like the type of security that you prefer to use when accessing the server. The Microsoft Jet 4.0 OLE DB Provider requires the least information for gaining access to the database.

6. Choose the Microsoft Jet 4.0 OLE DB Provider option, then click Next. You'll see the Connection tab of the Data Link Properties. This tab is where you specify the location of the database you want to access, along with a username and password.

7. Type the full path to the database, which is **\Chapter 08\Data\Food.MDB** in the example. (You can also use the Browse button to locate the database on your hard drive.)

8. Type a username and password in the appropriate fields. Neither value should be required for the example database.

9. Click the Test Connection button. You should see a Test Connection Succeeded dialog if you entered the information into the Connection tab properly. If you don't see the dialog, make sure you have all of the right values. More often than not, the problem is a mistyped password (something that's easy to do because Visual C++ replaces the password with asterisks).

10. Click OK. You now have a connection to the database that doesn't rely on a DSN.

11. Click OK to close the Database Options dialog. You should see a Select Database Object dialog like the one shown here. As you can see, you can choose from Views, Tables, or System Tables. (Note that this is an

improvement from the previous version of Visual C++, in which the dialog contained only table names.)

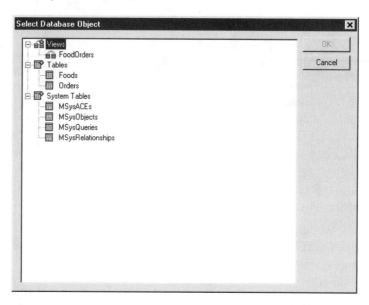

12. Highlight the FoodOrders view. You could have also selected a table. However, you'll normally use a query to access the contents of a database so that you can get just the data you want and in the order you want it. Click OK.

13. Select the Generated Classes tab. You'll see a dialog similar to the one shown next. There isn't anything to change on this dialog, but it's important to verify that the wizard has chosen COleDBRecordView in the Base Class field. This class will provide you with the functionality needed to make viewing your database easier.

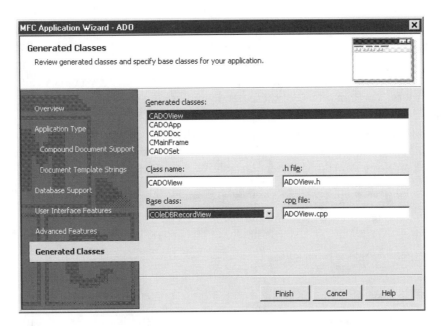

14. Click Finish. Visual C++ will create the new project for you.

Designing the Form View

It's important to remember that the document/view architecture of Visual C++ consists of two elements. The document is the data that you want to display, while the view is the presentation of that data. Consequently, you can create multiple views for a single document. In many cases, database management programs rely on this behavior to present the user with both an overview and the details of a database. With multiple views, each view can concentrate on a particular display feature. The form view of a database application contains the details of a single database record. It enables the user to view the details of a record without resorting to odd display manipulations. Complex database applications will often nest form views, with each view presenting more detail than the last.

Figure 8-1 shows the form used for this example. The IDD_OLE-DB_FORM contains fields for a single customer entry in a fictional database (FOOD.MDB). This database consists of two tables: Foods and Orders. The Food_ID field links the two tables. The example relies on a composite view of the two tables called FoodOrders. You can see all of these details by looking at the database on the source code CD.

You'll need to add member variables for each of the database fields in Figure 8-1. Do this by right-clicking the control, then choosing Add Variable from the context menu. You'll see an Add Member Variable Wizard similar to the one shown here:

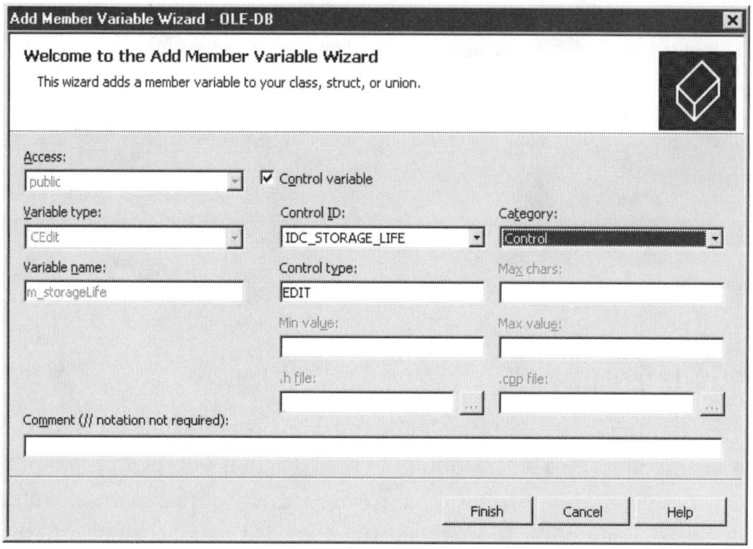

After you display the wizard, you'll need to select the type of member variable and give it a name. Table 8-1 provides a list of control names, types, and member variable names for IDD_OLE-DB_FORM.

Control Name	Type	Member Variable
IDC_FOOD_ID	Cedit	m_foodID
IDC_NAME	Cedit	m_name
IDC_PRICE	Cedit	m_price
IDC_PURCHASE_DATE	Cedit	m_purchaseDate
IDC_QUANTITY	Cedit	m_quantity
IDC_STORAGE_LIFE	Cedit	m_storageLife

Table 8-1   *IDD_OLE_DB_FORM Controls and Member Variables*

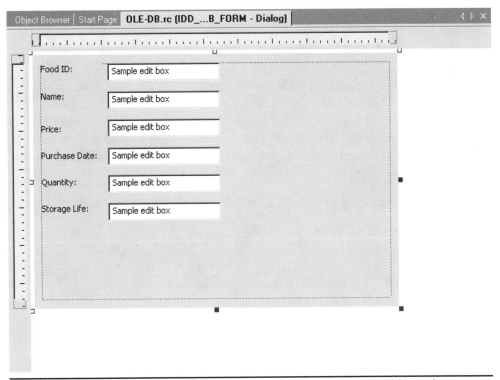

Figure 8-1 *IDD_OLE-DB_FORM shows a composite view of the two tables in the example database.*

The wizard creates a menu for you automatically. All of the options are common sense additions, such as the ability to print database records (something we'll discuss in the "Adding Print Capabilities to Your Application" section of the chapter). Visual C++ implements some items for you automatically, such as the Print options on the File menu. However, the print options won't do anything—the wizard enables these menu entries and then adds methods for them to your code.

The four Record menu entries (and associated buttons) perform many tasks automatically. However, if you want special behavior, you'll need to override them. Essentially, the four buttons will move the record pointer and call the appropriate methods to display the updated information. You can't add new records or perform other tasks using the defaults. We'll see how to add new records as the section progresses.

Adding Display Code to OLE-DB

One of the essentials of programming with Visual C++ .NET is that, as with its predecessor, Microsoft assumes nothing about your application. This way of thinking means you have to add code for almost everything in your application, or else it won't do anything. The example program won't display any information at this point, because we haven't defined a way to exchange data with the recordset. The fields in the form and the fields in the recordset require a connection in order to communicate. You'll need to modify the **DoDataExchange()** method as shown in Listing 8-1.

Listing 8-1

```
void COLEDBView::DoDataExchange(CDataExchange* pDX)
{
    // Verify that we're at the first record and not
    // at an empty record.
    if (m_pSet->m_FoodsFood_ID[0] == 0)
        m_pSet->MoveFirst();

    // Perform the default action.
    COleDBRecordView::DoDataExchange(pDX);

    // Perform data exchange between the recordset and the
    // text boxes on the form.
    DDX_Text(pDX, IDC_FOOD_ID, CString(m_pSet->m_FoodsFood_ID));
    DDX_Text(pDX, IDC_NAME, CString(m_pSet->m_Name));
    DDX_Text(pDX, IDC_PRICE, COleCurrency(m_pSet->m_Price));
    DDX_Text(pDX, IDC_PURCHASE_DATE, COleDateTime(m_pSet->m_Purchase));
    DDX_Text(pDX, IDC_QUANTITY, m_pSet->m_Quantity);
    DDX_Text(pDX, IDC_STORAGE_LIFE, m_pSet->m_Storage_Life);

    // Added for variables for each text box.
    DDX_Control(pDX, IDC_FOOD_ID, m_foodID);
    DDX_Control(pDX, IDC_NAME, m_name);
    DDX_Control(pDX, IDC_PRICE, m_price);
    DDX_Control(pDX, IDC_PURCHASE_DATE, m_purchaseDate);
    DDX_Control(pDX, IDC_QUANTITY, m_quantity);
    DDX_Control(pDX, IDC_STORAGE_LIFE, m_storageLife);
}
```

This method performs four essential tasks. First, it positions the record pointer to the first record if it isn't already there. OLE-DB often presents a NULL record when you first open the database (depending on the provider). This bit of code ensures the user doesn't see a blank screen when opening the application.

The second task is to perform the default data exchange. This act populates the pDX variable used for all other data exchange tasks. You need to populate pDX prior to performing any other task in the application.

The third task is to exchange data between the database and the data form. Microsoft chose not to update the **DDX_Xxx**() functions, so you will need to perform data conversions in many situations. For example, notice we must convert the TCHAR of the database to a string using the **CString**() class constructor. The same holds true for the price and purchase database fields where we use **COleCurrency**() and **COleDateTime**().

The fourth task is to exchange data between the form controls and local variables. The current method doesn't use these variables, but we'll need them in other areas of the example. It's normally a good idea to create member variables for the controls on the form.

Adding a Search Routine

Locating your data is at least as important as working with it in other ways (perhaps more important). The wizard doesn't create a search dialog or other essentials required when searching your database, so you need to create everything manually. Let's begin with the simple part of the new feature, adding a menu entry for searching the database. Open the IDR_MAINFRAME menu resource and add a new Find entry to the Edit menu, as shown here.

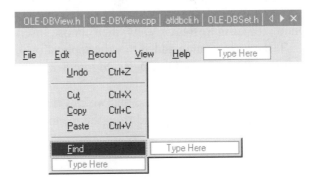

Give the new menu entry an ID of ID_EDIT_FIND. You'll likely want to change the prompt for this resource. Notice that Visual C++ assumes you want to find the selected text, but the example needs to locate a given record. Unfortunately, you can't change this property in the Properties window—you need to open the String Table resource, locate ID_EDIT_FIND, and then change the text associated with the prompt. This prompt includes two entries separated by a newline character (\n). The first appears on the Status Bar, while the second appears as balloon help. Here's an example of the String Table resource with a modified ID_EDIT_FIND.

ID	Value	Caption
ID_FILE_MRU_FILE12	57627	Open this document
ID_FILE_MRU_FILE13	57628	Open this document
ID_FILE_MRU_FILE14	57629	Open this document
ID_FILE_MRU_FILE15	57630	Open this document
ID_FILE_MRU_FILE16	57631	Open this document
ID_EDIT_CLEAR	57632	Erase the selection\nErase
ID_EDIT_CLEAR_ALL	57633	Erase everything\nErase All
ID_EDIT_COPY	57634	Copy the selection and put it on the Clipboard\nCopy
ID_EDIT_CUT	57635	Cut the selection and put it on the Clipboard\nCut
ID_EDIT_FIND	57636	Find the specified record in the database.\nFind a Record
ID_EDIT_PASTE	57637	Insert Clipboard contents\nPaste
ID_EDIT_REPEAT	57640	Repeat the last action\nRepeat
ID_EDIT_REPLACE	57641	Replace specific text with different text\nReplace
ID_EDIT_SELECT_ALL	57642	Select the entire document\nSelect All
ID_EDIT_UNDO	57643	Undo the last action\nUndo
ID_EDIT_REDO	57644	Redo the previously undone action\nRedo
ID_WINDOW_SPLIT	57653	Split the active window into panes\nSplit
ID_APP_ABOUT	57664	Display program information, version number and copyright\nAbc

The user will also need some means of entering a search value. While you can do this in a number of ways, the easiest way is to add a search dialog to the application. Right-click the Dialog folder in Resource View, then choose Insert Dialog from the context menu. You'll see a new dialog added to your application. Give this dialog a name—the example uses IDD_FIND_FOOD_ID. Figure 8-2 shows the construction of this dialog box.

We need to make this new dialog a class so that we can create an instance of it in the code when the user selects Edit | Find from the menu. Right-click the

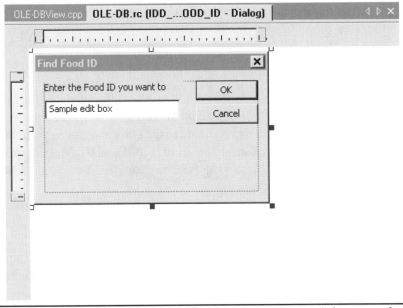

Figure 8-2   *The Find Food ID dialog box enables the user to search for a specific record.*

IDD_FIND_FOOD_ID form and choose Add Class from the context menu. You'll see an MFC Class Wizard dialog box similar to the one shown here.

Give your class a name of **CFindFoodID**. The wizard will automatically assign values to the other fields. Change the Base Class entry to CDialog (unless you really want to create a CHtmlDialog). Verify that the Dialog ID field has a value of IDD_FIND_FOOD_ID in it, then click Finish. Visual C++ will create the new class for you.

Now that you have a class associated with the dialog resource, you need to add a member variable to the CFindFoodID class. Make sure you create the class first; otherwise, you can't add the member variable to the class associated with the dialog resource. Give the member variable a name of **m_FindFoodID**. Make certain that you create this member variable as a value, not as a control. (You need a CString, not a CEdit for the example code.)

At this point, you have a new dialog class to display and a menu item to display it. We need to create some connection between the menu entry and the dialog resource. To make the connection, select the COLEDBView entry in Class View and click Events in the Properties window. You'll see a list of properties for various applications elements, including the ID_EDIT_FIND resource. Unfortunately, because we modified the purpose of ID_EDIT_FIND, you may see ID_EDIT_FIND as a numeric entry in the list, as shown here.

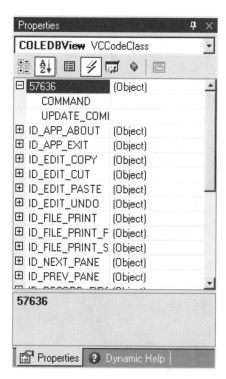

NOTE

Because of the way that Visual C++ mangles the ID of ID_EDIT_FIND, you'll probably need to change the message map entry near the beginning of the OLEDB-View.CPP file to read ON_COMMAND(ID_EDIT_FIND, COLEDBView::OnEditFind). Make sure you declare the method, if necessary.

Type **OnEditFind** in the COMMAND field, then press ENTER. It's time to add the code required to search the database. Listing 8-2 shows the code we'll use in this case.

Listing 8-2

```cpp
// Added for Find Food ID dialog support.
#include "FindFoodID.h"

void COLEDBView::OnEditFind()
{
    CFindFoodID     oFindIt;            // An instance of our dialog box.
    BOOL            lFound = false;     // Did we find a match record?
    BOOL            EndOfRowset = false; // End of the rowset?
    HRESULT         hr = S_OK;          // Operation Result
    COleCurrency    ProdPrice;          // Price of product.
    COleDateTime    ProdDate;           // Date of purchase.
    CString         cNumeric;           // Text form of numeric data.

    // Display the dialog and determine which button the user pressed to exit.
    if (oFindIt.DoModal() == IDOK)
    {
        // Go to the beginning of the query and search
        // for the Food ID entered by the user.
        m_pSet->MoveFirst();

        // Continue searching until we come to the end of the database
        // or we find a matching value.
        while (!EndOfRowset ^ lFound)
        {
            // Check if the value is equal.
            if (oFindIt.m_FindFoodID == CString(m_pSet->m_FoodsFood_ID))
                lFound = TRUE;

            // Go to the next record.
```

```
    else
        hr = m_pSet->MoveNext();

    // See if this is the last row.
    if (hr == DB_S_ENDOFROWSET)

        // If so, end the search loop.
        EndOfRowset = true;
}

if (!lFound)

    // Display an error message if we didn't find the record.
    MessageBox("Record not found!",
               "Database Error",
               MB_OK | MB_ICONERROR);

else
{

    // Display the data.
    m_foodID.SetWindowText(CString(m_pSet->m_FoodsFood_ID));
    m_name.SetWindowText(CString(m_pSet->m_Name));
    ProdPrice = COleCurrency(m_pSet->m_Price);
    m_price.SetWindowText(ProdPrice.Format(0, LANG_USER_DEFAULT));
    ProdDate = COleDateTime(m_pSet->m_Purchase);
    m_purchaseDate.SetWindowText(ProdDate.Format(0, LANG_USER_DEFAULT));
    itoa(m_pSet->m_Quantity, cNumeric.GetBuffer(10), 10);
    cNumeric.ReleaseBuffer(-1);
    m_quantity.SetWindowText(cNumeric);
    itoa(m_pSet->m_Storage_Life, cNumeric.GetBuffer(10), 10);
    cNumeric.ReleaseBuffer(-1);
    m_storageLife.SetWindowText(cNumeric);
    }
  }
}
```

Notice the #include added before the **OnEditFind()** method. You must include the header for the new dialog class we've created. The header contains the definitions used within the **OnEditFind()** method. Even though it's traditional to place all #include entries at the beginning of the source file, you can also place them immediately before the method that uses the class.

The first task is to display the dialog and allow the user to enter a value. If the user clicks OK, the code will continue processing input. Otherwise, the method ends and the display appears as it did before.

The code begins searching for the value entered by the user. If the search loop finds the value or it runs out of database entries to search, the loop ends. The code sets lFound to True if it finds the value. Otherwise, the code moves to the next record and determines if it's the last record in the database. If it's the last record, it sets EndOfRowset True.

Depending on the value of lFound, the code will display an error message or the data from the current record. Notice that we don't use the data exchange technique in this case, but merely place the data in the controls. The data exchange will take place if the user moves to another record. The **OnEditFind**() method must convert most of the database values into a CString acceptable for display in the controls. You'll see these methods used in other areas of the example because they work well for creating a common data format for all database values.

Adding Reports to an Application

Expect to create one or more reports for your database application. Even a small application like the one we've created in this chapter could benefit from multiple report types. For example, you might have an overview report that shows the database contents as a whole by summarizing like data (even the method of summarizing can create multiple reports) and a detail report that shows all of the records. In addition to the data that the report contains and the order in which you present it, there are other things to consider, like the appearance of the report from an aesthetic perspective. You may not want to take the time to print a report using the best-quality type and graphics for a workgroup meeting, but you can bet that such a report format will be required for a manager's meeting.

There isn't any way that I can tell you here about all the nuances of creating a report. This chapter will provide tips for creating a complex array of reports that include everything you'll need to view your data and will give an example of how to accomplish at least some of these goals in a programming example.

Printing Can Be Difficult

Trying to create the reports you need is difficult in some situations. You might be on a project where five managers each want their own set of reports added to the application, but you know that you only have time to create one or two report sets within the time allotted. Don't despair—you probably won't have to write all of those reports if you take a little time to analyze what the managers are looking for and add a little flexibility into the printing process.

Breaking down the reports you need into simple requirements is the first thing you should do when trying to reduce application complexity. It's a good idea to create a table with columns showing simple requirements and then listing the reports along the side. If you can find some comparable areas of the reports, you may be able to combine several of them into a single report and add configuration dialogs as needed. The following list gives you some ideas of what you can do to break down the reports into components parts.

▶ **Sort order**   Every report requires some type of sorting. Otherwise, you'll end up with a list of disorganized data that no one can understand. Remember that one of the main goals for any database is to organize the data it contains into something that's easier to understand. Your reports need to do the same thing. Sort order represents one of the easiest methods for combining two or more reports into a single programming task.

▶ **Groups**   There are times when you want a detail report that groups like items into a single heading. For example, you may create groups by ZIP code in a contact database. The ZIP code would appear as a heading, with all of the contacts in that ZIP code area in order beneath it. Groups aren't much different than sorting when it comes to organizing the data. However, it's very difficult to combine two reports with different groups even if the main part of the printout is the same. The reason is simple: you'd have to add a lot of complexity to the print routine to handle the inclusion of various header types. You can, however, combine two like reports where one includes groups and the other doesn't. All you need to do is include a switch to turn the heading on or off.

▶ **Group totals/summaries**   A lot of reports will provide a footer where the entire report or a related group of numbers is tallied. There are a lot of other statistical uses for footers, but a numeric tally is the most common type. As with group headings, it's difficult, if not impossible, to combine two reports that have different totals or summaries. You can, however, combine a report that doesn't use a footer of any kind with one that does as long as the columns are the same.

▶ **Report appearance**   If you have two reports with similar data but different requirements when it comes to final appearance, try combining them. It doesn't make sense to create two different printing routines if the only difference is the font used for presentation purposes and perhaps a little window dressing, like adding the company logo to the top of the report.

▶ **Level of detail**   Some reports are simply an overview of other reports. In other words, there are some reports that use the parent data only in its entirety. The child records are summarized in some way to provide an overview. It's easy to combine an overview report with one that shows the detailed contents of the database. Of course, there's the issue of what the reports contain. For example, if you have one report that shows every invoice for the month in salesperson order and another report that shows the total sales by individual salesperson, you can combine the two reports into one. A simple switch will determine whether the data is summarized or if every record in the child table gets printed as is.

▶ **Filtering**   It's very common for someone to ask for some, but not all, of the records in a database. If the only difference between two reports is the filtering used to determine which records get picked, then you can always combine them. Filtering is a function of the query you make to the DBMS, not a function of the code you write. In other words, all you need to do is change one or two lines of code to make the two reports.

At this point, you may be wondering why you don't just create a single report with a lot of configuration dialogs that will allow users to generate their own reports. There are several good reasons for not doing so. First, most users are going to be bewildered by the array of dialogs required to create a report. You'll find yourself spending a lot more time trying to get the user up to speed on creating the report than if you designed it yourself. In addition, as soon as you introduce custom reports, you'll also have to create some method for users to save those reports to disk so that they can create the same report later without a lot of fiddling around.

Another reason to avoid generic reports is the security risk involved. If you give the user too many different methods for creating custom reports, you may find that you've created security holes as well. Management normally wants some assurance that the company's confidential data won't get into the wrong hands. This means adding security and tightly controlling what gets printed—in addition to adding the right security to the database itself.

Adding Print Capabilities to Your Application

Now that we've looked at some of the complexities of writing a print routine for your database application, let's look at some ways to solve these programs. Fortunately, you already have three of the function shells you need in the OLE-DB application we've been using for example purposes up to this point. Just look at the COLEDBView class; there are three functions: **OnPreparePrinting()**, **OnBeginPrinting()**, and **OnEndPrinting()**.

▶ **OnPreparePrinting()**   Helps you to get your printer set up and to do any other preparatory tasks, like saving the current record number in the query so that you can return there after the print job completes.

▶ **OnBeginPrinting()**   Helps you to prepare the device context. Think of the device context as an artist's palette—you use it to draw the information you want to send to the printer. We'll run into this particular part of the Windows GDI (Graphics Device Interface) quite often in this example, so you'll have a good idea of what a device context is all about by the time we're done.

▶ **OnEndPrinting()**   Helps you to restore global application settings to their preprint condition. For example, this is where you'd return the query pointer to its preprint record.

One function is missing. We don't have a print routine to use to send data to the printer. The first thing we'll need to do is add an **OnPrint()** function to the program using the Overrides listing of the Properties window shown here.

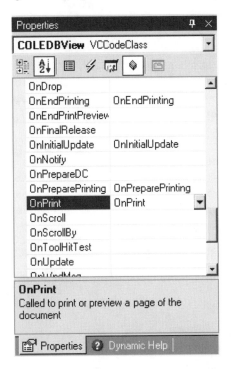

The **OnPrint()** function contains the code required to actually get the printed information out to the printer. This routine also gets called for other print-related tasks, like the Print | Preview command provided by most applications. To view this window, select COLEDBView in Class View, click Overrides in the Properties window, then locate the OnPrint entry. Click the drop-down list box for OnPrint and choose <Add> OnPrint from the list. Listing 8-3 shows the code you'll need to add to the **AddPrint()** method to enable your application to print.

Listing 8-3

```
void COLEDBView::OnPrint(CDC* pDC, CPrintInfo* pInfo)
{
    int             iRowCount = 1;        // Current print row count.
```

```
CString        cNumeric;                // Text form of numeric data.
CPen           oPen;                    // Pen for drawing.
CBrush         oBrush;                  // Brush for shading.
CFont          oTextFont;               // Text Font.
CFont          oHeadFont;               // Heading Font.
CFont          oColFont;                // Column Heading Font.
LOGFONT        lfFont;                  // Font characteristic structure.
CSize          oFontSize;               // Size of a font.
COLORREF       clrRef;                  // Color structure.
int            iRowPos = 120;           // Row position on printed page.
int            iTextHeight = 0;         // Current text height.
CRect          oDrawRect;               // Drawing area for printer.
int            iRecNumPos;              // Record number position.
int            iFoodIDPos;              // Food ID position.
int            iNamePos;                // Name position.
int            iPricePos;               // Price position.
int            iPurchasePos;            // Purchase Date position.
int            iQuantityPos;            // Quantity position.
int            iStoragePos;             // Storage Life position.
BOOL           EndOfRowset = false;     // End of the rowset?
HRESULT        hr;                      // Operation Result
COleCurrency   ProdPrice;               // Price of product.
COleDateTime   ProdDate;                // Date of purchase.

// Get the drawing area for our print routine.
oDrawRect = pInfo->m_rectDraw;

// Create a pen and select it into our device context.
clrRef = 0x00000000;
oPen.CreatePen(PS_SOLID, 2, clrRef);
pDC->SelectObject(&oPen);

// Create a brush and select it into our device context.
clrRef = 0x00C0C0C0;
oBrush.CreateSolidBrush(clrRef);
pDC->SelectObject(&oBrush);

// Create a heading font and select it into our device context.
oHeadFont.CreatePointFont(240, "Arial", pDC);
pDC->SelectObject(&oHeadFont);

// Display our heading.
```

```
oFontSize = pDC->GetOutputTextExtent("The ABC Company");
pDC->Ellipse(500,
    iRowPos - (oFontSize.cy / 2) - 10,
    oDrawRect.Width() - 500,
    iRowPos + (oFontSize.cy / 2) + 10);
pDC->SetBkMode(TRANSPARENT);
pDC->TextOut((oDrawRect.Width() - oFontSize.cx) / 2,
    iRowPos - (oFontSize.cy / 2) - 10,
    "The ABC Company");
pDC->SetBkMode(OPAQUE);

// Create the appropriate space.
oHeadFont.GetLogFont(&lfFont);
iRowPos = abs(lfFont.lfHeight) + 175;

// Create a text font.
oTextFont.CreatePointFont(120, "Arial", pDC);

// Get the current text font height.
oTextFont.GetLogFont(&lfFont);
iTextHeight = abs(lfFont.lfHeight) + 10;

// Create a font for displaying column headings.
lfFont.lfWeight = 700;     // Make it bold, normal is 400.
oColFont.CreateFontIndirect(&lfFont);
pDC->SelectObject(&oColFont);

// Compute the column spacings.  Set the first column to 1/2 inch.
iRecNumPos = int(oDrawRect.Width() / 17);
iFoodIDPos = iRecNumPos + 150 + pDC->GetOutputTextExtent("##").cx;
iNamePos = iFoodIDPos + 150 + pDC->GetOutputTextExtent("XXX00000XXX").cx;
iPricePos = iNamePos + 150 + pDC->GetOutputTextExtent("Perishable").cx;
iPurchasePos = iPricePos + 150 + pDC->GetOutputTextExtent("$00.00").cx;
iQuantityPos = iPurchasePos +
    150 + pDC->GetOutputTextExtent("Purchase Date").cx;
iStoragePos = iQuantityPos + 150 + pDC->GetOutputTextExtent("Quantity").cx;

// Display the column headings.
pDC->TextOut(iRecNumPos, iRowPos, "#");
```

```
pDC->TextOut(iFoodIDPos, iRowPos, "Food ID");
pDC->TextOut(iNamePos, iRowPos, "Name");
pDC->TextOut(iPricePos, iRowPos, "Price");
pDC->TextOut(iPurchasePos, iRowPos, "Purchase Date");
pDC->TextOut(iQuantityPos, iRowPos, "Quantity");
pDC->TextOut(iStoragePos, iRowPos, "Storage Life");

// Create a space between the column heading and the text.
iRowPos += iTextHeight;
pDC->MoveTo(iRecNumPos, iRowPos);
pDC->LineTo(oDrawRect.Width() - iRecNumPos, iRowPos);
iRowPos += 20;

// Select our text font into the device context.
pDC->SelectObject(&oTextFont);

// Determine the row height.
iTextHeight = 20 + pDC->GetOutputTextExtent("Xy").cy;

// Move to the first row.
m_pSet->MoveFirst();

// Print the records in a loop.
while (!EndOfRowset)
{

    // Display the current record number.
    itoa(iRowCount, cNumeric.GetBuffer(10), 10);
    cNumeric.ReleaseBuffer(-1);
    pDC->TextOut(iRecNumPos, iRowPos, cNumeric);

    // Print the data.
    pDC->TextOut(iFoodIDPos, iRowPos, m_pSet->m_FoodsFood_ID);
    pDC->TextOut(iNamePos, iRowPos, m_pSet->m_Name);
    ProdPrice = COleCurrency(m_pSet->m_Price);
    pDC->TextOut(iPricePos,
                 iRowPos,
                 "$" + ProdPrice.Format(0, LANG_USER_DEFAULT));
    ProdDate = COleDateTime(m_pSet->m_Purchase);
    pDC->TextOut(iPurchasePos,
                 iRowPos,
                 ProdDate.Format(0, LANG_USER_DEFAULT));
    itoa(m_pSet->m_Quantity, cNumeric.GetBuffer(10), 10);
```

```
cNumeric.ReleaseBuffer(-1);
pDC->TextOut(iQuantityPos, iRowPos, cNumeric);
itoa(m_pSet->m_Storage_Life, cNumeric.GetBuffer(10), 10);
cNumeric.ReleaseBuffer(-1);
pDC->TextOut(iStoragePos, iRowPos, cNumeric);

// Advance the row.
iRowPos += iTextHeight;
iRowCount ++;
hr = m_pSet->MoveNext();

// See if this is the last row.
if (hr == DB_S_ENDOFROWSET)
{
    // If so, end the printing loop.
    EndOfRowset = true;
    break;
}
}

//Perform the default action
COleDBRecordView::OnPrint(pDC, pInfo);
}
```

This looks like a lot of code, and it is. Working with printed output can get complicated without a lot of effort on your part. However, if you divide the task into smaller pieces, it's not too hard to figure out what's going on.

The first thing you need to know about is the mysterious pDC object of class CDC. I mentioned the device context earlier. It helps a lot if you think about pDC as your palette, the area in memory where you'll draw what you want to send to the printer. In fact, Microsoft has done just about everything it can to foster that view in the naming of functions and structures used with the GDI.

The first thing we do (besides produce what seems like thousands of variables) is create some drawing tools. You can't draw on a palette if you don't have the required drawing tools. In this case, I'll show you how to create the three basic drawing tools that you'll use in most of your programs: a brush, a pen, and a font. Pens can be any color and any one of a range of widths, and you can even choose a drawing pattern, such as dots. You use a pen for drawing lines, which includes outlines for objects. For example, a square doesn't necessarily need an outline, but most objects do. You could draw a square using just the fill color. That brings me to the brush. A brush provides fill color for solid objects. Brushes can also have a particular color, and you can choose to create a brush that has a pattern such as a crosshatch. Finally, you use a font to write something onscreen. It has many characteristics, most of them too arcane for the typical programmer's tastes. The source code in Listing 8-3 shows you a couple of ways to create fonts that don't require a complete knowledge of desktop publishing to use.

Just because you have a tool to draw with doesn't mean that you can use it. An artist might have a brush hanging from a nail in the wall, but that doesn't mean it's available for use in the current painting. Likewise, when you draw something in Windows, you have to select your tool first. That's what the **SelectObject**() function does. It allows you to select an object for drawing.

There's one brush, pen, and font object for each device context in Windows. Think of it as three hands, each one armed with a different tool. Before you can use another tool, you have to put the current one down and then select the new one. Windows takes care of putting a tool down for you automatically. Every time you use the **SelectObject**() function, you're putting the old tool down and picking up a new one.

Each of your tools is unique in many important ways. If you want an Arial 10 point font, you need a special font tool for that purpose. You'd have to create another font tool if you found that you needed the bold version of that font or if you suddenly wanted to write something in Times New Roman 12. Fortunately, you don't have to create a separate font for each color that you want to use—the device context controls that feature.

Another example of how each tool has a unique function is the pen. You need to create a pen for each width and style of line you want. Unlike with the font, you'll also need a pen for each color you want to create.

The bush is the most unique tool in some ways. While you can use the same function to create just about any font or pen you want, there's a different function call for each type of brush. For example, if you want to create a crosshatch brush, you need to use the **CreateHatchBrush**() function in place of the **CreateSolidBrush**() function shown in the code. It's important to realize the limitations of your existing tools and to create new tools as you need them.

NOTE

The drawing commands for this example are optimized for a printer that has a resolution in the range of 600 dots per inch. If you have a higher resolution printer, you may need to modify the location values to get a clear picture. However, no matter what resolution your printer is, you'll still be able to see how the commands work together to provide some form of output from your database application.

The first thing that we do in the way of drawing for this example is to create an ellipse using the **Ellipse()** function. As with most solid drawing commands, you need to specify the coordinates of the upper-left and lower-right corners of the graphics primitive. Windows assumes that you want to use the currently selected brush and pen, so you don't need to specify these values.

After drawing the ellipse, the code will place some text within it. The first thing we need to do is set the background drawing mode to transparent so that we don't erase any part of the ellipse. The other mode is opaque, which will replace the background color as well as add a drawing of some type in the foreground. Look at how the code uses the **GetOutputTextExtent()** function to determine the length of the text in pixels. This is about the only way to conveniently determine the length of a line of text so that you can center it on the page. The next line uses the **TextOut()** function to send the text to the printer. The very last line in this section of code resets the background drawing mode to opaque (the default setting) using the **SetBkMode()** function.

It's time to talk briefly about fonts. There are two convenient methods of creating fonts, and the next section of code shows both. The first method is to use the **CreatePointFont()** function. All you need is the name of a typeface and the size of the font you want to create in tenths of a point. So, if you wanted to create a 10-point font, you'd need to specify a font size value of 100.

Fonts use a special LOGFONT structure to pass all of the parameters they require. If you use the **CreatePointFont()** function, Windows creates this structure for you and makes certain assumptions in the process. What if you don't want those defaults? Well, you can create a simple font using **CreatePointFont()** (as we just did) and then use the **GetLogFont()** function to fill out the LOGFONT structure for you. Now you have a fully functional structure that you can modify slightly. I say *slightly* because you'll definitely shoot yourself in the foot if you try to make big changes in the structure that Windows just returned. I changed the weight of the font from normal to bold, which is an acceptable change as long as you don't make too big a difference in the font weight. Now you can use **the CreateFontIndirect()** function to create the bold version of the font. Just pass the LOGFONT structure provided by Windows with the lfWeight member change.

Notice that the code creates a bunch of headers using the bold font once it selects that font into the device context. Always remember to create the tool first and then select it as needed to draw on the device context. We also create a group of variables to track the positioning information for the columns. These positioning variables are used for both the headers and the detail information. Notice that the method used to derive the positioning information is device independent. In other words, it should look about the same whether you use a 300 dpi printer or one that's capable of 600 dpi. Of course, the random element here is how well Windows can determine the amount of space taken by the text we've provided using the current font. In most cases, you'll find that this calculation is accurate, but you may need to play around with it a tad to get a good presentation on all the printers in your company.

Drawing a line under the headings comes next. Notice that drawing a line is a two-step process. First, you use the **MoveTo()** function to move the pen to a specific point on the page, and then you use the **LineTo()** function to actually draw the line. Think of **MoveTo()** as moving with the pen up and **LineTo()** as moving with the pen down.

The last part of our print routine makes use of the data that's already available in the recordset (m_pSet). All that this code does is move from record to record in the recordset and print its contents to the printer or screen. Notice the use of data conversion routines to convert the data from a native database format to a CString. Also notice that the routines won't add a dollar sign ($) or other currency symbol to your output, so the example adds the "$" manually. How does the printed output of our application look? Figure 8-3 shows an example of what you should see when using the File | Print Preview command in the example application.

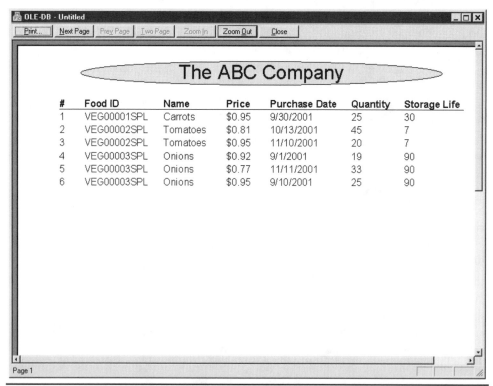

The ABC Company

#	Food ID	Name	Price	Purchase Date	Quantity	Storage Life
1	VEG00001SPL	Carrots	$0.95	9/30/2001	25	30
2	VEG00002SPL	Tomatoes	$0.81	10/13/2001	45	7
3	VEG00002SPL	Tomatoes	$0.95	11/10/2001	20	7
4	VEG00003SPL	Onions	$0.92	9/1/2001	19	90
5	VEG00003SPL	Onions	$0.77	11/11/2001	33	90
6	VEG00003SPL	Onions	$0.95	9/10/2001	25	90

Figure 8-3 *The print routine provides a tabular report of the content of the example database.*

Building Managed Database Applications

IN THIS CHAPTER:

Managed Database Application Scenarios

Understanding ODBC .NET

Writing a Managed Database Application

It's important to know how to create "old style" applications with Visual C++ because this is the only language where you can create native EXEs in Visual Studio .NET. The backward compatibility requirements alone warrant continued use of the techniques we discussed in Chapter 8. However, time marches on—everyone is looking toward the benefits of the managed .NET environment.

This chapter discusses two important new technologies: ODBC .NET and ADO.NET. The examples will show how to use both technologies for your next project. Generally, you'll find that Microsoft has oriented these managed technologies toward distributed application development. You can mix these technologies with protocols such as the Simple Object Access Protocol (SOAP) to provide solutions that span sites or even companies. Chapter 11 contains a discussion on SOAP and related technologies.

We'll also discuss which managed database applications work best. Many developers are confused about which technology to use in a given situation because Visual C++ .NET provides so many choices. As part of this discussion, we'll also consider the differences between ODBC and ODBC .NET. You'll find that ODBC .NET isn't a direct replacement for ODBC, but it does enable you to work with older applications in a managed environment.

NOTE

This chapter assumes you have a good understanding of how managed applications work and that you have some familiarity with the .NET Framework. Chapters 12, 13, and 14 contain a good overview of .NET and simpler examples than the example in this chapter.

Managed Database Application Scenarios

Visual Studio .NET has a strong emphasis on distributed application development. In fact, the distributed application takes precedence over any other application type. What this means to you as a developer is that you can create new application types that no longer depend on data appearing in one place. Users can grab data from multiple sources, even sources found in other companies.

The distributed application environment doesn't require the user to stay in one place. A user can access data with equal ease from a PDA on the road or a desktop machine at the office—the database application doesn't care about the user's location. All the application cares about is validating the user's identity and then responding to user requests. In short, the users can use data when and where they need it.

As technically appealing as these new capabilities are, they're unsuitable in some situations and overkill in others. For example, you wouldn't want to use distributed application techniques for an application that will only execute on a LAN and serve a small group of users. The performance costs of using distributed technologies, plus the additional development effort, make distributed programming techniques unsuitable.

NOTE

Microsoft also leaves out one important fact in their literature on ADO.NET and ODBC .NET—these technologies currently work only on Windows machines and don't even work with all versions of Windows. Microsoft's critics point this fact out regularly, and it bears repeating. If you use the managed application programming techniques in this chapter for your next project, the application is limited to platforms that provide the required support.

You'll also want to consider the importance of updating existing applications. In many cases, an existing application that works using older techniques won't benefit from an update. With this in mind, the following list contains some ideas on when distributed application development using managed code is ideal.

▶ **Users on the road**   This is the first use for distributed applications and the one that receives most use today. Supporting users on the road is problematic. The user requires constant updates of corporate data. In addition, the company will want to begin processing new user data as soon as possible. Using distributed application techniques means that an order the user takes today might ship tomorrow.

▶ **Business to Business (B2B) communication**   The Internet brought about the idea that businesses could communicate directly using a flexible technology that requires less custom programming. Current technology requires companies to create a custom interface for every business partner. Not only does this increase the complexity of application development and design, but it also slows the transfer of data from one part of the company to another. A managed application can rely on XML to send and receive data in plain text (getting rid of the problems with binary data transfer). In addition, the use of XSL and XPath enables the developer to translate between data formats without extensive programming.

NOTE

The costs of translating between data formats is so high that many companies invest in applications and servers whose sole purpose is to reduce the complexity of data transfers. For example, Microsoft's BizTalk server addresses this need. In most cases, creating a generic data translation utility is less expensive and easier to maintain than creating a custom data translation routine for each partner.

▶ **Special purpose** Many people are used to the image of a stockbroker whose desk is packed with monitors of various sizes and shapes. The reason for all of these monitors is that every exchange uses a different data format. New technologies such as the managed development strategies found in this chapter promise to cure this problem. Sometime in the future, your stockbroker will use just one monitor like everyone else.

▶ **Consumer Relationship Management (CRM)** As more business users gain access to wireless communication and use it regularly, the need and opportunity to create specialized distributed applications becomes more lucrative. Anything a company can do to make its services appear better than the competition helps the bottom line. Many developers will find themselves working on applications that push content to an unknown number of wireless devices in the near future. Examples of this type of application are the wireless communication projects currently under consideration by major airlines. Not only will these new wireless terminals enable a user to access the Internet while waiting in an airport, but the network could also have marketing implications and help the user to verify the status of services like flight times.

Understanding ODBC .NET

Open Database Connectivity (ODBC) has been one of the mainstays of database connectivity for Microsoft developers for a long time. When Visual Studio .NET appeared on the scene without a hint of ODBC, developers were understandably concerned (irate is more like it). After a lot of consideration, Microsoft determined that ODBC might be a good idea after all and began development of ODBC .NET. Unfortunately, ODBC .NET appeared on the scene well after the rest of Visual

Studio .NET and won't ship with the product—you'll need to download it as a separate product and install it on your system separately.

At the time of this writing, ODBC .NET is still in Beta 1. The current beta works only with Beta 2 of Visual Studio .NET and is completely invisible to the released product. All attempts to get ODBC .NET Beta 1 to work with the release version of Visual Studio .NET will fail, which is why I don't include an example of ODBC .NET in the chapter. However, Microsoft will eventually release ODBC .NET, and you'll be able to use it to access the same data sources that you've always used. The following sections describe the current form of ODBC .NET in more detail.

ODBC versus ODBC .NET

The biggest plus of using ODBC .NET is that you gain all of the benefits of a managed environment. You won't have to worry about memory management. In addition, ODBC .NET appears as part of the .NET Framework after you install it. You'll use the System.Data.Odbc namespace. ODBC .NET relies on the same techniques that you use with ADO.NET and OLE-DB to create code. Of course, the connection technology still relies on the Data Source Names (DSNs) that you've used in the past.

ODBC .NET doesn't add any new features to the world of ODBC. In fact, you'll find ODBC .NET imposes some new and not so exciting limitations because of the managed environment. For example, you'll have limited access to ODBC providers (which begs the question of why Microsoft changed this functionality). One of the big reasons to use ODBC in the past was that it was compatible with so many vendor products. ODBC .NET is only compatible with these providers:

▶ Microsoft SQL ODBC Driver

▶ Microsoft ODBC Driver for Oracle

▶ Microsoft Jet ODBC Driver

In many cases, the providers supplied with ODBC .NET are less capable than their unmanaged counterparts. While testing the beta, I found that many functions that would normally provide me with some content from the database would return the infamous E_NOTIMP or E_NOTIMPLEMENTED errors. Theoretically, Microsoft will fix these and many errors before they release ODBC .NET.

ODBC .NET provides access to four data access components that reflect its managed orientation. These are the same four objects that you use with other .NET database technologies and include.

Object	Description
Connection	Creates a connection between the application and the data source. You must establish a connection before doing anything else.
Command	Executes some action on the data source. You'll use this object after you create a connection to obtain data access. Commands also enable you to perform actions such as adding new records and performing database maintenance.
DataReader	Obtains a read-only, forward-only stream of data from the database. This is the object to use for disconnected application scenarios. You also use the DataReader when you want to display data without editing it.
DataAdapter	Obtains a read/write data stream from the database. The application can perform updates and add new records using this object. However, a DataAdapter requires a live connection to the database.

The ODBC .NET help file appears in the \Program Files\Microsoft.Net\Odbc.Net directory of your hard drive. Right now, you can't access it from the Start menu unless you add the link manually. The help file contains a good overview of ODBC .NET, but you'll want to augment this information with some Microsoft Knowledge Base articles. Here's the list of articles that I found most helpful. (Unfortunately, none of the coding examples rely on Visual C++, so you'll need to convert any examples from Visual Basic or C#).

▶ HOW TO: BETA: Use the ODBC .NET Managed Provider in Visual Basic .NET and Connection Strings
(**http://support.microsoft.com/default.aspx?scid=kb;EN-US;q310985**).

▶ HOW TO: BETA: Use the ODBC .NET Managed Provider in Visual C# .NET and Connection Strings
(**http://support.microsoft.com/default.aspx?scid=kb;EN-US;q310988**).

▶ HOW TO: BETA: Execute SQL Parameterized Stored Procedures Using the ODBC .NET Provider and C# .NET
(**http://support.microsoft.com/default.aspx?scid=kb;EN-US;q310130**).

▶ HOW TO: BETA: Execute SQL Parameterized Stored Procedures Using the ODBC .NET Provider and Visual Basic .NET
(**http://support.microsoft.com/default.aspx?scid=kb;EN-US;q309486**).

Installation Requirements for ODBC .NET

You must install a compatible version of Visual Studio .NET before you install ODBC .NET. The ODBC .NET installation program relies on the existence of the .NET Framework and you'll want the installation program to install any special features in the Visual Studio .NET IDE. ODBC .NET will also require Microsoft Data Access Components (MDAC) version 2.6. Microsoft provides the MDAC support as part of the Visual Studio .NET installation, so you won't need to perform a separate update of this product as indicated on the ODBC .NET download page.

BROWSER ALERT

Microsoft will very likely include ODBC .NET as part of the Microsoft Developer Network (MSDN) CD. You can also download the current version of ODBC .NET from http://msdn.microsoft.com/downloads/sample.asp?url=/MSDN-FILES/027/001 /668/msdncompositedoc.xml. Make certain that you read the online documentation for any late-breaking news before you download and install the product. Otherwise, you might find that the current product implementation breaks some part of your development environment.

One of the problems you could run into when working with ODBC .NET is that the installation program fails to update the providers correctly. The ODBC .NET installation program not only installs new providers, it updates the Microsoft ODBC Administrator to use the new providers as well. It's important to verify the presence of the new providers by opening the Microsoft ODBC Administrator and viewing the version numbers on the Drivers tab. Here's an example of a Microsoft ODBC Administrator display with updated providers.

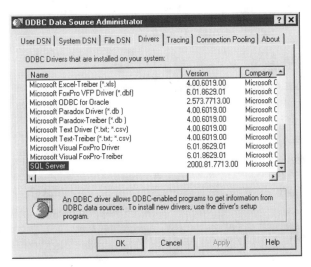

Writing a Managed Database Application

Managed database applications use the same basic structure and have the same features that other managed applications support. You still gain the benefits of automatic memory management, and you'll find it relatively easy to find the classes you need within the .NET Framework.

> **NOTE**
>
> *This example contains a lot of code, some of which won't appear in the text. The \Chapter 09\ ManagedDB folder on the source code CD contains the full source for this example. Make sure you check the source code for data declarations and other programming elements.*

Creating a .NET application does seem to require more code than unmanaged applications of similar complexity. The tradeoff is that you gain a little more flexibility and the resulting application is more scalable. The following sections show how to create a basic grid view application using managed code. We'll begin with the grid, look at what you need to create a connection between the database and the grid, and then develop a print routine for the application.

Creating the Grid View

The DataGrid control is one of the most flexible additions to the .NET Framework. You can use this control to display and manipulate any type of tabular data. In addition, Microsoft supplied both standard and Web versions of the DataGrid control with essentially the same characteristics, so it's relatively easy to move your code from the desktop to the Web. Of course, all of this flexibility comes at a cost—you need to perform substantial setup to obtain the maximum benefit from this control.

> **BROWSER ALERT**
>
> *The DataGrid control has become extremely popular for both Web and desktop development. You'll find a wealth of examples online. For example, if you want to see a simple and easy to understand version of the DataGrid control for ASP development, check **http://www.4guysfromrolla.com/webtech/122300-1.shtml**. You'll find a relatively good tutorial for using the DataGrid control with ASP .NET at **http://www.aspnextgen.com/tutorials.aspx?tutorialid=37**. The DevASP.NET Web site (**http://www.devasp.net/Net/Search/default.asp?c_id=317**) has a complete list of articles and tutorials for ASP development. You can also search for DataGrid examples on GotDotNet (**http://gotdotnet.com/**) and The Code Project (**http://thecodeproject.com/** or **http://www.codeproject.com/**).*

Creating the DataGrid

The example application uses a DataGrid control to display data from the same Access database we used in Chapter 8. (The example in that chapter presented a form view of the information.) Listing 9-1 shows the code you'll need to create and configure the DataGrid control for this example.

Listing 9-1

```
// Configure the data grid
dataGrid1->CaptionVisible = false;
dataGrid1->DataMember = "FoodOrders";
dataGrid1->DataSource = FoodDataSet;
dataGrid1->Dock = DockStyle::None;
dataGrid1->HeaderForeColor = SystemColors::ControlText;
dataGrid1->Name = "dataGrid1";
dataGrid1->Size = System::Drawing::Size(500, 361);
dataGrid1->Location = System::Drawing::Point(0, 40);
dataGrid1->TabIndex = 0;
dataGrid1->Select();
```

As you can see, we don't actually configure any part of the data presentation with this control. The DataGrid control acts as a data viewing mechanism for the most part. The DataSource property determines which data source the DataGrid control uses for display purposes. The example uses a dataset, but you can use other sources, such as a DataTable, DataView, or DataViewManager (among other data structures). You can even use a single dimensional array or a custom control as a source of data.

The other property that you must set to gain access to data is the DataMember property. A dataset can contain more than one table or view. The DataSource property selects every table the dataset has to offer. The DataMember property selects a particular table within the dataset for display purposes. Other input controls might not require the use of both the DataSource and DataMember properties, so you'll need to spend some time working with these properties if you're experiencing problems displaying data on screen.

Notice that the Location property setting places the DataGrid control below the top of the client area. Later in the example we'll add a ToolBar control that appears at the top of the client area. If you wanted to use the entire client area for the DataGrid control, you could use the Dock property to control its size and location.

Adding a Main Menu to the Application

This example makes use of a menu to enable the user to perform basic commands. In most cases, a database application will require a menu to avoid cluttering the screen with an endless array of buttons. The menu consists of a main menu with File and Record entries and two submenus to hold the File and Record options. Listing 9-2 shows the menu code for the example.

Listing 9-2

```
// Configure the main menu.
MenuItem *MainMenuItems[] = {mnuFile, mnuRecord};
mainMenu1->MenuItems->AddRange(MainMenuItems);
mnuFile->Index = 0;

// Configure the File menu.
MenuItem *FileMenuItems[] = {mnuFile_Print,
                             mnuFile_PrintPreview,
                             mnuFile_PageSetup,
                             menuSeparator,
                             mnuFile_Exit};
mnuFile->MenuItems->AddRange(FileMenuItems);
mnuFile->Text = "&File";
mnuFile_Print->Index = 0;
mnuFile_Print->Shortcut = Shortcut::CtrlP;
mnuFile_Print->Text = "&Print";
mnuFile_Print->add_Click(
   new EventHandler(this, mnuFile_Print_Click));
mnuFile_PrintPreview->Index = 1;
mnuFile_PrintPreview->Text = "Print Pre&view";
mnuFile_PrintPreview->add_Click(
   new EventHandler(this, mnuFile_PrintPreview_Click));
mnuFile_PageSetup->Index = 2;
mnuFile_PageSetup->Text = "P&age Setup";
mnuFile_PageSetup->add_Click(
   new EventHandler(this, mnuFile_PageSetup_Click));
menuSeparator->Text = "-";
mnuFile_Exit->Index = 4;
mnuFile_Exit->Text = "E&xit";
mnuFile_Exit->add_Click(
   new EventHandler(this, mnuFile_Exit_Click));

// Configure the Record menu.
MenuItem *RecordMenuItems[] = {mnuRecord_First,
                               mnuRecord_Previous,
```

```
                              mnuRecord_Next,
                              mnuRecord_Last};
mnuRecord->MenuItems->AddRange(RecordMenuItems);
mnuRecord->Text = "&Record";
mnuRecord_First->Index = 0;
mnuRecord_First->Text = "&First";
mnuRecord_First->add_Click(
    new EventHandler(this, RecordFirst_Click));
mnuRecord_Previous->Index = 1;
mnuRecord_Previous->Text = "&Previous";
mnuRecord_Previous->add_Click(
    new EventHandler(this, RecordPrevious_Click));
mnuRecord_Next->Index = 2;
mnuRecord_Next->Text = "&Next";
mnuRecord_Next->add_Click(
    new EventHandler(this, RecordNext_Click));
mnuRecord_Last->Index =3;
mnuRecord_Last->Text = "&Last";
mnuRecord_Last->add_Click(
    new EventHandler(this, RecordLast_Click));
```

As you can see, all of the standard entries require an Index and a Text property value. The only exception is the generalized menuSeparator entry, which contains only a Text property value of "-". In addition, you must assign an event handler to the menu entry or it won't do anything. Notice that mnuFile_Print also uses a Shortcut property value. This value enables the user to access the menu command using a keyboard shortcut. Even though the text for mnuFile_Print doesn't include the shortcut key entry, it will appear in the menu, as shown next:

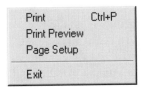

Once you create the individual menu entries, you need to add them to the host menu. Of course, the top menu in the hierarchy is the main menu. You add the submenus to the host menu by creating a MenuItem array that contains each of the submenus in the order you want them to appear in the resulting menu. The Index property of each menu should theoretically order the menus, but .NET doesn't order them in some situations. In addition, the generalized menuSeparator entry lacks an index, so you'll want to ensure that the order is correct so the separators appear in the right places. One way around the separator problem is to create a unique separator each time one is needed and assign it an Index value. Add the MenuItem array to the host menu by calling the **MenuItems->AddRange()** method.

Note that the main menu contains no positioning or size properties. The main menu always appears at the top of the application framework, and it reduces the size of the client area accordingly. You can't size the main menu and there's no option for docking it. In short, the main menu is part of the framework, not a control you use to augment the application using part of the client area. This distinction is important (as we'll see later in this section).

Adding a Toolbar to the Application

Most database applications sport a toolbar. The reason is simple. Using menu commands to move from record to record is painfully inefficient for the user. While a form view of the data could support movement buttons on the form, a grid view is less likely to support them. Toolbars typically contain options for printing as well, but the example application will concentrate on the buttons used for movement from record to record. Listing 9-3 shows the code you'll need to create a ToolBar control (we'll discuss resizing the form in the "Techniques for Resizing the Form" section that follows).

Listing 9-3

```
// Configure the toolbar.
toolBar1->Dock = DockStyle::None;
toolBar1->DropDownArrows = true;
toolBar1->Name = "toolBar1";
toolBar1->ShowToolTips = true;
toolBar1->Size = System::Drawing::Size(500, 39);
toolBar1->TabIndex = 1;
btnNext->Location = System::Drawing::Point(168, 8);
btnNext->Name = "btnNext";
btnNext->TabIndex = 4;
btnNext->Text = "Next";
btnNext->add_Click(new EventHandler(this, RecordNext_Click));
btnFirst->Location = System::Drawing::Point(8, 8);
btnFirst->Name = "btnFirst";
btnFirst->TabIndex = 2;
btnFirst->Text = "First";
```

```
btnFirst->add_Click(new EventHandler(this, RecordFirst_Click));
btnPrevious->Location = System::Drawing::Point(88, 8);
btnPrevious->Name = "btnPrevious";
btnPrevious->TabIndex = 3;
btnPrevious->Text = "Previous";
btnPrevious->add_Click(new EventHandler(this, RecordPrevious_Click));
btnLast->Location = System::Drawing::Point(248, 8);
btnLast->Name = "btnLast";
btnLast->TabIndex = 5;
btnLast->Text = "Last";
btnLast->add_Click(new EventHandler(this, RecordLast_Click));
```

NOTE

The order of control placement for a toolbar is important if you plan to use standard buttons, as shown in Listing 9-3. You don't place the controls in the ToolBar control as you would with a menu. The buttons reside on top of the ToolBar control, making it appear that the ToolBar control is containing them in some way. The reality is that the ToolBar provides a visual framework for standard Button controls. You can also create special ToolBarButton controls that appear as a collection within the toolbar. However, creating these buttons introduces extra coding, and they don't look different from a visual perspective.

As you can see, the example uses standard buttons, rather than the special ToolBarButtons designed for use with the Toolbar control. The order in which you place the controls in the code is important if you use this technique. The main advantage for using standard buttons is that you save some coding time for each control, and visually they don't look any different from the special ToolBarButtons. The standard buttons also provide easier access, because the ToolBar control relies on a collection and Visual C++ doesn't support the ForEach looping structure that other languages use to work with collections. The disadvantages of using this technique are that you now have to exercise care in the ordering of the buttons in the code and you must ensure the individual buttons have the proper configuration settings. In addition, you won't have the centralized button control that a toolbar can provide. For the Visual C++ developer, it's a definite trade-off.

As you can see from Listing 9-3, toolBar1 requires a minimum of configuration. All you need to do is provide a name and standard size. Notice that the example specifically sets the DockStyle property to DockStyle::None. You'll want to use this setting to avoid resizing problems caused by a multiple control scenario. Notice that the TabIndex property setting doesn't make any difference in this case, because the application automatically applies all tab movements to the DataGrid control.

Each of the buttons receives positioning information—the example uses the default button size. The code also sets the Name and Text properties as usual. Notice the technique used to assign an event handler to each of the controls. You can save coding effort by assigning each control the same event handler as its menu counterpart. Code sharing is also the reason for the somewhat generic name for the event handler methods.

Techniques for Resizing the Form

Normally, the controls on a .NET form can handle their own resizing needs, because the majority of the large controls provide some type of docking property. However, the example presents a challenge for the developer. The DataGrid control will observe the boundaries of a main menu, but you might experience problems combining it with other controls such as a ToolBar.

TIP

*The Dock property is a welcome addition to the DataGrid and other large .NET controls. If the DataGrid will consume all or a major part of the client area of the display, this property enables you to dock the control to one or all parts of the framework, making a separate **OnResize()** method unnecessary. You'll find that the Dock property uses different names with various controls depending on its purpose. For example, the ToolBar control implements it as the DockType property. The Dock property is a great feature, but you need to use it with care.*

If you set the DataGrid control to dock fully, it will consume the entire client area, and the ToolBar will likely hide part of the data (or the DataGrid will hide the ToolBar). On the other hand, if you choose to dock the DataGrid control with the side or bottom of the framework and dock the ToolBar with the other side or top of the framework, the two controls will resize together. The ToolBar and DataGrid will both increase in size. Because of these sizing problems, you'll want to override the default **OnResize()** behavior to make the grid look right when the user resizes the window.

The **OnResize()** method is part of the Form class. To add the **OnResize()** method, you need to declare **OnResize()** as public, or the compiler will complain that you can't override virtual methods using a private or protected declaration. You also need to declare any controls the **OnResize()** method will work with in such a way that **OnResize()** can access them. Here's the **OnResize()** method:

```
void MainApp::OnResize(EventArgs __gc *args)
{
    // Verify the data grid is accessible.
```

```
    if (MainApp::ActiveForm != 0)
    {
        // Resize the controls as needed.
        dataGrid1->Size =
            System::Drawing::Size(Width, Height - toolBar1->Height);
        toolBar1->Width = Width;
    }
}
```

The code must verify that the form is active. If it isn't active, any attempt to resize the form will result in an error. You can't resize controls on a form that doesn't exist. We need to resize both aspects of dataGrid1, so using the Size property is most appropriate. However, toolBar1 will remain the same height, so changing the width is fine. Notice that we don't need to do anything with the main menu because it isn't part of the client area of the form. You'll find that you need to declare both dataGrid1 and toolBar1 as protected, as shown here:

```
protected:
        // Protected display elements
        DataGrid    *dataGrid1;
        ToolBar     *toolBar1;
```

There are several good reasons for using a protected declaration, but the main reason is that you can't access private variables from a public event handler. Using protected variables enables you to maintain a level of data hiding. If the variables you access from a public method must remain private, you'll need to use properties to access them. While the use of properties does expose the data the variable contains to outside access, you can use the get and set methods to control access with greater accuracy.

Configuring the Application Form

You might think that configuring the form is going to be difficult because of all the display elements we've discussed so far. The form configuration is relatively simple because many of the control elements appear as part of something else. Here's the form configuration code for this example.

```
// Configure the form.
Text = "Managed Database Example";
FormBorderStyle = FormBorderStyle::Sizable;
StartPosition = FormStartPosition::CenterScreen;
```

```
Size = System::Drawing::Size(500, 400);
Menu = mainMenu1;
Controls->Add(dataGrid1);
Controls->Add(btnFirst);
Controls->Add(btnNext);
Controls->Add(btnPrevious);
Controls->Add(btnLast);
Controls->Add(toolBar1);
```

If we had used the ToolBarButtons instead of standard buttons for toolBar1, the code would have been even shorter. In the sections that follow, you'll learn that most of the magic of this example happens because of specialized data access controls. Creating the display elements is relatively simple compared to the data access controls.

Adding Some Data Access Code

You have many options when it comes to data access with Visual C++ .NET. Not only do you have a choice of access technology, but you also have a choice of methods for working with the database. The example uses a combination of a connection, data adapter, and a dataset to fill the data grid we created earlier. The data adapter also requires two commands, one for insert and a one for select. Here are the declarations of various data access elements:

```
// Data Elements
OleDbDataAdapter    *FoodAdapter;
OleDbCommand        *oleDbSelectCommand1;
OleDbCommand        *oleDbInsertCommand1;
OleDbConnection     *FoodConnection;
DataSet             *FoodDataSet;
```

Defining the Data Adapter

Once you declare and instantiate the various data objects, you need to configure them. You don't have to follow a specific order, but it does help, in some cases, to do so. For example, you can't fill a dataset before you configure the other data elements (this part of the project appears later in this section). Listing 9-4 shows the configuration code you'll need for the data adapter we use in this example.

Listing 9-4

```
FoodAdapter->InsertCommand = oleDbInsertCommand1;
FoodAdapter->SelectCommand = oleDbSelectCommand1;
DataColumnMapping *Food_IDColumn  =
   new DataColumnMapping("Food_ID", "Food Identifier");
DataColumnMapping *NameColumn  =
   new DataColumnMapping("Name", "Product Name");
DataColumnMapping *PriceColumn  =
   new DataColumnMapping("Price", "Price");
DataColumnMapping *PurchaseColumn  =
   new DataColumnMapping("Purchase", "Purchase");
DataColumnMapping *QuantityColumn  =
   new DataColumnMapping("Quantity", "Quantity");
DataColumnMapping *Storage_LifeColumn  =
   new DataColumnMapping("Storage_Life", "Storage Life (Days)");
DataColumnMapping *FoodOrdersColumns[] = {Food_IDColumn,
                                          NameColumn,
                                          PriceColumn,
                                          PurchaseColumn,
                                          QuantityColumn,
                                          Storage_LifeColumn};
DataTableMapping  *TempTableMapping  =
   new DataTableMapping("Table", "FoodOrders", FoodOrdersColumns);
DataTableMapping  *FoodAdapterMapping[] = {TempTableMapping};
FoodAdapter->TableMappings->AddRange(FoodAdapterMapping);
```

The OleDbDataAdapter control, FoodAdapter, provides a lot in the way of
configuration options. The code in Listing 9-4 represents a minimum implementation.
It provides command entries for the selection and insertion of data. While you might
be able to get by without the data insertion command, you must include a selection
command or the data adapter won't receive any input data. We'll see what the two
commands require in the way of configuration later in the chapter. For now, all you
need to know is that you should provide support for these two commands.

It's also important to tell FoodAdapter how to handle the data it receives from the
database. You'll need to create a set of DataColumnMapping objects. Each object
describes a field in the database. The dataset will eventually use this information as a

means for configuring the data grid. The first string contains the name of the field in the database. The string must match the name precisely. The second string contains the field name that you want to see in the data grid. If you don't provide a precise field name, the column will still appear in the data grid, but without the name you want to see. Here's what the fields look like for the example as a result of the mapping.

Food Identifier	Product Name	Price	Purchase	Quantity	Storage Life (Days)

After you create the column mappings, you need to combine them into a DataTableMapping. A data adapter can handle more than one table, so the table you create now could be just one of many. The final step is to add the DataTableMapping objects you create to FoodAdapter using the **TableMappings->AddRange**() method. Note that the process works similarly to the menu we created earlier in the chapter.

Configuring the Data Insertion Command

Most users will want the ability to add new records to the database, which means creating a data insertion command. You'll begin configuring oleDbInsertCommand1 by adding a CommandText property value that describes the action you want oleDbInsertCommand1 to perform. In this case, we want oleDbInsertCommand1 to create a new record, which means adding the record and giving it default settings. Here's the command text we'll use (you'll normally place the entire command on a single line in your source file):

```
"INSERT INTO FoodOrders(Food_ID, Name, Price, Purchase, Quantity, Stor
age_Life) VALUES (?, ?, ?, ?, ?, ?)";
```

Creating a SQL statement that defines what the database will do with the data once you send it isn't enough to create a new record. The command also requires a live connection to the database (supplied by FoodConnection in the example). You must also describe the data and how the Database Management System (DBMS) should react to it. For example, the DBMS needs to know that one value is a string, while the next is an integer or a special type such as currency. (The DBMS must support the special type you wish to store—the DBMS is unlikely to provide a conversion routine that will convert data it doesn't understand automatically.) Listing 9-5 shows the code you'll use to create a data field definition.

Listing 9-5

```
oleDbInsertCommand1->Connection = FoodConnection;
oleDbInsertCommand1->Parameters->Add(
```

```
    new OleDbParameter("Food_ID", OleDbType::VarWChar, 13, "Food_ID"));
oleDbInsertCommand1->Parameters->Add(
    new OleDbParameter("Name", OleDbType::VarWChar, 50, "Name"));
oleDbInsertCommand1->Parameters->Add(
    new OleDbParameter("Price",
                        OleDbType::Currency,
                        0,
                        System::Data::ParameterDirection::Input,
                        false,
                        ((System::Byte)(19)),
                        ((System::Byte)(0)),
                        "Price",
                        System::Data::DataRowVersion::Current,
                        0));
oleDbInsertCommand1->Parameters->Add(
    new OleDbParameter("Purchase", OleDbType::DBDate, 0, "Purchase"));
oleDbInsertCommand1->Parameters->Add(
    new OleDbParameter("Quantity",
                        OleDbType::Integer,
                        0,
                        System::Data::ParameterDirection::Input,
                        false,
                        ((System::Byte)(10)),
                        ((System::Byte)(0)),
                        "Quantity",
                        System::Data::DataRowVersion::Current,
                        0));
oleDbInsertCommand1->Parameters->Add(
    new OleDbParameter("Storage_Life",
                        OleDbType::SmallInt,
                        0,
                        System::Data::ParameterDirection::Input,
                        false,
                        ((System::Byte)(5)),
                        ((System::Byte)(0)),
                        "Storage_Life",
                        System::Data::DataRowVersion::Current,
                        0));
```

As you can see, the **Parameters->Add()** method does most of the work. The amount of data an entry requires varies by the type of data you want to supply. As a minimum, you must supply the name of the field, the field type, size of the field, and the name of the data source column in the database. In some cases, you must also determine

▶ Direction of data flow

▶ Whether the value can include a NULL value

▶ Number of digits to the left and right of the decimal point

▶ Version of the source data that you want to use

▶ Which object to use to represent the data value

Creating a Database Connection

The database connection, FoodConnection, provides the actual connection to the database. You need to configure only one property, ConnectionString, to make this object usable. Here's the connection string found in the example code:

```
"Provider=Microsoft.Jet.OLEDB.4.0;Password="""";User ID=Admin;Da
ta Source=D:\\0083 - Source Code\\Chapter 08\\Data\\Food.mdb;Mo
de=ReadWrite|Share Deny None;Extended Properties="""";Jet OLEDB:Sys
tem database="""";Jet OLEDB:Registry Path="""";Jet OLEDB:Data
base Password="""";Jet OLEDB:Engine Type=4;Jet OLEDB:Data
base Locking Mode=0;Jet OLEDB:Global Partial Bulk Ops=2;Jet OLEDB:Glo
bal Bulk Transactions=1;Jet OLEDB:New Database Password=""
"";Jet OLEDB:Create System Database=False;Jet OLEDB:Encrypt Data
base=False;Jet OLEDB:Don't Copy Locale on Compact=False;Jet OLEDB:Com
pact Without Replica Repair=False;Jet OLEDB:SFP=False"
```

Normally, you'll place this entire connection string on one line in the source code. You'll need to modify the Source portion of the string to match your system setup. In addition, the string doesn't have to be this long. The example shows the vast majority of the settings for a Access database connection. Visual C++ will work just fine with a short string—you just won't have as much control over the connection.

Configuring the Data Selection Command

The oleDbSelectCommand1 command requires two parameters as input. First, you need to tell the command which connection to use with the Connection property. The example uses a value of FoodConnection because that's the connection in this case. Next, you need to provide a command for selecting data from the database. Here's the command string used in this case (it would normally appear on a single line in the source code):

```
"SELECT Food_ID, Name, Price, Purchase, Quantity, Storage_Life FROM Food
Orders ORDER BY Food_ID, Purchase DESC";
```

As you can see, this simple SQL statement tells which fields to select from the
FoodOrders view and then tells how to order it. The DESC keyword tells Access to
order the Purchase field in descending order.

Filling the Dataset with Data

The configuration process is for naught without a single command to activate the
various objects. You must provide this line of code after the data connection is
completed or the data grid will remain blank:

```
FoodAdapter->Fill(FoodDataSet);
```

All that this command does is tell the data adapter to fill the dataset with data.
Without the command, the application will create a connection to the database, but
will never place anything in the dataset. Because the data grid relies on the dataset
for information, the data grid will assume there's no data to display.

NOTE

*You must perform all the database object configuration and fill the dataset before you begin
creating the data grid. The data grid code that appears in Listing 9-1 depends on a fully functional
database connection and a full dataset. In many cases, you'll obtain odd results if you create the
data grid first, then attempt to create the database connection. In a few cases, the application will
simply report the dataset is Null and refuse the run.*

Providing Record Movement Event Handlers

The user is going to want to move from record to record without manually clicking
the cell each time. In addition, you might need some method to move from record
to record when adding automation to the application. Developers normally provide
two or three methods of record pointer movement, all of which use the same code:
toolbar button, menu command, and keyboard shortcut. Listing 9-6 shows the record
movement code we'll use for this example.

Listing 9-6

```
void MainApp::RecordFirst_Click(Object* sender, EventArgs* e)
{
    // Move to the first record.
```

```
      dataGrid1->CurrentRowIndex = 0;
      dataGrid1->Select();
}


void MainApp::RecordPrevious_Click(Object* sender, EventArgs* e)
{
   // Validate pointer location.
   if (dataGrid1->CurrentRowIndex != 0)
      // Move to the previous record.
      dataGrid1->CurrentRowIndex--;
   else
      // Display an error message.
      MessageBox::Show("Already at first record!",
                       "Data Grid Pointer",
                       MessageBoxButtons::OK,
                       MessageBoxIcon::Exclamation);
   dataGrid1->Select();
}


void MainApp::RecordNext_Click(Object* sender, EventArgs* e)
{
   // Move to the next record.
   dataGrid1->CurrentRowIndex++;
   dataGrid1->Select();
}


void MainApp::RecordLast_Click(Object* sender, EventArgs* e)
{
   // Move to the last record.
   DataTable *Current = FoodDataSet->Tables->get_Item(0);
   dataGrid1->CurrentRowIndex = Current->Rows->Count - 1;
   dataGrid1->Select();
}
```

As you can see from the code, all of these methods share two features. First, the method changes the CurrentRowIndex property. Changing this property moves the record pointer. Second, the record movement method uses the **dataGrid1->Select()** method to highlight the new row.

Obtaining the current row so that you can change the CurrentRowIndex property isn't difficult when moving forward or backward. All you need to do is increment or decrement the pointer as needed. The data grid always uses a value of 0 for the first record index, so moving to the first record isn't that difficult either. However, gaining access to the value of the last record in the data grid can prove troublesome.

The only way to access the last row information is to create a DataTable object and fill it with the data for the table in question from the dataset (FoodDataSet). Because the dataset can contain more than one table, you need to track which table resides in each array position of the dataset. The Rows->Count property contains the 1-based value of the current record. However, the data grid uses a 0 base for its record number, so you need to subtract 1 from the value you obtain from Rows->Count. Figure 9-1 shows the final output of the application.

Adding Print Capabilities

As mentioned in Chapter 8, creating reports is an essential task for any database developer. Some people will never see the database application you create except through the reports that it generates. The .NET Framework provides drawing tools

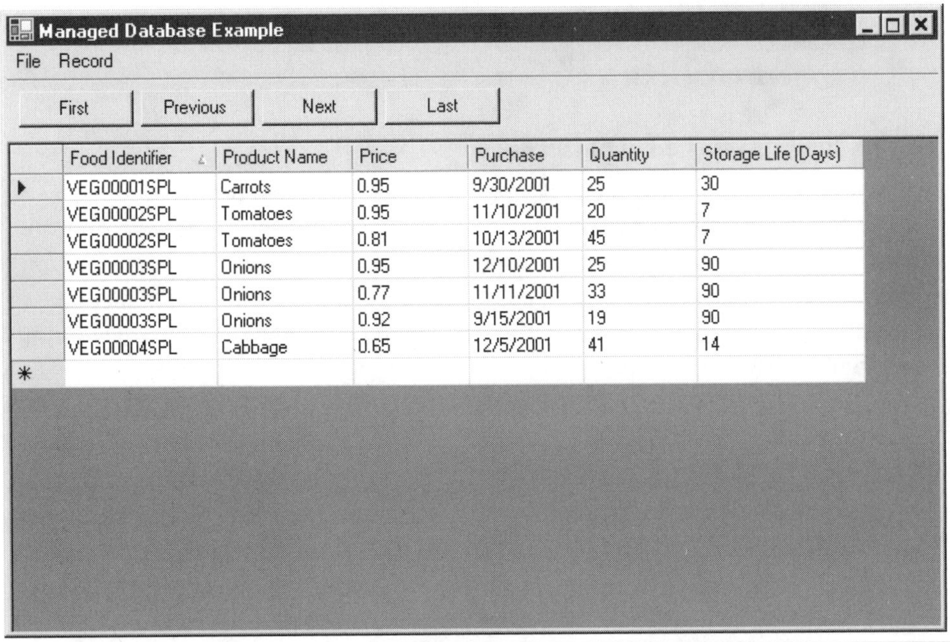
Managed Database Example
File Record
First
Previous
Next
Last
Food Identifier
Product Name
Price
Purchase
Quantity
Storage Life (Days)
VEG00001SPL Carrots 0.95 9/30/2001 25 30
VEG00002SPL Tomatoes 0.95 11/10/2001 20 7
VEG00002SPL Tomatoes 0.81 10/13/2001 45 7
VEG00003SPL Onions 0.95 12/10/2001 25 90
VEG00003SPL Onions 0.77 11/11/2001 33 90
VEG00003SPL Onions 0.92 9/15/2001 19 90
VEG00004SPL Cabbage 0.65 12/5/2001 41 14

Figure 9-1 *The example application produces a grid view of the data in the Access database.*

akin to those found in the Graphics Device Interface (GDI) API for Win32. In fact, Microsoft calls this support GDI+. The only problem with GDI+ is that it provides only two-dimensional drawing support. If you want to use three-dimensional drawing techniques for your reports, you'll need to use DirectX or some other unmanaged technology.

The example provides a simple text-only report that demonstrates basic GDI+ drawing capability. You also have access to drawing primitives such as ellipses. The following sections show you how to perform two essential reporting tasks. First, you must handle the menu commands for creating a report; second, you must generate the report document.

NOTE

Don't attempt to move your drawing code from unmanaged Visual C++ applications to the .NET environment. Microsoft has finally decided to bring some sanity to the drawing environment, so all of the languages now use the same drawing scale. For example, all fonts now use points as a unit of measure unless you specifically configure the application for something else. This standardization is good for developers as whole, because you don't have to guess about units of measure anymore. However, the change also means that some of your code will produce undesired results because of differences in the unit of measure.

Creating the Print Menu Event Handlers

As previously mentioned, you need to provide event handlers for the various print-related menu commands. The good news is that you can create several forms of a menu command using the same drawing code (discussed in the next section). Listing 9-7 shows the menu event handling code we'll use for this example. One of the elements you should look for in the two menu commands that produce output is the PrintPageEventHandler object.

Listing 9-7

```
void MainApp::mnuFile_PageSetup_Click(Object* sender, EventArgs* e)
{
    // Use the current printer settings (default if not set).
    PrnDialog->PrinterSettings = PrnSettings;

    // Show the printer setup dialog.
    PrnDialog->ShowDialog();
}
```

```
void MainApp::mnuFile_Print_Click(Object* sender, EventArgs* e)
{
    PrintDialog     *Dlg = new PrintDialog();    // Print Dialog
    PrintDocument   *PD = new PrintDocument();   // Document Rendering

    // Add an event handler for document printing details.
    PD->add_PrintPage(new PrintPageEventHandler(this, PD_PrintPage));

    // Set up the Print Dialog.
    Dlg->PrinterSettings = PrnSettings;

    // Obtain the print parameters.
    if (Dlg->ShowDialog() == DialogResult::OK)
    {
        // Set up the document for printing.
        PD->PrinterSettings = Dlg->PrinterSettings;

        // Print the document.
        PD->Print();
    }
    else
    {
        // Exit if the user selects Cancel.
        return;
    }
}

void MainApp::mnuFile_PrintPreview_Click(Object* sender, EventArgs* e)
{
    // Create a printer document and a dialog to display it.
    PrintDocument        *PD = new PrintDocument();
    PrintPreviewDialog   *ShowPreview = new PrintPreviewDialog();

    // Add an event handler for document printing details.
    PD->add_PrintPage(new PrintPageEventHandler(this, PD_PrintPage));

    // Assign the printer document to the dialog and then display it.
    ShowPreview->Document = PD;
    ShowPreview->ShowDialog();
}
```

The **mnuFile_PageSetup_Click**() event handler creates a printer configuration dialog box and displays it. Notice that this method assigns the PrnSettings object to the printer dialog. The same object appears in the **mnuFile_Print_Click**() event handler. In both cases, the object represents the current printer settings. The reason you want to use a field to hold this data is to allow the various print routines to coordinate their information. Using this technique means that a change in the **mnuFile_PageSetup_Click**() event handler will also show up in the **mnuFile_Print_Click**() event handler. You can set a variety of options for the printer dialog. Here's what the default print dialog looks like.

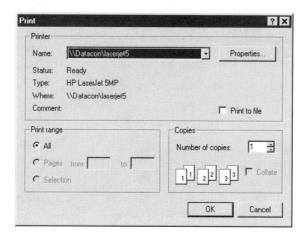

The **mnuFile_Print_Click**() event handler begins by assigning a PrintPageEventHandler object to the printer document. It then presents the user with a print dialog. If the user clicks Cancel in the print dialog, the routine exits. However, if the user clicks OK, The code assigns the printer settings from the print dialog to a print document (PD). The print document invokes the **PD_PrintPage**() print page event handler by executing the **Print**() method.

Creating a print preview still involves the **PD_PrintPage**() event handler. In this case, the print document (PD) becomes part of the ShowReview PrintPreviewDialog object. Printing begins when ShowReview executes the **ShowDialog**() method.

Creating the Print Page Event Handler

The **PD_PrintPage**() event handler is the centerpiece of printing for the example application. In a full-fledged application, you might have several of these event handlers in place. The example application outputs a simple tabular form. Listing 9-8 shows the code we'll use in this case.

Listing 9-8

```
void MainApp::PD_PrintPage(Object* sender, PrintPageEventArgs* ev)
{
    System::Drawing::Font    *docFont;       // Document Font
    System::Drawing::Font    *headFont;      // Heading Font
    System::Drawing::Font    *columnFont;    // Column Font
    float                    yPos = 20;      // Position of text on page.
    int                      Counter;        // Loop counter.
    DataTable                *Current;        // Data table array.

    // Create the font.
    docFont = new System::Drawing::Font("Arial", 12);
    headFont = new System::Drawing::Font("Arial", 24);
    columnFont = new System::Drawing::Font("Arial", 14, FontStyle::Bold);

    // Print the heading.
    ev->Graphics->DrawString("KATZ! Corporation",
                             headFont,
                             Brushes::Black,
                             20,
                             yPos);
    yPos = yPos + headFont->GetHeight() + 20;

    // Print the column headings.
    ev->Graphics->DrawString("Food ID",
                             columnFont,
                             Brushes::Black,
                             20,
                             yPos);
    ev->Graphics->DrawString("Name",
                             columnFont,
                             Brushes::Black,
                             150,
                             yPos);
    ev->Graphics->DrawString("Purchase Date",
                             columnFont,
                             Brushes::Black,
                             250,
                             yPos);
    ev->Graphics->DrawString("Price",
                             columnFont,
```

```
                                   Brushes::Black,
                                   430,
                                   yPos);
        ev->Graphics->DrawString("Quantity",
                                   columnFont,
                                   Brushes::Black,
                                   510,
                                   yPos);
        ev->Graphics->DrawString("Storage Life",
                                   columnFont,
                                   Brushes::Black,
                                   630,
                                   yPos);
        yPos = yPos + columnFont->GetHeight() + 20;

        // Continue printing as long as there is space on the page and
        // we don't run out of things to write.
        Current = FoodDataSet->Tables->get_Item(0);
        for (Counter = 0; Counter < Current->Rows->Count; Counter++)
        {
            // Print the line of text.
            ev->Graphics->DrawString(
                dataGrid1->get_Item(Counter, 0)->ToString(),
                docFont,
                Brushes::Black,
                20,
                yPos);
            ev->Graphics->DrawString(
                dataGrid1->get_Item(Counter, 1)->ToString(),
                docFont,
                Brushes::Black,
                150,
                yPos);
            ev->Graphics->DrawString(
                dataGrid1->get_Item(Counter, 3)->ToString()->Substring(0, 10),
                docFont,
                Brushes::Black,
                250,
                yPos);
            ev->Graphics->DrawString(
                dataGrid1->get_Item(Counter, 2)->ToString(),
                docFont,
                Brushes::Black,
```

```
            430,
            yPos);
        ev->Graphics->DrawString(
            dataGrid1->get_Item(Counter, 4)->ToString(),
            docFont,
            Brushes::Black,
            510,
            yPos);
        ev->Graphics->DrawString(
            dataGrid1->get_Item(Counter, 5)->ToString(),
            docFont,
            Brushes::Black,
            630,
            yPos);

        // Determine the next print position.
        yPos = yPos + docFont->GetHeight() + 10;
    }

    // Tell the application there are no more pages to print.
    ev->HasMorePages = false;
}
```

As you can see, the code begins by creating several drawing tools (fonts). You also have access to pens and brushes, just as you would for an unmanaged application. Unlike applications that use GDI, you don't need to create a device context or select the tools you want to use into the device context. The automatic creation of a device context and use of tools reduces the amount of code you need to write and the complexity of the print code.

After it creates the required tools, the code begins drawing strings on screen. The data won't appear on a printer (or on screen) until after the page is complete. GDI+ creates one page at a time. Each drawing command requires the data you want to output, some positioning information, and a brush or other drawing tool to use for drawing the image.

Notice how the code calculates the next line position. It uses the height of the current font, then adds a little to that number to provide separation between lines. If you use only the font height, the lines of data will stack one on top of another. Some print applications give the user control over this value, so the user can choose between readability and getting more data on one page. Figure 9-2 shows an example of the print preview output of this application.

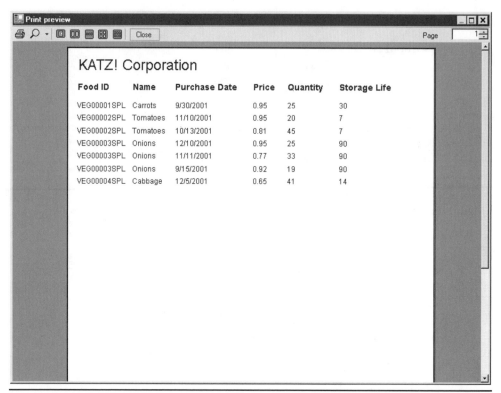

Figure 9-2 *The print preview output of this example shows the use of fonts and spacing between the lines of text.*

Visual C++ and Online Computing

OBJECTIVES:

- ► Learn how to work with PDAs

- ► Develop accessibility friendly Web sites

- ► Create a Web Services application

- ► Use ISAPI to build Web sites that perform well

- ► Create ISAPI Filter and ISAPI Extension Applications

- ► Discover how SOAP builds upon XML

- ► Learn the structure of SOAP messages

- ► Create a SOAP application

Building Applications for the Internet

IN THIS CHAPTER:

Working with PDAs and Other Alternative Devices

Understanding the Web Accessibility
Initiative (WAI)

Working with Web Services

Writing an Application with ASP.NET

There's little doubt that the Internet is going to be a major force in business communications of all types. Many businesses now have virtual private networks (VPNs) in place for employees on the road. Most are at least considering some form of customer relationship management (CRM) that relies on connections to the company's Internet site. You'll also find companies engaged in both business-to-business (B2B) and business-to-consumer (B2C) transactions. In short, the world today is one where distributed applications are a necessary part of business.

This chapter helps you begin the journey into a larger world of distributed application development. Part of that development is the use of alternative devices. We'll discuss the implications of the PDA and I'll show you how to use SOAP to create an application that will run on both your PDA and desktop machine. The use of component technology helps reduce the amount of code needed to perform any given task, and adding a browser front end just makes the job easier. Whenever you create an application that runs on multiple machine types without change, it's a big win for everyone from the client to the developer. As part of the browser-based application discussion, we'll look at the Web Accessibility Initiative (WAI), which is a new mandate to serve those with special needs.

We'll also discuss Microsoft's "not quite ready for prime time" Web Services. It's true that Web Services has a lot of promise, but you'll also encounter more than a few pitfalls when using it. During the Web Services discussion, you'll learn a few of the ins and outs of this new technology. Note that Web Services do run better on both C# and Visual Basic than they do on Visual C++.

Web page programming is a major issue for most developers. ASP offered developers a way to write Web applications quickly and easily. ASP.NET adds to that tradition by offering new features such as *code behind*. We'll discuss how ASP.NET can help you create Web-based applications more quickly. This section contains a simple application that demonstrates the functionality that ASP.NET has to offer.

Working with PDAs and Other Alternative Devices

The world is becoming more mobile all the time. It's nothing to see someone talking over a cell phone today—just a few years ago it was a novelty. When I first saw a Personal Digital Assistant (PDA) in 1998, I thought they might be a passing fad or a device of limited use. Today, that vision has changed significantly. Developers create applications for PDAs now that many people would have thought impossible even a year ago. Helping the wave of new PDA devices along is the proliferation of wireless services and browser clients that work on multiple machines.

SOAP is an excellent protocol for PDAs because the people who use them spend most of their time on the road. PDAs always perform remote communications with the company network, because vendors don't design them to communicate in any other way. In short, if you own a PDA, you need good remote communications of the sort that SOAP can provide.

Obviously, PDAs have special programming requirements. They don't have a hard drive in the normal sense of the word, lack a high-speed processor, and even memory is at a premium. The next section, "Special Needs for PDAs," examines the special programming requirements for PDAs. You'll find that you need to jump over some high hurdles to make some types of applications work on a PDA, even with the help of SOAP.

NOTE

At the time of this writing, Microsoft doesn't provide a toolkit that supports SOAP on a PDA, not even for Windows CE machines. The .NET Compact Framework is in beta testing, but it runs only on a very select few PDAs. Consequently, we'll examine several other SOAP toolkit choices in the "Getting SOAP for Your PDA" section of the chapter. We'll look at choices for several popular PDA operating systems.

Special Needs for PDAs

There's no free lunch—I often wish I had been the first one to say that because it's so true. Companies that want to gain the advantages of using PDAs also have to decide how to handle the special needs of these devices. A PDA isn't a single purpose device like a radio, but it isn't a full-fledged computer either; it's somewhere in between. A PDA has more to offer than the cell phones that some developers will eventually target. However, it can't process data as quickly as your desktop or laptop machine—which means you have to scale your applications down slightly to fit within the hardware confines of the PDA.

TIP

The easiest way to create an application that will run on both laptops and PDAs is to use a browser front end and a component or ASP.NET back end. Using SOAP combined with components offers greater flexibility and better performance. Using ASP.NET enables you to perform changes on the fly and develop the application faster.

After spending some time working with several PDAs as background for this chapter, I found it apparent that SOAP is even less ready for prime time when it comes to these devices than it is for the desktop. (The test machine is a Casio Cassiopeia.)

This makes sense, since software of this sort normally appears on the desktop first. However, it also means that you need to consider your PDA development plans carefully because there are many pitfalls. In all cases, you'll want to build a desktop version of your application before you attempt to create one for your favorite PDA.

NOTE

I also attempted to use a Palm VII as one of the devices for the book. A lack of functionality and dearth of third party tools restricts use of this device for SOAP applications today. Perhaps a third party will eventually create a SOAP client for the Palm, but a lack of tools makes it unusable as a distributed application device today.

Fortunately, you can create a SOAP application for your favorite PDA; it just takes a little more planning. The following sections examine the special needs of PDAs. It's important to note that most of these special needs are in addition to what you need to consider for a desktop application.

The Case for PDAs

Developing SOAP applications for PDAs will require considerable work. Many developers are unused to working with devices that have small screens; the memory limitations are problematic at best, and there's a limit to the number of available development tools. However, the need for PDA development is strong.

Consider the case of Sears. They recently purchased 15,000 PDAs for their business. The deal is worth between $20 and $25 million. That's a lot of PDA power for their staff. Each PDA is equipped with a built-in bar-code scanner and a wireless modem. The company plans to use these new devices for inventory management, price changes, and merchandise pickups. Some developer has a large programming task in the works as I write this. You can bet that such a serious investment comes with an equally serious need to affect the bottom line. In short, PDAs are becoming mainline systems for many different tasks.

Companies often cite two main reasons for switching to PDAs after using other devices. The first reason is that PDAs cost less to buy, operate, and maintain than many other devices. A PDA equipped with the right add-on devices can perform myriad tasks in an intelligent manner.

The second reason is ease of use. PDAs have a limited number of buttons on them, and the functions of each button are easy to understand. The user writes on the screen as they would using pen and paper—the PDA uses handwriting recognition to convert the handwritten information into text.

Sears may be looking toward the future as well. A customer could come into the store with their PDA, beam a product order to a sale clerk's PDA, and get their merchandise faster than ever before. Of course, this use is in the future; most shoppers today don't place their orders in a PDA. The point is that Sears and other companies like K-Mart are already planning for this eventuality.

Unlike older, single-function devices, PDAs are completely programmable. This means an investment in hardware today won't become an albatross tomorrow. Companies can extend the life of an investment by using the same PDA in more than one way. As the PDAs age, they'll handle applications with lower programming requirements.

Special Add-ons

Most vendors design PDAs as electronic versions of the calendar, address book, and personal note taker. Early versions of these products didn't include the mini word processors and spreadsheets you'll find in modern versions. In fact, you can extend many PDAs to double as cameras, scanners, and other devices now with special add-ons.

The PDA isn't exactly a standard device to begin with. There are many hardware implementations, more than a few operating systems, and even different capabilities to consider. When users start adding features to their PDA, you may find that it's nearly impossible to determine what features you can rely on finding. In short, standardization within the company is essential, even if there's chaos outside.

These special add-ons can also work to your advantage. Imagine creating an application to work with one of the camera attachments for a PDA. Each picture is automatically transferred to a remote processing center as the photographer takes pictures. SOAP could make this task relatively easy and automatic. The pictures would be ready for viewing by the time the photographer reaches the home office.

In sum, special PDA add-ons present problems because they create a nonstandard programming environment. On the other hand, these add-ons can create new productivity situations where a developer can provide functionality that no one has ever seen before. The optimum setup is to standardize features required to make SOAP work, such as the type of network interface card (NIC). On the other hand, it's important to consider specialization. Adding a camera to a PDA turns it into a direct image transfer device. PDAs provide the means to extend what computers can do as long as you configure them with application connectivity in mind.

Networking

SOAP relies on a connection between the client and the server. It's easy to create a connection when you're working with a desktop machine. If you can't create a direct connection using a LAN, there are always alternatives, such as using dial-up support. SOAP makes communications between a server and desktop machine easy because there are so many ways to create the connection.

A PDA may not offer much in the way of a network connection. In many cases, the network connection will offer a method to synchronize the PDA with the desktop. The synchronization process works with static data and won't provide you with a live connection to the network. It helps to have a wireless network setup when working with a PDA, since many vendors design PDAs to use this connection type. I was able to find a third party product for connecting a Pocket PC directly to the network using a special NIC.

Every PDA that I looked at does provide some type of modem support, but the modem is usually an add-on and doesn't come with the device. Again, you'll need to standardize the kind of modem support you need for your application. You'll also want to be sure that you can create the desired connection and view material using a browser if you decide to go that route.

The bottom line is that the original purpose of a PDA has little relation to the ways that some people use them today. Vendors design the PDA to provide electronic versions of calendars and address books. Yes, you can run SOAP on a PDA, but only if you have the required live network connection. Obtaining that connection can prove difficult, to say the least.

Operating System

You probably know about the major PDA operating systems on the market today. PDA vendors supply their own operating system. Windows CE is a favorite because it looks and acts much like Windows for the desktop. What you should realize is that the operating system the PDA package says it uses might not be the operating system you'll get. Small variations between machines make the difference between a SOAP toolkit that works and one that won't even install.

Windows CE allows for multiple levels of development. The operating system provides a subset of the features found in the Windows API. This means that you can use the programming techniques you learned in the past if you're already a Windows developer. There's even a special toolkit for working with Windows CE devices (**http://www.microsoft.com/catalog/display.asp?subid=22&site=763&pg=1/**).

NOTE

Unfortunately, about the only part of the current Windows CE toolkit of value for the Visual C++ developer is the emulator it provides. You can use the emulator to validate your application before you move it to the PDA. Microsoft should update this toolkit or provide other resources for PDA development in the near future.

Because Windows CE also contains Internet Explorer, you can interact with it using a browser application. In fact, this is the method that I recommend, because it opens a number of timesaving possibilities, not the least of which is the ability to develop the application on your desktop system before you move it to the PDA. Be warned, though, that the version of Internet Explorer that ships with Windows CE doesn't include full scripting support. You can use JScript (Microsoft's form of JavaScript), but not VBScript (see Internet Programming with Windows CE, **http://www.microsoft.com/mind/0599/webce/webce.htm**, for details).

Windows CE will simply ignore any script commands that it doesn't understand in the HyperText Markup Language (HTML) file. In addition to JScript, you also have access to some Internet Explorer functions, such as **Alert()**, and you can use standard HTML tags. The Windows CE version of Internet Explorer will also work with Java applets. This means that you can create complex browser applications that don't rely on VBScript.

Getting SOAP for Your PDA

If you're the lucky owner of a Pocket PC, getting a SOAP toolkit is relatively painless. Unfortunately, none of the other PDA choices on the market has a SOAP toolkit available as of this writing. (There are rumors of a SOAP toolkit for the Palm, but none of the potential toolkits have appeared on the market yet.) However, given the newness of this technology, you can expect other vendors to provide SOAP toolkit offerings for other platforms eventually. The SOAP::Lite site (**http://www.soaplite. com/**) contains a section of SOAP toolkit links you can check periodically for new additions. This list tells which toolkits will work with PDAs.

TIP

According to a recent Research Portal study, developers are most likely to favor handheld devices that use the Microsoft (32 percent) or Palm (27 percent) operating system. However, if you consider that these top two operating system choices control about 59 percent of the market, it's plain that developing for any given platform could be risky. There are two ways to get around this problem. First, ensure that your company adopts a single handheld device operating system as standard, if possible. Second, make sure you write most of the processing code for a PDA application to run on the server, rather than the client. This allows you to write for multiple PDA operating systems with less effort.

Although there's a long list of SOAP toolkits you find on the SOAP::Lite site, most of them aren't ready for prime time. The vast majority are in beta or not in any released state at all. The choices of usable toolkits for SOAP are extremely limited now, but you should see more choices as SOAP becomes entrenched within the corporate environment. The bottom line is that you not only need to find a SOAP toolkit for your PDA, but you need to find one that's fully functional.

BROWSER ALERT

*It's impossible to know, at this point, just how many SOAP-related specifications will eventually appear on the horizon. One of the best places to learn about new specifications is the XML Web Service Specifications page at GotDotNet (**http://www.gotdotnet.com/team/xml_ wsspecs/default.aspx**). Vendors are now trying to make all of these variations on a theme fit within a framework (**http://www.w3.org/2001/03/WSWS-popa/paper51**). The idea of a framework is to show how the pieces fit together into a cohesive whole. You can monitor progress on the framework as well as other XML projects at **http://www.w3.org/2001/ 04/wsws-proceedings/ibm-ms-framework/**.*

Three new specifications recently appeared on the standards groups agenda: Web Services Routing Protocol (WS-Routing), Direct Internet Message Encapsulation (DIME), and XLANG. Each of these three specifications is so new that there's little in print about them now. Here's the short overview of the three new specifications:

▶ XLANG (**http://www.gotdotnet.com/team/xml_wsspecs/xlang-c/ default.htm**) will allow developers to model business processes using a standardized syntax. Microsoft uses XLANG with their BizTalk Server product. You'll find the XLANG discussion group at **http://discuss. develop.com/xlang.html**.

▶ WS-Routing (**http://msdn.microsoft.com/ws/2001/10/Routing/**) makes it easier to move data using SOAP over transports such as TCP, UDP, and HTTP in one-way, request/response, and peer-to-peer scenarios. You'll also want to check the discussion group for WS-Routing (formerly known as SOAP-RP) at **http://discuss.develop.com/soap-rp.html**.

▶ DIME (**http://gotdotnet.com/team/xml_wsspecs/dime/default.aspx**) is used to package data using a binary format in a form called *payloads*. You'll find the DIME discusson group at **http://discuss.develop.com/dime.html**.

The following paragraphs provide a quick overview of some of the better SOAP toolkit choices for PDAs today. This list isn't exhaustive or even partially complete. I chose to concentrate on those toolkits that are close enough to completion that you can use them for development today.

pocketSOAP

This is the best choice if you own a Pocket PC. The same developer, Simon Fell, produces Simon's Soap Server Services for COM (4S4C) and pocketSOAP (**http://www.pocketsoap.com/**). You'll find desktop and PDA versions of pocketSOAP, making it easy to develop applications on your desktop machine and move them to your PDA later. This is especially true if you use scripts within a Web page, as we will for the examples in this chapter. The Pocket PC version is easy to install and works just as well within the confines of the Pocket PC's feature set.

Although this product is still in beta, you'll find that most applications work with few problems. The only major problem that I experienced during testing was an occasional HTTP timeout error. The developer has promised to keep working on the kinks, so you'll likely find this product an optimum choice for PDA development.

The only caveat when using pocketSOAP is that you need to create the message by hand. It doesn't support a high-level API as the Microsoft SOAP Toolkit does. However, this actually turned out to be beneficial when working with more than one platform (as we'll see in the examples). The bottom line is that you need to be prepared to spend a little more time coding when working with pocketSOAP, but the outcome is well worth the effort.

WASP

Web Applications and Services Platform (WASP) (**http://www.systinet.com/idooxoap.html**) is a fully developed desktop product. It currently comes in Java and C++ flavors, which many developers will find useful for both Web-based and desktop applications. The vendor is currently working on a version of WASP for the Pocket PC. Unfortunately, the PDA product wasn't ready at the time of writing.

One of the advantages of WASP is that it provides cross-platform support. The server part of the product runs on Linux or Unix. Eventually, it will run on Windows without modification as well. (There's a downloadable ISAPI package for WASP on the Web site, but you need to put the package together before you can use it.) The client runs on Linux, Unix, and all flavors of Windows (except Windows CE now).

TIP

WASP provides the best support for multi-part MIME messages. The support is only available on Linux and Unix machines now, but may become available on other platforms. Compatibility issues flaw the MIME support, but the vendor may have them fixed by the time you read this. You shouldn't count on MIME support for PDAs anytime soon, because of resource limitations. However, given the progress this particular vendor has made, the possibility of MIME support on a PDA does exist.

A major goal of this product is to provide the same programming experience no matter which platform you're using. Like pocketSOAP, this means that you should be able to move at least some of your code between platforms. However, the Java version is more likely to provide seamless support.

WASP also provides special support for the Tomcat server. You can download versions with or without Enterprise Java Beans (EJB). It was interesting to note that several of the specialty downloads included notes about daily product builds—an indicator of the volatility of the SOAP toolkit market.

Creating a Simple PDA Application

Now that you have a better idea of what creating a distributed PDA application involves, it's time to look at a simple example. The example queries the server for some server statistics. I didn't choose anything too exciting, but the information is typical of what a network administrator might want for a remote monitoring application.

The following sections provide a detailed look at the server code, client code, and application testing. The example uses a single component for data transfer, which means debugging should be relatively easy. We won't explore all of the intricacies of SOAP in this chapter. Make sure you look at the "An Overview of SOAP" and "Writing SOAP Applications" sections of Chapter 11 for more details.

NOTE

This example only runs with pocketSOAP. You must install pocketSOAP on both the development machine and the target PDA. In some cases, the example may not run, even on another Pocket PC, because of small differences in operating system and hardware implementation between vendors. The example will run definitely on a Casio Cassiopeia and likely on most Compaq PDAs.

Creating the Component Code

The component for this example retrieves the various computer name information from the server using the **GetComputerNameEx()** Win32 API call. Knowing which computer you're working with from a remote location is important, so this is a piece of information that everyone will want to know how to retrieve. Of course, a full-fledged application would supply a great deal more information than presented here, but this component represents a good starting point.

NOTE

You'll find the complete source code for this example in the \Chapter 10\CompName folder of the source code CD. The \Chapter 10\LocalCompNameTest folder contains a local test application you can use to validate that the component is properly registered and working correctly.

You'll need to create an ATL Project. Make sure you clear the Attributed option, select DLL as your server type, select Allow merging of proxy/stub code, and select Support MFC on the Application Settings tab. Once you create the project, add a new object named NameValues, then add two methods to it named GetCompName and GetAllNames. Listing 10-1 shows the input and output parameters for the component, along with the component code.

Listing 10-1

```
STDMETHODIMP CNameValues::GetCompName(MYCOMPUTER_NAME_FORMAT NameType, BSTR* Return)
{
   AFX_MANAGE_STATE(AfxGetStaticModuleState());

   CString oComputerName;  // Buffer to hold computer name data.
   ULONG   ulBufferSize = MAX_COMPUTERNAME_LENGTH + 1;

   // Setup data conversion.
   USES_CONVERSION;

   // See if there is a NetBIOS name for this item.
   if (GetComputerNameEx((COMPUTER_NAME_FORMAT)NameType,
      oComputerName.GetBuffer(MAX_COMPUTERNAME_LENGTH + 1),
      &ulBufferSize))
   {
      // Release the string buffer.
      oComputerName.ReleaseBuffer(-1);

      // Convert buffer contents to an OLE string.
      *Return = T2BSTR(oComputerName.GetBuffer(80));
      oComputerName.ReleaseBuffer(-1);
   }

   // If not, display a failure string.
   else
      *Return = T2BSTR("Value Not Available");

   // return the standard result.
   return S_OK;
}

STDMETHODIMP CNameValues::GetAllNames(BSTR* Return)
{
   AFX_MANAGE_STATE(AfxGetStaticModuleState());

   CString  AllNames;    // Return value array.
   BSTR     RetString;   // Return string from call.
```

```
//Fill the array with values.
USES_CONVERSION;
AllNames = "ComputerNameDnsDomain\t\t\t";
GetCompName(DnsDomain, &RetString);
AllNames = AllNames + CString(RetString);
AllNames = AllNames + "\r\nComputerNameDnsFullyQualified\t\t";
GetCompName(DnsFullyQualified, &RetString);
AllNames = AllNames + CString(RetString);
AllNames = AllNames + "\r\nComputerNameDnsHostname\t\t\t";
GetCompName(DnsHostname, &RetString);
AllNames = AllNames + CString(RetString);
AllNames = AllNames + "\r\nComputerNameNetBIOS\t\t\t";
GetCompName(NetBIOS, &RetString);
AllNames = AllNames + CString(RetString);
AllNames = AllNames + "\r\nComputerNamePhysicalDnsDomain\t\t";
GetCompName(PhysicalDnsDomain, &RetString);
AllNames = AllNames + CString(RetString);
AllNames = AllNames + "\r\nComputerNamePhysicalDnsFullyQualified\t";
GetCompName(PhysicalDnsFullyQualified, &RetString);
AllNames = AllNames + CString(RetString);
AllNames = AllNames + "\r\nComputerNamePhysicalDnsHostname\t\t";
GetCompName(PhysicalDnsHostname, &RetString);
AllNames = AllNames + CString(RetString);
AllNames = AllNames + "\r\nComputerNamePhysicalNetBIOS\t\t";
GetCompName(PhysicalNetBIOS, &RetString);
AllNames = AllNames + CString(RetString);

// Return the result.
*Return = T2BSTR(AllNames);

return S_OK;
}
```

As you can see from the listing, the code for **GetCompName()** isn't that complex. We retrieve the computer name value based on the type of value the user wants to retrieve. Windows supports several levels of network names, so knowing how to retrieve all of them is a real plus. After the code retrieves the computer name value, it returns it to the client. There are a few transitions that take place to ensure application compatibility, but that's about it. Notice that the method uses an odd input value named MYCOMPUTER_NAME_FORMAT. This is an enumeration found in the IDL file. It replicates the COMPUTER_NAME_FORMAT enumeration found in the various C++ header files. Here's the enumeration:

```
typedef enum MYCOMPUTER_NAME_FORMAT
{
    NetBIOS,
    DnsHostname,
```

```
    DnsDomain,
    DnsFullyQualified,
    PhysicalNetBIOS,
    PhysicalDnsHostname,
    PhysicalDnsDomain,
    PhysicalDnsFullyQualified,
    Max
}MYCOMPUTER_NAME_FORMAT;
```

The reason you want to include this enumeration is to provide non-Visual C++ clients with a list of acceptable input values. For example, Visual Basic users won't have access to the COMPUTER_NAME_FORMAT enumeration. The reason you have to use a different name and even different enumeration words is to avoid conflicts with the Visual C++ enumeration.

This component won't compile until you make one additional change. Open the stdafx.h file and look for the #define _WIN32_WINNT 0x0400 entry. Comment this entry out and add this one instead:

```
#define _WIN32_WINNT  0x0500
```

Creating the Client Code

The client code for this section is somewhat complex compared to other SOAP examples in the book because we have to use a third party toolkit. For one thing, we need to service two buttons instead of one. However, the Microsoft SOAP Toolkit also requires slightly different input than pocketSOAP, so there are differences in the message formatting code as well. Listing 10-2 shows the client source code for this example.

Listing 10-2

```
<HTML>
<HEAD>
<TITLE>CompName JScript Example</TITLE>

<SCRIPT LANGUAGE="JScript">
function cmdGetSingleName_Click()
{
    var SOAPEnv;     // SOAP envelope
    var Transport;   // SOAP transport
    var Param;       // Parameter list
    var SOAPParam;   // SOAP method call parameters.
    var RecData;     // Received data holder
```

```javascript
        // Create the envelope.
        SOAPEnv = new ActiveXObject("pocketSOAP.Envelope");
        SOAPEnv.MethodName = "GetCompName";
        SOAPEnv.URI = "http://tempuri.org/message/";

        // Create a parameter to place within the envelope.
        Param = SOAPEnv.CreateParameter("NameType",
            window.document.SampleForm1.comboName.value, "");

        // Send the request and receive the data.
        Transport = new ActiveXObject("pocketSOAP.HTTPTransport");
        Transport.SOAPAction = "http://tempuri.org/action/NameValuesProc.GetCompName"
        Transport.Send("http://WinServer/soapexamples/ComputerName/CompNameProc.WSDL",
            SOAPEnv.Serialize());
            RecData = Transport.Receive();
            SOAPEnv.Parse(RecData);

        // Display the result.
        RecData = SOAPEnv.Parameters.Item(0);
        window.document.SampleForm1.Results.value = RecData.Value;
    }

function cmdGetAllNames_Click()
{
    var SOAPEnv;     // SOAP envelope
    var Transport;   // SOAP transport
    var Param;       // Parameter list
    var SOAPParam;   // SOAP method call parameters.
    var RecData;     // Received data holder

    // Create the envelope.
    SOAPEnv = new ActiveXObject("pocketSOAP.Envelope");
    SOAPEnv.MethodName = "GetAllNames";
    SOAPEnv.URI = "http://tempuri.org/message/";

    // Create a parameter to place within the envelope.
    Param = SOAPEnv.CreateParameter("NameType",
        window.document.SampleForm1.comboName.value, "");

    // Send the request and receive the data.
    Transport = new ActiveXObject("pocketSOAP.HTTPTransport");
    Transport.SOAPAction = "http://tempuri.org/action/NameValuesProc.GetAllNames"
```

```
      Transport.Send("http://WinServer/soapexamples/ComputerName/CompNameProc.WSDL",
          SOAPEnv.Serialize());
      RecData = Transport.Receive();
      SOAPEnv.Parse(RecData);

      // Display the result.
      RecData = SOAPEnv.Parameters.Item(0);
      window.document.SampleForm1.Results.value = RecData.Value;
}
</SCRIPT>

</HEAD>

<BODY>
<!Add a heading->
<CENTER><H1>Computer Name Component Test</H1></CENTER>

<!Use a form to test out the VBScript.->
<FORM NAME="SampleForm1">

<!Create a text entry control.->
Select a single computer name if needed:<BR>

<select name=comboName>
<option value=0>ComputerNameNetBIOS
<option value=1>ComputerNameDnsHostname
<option value=2>ComputerNameDnsDomain
<option value=3>ComputerNameDnsFullyQualified
<option value=4>ComputerNamePhysicalNetBIOS
<option value=5>ComputerNamePhysicalDnsHostname
<option value=6>ComputerNamePhysicalDnsDomain
<option value=7>ComputerNamePhysicalDnsFullyQualified
<option value=8>ComputerNameMax
</select><P><P>

<!Define a place to put the results.->
Result values: <BR>
<TEXTAREA ROWS=11 COLS=60 NAME="Results">
</TEXTAREA><P><P>

<!-Create the two required buttons.->
<INPUT TYPE=button
       NAME=cmdGetSingleName
       VALUE="Get Single Name"
       ONCLICK=cmdGetSingleName_Click()>
<INPUT TYPE=button
       NAME=cmdGetAllNames
```

```
    VALUE="Get All Names"
    ONCLICK=cmdGetAllNames_Click()>

</FORM>
</BODY>
</HTML>
```

This example uses a five-step process for each function. First, you create an envelope. Second, you place data within the envelope. Third, you need to initialize the data. Fourth, you send and receive the data. Finally, you display the data on screen. The HTML code is difficult to optimize for a small screen because of the amount of data we need to display. We'll see later how you can overcome these problems without modifying the server side component.

TIP

Many developers now rely on the eXtensible HyperText Markup Language (XHTML) (http://www.w3.org/TR/xhtml1/) to work with PDAs. Using XHTML has the advantage of keeping the screens readable and small enough for a PDA. The disadvantage is that XHTML often makes desktop displays unusable or, at least, unfriendly. Make sure you choose between HTML and XHTML at the outset of your development project according to how you intend to use the Web pages later.

Testing the Application

The Computer Name example doesn't work quite the same on a PDA as it does on the desktop. The reason is simple—a PDA lacks the screen real estate to display this application fully. Part of the testing process is to ensure the screen remains close to the original (to keep training costs down) while ensuring readability. Figure 10-1 shows the output from this example if you click Get Single Name.

The application does work the same as a desktop application would from a functionality perspective. You still use a drop-down list box to select a computer name type. The buttons still produce the same results as before. Maintaining this level of compatibility between a desktop and PDA application is essential to the success of the application. Any application that requires the user to relearn a business process is doomed to failure, no matter how nice the display looks.

Fortunately, this example is reasonably small. Your testing process must include resource usage and other factors that affect PDA application performance. Complex database applications won't run very well on a PDA, because they require too many resources. Of course, you can always get around the problem by using more server side processing and presenting the PDA with semi-finished, rather than raw, results.

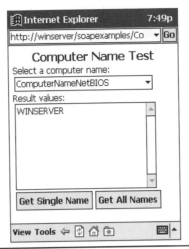

Figure 10-1   *Screen real estate makes a difference in appearance in some PDA applications.*

Addressing PDA Display Issues

Most developers realize before they begin their first project that working with a PDA is going to be a challenge. The problem is that the challenge usually turns out greater than expected. Small displays with limited color capability are something that most developers consigned to the past. The old techniques that developers used in order to conserve screen space are suddenly appearing again.

The following sections discuss several important display issues when working with a PDA. This section won't provide an in-depth treatise on the subject, but you'll walk away with some fresh ideas for your next SOAP application.

Screen Size

Many users today have 17 or 19 inch monitors capable of a minimum resolution of 1280×1024. Developers have taken advantage of the screen real estate to create better applications that display more data at one time. Even Microsoft uses higher resolutions as a baseline for applications—many of their application screens won't fit on a 800×600 display anymore.

Everything you want to do with your PDA has to fit within 320×200 pixels. That's a lot smaller than the typical computer screen. In addition, some PDAs use black and white displays in place of color, so you can't even use some of the modern tricks to make the display look nicer. In short, PDA screens tend to look a bit plain and developers normally find themselves feverishly cutting their application screens down to size.

No matter what you do, it's impossible to fit 1280×1024 worth of application screen in a 320×200 space in many cases. When this happens, you'll find that you need to make some compromises in the display. For example, even the computer name example in this chapter ran into problems displaying all of the information that it could provide. Here's an illustration that shows the results of some cutting that I performed to make the application data fit and still look reasonably nice:

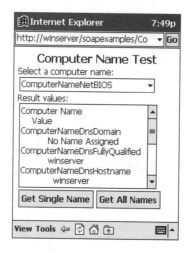

In this case, I indented the second line of each data entry to allow enough space for long entries. Notice that the data is still readable and the user won't have to guess about the formatting. Of course, this is still a less than perfect solution, since the data does appear on two lines.

It's important to keep every application element on a single screen if possible. The example application does this by sacrificing application data display space. The user can scroll through the data in the Result values field without moving other screen elements around. The stylus provided with a PDA doesn't lend itself to mouse-like movement.

Make sure you consider XHTML for complex applications with many elements. It allows you to display your application in segments with relative ease. Other options include using the Handheld Device Markup Language (HDML) (**http://www.w3.org/ TR/NOTE-Submission-HDML-spec.html**) or Wireless Markup Language (WML) (**http://www.oasis-open.org/cover/wap-wml.html**). Both of these technologies use the concept of cards and decks to break information up into easily managed pieces. Of course, the PDA you use has to provide support for these standards before you can use the tags within a document. As with XHTML, using either HDML or WML will prevent your page from appearing properly on a desktop machine.

Using Color

Developers have gotten used to seeing colors on their applications. Color dresses up a drab display and makes the application more fun to use. In addition, using color presents cues to the user. For example, many users associate green with a good condition and red with something bad. In short, most applications rely heavily on color today, and with good reason.

Depending on the PDA you use, you may not have any color at all. For example, many Palm models present the world in shades of gray. Even if a PDA does provide color support akin to the Pocket PC, the developer still has to use color carefully.

The problem for PDA users is that the screen is already small. If they get into an area with bright sunlight, seeing the screen might become impossible, especially if it's filled with colors that don't work well in such an environment. Notice that the PDA screenshots in this chapter are mainly black and white. The actual screens contain some color for the icons, but that's about it. Since these applications don't need color to present the information they can provide, it's possible to rely on a black and white image.

Using color to display icons or to convey a message is still a good idea, even in the world of the PDA. For example, a red icon could signal danger or tell the user to wait without using up screen real estate for words. Of course, you need to explain the meaning of the color changes within a manual or help file (preferably both).

Pointer Pointers

Most PDA users rely on a pointer to do all of their work. Sure, a few PDAs do offer a keyboard and mouse as separate items, but most of these offerings are bulky and difficult to use. Pointer use is one of the reasons that you want to keep your application on one screen or use multiple screens when necessary. Scrolling on a PDA screen is less than intuitive and requires some level of skill to master.

SOAP applications that you move from the desktop to the PDA will require some modification for screen size in many cases. While you're working on the screen, it might be a good time to add some pointer friendly features as well. For example, try to make as many tasks a "single pointer option" as possible. The user should be able to point to what they want and allow the PDA to complete it for them.

You can also build intelligence into the application. A SOAP application normally has a direct connection to the server. You can use some of the server's processing power to make things easier on the user. Most PDAs already include predictive logic as part of their setup. For example, as you write something, the PDA tries to guess the entire word. When it guesses the correct word, you can click on it and save some writing time. The same principle works for other activities as well. For example, a SOAP application could automatically display a data screen that the user needs most often, rather than force the user to dig through several screens to find it.

Pointer-friendly programs also make tasks "yes or no" propositions. Again, this allows the user to accomplish the task with a single click, rather than having to write something down. The point is to make the PDA as efficient as possible so the user doesn't get frustrated trying to do something simple.

Understanding PDA Security Issues

Many network administrators view the PDA with more than a little suspicion, and for good reason. The media has painted the PDA as a device that is so open that anyone can access it at any time, so that smart users keep all of their sensitive data on the company computer and just place lists of tasks on their PDA. Of course, such a view defeats the entire purpose of having a PDA in the first place. A PDA should be an extension of your workplace not a hindrance to avoid.

Many of the security concerns surrounding PDAs today are based on a perception that they're all wireless devices. Many PDAs use network or modem connections, not wireless connections. The PDAs that do provide wireless access tend to err on the side of safety whenever possible. Vendors realize that wireless access is both a blessing and curse for many companies. However, the wireless issue probably isn't much of a concern for the SOAP developer. Count on many of your users to rely on modem or direct network interface card (NIC) connections. For example, the Pocket PC provides a slot that will accommodate an Ethernet card that provides a direct network connection.

One of the biggest security issues for all PDA users is data storage. There are actually two threats to consider. The first is that someone could access sensitive data if they stole your PDA (or, at least, borrowed it for a while). Wireless or not, the person who has the PDA also has access to the data it contains. The second threat is data loss. Many PDAs lose all of their information once the main battery is exhausted. (Some PDAs provide a backup battery that retains the contents of memory until the user replaces or recharges the main battery.) Unless the user backs up on a regular basis while on the road, the data is lost.

SOAP can come to the rescue in this case by allowing the user to store all data on a central server in a secure location. The application remains on the client machine, but the data remains secure at the main office. Of course, there has to be some flexibility built into the security plan so that users can operate their PDA in a disconnected mode. PDA vendors will likely add some form of biometric protection to their PDAs in the future. For example, the user might have to press their thumb in a certain area in the back when starting the PDA so the PDA can check their identity.

Some security issues involve limitations in the PDA itself. For example, with a desktop application, users can be asked to enter their name and password. The application asks the server for verification before it requests any data access. The pointer PDA users must use to enter data hampers the security procedure. It's possible that they'll end up entering the password more than the three times that good applications normally allow. The next thing you'll hear is a frustrated user on the telephone asking why they can't get into their application. Security is required, but any attempt to implement security that causes user frustration is almost certain to fail.

Another PDA-specific security issue to consider is one of resources. Heavy security consumes many resources. A desktop user notices some slowing of their computer when they're working with a secure application. The slowing is due to the work of the security protocol in the background. With the limited resources of a PDA, you probably can't implement any level of heavy security without causing the application to run too slowly. The PDA already runs SOAP applications slower because it uses a browser-based application over a relatively slow connection. Adding to this problem is one way to lose user confidence in your application.

PDAs do suffer from every other security problem that SOAP applications normally experience. A lack of built-in security will allow prying eyes to see the data that the user transfers to the home office (at least if someone is actually looking). Unfortunately, the list of available security add-ons for PDAs is extremely limited. Theoretically, you can use technologies such as SSL with a PDA. We've already discussed the limitations of some of these technologies in previous chapters, so I won't go into them again here. Needless to say, using a PDA involves some security risk that you'll need to overcome.

Understanding the Web Accessibility Initiative (WAI)

The Web Accessibility Initiative (WAI) might seem like a foreign set of words, unless you work within the government. The WAI is a World Wide Web Consortium (W3C) specification that tells developers how to create Web sites that are friendly for those who have physical challenges. Most Web sites today don't work especially well with a screen reader because the various gizmos get in the way. Likewise, small hotspots and other oddities make Web sites so unfriendly that those with special needs can't use them.

BROWSER ALERT

You can find out more about WAI in several places. The first place to look is the W3C site at **http://www.w3.org/WAI/**. *You'll find more than just a set of guidelines here; the site provides real business reasons to adopt WAI for your next Web site. Webmonkey* (**http://hotwired.lycos.com/webmonkey/99/20/index0a.html**) *also has an in-depth review of WAI and why it's important to you as a developer. Finally, you'll want to check out the trace.wisc.edu* (**http://trace.wisc.edu/world/web/**) *Web site for a great overview of WAI as a whole.*

Many governments are under pressure to make their Web sites friendlier and easier to use for those with physical challenges. For example, government Web sites in the Unites States are required to meet the WAI specification. It won't be long before most government contracts will have to meet these requirements as well. However, WAI is for everyone. Every person who can't access your Web site is a potential customer, source of information, or partner prevented from communicating with you about your business.

What is WAI all about? This section can't provide you with a detailed view of precisely what you need to do to meet the requirements, but essentially WAI is about making your Web site usable. For example, when you place a graphic on your Web page, do you also include alternative text describing the graphic? Someone with poor vision might not be able to see the graphic, but could participate in the Web site by hearing a description of the picture.

The WAI requirements for participation become more intense as the media on your Web site becomes more complex. For example, you might include a movie clip on your Web site. Someone who can't see well won't be able to follow the presentation if every aspect of the movie clip relies on visual or aural presentation. To help someone in this situation, you'd need an audio description that tells the viewer what a sighted person would see. As another example, someone who can't hear well might not hear all of the sounds within the movie clip. You'd need to add something approximating closed captioning to meet this person's need.

Don't get the idea that WAI helps only those with physical challenges; it also helps you reach those who access your site using an alternative device. For example, someone who accesses your Web site with a telephone won't be able to see the information on screen. The same audio description that helps someone who has difficulty seeing will help those who want to access your Web site with a telephone.

Working with Web Services

Web Services—it's the new overused phrase in the computer dictionary. Visual Studio .NET provides support for Web Services on several levels, not all of which are obvious and many of which don't work right now. Let's begin with a basic definition. The loose interpretation that most people use for Web Services is an application component that's offered for use through an Internet connection. For example, most businesses that offer support through a SOAP connection meet the criteria of a Web Service. In fact, the Web Service Description Language (WSDL) file required for SOAP communication serves the purpose of advertising the Web Service and making it accessible to those who need it.

If you want to follow the common route to Web Services, then the SOAP example in this chapter and the one in Chapter 11 will help you get started. Many developers are using this route because other techniques that Microsoft would like you to use are simply too unstable now to provide a viable method for implementing applications of any complexity over a real Internet connection. Using the Microsoft SOAP Toolkit or one of the third party offerings mentioned in this chapter will work, even with Visual Studio .NET.

BROWSER ALERT

*Even though you'll hear a lot of conflicting information regarding Web Services, most developers would agree that the term indicates public exposure of code through some form of XML messaging over the Internet. Microsoft isn't the only company that's getting into Web Services, so it pays to look in other places to keep your options open. For example, a recent InfoWorld article (**http://www.infoworld.com/articles/tc/xml/01/12/03/011203tckylix.xml**) discusses what companies are doing for other platforms.*

Another level of Web Services is the .NET My Services (formerly Hailstorm) that Microsoft is currently offering to developers as a means of exposing their code. To some extent, this form of Web Services is simply a matter of packaging, not of technology. However, packaging is everything, in this case, because you're exposing a service to the public in the form of reusable code. One company, XDegrees, has already started using this peer-to-peer setup. (You can read about their solution at **http://www.infoworld.com/articles/hn/xml/01/11/13/011113hnxdegrees. xml?1114wewebservices**.) This solution makes use of Passport for verification. You can read more about .NET My Services at **http://www.microsoft.com/myservices/**.

Some of the promises of Web Services, at least for .NET, won't come true until Microsoft releases its line of .NET servers that will theoretically support XML natively. However, given that this is a new concept, it will probably take time for Microsoft to work out the bugs. In short, the Web Services support you get with your shiny new .NET server might be of dubious utility at best.

The final level of Web services, at least for this book, is the use of special Web Services projects from Visual C++ .NET. At the time of this writing, none of those projects will produce workable code. When Microsoft releases Visual Studio .NET, you will have a choice of using the ATL Server Web Service or the Managed C++ Web Service project. Both projects will help you create what amounts to another form of SOAP application, but hopefully with fewer glitches and compatibility problems.

Writing an Application with ASP.NET

Creating Web applications still belongs more in the art form department than the science department. Developers who can create great Web applications quickly are still somewhat rare in the development community. One of the most common technologies for developing applications quickly is Active Server Pages (ASP).

NOTE

The way Microsoft designed the ASP.NET designer makes it difficult to save the project in a manner that transfers easily to another machine. As a result, the example project (located on the source code CD) might not load in this case. You can, however, still access the individual source code files. If you can't access the project in this section, you'll need to create the project skeleton and transfer the code from the existing project on the source code CD.

Of course, ASP represents an earlier effort on Microsoft's part. ASP support is actually old news .NET. Developers have used ASP for several years now. During that time, developers have created a wish list of new features they consider essential. This is the basis for the improved form of ASP found in Visual Studio .NET, ASP.NET.

You can still use all of your existing ASP files with ASP.NET. Unlike some parts of the .NET upgrade (such as most of your database applications, as discussed in Chapters 8 and 9), ASP.NET provides full backward compatibility. However, it also provides all of those new features that developers want.

Two of the most important features are "code behind" and ASP controls. One of the biggest problems with ASP files right now is that they mix code and HTML elements. The mixture makes ASP files somewhat difficult to read. Code behind rids the developer of this problem by placing the script code for a page in a separate file. This technique also makes it easier to reuse existing code, because the code exists separately from the HTML elements used to render the results on screen.

Another problem with ASP is that it relies heavily on plain HTML tags to get the job done. The problems with HTML tags are that they don't work like the controls found in desktop applications and that they come with a wealth of limitations. ASP controls eliminate these problems by providing full control support for ASP development. The client still sees HTML tags, but the server side entity is a control. In short, ASP controls enable the developer to create applications faster and with better functionality, without requiring anything new on the part of the user.

Let's consider a very simple example consisting of a Test pushbutton and a label. When you click the Test pushbutton, the Web server displays a message within the label. Unlike with the managed Visual C++ environment, you actually gain access to Designer support for ASP.NET. Figure 10-2 shows the simple setup for this example.

Notice that the designer provides two tabs. The HTML tab shows you the code for the display shown in Figure 10-2. Figure 10-3 shows what this code looks like. Notice that most of it is the standard HTML tags you've used in the past. New to ASP.NET are the <asp> tags, which we'll discuss as the section progresses.

Now that you know a little bit about the Designer, let's talk about the code for this example. Listing 10-3 shows the ASPX (ASP eXtended) page required for this

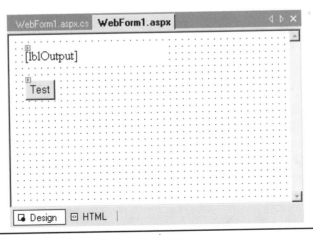

Figure 10-2   *A simple ASP.NET setup using the Designer*

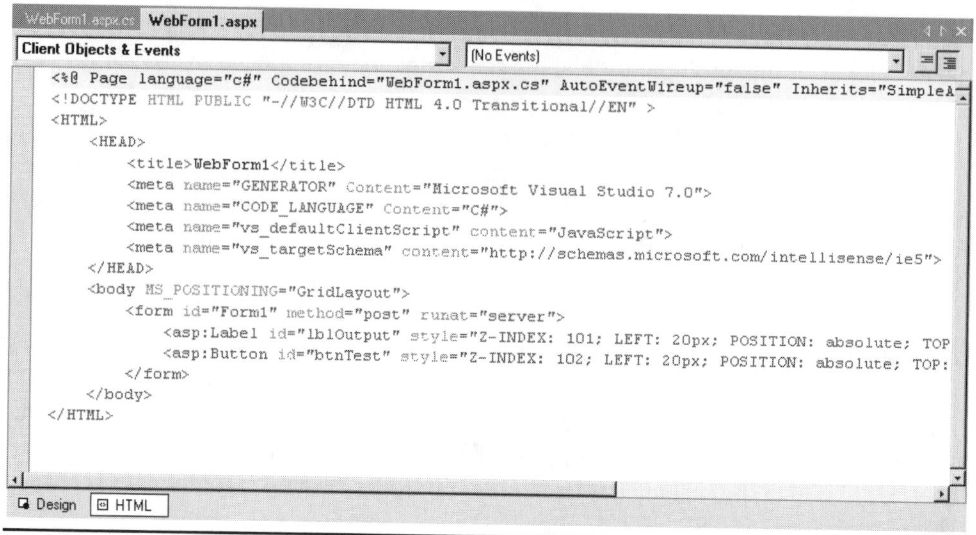

```
WebForm1.aspx.cs   WebForm1.aspx                                          ◀ ▶ ×
Client Objects & Events                    ▼  [No Events]                    ▼  ≡⟨≡
   <%@ Page language="c#" Codebehind="WebForm1.aspx.cs" AutoEventWireup="false" Inherits="SimpleA
   <!DOCTYPE HTML PUBLIC "-//W3C//DTD HTML 4.0 Transitional//EN" >
   <HTML>
       <HEAD>
           <title>WebForm1</title>
           <meta name="GENERATOR" Content="Microsoft Visual Studio 7.0">
           <meta name="CODE_LANGUAGE" Content="C#">
           <meta name="vs_defaultClientScript" content="JavaScript">
           <meta name="vs_targetSchema" content="http://schemas.microsoft.com/intellisense/ie5">
       </HEAD>
       <body MS_POSITIONING="GridLayout">
           <form id="Form1" method="post" runat="server">
               <asp:Label id="lblOutput" style="Z-INDEX: 101; LEFT: 20px; POSITION: absolute; TOP
               <asp:Button id="btnTest" style="Z-INDEX: 102; LEFT: 20px; POSITION: absolute; TOP:
           </form>
       </body>
   </HTML>

  ◀                                                                              ▶
 ⌨ Design  ⊞ HTML
```

Figure 10-3   *The HTML tab of the Designer shows the code behind the Designer display.*

example. (You'll find this project in the \Chapter 10\SimpleASP folder of the source code CD.)

Listing 10-3

```
<%@ Page language="c#" Codebehind="WebForm1.aspx.cs"
    AutoEventWireup="false" Inherits="SimpleASP.WebForm1" %>
<!DOCTYPE HTML PUBLIC "-//W3C//DTD HTML 4.0 Transitional//EN" >
<HTML>
    <HEAD>
        <title>WebForm1</title>
        <meta name="GENERATOR" Content="Microsoft Visual Studio 7.0">
        <meta name="CODE_LANGUAGE" Content="C#">
        <meta name="vs_defaultClientScript" content="JavaScript">
        <meta name="vs_targetSchema"
            content="http://schemas.microsoft.com/intellisense/ie5">
    </HEAD>
    <body MS_POSITIONING="GridLayout">
        <form id="Form1" method="post" runat="server">
            <asp:Label id="lblOutput"
                        style="Z-INDEX: 101;
```

```
                    LEFT: 20px;
                    POSITION: absolute;
                    TOP: 16px"
                    runat="server"
                    Width="173px">
        </asp:Label>
        <asp:Button id="btnTest"
                    style="Z-INDEX: 102;
                    LEFT: 20px;
                    POSITION: absolute;
                    TOP: 55px"
                    runat="server"
                    Text="Test">
        </asp:Button>
      </form>
   </body>
</HTML>
```

Notice that the page begins with a reference to WebForm1.aspx.cs. This statement is the glue that binds the Web page to the associated script. Code behind enables you to separate your code from the rest of the application. All that your ASPX file will contain is the actual display code—the logic behind the code appears in a separate file (a C# file in this case).

You should already recognize the tags within the <HEAD>. These tags remain unchanged from ASP for the most part. However, when you get to the <BODY>, you'll notice that some things have changed. The page now contains <asp:> tags that enable you to describe the page elements using the same properties as you'd use on a standard desktop application. In fact, when you work with the pages in the IDE, you'll use the same Toolbox that you would use for a desktop application. The feel of designing for the Web is the same as it is for the desktop.

The code behind page, WebForm1.aspx.cs, looks similar to any desktop application you create with C#. The application does use some namespaces we haven't discussed yet, and you'll find the control display code is missing—but otherwise it looks like a standard desktop application (see the file on the source code CD for details). Here's the simple event handler for displaying the test text within the label:

```
private void btnTest_Click(object sender, System.EventArgs e)
{
    // Output some text.
    lblOutput.Text = "Hello ASP.NET";
}
```

As you can see, the code looks the same as that which any desktop application would use. The only real difference is that it appears on a Web page. When you run this application, all you'll see is the Test button. Click Test and you'll see the message "Hello ASP.NET" in the label.

Working with Internet Information Server (IIS)

There are many different ways in which to work with IIS. Most of them are along the traditional static HTML route, which requires the use of scripts of various types. For example, you can use a CGI (Common Gateway Interface) script to query a database through a C/C++ program. The script would then format an HTML page containing the results of the query and upload it to the client.

We aren't going to cover any of these more traditional routes in this chapter, since there are entire books available on the topic. (Chapter 10 does mention Active Server Pages (ASP) briefly.) However, it's important to mention that the traditional methods exist, because they do work and you may find you need one when the newer methods we'll talk about in this chapter just don't fit the bill. For example, you may already have an existing infrastructure and it might not be cost effective to reprogram everything using new technology.

BROWSER ALERT

There's a fast way to learn the essentials of some types of IIS access techniques. Make sure you visit the Microsoft IIS FAQ site (sponsored by Stephen Genusa) at **http://www.genusa.com/iis/**, which includes topics like CGI. In addition, the KLV site at **http://www.adiscon.com/scripts/redir.asp?ShowURL=iis/main.asp** contains links for various Visual C++ programming considerations when using older technology. The same site includes links to places where you can find the latest information on Internet specification efforts and security concerns like user authentication.

One of the topics we'll discuss in this chapter is the Internet Server Application Programming Interface (ISAPI). More important, we'll look at some of the enabling technologies that go with ISAPI, like ISAs (ISAPI server applications). When you complete this chapter, you'll have a good overview of how this technology will work in a real-world situation. You'll also have a good idea of when you'll need to use those older technologies instead. I'll be sure to tell you about any problem areas you'll need to watch as you implement these new technologies on your own server. Knowing these pitfalls may help you decide whether to go the new technology route or stick with what you've used in the past.

BROWSER ALERT

The Internet provides many newsgroups you can visit to get help with your IIS, ASP, or ISA problem. In fact, there are too many to list in this chapter, so you'll want to spend a little additional time looking around. For the best Microsoft-specific support for IIS, take a look at *microsoft.public.inetserver.iis. There are other newsgroups in the **microsoft.public.inetserver** area that you'll want to look at too, but this one usually has the most messages. You'll find Microsoft-specific ASP help at **microsoft.public.inetserver.asp**. One of the more interesting non-Microsoft IIS sites is **comp.lang.java**. I was amazed to find message threads about everything from ASP to ActiveX on this site. Another good non-Microsoft site for IIS-specific help is **comp.infosystems.www.servers.ms-windows**. I found a great ISAPI thread on this newsgroup at the time of this writing. Needless to say, there are other **comp.infosystems.www** newsgroups you'll want to check out as well. If you're using Front-Page as one of your Web page maintenance tools, you'll want to take a look at **microsoft.public.frontpage.client** for ISAPI-specific help. It's hard to find out what the bugs are in some software, but you won't find it very difficult to do with IIS if you look at **comp.os.ms-windows.nt.software.compatibility**. Finally, if you're searching for that hidden ASP newsgroup, check **microsoft.public.activex.programming.scripting.vbscript.***

ISAPI is the basis of many new Microsoft technologies. For example, one way to implement the Simple Object Access Protocol (SOAP) on your IIS setup is to use an ISAPI listener provided as part of the SOAP toolkit. In case you haven't heard of SOAP, it provides the means to write distributed applications that work on more than one platform. SOAP is a superset of eXtensible Markup Language (XML). While XML merely provides a message formatting specification, SOAP defines a communication method. SOAP relies on a transport protocol such as Hypertext Transfer Protocol (HTTP) or Simple Message Transfer Protocol (SMTP) to transfer requests from a client to a server. While this chapter won't provide you with an in-depth view of SOAP, you'll learn enough to create a simple application that relies on the ISAPI listener. You'll learn how ISAPI and other technologies can work together in the distributed application environment of today.

An Overview of ISAPI (Internet Server API)

So, what is ISAPI? For the purposes of this book, ISAPI is a set of MFC extensions that allow you to work directly with IIS. We'll work with a new kind of project to implement ISAPI in this chapter, the ISAPI Extension Wizard. The five classes that we'll look at are CHttpServer, CHttpServerContext, CHttpFilter, CHttpFilterContext, and CHtmlStream. You'll use these classes to create ISAs—which are called by a whole variety of other names, like "ISAPI server extension DLLs" in the Microsoft documentation. We'll use ISA throughout the text just to keep things simple.

By necessity, ISAs rely on ISAPI. You'll use ISAPI classes to create ISA extensions and filters for IIS. However, you're not limited to ISAPI classes; there are also WinInet classes for controlling Internet communication and all of the standard MFC classes to provide things like an interface.

A filter allows you to keep something out or in by monitoring events on your server. For example, you could create an ISA filter that keeps people out of your Web site unless they enter the right password. Another type of filter could prevent files larger than a certain size from getting uploaded to the FTP server on your Web site.

Extensions are more like applications or background processes. For example, you could create an extension that allows the user to interact with a database without resorting to using scripts. The same extension could create Web pages dynamically based on the user input and the contents of the database on your server.

Before you can understand ISAPI, you have to understand where it fits into the Microsoft scheme of things. There are actually five levels of Internet support provided with Visual C++, three of which can reside on the server. The other two levels of support are client specific—you'll never see them on the server. The following list defines each level of support and tells where you'll find it.

▶ **ISAPI (server)**   This is the level of support we're discussing in this chapter. You need it to provide an extension or filter for the server itself. In other words, the client won't directly interact with this level of support; it'll merely see the results of the interaction.

▶ **WinInet (server or client)**   We don't cover this level of support in the book directly, but we do cover it indirectly. This set of classes allows you to use a specific method of data transfer between the client and the server. There are three levels of protocol support: HTTP, FTP, and Gopher. Essentially, you'd use these classes to create a session (CInternetSession), which is one connection to the server, and then specify a connection type (CFtpConnection, CHttpConnection, or CGopherConnection). After establishing a connection, the user can do things like look for a file (CFtpFileFind or CGopherFileFind). Normally, you don't have to interact with these classes directly because Visual C++ takes care of everything for you.

▶ **Asynchronous URL monikers (server or client)**   Asynchronous URL monikers allow you to perform tasks on the Internet without waiting. You simply tell the target application what you want, and then go on doing whatever else you wanted to do. The whole idea is that the Internet doesn't provide an instantaneous response in most situations. In the few situations where the Internet does provide fast response times, a long download could render the user's machine useless for hours at a time if you don't use asynchronous URL monikers in the application.

▶ **ActiveX documents (client)**   The distinction between individual applications is slowly disappearing. Creating an ActiveX Document application allows you to display a document in your browser. Once it's displayed, the user can make changes. The user saves the changed document locally or uploads it to the server (given the server provides the proper support).

▶ **ActiveX controls (client)**   Creating the basic elements of a Web page used to involve lots of scripting, and even then you got a static image. Using ActiveX controls on a Web site means that old technology and static displays no longer hold you back—your Web page can change to meet a specific situation.

BROWSER ALERT

*There are a lot of places you can visit on the Internet to find out more about IIS, ISAPI, and other Internet server–related technologies like ASP. The main Web site to visit for IIS information is **http://www.microsoft.com/windows2000/technologies/web/default.asp**. This Microsoft-supported Web site contains links to just about everything you'll need to use IIS itself and a few of the more common links for enabling technologies like ISAPI. If you value non-Microsoft help, look at the ISAPI Developer's Site at **http://www.genusa.com/isapi/**. This site contains a lot of helpful information about ISAPI and tells how you can use it for applications of all types. Another good place to look is the ASP Developer's Network at **http://www.aspdeveloper.net/**. This Web site contains a lot of valuable information about using Active Server Pages on your Internet server.*

Using ISAPI in the Real World

There a few things you need to know about ISAPI when it comes to a real-world production environment. For example, your ISA will be a DLL that loads on the server, just like any other DLL. This DLL will share the same address space as the HTTP server does, and you can unload it later if you need the memory it's consuming for something else. So what does that buy you? The following list tells you about the advantages of using ISAs when compared to other techniques like CGI.

▶ **Lower memory costs**   Since your ISA loads as a DLL on the server and uses the same memory space as the HTTP server, you won't have to waste the memory normally associated with CGI overhead. All you'll really need to load is the logic required to perform the task you're asking the ISA to do.

▶ **Speed**   Loading a DLL or C application the first time will take essentially the same amount of time, although the DLL will be slightly faster because of its smaller size. However, once you've loaded the DLL the first time, it'll stay in memory until you unload it, which means that you don't have to pay that loading cost more than one time if you don't want to. A CGI script will load the C application every time you call it. Reduced loading time is just the tip of the iceberg. Because the ISA DLL shares the same memory space as your HTTP server, you won't have to pay a time penalty for interprocess calls or any of the overhead normally associated with using a C application in a separate address space.

▶ **Code sharing**   All the server needs to do is load your DLL one time. Any application that requests the services of that DLL has access to it. Obviously, code sharing is one of the factors that leads to the lower memory costs and speed improvements over CGI mentioned in the first two points. However, code sharing results in some not-so-obvious benefits as well. For example, code sharing reduces administration time for your server, since the administrator only needs to replace one copy of any given DLL to affect every application that uses it. The C applications typically used by CGI have a lot of redundant code in them. Change a single routine and you'll need to change every C application that uses the routine on your server, which means greatly increased administrator time and the need for additional application tracking by the programmer.

▶ **Reliability**   C applications used by CGI scripts load and execute on the server without having much access to the server itself. Consequently, it's harder to create a C application that can monitor server events and recover from errors. What usually happens is that the server will terminate an errant CGI script and the client will end up with nothing. ISAs have full access to the server, which means that they can recover from errors more easily. Therefore, the client seldom (if ever) ends up having to make a request the second time.

▶ **Filtering capability**   You can't provide an event-driven equivalent to an ISA using CGI and a C application. The reason's simple: a C application gets called, does its work, and then unloads. There isn't any way that it can monitor server events over the long term.

► **Multiple tasks in one DLL**   Each task that you want CGI to perform requires a separate executable. As a result, you incur the overhead of calling each routine. ISAs, on the other hand, can contain multiple commands, each of which is a member of the CHttpServer class.

Getting these six capabilities doesn't mean that you have to pay a big price in either the learning curve or amount of coding. ISAs are just as easy to use as the CGI equivalent. Here's what the two lines of code would look like in an application:

```
<!-This is a call to a CGI routine with one parameter.->
http://aux/controls/sample.exe?Param

<!-This is a call to an ISA routine with one parameter.->
http://aux/controls/sample.dll?Param
```

As you can see, working with ISAPI doesn't have to be difficult. We called our ISA control using about the same code as we would a CGI routine. In fact, the only difference from a coding perspective is that our ISA control uses a DLL extension, while the CGI routine uses an EXE extension. Theoretically, you could switch your server to ISAs, make a few search-and-replace changes to your Web pages, and no one would notice the difference from an interface perspective. Of course, everyone would notice the higher efficiency of your Web site owing to the advantages of using ISAPI.

The last advantage that I mentioned for using ISAs was that you can perform more than one task with a single ISA. We'll see later how you implement this behavior. For right now, all you really need to know is that the calling syntax still doesn't differ much from standard CGI calls you may have used in the past. Here's an ISA routine call that specifies that you want to use the DisplayStr function:

```
<!-Call the DisplayStr function in an ISA routine with one parameter.->
http://aux/controls/sample.dll?DisplayStr?Param
```

As you can see, we called something other than the default task using a second question mark (?) in the calling string. The first parameter now tells which function you want to call within SAMPLE.DLL, and the second parameter contains a list of parameters. This method of calling functions is known as a *parse map*, which you'll learn how to create in the later section on creating an ISAPI extension.

ISAs do share some qualities that you'll find in CGI. For one thing, your application executes on the server, not the client. This makes updating your application easy—all you need to do is replace one DLL file on the server. (You do need to stop the service to update the DLL, but this is a small price to pay for the convenience of a one-machine update.) Obviously, this is a lot easier than trying to replace an application on every client machine that accesses your Web site. It's also one of the reasons that companies are taking a serious look at intranets to host things like a help desk and custom database applications—updating one server is a lot easier than updating a lot of clients.

TIP

IIS Versions 4 and above add some new capabilities that make working with ISAs easier. For one thing, you can tell the server to unload the ISA after each call. This means that you can try the ISA to see if it works and replace it with a new copy if necessary, all without stopping the service. The disadvantage of this new capability is that you'll see a slight performance hit because the server will need to reload the ISA every time it gets called by a client.

ISAPI versus ASP or ASP.NET

You might wonder why we haven't discussed ASP or ASP.NET in relation to ISAPI yet. Many developers compare ISAPI Extensions to Active Server Pages (ASP)—as if one could directly replace the other. In fact, many developers do use one technology to the exclusion of the other with great success. However, the two technologies don't necessarily compete.

ISAPI has the advantage of compiled code. It performs better and uses resources more efficiently than ASP in most cases. However, ISAPI is hard to modify because you need a compiler and special knowledge to do so. ASP requires an interpreter, so it can't compete from a performance perspective. (You can use ASP as a thin scripting layer, with most of your application compiled within components to gain a slight performance advantage.) However, ASP relies on scripts (plain text), so it's easy to modify, and most developers find it quite flexible. Combining ISAPI and ASP gives you the best of both worlds. It pays to use ASP for code that you'll modify regularly because it's so easy to do so. However, using ISAPI Extensions for code that must execute quickly provides you with a performance gain.

This brings us to Web Forms under ASP.NET. Web Forms provide a visual interface that relies on control-like programming functionality. You can view Web Forms as a halfway point between pure ASP and ISAPI. The managed environment compiles the ASPX files that Web Forms use. Therefore, the first time a user calls an ASPX, the load and execute time are similar to the interpreted ASP environment. After the first call, execute times are similar to ISAPI (albeit, not quite as fast with the current release). The developer also retains the ability to modify text files instead of writing code and compiling it as a DLL.

One problem you must overcome with Web Forms is that any ASP code you write will require complete revision. Web Forms rely on control-like interfaces that require special programming. These controls use a special <asp:> tag. You access the control properties much as you would in any application, and coding follows the same rules as standard application programming. A second problem is the managed environment. Not everyone will want to run their code in a managed environment. For example, if your Web setup still includes Windows NT servers, using a managed approach isn't the best solution. Chapter 10 provides a good example of using Web Forms, so we won't pursue the topic further in this chapter.

Choosing Between a Filter and an Extension

You don't have to spend a lot of time deciding whether to create an ISA filter or an ISA extension (or even both). The differences between the two types of ISA are easy to figure out. Once you do so, choosing the one you need becomes simple.

A filter will always react to events on the server itself. A user attempting to log into your Web site will generate an event that an ISA filter can monitor. You'll normally use it to modify the data flow between the client and server. For example, if your application saw an SF_NOTIFY_AUTHENTICATION event take place, it could display a dialog for the user to enter a name and password. If these were correct, the user would gain access to the Web site.

Extensions appear in the same situations as their CGI counterparts. For example, if you wanted to create an order entry system, you'd likely use an extension. The extension would receive data from a form that the user filled out, process the information, add it to the database, and finally send some type of receipt back to the user. Extensions rely on the same business process (data flow) as CGI; the only difference is that now you're using a DLL instead. Unlike a filter, an extension doesn't monitor events on the server—it acts in every way as an application would.

There are some situations when the choice of filter or extension doesn't really matter very much. For example, consider a simple Web counter. Every time someone accesses your Web site, you update the counter to show what number visitor that person is. You could call an ISA extension from the Web page to update this counter if so desired, or have a filter monitor the SF_NOTIFY_LOG event on the server and send the information automatically. The choice is a matter of personal taste.

You'll run into situations where you need to use both an extension and a filter. For example, you might want to display one Web page for an authorized Netscape user, another for an unauthorized Netscape user, and two others for authorized and unauthorized Internet Explorer users. This situation requires scripting within the

HTML form to detect the browser type, work on the part of the filter to determine user authorization level, and work on the part of an extension to generate the proper page. Using this combination of client scripting and ISA extensions to your server represents one way to fully extend your Web site and make it convenient for everyone to use.

Working with the Five ISAPI Classes

Previously, I mentioned that you'd be working with five new MFC classes in this chapter. These classes provide special capabilities you'll need to design an ISA filter or extension, so you'll use them in conjunction with classes you'd normally rely upon to create a DLL. The following list provides an overview of the classes that you'll work with in the sections that follow. Obviously, you'll get a much better view of these classes when we begin to work with the example code.

▶ **CHttpServer** This is the main class that you'll need to use to create either a filter or an extension. The CHttpServer class defines an object that works as a server extension DLL or an ISA. The main purpose of the CHttpServer object is to handle the messages generated by the server and the client. As a result, you'll find only one CHttpServer object in any ISA DLL.

▶ **CHttpServerContext** The CHttpServer class actually creates this object. It's a single instance of a single request from the client. In other words, you'll see one CHttpServerContext object for every active client request. The object gets destroyed when the client request has been fulfilled.

▶ **CHttpFilter** ISA filters require the use of a special CHttpFilter object to monitor server events. This object will look for all of the SF messages that the server generates as the client interacts with it. For example, the client will generate an SF_NOTIFY_LOG message every time a user tries to access the Web site.

▶ **CHttpFilterContext** The CHttpFilter object will create one CHttpFilterContext object for each active server event. The CHttpFilterContext class represents a single event generated by a single client during a specific session.

▶ **CHtmlStream** You'll use this class to manage data between the client and the server. The CHttpServer class will create an object of this type whenever it needs to transmit information between the client and the server. In most cases, there's only one of these objects per DLL. However, the CHttpServer object can create as many CHtmlStream objects as it needs to transfer data safely.

A typical CHtmlStream object contains data and all the tags required to create the content for an HTML page. For example, if you performed a search of a database, the resulting CHtmlStream object would contain not only the data, but the HTML tags required to actually create the Web page used to display the data as well.

An Overview of SOAP

Distributed application development has emerged from the Internet revolution as one of today's hottest new topics for developers. SOAP is one of the technologies that developers hope will make distributed application development easier. This section of the chapter provides the briefest overview of SOAP; a technology based on XML.

SOAP relies on XML to package data for transfer over the Internet. Essentially, two machines communicate with specially formatted text messages. SOAP is actually a one-way communication from the sender to the receiver. The format of the message enables the client and the server to engage in a request/response form of communication.

TIP

Working with the new capabilities provided by technologies like XML and SOAP means dealing with dynamically created Web pages. While it's nice that we can modify the content of a Web page as needed for an individual user, it can also be a problem if you need to troubleshoot the Web page. That's where a handy little script comes into play. Type javascript:'<xmp>'+document.all(0).outerHTML+'</xmp>' in the Address field of Internet Explorer for any dynamically created Web page and you'll see the actual HTML for that page. This includes the results of using scripts and other modern page construction techniques.

SOAP is a wire protocol similar in scope and purpose to other wire protocols such as DCOM. The difference between SOAP and these other protocols is that SOAP uses text messages, while DCOM and others rely on binary messages. This is the most important difference to remember, because the text format helps SOAP work better in distributed environments. For example, a Web server can easily check the content of the SOAP message for viruses.

A wire protocol isn't enough to create a message flow. The wire protocol describes the data package, but doesn't describe the method used to move the data from point A to point B. A SOAP message also relies on a transport protocol. The most popular transport protocol in use today is HTTP. SOAP messages can also rely on other transport protocols such as SMTP (for e-mail-type transfers) or HTTPS (if you require a secure connection). In fact, some developers are working on a Queued Component approach for SOAP that relies on SMTP to process the messages asynchronously.

Figure 11-1 shows a common SOAP message configuration. This is an actual SOAP message divided into its component parts for easy analysis. Notice the SOAP message formatting. This isn't the only way to wrap a SOAP message in other protocols, but it's the most common method in use today.

The next three sections are going to show you how a SOAP message actually appears during transmission. We'll use Figure 11-1 as an aid for discussion. It's the only time we'll explore a complete request or response, since you only need to worry about the SOAP message in most cases. The first section will look at the HTTP portion of SOAP. The second will help you understand where XML comes into play. Finally, we'll look at the SOAP message itself.

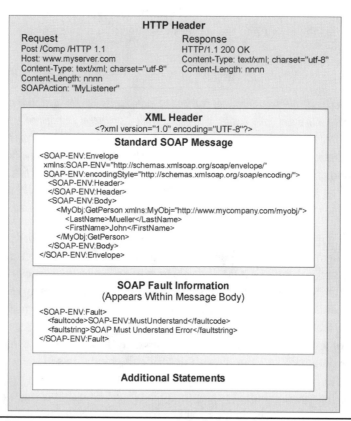

Figure 11-1   *SOAP messages appear as part of other protocols.*

Viewing the HTTP Portion of SOAP

The HTTP portion of a SOAP message looks much the same as any other HTTP header you may have seen in the past. In fact, if you don't look carefully, you might pass it by without paying any attention. As with any HTTP transmission, there are two types of headers: one for requests and another for responses. Figure 11-1 shows examples of both types.

As with any request header, the HTTP portion of a SOAP message will contain an action (POST, in most cases), the HTTP version, a host name, and some content length information. The POST action portion of the header will contain the path for the SOAP listener, which is either an ASP script or an ISAPI component. Also located within a request header are a Content-Type entry of text/xml and a charset entry of utf-8. The utf-8 entry is important right now because many SOAP toolkits don't support utf-16 or many other character sets (at least, not as of this writing).

You'll also find the unique SOAPAction entry in the HTTP request header. It contains the Uniform Resource Identifier (URI) of the ASP script or ISAPI component used to parse the SOAP request. If the SOAPAction entry is "", then the server will use the HTTP Request-URI entry to locate a listener instead. This is the only SOAP-specific entry in the HTTP header—everything else we've discussed could appear in any HTTP formatted message.

BROWSER ALERT

*Unicode Transformation Format (UTF) represents one standard method for encoding characters. One of the better places to learn about UTF-8 is **http://www.utf8.org/**. You can find a good discussion of various encoding techniques at **http://www.czyborra.com/utf/**. This Web site presents the information in tutorial format. The fact remains that you need to use the utf-8 character set when working with SOAP.*

The response header portion of the HTTP wrapper for a SOAP message contains all of the essentials as well. You'll find the HTTP version, status, and content length as usual. Like the request header, the response header has a Content-Type entry of text/xml and a charset entry of utf-8.

There are two common status indicators for a response header: 200 OK or 500 Internal Server Error. While the SOAP specification allows leeway in the positive response status number (any value in the 200 series), a server must return a status value of 500 for SOAP errors to indicate a server error.

Whenever a SOAP response header contains an error status, the SOAP message must include a SOAP fault section. We'll talk about SOAP faults later in this chapter. All you need to know now is that the HTTP header provides the first indication of a SOAP fault that will require additional processing.

Viewing the XML Portion of SOAP

All SOAP messages rely on XML encoding. SOAP follows the XML specification, and you can consider it a true superset of XML. In other words, it adds to the functionality already in place within XML. Anyone familiar with XML will feel comfortable with SOAP at the outset—all you really need to know is the SOAP nuances.

Although the examples in the SOAP specification don't show an XML connection (other than the formatting of the SOAP message), most real world examples will contain at least one line of XML-specific information. Here's an example of an XML entry:

```
<?xml version="1.0" encoding="UTF-8" standalone="no"?>
```

As you can see, the tag is quite simple. The only bits of information that it includes are the XML version number, the character set (encoding), and whether the message is stand-alone. As with the HTTP header, you'll need to use the UTF-8 character set for right now. The version number will change as new versions of XML appear on the scene. The stand-alone attribute determines if external markup declarations could affect the manner in which this XML document is processed. A value of **no** means external documents could affect the processing of this document.

BROWSER ALERT

*We won't discuss all of the XML tag attributes (declarations) in this chapter. You can find a complete listing of these attributes at **http://www.w3.org/TR/REC-xml**. For those of you who don't read specifications very well (or prefer not to), look at Tim Bray's annotated XML specification Web site at **http://www.xml.com/axml/testaxml.htm**. Another good place to look is the XML.com Web site at **http://www.xml.com/**.*

Some developers don't include all of the XML tag attributes in their SOAP messages. So far, I haven't seen any problems with leaving the encoding and stand-alone attributes out of the picture. You should, however, always include the XML version number, if for no other reasons than to document your code and ensure that there are no compatibility problems with future SOAP implementations.

Working with the SOAP Message

SOAP messages should look familiar to anyone who's worked with XML. The example shown in Figure 11-1 reveals several similarities between Web technology that you're already familiar with and SOAP. Notice that every entry has an opening and closing tag—that's the XML influence on SOAP, but this format also has it's roots in the HyperText Markup Language (HTML) we're all familiar with. A SOAP message always appears within an envelope. The envelope can have a header, just as an HTML document would, but this isn't required. The message must have a body. The message content appears within the body, as shown in Figure 11-1. We're making a request of the **GetPerson** function for a person whose last name is Mueller and first name is John.

You can extend all of these tags. In fact, you'll likely extend most of them when creating standard SOAP messages. For example, the envelope tag will probably look something like this in a real message.

```
<SOAP-ENV:Envelope xmlns:SOAP-ENV="http://schemas.xmlsoap.org/soap/envelope/">
```

The second parameter, in this case xmlns, is the namespace used for the envelope. A namespace reference tells where to find definitions for classes that contain functions used within the message. So, let's expand this principle to the **GetPerson** function mentioned previously. Here's what the body of the example message might actually look like:

```
<SOAP-ENV:Body xmlns:MyObj="http://www.mycompany.com/myobjects/">
    <MyObj:GetPerson>
        <LastName>Mueller</LastName>
        <FirstName>John</FirstName>
    </MyObj:GetPerson>
</SOAP-ENV:Body>
```

The xmlns tag contains the location of the MyObj object on your company server. This object contains the **GetPerson** function used in this example. As you can see, a SOAP message could quickly begin to look complex, but it's simple in design.

TIP

Remember that you must always pair all XML and SOAP tags; there's always an opening and closing tag. In cases when you don't need to include any data between tags, you can signify the closing tag by adding a slash at the end of the tag, like this example of a paragraph tag: <P />.

A standard browser can view the SOAP message you create. For example, Figure 11-2 shows the output from the sample code we looked at earlier. Since we didn't create an XSL file for this example, the browser uses the default template. This template will show you the content of the SOAP message with keywords and content highlighted in a variety of colors. Normally, you'd pass the SOAP response message to a client side application for interpretation and display. Note that you can click the "-" (minus signs) next to the various entries and collapse them to gain an overview of the message.

BROWSER ALERT

*Now that you have a taste of what SOAP is like, you might want to view the SOAP specification. The current specification, as of this writing, is version 1.1. You'll find it at **http://static.userland.com/xmlRpcCom/soap/SOAPv11.htm** (among other places). Not only will the specification fill you in on additional details, but you'll also see some example messages that contain the HTTP header, as well as the SOAP message. I chose to concentrate on just the SOAP portion of the message in my example listings.*

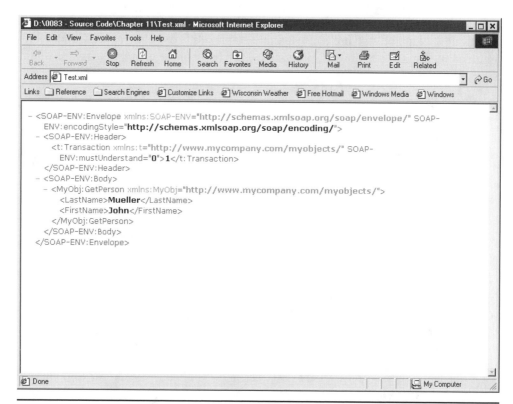

Figure 11-2   *Internet Explorer versions 5.5 and above can display SOAP messages in a simple format.*

Now that you have a summary of the SOAP message content, let's look at some particulars you'll need when working with SOAP. The following sections will fill you in on some technical details needed to understand the SOAP message fully. The first section tells you about the SOAP data transfer requirements as opposed to those supported by HTTP. The second section will tell you about a Web site that allows you to test your SOAP knowledge. The third section will explore SOAP fault messages. Finally, the fourth section will help you understand the HTTP Extension Framework.

HTTP and the SOAP Transfer

SOAP is essentially a one-way data transfer protocol. While SOAP messages often follow a request/response pattern, the messages themselves are individual entities. SOAP doesn't link the messages in any way. This means that a SOAP message is stand-alone—it doesn't rely on the immediate presence of a server, nor does the sender expect a response when a request message contains all of the required information. For example, some types of data entry may not require a response since the user is inputting information and may not care about a response.

The envelope in which a SOAP message travels, however, may provide more than just a one-way transfer path. For example, when a developer encases a SOAP message within an HTTP envelope, the request and response both use the same connection. HTTP creates and maintains the connection; SOAP has nothing to do with the connection. Consequently, the connection follows the HTTP way of performing data transfer, using the same techniques as a browser uses to request Web pages for display.

Testing Your SOAP Knowledge

Microsoft recently made two Web sites available to check your SOAP messages. The first accepts SOAP messages, parses them, and provides a check of their validity. You'll find it at **http://www.soaptoolkit.com/soapvalidator/**. Figure 11-3 shows what this Web site looks like.

As you can see, there are three panes in this display. The SOAP Message Text window contains a message that you want to verify. You can also choose one of the valid or invalid samples from the drop-down list boxes. These samples can teach you quite a bit about SOAP. They provide examples of what you can and can't do within a message and of the results that you'll get when performing certain actions. I've actually learned how to distinguish some error messages by using this Web site. You don't need to include the HTTP or XML headers in the SOAP Message Text window, just the SOAP message.

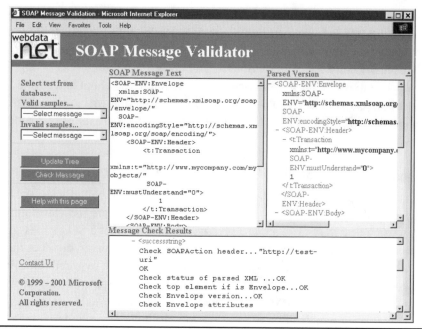

Figure 11-3   *The SOAP Message Validation site allows you to test your SOAP knowledge and learn about specific message types.*

The Parsed Version window shows what the message looks like after the SOAP listener parses it. This window doesn't tell you about the validity of the message, but it does help you understand the XML formatting better. You can use this window to determine if the message is well formed. The tags should form pairs that are easy to see in the pane. The use of text coloring also helps you to distinguish between specific text elements.

The Message Check Results window will show the results of diagnostics the site performs on your SOAP message. You'll see error messages in places where the SOAP message doesn't contain required entries or the entry format is incorrect. When all of the error messages are gone, the SOAP message is ready for use. Of course, this still doesn't mean the SOAP message will do anything. The Web site doesn't check the validity of the data within the SOAP message. You can create a perfect SOAP message that still doesn't work because the server-side component expects the data in a different format or even requires other arguments.

The second Web site is a generic SOAP listener. You can send a SOAP message to it using an application. The site will test the message much like the Message

Check Results window of the SOAP Message Validation site. You'll find this Web site at **http://www.soaptoolkit.com/soapvalidator/listener.asp**.

SOAP Fault Messages

Sometimes a SOAP request will generate a fault message instead of the anticipated reply. The server may not have the means to answer your request, the request you generated may be incomplete, or bad communication may prevent your message from arriving in the same state as you sent it. There are many reasons that you may receive a SOAP fault message. However, you can generally categorize them into four general areas, as shown in Table 11-1.

Message Type	Description
Client	The client generated a request that the server couldn't process for some reason. The most common problem is that the XML format of the SOAP message is incorrect (malformed). Another common problem involves the server not finding the requested component or the client not providing all of the information the server needs to process the message. If the client receives an error message of this type, it must recreate the message and fix the problems of the original. The server usually provides amplifying information if it can determine how the client request is malformed or otherwise in error.
MustUnderstand	This error only occurs when you set the SOAP message mustUnderstand attribute to 1. The error occurs when the client sends a request that the server can't understand or obey for some reason. The server may not understand a request when the client relies on capabilities of a version of SOAP that the server's listener doesn't provide. A server may not obey a client request due to security or other concerns. An upgrade of the listener or server side components will usually help in this situation.
Server	The server couldn't process the message even though the request is valid. A server error can occur for a number of reasons. For example, the server could run out of resources for initializing the requested component. In a complex application environment, the server may rely on the processing of another server that's offline or otherwise inaccessible. The client should definitely resubmit the same request later when this error occurs. The server usually provides amplifying information if it can determine the precise server side error that occurred.

Table 11-1   *General SOAP Fault Message Classifications*

Message Type	Description
VersionMismatch	SOAP doesn't have a versioning system. It does rely on the namespaces that you define to perform useful work. This error message occurs when the SOAP envelope namespace is either incorrect or missing. As of this writing, you should use a SOAP envelope namespace that points to **http://schemas.xmlsoap.org/soap/envelope/** (as shown in the source code examples in this chapter).

Table 11-1   General SOAP Fault Message Classifications *(continued)*

BROWSER ALERT

*It's possible to create other fault categories for SOAP messages. The list in Table 11-2 conforms to the SOAP specification. The only requirement for SOAP fault categories is that they follow the formatting requirements for XML namespaces. A good place to look for additional information about XML namespace formatting is the Namespace in XML document at **http://www.w3.org/TR/REC-xml-names/**.*

When a server returns a fault message, it doesn't return any data. A typical client fault message contains only fault information. With this in mind, the client side components you create must be prepared to parse SOAP fault messages and return the information to the calling application in such a way that the user will understand the meaning of the fault.

The fault envelope resides within the body of the SOAP message. A fault envelope will generally contain a faultcode and faultstring element that tells you which error occurred. All of the other SOAP fault message elements are optional. Table 11-2 provides a list of these elements and tells you how they're used.

TIP

You can use the presence or absence of various fault message elements to your advantage when determining the cause of an error. For example, if the faultactor element appears within the fault message, it's a good bet that the message passed between multiple servers. In some cases, this means that you can eliminate gross formatting errors from your list of things to check, because several machines parsed the message without generating an error. The absence of the detail element, on the other hand, may indicate that the error happened before the component on the server processed the request message. This means there's a problem with processing the message, rather than a problem with the server side component's handling of message data.

Element	Description
faultcode	The faultcode contains the name of the error that occurred. It can use a dot syntax to define a more precise error code. The faultcode will always begin with one of the classifications listed in Table 11-1. Since it's possible to create a list of standard SOAP faultcodes, you can use them directly for processing purposes.
faultstring	The faultstring is a human-readable form of the error specified by the faultcode entry. This string should follow the same format as HTTP error strings. You can learn more about HTTP error strings by reading the HTTP specification at **http://www.normos.org/ietf/rfc/rfc2616.txt**. A good general rule to follow is to make the faultstring entry short and easy to understand.
faultactor	The faultactor points to the source of a fault in a SOAP transaction. It contains a Uniform Resource Identifier (URI) similar to the one used for determining the destination of the header entry. According to the specification, you must include this element if the application that generates the fault message isn't the ultimate destination for the SOAP message.
detail	The detail element holds specific information about a fault when available. For example, this is the element that you'd use to hold server side component return values. This element is specific to the SOAP message body, which means you can't use it to detail errors that occur in other areas like the SOAP message header. A detail entry acts as an envelope for storing detail sub-elements. Each sub-element includes a tag containing namespace information and a string containing error message information.

Table 11-2   *SOAP Fault Message Elements*

Let's look more closely at the detail element. As stated, the detail element doesn't stand alone—it acts as an envelope for additional information. Here's a typical example of a detail element entry.

```
<detail>
    <e:additfault xmlns:e="http://www.mycompany.com/myobjects/">
        <message>Couldn't Create Object</message>
        <errorcode>429</errorcode>
    </e:additfault>
</detail>
```

Notice that detail information begins with a namespace entry. In this case, a component called AddIt that appears in the MyObjects directory on the server had an error. The error message is that it couldn't create a required object, while the associated error number is 429. The client side SOAP message parser could pass this information to the client application for additional processing. At least the user would have a better idea of what happened and could alert a network administrator to the problem.

Of course, the detail element isn't limited to a single component entry. Every component that has an error could make an entry. For that matter, you might include a single namespace entry for every error that a single component experiences. A component might actually provide several error messages that state an entire list of problems that it experienced in the processing of the SOAP message. For example, rather than return a single message at a time for faulty arguments, the component could parse all of the arguments and return a list of errors that covers all of them.

Writing an ISAPI Extension

OK, it's time to look at our first ISA. In this case, we'll create a very simple ISAPI extension using the ISAPI Extension Wizard. The whole purpose of this particular example is to get you used to the idea of working with ISAPI and show you some of the techniques you'll need to make ISAPI work. The example program will accept a string from the client, change it a little, and then display a new page showing the string that the client sent.

NOTE

You'll find a second example of how to create an ISAPI Extension on the source code CD. Look in the \Chapter 11\DateTime folder for this second example. The \Chapter 11 folder contains the required test Web page. This example shows how to retrieve server data and display it on screen for the user. Install the ISAPI extension on your server using the same techniques found in the "Running the Test Application" section of the chapter.

Creating the Program Shell

The following procedure will take you through all the steps required to create the sample ISA. You can use the same procedure to start any ISA extension that you need to create. I'm assuming that you already have Visual C++ running.

BROWSER ALERT

*One of the best places to look for ideas for your own ISAPI extension or filter is freeware produced by other programmers. The **alt.comp.freeware** newsgroup lists quite a few of these offerings. For example, at the time of this writing, AAIT Incorporated introduced a new freeware product named CGI Expert. It supports the CGI, win-CGI, ISAPI, and NSAPI interfaces simultaneously. Obviously, you'll want to use freeware products, like any other product, with care. However, they do provide excellent ideas on how to create your own custom extensions when needed — or a solution so you don't have to do any programming at all.*

1. Create a new MFC ISAPI Extension DLL project. The example uses a name of DispStr. You'll see the ISAPI Extension Wizard dialog box. This same wizard works for both ISAPI Filters and ISAPI Extensions.

2. Select the Object Settings tab. You'll see a list of choices for your extension or filter, as shown next. This is where you'll select the various characteristics for your ISA. Notice that there are three main areas to the dialog. You can choose to create a filter by checking the first checkbox and an extension by checking the second checkbox. The third area defines how you'll link MFC into your application.

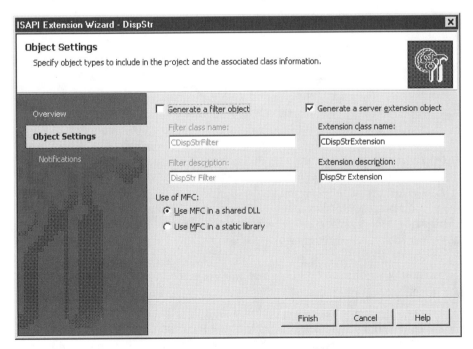

3. Check the "Generate a server extension object" option, and clear the "Generate a filter object option." You'll want to provide a short, concise statement of what your ISA does in the Extension Description field. The description appears as a string that you can use within the DLL as needed. This description won't show up in the Properties dialog when someone opens it for your ISA, so you'll want to add some additional text to the version information for your DLL as well.

4. Type **Display a string from the client.** in the Extension Description field.

5. Click Finish. The ISAPI Extension Wizard will create the required program shell for you.

Adding Some Code

At this point, we need to do three things to the skeleton that the ISAPI Extension Wizard has created for us to make the extension functional. The first task is to create a parse map for the new function we want to add. You'll find the parse map near the beginning of the DispStr.CPP file. Listing 11-1 shows the code you'll need to add to the parse map so that we'll be able to access the new function from the HTML page.

Listing 11-1

```
///////////////////////////////////////////////////////////////////
// command-parsing map

BEGIN_PARSE_MAP(CDispStrExtension, CHttpServer)
    // Our special DisplayStr parse command.
    ON_PARSE_COMMAND(DisplayStr, CDispStrExtension, ITS_PSTR)
    ON_PARSE_COMMAND_PARAMS("string='No String Supplied'")

    // Default parse command
    ON_PARSE_COMMAND(Default, CDispStrExtension, ITS_EMPTY)
    DEFAULT_PARSE_COMMAND(Default, CDispStrExtension)
END_PARSE_MAP(CDispStrExtension)
```

Even though you had to add only two lines of code to make this example work, we're actually concerned with three lines of code. The ON_PARSE_COMMAND() macro allows you to define a new function. Notice that we supply a function name, the class in which the function is supplied, and the type of parameters the function will use. The ON_PARSE_COMMAND() macro requires a parameter entry, even if you don't need any parameters to make the function work. Notice that the Default function uses a value of ITS_EMPTY since it doesn't need any parameters, but that our new function, DisplayStr, has a parameter of ITS_PSTR because it requires a string pointer.

That brings us to the ON_PARSE_COMMAND_PARAMS() macro on the next line. You have to tell Visual C++ how to deal with the parameters for your function. For example, if we had wanted to force the user to supply a string value for our function, we'd simply have "string" in the ON_PARSE_COMMAND_PARAMS() macro. Since we don't absolutely have to have the user supply a string to use our function, I've supplied a default value of "No String Supplied." Be aware that the query will fail if you require a parameter and the user doesn't supply it. Finally, you need to tell Visual C++ which function to use as a default using the DEFAULT_PARSE_COMMAND() macro. Since the Default function is just fine, in this case, I didn't change the default setting.

The second change you'll need to make to the code is to add the function entry to the DispStr.H file. Unless you modify the class specification to include your new function, Visual C++ won't know anything about it and the DLL won't compile. Fortunately, all we need is the single line shown in bold in Listing 11-2. I've included the surrounding code so that you know where to place the new entry.

Listing 11-2

```
class CDispStrExtension : public CHttpServer
{
public:
   CDispStrExtension();
   ~CDispStrExtension();

   // Overrides
public:
   virtual BOOL GetExtensionVersion(HSE_VERSION_INFO* pVer);
   virtual BOOL TerminateExtension(DWORD dwFlags);

   // TODO: Add handlers for your commands here.
   // For example:

   void Default(CHttpServerContext* pCtxt);
   void DisplayStr(CHttpServerContext* pCtxt, LPTSTR pszString);

DECLARE_PARSE_MAP()
};
```

As you can see, adding the function call declaration is a simple matter. At this point, though, you may be wondering where the CHttpServerContext* pCtxt part of the declaration came in. We certainly didn't declare it previously in any of the parse map macros. It turns out that the Web server passes the pCtxt parameter to your function by default. Remember from our previous discussion that the CHttpServer class automatically creates a CHttpServerContext object for every user request. This is where the parameter comes from. What you're getting is a pointer to the CHttpServerContext object associated with the user's call to your function. It's also the way that you keep multiple calls to your function separate—each call has a completely different object associated with it.

We need to perform one additional task to make this DLL function: add the function code to the DispStr.CPP file. I added the function code right after the existing **Default()** function code. Listing 11-3 shows the very short function that I created for this example. There isn't anything fancy here; the whole purpose is to show you how to put things together.

Listing 11-3

```
void CDispStrExtension::DisplayStr(CHttpServerContext* pCtxt, LPTSTR pszString)
{
    // Start sending information to the new Web page including a default title.
    StartContent(pCtxt);
    WriteTitle(pCtxt);

    // Display the body of the new page.
    *pCtxt << _T("<H3><CENTER>ISAPI Server Extension Example</CENTER></H3><P><P>");
    *pCtxt << _T("This was the string you entered:<P><EM>");
    *pCtxt << _T(pszString);
    *pCtxt << _T("</EM>");

    // End the display area.
    EndContent(pCtxt);
}
```

The function itself is easy to figure out. The first thing we do is tell Visual C++ to start a Web page. That's like adding the <HTML> and <HEAD> tags to a document. The second thing we do is output a title—just as if we were typing the <TITLE> tag into a document. The only way to override the default title is to override the **WriteTitle()** function—something that you can do if you'd like. Now that we've got a heading, it's time to create some body content. We have to use the stream operator to send the information. Notice that you can use any valid tags in this example, or even add client side script if desired. Anything you can do with a standard HTML document, you can do with your ISAPI extension. We'll see in just a few moments how all these tags work together to produce a Web page. You'll also want to notice that we send the string we got from the Web page back to the new Web page—you don't even have to convert the values to text to make them work. The final function call we use, **EndContent()**, tells Visual C++ that we're done sending information. It's like adding the </HTML> to the end of the document.

At this point, you can compile the ISAPI extension we've created. Once you successfully compile it, move the DLL to your Web server. There are several logical places to put the DLL, but the two most common would be a Scripts directory or a special Controls directory. I normally keep all my controls in one place in a Controls directory to make them easy to locate, but the actual location you use isn't that important. The only criteria are that the user be able to access the directory containing the DLL through your Web site and that you've marked the directory as executable using the Internet service manager provided with your Web server.

Running the Test Application

The test application for this example is a simple Web page. You'll find it in the \Chapter 11 directory of the source code CD as Extend.HTM. This Web page assumes that you've placed the DispStr.DLL in a Controls folder on your Web server, so you might need to change it slightly to work with your configuration.

TIP

HTML doesn't send any text after a space in a text box to the server. For example, if you type "Hello World" in the text box, the server will only receive "Hello." You must place plus signs (+) between words to send them to the server. For example, if you send "Hello+World" to the server, it'll see "Hello World" (the Web server log will still show the + sign, which indicates the + sign is replaced with a space after it arrives at the server). This means adding some text manipulation code not shown in the example program to replace the spaces in the text box with plus signs before sending the string to the server.

Open the test Web page and you'll see a Web page with two buttons and one text box. As previously mentioned, this is a test page, so I didn't add too much formatting code, in order to keep things simple.

NOTE

Make absolutely certain that the directory you use to store DispStr.DLL on the server is marked for execute privileges from within the Internet services manager for your Web server. Otherwise, you'll see any number of errors from the browser as it attempts to execute the file—most of which won't tell you that it can't execute the file (the most common error is that the service isn't supported). Marking the directory for execute privileges within the operating system isn't sufficient to allow a visitor to your Web site to use the ISA you've created. In most cases, you can avoid any problems by ensuring the ISA DLL appears in the script directory for your Web server (assuming it has one).

Let's test the DispStr.DLL. Begin by clicking the Default button. What you should see is a default string that the ISAPI Extension Wizard provides. (It tells you that you need to add some code to the default function.)

Click the Back button (or the equivalent on your browser) to get back to the Extend.HTM page. Now click the Display String button and you'll see a Web page containing a message stating that you didn't supply a string.

In this case, we called DispStr.DLL with the **DisplayStr** function, but since there wasn't any value in the text box, the function had to display the default string we defined as part of the ON_PARSE_COMMAND_PARAMS() macro. Now you can see the importance of providing a default value in most cases. Users don't have to worry about your ISA causing problems if they forget to provide a needed value. What they'll get instead is a return value that could help them troubleshoot their Web page. In this case, the user will know precisely what went wrong and can fix it in a matter of minutes instead of the hours that debugging normally takes.

Click the Back button again to get back to the Extend.HTM display. This time, type **Hello+World** into the Type a String Value field. Click the Display String button and you'll see a new Web page with the string you typed. In this case, we asked to use the **DispStr.DLL DisplayStr** function and provided it with "Hello+World" as a string value.

It's important to note that you must supply the plus sign between words when sending a string value to the server; otherwise, the resultingWeb page will contain only the first word. (You may want to experiment a little to see this for yourself— make sure you check the Web server logs as you try various combinations.) If you look at the Location field on the browser, you'll notice that we've supplied a plus (+) sign between words, yet the content of the page shows a space between the words. This happens because the Web server replaces the plus signs with spaces for you—that's why we didn't have to add any additional code to the ISA.

Writing an ISAPI Filter

Creating an ISAPI Filter is a little more complex than creating an ISAPI Extension. For one thing, you need to decide where to interrupt the message stream to view the data sent by the browser. Another problem is determining how to control the data stream. Filters don't necessarily modify the browser data or create content the client will see. In some cases, the filter will create log entries or perform other tasks that only the network administrator will understand. Because the filter works in the background, you also need to load it into the IIS environment. After the filter loads, you'll need to verify that it starts. Testing the filter after it starts might mean performing low-level checks instead of simply looking at a Web page for a result.

The following sections discuss how to create a simple filter that modifies the logs that IIS keeps for user activities. We'll begin with a discussion of the filter options. The next section shows how to construct the filter. Finally, we'll discuss how to test the filter.

NOTE

You'll find a second ISAPI Filter example in the \Chapter 11\LogOn folder of the source code CD. The \Chapter 11 folder contains the Web page required to test this example. You'll install the DLL using the same process as found in the "Installing the ISAPI Filter" section of the chapter. The second example shows how to force a logon screen to appear on the client machine.

Choosing Filter Options

The Notifications tab of the ISAPI Extension Wizard dialog is very important as far as filter designers are concerned, because it contains the options you'll need to set the filter's monitoring options. Following is an example of the Notifications tab for the example in this chapter.

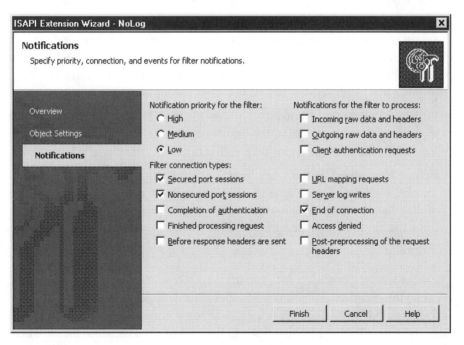

There are three sections of options on this page. The first section determines the filter priority—Low, the default, works just fine in most cases. You'll want to use this level for any kind of filter that performs a general background task. A security filter may require that you set the filter priority to Medium. After all, you don't want the filter to react after the event—a reaction during the event would be much better. Finally, you should reserve the High priority setting for emergency-level filters. For example, you might want to send a message out to everyone that the server is going down due to a power failure.

The second section of the Notifications tab contains five entries. These entries determine the filter environment—how it interacts with IIS. Microsoft calls this a filter connection because the connectivity determines the type of information the filter will see. The following list provides an overview of each entry.

▶ **Secured Port Sessions**   Enables you to monitor events when a user has a secure connection. For example, if you plan to provide extra services to a registered user that an anonymous user doesn't get, you may want to check this option.

▶ **Nonsecured Port Sessions**   Enables you to monitor events when a user doesn't have a secure connection to the server. That's the way most users will access your site if you have a general Web site on the Internet.

▶ **Completion of Authentication**   Notifies the filter when the client completes authentication. You could use this setting to perform additional post-authentication checks or to begin preprocessing client requests. For example, you might need to verify that the server has the resources to respond to a client request before you begin processing it.

▶ **Finished Processing Request**   Notifies the filter that the server has completed processing the client request, but hasn't begun creating the response message. You could use this option for data verification.

▶ **Before Response Headers Are Sent**   The response header determines how the client will handle the response. For example, if you send a result code of 200, the client will assume the request was successful. Other responses force the client to provide authentication information, while other responses signify errors.

The third section contains a list of notifications (events) that your filter will track. Every time the specified event happens, your filter will get called. However, there are two things that will affect when it gets called. If you set the priority of your filter to Low, then any High or Medium priority filters will get to react to the event first. In addition, your filter has to be set to monitor the event with the user's current security level. In other words, your filter won't get called at all if you set it to monitor nonsecured activity and the user is in secured mode.

Creating the Filter Shell

At this point, you should have a better idea of how notifications work. Learning which notifications to use to start your ISAPI Filter is an essential part of building one. This section will show you how to build your own ISAPI filter. The process for starting the ISAPI filter is just about the same as the one for creating an extension. The following steps will help you create a program shell.

1. Create a new MFC ISAPI Extension DLL project. The example uses a name of NoLog. You'll see the ISAPI Extension Wizard dialog box. This same wizard works for both ISAPI Filters and ISAPI Extensions.

2. Select the Object Settings tab. You'll see a list of choices for your extension or filter. This is where you'll select the various characteristics for your ISA. You can choose to create a filter by checking the first checkbox or an extension by checking the second checkbox.

3. Check the "Generate a filter object" option, and clear the "Generate a server extension object" option . You'll want to provide a short, concise statement in the Filter Description field of what your ISA does. The description appears as a string that you can use within the DLL as needed. This description won't show up in the Properties dialog when someone opens it for your ISA, so you'll want to add some additional text to the version information for your DLL as well.

4. Type **Classify some log entries for security reasons.** in the Filter Description field.

5. Select the Notifications tab. This is the tab you'll use to select the events and type of monitoring your filter will provide. There are three areas to consider. See the "Choosing Filter Options" section to get more details about these options.

6. Check the Server Log Writes checkbox, and clear the End of Connection checkbox. We want to activate our filter when the user requests specific kinds of access to the server since we're creating a simple filter to keep some log entries classified.

7. Click Finish. The ISAPI Extension Wizard will create the required program shell for you.

The coding portion of this example is short and to the point. Filters can quickly get out of hand in the complexity department, and debugging them is difficult. In most cases, you'll want to make your filter programs as short as possible. Modularization is a big help, as well, when it comes time to troubleshoot a faulty filter. Listing 11-4 shows the code you'll need to add to the **OnLog()** function to make it work.

Listing 11-4

```
DWORD CNoLogFilter::OnLog(CHttpFilterContext *pCtxt, PHTTP_FILTER_LOG pLog)
{
    // Check for a specific notification.
    if (strstr(pLog->pszTarget, "NoLog.htm") != NULL)
    {
        // Change the target information to Classified.
        pLog->pszTarget = "Classified Target";
        pLog->pszParameters = "Classified Parms";
    }

    // Pass control to the next filter.
    return SF_STATUS_REQ_NEXT_NOTIFICATION;
}
```

As you can see, we'll simply monitor the log entries for a particular target, which could include any number of objects, but is normally another Web page. Once we find the log entry we're looking for, we'll change two members, pszTarget and pszParameters, to their classified setting. Obviously, this whole idea is very simplified, but it does have practical uses. You might want to hide specific log entries from prying eyes, and this is one way to do it. The habit of crackers using log files they find on a server to dig deeper into a company's resources is justification enough, but you'll find other reasons, as well, for keeping some log entries classified. In some cases, you may even want to eliminate certain log entries totally, simply because you don't want to monitor them. Suffice it to say, you'll want to exercise care when using this kind of filter, but the security and privacy features it provides overcomes some of the problems the filter can create.

Installing the ISAPI Filter

You can now compile the new ISAPI filter. However, even after you move it to the Controls or Scripts directory on your server, you'll still have to perform one other task. Unlike an extension, an ISA filter gets loaded when you start the service. This means stopping the target service, making a registry entry, and then starting up the service again if you're using an older version of IIS. (You only need to use the registry method with IIS versions older than version 4.0—we'll cover a newer procedure for version 4.0 and above in a few paragraphs.) The filter will get loaded as part of the starting process.

The WWW service stores its filter entries in the following registry value: HKEY_LOCAL_MACHINE\SYSTEM\CurrentControlSet\Services\W3SVC\Param eters\Filter DLLs. You'll probably find one or more values in this location already. All you need to do is add a comma and then type the location of your new ISA filter. Make certain you perform this step before going on to the next section, or the filter won't load. In fact, you'll want to check this setting first if you have trouble getting the filter to work.

Users of IIS version 4.0 and above will really appreciate the fact that they no longer have to edit the registry manually to load an ISAPI filter. All you need to do is open the Microsoft Management Console, right-click on the Web site that you want to add the filter to, and choose Properties from the context menu. Select the ISAPI Filters tab and you'll see a dialog like the one shown here:

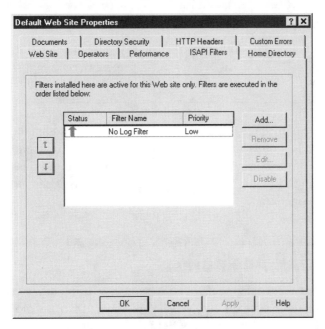

Click the Add button and you'll see a Filter Properties dialog. Type the human readable name in the Filter Name field. Use the Browse button to find the

NoLog.DLL file (or whatever ISAPI filter you want to add to the Web site). Once you select the file, its name will appear in the Executable field. Click OK once to close the Filter Properties dialog, and click OK again to close the Default Web Site Properties dialog. IIS will automatically load the filter for you.

Testing the ISAPI Filter

The filter requires three Web pages for testing. You'll find the Filter.HTM, NoLog.HTM, and LogIt.HTM files in the \Chapter 11 folder of the source code CD. The main Web page is Filter.HTM. You'll need to access it through a Web server connection (the one where you installed the filter).

When you access the Filter.HTM page, you'll see two links. Click Classified to activate the NoLog ISAPI Filter. Click Normally to log the request normally. Open the log file for your Web server. You'll find this log in the \WINNT\system32\LogFiles\ W3SVC1 (or a similar) folder. The exact name of the log will vary according to your logging options, so I can't provide an exact log name. Here's an example of what you should see in the Web server log:

Notice that the entries for Filter.HTM and LogIt.HTM contain the standard information. The NoLog.HTM entry contains "Classified Target" and "Classified Params" instead of the normal entries. (The exact format of the classified strings will vary according to the log format that you use.) The classified entries demonstrate the effect of the log entries.

Writing SOAP Applications

As companies begin exchanging data more frequently using the Internet, and employees spend more time off site, you'll find yourself writing more distributed application code. Because this is a new field of development, you'll find more than a few solutions to the problem of distributed application creation. One of the more popular development alternatives is SOAP. Using SOAP is relatively straightforward. Creating a SOAP application is similar to creating a desktop application with components, but with one important difference: the SOAP message. The easiest way to view SOAP is as a messaging system or a wire protocol (as stated earlier).

The following sections discuss a very simple SOAP application. We'll create a simple component and client application. The client will use SOAP to create an instance of the component on the server. The component adds two numbers together. The client will pass two variables to the component and request that it add them. The component will pass the result back to the client, which will display the result on screen.

NOTE

This section relies on the Microsoft SOAP Toolkit 2.0. You can download this toolkit from **http://msdn.microsoft.com/downloads/sample.asp?url=/msdn-files/027/001/ 580/msdncompositedoc.xml**. *The SOAP Toolkit must appear on both client and server machines.*

Creating the Component

The component we'll use for this example is extremely simple. (See Chapter 6 for detailed instructions for creating components.) Begin with a simple ATL Project named SOAPAdd. Use the default settings of Attributed and Dynamic-Link Library (DLL). Add an ATL Simple Object class named DoMath. Add a method to IDoMath called **DoAdd()** that expects two SHORT values as input and outputs a SHORT result (make sure you check both the out and retval attributes when creating the last argument). Listing 11-5 shows the source code for this example.

NOTE

You might need to modify the instructions for creating a SOAP component if you run into a bug currently found in Visual C++ .NET. First, don't use the attributed option when creating the project. Also, select merging of the proxy/stub code. When you create the project, you'll have to add the stdole32.tlb to the IDL file as shown here:

```
library SOAPAddLib
{
    importlib("stdole32.tlb");
    importlib("stdole2.tlb");
```

Why didn't I include these steps in the instructions? Microsoft has promised faithfully that they'll fix this problem for the final version. In addition, using the standard approach is faster and easier.

Listing 11-5

```
STDMETHODIMP CDoMath::DoAdd(SHORT Value1, SHORT Value2, SHORT* Answer)
{
    SHORT Temp; //Temporary value holder.

    // Add the two input values.
    Temp = Value1 + Value2;
    *Answer = Temp;

    return S_OK;
}
```

Creating a WSDL File

After you compile this component, move it to the server and register it using
RegSvr32 SoapAdd. Now we need to build a Web Services Description Language
(WSDL) file that contains an XML description of the component. The client
accesses this XML description to determine how to work with the component. The
use of a WSDL file also makes it easy to create a connection over the Internet.
Finally, you'll need the content of the WSDL file to create a connection to the
component. The following steps show how to create the WSDL file.

1. Start the WSDL Generator utility found in the SOAP toolkit. Click Next to
   get past the Welcome screen. The first screen will ask the name of the COM
   component to analyze.

2. Type a name for the Web service. This is the name you'll use for many access
   purposes, so choose something descriptive. The example uses SOAPMath.

3. Type or select the location of the component (SoapAdd.DLL in this case).
   Click Next. You'll see a list of services you can expose, similar to the one
   shown next.

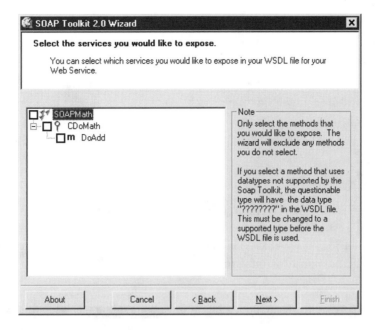

4. Check the methods you want to expose (**DoAdd()** for the example). Click
    Next. You'll see a SOAP Listener dialog. This dialog is where you'll choose
    the type of listener you want to create. The default setting is for an ISAPI
    listener, but you can also choose to use ASP. You also need to choose an
    XML Schema Definition (XSD) namespace. Newer is better unless you have
    compatibility concerns for older applications. SOAP is still under construction,
    so the schema changes as the standards groups define how SOAP should work.

5. Type the location of the listener files on your Web server. It generally pays
    to choose the same location as your component to keep the files together and
    reduce the number of debugging complexities. Most developers create a virtual
    directory on the Web server that has execute rights for their SOAP components.
    Select a Listener Type and XSD Schema Namespace year (the defaults work
    fine for the example).

6. Click Next. WSDL Generator will prompt for a WSDL and WSML file storage location. You can also choose between UTF-8 and UTF-16 for a character set (the example uses UTF-8).

7. Type or select a storage location for the files. Choose a character set. Click Next. You'll see a completion dialog.

8. Click Finish. Open the WSDL file you just generated and you should see a description of the component similar to the one shown in Figure 11-4.

Creating the Client

It's time to create the SOAP client. Begin with a dialog-based MFC application named SOAPTest. Add a Test pushbutton and three edit controls to the form (see the IDD_SOAPTEST_DIALOG on the source code CD for details). Create an event handler for the Test pushbutton. Create control variables for each of the edit controls

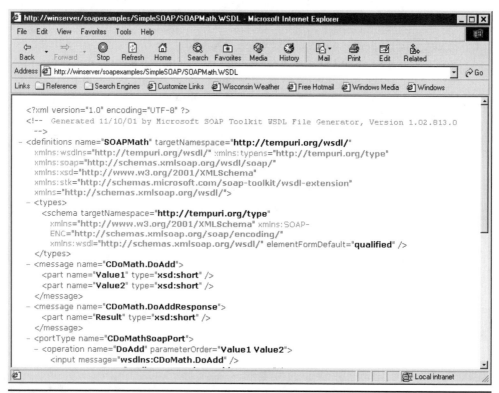

Figure 11-4 *Check the WSDL files for errors designated with a series of question marks.*

(m_Value1, m_Value2, and m_Answer) by right-clicking the associated control and choosing Add Variable from the context menu. That's all you'll need for the basic structure.

Because this is a SOAP application, you'll need to add both SOAP and XML support to your code. The SOAP library relies on the XML library for parsing and other needs. Listing 11-6 shows the code that you'll need to add. Note that the #import statements must appear on a single line, even though the MSSOAP1.DLL entry appears on multiple lines in the book. Otherwise, you'll see multiple errors during compilation. You'll also need to change the MSSOAP1.DLL location to match your setup.

Listing 11-6

```
// Add XML support to the application.
#import "msxml3.dll"
using namespace MSXML2;

// Add SOAP support to the application.
#import "D:\Program Files\Common Files\MSSoap\Binaries\mssoap1.dll"
exclude("IStream", "ISequentialStream", "_LARGE_INTEGER",
"_ULARGE_INTEGER", "tagSTATSTG", "_FILETIME")
using namespace MSSOAPLib;
```

Now it's time to add some code to the Test pushbutton. Listing 11-7 shows the code we'll use in this case.

Listing 11-7

```
void CSOAPTestDlg::OnBnClickedTest()
{
    CString          Value1;       // Input value 1
    CString          Value2;       // Input value 2
    CString          Result;       // Answer
    VARIANTARG       Values[2];    // Input parameters
    VARIANT          Answer;       // Output (return) value.
    HRESULT          hr;           // Result of operations
    ISOAPClientPtr   MyClient;     // Pointer to client interface.
    LPOLESTR         Function;     // Name of the method to retrieve.
    DISPID           dispid;       // Dispatch ID of DoAdd() method.
```

```
DISPPARAMS      DispParm;     // Dispatch call parameter struction.
EXCEPINFO*      Except;       // Exception information.
UINT            PErr;         // Number of dispatch argument errors.

// Initialize the COM environment.
CoInitialize(NULL);

// Initialize the Value1 parameter.
VariantInit(&Values[0]);
Values[0].vt = VT_BSTR;
m_Value1.GetWindowText(Value1);
Values[0].bstrVal = Value1.AllocSysString();
VariantChangeType(&Values[0], &Values[0], 0, VT_R8);

// Initialize the Value2 parameter.
VariantInit(&Values[1]);
Values[1].vt = VT_BSTR;
m_Value2.GetWindowText(Value2);
Values[1].bstrVal = Value2.AllocSysString();
VariantChangeType(&Values[1], &Values[1], 0, VT_R8);

// Initialize the Answer (result).
VariantInit(&Answer);

//Create the SOAP compoent.
hr = MyClient.CreateInstance(__uuidof(SoapClient));
if (FAILED(hr))
{
   AfxMessageBox("Failed to create SOAP component.");
   CoUninitialize();
   return;
}

// Initialize the connection.
hr = MyClient->mssoapinit(
   "http://winserver/soapexamples/SimpleSOAP/SOAPMath.WSDL",
   "SOAPMath",
   "DoMathSoapPort",
   "");
if (FAILED(hr))
{
   AfxMessageBox("Failed to create SOAP connection.");
   MyClient.Release();
```

```
   CoUninitialize();
   return;
}

// Get the dispatch ID of the DoAdd() method.
USES_CONVERSION;
Function = OLESTR("DoAdd");
hr = MyClient->GetIDsOfNames(IID_NULL,
                             &Function,
                             1,
                             LOCALE_SYSTEM_DEFAULT,
                             &dispid);
if (FAILED(hr))
{
   AfxMessageBox("Failed to obtain DoAdd dispatch ID.");
   MyClient.Release();
   CoUninitialize();
   return;
}

// Initialize Dispatch Parameters structure.
Except = NULL;
PErr = 0;
DispParm.cArgs = 2;
DispParm.cNamedArgs = 0;
DispParm.rgdispidNamedArgs = NULL;
DispParm.rgvarg = Values;

// Perform the math.
hr = MyClient->Invoke(dispid,
                      IID_NULL,
                      LOCALE_SYSTEM_DEFAULT,
                      DISPATCH_METHOD,
                      &DispParm,
                      &Answer,
                      Except,
                      &PErr);
if (FAILED(hr))
   AfxMessageBox("Method call to DoAdd() Failed.");
else
{
   // Convert the result and display it on screen.
   VariantChangeType(&Answer, &Answer, 0, VT_BSTR);
```

```
      Result = Answer.bstrVal;
      m_Answer.SetWindowText(Result);
   }

   // Clean up the variants.
   VariantClear(&Values[0]);
   VariantClear(&Values[1]);
   VariantClear(&Answer);

   // Uninitialize the COM environment.
   MyClient.Release();
   CoUninitialize();
}
```

The example code begins by initializing the variant structures used to hold the two input parameters and the single output parameter for the example. It's essential to initialize all of the values, including the output value. Note that the example doesn't check for a numeric input because the edit controls are set to accept only numeric input.

The next step is to create a soap client and initialize it. The initialization process requires that you create a connection to the WSDL file we defined earlier. The first piece of information you need is the URL to the WSDL file. Use localhost if you're testing the component locally, instead of on a two-machine setup. The second and third argument values come from the WSDL file, as shown here:

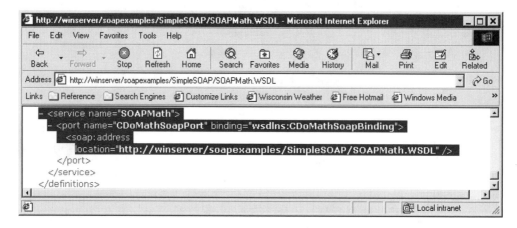

Notice the highlighted values that appear at the end of the WSDL file. You must include both the service name and the port name as shown in the illustration. The service name and port name provide binding to the component you want to access. At this point, you have access to any method the WSDL file contains for the specified service and port. This is an important consideration because some developers fall into a trap of updating their component, but not the associated WSDL file. The result is that you won't see any new methods the component contains.

Working with the methods is like working with any other component on your machine. The example code gains access to the dispatch ID for the **DoAdd()** method. Next, it creates a dispatch parameter list and invokes the **DoAdd()** method.

After making a successful call, the code converts the return value into a BSTR. The code places this value inside a CString, which it uses to place the answer on screen.

Notice all of the cleanup that takes place after making the call. Failure to clean up after your code will result in memory leaks. It also has a strange effect on the remote component. You'll find that you can't copy over it until IIS decides to release the component. In short, you need to perform cleanup even in the early stages of development.

Visual C++ .NET and Microsoft.NET

OBJECTIVES

▶ Learn how the managed environment differs from previous versions of Visual C++

▶ Learn about the differences between C++ and C#

▶ Understand how to convert existing code to .NET

▶ Create an application that invokes Win32 API calls from the managed environment

▶ Create a managed SOAP application and managed component

▶ Discover attributed programming, built-in and custom attributes, and reflection

▶ Learn how to work with assembly metadata

▶ Create an application that draws information from the command line

▶ Work with delegates and create an application that demonstrates their use

Working with the .NET Architecture

IN THIS CHAPTER:

An Overview of .NET

A Look at the Intermediate Language (IL)

Why Change a Great Language?

Visual C++ Versus C#

Understanding the Common Language Runtime for Visual Studio

Converting Your Existing Code to .NET

The .NET Architecture is the central piece of the new .NET programming environment for developers. It includes the .NET Framework, programming languages, and other pieces of the Visual Studio .NET package. In addition, the architecture includes operating system additions in the form of the Common Language Runtime (CLR), Global Assembly Cache (GAC), and other features. Future additions will likely include new operating system support when the .NET server makes its appearance, as well as add-ons such as ODBC .NET that won't ship with Visual Studio .NET. In short, the .NET Architecture represents a new way to create and use applications.

We've already looked at several managed coding examples in the book. You should know that managed code looks different from unmanaged code and can save you coding time in many situations. However, we haven't really discussed the differences up to this point, so you might not understand why .NET represents a better way to code certain types of applications. This chapter helps you understand the .NET architecture better. We'll discuss .NET from a Visual C++ developer perspective, and you'll learn why .NET is actually necessary in certain situations.

An Overview of .NET

Microsoft's marketing arm is something to behold—it's the reason that Microsoft is in the position that it is right now. However, many developers rightfully complain that it's this marketing staff that produces copious documentation with conflicting information. .NET doesn't have to be a mystery. For most Visual C++ developers, .NET is a combination of three elements.

- ▶   .NET Framework
- ▶   Attributed programming
- ▶   Use of an Intermediate Language (IL)

You've seen other examples of .NET (managed) applications throughout the book, but let's look at another example. Listing 12-1 shows a typical .NET application created with the Managed C++ Application project. You'll find this application in the \Chapter 12\Simple folder of the source code CD.

NOTE

The example code on the CD includes a few additions you won't find in the listing. For example, you still need to include a Version resource if you want to present a Version tab when someone opens the Properties dialog for your application. Likewise, you need to define assembly information so someone who looks at your code with a disassembler can find the required copyright and contact information. Resources are just as much a requirement for managed applications as they are for unmanaged applications—the wizards don't simply add them automatically.

Listing 12-1

```cpp
#include "stdafx.h"

// Import the required DLLs.
#using <mscorlib.dll>
#using <system.dll>
#using <System.Windows.Forms.DLL>
#using <System.Drawing.DLL>
#include <tchar.h>

// Add Required Namespace Access.
using namespace System;
using namespace System::Windows::Forms;
using namespace System::Drawing;

// Define the application namespace.
namespace Sample
{
   // Create a form-based class.
   public __gc class SimpleDialog : public Form
   {
   public:
      // Constructor must be public.
      SimpleDialog(void);

   private:
      // Form Control Listing.
      Button *btnOK;
      Button *btnTest;
```

```
    // Control Event Handlers.
    void OK_Click(Object* sender, EventArgs* e);
    void Test_Click(Object* sender, EventArgs* e);
};

SimpleDialog::SimpleDialog()
{
    // Create and configure the OK button.
    btnOK = new Button();
    btnOK->Text = "OK";
    btnOK->Location =
        ::Point(Width - btnOK->Width - 10, 10);
    btnOK->add_Click(new EventHandler(this, OK_Click));

    // Create and configure the Test button.
    btnTest = new Button();
    btnTest->Text = "Test";
    btnTest->Location =
        ::Point(Width - btnTest->Width - 10,
                btnOK->Bottom + 10);
    btnTest->add_Click(new EventHandler(this, Test_Click));

    // Create the application icon.
    ::Icon* MyIcon = new ::Icon("Icon1.ICO");

    // Configure the form.
    Text = "Simple Dialog Box Example";
    FormBorderStyle = FormBorderStyle::FixedDialog;
    StartPosition = FormStartPosition::CenterScreen;
    Icon = MyIcon;
    AcceptButton = btnOK;
    Controls->Add(btnOK);
    Controls->Add(btnTest);
}

void SimpleDialog::OK_Click(Object* sender, EventArgs* e)
{
    // Exit the application.
    Close();
}

void SimpleDialog::Test_Click(Object* sender, EventArgs* e)
{
```

```
      // Display a message.
      MessageBox::Show("This is a test message.",
                       "Test Message",
                       MessageBoxButtons::OK,
                       MessageBoxIcon::Information);
   }
}


// This is the entry point for this application
int _tmain(void)
{
   // Create a form instance.
   Sample::SimpleDialog *Dialog;
   Dialog = new Sample::SimpleDialog();

   // Run the application by displaying the form.
   Application::Run(Dialog);

   // Exit.
   return 0;
}
```

This application demonstrates all three parts of the .NET experience for the Visual C++ developer. Applications begin by importing one or more DLLs and then referencing the namespaces within those DLLs. The two-part technique makes it easier for you to create applications on the basis of the namespaces you select. Notice the way some DLLs use a dot syntax to designate their part in the .NET hierarchy.

TIP

You'll find all of the .NET Framework DLLs in the \WINNT\Microsoft.NET\Framework\v1.0.3215 folder of your hard drive. The Microsoft documentation doesn't include the required DLL names, in many cases, leaving it up to the developer to discover when the application requires a DLL. The \Framework folder might contain more than one version folder, so you'll need to be sure to check the right folder for the DLLs you need.

We created a managed console application in Chapter 2 (see the \Chapter 02\ Console5 folder for details). A console application is the only case where you can create a managed application without using namespaces and classes—at least if you want to avoid a lot of work. In most cases, your application will begin with the definition of a namespace and a class. You aren't required to use a namespace, but doing so avoids conflicts with applications from other developers.

The SimpleDialog class definition represents the first use of an attribute. All managed applications in Visual C++ require the use of a __gc attribute to show they support garbage collection. (We'll explore attributes in detail in Chapter 13.) Notice that the sample application derives from the Form class. Most of your GUI applications will derive from Form, but there are situations when you might use some other class as a starting basis.

Managed applications have the usual access to the public, protected, and private member access keywords. This example uses the standard keywords for simplicity. However, managed applications can also use member access keyword pairs, as shown in Table 12-1. Note that the table also includes the Common Language Specification (CLS) equivalencies where appropriate.

External Access	Internal Access	CLS	Result
public	public	public	Accessible by any code that accesses the class.
public	protected	famorassem	Limits accessibility to types in the same assembly or types derived from the containing type. A derived type doesn't have to appear in the same assembly.
public	private	assem	Only types within the same assembly have access.
protected	public	N/A	Accessible by code in any derived type and within the containing type. A derived type doesn't have to appear in the same assembly.
protected	protected	family	Accessible by code in any derived type. A derived type doesn't have to appear in the same assembly.
protected	private	famandassem	Only accessible by code in a derived type if the code appears in the same assembly.
private	public	N/A	Fully accessible from code within the containing type and subclasses.
private	protected	N/A	Fully accessible from code within the containing type and visible to subclasses.

Table 12-1   *Member Access Specifiers for Managed Code*

External Access	Internal Access	CLS	Result
private	private	private or privatescope	When used with a method, only accessible from code within the containing type. When used with a static variable, the member isn't accessible at all.

Table 12-1   *Member Access Specifiers for Managed Code* (continued)

Using the member access specifiers in Table 12-1 is the same as using member access specifiers in general. Here's a quick example.

```
public protected:
   int    MyInt;
```

In this case, any code within the same assembly can access the code, and any derived type can access it. Many developers find the use of double member access specifiers confusing, which is why Table 12-1 breaks them out as it does. The first specifier always defines external access, while the second specifier defines internal access. Note, also, that the table lists some combinations as not compatible with CLS. Generally, you should avoid using the member variable access combinations that lack a compatible CLS equivalent.

NOTE

The accessibility of the class determines the accessibility of the members it contains. For example, if the class is marked private, marking a method as public externally won't change anything. The compiler still views the external method access as private. If you find that an application, component, or control has accessibility issues, look for problems where the class accessibility level conflicts with that of the member elements.

The form for this application contains two buttons: OK and Test. The declarations and the event handlers for these buttons appear next. Note that you can declare the buttons within the class, but you must initialize them within a method. The example uses the constructor to initialize and configure the buttons. It also assigns an event handler for the click event of each button using the **add_Click**() method.

After the code initializes and configures the buttons, it configures the form. Adding an icon to the form means creating one using Resource View and then assigning the resulting file to an Icon control. Notice that you must assign the buttons to the form using the **Controls->Add**() method call. Here's what the resulting dialog box looks like:

A Look at the Intermediate Language (IL)

The previous section concentrated on the programming language aspect of the .NET Framework. It's important to realize that .NET is more than just a change to the programming language—it changes everything the language produces as well. That brings us to the IL. The IL is important because it defines a method for compiling the application that doesn't rely on a specific platform.

The IL represents a means for transporting the code to more than one platform in a manner similar to Java. Like Java, .NET relies on a platform-dependent runtime engine. Unlike Java, .NET compiles the application code. A Just-in-Time (JIT) compiler accepts the IL as input and creates a platform-specific executable. As a result, you only pay for the JIT compilation once and gain the full benefit of compiled code thereafter. We'll discuss the Common Language Runtime (CLR) in the "Understanding the Common Language Runtime for Visual Studio" section of this chapter.

As Visual C++ developers, you have more than a passing interest in the low-level features of the applications you develop. Many Visual C++ developers are as familiar with the assembler version of their code as they are with the C++ code. Disassembling Visual C++ so you can see how it works is part of many debugging sessions. That's the reason many Visual C++ developers will find managed code disconcerting—there isn't any native assembler code to view.

We initially discussed the Intermediate Language Disassembler (ILDASM) utility in Chapter 2. However, console applications, especially those with mixed code, don't lend themselves to easy disassembly. In addition, the console application output makes less sense than the output from a fully managed application. Figure 12-1 shows the results of using ILDASM with the example application in the previous section. Notice that the disassembly is laid out much the same as the application.

Each assembly element has a specific purpose and a symbol associated with it. For example, the red right arrow represents a module heading. ILDASM uses it for information directive, class declarations, and manifest information. Likewise, ILDASM uses a shield for namespaces, purple squares for methods, diamonds for fields, up arrows for properties, and down arrows for events.

If you double-click any of the entries shown in Figure 12-1, you'll see a disassembly of that element. The disassembly is useful only for managed code—you'll find it nearly useless for anything else, even in a mixed environment. Figure 12-2 shows an example of the disassembly for the **Test_Click()** event handler.

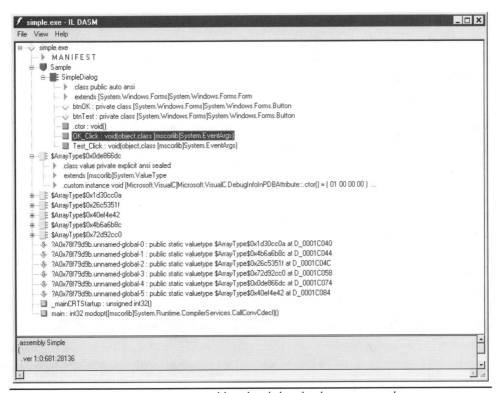

Figure 12-1   *Using ILDASM can reveal low-level details about your code.*

```
SimpleDialog::Test_Click : void(object,class [mscorlib]System.EventArgs)            _ □ ✕
.method private instance void  Test_Click(object sender,
                                          class [mscorlib]System.EventArgs e) cil managed
{
  // Code size         30 (0x1e)
  .maxstack  4
  IL_0000:  ldsflda     valuetype $ArrayType$0x40ef4e42 '?A0x78f79d9b.unnamed-global-5'
  IL_0005:  newobj      instance void [mscorlib]System.String::.ctor(int8*)
  IL_000a:  ldsflda     valuetype $ArrayType$0x0de866dc '?A0x78f79d9b.unnamed-global-4'
  IL_000f:  newobj      instance void [mscorlib]System.String::.ctor(int8*)
  IL_0014:  ldc.i4.0
  IL_0015:  ldc.i4.s    64
  IL_0017:  call        valuetype [System.Windows.Forms]System.Windows.Forms.DialogResult [System.


  IL_001c:  pop
  IL_001d:  ret
} // end of method SimpleDialog::Test_Click
```

Figure 12-2 *Use code disassembly to see how the compiler turns your code into IL.*

As you can see, the output really does look similar to assembly language. CLR uses a stack-based approach to working with data—there aren't any registers. If an application wants to add two numbers, it must first load the two numbers on the stack, then call the add routine. The add routine will pop the two numbers from the stack, add them, and then push the result back onto the stack. Of course, CLR also relies on memory to store objects—only values appear on the stack.

If you look at the source code for the **Test_Click()** event handler again, you'll notice it contains a single call to **MessageBox::Show()**. The call requires four arguments in this case. Look at the series of instructions shown in Figure 12-2. The LD* instructions load the stack with the data required for the call to **MessageBox::Show()**. However, there's more going on in the disassembly than a single call. Notice the LDSFLDA (load static field) instruction. The next instruction is a call to NEWOBJ. The NEWOBJ call "boxes" the static text found in the source code and creates a System.String object. The two LDC (load constant) calls push numeric values onto the stack. The final call is to the **MessageBox::Show()** method. This call is rather long, and you can't see the result in Figure 12-2. Here's the disassembled version of that call:

```
SimpleDialog::Test_Click : void(object,class [mscorlib]System.EventArgs)            _ □ ✕
ws.Forms.MessageBox::Show(string,
                          string,
                          valuetype [System.Windows.Forms]System.Windows.Forms.MessageBoxButtons,
                          valuetype [System.Windows.Forms]System.Windows.Forms.MessageBoxIcon)
```

Unlike with disassemblers you used in the past, creating IL file isn't a one-way trip. You can also use the Intermediate Language Assembler (ILASM) to compile the content of an IL file into working code. Theoretically, this would allow you to disassemble code, tweak it, and then compile it into an application again. Most developers will find using the standard .NET tools easier. It does bring up the possibility of third party developers writing compilers to create the required IL file and then calling ILASM to complete the task.

This section also demonstrates a potential problem with .NET. Many developers fear that third parties will steal their code by disassembling it. Worse still, some developers see the potential for crackers to distribute virus-ridden code in their name. Hopefully, Microsoft will find a cure for this problem in the near future. We'll see in Chapter 13 that there's a partial solution for the problem now in the use of strong names. You create a strong name by adding a key value to the AssemblyInfo.CPP file of a component or application.

Why Change a Great Language?

We still haven't discussed the reasons for using .NET. Yes, it helps you produce code relatively quickly and in a straightforward manner. The use of IL brings many advantages (and many disadvantages as well). However, new isn't necessarily better unless there's an overriding reason for the change. Some members of the press claim that Microsoft introduces many new things simply to generate income—an opinion shared by many developers as well. The need to update Visual C++ is real, but the need to replace it with a new language isn't. This section of the chapter discusses the "why" of .NET from a Visual C++ developer perspective.

It doesn't seem too long ago that Visual C++ was the new kid on the block, a time when many developers were wary of replacing their C compiler to gain the benefits of object oriented programming (OOP). Now, Visual C++ is the veteran programming language, and we have other new kids on the block. Unlike the old dog that couldn't be taught new tricks, Visual C++ is gaining new capabilities as part of Microsoft's .NET architecture. These new features will allow Visual C++ to remain a viable part of the corporate environment for some time to come.

However, some developers still question whether Visual C++ is the language for tomorrow's development. The fact that the Microsoft documentation tends to focus on Visual Basic and C# to the exclusion of everything else doesn't help matters. While everyone agrees that Visual C++ is still perfectly viable for existing project upgrades, some wonder whether it will be able to make the leap to a programming environment where the distributed application is king.

The concerns expressed by industry experts do have merit. Developers today have little time to study a language with a steep learning curve. In addition, as high-speed hardware becomes a commodity item, some developers question the need for a language that creates fast code at the expense of development time. The following sections are going to look at all of these issues. We'll talk about why developers occasionally look at Visual C++ as an old language without a future. The following sections will address these questions:

▶ What are the limitations of using Visual C++ for modern application development?

▶ Are there any reliability or stability issues to consider? (Yes, the *environment* is stable, but how stable are the resulting applications?)

▶ How does Visual C++ meet the requirements of distributed application development given Microsoft's plans for the .NET platform?

▶ How will Microsoft address needed changes to Visual C++ in order to keep it a viable development platform?

A Summary of Visual C++ Limitations in Today's Environment

There aren't any perfect languages. Even if someone were to develop a perfect language, it would be perfect only for a given set of circumstances. That's why it can be said that Visual C++ has limitations without implying that it's a poorly designed or implemented language. The fact is that Visual C++, like most languages, is very good at doing what Microsoft designed it to do and isn't particularly good for other tasks. The purpose of this section is to discuss those areas where Visual C++ is less suitable than other languages for a given purpose. We'll see how C# will address some of these issues in the "Visual C++ Limitations that C# Will Address" section of this chapter.

Many novice programmers shy away from Visual C++ because the low-level programming perception makes them think that this product is too hard to learn. In some respects, the current version of Visual C++ is a hard product to learn. As previously mentioned, Microsoft has made several missteps in creating the product, but chose to keep each product version intact to allow for backward compatibility. For example, you can currently write component code using two very distinct methods: Microsoft Foundation Classes (MFC) or Active Template Library (ATL). It's as if Microsoft embedded two different languages within the one language product. MFC and ATL represent two completely different methods for accomplishing the same task.

NOTE

You'll find that moving your Visual C++ 6 applications to Visual C++ .NET is a painful experience. Microsoft decided to make changes for the sake of standards compatibility and usability that render some Visual C++ 6 code unusable. We've discussed some of these instances throughout the book. The IDE will ask you to convert your application while loading it. The conversion process doesn't always work well and you might find it easier to reconstruct the project beginning with a fresh shell and moving your code from the old application to the new one. Even so, changes in the template language and modifications for the .NET Framework make compatibility a factor.

There are other problems when using Visual C++. For example, there are several incompatible versions of the MFC dynamic link library (DLL) file. Programs compiled with one version of the MFC DLL aren't necessarily compatible with newer versions. However, you need to look at the source of the compatibility problems. In many cases, developers chose to ignore Microsoft's warnings about using a specific programming technique. They may have ignored the warnings because the version of Visual C++ they were using had some limitation that the developer needed to work around to achieve a certain effect. Since Visual C++ is so flexible, it allowed the workaround, even though the coding technique led to compatibility problems later. In short, Visual C++ will allow a developer to work around problems, but with the possibility that the workaround could cause problems later. Another bonus of using Visual C++ is development flexibility, but the other side of the coin is potential compatibility problems.

In addition to providing many ways to accomplish the same task, Visual C++ uses a unique interface. There isn't anything wrong with this interface, but it's different from the interface used by other Visual Studio development platforms. Many developers view this difference as a problem, because it means they have to learn two different integrated development environments (IDEs). (An IDE is a combination of editor and compiler that allows a developer full control over application construction without leaving the environment.) However, in Microsoft's defense, the IDE currently in use by Visual C++ reflects its use as a low-level development language. The interface allows a developer to move around complex applications quickly. Therefore, while many developers have called for a unified Visual Studio IDE to reduce the product learning curve, developers stand to lose some of the flexibility provided by the current IDE.

The major complaint that everyone has about Visual C++ is the vast amount of code required to complete any given task. Even a small component requires many lines of code to accomplish the same thing you could with a few lines of code in Visual Basic. It's true that Microsoft provides Wizards to automatically write some code for the developer, but this technique brings problems of its own. Many developers don't understand what the Wizards do behind the scenes, with the result that modifications to standard behaviors become difficult. A Visual C++ developer can accomplish many tasks with an ease not found in other languages, but the price for this flexibility is coding time.

Stability Issues

Although the Visual C++ development platform is stable, some developers question the stability of the applications created using this product. There are several stability issues to consider. The first, and most important, is the use of completely incompatible programming techniques to achieve a given result. I've mentioned one of the worst offenders facing developers—the choice between creating applications quickly using MFC or relying on time intensive techniques that guarantee better results.

The MFC library is another source of concern. There are several versions of this library around, and each version tends to introduce new compatibility problems. Consequently, when a developer creates an application distribution package, he or she must include the MFC library and hope that the version used by their application doesn't interfere with anything else on the user's machine. The problem with the MFC library is a big one that Microsoft has chosen not to deal with.

Another potential problem is the need to use just the right set of add-ons to develop your application. For example, it's usually not enough to install the Platform SDK once when you set up your development machine. The Platform SDK constantly changes to meet changing Windows and environmental requirements. It also changes to reflect Microsoft's latest plans for new technology. This means you'll spend a few hours every three months (the release schedule for Platform SDK updates) modifying your setup and hoping that nothing breaks. From an application perspective, the use of the wrong SDK version could mean application stability problems on certain Microsoft platforms or with certain products such as database managers.

Memory management is another Visual C++ problem. When you write Visual C++ application code, you're also supposed to allocate and release memory in accordance with the rules that Microsoft has provided. The problem is that there are situations when the rules are less than clear, and few developers have a perfect track record for releasing all of the memory they allocate. The result is that many users experience memory leaks that rob their system of performance and eventually require a reboot. In a worst case scenario, memory management problems can actually cause the system to crash.

Challenges of the .NET Framework

The need to embrace the .NET Framework extends beyond developer productivity and the inherent problems in Visual C++ applications, such as memory leaks. Visual C++ developers face some interesting challenges as Internet computing becomes more pervasive. Remember that Visual C++ was designed at a time when the desktop application was king and remote computing was based on modem communications. Today, most companies are looking to build distributed applications. Not only do companies want employees to maintain constant communication with the home office, there are customers to support and business collaborations to consider as well. The Internet has significantly changed the face of business. Any developer creating an application today will need to consider remote communications as part of the development plan.

One of the first challenges that Microsoft faced in integrating Visual C++ with the .NET Platform is making a language product that was designed to build desktop applications that work within a distributed environment. They provided part of this support by adding COM+ and Queued Components to Windows 2000. Building a COM+ application doesn't require that much special coding, and the resulting application will work in a distributed environment if the developer follows certain guidelines. Queued Components enable a developer to add asynchronous request processing using a message-based technology. However, the distributed application support is neither automatic nor easy to incorporate—the developer has to plan in order for this approach to work.

Using COM+ doesn't fix all of the problems with Visual C++. It's important to remember that Visual C++ is designed to work with the Distributed Component Object Model (DCOM)—a protocol with Internet communication problems. DCOM uses multiple ports to communicate using binary data—both characteristics cause security problems in an environment where administrators have to reduce every potential problem. Contrast this with new languages like C# that get around Internet communication problems using new protocols such as eXtensible Markup Language (XML) and Simple Object Access Protocol (SOAP). We'll talk more about how C# fixes some problems with Visual C++ in the "Visual C++ Limitations that C# Will Address" section of the chapter.

You saw how to create a SOAP application using Visual C++ in Chapter 11. The code wasn't difficult to create, but you must admit there was a lot of it given the small size of the component. Imagine trying to create a database application using such code. Microsoft has bolted every available feature onto the unmanaged form of Visual C++, but development is still cumbersome in the unmanaged environment, partly because the environment can't perform the tasks that developers expect of it. Microsoft built the .NET Framework from the ground up for distributed applications.

BROWSER ALERT

*The best place to begin looking for XML-specific information is the Worldwide Web Consortium (W3C) Web site at **http://www.w3.org/XML**. Two of the better XML specific Web sites are The XML Cover Pages at **http://www.oasis-open.org/cover/sgml-xml.html** and XML.com at **http://www.xml.com/**. Two good places to look for SOAP information are the Microsoft Web site at **http://msdn.microsoft.com/soap/** and the DevelopMentor Web site at **http://www.develop.com/soap/**.*

Another potential problem area is the idea of managed versus unmanaged programming environments. The standard Visual C++ environment that everyone is used to today is unmanaged. This means that standard Visual C++ programs write to the Windows API directly through MFC or ATL. A managed environment is one where a framework, in this case the .NET Framework, manages the application. The framework controls everything from how the application creates objects to the way it allocates memory. An application talks to the framework, which determines if it can fulfill the request, and then the framework talks to the Windows API to complete the request. The addition of the .NET Framework allows better interoperability between languages, reduces errors due to common programming problems like memory management, and provides the means for creating better distributed applications.

Visual C++ provides managed and unmanaged projects. You also have a choice between ATL and MFC projects. All of the choices are there and you don't have to keep the environment pure—it's possible to mix managed and unmanaged code in the same application. However, one thing is clear—the developer still has to make a choice based on application requirements and individual needs. The developer needs to make a choice between functionality (the .NET Framework) and flexibility (direct Windows API access).

The existence of two environments, managed and unmanaged, increases the complexity of the Visual C++ development environment because now the developer has to determine when to use the managed environment. Determining when to use the managed environment is relatively easy. The following list details a few of the managed environment scenarios you need to know about.

▶ **Migrating Code**   At some point, you'll want to move code to the .NET Framework, or, at least, make the code accessible to other applications. Visual C++ will allow you to mix managed and unmanaged code in the same file.

Obviously, Microsoft would love it if you moved your application to .NET. A more practical solution is to create managed wrappers for existing code. This would allow you to maintain the existing code base and still make the code accessible from within the .NET Framework.

▶ **Component Access**   One of the problems with Visual C++ right now is that it takes a lot of extra coding to make a component visible and usable within Visual Basic. The .NET Framework is designed to aid in language interoperability. You can use managed code wrappers to expose the functionality of your component to any .NET language.

▶ **Accessing the .NET Framework**   Visual C++ contains managed code extensions—essentially attributes—that allow you to access the .NET Framework from within unmanaged code. This enables you to access the remote access features of technologies like ADO.NET. Of course, it's not always important to use the latest components. For example, Microsoft is actually recommending that people continue to use ADO if they need server-side cursor support. You'll find that using the same components that you always have will work better than using managed extensions when .NET has nothing new to offer.

How Does Visual C++ .NET Stack Up?

By now, you have some idea of why the .NET Framework is important and why you need to learn about managed code. Using managed code enables you to write code faster and with fewer bugs (at least of the memory variety). However, the wealth of existing code you own isn't going to modify itself, so you'll still need the unmanaged environment for quite some time to come. In this respect, Visual C++ .NET does well, but not great. You'll find that Microsoft has introduced a wealth of compatibility problems in order to move the language forward. Whether this makes life difficult or not depends on the kind of applications you create. Experience shows that database application development took the most significant hit in compatibility.

Many developers rightfully complain that Visual C++ still isn't standards compliant. For example, there are still problems with standard template language (STL) compatibility. (Microsoft has taken great strides in making Visual C++ more compliant.) Adding the .NET Framework hasn't affected the compatibility issues, but using the .NET Framework will definitely affect the compatibility of your code. Another choice you have is one of compatibility with the standards or using the latest technology for improving your productivity.

The bottom line is that Visual C++ has a lot to offer, but the offerings are confusing, to say the least. It's essential to weigh the benefits of moving your code to .NET before you make the attempt. In many cases, you'll find that moving your code isn't practical. If you decide not to move your code to .NET, then you need to consider the other problems that Visual C++ .NET presents. You may find situations when it's best to leave the old compiled code alone and simply build connections to it as needed.

Visual C++ Versus C#

There's a lot of talk going on about a new language, C#. This language looks a lot like Visual C++ at first, but then you begin to notice differences. Eventually, it becomes clear that C# is a combination of Visual C++ and Visual Basic, with some new object-oriented programming features (reminiscent of languages like Smalltalk and Eiffel, or even Java) thrown in for good measure. Most developers feel that C# is Microsoft's alternative to Java, and some have tried to make direct comparisons between the two.

NOTE

You might wonder why I'm including anything about C# in a Visual C++ book. Many developers have an affinity for their development language and will do anything to use that single language for every project. As previously mentioned, I feel that a good developer has multiple tools to use and C# is an excellent tool to add to your developer toolbox. I included this section in the book so you could gain a brief insight into the functionality that C# provides. You'll find that C# is an excellent language to use for Web page scripting, even if you don't use it for anything else. Visual C++ developers need a second language they can use for some of those distributed requirements of today's applications.

C# is a language designed to meet the requirements of new application development, especially when it comes to the .NET environment. You can also use it for updates of existing applications, but new application development is where this product shines. The following discussion provides you with an overview of how Visual C++ and C# differ so that you know when to use each of these languages.

Same Base Language, Different Development Environment

Programmers who are already familiar with Visual C++ development will have the shortest learning curve for C#. You'll find that creating variables is about the same and that C# uses many of the programming constructs that Visual C++ does. In fact, even a C programmer would understand many of the features of C#. For example, like any C program, C# applications begin with a **Main()** function. Listing 12-2 shows a simple C# application. The first thing you should notice is the similarity of this code to the managed Visual C++ application shown in Listing 12-1. Some of the differences between the two environments are due to the increased level of automation in C#. The IDE automatically maintains some portions of code for you as you use the form designer.

Listing 12-2

```csharp
namespace Sample
{
   using System;
   using System.Drawing;
   using System.Collections;
   using System.ComponentModel;
   using System.Windows.Forms;
   using System.Data;

   /// <summary>
   ///     Summary description for Form1.
   /// </summary>
   public class SimpleDialog : System.Windows.Forms.Form
   {
      private System.Windows.Forms.Button btnTest;
      private System.Windows.Forms.Button btnOK;
      /// <summary>
      ///     Required designer variable.
      /// </summary>
      private System.ComponentModel.Container components;

         public SimpleDialog()
         {
            //
            // Required for Windows Form Designer support
            //
         try
         {
            InitializeComponent();
```

```
      }
      catch (Exception e)
      {
      }


   }


   /// <summary>
   ///     Clean up any resources being used.
   /// </summary>
   protected override void Dispose( bool disposing )
   {
      if( disposing )
      {
         if (components != null)
         {
            components.Dispose();
         }
      }
      base.Dispose( disposing );
   }


   /// <summary>
   ///     Required method for Designer support - do not modify
   ///     the contents of this method with the code editor.
   /// </summary>
   private void InitializeComponent()
   {
      System.Resources.ResourceManager resources =
         new
System.Resources.ResourceManager(typeof(SimpleDialog));
      this.btnTest = new System.Windows.Forms.Button();
      this.btnOK = new System.Windows.Forms.Button();
      this.SuspendLayout();
      //
      // btnTest
      //
      this.btnTest.Location = new System.Drawing.Point(197, 36);
      this.btnTest.Name = "btnTest";
      this.btnTest.Size = new System.Drawing.Size(69, 20);
      this.btnTest.TabIndex = 1;
      this.btnTest.Text = "Test";
      this.btnTest.Click += new
```

```
System.EventHandler(this.Test_Click);
        //
        // btnOK
        //
        this.btnOK.Location = new System.Drawing.Point(197, 7);
        this.btnOK.Name = "btnOK";
        this.btnOK.Size = new System.Drawing.Size(69, 21);
        this.btnOK.TabIndex = 0;
        this.btnOK.Text = "OK";
        this.btnOK.Click += new System.EventHandler(this.OK_Click);
        //
        // SimpleDialog
        //
        this.AutoScaleBaseSize = new System.Drawing.Size(5, 13);
        this.ClientSize = new System.Drawing.Size(266, 237);
        this.Controls.AddRange(new System.Windows.Forms.Control[] {
            this.btnTest,
            this.btnOK});
        this.Icon =

((System.Drawing.Icon)(resources.GetObject("$this.Icon")));
        this.Name = "SimpleDialog";
        this.Text = "Form1";
        this.ResumeLayout(false);

    }

    protected void OK_Click (object sender, System.EventArgs e)
    {
        this.Close();
    }

    protected void Test_Click(object sender, System.EventArgs e)
    {
        MessageBox.Show(this, "This is a test message.",
                    "Test Message",
                    MessageBoxButtons.OK,
                    MessageBoxIcon.Information);
    }

    /// <summary>
    /// The main entry point for the application.
    /// </summary>
```

```
public static void Main(string[] args)
{
    Application.Run(new SimpleDialog());
}
    }
}
```

There are some significant coding differences between Visual C++ and C#. For one thing, C# is a managed code environment—you can't use it to write unmanaged code (at least, not in the sense of creating a native EXE). This means that the .NET Framework performs tasks like managing memory and keeping track of objects automatically. Whenever you create a variable, C# automatically allocates memory for it. You don't have to worry about releasing memory used by variables because the garbage collector automatically releases it for you. In addition, all variables can act like objects. C# performs a process called *boxing* to create an object out of a variable and *unboxing* to return it to a plain variable.

Developers build objects using the same techniques as those in Visual C++, but the resulting object acts differently in some cases. For example, when you release an object in unmanaged Visual C++, the system calls the destructor immediately. This allows the Visual C++ developer to count on certain activities at a specific time. Unlike with Visual C++, releasing an object in C# doesn't call the destructor immediately. The garbage collector calls the destructor when it detects that the system no longer needs the object. This means you can't count on the garbage collector to call destructor at a specific time—it could happen at any time after the application releases the object.

Pointers, one of the strong suits of Visual C++, are constrained under C#. You can't perform certain types of pointer math when working with C#. In fact, you must use the C# unsafe keyword to even work with pointers. (Note that you must use the /unsafe compiler option as well.) In many cases, the constraints in C# are there to counteract bad programming practices; but, in a very few cases, these constraints prevent the developer from executing safe procedures. However, some developers say that the unsafe keyword is so powerful that it makes C# the most flexible and extensible .NET language.

You'll find that some C++ statements act differently under C#. For example, the *new* keyword now means to "obtain a new copy of an object." When working with statements that test a Boolean condition, you must use a bool variable. C# won't automatically convert variables of type int into a bool for you. Switch statements no longer allow fall through—you must specify an action using either a *break* or a *goto* statement. You can use the new *for each* statement to iterate through objects and collections. The checked and unchecked keywords determine whether C# automatically detects overflows in mathematical computations. Objects have to have a definite value before you can use them. There are other differences, many of them subtle.

As you can see, even though C# looks a lot like both C and C++, it behaves differently in some situations. The base language you're familiar with is still there, but you need to be aware of how C# handles situations differently than C and C++ do. The real learning curve for C# from a Visual C++ developer's perspective, then, is learning a new set of rules for a language that the developer is already familiar with. The following list provides a summary of the C++ features that you won't find in C#.

- ▶ Const Member Functions or Parameters (You can use Const fields.)
- ▶ Conversion by Constructions
- ▶ Default Arguments on Function Parameters
- ▶ Global Variables
- ▶ Header Files
- ▶ Macros
- ▶ Multiple Inheritance
- ▶ Typedef

Visual C++ Limitations that C# Will Address

One of the biggest problems that Visual C++ developers run into is memory management. Many developers experience application memory errors because Visual C++ offers little in the way of automated management. Memory leaks are a common problem with Visual C++ applications. While you'll see errors if you don't allocate the memory required for a variable, deallocation of that memory will raise few alarms. As a result, the application exits with some memory in use, and Windows begins to suffer from memory leaks. When the memory leak problem becomes severe enough, the system can crash. C# addresses this problem by automatically initializing the variables you create. In addition, the garbage collector handles memory deallocation automatically. Memory management under C# is a snap.

Another problem that Visual C++ developers have is exception handling. A called function can raise exceptions in any number of ways. Here's a list of the more common methods in use right now.

- ▶ An HRESULT value contains an error code on return.
- ▶ The expected return value contains a NULL or other non-value.

▶ The caller doesn't report the error directly—you have to use a separate call to check for an error.

▶ The caller raises an exception that you have to trap.

There are several problems with this approach to error trapping, the most important being that it relies too much on the developer and not enough on automated techniques. A developer may not check for an error, even if one could occur. A second problem is that you have to have an in-depth knowledge of every call you make. Otherwise, you may miss the error. C# uses a "Try...Catch" structure to provide a consistent, exception-based, error reporting strategy that doesn't rely on the developer as much. Even if the developer doesn't handle the error, it still gets reported to the user. While Visual C++ does include the "Try...Catch" structure, it isn't implemented consistently.

Visual C++ isn't a very good prototyping environment because there isn't any way to provide instantaneous feedback. Microsoft is billing C# as a language where prototyping is as easy to do as it is using Visual Basic. Given the functionality of the .NET Designers, they may very well succeed. Visual Basic is a successful design platform because you can draw dialogs and other application features in their final form. The buttons won't work, but then you don't need them to work in the prototype stage. All you really need to do is show the customer what the final application will look like. A small change here or there can ensure the customer will be pleased with the result and save you hours of coding time.

Some people view Visual C++ as a non-standard implementation of the C++ language. It's true the Microsoft has added more than a few extensions and taken some liberties with the interpretation of the specification. C# is a new language that's going through the standards process as Microsoft develops it. The product you get from Microsoft will adhere to the standards, which means that you'll be able to rely on it for all types of development and may be able to use it on other platforms eventually. The point is that unlike Visual C++, C# won't have a lot of old baggage to carry around—it's the new language for the new age of development.

BROWSER ALERT

You can find out more about the C# standards effort at the ECMA Web site at http://www.ecma.ch/ecma1/NEWS/NEWS.HTM and http://www2.hursley.ibm.com/tc39/. There's a language reference at http://msdn.microsoft.com/library/en-us/csspec/html/CSharpSpecStart.asp.

It's relatively easy to break components in Visual C++ because it lacks versioning support as part of the IDE. C# will provide versioning support. The runtime handles member layout automatically, which means binary compatibility is no longer an issue. The runtime will even provide side-by-side versions, so that applications that rely on a specific component version will find the version they need. Finally, C# allows the developer to specify version information so that an application uses the correct version of a component even if that version is later superseded.

If you've ever lost track of a header file and therefore couldn't get your application to compile, you'll love the fact that all C# code appears in the same file. This means you won't worry about header files anymore. The use of inline code also means that C# applications compile faster and require less interpretation by the compiler. Less compiler interpretation means fewer chances for weird errors when the compiler uses the wrong header file or you forget to modify the header file to match the current application needs. The order of classes in a file doesn't make any difference either. You can place the classes in any order and won't need to make forward declarations in order to get your code to compile. Overall, you'll find that C# makes development a lot easier by removing some of the things developer's had to remember when working with C++.

Choosing a Language by Application Target

Adding yet another language to your arsenal can also add a new level of confusion to the development process. Some developers avoid the confusion completely by using a single language for every task, but that's not the most efficient way to program. Using a single language for everything reduces complexity at the cost of development time, which isn't a good trade in a time of short development cycles.

For some developers, Visual Basic and Visual C++ provide all that they need for desktop applications. Visual C++ is a great language for low-level operating system access. A lot of developers will place their low-level Visual C++ routines in DLLs or components. Visual Basic offers fast application prototyping and development, especially when working with database managers. By combining the strengths of both languages, a developer can create very robust applications in a short time.

Of course, there are other languages in most developer toolkits. Developers who need to work on the Internet will often add a language like Java to their arsenal. Java allows them to create components that execute within a browser in a platform-independent manner. Adding a scripting language like VBScript or JavaScript (now ECMAScript) makes Web programming even better. When a developer learns enough languages and knows how to combine them, creating an application becomes a lot easier.

So, where does C# fit into the picture? If desktop applications were limited to the local area network (LAN), then you might not need the capability that C# provides— at least, not to make applications work. C# makes it a lot easier to create components that will work both across a LAN and across the Internet. Using C# for certain types of component development, especially where remote access is a big concern, will greatly reduce development effort.

Another area where C# is the language of choice is when you need to create applications that rely on the .NET framework. Visual C++ provides .NET Framework support, but only if you add the required attributes. This is an error prone process that many developers will find increases the potential for application errors. While Visual Basic will include native .NET Framework support for the next edition, it doesn't provide the depth and flexibility that C# can provide. C# provides the new middle ground required for .NET applications. It allows you to perform tasks directly, rather than finding ways to work around problems.

C# also provides a managed environment by default. This actually makes C# a better choice for team development, because it forces members of the team to write code in a certain way. For example, C# uses strict data typing, which means there are fewer opportunities for error when performing type conversions.

It may sound like C# is the perfect language, but it isn't. You'll still want to use Visual C++ for unmanaged code situations, and Visual Basic is still the best choice for rapid application prototyping. You won't get rid of your scripting languages or Java any time soon either—all of these languages still have a place in your toolkit. C# is just another tool that every developer should learn about. As programming changes, you'll need new tools to create tomorrow's applications.

Determining When to Upgrade to C#

For many developers, C# sounds like a dream come true. It represents the next level of innovation for developers who need at least some type of access to the hardware and low-level operating system features. From a conceptual perspective, the change to C# may appear as an immediate requirement for all developers.

Any change made to a development environment incurs cost, and the upgrade to C# is no exception. The best course of action is to wait until the cost of upgrading is smaller than the benefits you'll receive. It may not be a good idea to switch when your company has too many projects partially completed, because you may not have the staff required to complete a changeover. Here are some of the potential cost centers you should consider before making the upgrade to C#.

▶ **Existing code base**   One of the hidden costs of a programming language update is the price of updating existing code. If you choose to keep the existing code in the current language, then you'll pay another cost by supporting two products. A transition between programming languages always means that your existing code base will cost you something—either as an anchor holding your development staff back or as a bottomless pit of code rewrites.

▶ **Staff training** An upgrade to C# will mean training your current staff to use this new language or training new staff who already know C# about company policies. In either case, you'll end up paying for staff training of some type. Since C# is a new language, trying to find trained personnel may be difficult. In addition, you'll pay a premium price for C# programmers, because they're relatively new on the market.

▶ **Software updates** Using a new language means upgrading your existing development suite. You already have a large investment in language products for Visual C++ that you'll need to replace when using C#.

▶ **Inconvenience** Visual C++ is an established product with known quirks and broad support by third party vendors. C# will eventually save your company time and effort during the development cycle because if offers many development shortcuts that Visual C++ doesn't. In the meantime, however, C# will prove inconvenient and actually cost you development time. The lack of third party support, trained staff, and a stable programming platform will definitely take a toll on your development budget.

As you can see, the costs for using C# right now are going to be high. One way around this problem is to use a phased approach for C# implementation. You could begin by training one or two persons to use the product. New projects could begin using C# as the application development language—relying on existing components developed in Visual C++ for support and preserving your investment. No matter which approach you use, transitioning to C# is going to be expensive, but well worth the cost in the long run.

Understanding the Common Language Runtime for Studio

The Common Language Runtime (CLR) is the engine behind managed applications created with Visual C++ .NET. In "A Look at the Intermediate Language (IL)" section of the chapter, we discussed how CLR (pronounced "clear") uses a stack-based approach to managing applications. In other words, the IL file contains directives for loading data onto the stack, performing an operation on the data, and then storing the data into memory. Because IL uses generalized instructions, the same file could potentially work on any platform. However, this is just a theoretical advantage now, because the only place you'll find .NET is as part of Windows (and not even all versions of Windows support it).

The central part of CLR is MSCOREE.DLL. Every managed application contains a reference to this DLL. MSCOREE.DLL performs a lot of work on behalf of the application by managing memory and enabling the developer to discover every aspect of every type (not just those that are exported from objects, as in COM). CLR calls all component assemblies, and each assembly contains one or more types. COM uses a separate 128-bit key to identify each type. CLR uses a 128-bit key for the assembly, then refers to each type within the assembly using a strong name. The effect of both techniques is the same, just different. Every type has a unique identifier, but CLR uses a different method to provide this identifier.

The fact that Visual C++ and Visual Basic use different techniques to describe types under Visual Studio 6 is a well-known problem with consequences both subtle and obvious for the developer. The use of text (IDL) and binary (TLB) forms of identification for Visual Studio 6 forced developers to spend untold hours looking for odd interface problems. Here's an example of the arcane IDL method of describing an interface:

```
[
    object,
    uuid(3B6BA6ED-589E-4047-8BC8-C7F90140E37E),
    dual,
    nonextensible,
    helpstring("IDoMath Interface"),
    pointer_default(unique)
]
interface IDoMath : IDispatch{
    [id(1), helpstring("method DoAdd")]
        HRESULT DoAdd([in] SHORT Value1,
                      [in] SHORT Value2,
                      [out,retval] SHORT* Answer);
};
[
    uuid(412E29AB-F18A-4F1E-BF9D-DE8FCCE5F194),
    version(1.0),
    helpstring("SOAPAdd 1.0 Type Library")
]
library SOAPAddLib
{
    importlib("stdole32.tlb");
```

```
importlib("stdole2.tlb");
[
   uuid(05C05F0C-E746-4783-A5BC-BF8535444886),
   helpstring("DoMath Class")
]
coclass DoMath
{
   [default] interface IDoMath;
};
};
```

CLR uses a single technique to describe types. The binary format enables all languages to gain access to type information. Here's the same interface described using managed Visual C++:

```
namespace SOAPAdd
{
   __interface IDoMath
   {
      short DoAdd(short Value1, short Value2);
   };
}
```

TIP

Don't use the Add | Add Method or Add | Add Property interface context menu entries for a managed Visual C++ component. The IDE produces an invalid entry in the interface code. Hand code the entries using the example in this section.

Anyone who's worked with components in an unmanaged environment knows about IUnknown and the VARIANT type. The first is the root type for all objects, while the second is the root type for all values. Both of these root types are gone under .NET. CLR uses a single root type, System.Object, for all types. Checking against a system- or a user-defined type enables you to detect the type of an incoming value, which is more convenient and error proof than previous techniques.

Given the number of differences between CLR and unmanaged code, MSCOREE must provide some means for translating between the two environments. Every time an application passes a value beyond the MSCOREE boundary, MSCOREE must translate that value in some way. The method used for objects is to create a Runtime Callable Wrapper (RCW) or a COM Callable Wrapper (CCW), depending on the direction of data flow. An RCW acts as a proxy for unmanaged applications, while a CCW acts as a proxy for managed applications. Values are treated differently from objects. MSCOREE can marshal all of the values in the following list directly:

- ▶ Single
- ▶ Double
- ▶ SByte
- ▶ Byte
- ▶ Int16
- ▶ UInt16
- ▶ Int32
- ▶ UInt32
- ▶ Int64
- ▶ UInt64
- ▶ Single dimensional arrays containing any of the previous types.

MSCOREE can't marshal some values directly—it must translate them before use. In most cases, this means conversion to a Win32 compatible type. Table 12-2 shows the values that require translation and describes the common method for translating them.

Value	Translation Method
Multi-Dimension Array	Marshals as a safearray, in most cases, or an interface in others.
Array of Complex Types	Marshals as an interface, in most cases, but can also use a safearray.
Boolean	Converted to a value of type VARIANT_BOOL or Win32 BOOL. The conversion depends on remote object requirements.
Char	Converted to CHAR for 8-bit values or WCHAR for multibyte values.
String	Converted to BSTR whenever possible. Converted to LPSTR for 8-bit values or LPWSTR for multibyte values if BSTR isn't possible. LPTSTR supported for platform invoke calls, but not for COM interoperation. Other conversions include ByValTStr and TBStr.
Object	Converted to a VARIANT for COM interoperation only.

Table 12-2 *Common Value Translation Methods Between Managed and Unmanaged Applications*

Sometimes the translation type for a value isn't clear at the outset. In this case, if you need a specific translation type, you can use the MarshalAs attribute to achieve a proper conversion. One of the most flexible types in this regard is the String. The following code shows how you can marshal strings as various types:

```
public static extern void MyFunction(
    [MarshalAs(UnmanagedType.LPStr)] String lpString,
    [MarshalAs(UnmanagedType.LPWStr)] String lpwString,
    [MarshalAs(UnmanagedType.LPTStr)] String lptString,
    [MarshalAs(UnmanagedType.BSTR)] String bstrString);
```

As you can see, CLR not only runs your managed applications, but also enables you to create a mixed environment with relative ease and data compatibility. CLR is the basis for running applications under the .NET Framework, and it therefore pays to know how to work with it. Make sure you read Chapters 13 and 14 to learn more about working with the managed environment and to see how attributes affect CLR operation.

Converting Your Existing Code to .NET

Most developers will begin learning about .NET by tinkering with small projects. The high learning curve for this product means spending time with small projects in order to understand what .NET is all about. Somewhere along the way, you'll want to become more involved with .NET. Many developers will begin by converting existing projects to use .NET. The problem is that .NET isn't the same as previous language updates—it uses an entirely different method for working with applications.

The first question is whether you want to convert your code at all. Even recompiling your code under Visual C++ .NET seems risky if there's no overriding reason to do so. In many cases, you'll want to create managed wrappers for existing components. A managed wrapper contains all of the calls necessary to access the existing component. In this way, you perform the work of importing the component into the managed environment only one time. Every other time you need to access the component, you call upon the services of the managed component instead.

If you do decide to move an application or component completely over to .NET, it's important to realize that none of the old code will work. All that you can move is your business logic. This means that you need to rewrite every report and every display routine and might even need to reformat the business logic to fit within the confines of .NET.

Sometimes you'll run into a problem where the .NET Framework doesn't provide an equivalent to a Windows API call. For example, you can't call DirectX using the .NET Framework (at least not in the current version). In this case, you'll need to retain the current calls in your code. However, you'll need to reformat them as Platform Invocation (PInvoke) calls. A PInvoke call relies on the DllImport attribute to gain access to a Windows API or other external function call. Here's a simple example of a PInvoke call at work:

```
#include "stdafx.h"

#using <mscorlib.dll>
#using <system.dll>
#include <tchar.h>

// Make sure you include the InteropServices namespace.
using namespace System;
using namespace System::Runtime::InteropServices;

// Import the MessageBeep function so we can use it.
[DllImport("User32", EntryPoint = "MessageBeep")]
bool MessageBeep(int uType);

// This is the entry point for this application
int _tmain(void)
{
    // Play the default beep.
    MessageBeep(-1);
    return 0;
}
```

If you compile and run this code, you'll hear the standard beep. However, the important consideration is that you now have access to the **MessageBeep()** API call found in User32. The same technique works well for other API calls as well.

Visual C++ users can salvage a few items from their old applications. For example, the Version and String resources work fine under the new version of Visual C++. You can also use icons, cursors, HTML, and bitmaps from older applications. Dialog layouts will import into Visual C++ .NET, but you can't use them within the managed environment (see Listing 12-1 for details on how .NET works with dialog boxes). Likewise, you'll need to create new menus and accelerators for your applications. None of these items import into a .NET application particularly well.

Attributes and Visual C++ Programming

IN THIS CHAPTER:

Why Attributes?

Understanding the Attribute Types

Working with Attributes

Avoiding Problems when Using Attributes

Attributed Programming and Debugging

V isual C++ .NET includes a new feature called *attributed programming*. Developers have many reasons to use attributes—most notably as a means for describing code in a way that other developers can understand with ease. In some respects, attributes are an extension of what Visual C++ developers already do in the IDL files for an application. The difference is that, with attributed programming, the developer performs tasks within the code file, rather than a separate IDL file. Attributes are also more powerful than IDL entries of the past. You use attributes to control the application, the compiler's behavior, and optional environmental behaviors.

So, why is this feature so important? Imagine writing the components you always have in the past, but with as little as 25 percent of the code you use today. Less code means fewer potential errors and a shorter development time. Programmers from all walks are finding they have a hard time meeting delivery dates given shorter deadlines and increasing application complexity. Any technology that promises to reduce development time using a tool that you're already familiar with is a welcome relief. As you'll see in this chapter, attributed programming is the must-have feature for Visual C++ .NET. Other improvements to Visual C++ will provide incremental speed increases—only attributed programming promises to reduce development time by an order of magnitude.

We'll look at attributes in detail in the following sections. The beginning of the chapter will cover a combination of usage and theory topics, such as why you'd want to use attributes in your next application. The theory sections will tell you about the various attributes and provide some code snippets showing their use. The "Working With Attributes" section contains two component examples that rely on attributes. In addition, one of the component examples will use managed (in contrast to unmanaged) coding techniques. Finally, we'll discuss how you can avoid problems when using attributes in your next project and how attributes work within the debugger.

TIP

*Attributes represent a new and interesting way to produce application code quickly and with fewer errors. However, they also represent an unknown for many developers, which means the learning curve will be high. If the content of this chapter whets your appetite for updated information, you may want to look at Microsoft's white papers at **http://msdn.microsoft.com/vstudio/ nextgen/technology/introcom.asp**. As attribute use evolves, it's almost certain that Microsoft will provide additional information at this site.*

Why Attributes?

One of the main problems that developers want to avoid today is added complexity. The development environment of today is much more complex than even a few years ago. Developers will likely design an application to perform more tasks using multiple single-task components, and they'll find they must create these applications in a shorter time. Anything that adds complexity to an already complex environment is unwelcome, to say the least.

It's important, therefore, to understand how using attributes can save development time, make debugging easier, and shorten the update cycle. The following list will help you understand how you can use attributes to reduce application complexity. Although the use of attributes means learning yet another programming concept, the effort is well worth the benefits that you'll gain.

▶ **Easier to read**   Attributes makes it easier for developers to understand code created by others. In actuality, there's less code—you'll see only the important code, not the glue code of the past. The reduced level of glue code allows other people to concentrate on the important elements.

▶ **More efficient code**   Using attributes helps the compiler to make specific types of optimizations. The result is code that runs faster and consumes fewer resources. There isn't any real magic in this case. You could compare attributes to macros to an extent—the optimization comes from using code that's already debugged and written efficiently.

▶ **.NET framework access**   You must use attributes to switch between managed and unmanaged code. Remember that only managed code has access to .NET Platform features—an important consideration for new application development.

▶ **Quicker development**   Using attributes enables developers to write code faster. An attribute can replace some of the code that developers currently use to get around problems in the Visual C++ environment.

▶ **Reduced debugging time**   Attributes can act as hints about the normal or anticipated operation of an application. Knowing the expected behavior can significantly reduce debugging time.

▶ **Custom attributes**   You can also create custom attributes to define specific Visual C++ actions. Using custom attributes enables you to automate repetitive tasks. However, at the time of this writing, creating attributes using Visual C++ is an error-prone process that can be done only with managed code. Creating custom attributes in other .NET languages such as Visual Basic is easier.

Understanding the Attribute Types

Attributes fall into categories. It's important to know that each attribute affects application functionality at a specific level. For example, some attributes affect the way the compiler looks at the code during the compilation process. Attributes can allow certain types of optimizations to occur that the compiler may not normally use. They can also prevent inadvertent bugs by shutting off compiler optimizations in areas where the optimization may have unexpected results. With this in mind, let's look at the various kinds of attributes that the latest version of Visual C++ will place at your disposal.

ATL Server

These attributes affect the new ATL Server classes included in Visual Studio .NET. An ATL Server class helps you create Web applications, Web services, Web clients, message queuing-enabled applications, cryptographically protected applications, Simple Mail Transfer Protocol (SMTP) clients, and other server-side applications. In some respects, you can equate the ATL Server classes to a new form of COM+ programming. These classes enhance the ability of the developer to create distributed applications. For example, with the addition of a simple attribute, you can tell the server that an ATL component is able to handle HTML requests, as shown here:

```
[ request_handler( name="MyRequestHandler" ) ]
class CMyClass
{
   void MyMethod(void);
};
```

Note that the request_handler attribute can include up to two optional parameters. The first is the name of the request handler. If you don't specify a name, Visual C++ automatically assumes you want to use the class name. In this case, the name of the request handler is MyRequestHandler. The second parameter is the Service Description Language (SDL) entry. You won't need to provide this parameter unless the class in question also provides SOAP handling capability.

As you can see, the main purpose of this attribute type is to add distributed application handler support not available in previous versions of Visual C++. You'll use these attributes when working with SOAP, in most cases, but you can use them for something as simple as a specialized HTML parser. Of special interest is the inclusion of performance monitor attributes that allow you to create counters with far less code and fewer headaches. Table 13-1 contains the entire list of attributes of this type. In most cases, you can combine these attributes to attain special effects. However, be aware that you may need to use special parameters, like the SDL in our example, to achieve the desired results.

Attribute	Description
perf_counter	Adds performance monitor counter support to a class member variable. The parameters for this attribute include the counter name, help string, type, scale, and size.
perf_object	Adds performance monitor object support to a class. The parameters for this attribute include the number of instances that you want to allow and the CPerfMon class to which this object applies.
perfmon	Adds performance monitor support to a class. There are only two parameters for this attribute. The first is the name of the performance monitor object, while the second determines if the object is registered.
request_handler	Exposes a class as an ATL Server request handler. Allows the class to handle HTML requests. As previously mentioned, this attribute accepts two parameters—the name of the handler and the SDL entry used for SOAP processing.
soap_handler	Exposes a Web service class as an ATL Server request handler. Allows the class to handle SOAP requests through HTTP. This attribute accepts three parameters as input. The first is the name of the Web service. The second is the XML namespace used to identify the Web service, methods, and data. The third is the protocol used to access the Web service—"soap" is the only acceptable value as of this writing.
soap_header	Maps a member of a Web service class to a SOAP header. The two parameters for this attribute are "name" and "required." The name parameter determines the name of the SOAP header. The required parameter determines if this is a required SOAP header.
soap_method	Exposes a Web service class member as a public SOAP method. The only parameter for this attribute is the name of the method.
tag_name	Allows a request handler method to act as a replacement for a method associated with an HTML tag name. There are only two parameters for this attribute. The first is the name of the tag name replacement handler, while the second is the name of a method used to parse data for the tag name replacement handler.

Table 13-1   *ATL Server Attributes*

COM

If you've ever had to deal with the vast number of macros required to create a component, you know that they can become confusing. While the Visual C++ wizards attempt to write as much of the code for you that they can, there are always additions that you need to make. Unfortunately, figuring out where to make the entries and how to format them is often more like some kind of black art than science. In addition, if you make a mistake in filling out the wizard entries, trying to overcome the problem can prove difficult, because the wizard-generated code is difficult to read. The COM attributes overcome these problems by replacing large numbers of macro entries with easier to read attributes. Consider this example:

```
[ progid("CAgClass.coclass.1"), aggregates(__uuidof(CAgClass) ]
class CMyClass
{
   void MyMethod(void);
};
```

The progid attribute specifies the program identifier—the human-readable dot syntax name of an object. The compiler uses this information to locate information about the object in the registry and learn more about it. You'll use this attribute when creating external references to other objects on the client machine.

The aggregates attribute allows you to aggregate an existing component into the current component. In this case, CAgClass will become part of CMyClass. Notice that we use the __**uuidof**() function to obtain the universally unique identifier (UUID) of the existing class from the registry. You could also enter the UUID directly.

TIP

You can't use the aggregates attribute alone—this attribute is always preceded by the coclass, progid, or vi_progid attributes. (If you use one of the three, the compiler will apply all three.) The progid and vi_progid descriptions appear in Table 13-2. We'll discuss the coclass attribute in the IDL section. However, it's important to realize that some attributes have dependencies—you can't use them alone. Always check for dependencies before using an attribute in your code.

The COM attributes are one of the more complex attribute groups. They're also one of the best ways to improve developer productivity over the methods provided in previous versions of Visual C++. You'll find that these attributes will at least halve the amount of code you write for even simple code and will make your code infinitely easier to understand. Table 13-2 provides a list of common COM attributes and associated descriptions.

Attribute	Description
aggregatable	Determines whether another control can aggregate this control. A component can disallow aggregation, allow both stand-alone and aggregated use, or require aggregated use.
aggregates	Shows that this control is aggregating another control.
com_interface_entry	Adds an interface to the current class. You define the interface separately from the class code. We'll discuss this issue in the IDL section.
implements_category	Identifies component categories implemented by the target class—in other words, the areas of functionality that the component supports.
progid	Specifies the program identifier of a control.
rdx	Creates or modifies a registry key. The parameters for this attribute include the key, value, and value type.
registration_script	Allows execution of a custom registration script.
requires_category	Identifies component categories required by the target class—in other words, the areas of functionality that a container must provide to use this component.
support_error_info	Specifies that the component will return detailed context-sensitive error information using the IErrorInfo interface.
synchronize	Synchronizes access to a method within the target class.
threading	Determines which threading model a class uses. Standard values include apartment, neutral, rental, single, free, and both.
vi_progid	Specifies the version-independent program identifier of a control.

Table 13-2   *COM Attributes*

Compiler

You won't currently find compiler attributes that control every aspect of compiler behavior. However, you'll find attributes that provide access to the functionality required for new features of Visual C++ and reduce the complexity of changing some existing features. You need to know about this attribute category if you want to work in a managed code environment. In short, the compiler attributes affect only certain compiler operations, but they're very important operations. Many of these attributes appear at the beginning of the file or in conjunction with specialty classes. Table 13-3 contains a list of the compiler attributes.

Attribute	Description
emitidl	Determines if the compiler generates an IDL file based on IDL attributes (described in the IDL section). There are four possible emission conditions: true—the IDL is generated. false—the IDL isn't generated. restricted—allows IDL attributes without a module attribute—no IDL file generated. forced—overrides the restricted condition and forces the file to contain a module attribute.
event_receiver	Creates an event receiver. The event receiver can use the native, COM, or managed models for receiving events. The managed option will enforce .NET Framework requirements such as use of the garbage collector.
event_source	Creates an event source. The event source can use the native, COM, or managed models for sending events. The managed option will enforce .NET Framework requirements such as use of the garbage collector.
export	Places the target union, typedef, enum, or struct in the IDL file.
importidl	Allows placement of the target IDL file within the generated IDL file.
includelib	Defines the name of an IDL or H file that you want to place within the generated IDL file.
library_block	Places a construct, such as an interface description, within the generated IDL file. This ensures the construct is passed to the type library, even if you don't reference it.
no_injected_text	Prevents the compiler from injecting text as the result of using attributes within the code. This option assumes that the text is either not needed or that you injected it manually. For example, the /Fx compiler option uses this feature when creating merge files.
satype	Specifies the data type for a SAFEARRAY structure.
version	Specifies a class version number.

Table 13-3   *Compiler Attributes*

IDL

If you've ever spent an hour trying to debug a component only to find the IDL file has one bracket out of place, you know the frustration that IDL attributes will prevent. Using attributes, you can create components using far less code than ever before and you can ignore the IDL file completely. For example, you can create an interface within the main code file using just a few lines of code, as shown here:

```
[ dual ]
__interface IMyInterface : IDispatch
{
    [id(1) HRESULT MyMethod(void);
};
```

This dual interface contains a single method named MyMethod. The [dual] attribute defines the type of interface, while the __interface function defines the interface name (IMyInterface). Visual C++ automatically defines all of the required glue code for you. Of course, you can still use optional attributes to define alternative behaviors for both the interface and bundled methods.

The IDL file has always been an important and misunderstood part of the COM picture for Visual C++ developers. Let's look at another example of IDL attributes you'll see in Visual C++ .NET.

```
[ module( name="MyObject", type="EXE", version="1.1" )]
[ coclass, aggregatable( never ) ]
class CMyObject
{
    void MyMethod(void);
};
```

We're using several attributes in this case. The module attribute defines a library entry in the IDL file. You don't need to make the entry—Visual C++ handles it automatically for you. The library block will include an object name, type, and version in this case. The type property is interesting because it allows you to define the kind of component that you create. The example code will create an out-of-process server. If I had specified a property value of DLL, then the compiler would create an in-process server.

The second line of code includes two attributes that are being used together. The coclass attribute makes several important basic component entries in the IDL file. For example, it automatically creates code to register the component and to implement the IUnknown interface. The aggregatable attribute determines if you can use this component as part of a larger component. The example code shows that this will never happen with the component in question. You can also choose to allow both stand-alone and aggregated use or to disallow stand-alone use (the developer must incorporate the component into a greater whole).

As you can see, Microsoft designed the IDL attributes to reduce the amount of code you write and the opportunities for error. In addition, your code will compile faster and you have one less file to worry about (the IDL file) per class. Decreased coding is one of the most practical benefits of attributes since it has the greatest effect on developer productivity. Table 13-4 contains a list of the new IDL attributes—I haven't included attributes that appeared in the IDL files of older versions of Visual C++. The difference between the old IDL attributes and the new version of the same thing supplied with Visual C++ .NET is that you can now use the attributes within the application code.

Attribute	Description
coclass	Creates a COM class. You'll use this attribute with many other attributes described in this chapter. In most cases, you must create the COM class before you can perform any other COM-related tasks. Whenever you use this attribute, Visual C++ will automatically generate the progid, threading, uuid, version, and vi_progid attributes if you don't specify them with the coclass attribute.
dispinterface	Defines an interface as a dispatch interface within the IDL file. There are many requirements for using this attribute. Make sure you understand dispatch interfaces before you use this attribute within your code. The usage of this attribute is a little different from the MIDL version with respect to formatting and coding requirements.
dual	Specifies the interface is a dual interface. This attribute affects the entries the compiler places in the IDL file for the target interface.
idl_module	Defines many of the base information items for a DLL, including the module name, DLL name, UUID, and help information. This attribute can also determine whether to hide the library elements or restrict element use. This attribute is similar to the MIDL module attribute, but there are differences in use and implementation.
idl_quote	Allows use of attributes not supported by the current version of Visual C++. The quoted attribute will pass through to the IDL file without generating a compiler error.
module	Defines the library block within an IDL file. This information includes the module type, name, UUID, version, help context and files, along with other identifying information. Module types include DLL, EXE, service, console, and unspecified. The automatic entries that Visual C++ makes for you vary by module type, especially when working with ATL components.

Table 13-4   *IDL Attributes*

Attribute	Description
object	Creates a custom interface. Visual C++ automatically places the interface description within the IDL file. Custom interfaces must derive from IUnknown—the compiler will automatically derive a new interface from IUnknown if none of the base interfaces inherit from IUnknown.

Table 13-4   *IDL Attributes* (continued)

OLE-DB Consumer

Database management is a mainstay of most developers. Somewhere along the way, most developers end up spending at least some time working with databases. That's why the inclusion of OLE-DB consumer attributes is so important. Using attributes in a database application can greatly reduce the amount of coding you need to do to perform simple and common tasks. Here's a simple example of what you might see within a method designed to work with databases:

```
HRESULT MyDataAccess()
{
   [ db_source(
      db_source="DSN=FoodOrdersData",
      name="FoodOrder",
      hresult="hr" ]

   if (FAILED(hr))
      return hr;

   [ db_command(
      db_command="SELECT * FROM FoodOrders",
      name="FoodOrderRowset",
      sourcename="FoodOrder",
      hresult="hr" ]

   if (FAILED(hr))
      return hr;

   return S_OK;
}
```

In this case, data access consists of a db_source and a db_command attribute. The db_source attribute allows us to gain access to the database connection defined by the FoodOrdersData data source name (DSN). The connection receives a name of FoodOrder, and the result of the call appears in hr. Note that we don't create hr— Visual C++ automatically creates the HRESULT variable. The db_command attribute accepts a standard SQL command. The results of this command appear in FoodOrderRowset. Access to the database requires a connection, which is supplied by the sourcename parameter.

Microsoft has gone to great lengths to simplify database access in Visual C++ by using attributes. In fact, you'll find that most activities require only two or three of the six database attributes. Table 13-5 lists the attributes and describes them for you.

Attribute	Description
db_accessor	Binds the columns in a rowset to the corresponding accessor maps. You must provide an accessor number as the first parameter. The second parameter can contain a Boolean value that determines if the application automatically retrieves the accessor.
db_column	Binds a column to a rowset. You must provide a column name or the ordinal number of the column within the rowset to use for binding. Optional parameters include the data type, precision, scale, status, and length of the data.
db_command	Allows execution of database commands on an open connection. You must provide a database command as the first parameter. Optional parameters include the rowset name, source name, return value variable name, bindings value, and bulk fetch value.
db_param	Creates a connection between a member variable and an input or output parameter. You must provide a column name or the ordinal number of the column within the rowset to use for binding. Optional parameters include the parameter type, data type, precision, scale, status, and length of the data.
db_source	Opens a connection to a data source using a data provider. You must provide the name of a data source. Optional parameters include a name for the connection and the name of a return value variable. The connection string can take a number of forms—it's not necessary to use a DSN.
db_table	Opens an OLE-DB table. You must provide the name of the table you want to open. Optional parameters include a name for the table that the call returns, a data source name, and the name of a variable to receive the results of the operation.

Table 13-5   *DB-OLE Consumer Attributes*

Working with Attributes

There are several ways to work with attributes. The first method is to add them to your code automatically using a wizard. The various component wizards will now contain checkboxes that allow you to work with attributes. Check the required box and Visual C++ will automatically add the required attributes for you. Of course, there are some cases when you'll need to add an attribute manually. For example, you may want to override a default behavior. All you need to do, in such a case, is add the attribute in square brackets right before a class or other declaration, like this:

```
[ event_receiver(com) ]
class CMyClass
{
public:
    HRESULT MyMethod();
    {
        printf("You called the event handler.");
        return S_OK;
    }
};
```

This bit of code says that a class named CMyClass will receive events. You'll use the **__hook** function to hook one of the methods within CMyClass as an event handler from an event source. For example, if you want to call MyMethod every time a pushbutton generates a click event, you'd use the **_hook** function to make the linkage. The important consideration is that using attributes keeps you from spending hours writing macros and a lot of glue code that you normally need to write.

Now that you have a better idea of how attributes work, let's see them in action. The first example that follows is a managed component. The unique aspect of this component is that you can call it with equal ease from the managed and unmanaged programming environment. This technique is useful because it enables you to create managed components that you can use with your existing applications. The second example demonstrates how you'd create the PButton control using attributed ATL code. Compare the code used for this example to the code in Chapter 6 and you'll instantly see why attributes are such as a big deal.

Managed Component Example

The managed coding example requires some special configuration and coding techniques that differ from any coding example shown so far. For one thing, the managed component relies on the .NET Framework, which means you can't use it on machines that lack this support. However, you'll find that the actual coding process is both faster and easier. Begin by creating a Managed C++ Empty Project. The example uses DoSomething as a name. What you'll get is an empty framework without any files.

We need to change a few features of this control. For one thing, Visual C++ always assumes you want to create an EXE file. Our control will require a DLL, so you'll need to highlight DoSomething in Class View, use the Project | Properties command to display the DoSomething Property Pages dialog, and then change the Configuration Type field on the General tab to Dynamic Library (.dll). Open the Linker folder and select the General tab. Change the Output File to $(OutDir)/DoSomething.dll.

NOTE

You'll find that working with components is easier if you add the \WINNT\Microsoft.NET\ Framework\v1.0.3215 and \Program Files\Microsoft Visual Studio .NET\FrameworkSDK\Bin paths to the Path environment variable for your Windows setup. (Using the Visual Studio .NET Command Prompt shortcut automatically adds these paths, but requires you that you open the command prompt using a particular shortcut.) The command line utilities used in the sections that follow rely on these two path additions. Make sure you substitute the most current framework version number for the one listed in this note. The \WINNT\Microsoft.NET\Framework folder might contain more than one version of the .NET framework, and you should normally use the most current version for any applications that you create.

Adding Files and Code

Because our project lacks any files, you'll need to add one. Right-click DoSomething in Solution Explorer and select Add | Add New Item from the context menu. You'll see an Add New item dialog like the one shown next.

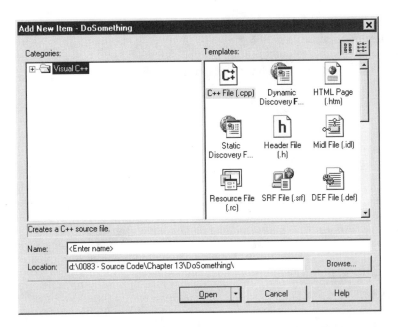

Select the C++ File (cpp) icon. Type **DoSomething** in the Name field and then click Open. Listing 13-1 shows the source code for DoSomething.

Listing 13-1

```
// Add the requited DLL support.
#using <mscorlib.dll>
#using <System.DLL>
#using <System.Windows.Forms.DLL>
```

```
// Add the required namespaces.
using namespace System;
using namespace System::Windows::Forms;
using namespace System::Runtime::InteropServices;

// Create the namespace.
namespace DoSomething
{
   // Begin the class declaration.
   // Managed controls only support public inheritance.
   [ClassInterface(ClassInterfaceType::AutoDual)]
   public __gc class SayHello
   {

   public:

      // You only need a constructor.
      SayHello(void);

      // Class methods.
      void DisplayMsg(void);
   };

   SayHello::SayHello(void)
   {

   }

   void SayHello::DisplayMsg(void)
   {
      // Display a simple dialog box.
      MessageBox::Show("Hello World");
   }
}
```

As you can see, the component code is extremely simple. This is all you need to create a component in the managed environment. Notice there's no destructor—you don't need one in the managed environment. The one important piece of code is the attribute added to the class declaration. You could access this component from within the managed environment, even without this attribute. However, the text program is unmanaged. The ClassInterface attribute tells Visual C++ how to generate the class interface information. Without this attribute, your class won't register correctly and you won't be able to access it from an unmanaged application. The acceptable interface types include dual, dispatch, and none.

You'll need to create a second CPP file at this point. Give this file a name of AssemblyInfo.CPP. This file contains identifying information for your assembly. It also contains an extremely important entry that enables you to give your assembly a strong name. A *strong name* essentially means Visual C++ encrypts the assembly using a key we'll generate later in this section. The idea is that an encrypted component is less susceptible to modification by third parties. Assemblies must have a strong name before you can add them to the Global Assembly Cache (GAC). Listing 13-2 shows the code for the AssemblyInfo.

Listing 13-2

```
#pragma once

#using <mscorlib.dll>
using namespace System::Reflection;
using namespace System::Runtime::CompilerServices;

// Add the general assembly information.
[assembly:AssemblyTitleAttribute("Say Hello Demonstration")];
[assembly:AssemblyDescriptionAttribute("Tell the world hello.")];
[assembly:AssemblyConfigurationAttribute("DoSomething Version 1.0")];
[assembly:AssemblyCompanyAttribute("DataCon Services")];
[assembly:AssemblyProductAttribute("DoSomething.DLL")];
[assembly:AssemblyCopyrightAttribute("Copyright 2001")];
[assembly:AssemblyTrademarkAttribute("")];
[assembly:AssemblyCultureAttribute("")];

// Add a version number to the assembly.
[assembly:AssemblyVersionAttribute("1.0.*")];

// Sign the assembly so we can give it a strong name.
[assembly:AssemblyDelaySignAttribute(false)];
[assembly:AssemblyKeyFileAttribute("MyKey")];
```

As you can see, the assembly information consists entirely of attributes. Note that although this information looks similar to the version information used for unmanaged components, it doesn't produce the same results. You'll learn how to work with standard resources in the Resource Requirements section. For now, you need to keep the assembly information separate from the version resource.

All of the entries in Listing 13-2 are standard. However, notice that the version number has an asterisk. The position of this asterisk means that the build number and revision will change for every build, while the major and minor version numbers remain the same. You must also set the AssemblyKeyFileAttribute attribute to a key name. We'll generate the key later—the key must exist before this example will link.

Resource Requirements

Managed components can use the same resources that unmanaged components use. The difference is that the managed component wizards assume you won't use them, so it doesn't include them in the project. At a minimum, you should add a Version resource so that other developers can identify your component.

To add a Version resource, open Resource View. Right-click DoSomething and choose Add | Add Resource from the context menu. Highlight the Version icon in the Add Resource dialog and click New. Visual C++ will add a new Version resource to your component. Fill out the various Version strings as you would for any component. Using the assembly information we discussed earlier as a source of information helps create consistent component information.

Key Generation and Registration

Before you can link the example code, you need the key referenced in the AssemblyInfo.CPP file. To generate a key, open a command prompt in the source code directory for the component. Type **SN -k MyKey** at the command prompt and press ENTER. The SN utility will generate a key pair that the linker will use to sign the component. The signing process gives the component a strong name.

NOTE

Make sure you compile and link your component before you proceed. Otherwise, the component won't register.

After you compile and link the component, you can open a command prompt in the component directory (usually \Debug or \Release). Registering your component will require two steps. First, type **RegAsm /TLB:DoSomething.TLB DoSomething.DLL** at the command prompt and press ENTER. This step creates a registry entry for the component. It also outputs a type library that programming environments such as Visual Basic use to access the component.

The second step is to type **GacUtil -I DoSomething.DLL** at the command prompt and press ENTER. You must add the component to the GAC if you want to access it with ease from any other application. As an alternative, you can always place a copy of the component in the same directory as the application.

TIP

Make certain you unregister a component before you remove it from your drive. Otherwise, you'll end up with a mountain of registry entries that you'll have to remove manually. The unregistration process requires two steps. First, type **GacUtil -u DoSomething** *at the command prompt and press* ENTER. *Don't add the file extension. Second, type* **RegAsm /unregister DoSomething.DLL** *at the command prompt and press* ENTER. *You can remove the component.*

At this point, you can access the component from an unmanaged application. It pays to verify that everything went as planned, because the various utilities don't always tell you if something went wrong. The best utility to verify the presence of your new component in the registry is OLE/COM Object Viewer. Look under the .NET Category folder and you should find the DoSomething.SayHello component shown in Figure 13-1. If you can't see the component, then the registration process failed or you forgot to add the ClassInterface attribute.

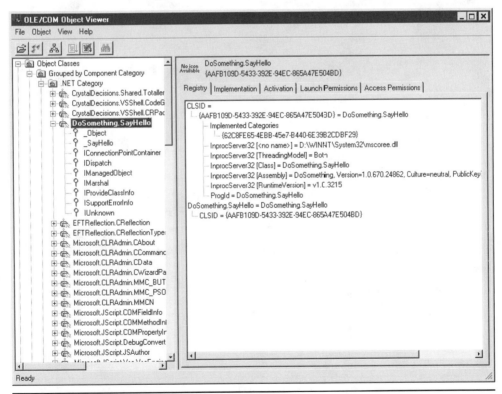

Figure 13-1 *Always verify proper component registration.*

Make sure you create an instance of the component with OLE/COM Object Viewer by clicking the plus sign next to the component entry, as shown in Figure 13-1. If the component entry appears in the list, but OLE/COM Object Viewer fails to instantiate the component, it means that the Common Language Runtime (CLR) can't find the component. A failure of this type normally indicates a failure of the GacUtil to register the component properly. You can verify proper component registration by looking in the Windows Assembly folder. Figure 13-2 shows the example component.

If you see the component is properly registered, but still won't instantiate in the OLE/COM Object Viewer, it normally signifies a major problem in your code. For example, you must always include a constructor, even if the constructor is empty. Likewise, managed components don't normally require a destructor, so you don't need to include one. You can also run into problems by not making your namespace or class public, or by not including the __gc attribute as needed.

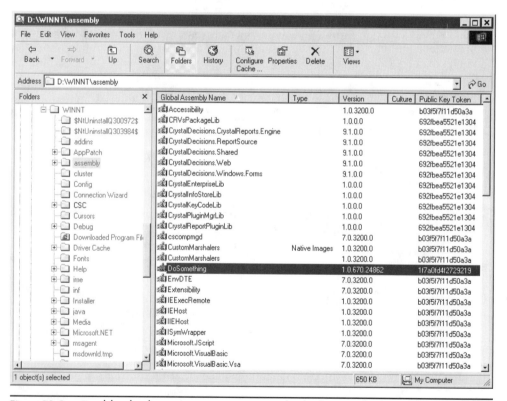

Figure 13-2   *Double-check component registration by looking in the Assembly folder.*

Testing the Component

One of the challenges that most Visual C++ developers will face is integrating managed components into existing unmanaged applications. That's why this chapter relies on a simple dialog-based MFC application. We created one of these applications in Chapter 2, so I won't discuss all the details in this section of the chapter. The test application appears in the \Chapter 13\DoSomethingTest directory of the source code CD.

The test application includes a Test pushbutton. Clicking this button will create an instance of the managed component and will execute the **DisplayMsg()** method. Listing 13-3 shows you how.

Listing 13-3

```
void CDoSomethingTestDlg::OnBnClickedTest()
{
    HRESULT     hr;             // Operation result.
    CLSID       clsid;          // Object ClassID.
    LPUNKNOWN   punk = NULL;    // IUnknown pointer.
    IDispatch   *pdisp = NULL;  // IDispatch pointer.
    DISPID      dispid;         // Dispatch ID of the function.
    LPOLESTR    MyFunction;     // Function name.
    EXCEPINFO*  pexcep;         // Exception information.
    DISPPARAMS  dispparams;     // Dispatch parameter list.
    UINT        perr = 0;       // Number of argument with an error.

    // Initialize the COM environment.
    OleInitialize(NULL);

    // Get the DoSomething ClassID.
    hr = CLSIDFromProgID(OLESTR("DoSomething.SayHello"), &clsid);
    if(FAILED(hr))
    {
        AfxMessageBox("Retrieval of DoSomething Program ID failed.");
        return;
    }

    // Create an instance of the object.
    hr = CoCreateInstance(clsid,
                          NULL,
                          CLSCTX_ALL,
                          IID_IUnknown,
                          (void**)&punk);
    if (FAILED(hr))
    {
        AfxMessageBox("Failed to create object.");
```

```
      return;
   }

   // Gain access to IDispatch.
   hr = punk->QueryInterface(IID_IDispatch, (void**)&pdisp);
   if (FAILED(hr))
   {
      AfxMessageBox("Failed to access IDispatch");
      punk->Release();
      return;
   }

   // Get the dispatch ID of the function.
   MyFunction = OLESTR("DisplayMsg");
   hr = pdisp->GetIDsOfNames(IID_NULL,
                             &MyFunction,
                             1,
                             LOCALE_SYSTEM_DEFAULT,
                             &dispid);
   if (FAILED(hr))
      AfxMessageBox("Function doesn't exist.");

   // Initialize the variables.
   pexcep = NULL;
   dispparams.cArgs = 0;
   dispparams.cNamedArgs = 0;
   dispparams.rgdispidNamedArgs = NULL;
   dispparams.rgvarg = NULL;

   // Execute the function.
   hr = pdisp->Invoke(dispid,
                      IID_NULL,
                      LOCALE_SYSTEM_DEFAULT,
                      DISPATCH_METHOD,
                      &dispparams,
                      NULL,
                      pexcep,
                      &perr);
   if (FAILED(hr))
      AfxMessageBox("Failed to execute function.");

   // Release the object pointers.
   punk->Release();
   pdisp->Release();
```

```
    // Uninitialize the COM environment.
    OleUninitialize();
}
```

Notice that the example code uses the dispatch method for accessing the component. You can use this method with any component, but at the time of this writing it appears to provide the only access method for managed components. Unlike with Visual C++ unmanaged components, the compiler doesn't automatically generate the interface (*_i.c) or the proxy (*_p.c) files. You can generate these files by hand, but it's a time consuming process. Likewise, many developers are used to using the #import directive to create a smart pointer to a component. This technique still produces the TLH and TLI files with a managed component, but the results are error prone and generally won't compile.

As you can see from Listing 13-3, the code follows a multipart process to access the methods and properties within the component. Generally, the application will gain access to IUnknown then use **QueryInterface()** to access IDispatch. Once you have a pointer to IDispatch, you can use **GetIDsOfNames()** to obtain a pointer to a particular method or property. **Invoke()** provides access to the method.

When using the dispatch method of accessing a component, you always provide a DISPPARAMS structure, even if the method call doesn't require any arguments. At a minimum, you have to tell IDispatch that the method doesn't require any arguments by setting the cArgs member to 0. As the code shows, you should also initialize the other structure members. If you fail to provide a DISPPARAMS structure, then you'll receive a nebulous E_POINTER return error. You can set other **Invoke()** arguments to NULL, such as the return value (as shown in Listing 13-3), if you don't need them.

Attributed ATL ActiveX Control Example

In the "ATL ActiveX Control Example" section of Chapter 6, we discussed the method for creating a simple ATL component. Chapter 6 showed you the standard method for creating this component—without the benefit of attributes. If you use attributes, you'll find that you can shave a substantial amount of time from the development process. In addition, you'll have fewer files to work with because the use of attributes precludes the need for an IDL file.

The control in this section uses the same test application found in Chapter 6. In general, the functionality of the control in this chapter is precisely the same as the one in Chapter 6, so you can make easy comparisons between the two. You'll also find the version of the test application for this control on the source code CD. I named the example PButton3 (and changed the class names as appropriate) to avoid confusion. The control code on disk is more robust than the code shown here. For example, the code in the chapter doesn't show how to add an About Box, but you can see this code on the source code CD.

Use the Chapter 6 instructions to create the control in this chapter. There are two simple changes, though, that you need to observe. The first difference is to keep the Attributed option selected on the Application Settings Tab. This change means you can't select the Allow merging of proxy/stub code option. The second difference is that you won't make the Click event operational in the same way. You'll modify the **OnBNClicked**() method found in PButton3Ctrl.h, as shown here.

```
LRESULT OnBNClicked(WORD /*wNotifyCode*/,
                    WORD /*wID*/,
                    HWND /*hWndCtl*/,
                    BOOL& /*bHandled*/)
{
   // Fire the Click event whenever the user clicks the button.
   Click();

   // Return the standard result.
   return 0;
}
```

After you create the PButton3 example, you'll notice several differences from the PButton2 example in Chapter 6. First, there are fewer files, because you don't have a permanent IDL file to consider. However, you'll notice that Visual C++ creates temporary IDL files automatically during the link process. Visual C++ generates these files on the fly—they don't remain as a permanent part of the project. Of course, you still need to specify the information contained in the IDL file in some way. That information now appears as attributes in the various H files associated with the project. For example, Listing 13-4 shows a small part of the code used to define the PButton3 control interface and associated properties.

Listing 13-4

```
[
   object,
   uuid(A69123CC-DBD8-4EFD-8826-B20866B52C6B),
   dual,
   helpstring("IPButton3Ctrl Interface"),
```

```
      pointer_default(unique)
]
__interface IPButton3Ctrl : public IDispatch
{
    [propputref, bindable, requestedit, id(DISPID_FONT)]
    HRESULT Font([in]IFontDisp* pFont);
    [propput, bindable, requestedit, id(DISPID_FONT)]
Additional Properties...
};
```

If you look at the PButton3Ctrl.h closely, you'll find three attribute blocks. The first defines the interface used for properties. The second defines the interface used for events. The third block defines the control attributes. These three blocks provide all of the entries you used to find in a combination of the header and IDL files.

You also need to consider another factor in working with attributed controls. Remember that PButton2 includes two enumerations that the client requires in order to work with the control: ModalType and StdButton. Fortunately, you can use the export attribute to enable client access to the enumerations. In short, you now need only one copy of the enumeration, not two. Using attributes means the enumerations will always stay in sync. You no longer have a separate enumeration in the header and IDL files, so both client and control use the same enumeration—reducing potential errors. The export attribute applies only to union, typedef, enum, struct, or interface, which means you can't apply it to class. Using the export attribute is easy. Here's an example for the ModalType enumeration.

```
// Define the valid ModalResult property values.
[export]
typedef enum ModalType
{
    mrNone = -1L,
    mrOK = 1L,
    mrCancel = 2L,
    mrAbort = 3L,
    mrRetry = 4L,
    mrIgnore = 5L,
    mrYes = 6L,
    mrNo = 7L,
    mrOn = 8L,
    mrOff = 9L,
};
```

Avoiding Problems when Using Attributes

Learning to use attributes is like any other programming endeavor—practice makes perfect. Some developers will tend to resist using attributes or will try to mix old and new coding methodologies. Whether you use attributes in your code is a personal matter, unless you're part of a team development project that calls for the use of attributes to make the team's code easier to read and faster to develop. However, mixing old and new programming techniques in a single application is probably an invitation to disaster. Sure, Visual C++ allows you to do it, but using a single strategy is the best way to go to prevent confusion both to yourself and to others who may look at your code.

Another potential problem area is attributes that sound similar, but perform completely different tasks. Consider the COM vi_progid attribute and the IDL v1_enum attribute. When you look at them in this paragraph, they look completely different. However, in the heat of programming with a new technology, you might confuse the two. Make sure you know which attribute to use in a given situation.

One of the major reasons to use attributes is to reduce the amount of coding you have to perform. It doesn't make sense then to use every attribute available because it might do something interesting for your project. Use only the attributes that you actually need when creating an application. Likewise, most attribute properties have default values. Specify a property only if you need to change the default behavior or make a standard behavior clear in your code.

Attributed Programming and Debugging

Attributes add a lot to the Visual C++ programming environment. Some developers may feel that macros could handle at least a few of these capabilities. There's one way in which attributes are decidedly better than macros—debugging. Unlike with macros, Visual C++ fully expands attribute code in place during the compile process. Therefore, although you don't see this additional code as you write the application, the code is available during the debugging process. You can better see how your code is supposed to work because you can trace into an attribute (unlike with macros, which are nearly impossible to debug).

Working in the Managed Code Environment

O ne of the best reasons to move to Visual Studio .NET is to gain access to the .NET Framework. The .NET Framework enables you to create applications faster and with less code. You can also avoid problems such as "DLL hell." The .NET Framework also provides additional security. For example, the managed control example in Chapter 13 showed you how to sign your controls by assigning them a strong name.

We've already looked at several managed coding examples in the book. For example, you learned how to build a managed console application in Chapter 2. In Chapter 4, you learned how to work with graphics in a managed environment.

This chapter is going to fill in many holes in your managed coding experience. We'll discuss several applications throughout the chapter that demonstrate managed code application and component development. For example, the first section shows how to work with forms in the .NET Framework. The example given is the equivalent of the SDI application in Chapter 2. You'll also learn about one of the benefits of using that managed environment—language interoperability.

The important idea to take away from this chapter is that the .NET Framework makes life a lot easier for the developer, so long as the user can work within the .NET environment. The problem is that this environment is far from ubiquitous. The Visual C++ developer will need to continue working with native EXEs so long as users lack the resources to use the .NET Framework on their machine. Given the current spending habits of IT, you might be working with mixed applications for quite some time.

Working with Windows Forms

Most of the applications you create will rely on a form of some type. The application might be a dialog-based, single document interface (SDI) or a multiple document interface (MDI) application, but it will still rely on at least one form. Consequently, you'll want to know how forms work in the Visual C++ managed environment and how to create them.

Unfortunately, there's some bad news for Visual C++ developers. This version of Visual C++ .NET won't contain a form designer. Microsoft has promised to add this feature for the next version, but in the meantime you need to create forms by hand using standard code. Fortunately, the process of creating a form isn't too difficult.

You'll also need to overcome some fit and finish problems with the default project. For example, it would be nice to get rid of the console dialog box that appears every time the application starts. The example in this section shows you how.

Begin by creating a Managed C++ application. The example uses a name of CommandLine. After you create the application, open the CommandLine.CPP file. You'll want to change the **_tmain()** function as shown in Listing 14-1.

Listing 14-1

```
// This is the entry point for this application
__stdcall WinMain(Int32 hInstance,
                  Int32 hPrevInstance,
                  char* lpCmdLine,
                  int nCmdShow)
{
   // Create a form instance.
   Sample::DirectForm *Dialog;
   Dialog = new Sample::DirectForm(lpCmdLine, nCmdShow);

   // Run the application by displaying the form.
   Application::Run(Dialog);

   // Exit.
   return 0;
}
```

Listing 14-1 shows the coding for a Windows application. Notice that you receive a handle for the current instance of the application, the previous instance of the application (so you can check for multiple running copies), command line arguments, and the starting display method. As you can see, **WinMain()** creates an instance of the form, as usual, but passes the command line and display method parameters.

You'll also need to change one of the linker options. Right-click CommandLine in Solution Explorer and choose Properties from the context menu. Select \Linker\System. Click the down arrow in the Subsystem field and you'll see a list of options like the ones shown next.

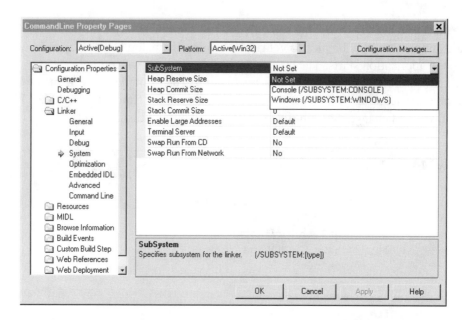

Select the Windows (/SYSTEM:WINDOWS) option. This option enables your application to start without the console window.

Windows uses one of several display methods for starting your application. It's interesting to see how this constant changes based on the method you use to start the application. For example, if you start the application within the debugger, Windows will simply tell the application to show itself. Starting from the command line results in a default show request, while the default method from within Windows is to show the window in normal size. The application relies on a set of constants to discover the display mode. You'll want to place these constants outside the class so they'll be generally available. Here are the constants we'll use for this example.

```
// Window show constants.
const SW_HIDE = 0;
const SW_SHOWNORMAL = 1;
const SW_NORMAL = 1;
const SW_SHOWMINIMIZED = 2;
const SW_SHOWMAXIMIZED = 3;
const SW_MAXIMIZE = 3;
const SW_SHOWNOACTIVATE = 4;
const SW_SHOW = 5;
const SW_MINIMIZE = 6;
const SW_SHOWMINNOACTIVE = 7;
const SW_SHOWNA = 8;
```

```
const SW_RESTORE = 9;
const SW_SHOWDEFAULT = 10;
const SW_MAX = 10;
```

All of the code used to decipher the command line and display method appears in the constructor for the DirectForm class. Listing 14-2 contains the constructor code.

Listig 14-2

```
DirectForm::DirectForm(char* lpCmdLine, int nCmdShow)
{
    String    *Temp;                // Temporary String
    String    *Entry[];             // Command Line Entry Array
    Char      Separator[] = {' '};  // Separator Character
    int       Counter;              // Loop counter.
    String    *DispString;          // Display String

    // Create and configure the OK button.
    btnOK = new Button();
    btnOK->Text = "OK";
    btnOK->Location =
        ::Point(Width - btnOK->Width - 10, 10);
    btnOK->add_Click(new EventHandler(this, OK_Click));

    // Create and configure the first static text.
    lblStatic1 = new Label();
    lblStatic1->Text = "Window Show Type:";
    lblStatic1->Width = 200;
    lblStatic1->Location = ::Point(10, 10);

    // Create and configure the Window Type text box.
    editWindow = new TextBox();
    editWindow->Location = ::Point(10, 30);
    editWindow->Width = 200;

    // Display text box information based on the
    // window show type.
    switch (nCmdShow)
    {
    case SW_SHOWNORMAL:
        editWindow->Text = "SW_SHOWNORMAL or SW_NORMAL";
        break;
```

```
   case SW_SHOWMINIMIZED:
      editWindow->Text = "SW_SHOWMINIMIZED";
      break;
   case SW_SHOWMAXIMIZED:
      editWindow->Text = "SW_SHOWMAXIMIZED or SW_MAXIMIZE";
      break;
   case SW_SHOWNOACTIVATE:
      editWindow->Text = "SW_SHOWNOACTIVATE";
      break;
   case SW_SHOW:
      editWindow->Text = "SW_SHOW";
      break;
   case SW_MINIMIZE:
      editWindow->Text = "SW_MINIMIZE";
      break;
   case SW_SHOWMINNOACTIVE:
      editWindow->Text = "SW_SHOWMINNOACTIVE";
      break;
   case SW_SHOWNA:
      editWindow->Text = "SW_SHOWNA";
      break;
   case SW_RESTORE:
      editWindow->Text = "SW_RESTORE";
      break;
   case SW_SHOWDEFAULT:
      editWindow->Text = "SW_SHOWDEFAULT or SW_MAX";
      break;
}

// Create and configure the first static text.
lblStatic2 = new Label();
lblStatic2->Text = "Command Line Parameters:";
lblStatic2->Width = 200;
lblStatic2->Location = ::Point(10, 60);

// Create and configure the Command Line text box.
editCommand = new TextBox();
editCommand->Location = ::Point(10, 80);
editCommand->Multiline = true;
editCommand->Width = 200;
editCommand->Height = 100;
editCommand->ScrollBars = ScrollBars::Both;

// Parse the Command Line.
```

```
Temp = lpCmdLine;
Entry = Temp->Split(Separator);
DispString = Entry[0];
for (Counter = 1; Counter < Entry->Length; Counter++)
{
   // Create one dipslay string for each command line entry.
   DispString = DispString->Concat(DispString, "\r\n");
   DispString = DispString->Concat(DispString, Entry[Counter]);
}

// Place the result in the text box.
editCommand->Text = DispString;

// Configure the form.
Text = "Command Line Processing Example";
FormBorderStyle = FormBorderStyle::FixedDialog;
StartPosition = FormStartPosition::CenterScreen;
AcceptButton = btnOK;
Controls->Add(btnOK);
Controls->Add(lblStatic1);
Controls->Add(editWindow);
Controls->Add(lblStatic2);
Controls->Add(editCommand);
}
```

The code in Listing 14-2 begins by creating some basic controls. Notice that the OK button has the usual event handler (you'll find the code in the \Chapter 14\CommandLine folder on the source code CD). It's interesting to note the technique used to place the button on the form. In many cases, you'll need to use control placement techniques such as the one shown in Listing 14-2, because Visual C++ .NET lacks designer support.

The first text box contains the display method used to start the application. In some cases, you might choose to trap this information in your application so that you can override the default settings. For example, you might not want to allow the user to start the application maximized. In this example, all we do is show the display method on screen. Notice that some display methods use different constants, but end up doing the same thing. For example, SW_SHOWMAXIMIZED and SW_MAXIMIZE are essentially the same value, so all you really need to do is check for one of them.

The second text box is a little more complex. We need to parse the command line, then display the individual elements. This means creating a multi-line control. Notice that the code also enables the use of scrollbars to ensure that the user can see everything in the text box for long command line entries.

TIP

*You might wonder why I didn't use the **AppendText()** method for the text box, rather than the convoluted technique shown in Listing 14-2 for concatenating the string. The fact is that this method works fine in some places, but not in this one. Even though you should theoretically use **AppendText()** to reduce the amount of coding, the **AppendText()** method always displays an exception message. Microsoft is currently working on a fix for this problem.*

Parsing the command line is relatively easy. The example begins by creating an array of individual strings using the **Split()** method. Notice the use of the Separator variable, which contains a single value—in this case, the space. However, the **Split()** method does enable you to split strings based on other separator characters. It's one of the more versatile additions that .NET brings to the development environment. A For loop combines the individual command line entries with linefeeds, so they appear on separate lines. Here's what you'll see when you run the application from the debugger using the default command line entries of "One Two Three Four."

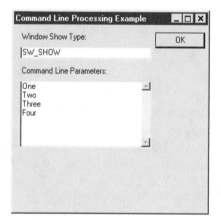

At this point, you might wonder how to supply command line arguments while in the debugger. Right-click CommandLine in Class View and choose Properties from the context menu. Select the Debugging folder and you'll see a list of debugging entries, including the Command Arguments entry shown next.

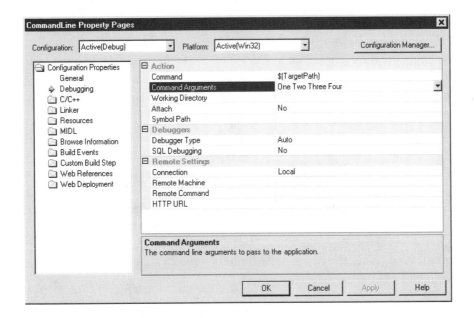

Working with Delegates

Delegates are the new event class for .NET. Using a delegate is somewhat different from an event because delegates require a special coding technique. In some respects, using a delegate affords greater flexibility than does using events. For example, delegates can address the needs of more than one handler, and the delegate can address those needs in a unique way, if necessary. However, given the differences between delegates and events, most experienced programmers find them confusing, to say the least.

NOTE

The example in this section requires a substantial amount of code for the form and other features. The listings present only the code essential for creating a delegate, so you'll want to view the source on disk to learn how to create the controls. The source code for this section appears in the \Chapter 14\Delegate folder of the source code CD.

Delegates can take many forms, and one of the easiest to understand will be discussed in this section. In addition, delegates often provide support for multiple handlers. This section will look at two forms of handlers, but we'll discuss them separately. In a multiple handler scenario, the delegate actually receives a linked list of handlers that it calls in order.

You begin creating a delegate by declaring the form the delegate must take. The __delegate keyword creates a special type of class that enables you to define delegate prototypes. Here's the code you'll normally use to declare a delegate:

```
// Create the delegate.
public __delegate void DisplayMessage(String *Subject, String *Title);
```

As you can see, the code is relatively simple. Notice that the delegate relies on the __delegate keyword instead of __gc, which most of the classes in the book use to indicate a managed state. You define the return value (normally Void), the delegate name, and any arguments the delegate will require. It's important to note that this one line of code represents an entire class. Visual C++ creates the class for you behind the scenes. As a result, the delegate definition normally appears within a namespace, but outside of a class.

NOTE

Single-cast delegates can have a return value. While a multicast delegate can have a return value, it doesn't make sense to provide one because each client would expect a different return. In addition, there is no way for the delegate to anticipate client requirements.

Delegates require an external entity that stores data for processing and the list of handlers for the delegate. These entities normally appear in a separate class. The class could provide something as complex as database manipulation, or as simple as managing a list in memory. For that matter, you can keep track of data members one at a time, but that technique doesn't demonstrate the power of delegates fully. Listing 14-3 shows the ProcessMessageClass for the example.

Listing 14-3

```
public __gc class ProcessMessageClass
{
private:
   // Using this struct makes it easier to store the
   // Subject and Title values.
   __gc struct Message
   {
   public:
      String   *Subject;
```

```
   String    *Title;

   Message(String *_Subject, String *_Title)
   {
      Subject = _Subject;
      Title = _Title;
   }
};

// Create an array to hold the message values.
ArrayList    *Msg;

public:
   // Add an event recipient.
   void add_Message(String* Subject, String* Title);

   // Fire the event.
   void ProcessMessage(DisplayMessage *Del);
};

void ProcessMessageClass::add_Message(String* Subject, String* Title)
{
   if (!Msg)
      Msg = new ArrayList();

   Msg->Add(new Message(Subject, Title));
}

void ProcessMessageClass::ProcessMessage(DisplayMessage *Del)
{
   Message* Current;
   int      Counter;

   // Process each message in the message list.
   if (Msg)
   {
      for (Counter = 0; Counter < Msg->Count; Counter++)
      {
         //Current = (Message*)Msg->get_Item(Counter);
         Current = __try_cast<Message*>(Msg->get_Item(Counter));
         Del(Current->Subject, Current->Title);
      }
   }
}
```

As you can see, the example uses a struct named Message to act as a means for storing the data elements exposed to the handlers. Notice that Message appears as a subclass within ProcessMessageClass. Any struct must begin with the __gc attribute, just as a class would. The example will store a message subject (content) and title. The ArrayList data member Msg is the in-memory database for the example. It holds every addition the code makes to the list of messages the user wants processed. The final piece of the database is **add_Message()**. This method adds new messages to Msg. Notice that the method also verifies that Msg is instantiated before it begins using it. You can't instantiate Msg outside of the method call, so this extra piece of code is always necessary.

TIP

You must add the System::Collections namespace to your project in order to use the ArrayList data type. The ArrayList data type provides an extremely flexible method for creating an in-memory database for your application. Of course, you'd need to provide storage on disk for any permanent data.

ProcessMessage() is the active part of the delegate processing mechanism. It receives an implementation of the delegate we discussed earlier (the handler) and sends the handler the data in Msg to process. **ProcessMessage()** has no idea at the outset if it will receive one or multiple handlers, nor does it care which handler processes the data. In short, it's completely disconnected from the client portion of the application until the code creates the required connection.

Notice how **ProcessMessage()** handles the data request. First, you must ensure that Msg contains data to process (otherwise, you get a Null reference error). The data stored within Msg is in object format. The __try_cast keyword enables the code to convert the object to a Message pointer. You can still use C-style casts, as shown in the commented code, but Visual C++ .NET will flag the entry with a warning in a managed environment.

Let's discuss the process of adding entries to the database. The test form contains two textboxes that tell the application what data to store for presentation later. You must also create and instantiate a PorcessMessageClass object. The example uses MyMsg as the object name. The following code shows how the application sends the information contained in two textboxes to the database for processing.

```
void DelegateTest::AddMessage_Click(Object* sender, EventArgs* e)
{
    // Add new messages to the message list.
    MyMsg->add_Message(txtSubject->Text, txtTitle->Text);
}
```

First we need to create an instance of the data handling class, the ProcessMessageClass. Whenever the user clicks Add, the application calls **add_Message()** with the values from the two textboxes. The **add_Message()** method adds these entries to the ArrayList Msg.

At this point, we have a delegate, a database, and a means for handing the data off for processing. The handlers come next. A handler is an implementation of the delegate we discussed earlier. The code in Listing 14-4 demonstrates that it's the form of the handler, not the code inside, that's important.

Listing 14-4

```
// Create a dialog-based message handler.
void DelegateTest::PrintMessage(String *Subject, String *Title)
{
    // Display the message.
    MessageBox::Show(Subject,
                     Title,
                     MessageBoxButtons::OK,
                     MessageBoxIcon::Information);
}

// Create a textbox-based message handler.
void DelegateTest::ListMessage(String *Subject, String *Title)
{
    // List the message in the textbox.
    txtOutput->AppendText(Subject);
    txtOutput->AppendText("\t");
    txtOutput->AppendText(Title);
    txtOutput->AppendText("\r\n");
}
```

These two handlers don't do anything spectacular, but they do process the data. The first displays a message box for every data element in the database. The second places each data element on a separate line of a multiple line textbox.

The handler and the data processing elements exist, but there's no connection between them. We need something to fire the event. Listing 14-5 shows this last part of the puzzle.

Listing 14-5

```
void DelegateTest::FireMessage_Click(Object* sender, EventArgs* e)
{
   // Fire the event and put the message handler into action.
   MyMsg->ProcessMessage(new DisplayMessage(0, PrintMessage));
}

void DelegateTest::FireList_Click(Object* sender, EventArgs* e)
{
   // Clear the old content from the Output textbox.
   txtOutput->Clear();

   // Fire the event and put the message handler into action.
   MyMsg->ProcessMessage(new DisplayMessage(this, ListMessage));
}
```

As you can see, the code calls **ProcessMessage()** with the handler of choice. Notice how we pass the name of the handler to the delegate as if we're creating a new object. This process is how delegates create the connection. Here's some typical output from this example:

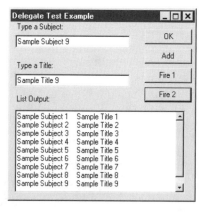

Working with Metadata

All .NET applications include metadata as part of the assembly. The metadata describes the assembly, making it easier to learn about the assembly after it's put together. The Visual C++ compiler automatically adds some types of metadata to your assembly. For example, it includes a list of the assemblies used to construct the current assembly.

A developer can also add metadata to the assembly. Many of the attributes you use will automatically add descriptive metadata. In addition, a developer can create custom attributes to assist in the documentation of the assembly. Custom attributes could also perform tasks such as sending application documentation to a server for storage. The point is that metadata is another form of essential documentation.

The following sections will show you how to create a custom attribute that adds metadata to an assembly. We'll look at the resulting metadata. The final section will show you how to use reflection to view the metadata from within your application. Using this technique enables you to build utilities to manage your applications. For example, a search utility could help you find and reuse code.

Creating a Custom Attribute

In Chapter 13, we discussed attributes and how you can use them within your applications to produce certain effects. .NET comes with a lot of built-in attributes that meet common needs for all developers. However, you'll find that .NET doesn't cover every base, and the attributes it does supply aren't always complete. You'll also want to create some custom attributes just to ensure you can work with attributes in the way that's most convenient for you.

Interestingly enough, you use an attribute to begin creating a custom attribute. Here's an example of an attribute we'll use for the example in this section:

```
[attribute(All, AllowMultiple=true, Inherited=false)]
```

The [attribute] attribute has only one required parameter: the types that the attribute will affect. The optional AllowMultiple parameter determines if a user can have more than one attribute placed in front of a given entity. For example, you'd only want to allow one attribute that determines the configuration of a component. However, you'd want to allow multiple copies of an attribute that provides documentation for a class. The optional Inherited parameter determines if other attributes can inherit the features of the custom attribute. Here's a list of the types that you can support using attributes:

- ▶ Assembly
- ▶ Module
- ▶ Class
- ▶ Struct
- ▶ Enum
- ▶ Constructor
- ▶ Method

- ► Property

- ► Field

- ► Event

- ► Interface

- ► Parameter

- ► Delegate

- ► ReturnValue

- ► All

Creating a custom attribute is relatively easy once you know about the [attribute] attribute. You can use either a struct or a class. Using a struct has certain performance and memory advantages; using a class affords greater flexibility, especially if you plan to use inheritance to create variations of an attribute. Listing 14-6 shows the code for the custom attribute used in this section. The example will enable developers to describe entities in various ways. For example, you could use the attribute to describe additional work the assembly requires to provide a list of bugs within the entity.

Listing 14-6

```
[attribute(All, AllowMultiple=true, Inherited=false)]
public __gc struct EntityDescribe
{
private:
    String    *_Date;       // The date the comment is made.
    String    *_Author;     // Comment author.
    String    *_Purpose;    // Purpose of the element.
    String    *_Comment;    // Comment about the element (optional).

public:
    EntityDescribe(String *Date, String *Author, String *Purpose)
    {
        // These three values are mandatory and appear as part of
        // the constructor.
        _Date = Date;
        _Author = Author;
        _Purpose = Purpose;
    }

    // The comment field is optional,
```

```
    // so it gets treated as a property.
    __property String* get_Comment(void)
    {
       return _Comment;
    }
    __property void set_Comment(String *Value)
    {
       _Comment = Value;
    }

    // Accessors for the mandatory fields.
    __property String* get_Date(void)
    {
       return _Date;
    }
    __property String* get_Author(void)
    {
       return _Author;
    }
    __property String* get_Purpose(void)
    {
       return _Purpose;
    }
};
```

As you can see, the code is relatively simple. However, you need to know about a few nuances of attribute construction. Notice that only three of the properties—Date, Author, and Purpose—appear in the constructor. These three properties represent the required entries for using the attribute. The Comment property is separate and is therefore optional.

Because Comment is optional, you need to provide it with both a get and a set property, as shown in the listing. You could add anything here that you wanted such as range checking. The main thing that the "get" and "set" routines have to provide is some means of storing the data provided by the user as part of the custom attribute.

The final task is providing accessors for the three mandatory properties. The assembly will still contain the data if you don't provide an accessor, but you won't be able to read it from within your code. In short, the data will become lost within the assembly, never to see the light of day.

Viewing the Metadata

The custom attribute from the previous section is ready to use. All we need to do is add one or more entries to another class to see it at work. The example places attributes in two places to make it easier to discuss the effect of the attribute on application metadata. However, the three most important entries appear at the class level, because we'll use reflection to read them in the next section. Here are the three entries we'll add to the class:

```
[EntityDescribe("11/27/2001",
                "John",
                "Created the new form for test application.")]
[EntityDescribe("11/28/2001",
                "Rebecca",
                "OK Button Click Event Handler",
                Comment="Needs more work")]
[EntityDescribe("11/29/2001",
                "Chester",
                "Added Attribute Test Button")]
public __gc class QuickForm : public Form
```

As you can see, the three custom attribute entries all describe aspects of the target class, QuickForm. One of the entries also makes use of the optional Comment property. Notice that you need to provide the name of the custom property to use it.

After you add some custom attribute entries to the application, you can compile it. Open the application using the ILDASM utility (discussed in several places in the book). Figure 14-1 shows the results of the three entries we made to the class. Notice that ILDASM doesn't make them that readable, but you can definitely see them in the list (starting with the highlighted entry in the figure).

If you want to see the full effect of an attribute entry, you need to attach it to a data member such as a pushbutton. Open the disassembly of the data member by double-clicking it in ILDASM. Figure 14-2 shows an example of the [EntityDescribe] attribute attached to the btnOK object. Notice that you can see all three of the default entries.

It's important to realize that the compiler stores the property values as they appear for the constructor. In other words, the compiler doesn't change the attribute in any way. The data you add to an assembly is readable in the disassembly, even if the attribute would normally encrypt the data. This security problem means you shouldn't store company secrets in the attributes, and you might want to remove

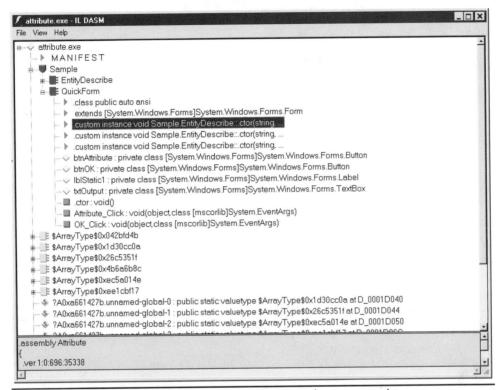

Figure 14-1   *ILDASM allows you to see any custom attributes you make.*

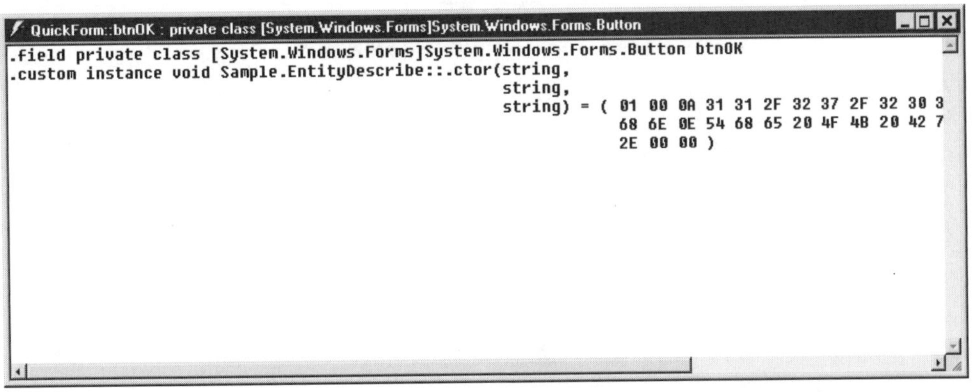

Figure 14-2   *Use a disassembly to see the full effect of any custom attribute you create.*

attributes from applications before you send them to a customer. Here's an example of the readable data for the btnOK object:

```
/ QuickForm::btnOK : private class [System.Windows.Forms]System.Windows.Forms.Button  _ □ X
rms.Button btnOK


 ( 01 00 0A 31 31 2F 32 37 2F 32 30 30 31 04 4A 6F    // ...11/27/2001.Jo
   68 6E 0E 54 68 65 20 4F 4B 20 42 75 74 74 6F 6E    // hn.The OK Button
   2E 00 00 )                                          // ...
```

Using Reflection

One of the reasons to include metadata within an assembly is to document the assembly's features and problems. Of course, reading these comments with ILDASM is hardly the best way to make use of the information. You could easily view the source code instead and probably save time by doing so. Reflection enables an application to read its own metadata and the metadata contained in other assemblies. This feature enables you to create utilities to read the metadata and do something with it. The nice part of this feature is that it also applies to the Microsoft assemblies, which means you can finally search them for tidbits of information.

Creating an application that relies on reflection isn't difficult, but it does look at tad strange at first. Listing 14-7 shows an example of reflection at work. In this case, clicking the Attribute button on the example application will fill the txtOutput textbox with the content of the higher level attributes for the sample application.

Listing 14-7

```
void QuickForm::Attribute_Click(Object* sender, EventArgs* e)
{
    Object          *Attr[];    // Array of attributes.
    EntityDescribe  *CurrAttr;  // Current Attribute.

    // Gain access to the member information for the class.
    MemberInfo  *Info = __typeof(QuickForm);

    // Grab the custom attribute information.
    Attr = __try_cast<Object*[]>(Attribute::GetCustomAttributes(Info,
                            __typeof(EntityDescribe)));

    // Look at each attribute in the array.
    for (int Counter = 0; Counter < Attr->Length; Counter++)
    {
```

```
    // Obtain the current attribute.
    CurrAttr = __try_cast<EntityDescribe*>(Attr[Counter]);

    // Display the information.
    txtOutput->AppendText(CurrAttr->Date);
    txtOutput->AppendText("\t");
    txtOutput->AppendText(CurrAttr->Author);
    txtOutput->AppendText("\t");
    txtOutput->AppendText(CurrAttr->Purpose);
    txtOutput->AppendText("\t");
    txtOutput->AppendText(CurrAttr->Comment);
    txtOutput->AppendText("\r\n\r\n");
  }
}
```

The first task is to gain access to the member information that you want to use to search for attributes. In this case, we'll gain access to the QuickForm class and view the class level attributes. The Info variable contains this information.

The next task is to search for the attributes. You'll find a number of overrides for the **GetCustomAttributes**() method. Listing 14-7 shows just one option. In this case, we'll search for all of the EntityDescribe attributes found in the QuickForm class. Notice the use of the __try_cast attribute. You need to order the statements as shown in the listing or Visual C++ will display an error message during the compile cycle and not provide much in the way of a helpful answer about what's wrong with the code. (In short, the precise sequence of events is important.)

NOTE

*The .NET Framework actually provides two methods for gaining access to a custom attribute's information. The first is **GetCustomAttribute()**, which returns a single attribute — the first one it finds. The second is **GetCustomAttributes()**, which returns an array of all of the attributes that fit within the search criteria.*

After you gain access to the attributes, you need some way to convert them to readable or storable data. The first step in the For loop is to cast the individual attribute entry into a EntityDescribe data type. After that, you can use the data to display information on screen, send it to the printer for a report, or place it within a database for later use. In this case, we'll use the **AppendText**() method to place the data in the txtOutput textbox. Following is the output from the application.

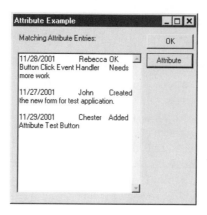

State Information Maintenance

Metadata fill one other purpose that you've probably already thought about. Look again at the disassembly in Figure 14-1. You'll notice that the attribute saves the initial state of the information, not the final state. In some respects, this means that the session state information appears as part of the metadata. The use of raw information means that metadata can come in handy for determining how some part of the application is stored after compilation.

Theoretically, you can use this information to restore an errant application, or you can use it for debugging purposes. The debugger that comes with Visual Studio .NET does a phenomenal job in analyzing common application problems (and some of those that aren't quite so common). However, most developers are still going to need to search through the disassembly of their applications from time to time to find that one clue needed to rid an application of a stubborn bug. Using attributes correctly could help in the debugging process by showing you how Visual C++ interprets the final state of an application.

Consider metadata the next time you need to determine the state of your application. A look at the metadata can reveal problems that you might never find by looking at the code. For example, an attribute could record some flaw in logic on the part of the designer. It could also tell you that there's nothing wrong with the code and that you need to send a bug report into Microsoft about the problem.

Accessing the Property Browser

The Property Browser is no longer under Visual Studio .NET. You now have access to a Property Window of the same sort used by Visual Basic in previous incarnations of Visual Studio. This change might not seem like such a big deal until you begin working with controls regularly. The Visual Basic method does have certain advantages. For example, all you need to do is click on an object to see its properties. However, for those of us who are used to working with property pages and the tabbed interface they provide, Visual Studio .NET is a slight step backward in at least one way—no more property pages.

NOTE

You'll notice there's a Property Pages button in the Properties window. However, few controls activate the button. Of the few that do activate the button, many don't display their property pages correctly. In short, the feature is potentially available for a small subset of the controls, but generally not available for regular use.

Fortunately, the Property Window is a big step forward in other ways. When you click on a control in the design window (when working with unmanaged code), you can access the properties and events for the control. Creating an event handler is as easy as finding it in the list and selecting the suggested method name from the drop-down list. Selecting multiple controls enables you to change the common properties for them. Of course, you can't change unique properties, such as the control name, when you select multiple controls in the design window.

TIP

You can list properties by category or in alphabetic order. Depending on the skill of the control creator, using alphabetic order is normally faster if you already know the name of the property that you want to change. Category order is useful for learning about the properties of a new control.

The Property Window is handy in other ways. If you click on a class name within Class View, you'll see additional buttons in the Property Window. You can use these buttons to list the overrides and messages for the class. As with events, creating a new override or message handler is as easy as selecting the method name in the drop-down list box. Of course, you still have access to properties and events for the class.

TIP

You can show and hide the Description pane of the Properties window. Right-click anywhere within the Properties window and either select or deselect the Description option from the context menu. The context menu also contains a Reset option that enables you to restore a property to its normal state. The default state is the state that the control designer provided during the control creation process or a default state for the type of property data if the control designer didn't provide a default.

No More Property Pages

All of the controls used in this book have had property pages. However, if you're planning to use just Visual Studio .NET, you really don't need to add property pages to your control; the IDE handles this functionality for you by examining the control when you load it. From a purely developer-productivity perspective, managed controls have one fewer problem areas to contend with, and a developer will have more time for important coding issues. Coding a property page doesn't take much time, but it does require some coding and testing.

Another good reason to remove property pages from your controls is size. You can reduce the size of a control by removing the property page. In addition, removing the property page will also provide a small improvement in memory usage and could reduce load time. The gains you'll receive are going to be noticeable but small, so removing a property page solely for performance reasons is ill advised.

Unfortunately, property pages are still important for several reasons. Whether you need to add property pages to your control depends on whether you fit within a pure .NET profile. For example, many developers rely on the ActiveX Control Test Container to test their controls. If your control lacks the requisite property pages, you'll find it difficult to test your control. Notice that I didn't say you'd find it impossible. You can still change property values using the get/set methods contained within the control, but doing so in this hostile environment for testing will likely waste more developer time than leaving the property page out saved.

Chapter 13 also demonstrated how to use a managed component within an unmanaged application. You can also use unmanaged controls within a managed application. This scenario will happen quite often for the next few years. A developer needs to consider both managed and unmanaged environments during control development. In short, you might need to add a property page to your control to support older application environments.

The bottom line is that you need to determine where you'll use a control. If you plan to use it only in the new environment, creating a property page is a waste of time. Otherwise, you'll probably want to add one with an eye to removing it later.

Understanding Type Conversion

The Properties window has some advantages that the previous Visual C++ IDE doesn't provide. One of those advantages is automatic type conversion. The .NET Framework as a whole provides a wealth of type conversion features. The Visual Studio .NET IDE makes use of this feature to create a friendly environment for the developer. For example, if you type a 1 into a property designed to provide a bool, the IDE will often convert the value to True for you (False is 0 in the .NET world).

It's important to understand that the type conversion features also extend to the development world. One of the most common ways to convert any value into something that you can print is to use the **ToString()** method. This particular method appears as part of almost every object. If you have an int that you want to convert to a string for printing, just use the **ToString()** method to do it. Unfortunately, while **ToString()** does exist for every object, it doesn't always do something useful. For example, you might receive a string with the object name or type and nothing more. If you want the **ToString()** method to do something useful in these situations, you need to override the code for a derived class and provide a different implementation.

Sometimes you need a little more control over the string format. In this case, you can use the **String::Format()** method. This method provides modifiers you can use to present data, especially numbers, in a particular format. For example, if you typed

```
String::Format("\n\nCurrency:\t{0:C}", myInt);
```

Visual Studio .NET would convert myInt from an integer to a currency format. Notice the use of the curly braces to contain the variable number and the format you want to use with it. You can convert to a number of other formats as well.

Of course, data conversion isn't just a matter of converting some data into a string. Sometimes you need to convert from a string into a number. The .NET Framework provides several means to perform a conversion of text to another type. The first place to look is the System::Convert namespace. You'll find methods there such as **ToInt32()**, **ToBoolean()**, and **ToDateTime()**. Here's an example of the System::Convert namespace in action.

```
int myInt = System::Convert::ToInt32(myString);
```

You can also use the **Int32::Parse()** method to convert a string into its numeric counterpart. It turns out that there are other **Parse()** methods available such as **Int16::Parse()**. The point is that you have multiple ways to convert one value to another when working with .NET.

The Developer View of Visual C++ .NET

OBJECTIVES

▶ Learn how to design your applications with security in mind

▶ Understand the Windows Security API including cryptography

▶ Learn about the various security standards in use today

▶ Understand the need for administrative tools that use a common interface

▶ Create an MMC snap-in

▶ Learn how to build various help file types

▶ Create a help file and attach it to an application

▶ Obtain an overview of the various application packaging types

▶ Create installation files using various techniques including Windows installer

Designing with Security in Mind

IN THIS CHAPTER:

Making Windows 2000 Security Work for You

Understanding the Windows Security API

Ensuring the Safe Download of Internet Code

Security Standards

J ust about everyone knows what kinds of problems the network administrator faces trying to enforce security on a network today. We all know that short and/or common passwords, users who don't understand security procedures, and outright neglect on the part of the administrator can all work toward making your LAN a security risk. Fortunately, operating systems like Windows 2000 and the new Windows eXPerience (XP) make it much easier to enforce security on the local machine and the LAN, regardless of user habits. Knowing how to access these security features and build them into your applications is essential to ensuring the safety of both your data and applications.

Security is also one of the major issues facing anyone building an Internet or intranet site today. It's hard to know who's harder pressed: the company building a public access Internet or the one trying to hide its presence with an intranet. No matter which environment you work in, third party vendors are preparing tools of various kinds and capabilities to address the needs of those who want to protect their data from harm. Unfortunately, using great tools won't prevent you from shooting yourself in the foot when building your own controls and application programs. (These tools also don't work very well when you use them in the wrong way.) Again, knowing the security features that Windows 2000 provides can help you improve the security of remote access technologies.

What you shouldn't be looking for in this chapter are concrete answers that are going to work in your specific situation. It would be silly to try to cover in one chapter all of the various technologies available today or every security issue you'll ever run into. What we'll concentrate on instead is the programmer's perspective on security matters. We'll talk about the technologies that are available to you as a programmer, but we won't get into specific solutions to a specific problem. The solution you finally decide to use will have to be based on your company's needs and the tools you have at your disposal.

The first part of this chapter will discuss how you can make Windows 2000 security work for you. We'll discuss built-in security features such as access tokens and security descriptors. One section will show how to use the Access Control Editor, while another looks at the Security Configuration Editor. We'll also talk about the Windows logon features.

The second part of the chapter contains a Windows Security application programming interface (API) overview. It tells you how to use this API to make your applications safer. Given that much of the data that you'll work with ends up on the Internet today, we'll also talk about the Cryptography API. This API allows you to encrypt and decrypt data exchanged between client and server.

Speaking of the needs of the Internet, the third section of the chapter tells how you can ensure the safe download of code from the Internet. Many in-house development efforts still rely on the use of ActiveX controls embedded on Web pages. You can also see the use of controls on commercial Web sites, such as Microsoft's Windows Update Web site. While controls do have limited appeal, in many cases, they're indispensable in others.

The fourth section of the chapter will tell you about the various security standards that you'll deal with as a developer. The addition of security standards ensures that data can flow from one site to another without many problems. However, the existence of an ever-increasing number of standards also means that developers have to spend more time learning the new methods for ensuring that data remains safe.

The final section of the chapter will look at Distributed Component Object Model (DCOM) security issues. We'll discuss how you can secure a DCOM application at various levels. DCOM offers extensive security features, which makes it one of the safest ways to move your data. However, the complexity of these security features leaves many developers with significant implementation problems. This section will help clear up some of those problems.

NOTE

Microsoft has produced a plethora of Windows operating system versions. For the purposes of this discussion, we'll divide those versions into two categories. I'll refer to Windows 95/98/ME as Windows 9x throughout the chapter. Likewise, I'll refer to Windows NT/2000/XP as Windows 2000 throughout the chapter. If I need to refer to a specific operating system version so that I can point out a new or interesting feature, I'll refer to the operating system by name. We'll discuss the reason for this operating system division in the "Built-In Security Features" section of the chapter.

Making Windows 2000 Security Work for You

Windows 2000 ships with a wealth of security features. Network administrators can set security in a number of ways. For example, they can define individual security settings for objects or use group policies to control how more than one user interacts with a single object. The point is that network administrators have a lot of choices, and those choices will only become greater with Windows XP on the scene.

The following sections will help you discover several important facets of Windows 2000 security. We'll examine how you can access these features within your applications. The first section begins with a look at the built-in Windows security features. Next, we'll look at the Access Control Editor and the Security Configuration Editor. You can affect how these editors interact with your components by adding the correct code. Finally, we'll talk about how you can work with Windows Logon to make the entire Windows environment more secure.

Built-In Security Features

Microsoft receives a lot of bad press about security problems in their operating systems and other products. You may even wonder how useful the built-in security features of an operating system like Windows 2000 will be. After all, crackers break into Windows machines seemingly at will. However, Windows does have a lot to offer in the security department, more than most developers realize until they actually get into the internals of the security API. You may even find that Windows 2000 provides more security than your application requires.

Whether you're creating a control or an application, whether the code will run on the Internet, local drive, WAN, or LAN, you'll find that a good understanding of the underlying network security architecture is essential. Windows 9x doesn't provide the same level of security that Windows 2000 does, so you'll find yourself doing without added security under Windows 9x at times. However, when Windows 9x does provide a security feature, it uses the same setup as Windows 2000, so one security module will work with both of them. (In other cases, you'll definitely want to use a separate module for Windows 2000 to make better use of its enhanced security capabilities; see the following note for details.)

NOTE

Windows 2000 does support a lot more Windows security API calls than Windows 9x does, because its security is much more robust. In fact, you'll find that your ability to manage security when using Windows 9x is severely hampered by its lack of support for Windows 2000 security features. For example, you can't use the GetUserObjectSecurity call under Windows 9x. Most of the access token calls that we'll look at in the next section won't work either. The best way to figure out whether a call is supported or not is to test it. If you get ERROR_CALL_NOT_IMPLEMENTED (value 120) returned from the call, you know that you can use it only under Windows 2000.

Windows 2000 and Windows 9x both use the term "object" rather loosely. It's true that many objects are lurking beneath the surface, but you may find that they don't fit precisely within the C++ usage of the term. In the next few sections, we'll look at an object as the encapsulation of code and data that performs a specific security task. In other words, each security object is a self-contained unit designed to fulfill a specific role. (In many places in both Windows 9x and Windows 2000, Microsoft chose to use the full C++ version of an object, mainly because it implemented the required functionality as part of the Microsoft Foundation Classes (MFC). However, when reading either the Microsoft documentation or this chapter, you shouldn't depend on the definition of an object to mean a strict C++ object—think of objects more in the COM sense of the word.)

Knowing that everything is an object makes security a bit easier to understand— at least it's a starting point. However, an object *is* just a starting point. Users are the other part of the security equation. Users access objects, so security in Windows is a matter of comparing the object security level to the user's rights. If the user has sufficient rights (rights that meet or exceed those of the object), then he or she can use the object. The Windows documentation refers to the object security level as a *security descriptor.* This structure tells the security system what rights a user needs to access the object. Likewise, the user has an *access token,* which is another structure that tells the security system what rights a user has in a given situation. "Token" is a good word here, because the user will give Windows 2000 the token in exchange for access to the object. (Think of the object as a bus, with Windows 2000 as the driver and the user presenting the required token to board.) Figure 15-1 shows both of these structures.

This is the quickest look you can take at security under either Windows 9x or Windows 2000. Simply knowing that there are security objects and user tokens will go a long way toward making sense out of the Windows security API calls. In the following sections, we'll define what a token is and how it works. We'll also discuss security descriptors. You don't have to know this information to implement security if your only interest is the Internet, but knowing it can help you design applications and controls of a more general nature and wider appeal.

Understanding Access Tokens

You'll find that there are two ways of looking at a user's rights under Windows; both relate to objects in one form or another. The user's access token has a security identifier (SID) to identify the user throughout the network—it's like having an account number.

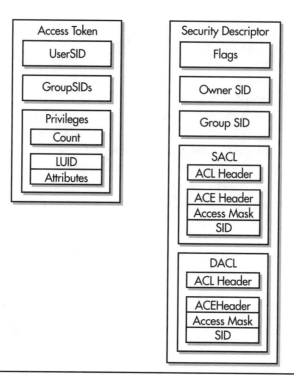

Figure 15-1   *Access tokens define the user's rights, while security descriptors define the protection level for a process.*

The user token that the SID identifies tells what groups the user belongs to and what privileges the user has. Each group also has a SID, so the user's SID contains references to group SIDs that the user belongs to, not to a complete set of group access rights. You'd normally use the Local Users and Groups or the Active Directory Users and Computers Microsoft Management Console (MMC) snap-in under Windows 2000 to change the contents of this access token.

Let's talk about the "privileges" section of the access token shown in Figure 15-1. It begins with a count of the number of privileges that the user has—the number of special privilege entries in the access token. This section also contains an array of privilege entries. Each privilege entry contains a *locally unique identifier* (LUID)— essentially a pointer to the entry object—and an *attribute mask*. The attribute mask tells what rights the user has to the object. Group SID entries are essentially the same. They contain a privilege count and an array of privilege entries.

One of the things that you need to know as part of working with objects is that object rights flow down to the lowest possible node unless overridden by another SID. For example, if you give a user read and write rights to the \Temp directory on a hard drive, those rights would also apply to the \Temp\Stuff directory unless you assigned the user specific rights to that directory. The same holds true for containers. Assigning a user rights to a container object like a Word document gives the user the right to look at everything within that container, even other files in most cases. It's important to track a user's exact rights to objects on your server through the use of security surveys, since you could inadvertently give the user more rights than he or she needs to perform a certain task.

Using Access Tokens

Let's talk briefly about the token calls in the security API, since they're the first stepping-stones you'll need to know about. To do anything with a user's account—even if you just want to find out who has access to a particular workstation—you need to know about tokens. As previously stated, tokens are the central part of the user side of the security equation. You'll usually begin accessing a user account with a call to OpenProcessToken. Notice the name of this call—it deals with any kind of a process, user or otherwise. The purpose of this call is to get a token handle with specific rights attached to it. For example, if you want to query the user account, you need the TOKEN_QUERY privilege. (Your access token must contain the rights that you request from the system, which is why an administrator can access a token but other users can't.) Any changes to the user's account require the TOKEN_ADJUST_PRIVILEGES privilege. There are quite a few of these access rights, so we won't go through them all here.

Once you have an access token handle, you need to decide what to do with it. For example, you can change a user's privilege to do something by accessing the LUID for the privilege you want to change. All of these appear in the WINNT.H file with an "SE_". For example, the SE_SYSTEM_PROFILE_NAME privilege allows the user to gather profiling information for the entire system. Some SE values don't relate to users (for example, the SE_LOCK_MEMORY_NAME privilege that allows a process to lock system memory). You get the LUID for a privilege using the LookupPrivilegeValue call. Now you can combine the information you've gotten so far to change the privilege. In general, you'll use the AdjustTokenPrivileges call to make the required change.

Querying the user's account (or other token information) is straightforward. You use the GetTokenInformation call to retrieve any information you need. This call requires a token class parameter, which tells Windows the type of information required. For example, you would use the TokenUser class to learn about a specific user. You'll also supply an appropriate structure that Windows can use for storing the information you request—which differs by token class.

Understanding Security Descriptors

Now let's look at the security descriptor. Figure 15-1 shows that each security descriptor contains five main sections. The first section is a list of flags. These flags tell you the descriptor revision number, format, and ACL (access control list) status.

The next two sections contain SIDs. The owner SID tells who owns the object. This doesn't have to be an individual user; Windows allows you to use a group SID here as well. The limiting factor is the group SID must appear in the token of the person changing the entry. The group SID allows a group to own the object. Of the two SIDs, only the owner SID is important under Windows. The Macintosh and POSIX security environments use the group SID.

The final two sections contain ACLs. The security access control list (SACL) controls Windows' auditing feature. Every time a user or group accesses an object when the auditing feature for that object is on, Windows makes an entry in the audit log. The discretionary access control list (DACL) controls object use. You can assign groups and users to a specific object.

NOTE

There are two types of security descriptors: absolute and self-relative. Absolute security descriptors contain a copy of each ACL within its structure. Use this type of security descriptor for objects that require special handling. The self-relative security descriptor contains only a pointer to the SACL and DACL. This type of descriptor saves memory and reduces the time required to change rights for a group of objects. You'd use it when all objects in a particular group require the same level of security. For example, you could use this method to secure all threads within a single application. Windows requires that you convert self-relative security descriptors to absolute form before you save them or transfer them to another process. Every descriptor you retrieve using API calls is of the self-relative type. You can convert a security descriptor from one type to another using the MakeAbsoluteSD and MakeSelfRelativeSD API calls.

An ACL consists of two entry types. The first is a header that lists the number of access control entries (ACEs) in the ACL. Windows uses this number to determine when it's reached the end of the ACE list. (There isn't any end-of-structure record or other way to determine the size of each ACE in the structure.) The second entry is an array of ACEs.

CAUTION

Never directly manipulate the contents of an ACL or SID — Microsoft may change its structure in future versions of Windows. The Windows API provides functions to change the contents of these structures. Always use an API call to perform any task with either structure type to reduce the impact of changes in structure on your application.

An ACE defines the object rights for a single user or group. Every ACE has a header that defines the type, size, and flags for the ACE. It includes an access mask that defines rights a user or group has to the object. Finally, there's an entry for the user or group SID.

Windows uses three out of the four ACE header types. The access-allowed type appears in the DACL and grants rights to a user. Use it to add to the rights a user already has to an object on an instance-by-instance basis. For example, you might want to prevent the user from changing the system time so that you can keep the machines on the network synchronized. However, there might be one situation—such as daylight savings time—when the user would need this right. You could use an access-allowed ACE to allow the user to change the time in this one instance. An access-denied ACE revokes rights a user has to an object. You can use it to deny object access during special events. For example, you could deny access rights to a remote terminal while you perform an update on it. The system audit ACE type works with the SACL. It defines which events to audit for a particular user or group. The currently unused ACE type is a system alarm ACE. It allows either the SACL or DACL to set an alarm when specific events happen.

Using Security Descriptors

Understanding what a security descriptor is and how the various structures it contains interact is only one part of the picture. You also need to know how to access and use security descriptors to write a program. Unlike tokens, Windows doesn't generalize security descriptors. You can't use a standard set of calls to access them. Windows includes five classes of security descriptors, each of which uses a different set of descriptor calls to access the object initially. (You must have the SE_SECURITY_ NAME privilege to use any of these functions.)

NOTE

Only NTFS provides full security—VFAT provides a lesser degree. You can't assign or obtain security descriptors for either HPFS or FAT file systems. The FAT file system doesn't provide any extended attribute space, one requirement for adding security. The HPFS file system provides extended attributes, but they don't include any security features. Of all the file systems described, NTFS is the most secure. However, never assume that any file system is completely secure.

▶ **Files, directories, pipes, and mail slots**   Use GetFileSecurity and SetFileSecurity.

▶ **Processes, threads, access tokens, and synchronization objects**   Use GetKernelObjectSecurity and SetKernelObjectSecurity. All these objects, even access tokens, are kernel objects. As such, they also have their own security descriptor.

▶ **Window stations, desktops, windows, and menus**   Use GetUserObjectSecurity and SetUserObjectSecurity. A window station is a combination of keyboard, mouse, and screen. Desktops contain windows and menus. These four objects inherit rights from each other in the order shown. In other words, a desktop will inherit the rights of the window station.

▶ **System registry keys**   Use RegGetKeySecurity and RegSetKeySecurity. Notice that these two calls start with Reg, just like the other registry-specific calls Windows supports.

▶ **Executable service objects**   Use QueryServiceObjectSecurity and SetServiceObjectSecurity. For some strange reason, neither call appears with the other security calls in the Windows API help file. An executable service is a background task such as the UPS monitoring function.

Once you do gain access to the object, you can perform a variety of tasks using generic API calls. For example, the GetSecurityDescriptorDACL retrieves a copy of the DACL from any descriptor type. The descriptors for all of these objects follow roughly the same format—although the lengths of most of the components differ. One reason for the differences in size is that each object will contain a different number of ACEs. The SIDs' sizes differ as well.

The next step to query or modify security descriptor content is to disassemble the components. For example, you could view the ACEs within a DACL or a SACL using GetACE. You could also use the owner and group SIDs for a variety of SID-related calls. In essence, any security descriptor access will always consist of the same three steps:

1. Get the descriptor.
2. Remove a specific component.
3. Modify the contents of that component.

To change the security descriptor, you reverse the process. Use a call like AddACE to add a new ACE to an ACL, use SetSecurityDescriptorSACL to change SACL within a descriptor, and, finally, save the descriptor using a call like SetFileSecurity.

ACEing Security in Windows

Once you know how Windows evaluates the ACEs in the DACL, you'll discover a few problem areas—problems that the Windows utilities address automatically. You'll need to program around these problems to derive the same result. You'll experience the same problems when you work with the SACL, but the SACL affects only auditing, so the effect is less severe from the system security standpoint.

Windows evaluates the ACEs in an ACL in the order in which they appear. At first, this might not seem like a very big deal. However, it could become a problem in some situations. For example: What if you want to revoke all of a user's rights in one area, but his or her list of ACEs includes membership in a group that allows access to that area? If you place the access-allowed ACE first in the list, the user would get access to the area. The bottom line is that you should place all your access-denied ACEs in the list first, to prevent any potential breach in security.

Also, use care in the ordering of group SIDs. Rights that a user acquires from different groups are cumulative. This means a user who's part of two groups, one that has access to a file and another that doesn't, will have access to the file if the group granting the right appears first on the list. In addition, if one ACE grants read rights and another write rights to a file, and the user is asking for read and write rights, Windows will grant the request.

Obviously, you could spend all your time trying to figure out the best arrangement of groups. As the number of groups and individual rights that a user possesses increases, the potential for an unintended security breach does as well. That's why it's important to create groups carefully and limit a user's individual rights.

Potential Programming Pitfalls When Using Windows 2000 Security

There are two other concerns when you look at security under Windows 9x or Windows 2000: data protection and server protection. The first deals with a client's ability to access data through a server. (I'm not talking about a file server here, but some type of DDE or other application server.) Think about it this way: What if a client didn't have rights to a specific type of data, but accessed the data through a DDE call to a server that did have the required rights? How could the server protect against the security breach?

Windows provides several API calls that allow a server to impersonate a client. In essence, the calls allow a server to assume the security restrictions of the client in order to determine whether the client has sufficient rights to access a piece of data or a process. For example, a Word for Windows user might require access to an Excel data file. The user could gain access to that file using DDE. In this case, the server would need to verify that the Word for Windows user has sufficient rights to access the file before it sends the requested data. A server might even find that the client has superior rights when he or she uses this technique.

This set of API calls supports three different types of communication: DDE, named pipes, and RPCs. You need to use a different API call for each communication type. For example, to impersonate a DDE client, you'd use the DDEImpersonateClient call. Windows places limitations on the level of impersonation support it provides. For example, it doesn't support TCP/IP, so you have to use other methods to verify access rights in this case.

The other security concern is protecting the server. What prevents a user who calls Excel from Word for Windows from using Excel to damage the server? Ensuring you address security concerns isn't difficult with files and other types of named structures, since the server automatically attaches a security descriptor to these objects. (A DDE server like Excel wouldn't need to do anything because the file is under server control.) However, DDE and application servers use unnamed private objects that require special protection. Windows also provides API calls to protect a server. For example, the

CreatePrivateObjectSecurity call allows the server to attach a security descriptor to any private object—a thread or other process. The security descriptor prevents anyone other than the server from accessing the private object.

Using the Access Control Editor

The Access Control Editor is a COM control that allows you to add a standard interface to your application—allowing administrators to set application security as needed. These are the same property pages that Microsoft uses within Windows 2000 to set security. The Access Control Editor uses two sets of property pages. The user will normally see this simple property page dialog:

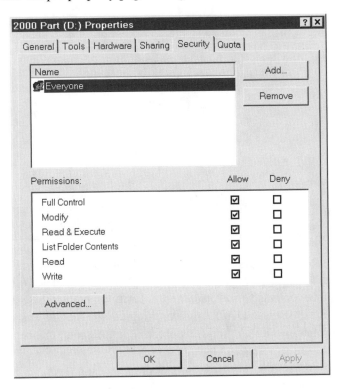

I chose this particular example so that you'd see the dialog in action. The content of the dialog changes to meet object requirements. The Administrator will normally use the advanced property page shown here:

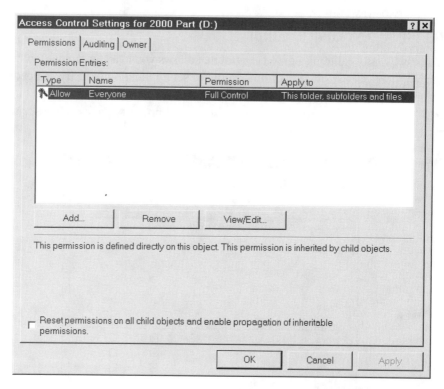

As you can see, both property pages allow the administrator to work with the security settings for an application with relative ease. Notice the advanced dialog provides complete controls for setting every security aspect for this particular object. The Permissions tab sets the DACL, the Auditing tab the SACL, and the Owner tab the owner information. The only missing element is the group information, which isn't important at the user level in many cases.

Now that we've seen the Access Control Editor user interface, let's look at development. You create Access Control Editor property sheets using the ISecurityInformation interface. There are two main methods used to call on this interface: **CreateSecurityPage()** and **EditSecurity()**. The **CreateSecurityPage()** method is used to add a Security tab to an existing property sheet. You can use the **PropertySheet()** function or the PSM_ADDPAGE message to add the resulting property page to the existing property sheet. The **EditSecurity**() method displays the Security property page on a property sheet that's created specifically to display the Access Control Editor.

Some two-way communication takes place between your application and the Access Control Editor. The Access Control Editor doesn't know anything about your application when you first start it, so you have to supply this information. This means implementing several methods of the ISecurityInformation interface within your application. The following table provides a very brief description of these functions.

Function	Description
GetObjectInformation	Obtains the information to initialize the Access Control Editor.
GetSecurity	Obtains the object security descriptor.
SetSecurity	Returns an updated security descriptor to the object after the user completes the editing process Access Control Editor dialog.
GetAccessRights	Obtains the object access rights.
MapGeneric	Asks the object to map the generic rights in an access mask to the standard and specific rights equivalents.
GetInheritTypes	Asks how child objects can inherit the ACEs owned by the requesting object.
PropertySheetPageCallback	Tells the object that Windows is about to create or destroy the property page.

TIP

The Access Control Editor provides you with control over the security environment it creates. In fact, you can set one of the flags to allow the user to view only the object security information. This means a user could look at what rights they had to an object in your application, then request help from an administrator if needed.

The **GetObjectInformation**() method implementation is important. You create an SI_OBJECT_INFO data structure and pass it to Access Control Editor. The data structure includes security dialog configuration information. For example, you can choose which features the user will see. You can also disable the Advanced button, making it impossible to change auditing options or the object owner. In addition, this data structure defines property page elements like the title bar contents, the name of the object, and the name of a server that Access Control Editor uses to look up object security information.

Using the Security Configuration Editor

The Microsoft Security Configuration Editor is an administration tool that reduces both security management and analysis time. Initially, you'll use this tool to configure the operating system security parameters. Once these parameters are in place, you can use the Security Configuration Editor to schedule periodic tests.

NOTE

Windows NT provides one MMC snap-in for the Security Configuration Editor called the System Configuration Manager. You can use the System Configuration Manager to work with the security database (SDB) and security configuration (INF) files you create using the Security Configuration Editor. Windows 2000 divides the Security Configuration Editor into two parts. The Security Configuration and Analysis MMC snap-in allows you to work with the security database, while the Security Templates MMC snap-in allows you to work with the security configuration files. Both operating systems provide similar functionality. Windows 2000 does provide some advanced features. All screenshots in this section of the chapter depict the Windows 2000 setup.

The overall goal of the Security Configuration Editor is to provide a single place to manage all of the security concerns for a network. However, it doesn't actually replace all of the tools you used in the past—the Security Configuration Editor augments other security tools. The Security Configuration Editor also provides auditing tools that Windows has lacked in the past.

One of the unique ideas behind the Security Configuration Editor is that it's a macro-based tool. You'll create a set of instructions for the Security Configuration Editor to perform, then allow it to perform those instructions in the background. Obviously, this approach saves a lot of developer time, since the developer doesn't have to wait for one set of instructions to complete before going to the next set. You can also group tasks, which saves input time.

At this point, you may wonder why a developer should care about this tool at all. After all, configuring network security is a network administrator task. That idea used to be true—a network administrator was responsible for all security on the network. However, as computer networks became more complex and the technologies used with them more flexible, part of the responsibility for network security has shifted to the developer. As a developer, you need to know how this tool works so that you can test the applications you create.

Creating a security setup begins when you choose an existing template or create a new one using the Security Templates MMC snap-in. If you want to use an existing template as a basis for creating a new one, you can right-click on the desired template and use the Save As command found on the context menu. Microsoft supplies a variety of templates designed to get your started in creating this security database as shown in Figure 15-2.

Each of the security templates is designed for a different purpose (which is indicated by the name). The one I'll use in this section is the basic workstation template (basicwk), but all of the other templates work about the same as this one. All of the templates contain the same basic elements shown in Figure 15-3. The following list describes each of these elements for you.

▶ **Account Policies**: Defines the password, account lockout, and Kerberos policies for the machine. Password policies include items like the minimum password length and the maximum time the user can use a single password. The account lockout policy includes the number of times a user can enter the wrong password without initiating a system lockout. Kerberos policies feature elements like the maximum user ticket lifetime.

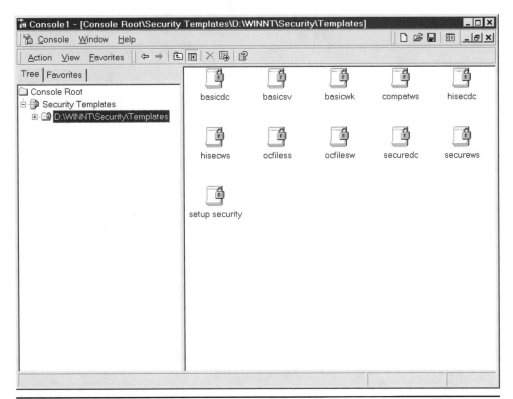

Figure 15-2   *The Security Configuration Editor provides a number of standard templates to use when creating your security setup.*

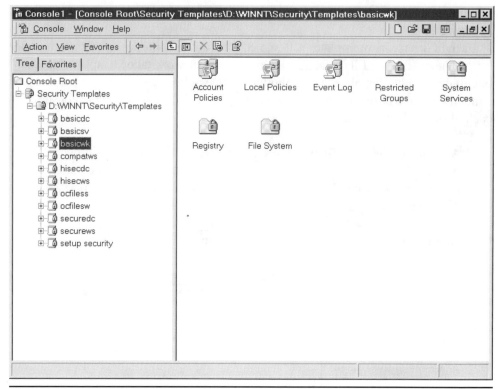

Figure 15-3   *Each of the security templates contains the same security elements.*

▶ **Local Policies**   Defines the audit policy, user rights assignment, and security
   options. Audit policies determine the types of data you collect. For example,
   you could audit each failed user logon attempt. User rights assignments are of
   special interest since this policy affects the rights you can assign to a user (the
   access token). The security options policy contains the elements that determine
   how the security system will react given a particular set of circumstances. For
   example, one policy will log a user off when their usage hours expire.

▶ **Event Log**   Defines how the event log stores data and for how long. These
   policies also determine maximum event log size and event log viewing rights.

▶ **Restricted Groups**   Defines groups that can't access the workstation or server
   at all or restricts the amount of access they can obtain.

▶ **System Services**   Displays a list of the system services on the target machine.
   Double-clicking a service displays a dialog that allows you to set the policy for
   that service and to adjust the startup mode for the service. Normally, you'll leave

the icons in this policy alone. However, you can safely change any system service DLLs you create.

▶ **Registry**   Contains all of the major registry hives. Double-clicking a branch displays a dialog you use to set the security for that branch. In addition, you can choose the method of security inheritance by children of this branch.

▶ **File System**   Contains protected file system entries. You can add new files to the list or modify exiting entries. Double-clicking a file system entry displays a dialog you use to set the security level for that file system member. In addition, you can choose the method of security inheritance by children of this file system entity (applies only to folders).

▶ **Active Directory Objects**   Allows you to edit the security settings for any Active Directory objects, including users and groups. This entry is available only if you have Active Directory enabled (which means you must have a domain controller set up).

BROWSER ALERT

You can learn more about the Security Configuration Tool Set at **http://www.microsoft.com/ WINDOWS2000/techinfo/planning/security/secconfsteps.asp**. *This site provides step-by-step usage instructions and provides you with links to related sites. You'll also learn about updates on this site—an important consideration in a world where security changes on a daily basis.*

Working with Windows Logon

Most people take the logon dialog for granted. It becomes almost second nature to type a name and password when you first start the system. Familiarity with the Windows logon dialog creates problems for network administrators. For one thing, passwords aren't exactly secure. Just about every company has one or more users who record their password, then leave the password where anyone can see it.

At the same time that users are getting lax, crackers are getting more proficient at barreling their way past firewalls and other forms of protection on the network. As a result, break-ins are becoming more common—common enough, in fact, that even the FBI experienced a security problem on its Web server. With this in mind, Microsoft provides four technologies that a developer can use to enhance both workstation and server security on a network. The following list provides an overview of all four technologies.

▶ **Password Filters**   Allows password policy enforcement and password notification.

▶ **Winlogon User Interface**   Provides interactive logon support.

▶ **Network Provider API**   Allows communication between the Multiple Provider Router (MPR) and the network providers.

▶ **Local Security Authority (LSA) Authentication**   Authenticates and logs the user into the system.

Password Filters

One problem administrators have is getting users to create passwords that are difficult to guess, yet easy to remember. For example, many administrators will use a password policy of a word, followed by a number or special character, followed by another word. While this policy won't keep crackers at bay forever, it does slow them down. In addition, two words with a special symbol in-between are easy to remember compared to the arcane jumble of digits and numbers some administrators use.

Unfortunately, Windows doesn't provide any way to implement such a policy through configuration or other standard features. However, you can provide this feature by writing a password filter. This is a DLL that Windows calls as part of the logon process or any other time a user needs to enter a new password.

Every time a user changes his or her password, the LSA calls each password filter twice. The first time the filter verifies the new password. Your filter gets a chance to see what the user wants to use for logging into the system. If the password doesn't meet the corporate policy, you can request a password change. The second time the filter sees the final password. The LSA calls each password filter to provide notification of the password change.

Microsoft provides a default password filter, PASSFILT.DLL or AUTHFILT.DLL. This filter ensures that passwords are at least six characters long, contain a combination of uppercase letters, lowercase letters, numbers, and punctuation marks (you only have to use three out of the four categories), and don't include the user's name. Fortunately, you can use this default filter and a custom filter in combination.

You'll need to install the filter in the SYSTEM32 folder and add a registry entry to the HKEY_LOCAL_MACHINE\SYSTEM\CurrentControlSet\Control\Lsa\ Notification Packages key (this is the Windows 2000-specific location). If you don't see the Notification Packages key, then add it. All this means is that there aren't any other notification packages installed on the client machine. Finally, add the name of the filter as a string value to the key. You can add more than one password filter to the Notification Package key. Windows calls each filter in turn to verify the password added by the user.

Creating a password filter is easy. Start by creating a standard DLL project. The DLL you create has to export three functions. The following list provides a description of each function.

- ▶ **InitializeChangeNotify()**   This function returns TRUE if the password filter DLL is loaded, FALSE if it isn't.

- ▶ **PasswordChangeNotify()**   This function is called by the LSA after a password change is made. The password filter will receive, as input, the username, RID, and new password. The default return value is STATUS_SUCCESS.

- ▶ **PasswordFilter()**   This function is called by the LSA prior to a password change so the filter can verify the new password. The LSA provides the account name, username, new password, and operation type as input. The operation type is set to TRUE if the password is being set (normal for a new user) rather than changed. A return value of TRUE indicates that the password is good.

WinLogon User Interface

The Windows logon dialog we're all used to seeing is the one that appears when Windows first starts. Windows registers the CTRL-ALT-DELETE key sequence as the one that will initialize Winlogon, which means that Windows uses Winlogon in more than one place. In fact, these places are defined through the desktops that Winlogon creates as part of the Windows initialization process: Winlogon, application, and screen saver. Windows protects all three desktops by any access except for Winlogon and protected system processes. When the user presses CTRL-ALT-DELETE and sees the Windows Security dialog, what they're seeing is the Winlogon desktop.

The DLL associated with Winlogon is GINA.DLL (MSGINA.DLL is the default GINA.DLL in Windows 2000). GINA stands for graphical identification and authentication. This application performs the logon process, and you can replace it with your own version of the DLL. For example, you might want to create a version of GINA that polled a smart card reader or a retinal scanner instead of presenting the usual logon dialog.

Adding your custom GINA.DLL to Windows is easy. All you need to do is add a value named GinaDLL to the HKEY_LOCAL_MACHINE\SOFTWARE\Microsoft\ Windows NT\CurrentVersion\Winlogon key. This value should contain the name of your GinaDLL (normally GINA.DLL).

Since the Winlogon.EXE and GINA.DLL are called before there's a session you can use for debugging purposes, Microsoft provides a special way for you to enter debug mode when working with this kind of DLL. All you need to do is add a heading to WIN.INI named [WinlogonDebug]. Windows includes many switches you can use to debug your GINA.DLL, including one that allows you to bypass the normal Winlogon process. (You need this back door in case the DLL fails to function in order to change the registry settings.)

When creating a GINA.DLL, you use a standard DLL project. A GINA.DLL must export specific functions because Winlogon.EXE will call those functions during the logon process (and at other times when the system needs to verify the identity of the user). Table 15-1 provides a brief overview of the various functions that a GINA.DLL must export.

Function Name	Description
WlxActivateUserShell	Starts the user shell program, which is normally Explorer.EXE.
WlxDisplayLockedNotice	Displays a message telling the user that the workstation is in the locked state. This message could say who locked the workstation and when they locked it.
WlxDisplaySASNotice	Displays a message and dialog showing that no one has logged onto the machine. You could include instructions for logging into the machine, such as telling users to swipe their security card through the smart card reader if you chose to use that system.
WlxInitialize	Initializes GINA.DLL for use. Windows calls this function once for each window station present on the computer.
WlxIsLockOk	Verifies that the workstation lock is still functional.
WlxIsLogoffOk	Verifies that it's all right for the user to log off the system.
WlxLoggedOnSAS	Called when a security attention sequence (SAS) occurs when there's a user logged onto the workstation and the workstation is unlocked. For example, Windows calls this function if the user presses CTRL-ALT-DELETE or if they insert a smart card into the smart card reader.
WlxLoggedOutSAS	Called when a SAS occurs when there isn't any user logged into the workstation.
WlxLogoff	Indicates the user request or the system initiated a logoff sequence.
WlxNegotiate	Indicates whether the current version of Winlogon.EXE works with the GINA.DLL that's loaded.
WlxNetworkProviderLoad	Called when Winlogon requires user authentication information from GINA.DLL. Winlogon will pass this information along to the network provider for verification purposes.

Table 15-1   *GINA.DLL Exported Functions*

Function Name	Description
WlxRemoveStatusMessage	Returns a status value indicating whether something removed a status message for the window station provided by Winlogon.
WlxScreensaverNotify	Allows GINA.DLL to interact with the screen saver before the screen saver becomes active so it can set security as required.
WlxShutdown	Called before the system shuts down. Allows GINA.DLL to perform tasks like ejecting a smart card from a smart card reader.
WlxStartApplication	Called during emergency application start situations. For example, Windows uses GINA.DLL to restart Explorer.EXE if it stops unexpectedly. Windows also calls this function if the system needs to run the extended task manager. Theoretically, this function should be able to run any application on the user's machine.
WlxWkstaLockedSAS	Called when a SAS occurs when the workstation is locked (even if a user is logged into the system).

Table 15-1   *GINA.DLL Exported Functions* (continued)

Network Provider API

There are many network provider types, and talking about all of them would be outside the scope of this book. However, we can talk about a *credential manager provider*. The main reason you'd implement a credential manager is to add checks of the user's credentials beyond those performed by network-specific providers, such as the ones used to access Windows 2000.

Full-fledged network providers perform several tasks, including device redirection, resource enumeration, connection-related activities, administrative functions, and credential checks. You'll implement a credential manager as a DLL. A credential manager only needs to export two functions as shown in the list that follows.

▶ **NPLogonNotify()**   Windows calls this function to notify the credential manager of a logon event. The credential manager supplies the MPR with a logon script.

▶ **NPPasswordChangeNotify()**   This function notifies the credential manager of a change in authentication information. Information provided as input includes the username and password. The credential manager replies with any of a number of responses, including WN_SUCCESS, which signifies a successful authentication update.

LSA Authentication

The Logical Security Authority (LSA) and GINA work hand-in-hand. The functions provided by this part of the security API allow GINA to verify users' identities and log them into the system. LSA connects to many areas of the system. For example, all Security Support Providers (SSPs) work with LSA and use it as a conduit when working with GINA. In short, LSA is really glue code that holds many of the security elements in Windows 2000 together. We'll talk about functions with a direct relation to GINA in this section. Table 15-2 contains a list of the functions that you can call within a GINA.DLL.

Understanding the Windows Security API

The Windows security API is vast and performs many functions within the operating system and the applications it supports. We're going to talk about two essential topics in this portion of the chapter.

The first section is an overview of the security API from a programmer's perspective. While users may be faintly aware that there's a security API, they're unlikely to use it or even care that it exists. As a programmer, you need to be very aware of this part of Windows 2000 and know how to use the various API calls to make your applications secure.

Function Name	Description
LsaRegisterLogonProcess	Verifies the caller is a legitimate logon application after connecting to the LSA server.
LsaLogonUser	Verifies the identity of a user. If the user authentication information is valid, then LSA creates a new user session and returns an access token.
LsaLookupAuthenticationPackage	Returns the identifier for an authentication package.
LsaFreeReturnBuffer	Frees the memory used by a buffer.
LsaCallAuthenticationPackage	Allows a logon application to communicate with an authentication package. You'll use this function to run dispatch routines provided by the authentication package.
LsaDeregisterLogonProcess	Deletes a logon application context. Call this function after the application runs and doesn't require access to system resources.
LsaConnectUntrusted	Creates an untrusted connection to the LSA server. The untrusted connection has limited rights on the LSA server.

Table 15-2   *GINA-Related LSA Functions*

BROWSER ALERT

*The computer industry is constantly creating new APIs. A new security API relies on biometrics, the use of human body elements such as the iris and fingerprints, for identification purposes. The Biometrics API (BAPI) allows programmers to embed biometric technology into applications. A consortium of vendors including IBM, Compaq, IO Software, Microsoft, Sony, Toshiba, and Novell originated BAPI. Learn more about BAPI at the IO Software Web Site (**http:// www.iosoftware.com/**). You can download an overview, general information, technical information, and the BAPI Software Development Kit (SDK). Lest you think that all of these APIs are vendor-specific, you can also find a biometrics standards Web site at the Biometrics Consortium Web site (**http://www.biometrics.org/**).*

The second section highlights the cryptography API. This API allows you to encrypt and decrypt messages under Windows 2000. It provides the built-in cryptography support used by many applications. Of course, you can also buy third party alternatives.

Windows 2000 Security API Overview

The Windows security API is large and cumbersome in some respects. Let's begin with the user end of the picture. It's important to understand that the user's access is limited to the combination of groups and individual rights that the administrator assigns. However, most of the configuration options available to the administrator affect Windows as a whole, not your particular application. If you want the administrator to set user level access for your application in particular, then you need to provide the ability to set individual user access for each object or task your application provides.

User level access depends on a security ID (SID). When the user first logs into the system, Windows assigns an access token to the user and places the user's SID (stored on the domain controller or other security database) within it. The user object carries both the access token and the SID around for the duration of the session. An access token also contains both a DACL and an SACL. The combination of ACLs and SID within the access token is a key that allows the user access to certain system resources. Table 15-3 contains a list of the various API functions that you'll commonly use to change the user's access token. This list provides only an overview, and not a detailed description, of each API function.

NOTE

The tables in this section don't provide a complete list of all of the functions in the security API. Functions were chosen because they're unique, new, modified, or a representative example of a larger group of functions within Windows 2000. You'll use these functions most often to secure your applications.

Function Name	Description
AdjustTokenGroups	Allows you to adjust one or more group flags that control group usage within the access token. For example, you can use this function to replace the group's owner.
AdjustTokenPrivileges	Allows you to adjust one or more privileges within the access token. This function enables or disables an existing privilege; you can't add or delete privileges from the access token.
AllocateLocallyUniqueId	Creates a new LUID. The LUID is unique only for the current computer session on a particular computer. Unlike a GUID, a LUID is temporary.
BuildExplicitAccessWithName	Creates an EXPLICIT_ACCESS data structure for the named trustee. This data structure defines the trustee's ACL information. Use this data structure with API functions like SetEntriesInAcl to define a trustee's access level to objects. The EXPLICIT_ACCESS data structure can affect either the SACL or DACL depending on the access mode you set for it.
BuildTrusteeWithName	Creates a TRUSTEE data structure used to identify a specific trustee. You supply a trustee name and Windows fills the other data structure elements with default values. You'll need to modify the data structure before using it.
BuildTrusteeWithSid	Creates a TRUSTEE data structure that relies on a SID, rather than a trustee name. Windows modifies the default data structure values appropriately.
CheckTokenMembership	Determines whether a SID appears within an access token. This can help you to determine if a user or process belongs to a particular group.
CreateRestrictedToken	Creates a duplicate of an existing token. The new token will have only a subset of the rights within the existing token. You can't use this function to add new rights to the resulting token.
DuplicateToken	Creates a copy of an existing token. Using this technique allows you to create a new token that varies from an existing token by one or two privileges.
DuplicateTokenEx	Creates a duplicate of a token. This function allows you to create either a primary or impersonation token. You can set access rights to the new token as part of the duplication call.

Table 15-3   *Common User Access Token Function Overview*

Function Name	Description
GetAuditedPermissionsFromAcl	Returns a list of ACL entries that result in an audit log entry for the specified trustee. These include ACL entries that affect the trustee as well as groups to which the trustee belongs. You get a complete list of all audit generating access events, not just those associated with the trustee. Windows returns the audited access in an ACCESS_MASK data structure.
GetEffectiveRightsFromAcl	Returns a list of ACL entries that list the effective rights for the specified trustee. Windows returns the effective rights in an ACCESS_MASK data structure.
GetExplicitEntriesFromAcl	Returns an array of EXPLICIT_ACCESS data structures that define the level of access each ACE within an ACL grants the trustee. The data structure provides information like the access mode, access rights, and inheritance setting for each ACE.
GetTokenInformation	Returns a data structure containing complete information about the access token. This includes the token's user, groups that appear within the token, the owner of the token, the impersonation level, and statistics associated with the token.
GetTrusteeForm	Returns a constant from one of the TRUSTEE_FORM enumeration values for a trustee. In most cases, the constants indicate whether the trustee is a name, a SID, or an object.
GetTrusteeName	Returns the name associated with a name trustee. If the TRUSTEE data structure that you provide is for a SID or object, Windows returns a NULL value.
GetTrusteeType	Returns a constant from one of the TRUSTEE_TYPE enumeration values for a trustee. In most cases, the constants indicate whether the trustee is a user, group, domain, or alias. There are also values to show deleted or invalid trustees.
IsTokenRestricted	Detects whether the access token contains one or more restricting SIDs.
LookupPrivilegeDisplayName	Converts a privilege name listed in WINNT.H to human readable form. For example, SE_REMOTE_SHUTDOWN_NAME might convert to "Force shutdown from a remote system."

Table 15-3   *Common User Access Token Function Overview* (continued)

Function Name	Description
LookupPrivilegeName	Allows you to convert a privilege name specified by a LUID to one of the constant forms listed in WINNT.H.
LookupPrivilegeValue	Allows you to convert a privilege name as listed in WINNT.H to a LUID.
OpenProcessToken	Opens a token associated with a process (application). As with a file, you need to specify a level of access to the token. For example, the TOKEN_ALL_ACCESS constant gives you complete access to the token.
OpenThreadToken	Opens a token associated with a thread within an application. As with a process token, you need to request a specific level of access when making the request.
SetEntriesInAcl	Creates a new ACL by merging new access control or audit control information into an existing ACL. You can use this function to create an entirely new ACL using the ACL creation function, BuildExplicitAccessWithName.
SetThreadToken	Used mainly to implement impersonation within a thread. Use this function to give different rights to a single thread within an application. This allows the thread to perform tasks that the user may not have the rights to perform.
SetTokenInformation	Sets the information contained within an access token. Before you can set the information within the token, you have to have the required access rights. The three data structures associated with this function allow you to adjust owner, primary group, and DACL information.

Table 15-3   *Common User Access Token Function Overview* (continued)

Normally, you'll never work with SIDs directly. The reason is that you can address users by their login name and make your code both easier to debug and understand. However, there are certain situations when you'll want to work with SIDs. The most important of these situations is when you're dealing with common SIDs like the one for the World, which has a SID of S-1-1-0. The SID for the World always remains the same, but the name for the World could change from country to country. Always refer to common, universal SIDs by their SID rather than a common name. With this in mind, you'll want to know about the SID-related functions for those times you want to work with common SIDs. Table 15-4 contains a list of SID-related functions.

Function Name	Description
AllocateAndInitializeSid	Creates and initializes a SID with up to eight subauthorities.
ConvertSidToStringSid	Converts a SID to a string in human-readable format. This format consists of values in the form S-R-I-SA, where S designates the string as a SID, R is the revision level, I is the identifier authority value, and SA is one or more subauthority values. Note that the dashes between SID values are always part of the SID string.
ConvertStringSidToSid	Converts a specially formatted string into a SID.
CopySid	Creates a duplicate of an existing SID.
EqualPrefixSid	Compares two SID prefixes for equality. A SID prefix is the SID value minus the last subauthority value. This test is useful for detecting two SIDs in the same domain.
EqualSid	Compares two SIDs for equality in their entirety.
FreeSid	Deallocates the memory used by a SID previously created using the AllocateAndInitializeSid function.
GetLengthSid	Returns the length of a SID in bytes.
GetSidIdentifierAuthority	Returns a pointer to a SID_IDENTIFIER_AUTHORITY data structure that contains an array of six bytes that specify the SID's top-level authority. Predefined authorities include NULL (0), local (1), world (2), creator (3), and Windows NT/ Windows 2000 (5).
GetSidLengthRequired	Returns the length of a buffer required to hold a SID structure with a specified number of subauthorities.
GetSidSubAuthority	Returns the address of a specific subauthority within a SID structure. The subauthority is a relative identifier (RID).
GetSidSubAuthorityCount	Returns the address of a field used to hold the number of subauthorities within the SID. Use this address to determine the number of subauthorities within the SID.
InitializeSid	Sets the identifier authority of a SID structure to a known value using a SID_IDENTIFIER_AUTHORITY data structure. Subauthority values aren't set using this function. Use the AllocateAndInitializeSid function to initialize a SID completely.
IsValidSid	Determines the validity of a SID structure's contents. This function checks the revision number and ensures the number of sub-authorities doesn't exceed the maximum value.
LookupAccountName	Retrieves the SID (and accompanying data) for a specific account. You must supply an account and system name.
LookupAccountSid	Retrieves the name and machine associated with a given SID. It also returns the name of the SID's first domain.

Table 15-4   *Common SID-Related Function Overview*

Security isn't this one-sided. Once Windows determines the rights a user or other object has, it must match those rights to the access requirements of the system resource. This means working with security descriptors. A *security descriptor* is a lock on the object or other system resource. The key (access token) fits the lock or it doesn't. Windows grants or denies access when the key fits the lock. Table 15-5 is an overview of the security descriptor API functions.

By now, you should have some idea of how to work within the security API Windows 2000 provides. The divisions I set up within the tables are artificial; they're for description purposes to make the functions easier to comprehend and use. In a real-world application, you'll combine elements of all three tables to create a complete security picture.

Function Name	Description
ConvertSecurityDescriptorToString SecurityDescriptor	Converts a security descriptor to string format. Flags determine the level of information returned in the string. A complete string contains the owner SID, the group SID, a DACL flag list using coded letters, a SACL flag list using coded letters, and a series of ACE entries.
ConvertStringSecurityDescriptorTo SecurityDescriptor	Converts a specially formatted string into a security descriptor.
GetNamedSecurityInfo	Returns the security descriptor for the named object provided as input. Flags determine what kind of information to retrieve.
GetSecurityDescriptorControl	Returns the security descriptor control information and revision number for the security descriptor structure provided as input.
GetSecurityInfo	Returns the security descriptor for an object specified using an object handle. Windows 2000 provides flags that determine which security descriptor entries to retrieve.
SetNamedSecurityInfo	Modifies the security descriptor information for an object specified by name.
SetSecurityDescriptorControl	Modifies the control bits of a security descriptor. Functions related to this one include SetSecurityDescriptorDacl, which allows you to set other control bits of the security descriptor.
SetSecurityInfo	Modifies the owner, group, SACL, or DACL within the security descriptor for an object. Each information type requires a separate data structure. Flags to tell Windows 2000 which elements to change. A handle and object type descriptor identify the object.

Table 15-5   *Security Descriptor Function Overview*

Cryptography API—Overview

Data protection is sometimes more a matter of adding hurdles that discourage theft than preventing the theft from occurring. Encrypting data at several levels adds "doors" the cracker must pass through to get to the data. Put enough doors between your data and the cracker, and the cracker will find something easier to break.

Microsoft's CryptoAPI provides a means of adding yet another layer of protection to your sensitive data. While a cracker could break the encryption techniques Microsoft supplies, the time required for someone to unlock your data and read it would be extended. Using the CryptoAPI routines will help you better protect the data transferred between a client and server in any environment.

BROWSER ALERT

*You can find many of Microsoft's security solutions at **http://www.microsoft.com/ technet/security/default.asp**. This site includes a link for additional CryptoAPI information. You'll also find valuable operating system and other security technology links.*

The CryptoAPI is a general-purpose tool that allows data encryption in any environment. For example, you could build an application that stores data using the same encrypted format whether the information is stored locally, transferred through a modem, uploaded to a Web site, or sent through the mail on a disk. That's a big advantage to your company. Using encryption all the time means a cracker breaking into your system will find that the job has suddenly gotten harder, while at the same time a single encryption technique means users won't have to learn new ways to work. You can bet that a user is more likely to use encryption when it's convenient (and for the most part automatic).

Microsoft used a modular approach when designing the CryptoAPI, much as it has for other portions of Windows. You could compare the CryptoAPI to the GDI (Graphics Device Interface) API under Windows. Any vendor can add a new device driver that tells the GDI how to work with a particular display adapter. The same holds true for the CryptoAPI. It uses the idea of a Cryptographic Service Provider (CSP) that vendors can update using techniques similar to device driver replacement. Windows comes with one CSP—the one provided by Microsoft. However, if Microsoft's encryption feature set doesn't meet your needs, you could either design a new CSP yourself or buy one from a third party.

NOTE

This section of the chapter shows the unmanaged way to use the CryptoAPI. Microsoft also provides a managed way to use the CryptoAPI using the System.Security, System.Security.Cryptography, System.Security.Cryptography.X509Certificates, System.Security.Cryptography.Xml, System.Security.Permissions, System.Security.Policy, and System.Security.Principal namespaces. Many developers plan to continue using the unmanaged route for performance reasons. In addition, many companies have a big investment in existing cryptographic code. If you're writing new security code, don't require the fastest performance, and would like the convenience of working with managed code, these are the namespaces you'll want to investigate.

One of the easiest ways to show you the functionality provided by the CryptoAPI is to provide an example. Encrypting a file is simple. Microsoft follows a straightforward procedure using an eight-step process (six of the steps involve cryptographic-specific calls). You begin by opening a source and destination file, just as you would in any program. Once you have valid file handles, you need to get the handle for a CSP, like this:

```
// Get handle to the default provider.
if(!CryptAcquireContext(&hProv, NULL, NULL, PROV_RSA_FULL, 0))
{
    MessageBox("Error during CryptAcquireContext", NULL, MB_OK | MB_ICONEXCLAMATION);
    PostQuitMessage;
}
```

NOTE

You'll find a complete list of cryptography-related functions, structures, and defines in the WINCRYPT.H file.

CryptAquireContext() can accept up to five parameters, but only two of them are essential. The first required parameter stores a handle for the CSP. The second required parameter (fourth argument) specifies the type of CSP that you're looking for. Every CSP has both a name and a type. For example, the name of the CSP currently shipped with Windows is Microsoft Base Cryptographic Provider, and its type is PROV_RSA_FULL. The name of each provider is unique; the provider type isn't. The second argument contains the key container name. If you specify a value here, Windows will look for a specific key container. A vendor can store the key container in hardware, within the registry, or on the hard drive, so you normally won't know the name of the key container. Using NULL (as shown) tells Windows to return the default key container. The third argument contains the name of a CSP. You can retrieve the values of any installed CSPs using the **CryptGetProvParam**() function. Supplying a NULL value returns the default CSP. The final argument contains one or more flags. Normally, you'll set this value to 0 unless the CSP provides specific flag values for you to use. (Microsoft does provide some default flag values, but they're for administrative purposes only.)

The next step is either to encrypt the file using a random key or to generate a key using a password. The random key method is the one you'll probably use most often, so that's the one described here. The password method is similar and actually requires fewer steps than the random key method.

```
// Create a random session key.
if(!CryptGenKey(hProv, ENCRYPT_ALGORITHM, CRYPT_EXPORTABLE, &hKey))
{
    MessageBox("Error during CryptGenKey", NULL, MB_OK | MB_ICONEXCLAMATION);
    PostQuitMessage;
}
```

The **CryptGenKey**() function provides you with a unique key. The first parameter is the CSP handle obtained in the previous step. The second parameter is an encryption algorithm name. Microsoft supports two: CALG_RC2 (block cipher) and CALG_RC4 (stream cipher). The algorithm names vary by vendors, so it's important to know which vendor the user will use as a CSP. The third parameter contains flags. CRYPT_EXPORTABLE tells Windows that it can export the random key value as a blob. CRYPT_CREATE_SALT tells Windows to use a non-zero random key seed. Finally, CRYPT_USER_PROTECTED tells Windows to notify the user when certain actions take place while using this key. Each CSP defines a unique set of actions. The last parameter is a container for the returned random key.

The user received a public key as part of obtaining a certificate. The CSP stores this key in a central place—it identifies the user. To make data transfers safe, it's important to get a copy of the user's public key to use in the encryption process. That's what we do in the next step.

```
// Get handle to key exchange public key.
if(!CryptGetUserKey(hProv, AT_KEYEXCHANGE, &hXchgKey))
{
    MessageBox("Error during CryptGetUserKey", NULL, MB_OK | MB_ICONEXCLAMATION);
    PostQuitMessage;
}
```

The first parameter is the handle to the CSP. The next parameter tells what kind of key to retrieve from that provider. Every CSP supports two keys: AT_KEYEXCHANGE (exchange the public key provided for a personal certificate used in an application like a browser) or AT_SIGNATURE (get a signature key used for objects such as ActiveX controls). The third parameter stores the key returned by the function.

Now comes the fun part. We take the random key and the user's public key and mix them together. Mixing them means that even if the user's key is compromised, the data is still encrypted in a way that forces the cracker to start from scratch every time. The random element makes this encryption technology at least a little more secure than other methods.

```
// Determine size of the key blob and allocate memory.
if(!CryptExportKey(hKey, hXchgKey, SIMPLEBLOB, 0, NULL, &dwKeyBlobLen))
{
    MessageBox("Error computing blob size.", NULL, MB_OK | MB_ICONEXCLAMATION);
    PostQuitMessage;
}
if((pbKeyBlob = malloc(dwKeyBlobLen)) == NULL)
{
    MessageBox("Error allocating memory for blob.", NULL, MB_OK | MB_ICONEXCLAMATION);
    PostQuitMessage;
}

// Export session key into a simple key blob.
if(!CryptExportKey(hKey, hXchgKey, SIMPLEBLOB, 0, pbKeyBlob, &dwKeyBlobLen))
{
    MessageBox("Error during CryptExportKey", NULL, MB_OK | MB_ICONEXCLAMATION);
    PostQuitMessage;
}
```

Exporting the blob key (the combination of the user's public key and the random key) is a three-step process. You call **CryptExportKey()** twice. The first two values are the keys: random and user. The third parameter tells Windows what kind of blob to create. Most CSPs support two values: SIMPLEBLOB or PUBLICKEYBLOB. The fourth parameter is for flags. Always set this value to 0 unless a CSP uses it for some purpose. The fifth parameter points to a buffer used to store the blob. If you call **CryptExportKey()** with a NULL value, it returns the buffer size in the sixth parameter. That's what we've done in the first call to the function. The sixth parameter normally contains the size of the buffer when you actually call **CryptExportKey()** to create the blob. (The source code displayed here also contains a memory allocation function call.)

Now that we have a blob to work with, it's time to do a little maintenance. Make sure you destroy the user's public key first. Just think about a cracker looking around in memory for some way break your code. Leaving the key in memory is one of the fastest ways to do this. Killing the key is a necessary part of maintaining a secure environment. The following source code calls the **CryptDestroyKey()** function to get rid of the public key.

```
// Release key exchange key handle.
CryptDestroyKey(hXchgKey);
hXchgKey = 0;
```

It's time to send the blob to a destination file. The blob forms a header the recipient will use later to decrypt the file. However, a header isn't much good without some data. First you'll want define a block size for the data. If you're using a block cipher, the CSP provides a block size for you to use. A block cipher normally requires one additional blank block at the end of the file as well. When using a stream cipher, you can define any convenient block encryption size (Microsoft recommends a block size of 1,000 bytes). Read the data into a buffer one block at a time, use the following code to encrypt it, and write the block to the destination file.

```
// Encrypt data.
if(!CryptEncrypt(hKey, 0, eof, 0, pbBuffer, &dwCount, dwBufferLen))
{
    MessageBox("Error during CryptEncrypt", NULL, MB_OK | MB_ICONEXCLAMATION);
    PostQuitMessage;
}
```

You can process the data in a loop until you run out of blocks. Make sure you pad the end of any incomplete blocks. The CryptoAPI depends on an even block size as part of the decryption process.

Ensuring the Safe Download of Internet Code

At least a few vendors besides Microsoft use ActiveX controls to provide code on the Internet. For example, the Adobe Acrobat Reader is a common ActiveX control used to read documents online in PDF format. Trying to keep this code virus-free could cause vendors major problems. In this section, we'll look at the Microsoft solution for the problem, the Windows Trust Provider Service API. You'll get an overview of how this technology works and some suggestions of places to go for detailed information.

We'll also look at the Windows Software Publishing Trust Provider in this section—a Windows Verify Trust API add-on that verifies the trustworthiness of downloaded components. It uses several methods that include checking local rules (such as the security-related check boxes in your browser) and cryptographic information in the file itself (such as digital signatures).

Finally, you'll learn how to sign your ActiveX controls. Signing your control removes the "not trusted" messages users see each time they download a page containing the ActiveX control.

Using the Windows Verify Trust API

The Windows Trust Verification API is a general method for determining the trustworthiness of any Windows object. It doesn't matter whether the object is a client requesting services, a server requesting information, a downloaded document, or an ActiveX control. Like most of the APIs supported by Windows, the Windows Trust Verification API is extensible—you can add new features to perform extended checks. One extension that comes as part of Internet Explorer is the Windows Software Publishing Trust Provider. We'll look at it in the next section.

The Windows Trust Verification API uses several methods to check the trustworthiness of a file. The two most common methods are checking system rules and verifying any certificates or digital signatures accompanying the object. The Windows Trust Verification API also relies on external certificates. For example, many popular Internet encryption standards currently use public and private keys. Applications pass the public key around in the header of a file (to see one example of how this works, look at the section on encrypting a file earlier in this chapter). The private key resides on the user's machine. To decrypt a file, you need the public and private keys. Since only the user has the private key, no one else can view the file. Some schemes also add a random key, which, when combined with the public key, makes it nearly impossible for a cracker to break into more than one file without individually decrypting each one.

System rules could reside in a number of places. For example, browsers store their "trust" information as part of a configuration file or within the registry. The system administrator also sets policy within an individual user's registry file or the domain settings used by everyone. The exact placement of a policy depends on which version of Windows you're using, whether you have multiple users enabled (under Windows 9x), and the type of policy the system administrator wants to implement (system or individual). You also have the trust provider (CPS) rules to work with. (The precise term used by the specification is "trust provider," since the source of rules could be any trusted authority, not just a CPS.) For example, telling your browser that anyone certified by a certain trust provider is trustworthy places the burden for verification on the trust provider. A trust provider will define a specific object type, level of trust provided, and list of owner names as part of the trust verification rules. User actions also affect the rules that the Windows Trust Verification API uses. For example, when a user tells the system that a certain vendor is trustworthy, Windows places the information in the registry. Every time the Windows Trust Verification Service sees that vendor's name on a certification from that point on, it passes the object without checking further.

Now that you have an overview of what this API will do for you, let's take a quick look at the API itself. The call that you'll be most interested in is this:

```
WinVerifyTrust(HWND hwnd, DWORD dwTrustProvider, DWORD dwActionID,LPVOID ActionData);
```

As you can see, the call requires four parameters. The first parameter is a handle for the current window. The purpose of this parameter is to tell **WinVerifyTrust()** there's a user available to make decisions. For example, the call may want to ask whether to download an unsigned file. It's possible to check the trustworthiness of an object without the user by substituting INVALID_HANDLE_VALUE for the window handle. Use a value of 0 if you want the user's desktop to take care of any interaction instead of the current application. The second parameter defines whom to ask regarding the matters of trust. Windows recognizes two values by default: WIN_TRUST_ PROVIDER_UNKNOWN (find a trust provider based on the action you want performed) or WIN_TRUST_SOFTWARE_PUBLISHER (an actual software publisher). If you choose the WIN_TRUST_PROVIDER option, Windows will try to find a registry entry containing the action you want performed. If it can't find such an entry, the **WinVerifyTrust()** function will return TRUST_E_PROVIDER_ UNKNOWN. The third parameter specifies an action. It tells the trust provider what you want to do. Since each trust provider is different, you'll have to check trust provider documentation for a list of valid actions. The content of the final parameter is also dependent on the trust provider you use. In most cases, you'll tell the trust provider at least what data you want checked. Some trust providers may also request information about the level of trust required or context for the trust decision.

Once you make a call, WinVerifyTrust will return a trust provider-specific value. In some cases, it could also return one of four standard values. You'll notice that all four of them are error values—the Windows Trust Verification API doesn't define any default success message. The following list shows the four values and provides an explanation for each one.

▶ **TRUST_E_SUBJECT_NOT_TRUSTED**   Normally, the trust provider uses a more specific error message than this one. This return value states that the object wasn't trusted for the action specified. Unfortunately, you'll need to call **WinVerifyTrust()** once for each action unless the trust provider supplies a generic action or you need to perform only a single action with this particular object.

▶ **TRUST_E_PROVIDER_UNKNOWN**   Windows returns this error message when it can't find a specific trust provider on the basis of the action you requested.

▶ **TRUST_E_ACTION_UNKNOWN**   Windows returns this error value if the trust provider doesn't support the requested action. WinVerifyTrust relies on registry entries instead of querying the trust provider to verify valid actions. In short, a damaged registry could prevent use of a trust provider for specific actions.

▶ **TRUST_E_SUBJECT_FORM_UNKNOWN**   You'll normally see this error if the data parameter isn't formatted correctly or contains incomplete information. A trust provider may not be able to find the object you want verified and will then return this message as well.

Understanding the Windows Software Publishing Trust Provider

The Windows Software Publishing Trust Provider is a Windows Trust Verification API add-on that allows an application to check a component for digital signatures or certificates. Either of these items will identify the file as authentic software released by a publisher trusted on the user's system. As with the Windows Trust Verification API, this API uses many techniques and information sources to determine document trustworthiness.

The Windows Software Publishing Trust Provider also uses **WinVerifyTrust()**. There are a few differences, however. First, always use the WIN_TRUST_ SOFTWARE_PUBLISHER trust provider unless the trust provider supplies a different value. If you use WIN_TRUST_PROVIDER_UNKNOWN, Windows will select the default trust provider. Second, Windows defines two actions: WIN_SPUB_ ACTION_TRUSTED_PUBLISHER (checks to see that the publisher of the document is in the trusted list) and WIN_SPUB_ACTION_ PUBLISHED_SOFTWARE (checks the document itself for the proper verification certificate). Windows Software Publishing Trust Provider doesn't currently support the WIN_SPUB_ ACTION_TRUSTED_PUBLISHER action. If you select the WIN_SPUB_ACTION_ PUBLISHED_SOFTWARE action, then **WinVerifyTrust()** will also expect the WIN_TRUST_ACTDATA_SUBJECT_ONLY data structure shown here:

```
typedef LPVOID WIN_TRUST_SUBJECT

typedef struct _WIN_TRUST_ACTDATA_SUBJECT_ONLY
{
   DWORD                 dwSubjectType;
   WIN_TRUST_SUBJECT     Subject;
} WIN_TRUST_ACTDATA_SUBJECT_ONLY , *LPWIN_TRUST_ACTDATA_SUBJECT_ONLY
```

The structure contains two variables, and dwSubjectType defines the type of object you want to verify. You can choose either WIN_TRUST_ SUBJTYPE_ RAW_FILE for most data file types or WIN_TRUST_SUBJTYPE_ PE_IMAGE executable files (including DLLs and OCXs). The Subject structure points to the object that you want to verify. It has the following format.

```
typedef struct _WIN_TRUST_SUBJECT_FILE
{
   HANDLE                hFile;
   LPSTR                 lpPath;
} WIN_TRUST_SUBJECT_FILE, *LPWIN_TRUST_SUBJECT_FILE;
```

As you can see, the two variables in this structure point to the file and file path. In most cases, you'll find the file in the browser (or other application) cache folder.

Now that you have all of the information together and have made the call to **WinVerifyTrust()**, how does Windows verify the document? First, it looks for a PKCS #7 signed data structure. This is the data structure that we'll create in the upcoming section on signing your control. Second, it looks for a series of X.509 certificates. In the current implementation of Windows Software Publishing Trust Provider, you must provide a root private key along with the software publisher's public key. In the future, Windows Software Publishing Trust Provider will also look for appropriate X509.3 extensions defining key-usage restrictions and other attributes of the certified parties. If the PKCS #7 data structure and X.509 certificates are correct, WinVerifyTrust returns a success message to your application.

Internet Component Download Mechanics

You could also entitle this section "Signing Your Code." There are four parts to this process, and you may have to repeat them several times to get the right results.

1. Create a document that uses your ActiveX control on a local Web server. You need to access the server as an Internet site, or any testing you do won't mean a thing. (See Chapter 6 for details.)

2. Unregister your ActiveX control. Most programming languages automatically register the control. Even if they didn't, you'd have to register it as part of the testing process discussed in Chapter 6. Unregistering the control removes all of the registry entries that **WinVerifyTrust()** would use to look for a local copy of the control. Since it won't find any, you'll see the same trust screens that the user will.

3. Sign your ActiveX control. This is the first step we perform in this chapter.

4. Visit your test Web site and look at the page. This action will download the control and allow you to test the signing process. You may need to perform these last three actions several times before you get the signing process right.

Signing Your Control

Signing your control is a four-step process. First, create an X.509 certificate (we talked about this certificate in the previous section on the Windows Software Publishing Trust Provider). Use the MAKECERT utility as follows to create a basic certificate.

BROWSER ALERT

*Make sure you use the latest versions of all tools discussed in this section of the chapter. You'll find the latest tools in the Platform SDK. Find out more about this product at **http://www.microsoft.com/msdownload/platformsdk/setuplauncher.asp**. The MSDN subscription also comes with the latest version of the Platform SDK. The ActiveX SDK (**http://download.microsoft.com/msdownload/sbn/activex/activex.exe**) is also a reliable source for code signing tools. Look at **http://msdn.microsoft.com/downloads/default.asp?URL=/code/topic.asp?URL=/msdn-files/028/000/123/topic.xml** if you want to see the main ActiveX SDK page and list of associated SDKs.*

```
MAKECERT -u:AKey -k:AKey.PVK -n:CN=MyCompany -d:A-Company TESTCERT.CER
```

This command line creates a random public/private key pair and associates the key pair with a friendly name. It also creates a private key file (PVK) that holds a copy of the private key. Once you create a certificate, combine it with a root X.509 certificate from a CSP such as VeriSign (this is step 2). You can also generate a certificate using Windows 2000 Certificate Services or use the test certificate in the ActiveX SDK called ROOT.CER.

Use the CERT2SPC (certificate to Software Publishing Certificate) utility to place both certificates into a PKCS #7 signature block object. This object acts as a holder for any certificates included within a signed object. Normally, there are only the two certificates that we've described so far. You use the CERT2SPC as follows:

```
CERT2SPC ROOT.CER TESTCERT.CER TESTCERT.SPC
```

The three parameters are the root certificate, the certificate created in the first step, and the name of a file used to store the PKCS #7 signature block object. Now that you have a completed certificate, place it within the ActiveX control (step 3) using the following command line.

```
SIGNCODE -prog EXMPL.OCX -spc TESTCERT.SPC -pvk MYKEY.PVK
```

This command line performs quite a few tasks. First, it creates a cryptographic digest of the image file (EXMPL.OCX in this case) and then signs it with the private key found in MYKEY.PVK. This cryptographic digest allows the client to compare the current state of the image file with the received state. The client uses this comparison to detect any tampering along the way. Next, SIGNCODE removes any X.509 certificates it finds from the SPC file. It creates a new PKCS #7 digital signature object using the serial number of the X.509 certificate and the signed cryptographic digest. Finally, it embeds the new PKCS #7 digital signature object along with the X.509 certificates into the image file.

Performing a Test

You'll want to check the signed control for flaws. First, check the digital signature implantation. Use the PESIGMGR utility to do this. All you need to supply is the name of the file you want to check. If you get a success message, check that the digital signature object properly represents the executable code by using the CHKTRUST utility. This utility performs the same steps a user's browser will. It examines the digital signature object and then the X.509 certificates. If they both check out, CHKTRUST will also check image file code to see if it compares with the signed cryptographic digest. CHKTRUST performs one final act not usually performed by your browser. It checks the linkage between the various certificates and makes sure that the dependency chain eventually ends up at the root. Windows 2000 (and later) users can also check the certificate visually by right-clicking the file and choosing Properties. Signed files will have a Digital Signatures tab that you can view.

The last verification step is to use the control. You have to do this over an Internet or intranet connection; nothing else will do. Move the control to your Internet server, unregister it at your local machine, and then view the test page using your browser. If everything works right, you should see a certificate displayed when your browser downloads the control.

Your test can fail even with a properly signed control. First, look for an improperly formatted <OBJECT> tag. Make sure your CODEBASE attribute points to the location of the control. In addition, use an URL instead of a directory location on your machine. For example, if your control is located in the CONTROLS subdirectory of the Web site root, use an URL like **http://www.mycompany.com/CONTROLS/ EXMPL.OCX** with the CODEBASE attribute.

Double-check your control after signing locally as well. It's unlikely that the signing process will damage the control, but it could happen. Make sure the control works on your local test page if it doesn't work properly the first time you test it at the remote location.

Security Standards

Security is an ongoing problem, and vendors are constantly seeking new ways to overcome problems created by crackers. One way they do this is by creating standards groups to study the problem and define new solutions. Standards groups are working even as you read this to create new methods for protecting data. Learning about the standards will save considerable time. You won't have to reinvent the wheel and create everything from scratch. In addition, your security methods will mesh with those used by other developers, reducing the user learning curve and making it possible for you to use tools developed for other programmers.

I could write an entire book on just security standards, so consider the information in the sections that follow just the tip of the iceberg. The standards that follow are those that you'll want to use most often to create applications today.

Windows 2000 Authentication Over HTTP

Windows 2000 authentication is less a programmer issue and more a network setup issue. However, you should know about authentication issues, especially if you plan to work with intranets or Internets. Windows 2000 supports two basic types of authentication.

The first method of authentication is Windows 2000 Challenge/Response. This method relies on communication between the server and the client without any form of user input. The server asks the client to provide the username and password the user supplied during initial login to the system. The client provides a specially encrypted username and password. It must also supply a domain name since the client must be part of the server's domain or exist in one of the trusted domains that the server recognizes. Since Windows 2000 Challenge/Response automatically uses encryption to pass information between the client and server, it's more secure than the basic authentication provided by the server.

How does the client know to send the username and password to the server? The server requests the information as part of a header. The server sends an error message (401 Access Denied) that tells the client to request secure access. It's important to realize that what you see in the browser doesn't include everything that the browser actually receives from the server. What you see in the browser is the information that the server wants you to see after the browser strips off any header information. For example, the server tells the browser what type of information it's receiving so that the browser can activate a helper application if necessary.

The second method relies on a digital signature technology known as SSL (Secure Sockets Layer). Windows 2000 requests a digital certificate from the client machine. The client can likewise request a digital certificate from Windows 2000. The client and server obtain these digital certificates from a third-party vendor such as VeriSign. (See the "Working with SSL" section later in this chapter for details on how SSL works.)

CAUTION

If you choose to implement basic security on your Internet site, you must use Secure Sockets Layer (SSL) to ensure secure transmission of username and password information. Using basic security without SSL transmits the username and password in plain text, making it very easy for someone to intercept the username and password and use them to gain access to your secured Internet site.

Using Digital Signatures

Many developers refer to digital signatures as certificates. Whichever term you use, think of digital signatures as you would a driver's license, since it has the same function. A digital signature identifies some Internet object—who created it and when—and could potentially provide other information. If the object is a client or server, a digital signature shows the current owner of that object. The digital signature, like a driver's license, also expires—forcing vendors to keep proving their identity. The expiration date also gives crackers a lot less time to figure out how to steal the certificate. (Since each certificate is a separate item, learning to steal one won't necessarily buy the cracker anything.) Using a digital signature helps to keep everyone honest, because it forces everyone to go through a central verification point. A digital signature avoids the one big problem with the honor system used by the Internet to date: it doesn't rely on one person to maintain the security of your machine.

Of course, digital certificates aren't perfect. The VeriSign debacle (see the InfoWorld article at **http://www.infoworld.com/articles/hn/xml/01/03/22/ 010322hnmicroversign.xml** for details) leaves the integrity of digital certificates in doubt. Fortunately, the release of a false digital certificate is still extremely unlikely. You can trust the integrity of the digital certificate in most cases. Still, it pays to provide additional security in an application that forces the user to acknowledge trust in the vendor's certificate.

Implementing a digital signature—especially from the client end—is straightforward. In most cases, you'll find that vendors provide a standard certificate recognized by any browser or server with that capability, but there are some differences in the way the certificates actually accomplish the task. VeriSign offers several levels of digital certificate. Make sure you get the right level for the job at hand. Unfortunately, this information changes from time-to-time, so you'll want to visit the VeriSign site at **http://www.verisign.com** for details. See the "Internet Component Download Mechanics" section of this chapter for information on using digital certificates to sign your controls.

Kerberos

Kerberos is a private key protocol. This means Kerberos is limited to use between sites that know each other, since the sites have to agree on keys in advance. In other words, you'll normally restrict your use of Kerberos to the local network, a virtual private network (VPN), or intranet communications.

NOTE

Microsoft is always looking for ways to enhance the security that Windows provides. One of the new features for Windows 2000 is an authentication requirement. Windows must authenticate users before they gain access to an NTFS partition. In addition, NTFS uses the Kerberos 5 Protocol to secure data on the drive. These protection upgrades reduce the probability that someone will steal data from your drive. It's always important to combine security monitoring with new security features.

The concept behind Kerberos operation is simple. Kerberos uses tickets to enforce security. The user must have a ticket for each service that he or she wants to access. The following sequence of events occurs every time a user requires access to the local server using Kerberos.

1. The user requests access to a server or other resource.

2. The server, in turn, asks for the user's identification.

3. Once the server has gotten the user's identification, it sends the information to the Key Distribution Center (KDC).

4. The KDC checks the user's identity.

5. If the user has the required permissions, the KDC provides tickets for each of the required services or resources.

6. The user provides a ticket for each service or resource needed. This ticket identifies the user and optionally carries the users access level information so that the service or resource doesn't provide too much access.

Keberos represents the primary authentication method for Windows 2000, which is a departure from the NTLM authentication used in the past. The version of Kerberos used in Windows 2000 is mostly compatible with the Version 5 Kerberos used for authentication on other platforms. Windows 2000 does use nonstandard Kerberos extensions (you can read about problems they cause at **http://www.cnn.com/2000/TECH/computing/05/10/w2k.brew.idg/**). The security community is more than a little upset about the extensions to an approved standard, and you'll find that they do cause platform compatibility issues. These nonstandard extensions also make it possible to expand Kerberos to allow for nonstandard methods of user identification. For example, you can use smart cards in place of a username and password for identification purposes. As a developer, you'll need to make a choice about Windows 2000 Kerberos support. If you're running an all-Windows shop, the decision should be painless.

BROWSER ALERT

*Kerberos is an internationally approved authentication standard from the Internet Engineering Task Force (IETF). You can find out more about Kerberos at: **http://www.ietf.org/rfc/rfc1510.txt**. Another good place to look for non-Microsoft Kerberos information is the MIT site at: **http://web.mit.edu/kerberos/www/**. The information on this second Web site isn't as technically intense as the IETF information, but it is a lot more readable.*

The KDC runs on a domain controller (DC) as a privileged process. Every DC replica will have access to its own KDC to reduce the time required for user authentication. The actual user identification information is contained within the Active Directory, which also runs on the DC as a privileged process. It takes the combination of these two processes to perform user authentication.

Active Directory also performs other Kerberos-related tasks. For example, it performs multiple master update and replication so it can add new users at any DC. This same feature allows the administrator to make changes to the user's group membership or change the user's password.

Public Key Infrastructure (PKI)

We'll discuss three PKI components. The first is SSL. SSL relies on encryption and digital certificates to do its work. If you're paranoid about security, you can even combine these two security methods—they're not mutually exclusive.

The second component is Private Communication Technology (PCT). Microsoft and the IETF have worked together to create this low-level protocol. Like SSL, PCT prevents crackers from eavesdropping on communications between a client and server using encryption, authentication, and digital signatures. As with SSL, client authentication is optional.

The third component is Transport Layer Security (TLS). This is yet another technology based on SSL that's supposed to cure the woes of data communication on the Internet. The main benefit of TLS is privacy. It provides the means to detect message tampering, interception, and forgery.

Working with SSL

SSL is an easy protocol to understand. Windows 2000 requests a digital certificate from the client machine. The client can likewise request a digital certificate from Windows 2000. A third-party vendor, such as VeriSign, that can vouch for the identity of both parties issues the digital certificate. However, the certificate exchange procedure is more complex than sending a digital certificate from one machine to another. Here's the six-step SSL authentication process.

1. The client sends Windows 2000 an unencrypted random message along with its VeriSign-issued certificate (which contains the client's public key). VeriSign encrypted the certificate using its private key. Since everyone has VeriSign's public key, Windows 2000 can decrypt the certificate and check it for accuracy.

2. Once Windows 2000 confirms that it's received a valid certificate and public key from the client, it tells the client to send an encrypted version of its original message.

3. The client computes a digest of its original random message and then encrypts it using its private key.

4. Windows 2000 uses the client's public key to decrypt the digest.

5. Windows 2000 compares the decrypted digest to a digest it generates from the random message originally sent in unencrypted form by the client.

6. If the two digests match, Windows 2000 authenticates the client.

Working with PCT

PCT assumes that you have a reliable transport protocol in place such as TCP. Some people look at TCP/IP as a single protocol, but it isn't. TCP is the transport part of the protocol, while IP is the data transfer portion of the protocol. IP doesn't provide any form of data encryption. When you use TCP/IP, your data is open to anyone who wants to see it. Using a protocol such as TCP/PCT or TCP/SSL makes your communications secure. PCT corrects several problems with SSL, as described in the following list.

▶ **Simplified message and record structures**   Reconnected sessions require a single message in each direction if you don't enable client authentication. Even with client authentication, a reconnection requires only two messages in each direction.

▶ **Extended cryptographic negotiation**   PCT supports more algorithms than SSL. This means that it can support a broader range of protocol characteristics and that it negotiates those characteristics individually. For example, the common characteristics include cipher type, server certificate type, a hash function type, and a key exchange type.

▶ **Improved message authentication keys**   The message authentication keys are separate from the encryption keys under PCT. This means messages can use a long key, ensuring secure transmission even if the encryption key is short or nonexistent.

▶ **Patched security hole**   PCT uses a client authentication based on the cipher negotiated during a session. This prevents someone from capturing the client authentication key, disconnecting the original client, and then reconnecting to the server using the stolen key. The client must know both the cipher and the key to gain access to the server.

▶ **Addition of Verify Prelude field**   During the initial handshaking process, communication between the client and server occurs in the clear. This field makes it possible for the client and server to detect any tampering with these "in the clear" communications.

NOTE

Even though SSL version 3 also provides a Verify Prelude field type capability, a cracker can get around it by changing the protocol version number to 2, which didn't include this feature. Since SSL version 3 is fully version 2 compliant, neither client nor server will notice the change.

Now that we have a few of the basics down, let's look at how PCT works. PCT uses variable-length records as a means of communication. Every record contains a header that defines the kind of message it contains. There are two kinds of messages: application and protocol messages. Application messages always contain data and can use the standard PCT or datagram formats. A protocol message contains key management, error, or handshake information.

BROWSER ALERT

*If you want to find out about the status of PCT, check the W3C Web site at: **http://www.w3.org/Security/**. This site has details on current Internet security technologies, including TLS, PCT, and SSL. You can find Microsoft information on the subject at **http://msdn.microsoft.com/library/psdk/secpack/schannel_6x4c.htm**.*

A PCT protocol connection begins with a handshake phase. This is where the handshake management message type comes into play. The client and server exchange several pieces of information, beginning with the negotiation of a session key for the connection. In other words, the client and server decide on a secret password to use for talking to each other. The client and server authenticate each other during this time as well. Once the client and server determine that they can trust each other, they decide on the master key used for encrypting all other messages.

Working with TLS

The details of TLS are sketchy as of this writing. The Microsoft documentation at **http://msdn.microsoft.com/library/psdk/secpack/schannel_4sa4.htm** is marked as preliminary, so the material in this section will likely change. However, as previously mentioned, TLS cures some of the privacy woes of current Internet communication by detecting certain types of message tampering.

As with every other protocol on the market, TLS relies on careful handshaking to connect the client and server. TLS uses a four-step connection process, as outlined here:

1. Create a connection between client and server to negotiate a cipher suite.

2. Authenticate the client and server so that both parties can identify each other. The cipher suite determines the method and form of negotiation. However, the client and server will normally exchange digital certificates as part of the authentication process.

3. Exchange a key used to encrypt data. The client and server independently create random numbers. They exchange these numbers, perform some manipulation with them, and create a Master Secret key. This key allows secure data encryption, since it doesn't rely on the client or server alone.

4. Begin exchanging data between the client and server. The data exchange relies on a record format similar to PCT. The client or server encrypts each record individually.

Distributed Password Authentication (DPA)

DPA is a challenge/response password-based security methodology that relies on a trusted third party authentication server. It's part of the Microsoft Commercial Internet System (MCIS). MCIS is used as a back-end Internet service that multiple sites can link to, allowing a user to move from one membership site to another without reentering any authentication information (unless required for higher level access).

When using this protocol, the user provides a username, which isn't necessarily unique to that user, along with a valid password when requested to do so by a server. The server then requests validation from the authentication server before granting access to the user.

There are actually three different levels of username supported by DPA: single user, group name, and generic name. The generic name option is the most interesting, since it allows the server to access usernames like WORD_USERS, in place of a specific username like Tom. In addition, generic names don't have to appear on the server as a specific group as Administrators would.

CHAPTER 6

Creating
Administrative Tools

IN THIS CHAPTER:

An Overview of Tool Types

Determining Which Tool Type to Use

Providing Internet Access to Your Tool

Writing an MMC Snap-In

Writing an HTML Accessible Tool

L ook through any trade press or browse any technical magazine and you're likely to find more than a few vendors hawking administration tools of various types. Network administrators, developers, management, and anyone else who works on large computer networks need tools to get anything done. Unfortunately, no matter how well a third party vendor designs a tool, it's still a generic tool made for a target audience. Vendors don't make money by customizing tools for an individual company's needs (unless that's their main business and they get well paid for the effort).

Windows 2000/XP ships with a generic tool that you can easily customize called Microsoft Management Console (MMC). This tool is actually nothing more than a framework with a well-documented interface. The method someone uses to interact with the framework is up to them. Of course, that level of flexibility opens new doors for the developer who wants to create custom tools that really do what a company needs them to do.

This chapter is going to look at creating administrative tools. The first three sections will discuss three issues that I consider important when building a tool. First, we'll talk about the kinds of tools that you can create. MMC is extremely flexible, but even it can't support every potential tool type on the market. Second, we'll talk about how you can determine the right tool for the job. In other words, we'll talk about how you can design an MMC snap-in with a particular use in mind. Third, we'll talk about Internet access. The world of network administrators is no longer tied to LANs or WANs. Developers need to plan for network administrators who could potentially require access to computers anywhere in the world.

The fourth section of the chapter will show you how to create an MMC snap-in. This snap-in is a server information display. You'll find that getting information is one of the reasons to design a new administrator tool. Network administrators need displays that tell them what they need to know quickly. Many MMC snap-ins aren't organized very well. The network administrator suffers from information overload from displays that contain a lot of information that *someone* might need, just not that administrator. Creating a useful informational MMC snap-in is a good place to start because you don't need to worry much about user interaction requirements.

The final section of the chapter will talk about HTML-based tools. Not only do developers need to consider the Internet, they need to think about the size of some of the tools that network administrators will use in the future as well. Some tools will have to work on PDAs or perhaps even a telephone in the future. Using HTML-based tools provides one way to scale a tool up or down to meet the need of the moment.

An Overview of Tool Types

You can classify the tools that administrators commonly use on a network in many different ways. The job that the tool is required to perform will affect its appearance—what capabilities the tool possesses. The following sections will help you understand the various tool types. These sections will provide you with some basic ideas for building your own tools. Knowing what kind of tool you want to build is the first step to creating it.

Categorizing by Usage

An obvious method of classifying a tool is to determine what you'll use it for in a general way. For example, do you want a tool that will monitor the network and alert you to possible problems, or do you need a proactive tool that performs maintenance on a regular basis so there won't be any need for monitoring? The following list describes some of the ways to define tool type by general usage.

▶ **Monitor**   This is the type of software that administrators use on a daily basis. It helps them keep track of the current status of the network. For example, monitor software can tell an administrator how much memory the server has left or the current status of the hard drives.

▶ **Analysis**   Knowing network statistics tells you about the network, but statistics don't help you make a decision about the network. Analysis software takes raw input from monitoring software, performs studies on it, and then returns the result. For example, an analysis tool might try to predict hardware failures based on certain network trends, like the number of errors found while doing normal hard disk maintenance.

▶ **Event**   Tools don't always provide some type of proactive feature; they may be reactive instead. A hard drive failure is something that you can prepare for and even anticipate, but it's not something that you can predict with absolute accuracy. As a result, a hard drive failure is an event you might want to monitor using some type of tool.

▶ **Automated maintenance**   There are some maintenance tasks that you need to perform daily that don't require any form of administrator input. For example, tape backup software has been automated for quite some time. The administrator only needs to set up the parameters once, then the software can automatically perform this maintenance from that point on. Any time you can automate a maintenance task, it increases network administrator efficiency and reduces the chance of error.

▶ **Manual maintenance**   Testing software was probably one of the first administrator tools created. It's important to test the network and verify that it actually works as intended—that there isn't some hidden flaw waiting to cause data corruption or other problems. Some of these testing tasks require constant monitoring, input, or even analysis on the part of the network administrator. These kinds of tasks are perfect candidates for manual maintenance utilities.

▶ **Configuration**   Software today is more flexible than ever before, which means that there are more configuration options than before. Sometimes an operating system vendor will hide some of the more powerful configuration options because they fear the user will handle the options incorrectly. This problem happens all of the time with Windows. Power Toys, a set of utilities designed by some Microsoft engineers, is a perfect example of a tool designed to overcome the limitations of the built-in configuration options of the operating system.

▶ **Installation**   Administrators perform all types of installations—everything from word processors to new operating systems. As a result, this is one area where even a small amount of automation can produce a large increase in administrator productivity.

▶ **User assistance**   Most software companies have come to the same conclusion about user support: It's less expensive to write software to do the job than to hire support personnel. Witness the automated methods vendors employ to direct your attention to some other source of help. Telephone lines have menu systems that offer everything from fax-back support to recorded message help. Online sites provide complex search systems that allow the user to find information, rather than depend on human support. Once you look at large vendor offerings and analyze why they go through the trouble to set up non-human user assistance, it's obvious you might need to do the same thing at your company.

▶ **Tracking**   Records are the mainstay of many administrators. Unfortunately, few administrators have the time to keep records that are both complete and up-to-date. Automating the task of tracking various maintenance and error events on a server makes it easier for an administrator to locate problems based on the history of the system.

Categorizing by User and Environment

Another way to look at tools is to consider where they'll be used and by whom. For example, you'd need a tool with an extensive help system and limited potential for harming the network if the person using it was a novice administrator or trainee. On the other hand, an expert administrator who needs remote server control would want a tool with robust features, a minimum-size help system, and a small footprint. The following list looks at ways of classifying tools by location and user level.

▶ **Distance**   The distance between your workstation and the server makes a great deal of difference in the type of tool you create. A tool that's used on a LAN doesn't have to be as small or network bandwidth-efficient as one created for use on the Internet. In some cases, this means that a single large tool designed for LAN use could combine several functions and would be preferred to a number of smaller single-use tools that are easy to download.

▶ **Level of expertise**   A tool designed for new administrators will require more in the way of assistance features. For example, the tool may include more dialogs designed to alert the administrator to potential risks and help screens designed to describe tool features fully. Unfortunately, adding these types of features can increase the size of the tool and make managing the network a frustrating experience for experienced users. You'll normally create tools that consider the level of administrator expertise.

▶ **Communication media**   LANs are normally high-speed connections, so creating a tool that communicates with the server a lot isn't a big problem. On the other hand, a dial-up connection is almost ridiculously slow, so you'll want to optimize communications for the remote administrator who uses a dial-up connection. In some cases, this may even mean cutting features in exchange for speed.

▶ **Data sensitivity**   Adding security to an application slows it down; it doesn't matter if the application is an administrator tool. Some tools you design will handle sensitive data like user passwords, while other tools will handle nonsensitive data like server processing speeds. The sensitivity of the information the tool handles determines if the data requires encryption, which in turn determines things like the tool's processing speed.

▶ **Management requirements**   A tool that monitors network statistics is less complex to build than one that uses statistics to predict things like hardware failures. The complexity of the management task determines the characteristics of the tool.

Determining Which Tool Type to Use

In some cases, the choice of tool type is relatively easy to make. For example, a sole administrator who works with a small company with three shifts will definitely want a set of tools that work well over a dial-up connection. The administrator may want a tool that checks the current level of processor usage or that can determine whether a hardware failure has occurred. However, some choices aren't easy because you don't know what an administrator will require in the future. For example, just because the administrator performs all network maintenance on the job site today doesn't mean that this will be true in the future.

Unless the use, location, and required level of expertise for a tool is well known, it pays to spend some time looking at both current and potential future needs. Custom tools take time to build; longer, in many cases, than custom applications, so assessing the requirements for the tool up front is critical. Part of the tool type determination process, therefore, is to figure out how the administrator will use the tool in the present and in the future.

Obviously, part of your consideration will focus on how long you expect to use the tool. A tool designed to answer a shortcoming of one version of an operating system may not be needed for very long. On the other hand, a special monitoring tool may be useful through several server software updates.

Another problem is determining how much and what type of information the administrator actually requires. For example, you may build a monitoring tool that uses existing server data only to find out that the administrator ends up calculating the value that's really needed. In some cases, an analysis tool that does some or all of the calculation work for the administrator is a better choice than the easy-to-build monitoring tool.

There's also a question of how much automation a tool really needs. Too much automation may give the administrator a false sense of security, making it possible that the tool won't actually prevent the catastrophe it's designed to prevent. Automation should relieve an administrator of needless tedium, not the responsibility of making decisions based on all of the available facts.

Defining the expertise level is something that can be difficult. Even expert administrators may have educational or experiential gaps that prevent them from getting full use from a custom tool. If portability is a concern, but the administrator's true level of expertise is in question, you might consider making a Help option part of the tool. The administrator could always download just the amount of help he or she needs to do the required work.

As you can see, it's not only important to determine exactly what kind of tool to create, but to specify the range of its operation as well. In many cases, a custom built tool starts out as a handy gizmo on the programmer's desktop and ends up in the hands of a user who may not have any idea of what it does. Designing a tool properly from the outset reduces the risk of improper use. Always choose the tool type based on who will use it, rather than on the person who designed it.

TIP

Password protection is a requirement for administrative tools. Adding password protection doesn't require much code and can take dangerous tools out of the hands of novice users. The kind of security you add depends on the tool's potential for harm. It always pays to err on the side of security rather than discover your tool caused a server failure.

Providing Internet Access to Your Tool

There isn't any doubt that you'll use any tool you create on the LAN to get work done, but many administrators are no longer limited to just working at the office. That's where things like dial-up connections come into play. You could conceivably use products like PC Anywhere to create a remote session with your workstation and administer the network that way. However, what happens when work is no longer a local call? At that point, it may be time to look at the Internet solution of a virtual private network (VPN).

TIP

While this section of the chapter discusses technologies that are available today, you should also consider technologies that vendors are currently developing. For example, the Simple Object Access Protocol (SOAP) provides a simple means of transferring data from a remote location to a server. SOAP has many advantages in an HTTP environment and none of the disadvantages of older technologies such as DCOM. Of course, SOAP is the new technology on the block, so it's an unproven ally in software development.

Creating a tool that can monitor the server's current temperature or determine whether a hard drive is bad isn't as hard as it used to be. Not only has Microsoft added APIs and various counters to help you out, but some hardware vendors now include the sensors needed to perform some types of monitoring activities as well. As a result, you can get more information about your server than ever before from a remote location.

Of course, getting this information through an Internet connection isn't quite the same as getting it from the server to your workstation on the LAN, but there's a common solution to both problems that will reduce your workload. You can monitor your server from any location if you build the right type of components and install them the right way. All you really need is a counter, a DCOM component, and an application that's built to access the remote component.

Gaining access to the information you require isn't the only problem. A tool designed for Internet use also has to be small enough to download if necessary. If you plan to use a browser to access the component on the server, a download may very well be necessary. Using ATL-base COM components is probably the method of choice in such cases, since you'll want to create the smallest possible implementation without losing much in the way of component flexibility.

Another potential problem for tools that can work on the Internet is security. You need to worry about three levels of security.

▶ The first security issue is *unauthorized access*. You don't want just anyone to be able to access your server to perform maintenance. Some people might perform maintenance of the unhealthy sort if you do allow them to gain access.

▶ The second security problem comes in the form of *data transmission*. Someone with a sniffer could learn your company's most sensitive secrets if you don't protect the flow of information from the remote workstation to the server and back. Encryption is one way to take care of the problem, but you'll also want to minimize the information you transfer from one place to another. In other words, you need to design your tool in such a way that it doesn't request any more information than necessary to get the job done.

▶ The third security problem is *the tool itself*. Allowing someone to remove an administrative-level tool from the work site is one sure way to invite them to take it apart to see how it works. Theoretically, someone could gain quite a bit of knowledge by looking at how a tool is put together and analyzing the methods it uses to garner information from your company's server.

Fortunately, Microsoft provides answers to the first two problems as part of Internet Information Server (IIS). You can secure your Web site and require the user to log in using the same methodologies used for logging in to the local network. Since their name and password is encrypted (at least if you use the Windows 2000/XP specific security), there's little chance someone else will discover who they are. Once the user is logged in, you can establish a secure connection with them using certificates. This means that the data will be kept secure as well.

The third problem isn't as easy to solve. You either have to trust the employee or you need to find a way to allow access without giving them the control. Using a Web page is one way to get around the problem. A Web page can act as a front end for the administrator, with all work being done on the server, rather than the client. This solution is limited because everything will get downloaded each time the administrator needs to do anything with the server from a remote terminal. The biggest problems with this solution are speed and flexibility.

Writing an MMC Snap-In

Windows 2000/XP includes Microsoft Management Console (MMC). This utility allows you to add snap-ins to adjust its current feature set and add functionality. In this section, you'll learn how to build a simple MMC snap-in, which uses two new Windows 2000/XP functions to display and change the names of network servers you've installed. The **GetComputerNameEx()** function allows you to display the computer's NetBIOS and DNS names. Likewise, the **SetComputerNameEx()** function will allow you to change these names.

NOTE
*As of this writing, it's uncertain whether Microsoft will include the ATL MMC SnapIn Wizard as part of the Visual C++ .NET package. However, they'll include the required wizard as part of the Platform SDK (**http://www.microsoft.com/msdownload/platformsdk/ setuplauncher.asp**).*

An Overview of the Interfaces

Writing an MMC snap-in requires knowledge of the many interfaces that you can use. Unless you know which interfaces are available and how to use them, you can't communicate with MMC. The first part of the equation is MMC. It's important to know what you can expect in the way of services for your component. Table 16-1 outlines the interfaces that MMC supports.

Interface	Description
IConsole2	Allows the component to communicate with the console to perform tasks such as setting the Result View Pane column heading text. You'll get a pointer to this interface through the **IComponent::Initialize()** and **IComponentData::Initialize()** methods.
IConsoleNameSpace2	Enumerates subcontainers within the Scope Pane. For example, you might create a main node for all of the employees in your company and subcontainers containing employee name and other information.
IConsoleVerb	Requests actions from the console such as cut, paste, copy, delete, properties, rename, refresh, and print. Think of action words when you think about this interface.
IContextMenuCallback	Adds menu items to a context menu. There's one default context menu associated with the Scope Pane and the Result View Pane within MMC. The default context menu normally contains a Help entry. You'll need to implement any additional context menu items separately.
IContextMenuProvider	Creates custom context menus for your snap-in. Use this if the default context menu requires too many changes to implement a property for an item in either MMC pane. For example, you might write a wrapper for an ActiveX control that requires a different context menu than the main snap-in does.
IControlbar	Creates control bars for your snap-in. Control bars work just like any application control bar—the main difference is that you're implementing them within MMC instead of a standard application frame.
IDisplayHelp	Adds custom help for your snap-in to the main MMC Help. Not every snap-in requires extensive help, but you should at least provide instructions on how to use the snap-in and element descriptions. As far as the user is concerned, the help you add is part of the main MMC Help file.
IHeaderCtrl	Modifies and manipulates the Result View Pane column headings. You can add or remove columns, change the text they contain, and change their width using the methods in this interface.

Table 16-1 *MMC Interface Descriptions*

Interface	Description
IToolbar	Creates toolbars for your snap-in. These toolbars work just like any application toolbar—the main difference is that you're implementing them within MMC instead of a standard application frame.
IImageList	Contains the list of images used to display items in both the Scope Pane and Result View Pane. You'll need a minimum of two icons: a 16 X 16 pixel image for small icon item displays and a 32 X 32 pixel image for large icon item displays. In addition, you may want to add an icon for each of the node types you add to the MMC display. The image list uses virtual index numbers because MMC shares it with all of the currently loaded snap-ins. MMC maps the index number you provide to the real number within the image list automatically.
IMenuButton	Allows you to add, delete, or modify custom buttons on the menu bar. These buttons are associated with your snap-in and allow the user to perform special tasks within your snap-in without using menu entries.
IPropertySheetCallback	Adds (or removes) a property page to (or from) the property sheet for your snap-in.
IPropertySheetProvider	Creates, finds, or shows a property sheet for your snap-in. Extension snap-ins can also use this interface to add extension property sheets to the property sheet created by the main snap-in.
IResultData	Contains the methods required to add items to the Result View Pane. It also provides item management methods, defines the total number of items displayed in the Result View Pane, and performs visual modifications, such as sorting the items displayed in the Result View Pane.
IRequiredExtensions	Adds and enables any extension snap-ins required by your snap-in.

Table 16-1   *MMC Interface Descriptions* (continued)

COM communication is a two-way street. You have to implement certain interfaces in your snap-in to make it work at all. You can also implement optional interfaces to extend the functionality of your snap-in. As we've seen in other chapters, the interfaces you implement determine the functionality of your component and give it a unique personality when compared to other components of the same type. Table 16-2 provides an overview of the commonly used required and optional interfaces for an MMC snap-in.

Interface	Required/Optional	Description
IComponent	Required	Allows MMC to communicate with your component. Override the methods in this interface to provide a unique implementation of the Result View Pane. The two most commonly overridden methods are **Initialize()** and **GetDisplayInfo()**. This interface corresponds to the "view" level of Microsoft's document/view architecture. Most snap-ins use this interface to modify the MMC Result View Pane.
IComponentData	Required	Allows MMC to communicate with your component. Override the default methods to allow MMC to work with the data provided by your component. This interface corresponds to the "document" level of Microsoft's document/view architecture. Most snap-ins use this interface to modify the MMC Scope Pane.
IExtendContextMenu	Optional	Adds new entries to a context menu.
IExtendControlbar	Optional	Adds a custom control bar to MMC.
IExtendPropertySheet2	Optional	Adds property pages to the property sheet for an item. You can also use the methods in this interface to query existing pages and to obtain the watermark and header information for existing property pages.
IEnumTASK	Optional	Enumerates the tasks that will get added to a taskpad. Use this interface with the IExtendTaskPad interface.
IResultDataCompare	Optional	Compares items in the Result View Pane against one another when they're in sorted order.
ISnapinAbout	Optional	Allows the snap-in to display information about itself so that the user can learn more about the snap-in without too much difficulty. This interface isn't required from a strict functionality perspective, but most snap-ins implement it. The information obtained using this interface is simple. For example, MMC can call upon the **GetProvider()** method to learn who created the snap-in.
IResultOwnerData	Optional	Allows you to create virtual lists. While it does take some time to implement this interface, you'll see a performance increase in some data-intensive snap-ins by doing so.

Table 16-2   *MMC Snap-in Optional and Required Interfaces*

Interface	Required/Optional	Description
ISnapinHelp	Optional	Defines the location of the snap-in Help file. MMC adds the file to the main MMC Help file so the user can locate snap-in information while searching the standard Help file.
IToolbar	Optional	Creates, deletes, and manipulates toolbars associated with your snap-in. MMC creates each toolbar in its own band on the control bar.

Table 16-2 *MMC Snap-in Optional and Required Interfaces* (continued)

Creating the Snap-In Shell

This section shows you how to create the ATL shell for the MMC component. Once we have a shell in place, we can add an MMC component to it. This is a simplified version of the procedure we followed in Chapter 6.

1. Use the File | New | Project command to display the New dialog. Highlight the ATL Project icon in the Visual C++ Projects folder.

2. Type a project name in the Project name field. The example uses **ComputerName** as the project name.

3. Click OK. You'll see the ATL COM AppWizard. Select the Application Settings tab. Clear the Attributed check box if necessary.

4. Check "Allow merging of proxy/stub code" so there's only one component file.

5. Choose the Dynamic Link Library (DLL) option. Remember, we're creating an in-process server that will execute as an extension of the MMC framework.

6. Check Support MFC. While this will make the component larger and harder to distribute, it will also reduce the amount of work you need to do to create the component in the first place.

7. Click Finish. Visual C++ creates the new project for you. Remember this shell is essentially blank; there aren't any objects included in it. The next step is to add an object.

8. Right-click ComputerName in Solution Explorer and select Add | Add Class from the context menu. You'll see an Add Class dialog.

9. Highlight the ATL MMC SnapIn icon, then click Open. You'll see the ATL MMC SnapIn Wizard dialog shown in Figure 16-1. This dialog should look somewhat familiar to those of you who used the ATL Object Wizard in Visual C++ 6.

10. Type **CompName** in the Short Name field. The ATL Object Wizard will automatically add appropriate entries to the rest of the fields.

11. Click the MMC tab. You'll see a dialog like the one shown in Figure 16-2. This is where you'll define additional features for the MMC snap-in. Like most COM objects, an MMC snap-in depends on interfaces to define its functionality. In this case, there are special interfaces you can implement to augment the basic snap-in functionality. Notice that you can also make a snap-in an extension of an existing node (another snap-in). A snap-in will default to providing persistent storage and an About dialog. In this case, we have no need for persistent storage since the result we'll create is immediate.

12. Clear Supports Persistence. This will slightly reduce the complexity of creating the snap-in.

13. Click Finish. Visual C++ will create the snap-in.

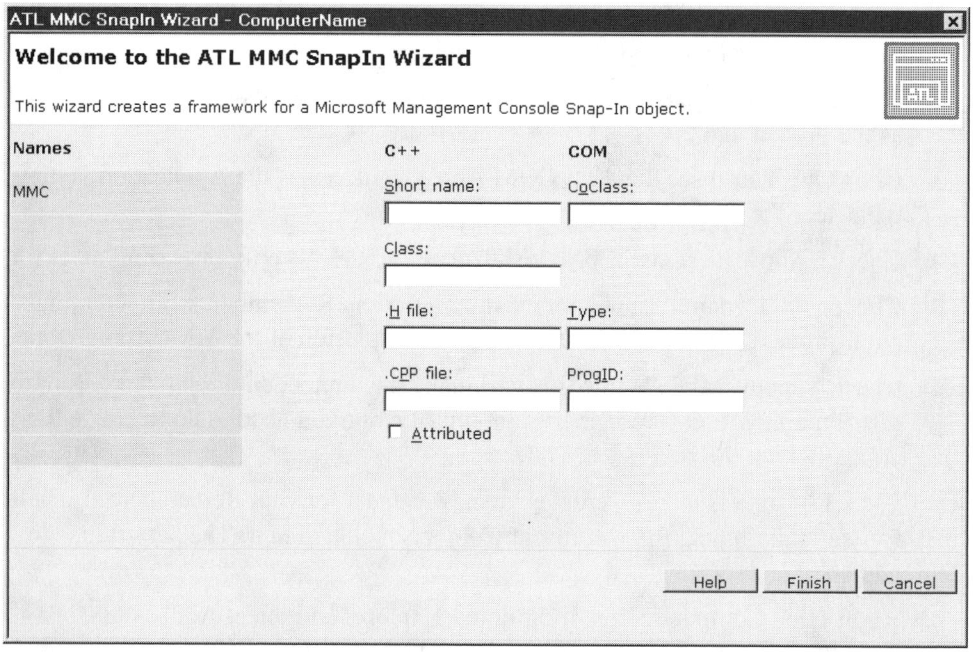

Figure 16-1   *The ATL MMC SnapIn Wizard helps you configure your MMC snap-in.*

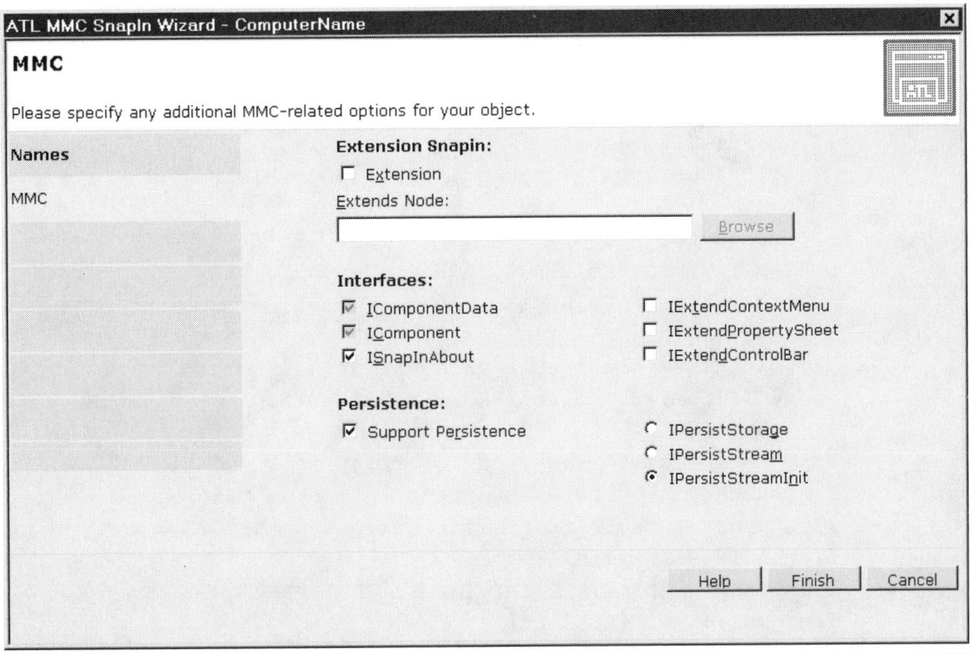

Figure 16-2   *The MMC tab allows you to configure MMC specific settings.*

Adding Some Code

This example shows you how to create a simple single-node MMC snap-in that displays **GetComputerNameEx()** outputs. As a result, we won't be doing anything with the MMC Scope Pane.

There are two main sections of code for this example. The first processes the event MMC requests. The second displays the requested data. In most circumstances, you could combine these two tasks into one method call. However, MMC uses a callback mechanism to display items within the Result View Pane. Each item is processed on a column-by-column basis. The callback function will need to detect the current column and provide only the string required for that column, rather than fill in all of the columns at one time. Add the following source code (in bold type) to the MMCN_SHOW event handler in the **CCompNameData::Notify()** method.

```
switch (event)
{
```

```
case MMCN_SHOW:
    {
        RESULTDATAITEM    Item;    // Result data variable.

        CComQIPtr<IResultData,
            &IID_IResultData> spResultData(spConsole);

        // Create two headers.
        spHeader->InsertColumn(0, L"Name Type", 0, 250);
        spHeader->InsertColumn(1, L"Name Value", 0, 150);

        // Initialize the result data variable.
        memset(&Item, 0, sizeof(RESULTDATAITEM));

        // Create entries required for first item.  Include
        // constants for relevant items in mask.  Make sure
        // you use a callback for strings.  Set the image to
        // the 16 X 16 pixel image.
        Item.mask = RDI_STR | RDI_IMAGE | RDI_PARAM;
        Item.str = MMC_CALLBACK;
        Item.nImage = 0;
        Item.lParam = 0;
        Item.nCol = 0;

        // Display the first item.
        spResultData->InsertItem(&Item);

        // Modify lParam member for second query.
        Item.lParam = 1;

        // Display the second item.
        spResultData->InsertItem(&Item);

        // Perform the same two steps for subsequent items.
        Item.lParam = 2;
        spResultData->InsertItem(&Item);
        Item.lParam = 3;
        spResultData->InsertItem(&Item);
        Item.lParam = 4;
        spResultData->InsertItem(&Item);
        Item.lParam = 5;
        spResultData->InsertItem(&Item);
```

```
        Item.lParam = 6;
        spResultData->InsertItem(&Item);
        Item.lParam = 7;
        spResultData->InsertItem(&Item);

        hr = S_OK;
        break;
    }
case MMCN_EXPAND:
```

Responding to MMC's request to show the component's data is straightforward. The code begins by adding two headers to the MMC display. It doesn't matter what view MMC is currently using; you'll definitely want the headers available if the user decides to use the Detail view, rather than one of the other views like Large Icon. In fact, the Detail view is the only useful view for this component, since the other views hide the data and we haven't implemented a dialog that could be used to display the data instead.

Once the two column headings are displayed, the next step is to initialize the RESULTDATAITEM data structure variable, *Item*. Notice that this is accomplished in three steps. First, the RESULTDATAITEM sets aside the memory required for the data structure. Second, the call to the **memset()** function zeroes the memory. Then, the code fills the data structure elements in. A special data structure element named *mask* contains constants that indicate which of the other data structure elements contain information. In this case, we'll use the **str**, **nImage**, and **lParam** data members to hold information. You'll also initialize *nCol* to 0 to ensure the component starts displaying information at the right column.

Notice that the **str** input value is MMC_CALLBACK. The Microsoft documentation seems to say you could place a string in this data member if the output consists of a single column of data, rather than rely on a callback function. However, it's safer and more flexible to rely on a callback function. You must use a callback function when displaying more than one column of data.

Adding the data to the MMC display comes next. You'll use the **InsertItem()** method to add new data items to the display. This method requires a single argument as input and a pointer to the item that you want to add, which must be a RESULTDATAITEM data structure. There are also methods for removing and modifying existing items should you wish to do so.

The rest of the code performs two tasks. First, it places a new value in **lParam** to indicate which kind of data to display. Second, it uses **InsertItem()** to add the item to the display.

The ATL COM AppWizard doesn't automatically provide a callback function to use for displaying the items on screen, so you'll need to add it. However, you must add the callback function, **GetDisplayInfo()**, to the class that implements either the IComponent or the IComponentImpl interfaces. If you use the ATL COM AppWizard that's provided with Visual C++, then you'll find this interface in the C<Component Name>Component class. However, this interface could appear anywhere (as witnessed by the Microsoft examples provided with products like MSDN). Since there isn't any consistent place for this interface to appear, you'll need to check your source code before adding the **GetDisplayInfo()** function.

Once you do find the class that implements the IComponent or IComponentImpl interface, right-click on the class folder and choose Add Function from the context menu. You'll see a "Welcome to the Add Member Function Wizard" dialog. Type **STDMETHODIMP** in the Return Type field and **GetDisplayInfo** in the Function Name field. You'll need to add one parameter with a RESULTDATAITEM* parameter type and *pResultItem* as the parameter name. Click Finish and Visual C++ will add the function to class for you. Double-click the new GetDisplayInfo entry in ClassView. Here's the code you'll need to implement the new member function.

```
STDMETHODIMP CCompNameComponent::GetDisplayInfo
  (RESULTDATAITEM *pResultItem)
{
  CString oComputerName;  // Buffer to hold computer name data.
  ULONG   ulBufferSize = MAX_COMPUTERNAME_LENGTH + 1;

  // If the caller sent some information.
  if (pResultItem)

    // If that information contains a string.
    if (pResultItem->mask & RDI_STR)
    {

      // Check which string the caller is requesting.
      switch (pResultItem->lParam)
      {
      case 0:

        // Display the NetBIOS name item.
        if (pResultItem->nCol == 0)
           pResultItem->str = (LPOLESTR)L"NetBIOS Name";
        else
        {
```

```cpp
      // See if there is a NetBIOS name for this item.
      if (GetComputerNameEx(
        ComputerNameNetBIOS,
        oComputerName.GetBuffer(MAX_COMPUTERNAME_LENGTH + 1),
        &ulBufferSize))
      {
        // Release the string buffer.
        oComputerName.ReleaseBuffer(-1);

        // Convert buffer contents to an OLE string.
        USES_CONVERSION;
        pResultItem->str = T2BSTR(oComputerName.GetBuffer(40));
      }

      // If not, display a failure string.
      else
        pResultItem->str = (LPOLESTR)L"Value Not Available";
    }
    break;

  case 1:

    // Display the DNS Host name item.
    if (pResultItem->nCol == 0)
      pResultItem->str = (LPOLESTR)L"DNS Host Name";
    else
    {

      // See if there is a DNS Host name for this item.
      if (GetComputerNameEx(
        ComputerNameDnsHostname,
        oComputerName.GetBuffer(MAX_COMPUTERNAME_LENGTH + 1),
        &ulBufferSize))
      {
        // Release the string buffer.
        oComputerName.ReleaseBuffer(-1);

        // Convert buffer contents to an OLE string.
        USES_CONVERSION;
        pResultItem->str = T2BSTR(oComputerName.GetBuffer(40));
      }

      // If not, display a failure string.
```

```
      else
        pResultItem->str = (LPOLESTR)L"Value Not Available";
    }
    break;

case 2:

    // Display the DNS Domain item.
    if (pResultItem->nCol == 0)
      pResultItem->str = (LPOLESTR)L"DNS Domain";
    else
    {

        // See if there is a DNS Domain for this item.
        if (GetComputerNameEx(
          ComputerNameDnsDomain,
          oComputerName.GetBuffer(MAX_COMPUTERNAME_LENGTH + 1),
          &ulBufferSize))
        {
          // Release the string buffer.
          oComputerName.ReleaseBuffer(-1);

          // Convert buffer contents to an OLE string.
          USES_CONVERSION;
          pResultItem->str = T2BSTR(oComputerName.GetBuffer(40));
        }

        // If not, display a failure string.
        else
          pResultItem->str = (LPOLESTR)L"Value Not Available";
    }
    break;

case 3:

    // Display the Fully Qualified DNS Host name item.
    if (pResultItem->nCol == 0)
      pResultItem->str =
        (LPOLESTR)L"DNS Host Name (Fully Qualified)";
    else
    {

        // See if there is a Fully Qualified
```

```
    // DNS Host name for this item.
    if (GetComputerNameEx(
      ComputerNameDnsFullyQualified,
      oComputerName.GetBuffer(MAX_COMPUTERNAME_LENGTH + 1),
      &ulBufferSize))
    {
      // Release the string buffer.
      oComputerName.ReleaseBuffer(-1);

      // Convert buffer contents to an OLE string.
      USES_CONVERSION;
      pResultItem->str = T2BSTR(oComputerName.GetBuffer(40));
    }

    // If not, display a failure string.
    else
      pResultItem->str = (LPOLESTR)L"Value Not Available";
  }
  break;

case 4:

  // Display the Physical NetBIOS name item.
  if (pResultItem->nCol == 0)
    pResultItem->str = (LPOLESTR)L"NetBIOS Name (Physical)";
  else
  {

    // See if there is a Physical NetBIOS name for this item.
    if (GetComputerNameEx(
      ComputerNamePhysicalNetBIOS,
      oComputerName.GetBuffer(MAX_COMPUTERNAME_LENGTH + 1),
      &ulBufferSize))
    {
      // Release the string buffer.
      oComputerName.ReleaseBuffer(-1);

      // Convert buffer contents to an OLE string.
      USES_CONVERSION;
      pResultItem->str = T2BSTR(oComputerName.GetBuffer(40));
    }

    // If not, display a failure string.
```

```
          else
            pResultItem->str = (LPOLESTR)L"Value Not Available";
        }
        break;

    case 5:

        // Display the Physical DNS Host name item.
        if (pResultItem->nCol == 0)
          pResultItem->str = (LPOLESTR)L"DNS Host Name (Physical)";
        else
        {

          // See if there is a Physical DNS Host name for this item.
          if (GetComputerNameEx(
            ComputerNamePhysicalDnsHostname,
            oComputerName.GetBuffer(MAX_COMPUTERNAME_LENGTH + 1),
            &ulBufferSize))
          {
            // Release the string buffer.
            oComputerName.ReleaseBuffer(-1);

            // Convert buffer contents to an OLE string.
            USES_CONVERSION;
            pResultItem->str = T2BSTR(oComputerName.GetBuffer(40));
          }

          // If not, display a failure string.
          else
            pResultItem->str = (LPOLESTR)L"Value Not Available";
        }
        break;

    case 6:

        // Display the Physical DNS Domain name item.
        if (pResultItem->nCol == 0)
          pResultItem->str = (LPOLESTR)L"DNS Domain (Physical)";
        else
        {

          // See if there is a Physical
          // DNS Domain name for this item.
```

```
    if (GetComputerNameEx(
      ComputerNamePhysicalDnsDomain,
      oComputerName.GetBuffer(MAX_COMPUTERNAME_LENGTH + 1),
      &ulBufferSize))
    {
      // Release the string buffer.
      oComputerName.ReleaseBuffer(-1);

      // Convert buffer contents to an OLE string.
      USES_CONVERSION;
      pResultItem->str = T2BSTR(oComputerName.GetBuffer(40));
    }

    // If not, display a failure string.
    else
      pResultItem->str = (LPOLESTR)L"Value Not Available";
  }
  break;

case 7:

  // Display the Physical Fully Qualified DNS Host name item.
  if (pResultItem->nCol == 0)
    pResultItem->str =
      (LPOLESTR)L"DNS Host Name (Fully Qualified & Physical)";
  else
  {

    // See if there is a Physical Fully Qualified
    // DNS Host name for this item.
    if (GetComputerNameEx(
      ComputerNamePhysicalDnsFullyQualified,
      oComputerName.GetBuffer(MAX_COMPUTERNAME_LENGTH + 1),
      &ulBufferSize))
    {
      // Release the string buffer.
      oComputerName.ReleaseBuffer(-1);

      // Convert buffer contents to an OLE string.
      USES_CONVERSION;
      pResultItem->str = T2BSTR(oComputerName.GetBuffer(40));
    }
```

```
              // If not, display a failure string.
              else
                pResultItem->str = (LPOLESTR)L"Value Not Available";
            }
          break;
        }
    }


    return S_OK;
}
```

While this code may appear long, it actually contains a few processing steps that get repeated using different values depending on the item that the caller wants to display. Since I wanted to show you everything that the new **GetComputerNameEx()** function is capable of doing, we'll need to call the function in eight different ways. This example requires two variables, one of which is initialized to MAX_COMPUTERNAME_ LENGTH + 1. You need to initialize the buffer length to the maximum computer name string size and then add 1 for a **NULL** termination in order to ensure you can display the entire computer name. In addition, the Microsoft documentation warns that using a shorter string can have unexpected results under Windows 95.

The next task is to check whether the caller has provided a filled (or at least initialized) RESULTDATAITEM data structure. The code also verifies that the data structure contains an initialized **str** data element. The reason is simple: This component provides text output, so the **str** data element is absolutely essential. Figuring out what to display comes next; as previously stated, there are eight different computer name values that you can obtain using the **GetComputerNameEx()** function.

The processing sequence for all eight outputs is the same, so I'll only describe one of them. There are two columns for data output. The first column contains a string that shows what type of computer name data we're displaying. Since this value is constant, we can simply place it into the **str** data element for immediate display. Notice that the code outputs an OLE string, not a standard C string. Make sure you perform any required data conversions before you place a value in the data structure or you'll get memory-read errors when using MMC.

The second column contains the actual value for the computer name type that we want to display. For this we need to use the **GetComputerNameEx()** function, which requires three inputs: a constant containing the type of name we want to retrieve, a pointer to a buffer that can accept the name, and size of the buffer provided. Once the **GetComputerNameEx()** function returns, you'll need to release the *CString* variable buffer that we provided as part of the **GetComputerNameEx()** input. Finally, the code converts the *CString* variable contents to an OLE string for output. Make sure you add the USES_CONVERSION macro if you use the **T2OLE()** function to perform the conversion.

Not every attempt to get a computer name is going to be successful. In most cases, there isn't a name to get. With this in mind, you'll need to provide an alternative string for the user. In this case, the component displays a simple "Value Not Available" string.

Modifying the Resource Strings

Unlike many application programming projects where customizing the various resource strings isn't a very big deal, you'll definitely want to perform this task when working on an MMC snap-in. The reason is simple: The resource string contents get displayed when the administrator adds the snap-in to MMC. In other words, instead of being hidden, these resource strings are the very first thing that the administrator will see.

Two strings in particular are important. IDS_COMPNAME_DESC and IDS_COMPNAME_PROVIDER. The first provides a description of the component so the administrator has some idea of what the component will do when installed. The second provides the name of the individual or company that created the component.

Modifying these strings is easy. Just click the ResourceView tab in the Workspace window, open the String Table folder, then double-click the String Table entry. At this point, you can double-click the entry you want to change, type a new value, then click the Close button. The suggested string values for this example are shown here.

ID	Value	Caption
IDS_PROJNAME	100	Computer Name Display Component
IDS_COMPNAME_DESC	103	This is a very simple MMC Snap-In
IDS_COMPNAME_PROVIDER	104	DataCon Services and John Mueller
IDS_COMPNAME_VERSION	105	CompName Version 1.0

ComputerName.rc (String Table (group))*

Testing the Snap-In within MMC

Compile the MMC snap-in and place it on the target server. Use **RegSvr32** to register the component so that MMC will see it. Make sure you get a registration success message after you register the component.

It's time to see what the component looks like in action. The following procedure will help you test the ComputerName component.

1. Start MMC using the Start | Run command. Type **MMC** in the Open field and click OK. You'll see a blank MMC window.

2. Use the Console | Add/Remove Snap-In command to display the Add/Remove Snap-In dialog.

3. Click Add. You'll see an Add Standalone Snap-In dialog like the one shown next. Notice that the figure shows the CompName component highlighted. To the right of this component is the provider string (IDS_COMPNAME_PROVIDER) from the Sting Table. Likewise, you'll see the description (IDS_COMPNAME_DESC) in the Description field of the dialog.

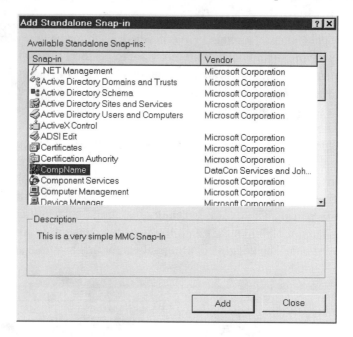

4. Click Add, then Close. You'll see the new snap-in added to the Add/Remove Snap-in dialog. Highlight the snap-in and you'll see text added to the Description field.

5. Click OK. You'll see the CompName component added to the Component Services display. Figure 16-3 shows an example of this component in action.

6. Select Console | Exit to exit MMC. MMC asks if you want to save the current settings.

7. Click No. The Component Services dialog will close.

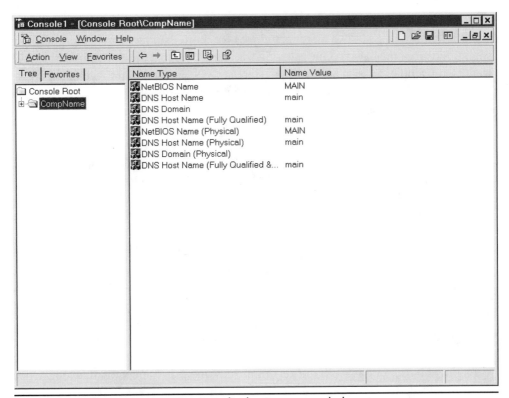

Figure 16-3   *The Component Services display is one good place to see your MMC snap-in in action.*

Writing an HTML Accessible Tool

Browsers form the basis of many tools, not just tools for administrators. The reason is simple: A browser displays many types of information, provides a method for exchanging information, and requires little interface design work on the part of the developer. Of course, the biggest reason that browsers are gaining in popularity is that you can use them in a variety of locations, both local and remote. (A browser still isn't the perfect tool, because there are limits to what you can do with its interface, but the latest browsers are a big improvement over those originally used to cruise the Internet.)

We've already looked at all of the pieces you need to create an HTML-accessible tool. You can use these techniques for more than just application to server communication, they also come in handy for many component-level applications as well. For example, instead of creating a standard EXE as in the past, we could create a client-side ATL component. This component can appear within an application, a Web page, or any other location where the user could easily access components.

The point is that all you really need to build an administrator tool that relies on HTML instead of standard applications is a component and some type of Web page. Using an ASP script provides you with the ultimate flexibility that scripts can provide and the security of using a component. In sum, the ability to create useful HTML tools for the administrator isn't any more complex than what you've done in the past for the user. The only real difference is the mind set required to build such an application.

Of course, there are some differences that you do have to take into account that have little to do with the application itself. The most important difference is the amount of security required to ensure secure communications. Obviously, if you can get onto the network from a remote location, someone with enough tenacity to break any security measures you have in place will be able to gain access to the network as well.

While it's important to ensure that you have proper login security and that you encrypt the data before transmitting it, make sure you take a proactive approach to managing the network as well. For one thing, assume that someone will eventually break into the network, rather than the opposite. It'll definitely help if you keep good logs of network activity in secure locations and create administrative tools that help you detect break-ins. Never assume that remote access is anything but a non-secure method of working with the network. Build the tools that you want to use from a remote location with this limitation in mind.

CHAPTER 7

Building a Help File

IN THIS CHAPTER:

Deciding What Type of Help to Create

Outlining Your Help File

The Importance of a Glossary

Using the Microsoft Help Compiler

Using the Microsoft Help Workshop

Adding Standard Help to Your Application

Creating an HTML-Based Help Package

M ost developers hate writing documentation, yet documenting your application is a necessary and important task. If you think about it for a few seconds, the help file that comes with your application is just as important as the application itself. Are the users really going to care about that nifty new sort routine you added to the program if they can't figure out how to use the program? What about all those new features you added—will the users really care if they can't find them? Help files should be as well-constructed and easy to use as your application.

You'll spend some time writing help files—there just isn't any way around it. The bigger your application, the larger and more complex the help file you'll need. In fact, a good rule of thumb is to allocate one help file development hour for every four programming hours. You might be able to get by with less than that, but not much less. The nice part about creating a good help file is that you can use it as the basis for the application's manual. Some people I know use a single file for both purposes.

BROWSER ALERT

*Do you need help creating help files? This chapter will answer the major questions, but you may need assistance from other programmers. Developers discuss help files in all the places we've talked about so far. For example, you'll want to look at the **comp.os.ms-windows.programmer.win32** and **microsoft.public.win32.programmer.tools** newsgroups. However, developers also discuss help files in less common places like **microsoft.public.access.chat**—a good place to talk about database application help file requirements. Visit **comp.lang.java.programmer** or **microsoft.public.internet.news** if you intend to create a help file for the Internet. (You can use either HTML-based help or Windows Help on the Internet, but HTML-based help is the better choice.) You'll even find help files discussed in general programming newsgroups like **comp.programming**.*

The following sections are going to help you get over many of the hurdles you'll face when creating a help file of your own. There's more than one kind of help in common use today, so the first issue you'll need to decide is what type of help best suits your needs. The first section of this chapter talks about two kinds of help and provides you with some ideas of when to use one over the other. Obviously, there isn't any way that I can create a set of hard-and-fast rules for you to follow, but you'll at least have some idea of where each kind of help works best.

As with any programming project, the next step in creating a help file is organizing the help file content. You'll find that help files, like applications, are a lot easier to create when you organize your thoughts first. In fact, you'll replace the pseudocode used to represent program flow with a specially designed outline meant to show help file flow.

The next two sections discuss help file implementation. The first shows you how to use the Help Compiler with a rich text format (RTF) file. This method works well if you plan to add unique features to your help file and want the added flexibility it provides. The second method relies on the Microsoft Help Workshop. This method is faster and requires less time to learn.

Building a great Windows Help file isn't much use unless you integrate it into your application. That's what the next section of the chapter discusses. We'll look at several different ways to incorporate Windows Help into the single-document application from Chapter 2. This section shows that adding context-sensitive Windows Help to an application is relatively easy.

HTML-based help requires an implementation phase as well. However, creating HTML-based help is more akin to building a Web page than you might think. This next section of the chapter will discuss special considerations for creating HTML-based help files.

The final section of this chapter shows how to add HTML-based help to the application from Chapter 2. Adding HTML-based help to an application isn't hard, but it's different than adding Windows Help to an application. There are limitations to making HTML-based help truly context-sensitive, but you can get around most problems with a little planning. Finally, this section of the chapter shows why so many vendors like using HTML-based help.

Deciding What Type of Help to Create

Microsoft would have you believe that HTML-based help is the best documentation aid to come on the market —that it's the only form of help to use for new applications. Nothing could be further from the truth. You should base the form of help included with an application on a number of factors instead of the latest fashion statement to come out of Redmond. How do you decide what form of help to use? The following list tells you some of the reasons that you'd want to use HTML-based help over Windows Help.

NOTE

Look for HTML-based help to become the de facto standard for commercial software because it's easy to create, which reduces the cost of creating the documentation. However, reduced documentation costs don't necessarily result in better documentation.

▶ **Upgradeability**   When you write a Windows Help file and include it with your application, you're creating a static help file that can't easily be upgraded because it resides on the user's machine. HTML-based help can reside on a Web site, making it possible to provide the user with upgraded help by changing the contents of one file.

▶ **Reduced learning curve**   As businesses move to the Internet or create intranets, it becomes likely that someone on staff will know how to create Web pages. Windows Help files, on the other hand, require the programmer to learn an entirely new set of tags.

▶ **Fewer language/special needs concerns**   There are a lot of ways to make HTML-based help more language-friendly and accommodating of special needs without incurring the usual programming penalty imposed by Windows Help. You can ask users which language they want to use, store the required information in a cookie, then use the information to redirect users to a help page in the desired language. Language support becomes automatic without the need to build special language features into each application you write.

▶ **Enhanced customization opportunities**   The open structure of HTML files makes it easier to customize help files. Unlike Windows Help files, where all graphics are in the compiled file, you can substitute graphics in an HTML-based help file. This makes it easy to customize a help file with a client company's logo without having to re-create the help file.

Using HTML-based help won't solve *all* of your problems. In fact, it'll introduce a few new ones. The following list describes some features you'll give up to use HTML-based help.

▶ **Security**   A Windows Help file allows you to hide information about application features available only to the administrator. Since HTML-based help is in plain text, anyone can learn that administrator features exist—making it likely someone will find a way to access them.

▶ **Size**   You can compress a Windows Help file to consume a fraction of the disk space that the text and graphics would take.

▶ **Remote access**   Windows Help is always available since it's located on the local hard drive. A few vendors make HTML-based help available only through an Internet connection, which can make help inaccessible while on the road.

▶ **No annotation/reduced bookmark support**   The ability to add notes to help files is extremely important, yet this feature is missing with HTML-based help. Theoretically, you could add an application feature that would allow the user to modify the original HTML files, but this would create more work than using

Windows Help. Likewise, even if you incorporate a "Favorites" feature into your HTML-based help file (akin to the Favorites feature in Internet Explorer), the user could save only the location of the page itself. Windows Help allows you to mark a specific location on a page, making the bookmark a lot more useful.

▶ **Reduced search capability**   Windows Help allows you to look for specific words in the help file. The use of keywords allows you to create custom search criteria for the user as well. HTML-based help makes it hard to provide search capabilities anywhere near those found in Windows Help. You definitely won't get the ability to search for single words or keywords.

BROWSER ALERT

*Sometimes a third party product can do a better job of helping you organize the information for your help file than the tools provided with Visual C++ .NET. One such tool is DocBuilder (**http://www.gfai.de/produkte/docbuilder/e_index.htm**). This product relies on scripts to search your application and create documentation automatically. Of course, this product is oriented more to the developer than to the end user. DocBuilder is freeware at the time of this writing. It has a definite German slant, but you can easily modify it for use with English by changing the configuration files. I tried using this product on the SayHello example in Chapter 1. You'll find the results in the \Chapter 17\DocBuilder folder of the source code CD-ROM. For the most part, this product completely documented my application from a developer perspective, which comes in handy when you want to share applications and components with other developers.*

Outlining Your Help File

There are many ways to design a help file. Organization is the first issue you'll need to tackle. The way that you organize a help file determines how easy it is to use. For example, a help file that's task oriented will help users get specific tasks done more quickly—assuming of course, that you know precisely what tasks they intend to perform with your application. On the other hand, a menu-oriented help file can make searching for specific items faster.

The type of help file you create also affects its organization. For example, since a Windows Help file provides superior search capabilities, you can use a task-oriented organization more often, because users are able to find the command information they need easily. In addition, it's difficult to create a help file with a tutorial organization using an HTML-based help file. On the other hand, you'll find it's easy to use a menu-flow organization with HTML-based help files, because adding new menu options is trivial when compared to the same operations in Windows Help files.

It's important to begin the help file writing process by composing an outline of what you want the help file to contain. The outline should reflect the user orientation that you'll pursue when writing the help file. For example, when using the menu orientation, your first level headings should be the entries across the menu bar, while second level headings contain the content of each initial menu. Given a typical Windows application, File is a first-level heading, while Open is a second-level heading. Doing this will help you organize the file from the beginning and focus your thoughts on each segment as you write it.

Once you create an outline, fill it in with some meaningful text. There are a few rules that you should follow. First, keep each help topic entry in the file down to one screen. (The one-screen rule is especially important if you want to use HTML-based help, since the user won't have access to bookmarks or annotations to make finding information easier.) Users won't want to page up and down in the help file as they look for critical information. In many cases, you can break a large piece of the help file into subtopics, making the file easier to read. In today's computing environment, you'll want to keep a single screen down to what you can see at 800×600 resolution (although 1024×768 resolution displays are becoming more common). Although many developers have large displays, many people still use small ones. In addition, many older laptops provide an 800×600 or even a 640×480 display.

There are exceptions to the one-screen rule. For example, don't divide a procedure into subtopics. It's annoying to use a help file organized this way. Such files have instructions like "create a mail merge file—see help topic 3A for instructions on how to do this." Satire about everyday pieces of equipment like the stereo point to the existence of this type of procedure. I know you've all heard the expression "This reads like stereo instructions."

You'll also want to exceed a single-screen help topic if there isn't any way to break it into parts conveniently. For example, procedures that require graphics for explanatory purposes often require more than one screen. Complex procedures also call for more than one screen. Don't use the complexity of a procedure to avoid using subtopics, though; look for places to simplify a procedure whenever possible. It's important to reach a balance between the use of full procedures and breaking the procedure into subtopics. Make sure that the screen reads well without the subtopics. Place amplifying information in the subtopic area. That way an advanced user can look at a single help screen and get the information he or she needs.

The entire process I've just described could be termed "building a script." You're creating what amounts to a book, but not in book form. One topic doesn't necessarily flow into the next, as it would in a book. (It's irritating to use a help file written as a book—you'll get screens that introduce a topic but don't really lead anywhere.) Design each topic to stand on its own. Of course, adding continuity between topics in a help file will always make it easier to use.

Creating a script is about half the process of building a help file. Another third of the process is to convert that script into something that the Windows Help engine or HTML browser can use to display information to the users of your application. You'll need to break the outline into screens and add hypertext links as required. Some help compilers also require the equivalent of a *make* file. The make file tells the compiler which script files to include in the help file and can add optional features like buttons.

Now that you understand the outlining process, let's talk about organizational techniques. The following sections provide some of the organizational techniques that I've used in the past.

Menu Flow

The menu flow technique starts with the application menu system and works down from there. Simply list all of the menu items in hierarchical format. Once you have all the menu items listed, start listing any dialogs. List each dialog in order along with the controls that it contains. Finally, list the Main window and any components it contains.

Using this organizational method has the advantage of fast access to specific program features. The disadvantage is that you're not telling the reader how to accomplish a specific task, just how to use the menu item.

Limit this approach to situations where users are apt to have at least a moderate level of expertise—give them quick access to application functionality without burdening them with information they already know. Use this type of help file with utility programs, since users will understand what to do when they buy the application. It also works well with configuration modules where users have straightforward questions, but they need a little help answering them.

Task

Most users I've talked to don't care about the latest "gee whiz" feature in a program. All they know is that they have to get a particular job done in a limited amount of time. This is especially true of people who crunch numbers all day or those who perform some of the more mundane office chores in a company. They don't have time to figure out how to do something—you have to tell them.

This kind of help file is most useful in rushed environments. You work out a list of tasks the user will perform, and then explain each one in detail. It's good to start with an explanation of the task. You need to answer the question: "What will the user accomplish?" Then provide a procedure to get the job done.

You should expect this kind of user to have few computer-related talents and little desire to learn new ones. This particular technique works well with data entry or other programs that perform a fixed number of tasks. Once you start getting into the freewheeling world of the word processor or other general-purpose applications, you need to take a different approach.

Generalized Menu/Task Approach

Some applications perform many tasks. For example, most people use a word processor for more than one task. Writing hard and fast rules for accomplishing tasks, in this case, would do both the user and the developer a disservice.

What I usually do is provide a list of task explanations that demonstrate product features, along with an overview of the menu system. The user gets a general feel for what the application can do without absorbing too many preconceived ideas from the developer. Follow this up with ample "cloud" help—the balloons that appear near a control when you place the mouse cursor on top of it for a few seconds.

Reference

Compilers and applications that provide their own macro language often include a reference-type help file. In this case, you're looking at the program not from a physical perspective but from a control perspective. It doesn't really pay to do much more than list the macro commands for a word processor in alphabetical order, because there isn't any way to know how the user will use them. Describe the command, tell what each parameter will do, and then provide some kind of example of how to use the command. You can also add other information, such as hints and version-specific differences. Users find it extremely helpful to have tips that say: "If you want to do X, then use this command; otherwise, use command Y—it's more efficient".

Tutorial

Tutorials are special-purpose help files used with applications designed for novices. You'll use the help file to teach someone how to use your application. Most programmers find this kind of help file effective in places where the user hasn't had previous experience using the application. A minimal amount of experience with the computer and operating system is essential to making this type of help file work.

Data entry users find this type of help file useful. Provide a short, task-oriented text section, followed by a question-and-answer section. An interactive help session where the user works with a mock-up of the real application is also helpful.

You can use help file macros to provide tutorial automation. The help file monitors user input for correct responses. This type of help file is unfortunately difficult to put together and provides little benefit to the user over the long haul. You'd be better off convincing a company to hire a trainer or two instead of taking the time to put one of these together.

Functional Area

Some applications lend themselves to organization by functional area because of the way that they're used. CAD and other drawing programs fall into this category because you can group the tasks they perform into functional areas. A CAD program provides some commands for drawing, others that control the color palette, and still others that allow you to manipulate the drawing size and shape. Grouping like items will help users find what they need quickly. The reason is simple: When users are creating the drawing, they look for drawing commands. Later, as they embellish their work of art, they'll want to know about color- and texture-related commands.

The Importance of a Glossary

Those of us who spend every hour of the workweek immersed in programming or other computer-related activities learn even arcane terms quickly. A new term is something to spice up the day, not a hindrance to communication.

On the other hand, most users look at the computer as a mere acquaintance—something they use to do their job. (A good friend of mine even says that she's "computer hostile"—how's that for a descriptive term?) For the typical user, a new term is an insurmountable obstacle to getting work done. Help files filled with undefined jargon are always worse than no help file at all. The user can read the file but doesn't understand what it means.

Let's face it, there's no way to completely avoid jargon when writing a help file. We're working in an industry that seems to invent yet one more new term (and sometimes more) every day. You should do your best to avoid jargon when writing help files, but it's impossible to avoid using standard computer terms.

Always script help files before committing them to final form. Create an outline and then fill in the blanks. Ask one or two people who haven't seen the file before to read it and write down any terms they don't understand. Picking non-technical types is best, because you'll get better input. When they're finished, take the list of "unknown" words from each reader and define them. Now you have a glossary that's hand-tuned to meet user needs.

The last step in the process is to add hot links from every occurrence of an unknown word in the text to its entry in the glossary. Users can click the link for a definition when they don't know what a term means.

Using the Microsoft Help Compiler

This section provides an overview of the Microsoft Help Compiler (MHC)—it describes the commands you'll use most often and presents a simple example of how you could create a help file using a standard word processor and the MHC. This section represents the method that most of us used until better tools arrived on the market. It also represents the most flexible way to create a help file, since you have the most control over the contents of the help scripts you create.

Visual C++ requires that you perform an extra step before you create a help script or make file. Fortunately, that extra step will save you some time later, especially if you remember to do it before you start working on the RTF or make files. Use the MakeHM (make help map) utility located in the Program Files\Microsoft Visual Studio.NET\Common7\Tools directory to create a help map before you do anything else. All you need to do is type the following at the command prompt to create the help map you'll need later to link the help file to the application.

```
MAKEHM ID_,HID_,0x10000 RESOURCE.H MY.HM
```

You'll get a listing of the help IDs in your application. Help identifiers allow you to make the link between Visual C++ and your help file, as we'll see later. For right now, all you need to know is that you'll include that list of help IDs in your help file. You'll also use the help ID names in your help script. Listing 17-1 shows a list of help identifiers for the Sngl_Doc application from Chapter 2.

Listing 17-1

```
HID_CANCEL_EDIT_CNTR               0x18000
HID_CANCEL_EDIT_SRVR               0x18001
HID_UNDERLINE                      0x18006
HID_STRIKETHROUGH                  0x18007
HID_BOLD                           0x18008
HID_ITALIC                         0x18009
HID_FONT_DIALOG                    0x1800A
HID_VIEW_FORMATTOOLBAR             0x1800B
HID_FORMAT_FONT2                   0x18010
HID_HELP_CONTENTS                  0x18012
HID_HELP_WHATSTHIS                 0x18013
```

The Microsoft Help Compiler requires a minimum of two files: the help script and a make file. I use Microsoft Word to create the help script, since it provides full RTF support and it's my word processor of choice. You'll want to separate the help file sections. Do this by adding a hard page break (\page statement) before each new section. (I'll include some common RTF statements in my discussion so you can troubleshoot problems in your RTF file.)

BROWSER ALERT

*If the Microsoft utilities don't fulfill your help file writing needs, then look at the Help Maker Plus utility **http://www.exhedra.com/exhedra/helpmakerplus/default.asp**. The vendor promotes this utility as a replacement for the Microsoft Help Compiler. Dave Central (**http://www.davecentral.com/**) is a great place to look for programmer utilities. Richard Hendricks site (**http://ourworld.compuserve.com/homepages/ RHendricks/whelpdev.htm**) contains helpful tips for both HTML help and WinHelp.*

Adding one or more footnotes to each heading comes next. The help compiler uses footnotes for a variety of hyperlink functions. For example, the search words for your index will come from this source. You'll also use footnotes to define links between words in the glossary and the help file. Table 17-1 shows a partial list of footnotes—the footnotes you use most often. You should also check the documentation for the Microsoft Help Compiler for additional ideas.

Footnote Type	Purpose
*	You'll eventually end up with many RTF files and may not want to include all of the topics they contain in every help file. For example, one help file I include with communication programs talks about online courtesy. It's generic and most users find it helpful when figuring out acronyms they see online. It appears in an RTF file of general topics. While I wouldn't want to include online courtesy in a utility program, the general file does have topics I do want to include. This footnote defines a build tag. It works in concert with the help project (HPJ) file (I'll describe this later). The help compiler looks at the list of help topics you want to include and then looks at the build tags in the RTF file to find them. You must include this footnote as the first footnote for a topic. Build tags are case insensitive, but I type mine in uppercase so future changes to the way that Microsoft handles help files won't break mine. A typical build tag in an RTF file looks like this: *{/footnote BUILD_TAG}.

Table 17-1 *Standard Footnote Styles for the Microsoft Help Compiler*

Footnote Type	Purpose
#	This is a topic identifier footnote. It's similar to a label used by a GOTO statement. Whenever you "call" a topic identifier, Windows Help changes the focus to the target footnote. This is the first half of a hyperlink within the help file. You can use hyperlinks for tasks such as creating menus or links to a glossary. Like build tags, topic identifiers are case insensitive. One example of a topic identifier footnote in an RTF file is: #{\footnote SOME_LINK}.
$	Use this footnote type to create a topic title. The topic title appears in the gray area above the help text in the help window. You'll also see the topic title in the Topics Found and the History dialogs. This footnote accepts any kind of text. For example, you could use ${\footnote This is a title.} as a topic title.
+	The browse-sequence identifier footnote creates a sequence of help topics to allow the user to move from one area of the help file to another with ease. For example, a lengthy procedure may require more than one screen. This footnote allows you to break the procedure into window-sized elements and allows the user to browse from one window to the next. It activates the two Browse buttons >> and << in the help window. (You have to enable the Browse buttons by adding a BrowseButtons macro to the HPJ file.) Windows allows you to use any identifier for a browse sequence—it sorts the identifiers in alphabetical order to determine which sequence to display next—but I usually use a page-numbering sequence. For example, +{/footnote Page:1} is the first page in a sequence. The only usage limitation is that you can only have one browse-sequence identifier per topic. The browse sequence identifier is one of the handier help file footnotes because you can use it to break up long sections of text without causing any confusion for the user. I also find it essential when I need to display a multipage graphic, like a hierarchical chart. For example, one of the help files I created contained a complete hierarchical chart of all the Novell forums. Since the chart requires more than one page, I used a browse sequence to make it easy for the user to move from one area to the next. You could also use this feature in a reference-type help file to move from one command to the next. The applications for this particular footnote are almost unlimited.

Table 17-1 *Standard Footnote Styles for the Microsoft Help Compiler* (continued)

Footnote Type	Purpose
K	The search capability of your help file depends on the keyword footnote. You define one or more descriptive words for each topic and subtopic in your help file. The keywords you define appear in the Index page of the Search dialog. A keyword can contain any sequence of characters including spaces. Windows also preserves the case of your keywords—making it easier for you to define descriptive terms the user can identify easily. One topic can also have more than one keyword separated with semicolons. One example of a keyword footnote is: K{/footnote Control;Exit Pushbutton;Leaving the Program}. In this case, the user could find the same help topic using three different keywords: Control, Exit Pushbutton, and Leaving the Program. You'll find it easier to build a comprehensive yet consistent help file if you maintain a sorted list of keywords as you build the RTF files. Make sure you use the same keyword every place a topic appears. For example, if you say "Control" in one place, don't use the plural form in another place. A user can adapt to a consistent help file—help files that use terms inconsistently cause problems.
@	Help files can get quite complex. You could easily forget why you added a macro or did something in a particular way between editing sessions. The author-defined comment footnote solves this problem. It's like adding comments to your help file. The only difference is that you won't see the comment until you open the footnote for viewing (assuming you use a standard word processor to create the file). A typical author-defined comment footnote looks like this: @{/footnote This is a comment.}.

Table 17-1   *Standard Footnote Styles for the Microsoft Help Compiler* (continued)

What do you type in the footnote? It depends on the kind of footnote. For example, you add the name of a hyperlink when using the # footnote. Make sure you read the text that follows each footnote in the table to learn about any requirements for using them. It's extremely important to create unique names for each of your footnotes. Descriptive names are also essential so you'll remember what the names mean later. Remember that hyperlink names, like variables, don't contain spaces. Footnotes are symbolized by the <footnote type>{\footnote <text>} RTF file statement.

It's time to compile a list of the topic identifier (#) footnotes you've created. Armed with this list, you can go through the rest of the help file and create the appropriate hyperlinks. Just how do you go about doing this? When you look at a standard help file and see the green text that signifies a hyperlink, what you're looking at is a double underline (/uldb in an RTF file) or a strike-through (/strike in an RTF file). You should double-underline or strike-through the text that you want the user to see as green text, then add the topic identifier of the hyperlink in hidden text (use the /v statement in an RTF file). This is the same identifier that you typed in the # footnote.

You can dress up your help file once the hyperlinks are in place. For example, you could add graphics. A few graphics in the right places can go a long way toward making your help file truly user friendly. Some people like to add sound or other multimedia. Unless you're proficient at using these mediums, I'd avoid them for the first few projects. You'll also need to decide what types of information to include in your make file. The following sections provide you with the details of completing your help file. We'll discuss the options you have and what I normally do with specific types of help files.

Adding Special Effects to a Help File

You can add many enhancements to a help file. For example, you can grab a screen shot of your application and then define hotspots on it with the Hotspot Editor utility (SHED.EXE). You can use BMP, DIB, WMF, and SHG graphics formats with the Hotspot Editor. Files containing hotspots always use the SHG extension.

TIP

One of my favorite graphics additions to tutorial-style help files are Answer buttons. They look like standard Windows buttons that I create as a graphics image. Users read the question, mentally answer it, and then click the Answer button to see the correct response. You can also use this technique to simulate other application controls—the Windows Help utility doesn't provide very much help in this regard. It does, however, provide the {BUTTON [LABEL], Macro1[: Macro2: ... : MacroN]} macro that allows you to create a standard button. Label contains the caption you want to see on the button. The macro parameters allow you to attach one or more macros to the button.

Figure 17-1 shows a typical view of the Hotspot Editor. I've opened a screen shot of the example program we'll use later to test the help file. In this case, we're looking at a picture of the main form. I'll add hotspots for each control to make it easy for the user to learn about the application. You can't use the Hotspot Editor to create a new drawing—you'll need a graphics application to do that. The purpose of using the Hotspot Editor is to add places where the user can point and expect something to happen. Every time you see the cursor change from a pointer to a pointing hand in a help file, you're seeing the effect of using the Hotspot Editor.

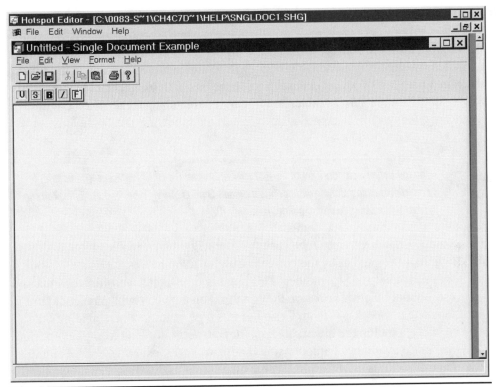

Figure 17-1   *The Hotspot Editor lets you add hotspots to drawings, but doesn't create new drawings.*

Creating a new hotspot is as easy as dragging the mouse. All you need to do is create a box. The area within the box is the hotspot. Once you create a hotspot, you need to define it. Just double-click on the hotspot and you'll see the Attributes dialog shown here.

There are three mandatory entries in this dialog: Context String, Type, and Attribute. A context string works the same as the double-underlined (or strike-through) text in the previous section. The context string acts as the second half of a hyperlink. When the user clicks on the hotspot, Windows Help will set the focus to the place in the help file that you've defined. You can choose to make the box surrounding the hotspot visible or invisible. I make them invisible, and I've never seen anyone else do otherwise. There are three types of hotspots as described in the following list.

TIP

You can define a standard set of hotspot attributes using the Edit | Preferences command. A Preferences dialog allows you to define a default Context String, Type, and Attribute. You can also use this dialog to define a default Hotspot ID.

▶ **Jump**   Windows Help replaces the contents of the current window with the help topic pointed at by the context string. A jump moves the user from one area of the help file to another. This hotspot type works well for icons that tell users about other information they can find on a given topic. You could use it to create a "See Also" icon. I also use this type of jump when creating links between a multipage hierarchical chart. Hotspots allow the user to jump from one place to another without using the Browse buttons. I also use this jump to control pictures used to simulate the display the user will find in an application.

▶ **Pop-up**   You'll find that this kind of a jump is used most often with control descriptions or other pictorial-type hotspots. Windows displays the help topic associated with the hotspot in a pop-up window. Since the user doesn't leave the picture, he or she can easily select other controls. I also use this hotspot in tutorial-type help files in the question-and-answer section. The Answer button displays a pop-up window containing the answer to a question.

▶ **Macro**   The macro hotspot allows you to play back a predefined macro. You'll find that macros are a powerful (and underused) feature of Windows help. You can even use macros to call programs or reprogram the way that Windows help works.

TIP

The Microsoft Help Compiler provides many predefined macros. For example, you can use the SetPopupColor macro to change the color of a pop-up window. Attaching macros to a button or menu will give users control over the help window and enhance their ability to use it. One way to combine a macro with a bitmap is to create a bitmap of colored squares. When a user clicks on a colored square, the color of the help windows changes.

The Attribute dialog contains a few optional entries. One is the Hotspot ID field. It tells the Hotspot Editor how to identify this particular hotspot. The other four entries define the bounding box for the hotspot. You can use these entries to fine-tune a box's position or size. However, the user won't notice if the hotspot is a pixel or two off, as long as the hotspot is available for use.

You may need to redefine a hotspot. Hotspots are easy to find if you make them visible, but I've already noted that most people don't. So how do you find a hidden hotspot on a complex drawing? The Edit | Select command provides the answer. It displays the Select dialog.

The Select dialog lists the hotspots in the current drawing by hotspot identifier, not by context string. Selecting a particular hotspot will display its context string so that you can be sure you have the right one without going to that location on the drawing. The Select dialog also displays the jump type and attribute information.

After you define the hotspots, you may be tempted to save your graphic using the File | Save command. I always save it with an SHG extension using File | Save As. The Hotspot Editor doesn't insist that you do this. However, if you don't, you'll find that you've overwritten your drawing with information that some drawing programs can't read. Since you can't modify your drawing within the Hotspot Editor, you're stuck with an image that you can't change.

Now that you have a drawing (or other multimedia element), you can add it to your help file. Microsoft defined commands that allow you to add graphics or other elements to your help file. The same commands provide control over the placement of these graphics, but I find the positioning mechanism is crude at best. Table 17-2 shows a complete list of the commands you'll use to add multimedia elements to your help file.

TIP

You can add a T (for transparent) to the three graphics commands listed in Table 17-2. This changes the background color of the image to match that of the help window. For example, the {BMRT FIGURE.BMP} command would display a bitmap named "figure" on the right side of the screen and change its color to match that of the help window. Windows help allows you to use this feature only with 16-color graphics.

Command	Description
{BMR <Filename>}	Displays a graphic on the right side of the display window. You must provide a full filename and extension. Windows Help recognizes bitmaps (BMP, DIB, and WMF files), multiple-hotspot bitmaps (SHG files), and multiple-resolution bitmaps (MRB files).

Table 17-2 *Multimedia Element Help Commands*

Command	Description
{BMC <Filename>}	Displays a graphic in the center of the display window.
{BML <Filename>}	Displays a graphic on the left side of the display window.
{MCI_LEFT [<Options>,] <Filename>}	Displays a media control interface (MCI) file on the left side of the display. There's a mistake in the Microsoft Help Workshop help file that says you can use this option only with AVI files. The current version of Windows Help supports all MCI formats, including WAV, MID, and AVI files. Sticking with these three formats is probably a good idea unless you know the target machine supports other formats. You can also specify one or more options with this command, including EXTERNAL, NOPLAYER, NOMENU, REPEAT, and PLAY. The EXTERNAL option keeps the file outside the help file, reducing the amount of memory the help file consumes when the user loads it. The downside of this option is that you must include the multimedia file as a separate item. Normally, Windows Help displays a multimedia player when it displays the file—you can use the NOPLAYER option to prevent this. This option comes in handy if you want to automatically play or repeat a multimedia file. The NOMENU option displays a play bar without the menu button, effectively keeping the display elements of the play bar but removing the user's ability to control playback. The REPEAT option tells Windows Help to play the file again when it finishes playing the first time. The PLAY option automatically plays the file.
{MCI_RIGHT [<Options>,] <Filename>}	Displays an MCI file on the right side of the display.

Table 17-2 *Multimedia Element Help Commands* (continued)

TIP

You can specify more than one bitmap within a single command to compensate for differing display capabilities of the machines that use your help file. Windows Help chooses the bitmap that most closely matches the color capabilities of the machine and displays it. For example, the command {BMR CAT016.BMP;CAT256.BMP;CAT024.BMP} allows computers to display bitmaps in 16-, 256-, and 24-bit colors. You can further enhance the flexibility of your help file by using MRB files to compensate for differences in resolution. The upside of this approach is that you gain the ability to display detailed information to those users who have a machine capable of displaying it. The downside is that this approach increases the size of the help file and its corresponding memory requirements.

It doesn't take long to learn you can include a lot of bells and whistles in your help file. Almost any feature you can include in an application will also go into a help file. You need to consider some facts before you go overboard in making your help file look like someone's idea of a nightmare. A little multimedia goes a long way. Use graphics and sounds only where they really fit—where they enhance the appearance of your help file.

NOTE

If you don't see everything you want in regard to multimedia capability, Microsoft also provides a special help statement you can use to further enhance a help file. The {EWx <DLLName>, <WindowName>, <Data>} statement allows you to access routines in an external DLL. The x in EWx specifies left (l), right (r), or center (c) placement of the output from the DLL. WindowName contains the name of the current help file window—it's the $ footnote we covered earlier. The Data parameter allows you to send data to the DLL for processing.

Also, consider memory consumption when writing help files. Windows Help loads an entire help file when the user tries to access it. One of the ways to reduce the memory load on the machine is to use external files—you can break the help file into pieces and store any multimedia externally. In the end, though, a modicum of restraint when using graphics and sounds in your help file is what you'll need to make it efficient as well as fun to use.

Creating the Make File and Compiling Your Help File

Unlike the make (project) files you use when writing an application, the make file used with a help compiler usually contains more than just a list of files to compile. I'm going to show you the manual method of creating a make file in this section. The Microsoft Help Workshop utility provides an automated method, which I'll show you later. It's handy to know what a make file contains so that you can manually tune some features like macros if necessary.

Let's begin by looking at a typical make file. Listing 17-2 contains a make file for the example help file. Note that you could create this file using the Microsoft Help Workshop. I've included features such as macros in this example that you may not want to include in a typical help file.

Listing 17-2

```
[OPTIONS]
COMPRESS=12 Hall Zeck
ERRORLOG=HELP.LOG
```

```
LCID=0x409 0x0 0x0 ;English (United States)
REPORT=Yes
CONTENTS=CONTENTS
TITLE=Single Document Application Help File Example
COPYRIGHT=2001 Some Company
CITATION=Copyright 2001 - Some Company (Not for Distribution)
HLP=.\Sngl_Doc.hlp


[FILES]
.\Sample.rtf
.\Glossary.rtf


[MAP]
#include ..\Resource\my.hm
CONTENTS=1                ; Main help file menu.
FORMAT_TOOLBAR=2          ; Format Toolbar explanation shortcut.
GLOSSARY=3               ; Glossary window shortcut.
HID_FORMAT_FONT=0x1E160; Added for ID_FORMAT_FONT in AFXRes.h file.


[WINDOWS]
; This is the Main window.
Main="A Sample Help File",(0,0,800,600),52484,(r14876671),(r12632256),f7


; The direct Glossary help window.
Glossary="A Sample Help File - Glossary",(50,50,850,650),52484,(r14876671),(r12632256),f7


[CONFIG]
; Add a Glossary button to the display.
CB("glossary", "&Glossary", "JI(`SNGL_DOC.HLP>glossary', `GLOSSARY')")
; Add a jump to the controls bitmap button.
CB("controls", "C&ontrols", "JI(`SNGL_DOC.HLP>main', `FORMAT_TOOLBAR')")


; Enable (or disable) a menu item.
RegisterRoutine("USER", "EnableMenuItem", "uuu")
; Get the name of a submenu.
RegisterRoutine("USER", "GetSubMenu", "u=uu")
; Get a menu name.
RegisterRoutine("USER", "GetMenu", "u=u")
; Get the active window name.
RegisterRoutine("USER", "GetActiveWindow", "u=")
; Instruct Windows Help to draw a menu bar.
RegisterRoutine("USER", "DrawMenuBar", "u")


; Disable the Copy option of the Edit Menu.
EnableMenuItem(GetSubMenu(GetMenu(GetActiveWindow()), 1), 0, 1027)
; Redraw the menu when we're through.
DrawMenuBar(GetActiveWindow())
```

As you can see, the make file can look a bit overwhelming the first time you view one. It helps to take the file one section at a time. The OPTIONS section tells you how

For example, the COPYRIGHT statement appears in the About dialog of Windows Help when the user loads the help file. The COMPRESS statement defines whether the help compiler compresses the file and what technique it'll use to do so. The one entry you have to pay special attention to is HLP. Notice that the name of the help file is going to be the same as the name of our Visual C++ application. While this isn't an absolute requirement, you'll find that adding help to an existing application is a lot easier if you take this simple step. MFC helps you implement help in your application if you give your application and help file the same name.

You'll use the MAP section of the help project file to define the help context property settings that Visual C++ requests. Each word appears as a topic identifier (# footnote) in one of the script files. Associating a number with each exported jump makes the topic accessible from a control. All the user needs to do is select the control and press F1 to get help on that particular control. Notice that we haven't listed all of the controls in the example application—instead we included the HM file we created earlier in the chapter. Using an HM file will not only save you time typing; it can also actually help you find gaps in your help file (as we'll see in the next section).

There's more than one way to display the data in your help file. I usually display main topics in their own window. Notice two windows appear in the WINDOWS section. One is the Main (initial) window, while the other is a special glossary window. If users click Glossary on the speed bar, they'll see this window. It allows them to find a word without losing their current position in the help file. I don't display this window every time the user accesses the glossary. If the user hot-links to the glossary by clicking on a highlighted word in the help file, Windows Help displays the glossary in the Main window.

The CONFIG section is where you'll spend the most time when creating your make file because it offers the greatest flexibility. There are three events in the example make file: button creation, function registration, and a set of Windows API calls. You could add any number of events to your file, but let's look at this simple example.

The code begins by creating two new buttons. The first is the Glossary button. Notice I use two macro calls to get the job done. One call creates the button. I tell the help compiler to call this button "glossary," to use the word "Glossary" for the button label, and to underline the G. This button provides a jump to the identifier returned by the JI macro call. The JI macro call requires three parameters. The "SNGL_DOC.HLP>glossary" argument provides two parameters (pieces of information): what help file to look into and which window to use to display the help topic. The other parameter provides the name of a topic identifier—remember that's a # footnote.

It's time to register some DLL functions with Windows Help. You can use any DLL function as long as you register it first. Registering a DLL function is a three-step process. First, tell Windows Help what DLL to look in. Windows Help assumes the DLL is in the SYSTEM directory, so you'll need to either place the DLL there if it isn't already there or provide path information. Second, provide the name of the function you want to use within the DLL. Make sure you use the same capitalization that the DLL uses—I've had strange results when I didn't do this in the past. Third, tell Windows Help about the function parameters. That's what the "u=uu" is all about when I register the **GetSubMenu** function. In this case, I'm telling Windows Help that the **GetSubMenu** function requires two unsigned numbers as input and returns an unsigned number as output. You can specify four types: unsigned number (u), signed number (i), string (s), or unknown (v). The equals sign (=) delimits input values from output values.

Once you register the menu handling functions, you can make changes to the help display. In this case, I disable the Edit | Copy command. You can still see it, but it's grayed out. Notice that I use the **DrawMenuBar** function to redraw the menu bar when I'm done. If you don't do this, there's a good chance that any menu changes you make won't show up.

Using the Microsoft Help Workshop

The Microsoft Help Workshop aids you in creating help project files (the help make file that we visited in the previous section) and compile them from within Windows. Let's look at how this tool can help reduce the complexity of creating that make file we looked at in Listing 17-2. We'll use the RTF files found on the source code CD-ROM in this section, but you'll normally need to create them first. The first step is to create a new project. Use the File | New command to display the New dialog. Select Help Project and click on OK to complete the action. The project starts out as a blank page that you fill in with the characteristics of your help file.

Defining a Project's Options

You'll start a project by defining some of the project options. For example, you should give your help file a name and add copyright information. I always use "contents" as my main topic, so adding that entry at the beginning is a good idea as well. Click Options and you'll see the Options dialog shown here.

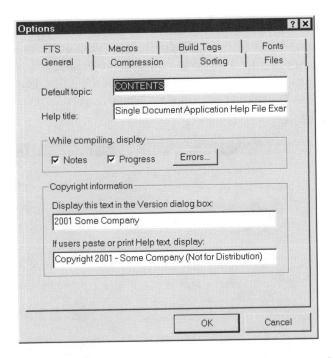

Most of these options should look familiar since I described most of them as part of the make file discussion in the previous section. (You'll find that the options on the Compression tab look familiar, too—they define the type of compression you'll use to reduce the size of your help file.) As you can see, this dialog provides a simple form for you to fill out; no longer do you need to remember what statements to use to accomplish a specific task.

The Sorting tab of the Options dialog contains several options. Windows Help uses the Language option to determine how to sort entries. The Non-spacing marks option allows you to ignore non-spacing characters. For example, the circumflex (^) that appears in ê would affect the sort order if you didn't select this option. Another option tells the help compiler to ignore any symbols in the help file when sorting. This is handy if you want to create a nonspecialized index for a data entry program or other general application. On the other hand, it would actually get in the way when creating an index for a reference help file. Many C functions begin with an underscore. Ignoring those underscores would make the function difficult to find. Finally, you can choose something other than commas and colons to separate index entries. The only time you'd need this feature is if you wanted to create a help file based on the output of another application that doesn't support the standard separators.

The Files tab of the Options dialog determines which files you use for a given task. You can change the name of the help file by changing the contents of the Help File field. The help compiler uses the name of the project file as a basis for naming the help file. The Log File field contains the name of a log file. This option isn't required with the help compiler since it also displays errors on screen. Here's what the Files tab looks like.

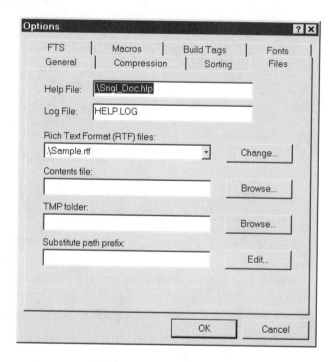

One of the most important fields on the Files tab is the Rich Text Format (RTF) files list box. You'll find a list of the files for the current help project here. Clicking the Change button next to the field displays the Topic Files dialog. This is where you add and remove topic files from the list in the FILES section of the project file. The two check boxes at the bottom of this dialog control how the help compiler reacts to your RTF files. The first option allows the help compiler to automatically implement any changes you make to the RTF files during the next compile. If you leave this box unchecked, the help compiler will ignore any changes. The second option is important if you use a double-byte character set (DBCS) within your help file. This option changes the way the help compiler works with your file and allows it to preserve the special characters.

There are other options on the Files tab of the Options menu. One of them is the Contents File field. If you're creating a project from scratch, Help Workshop fills it in automatically when you create the Contents page. You can add an entry if you already have a contents page that you want to use with the current project. The TMP Folder field comes into play only when your help file gets over 8 MB. It specifies another directory for the temporary files that Help Workshop creates when it compiles your help file. Use the Substitute Path Prefix field if you move the files used to create the help file and don't want to change the path information in the project file.

Windows Help offers full text search (FTS)—a database created when you select the Find page of the Help Topics dialog. FTS allows you to search an entire help file word by word. The FTS tab of the Options dialog contains an option to generate this file when you compile the help file. Since Windows creates a GID file on the user's machine by default, I leave this option blank. The GID file that the help compiler creates takes up a lot of room on the distribution disks and increases compile time considerably.

You'll want to spend some time learning to use the Macros tab. It allows you to define keyword macros to use on a file-wide basis. These macros also appear on the Index page of the Help Topics dialog when the user searches for a particular topic.

Clicking Add displays a Keyword Macros dialog containing three fields. The first field contains the name of the macro. The second field contains the macro itself. The third field contains a string that tells Help Workshop how to display the macro on the Index page. Use this entry when you have more than one help file and want to display a particular keyword file-wide. For example, I often place the glossary and list of acronyms in a separate file and then use the JI macro to create a file-wide jump to them. The keyword macro is the method I use to do this. The user never even realizes that he or she has loaded another file—it's that transparent.

I previously discussed the * footnote. The Build Tags tab of the Options dialog is where you use this feature. The main idea is to provide Help Workshop with a list of build tags that you want to include in a help file. Even if an RTF file contains other topics, it won't include them in the help file if you don't include the build tag. If you leave this page blank, Help Workshop assumes you want to include all RTF file topics as part of the final help file.

The Fonts tab of the Options dialog is your first chance to customize the look and feel of your help file. If you're creating an RTF file using a text editor, this feature can save you some time. The Character Set field selects a character set for your help file; the default is ANSI. You can also choose from language types such as Arabic. The Font in WinHelp Dialog Boxes field defines a default font type. Click Change and you'll see a Font dialog containing three fields. The first defines the font name, the second the font point size, and the third defines the character set. The list box below the Font in WinHelp Dialog Boxes field changes the general fonts used within the Windows Help file. It lets you substitute one font for another. The Add button displays an Add/Edit Font Mapping dialog that contains two groups of three fields. The three fields are the same as the ones used in the Font dialog I just described. The only problem is the settings on this tab won't work if your word processor overrides the settings—something that generally happens if you use a product like Word for Windows.

Defining Windows

Defining options is only the first phase of creating a project file—you need to define some windows to display your data. I always create one window called Main. Ancillary windows may include a Glossary window to display terms.

Creating a window is simple. Click Windows in the Main window to display the Window Properties dialog shown here.

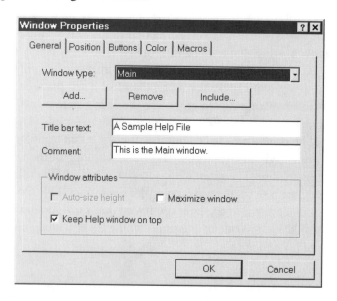

The General tab is where you'll start. Click Add and you'll see an Add a New Window dialog with two fields. One field contains the name of the window. The other field contains the window type. Help Workshop creates three window types: procedural, reference, and error message. There's little difference between the procedural and reference windows. Both auto-size and contain the three system buttons. The big difference between the two is their placement on screen—which you can override with the settings I'll show you next. The error message window differs from the other two in that it doesn't include the three system buttons. It looks somewhat like a dialog.

The Title Bar Text field on the General tab determines what Windows Help places on the title bar. This entry doesn't affect the appearance of the topic title area of the help window. The Comment field allows you to place a comment next to the entry in the project file. There are also three attribute check boxes. Help Workshop may disable one or more of these check boxes, depending on the situation. For example, you can't make the main help window an auto-sizing window. If you make an ancillary window auto-sizing, you can't maximize it when it opens. Most procedural windows default to staying on top.

TIP

Turn the Auto-Size Height feature off to provide better control over the appearance of a window on screen. The options on the Position page that we'll look at next provide you with full control over the appearance of your help window on screen.

You'll usually want to spend some time working with the Position tab of the Window Properties dialog. The name of this tab is a bit deceiving because it provides more functionality than you might expect. While it does control the starting position and size of the help windows you create, this dialog provides some other features that you'll find handy. Here's what the Position tab looks like.

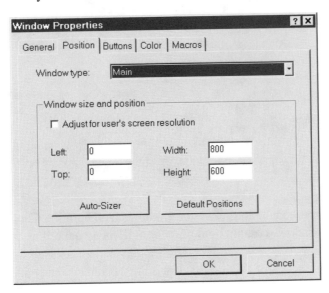

There are four fields on the Position tab: Left, Top, Width, and Height. These control the size and position of your window. I normally position my first help window in the upper-left corner and use a size of either 640×480 or 800×600, depending on the capabilities of the target machine for my application. This may seem a bit small, but the user can always resize the window as needed. Trying to find a help window on an older display when the programmer positions it near one of the edges is frustrating, to say the least. I really like the Adjust for User's Screen Resolution option on this page because it prevents the help window from becoming totally hidden when the user has a low-resolution display.

There's one special feature on this page, and you may not notice it at first. Look at the Auto-Sizer button. Clicking on this button displays an example window. If you change the window's position, the Left and Top field values also change. Resizing the window changes the value of the Width and Height fields. This graphic method of changing window size reduces the number of times you have to recompile the help file to take care of aesthetic needs.

There are situations where you may not want to add all of the default buttons normally provided by Windows Help to your help file. For example, the Browser buttons aren't important if you don't define a browse (+ footnote) in one of your RTF files. The Buttons tab, shown here, allows you to define the buttons used with your help window.

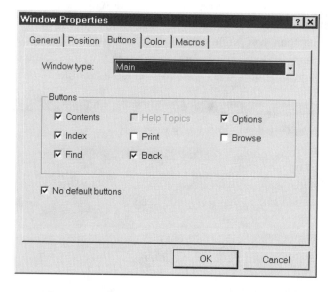

All ancillary procedure and reference windows lack both the Contents and Index buttons. Main windows contain both of these buttons by default as well as the Print and Back buttons. On the other hand, a Main window won't allow you to select the Help Topics button. Unlike other window types, an error message window has no restrictions. You can include any of the default buttons that you like on it.

The Color tab contains two fields: Nonscrolling Area Color and Topic Area Color. Each has a Change button. Click Change to display a color palette. Selecting a different color from the palette changes the appearance of the help window.

The Macros tab displays the macros defined for your help file. The Main window always uses the macros in the CONFIG section of the project file. The macros you see in this section are self-executing—that's why Help Workshop adds the macros in the CONFIG section to the Main window. Adding a new macro to the Main window always adds it to the CONFIG section of the help project file. Adding macros to other windows changes the way those windows appear in comparison to the Main window. For example, if you add a browse to one of the ancillary windows, you might need to add macros to handle new conditions. Each ancillary window has a special CONFIG-<window name> section in the help project.

TIP

Another way to access the Macros dialog for the Main window is to click on the Config button on the Main window.

Mapping Help Topics

If you don't map the topic identifiers in your help file to a help context number, you can't attach context-sensitive help to the controls in your application. You'll see how this works in the section that follows on adding context-sensitive help to your application.

Adding a map is easy. Click Map to display the Map dialog. This is where you define the relationship between a topic identifier and a context number. The topic identifier is set equal to a help context number. It's followed by a comment that describes the entry.

There are many ways to keep the context numbers straight. I usually start at 1 and count up until I reach the last topic identifier for small help files. Large help files require something a bit more complex to avoid reusing numbers. Use a three- or four-digit number in these situations. The first two numbers are the position of the control or menu item described by the help context within the application. For example, the File menu is normally 01, and the Edit menu is 02. A description of the File | New command would receive a help context number of 0101, since the New option is usually the first entry on the File menu. I assign a value of 0001 to the first non-application topic. For example, the glossary would fall into this category. The first two numbers for a control on the form of an application would be one greater than the last menu item. I use the tab order for the last two numbers, since it's unlikely that a label or other nonactive component would ever appear in the help file.

Add a new map entry by clicking Add. You'll see the Add Map Entry dialog. This dialog contains three fields: a topic identifier, a mapped numeric value (help context number), and a comment. Fill out the three fields and click OK to add a new map to the project.

You'll want to include an HM file with your help file to reduce the amount of work you do and to provide a quick and easy method for checking your work. Nothing is more frustrating than to release a help file that you thought was complete at the time of testing that turns out to be missing one or more crucial entries after you release it. Click Include to include a file. You'll see an Include File dialog. This dialog provides a Browse button so you can search for your Include file on the hard drive. The Browse button opens a standard Open dialog, just like the ones you've used with other applications.

Compiling Your Help File

Once you get a help project file put together, it's time to try to compile it. Click Save and Compile at the bottom of the Main window. The Help Workshop window will minimize while it compiles the help file. This allows you to work on something else (compiling a large help file can take a long time). Once the compilation is complete, you'll see a window similar to the one shown in Figure 17-2.

You should notice something almost immediately about this dialog—it shows that there are errors in the help file (actually they're notes, but you'll still want to count them as errors). We didn't define help file entries for every entry in the HM file. This means there are holes in the coverage provided by the help file. As you can see, using the HM file is a great help because it reduces the chance you'll miss an important topic.

However, using an HM file doesn't guarantee perfect coverage. Take another look at Listing 17-2 and you'll see I had to add a Map entry for ID_FORMAT_FONT. This is a standard identifier for MFC that appears in the AFXRES.H file, not the RESOURCE.H file that contains the IDs for your custom controls. You'll need to remember to add support for standard controls—the HM file can't help you in that case.

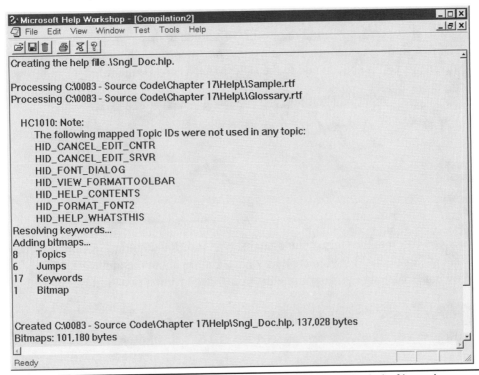

Figure 17-2   *This compilation screen shows the current status of the help file and any error messages.*

Adding Standard Help to Your Application

It's time to add help support to our application. I chose the Single Document project we started in Chapter 2. I also chose it because we didn't do anything to add help support to this program. Most of the work required to add help support to your application is in the help file itself. We'll add help support to the Single Document example program using a little code.

We'll actually look at two methods for adding support. One is automatic—you'll add a menu entry and one manual entry to the beginning of the MainFrm.CPP file. Use this method, in most cases, because it's the most efficient way to work and you won't gain much using the second method. The second method requires a little more work but offers more flexibility in return. You'll hand-code the help access into your program. However, you'll find there still isn't much to do.

The first thing we need to do is add some menu entries. Shown here are the two menu entries you'll need to add to the IDR_MAINFRAME menu.

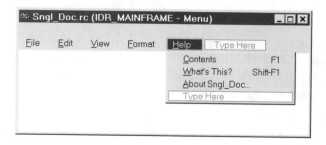

As you can see, the Help menu contains two additional entries: "Contents" and "What's This?" that will help the user find out more about the application. The following table contains the parameters you'll need for the two entries.

ID	Caption	Prompt
ID_HELP_CONTENTS	&Contents\tF1	Displays the Main Help File\nHelp
ID_CONTEXT_HELP	&What's This?\tShift-F1	Click here for context-sensitive help.\nContext Help

Notice that the ID for the What's This? menu entry doesn't use the normal convention. You'll see why in a few moments. Just remember that we're not using the standard ID (it's important if you want to implement the MFC help features automatically).

You'll also want to change the Help button on the IDR_MAINFRAME toolbar. Right now, it displays the About dialog, which is fine if you don't have help added to your application. Since we're adding help, open the IDR_MAINFRAME toolbar, double-click on the Help button, and change its ID to ID_HELP_CONTENTS.

The two menu entries also have accelerators associated with them, so open the IDR_MAINFRAME accelerator. Add a new accelerator for the ID_HELP_CONTENTS menu entry and another for the ID_CONTEXT_HELP menu entry, as shown in the following table.

ID	Key	Type
ID_HELP_CONTENTS	VK_F1	VIRTKEY
ID_CONTEXT_HELP	Shift + VK_F1	VIRTKEY

Adding the accelerators is easy. Double-click the last blank entry and you'll see a blank accelerator entry added to the list. Choose the ID you want from the drop-down ID list box and select the behavior options you want. In this case, assign F1 to ID_HELP_CONTENTS and SHIFT-F1 to ID_CONTEXT_HELP.

Remember that we'll implement one of these help options without writing code. MFC supports four default help actions: contents, find, index, and context sensitive. We'll implement the context-sensitive option using the built-in MFC features. All you need to do is add a line of code to MainFrm.CPP, such as the bold code shown in Listing 17-3. Adding this one line of code activates a built-in MFC function for context-sensitive help.

Listing 17-3

```
BEGIN_MESSAGE_MAP(CMainFrame, CFrameWnd)
    //{{AFX_MSG_MAP(CMainFrame)
    ON_WM_CREATE()
    ON_COMMAND(ID_BOLD, OnBold)
    ON_COMMAND(ID_ITALIC, OnItalic)
    ON_COMMAND(ID_STRIKETHROUGH, OnStrikethrough)
    ON_COMMAND(ID_UNDERLINE, OnUnderline)
    ON_COMMAND(ID_VIEW_FORMATTOOLBAR, OnViewFormattoolbar)
    ON_COMMAND(ID_HELP_CONTENTS, OnHelpContents)
ON_COMMAND(ID_CONTEXT_HELP, OnContextHelp)
//}}AFX_MSG_MAP
END_MESSAGE_MAP()
```

We'll add a function to implement the Contents menu option. Click CMainFrame ClassView and locate ID_HELP_CONTEXT in the Events list in the Properties window. Select <Add> OnHelpContents. Here's the code you'll need to add to make the Contents menu option work.

```
void CMainFrame::OnHelpContents()
{
    // Call WinHelp to display the main help window.
    WinHelp(0, HELP_CONTENTS);
}
```

As you can see, the code for implementing the required level of help isn't hard. All you need to do is call **WinHelp()** with the required define: HELP_CONTENTS. We didn't need to provide any supplementary information, so the first parameter is set to 0.

Creating an HTML-Based Help Package

HTML help is composed of Web pages like its informational counterpart on the Internet. However, HTML help doesn't end with a simple Web page; there are other elements to consider. For example, you need to consider the organization of the help file from an access perspective. The following sections help you create a help file setup that's both efficient and practical.

NOTE

The source code CD-ROM includes a complete HTML-based help file application in the \Chapter 17\ HTMLHelp directory. This example shows you how to create an application that relies on HTML help, even though the application itself is a standard Windows application.

Multipage or Single-Page Files?

One of the more important considerations is how to put your help file together. When you use Windows Help, you create a single file containing many pages of information. This kind of approach won't work with HTML-based help, because it doesn't use a master file approach. You have to figure out how to put multiple pages of information into one package yet be assured that the package you create will contain multiple files.

Remember that your help file uses an outline. What you need to decide is where to block text for placement in a file. Table 17-3 describes the file layout options and their pluses/minuses.

Layout Method	Description	Pluses	Minuses
Topic	Each file contains one help file topic. For example, you might have a file on data entry methods.	Users who want to find out a lot of information about a specific topic will get fast access, since all of the information will arrive in one download.	Remote users who require information on menu-related items will end up waiting for each item to download. Information is difficult to update since you'll need to look through several files for one menu change.

Table 17-3   *HTML File Layout Methods*

Layout Method	Description	Pluses	Minuses
Large Menu/Dialog Control	All dialog controls or menu tree entries appear in one file. Anchors allow the user to move from topic to topic. Users rely on a table of contents to go directly to a topic.	First-time users will find it easy to explore the application. In addition, the layout makes the help file read more like the manual it's designed to replace. The use of a table of contents makes information easy to find.	The large file size will cause some users to think twice before downloading the file. In addition, some users will find it cumbersome wading through all the menu entries contained in one file. Updates are harder because you may have to make the same change to multiple files.
Small Menu/Dialog Control	Each menu item or dialog box control appears in a separate file.	Short download times will allow users to use help even when connected through a dial-up line. Users will find information fast since they see only one screen. Updates are faster and more reliable since the information appears in only one file. Reduced help file size on the server.	First-time users will find the constant download of information for each menu item or dialog control frustrating, especially when a dial-up connection is used. A table of contents won't be an automatic feature and will require separate maintenance time.
Large Task	Each file contains a complete description and procedure for performing a specific task. For example, you may create a file for creating a new document.	New users will find that they can perform tasks easier. You can test each task separately, reducing the possibility of mistakes. Large task files allow the writer to include specific screen shots and enhanced graphics. This is the only layout that works for tutorials, although bandwidth and reliability limitations of the Internet reduce the level of training you can provide.	Advanced users have to wade through entire procedures to find one piece of information. The lack of common sub-procedures will increase the user learning curve since they won't see common subtasks involved in performing a specific task. Help files are harder to update and will require more space on the server. Remote downloads will take a long time due to increased file size.

Table 17-3   *HTML File Layout Methods* (continued)

Layout Method	Description	Pluses	Minuses
Small Task	You create a hierarchical table of contents and a list of tasks. Each task is broken into a series of common subtasks. A task overview page covers any special events.	The table of contents makes information easy to find. The hierarchical format allows users to drill down to the information they need. Short download time encourages everyone to use help rather than call the help desk for information. Updates consist of changing the information in a single subtask folder.	There's a possibility of introducing subtle errors into the task procedures. For example, a menu entry may change in one part of the application but not in another. Some novice users will find the subtask orientation difficult to understand.

Table 17-3   *HTML File Layout Methods* (continued)

Connection Type

It's interesting to note that some vendors who use HTML-based help assume that everyone has a T1 connection to the Internet. The truth is that many users rely on a dial-up connection to download their files. Help files are an essential application, unlike many sites that users surf to on the Internet. This means you need to keep HTML help fast, or the support desk will hear about it. The following list will help you optimize your help file for dial-up connections.

▶ Use graphics, sounds, and multimedia sparingly. Keep file sizes small by reducing resolution, color depth, or other features.

▶ Allow users to choose a text-only presentation.

▶ Reduce content whenever possible, but allow the user to click links that provide additional information.

▶ Use the right HTML file layout.

Search Capability

Searching a help file for valuable information is what most users do once they get past the novice level. They'll look for some tidbit of knowledge that they need in order to accomplish a task or for an explanation of some control on a dialog box. You can't completely duplicate the search features of Windows Help using HTML help, but there are ways you can mimic the search capability of Windows Help. The following list provides a few ideas you can use.

- ▶ Create an index.
- ▶ Define additional links.
- ▶ Add a table of contents.
- ▶ Produce a hot topics list.
- ▶ Add a Search page that relies on the search capabilities of your server.

It's unlikely that you'll create a word-for-word index like the one provided with Windows Help. This means the user will always have some question that you didn't anticipate and that the search features of your HTML-based help file won't be able to answer. It always pays to provide a comment page so users can request additional links.

Packaging Your Application

IN THIS CHAPTER:

Understanding Various Packaging Types

Gathering the Files

Using InstallShield

Using Windows Installer

Setup and Deployment Projects

ackaging an application—sounds like you're going to shrink-wrap it and
send it off to the store. From a programmer's perspective, packaging has
nothing to do with stores, but it does have everything to do with how well
an application is received by the user. When users install your application and see
that the setup program provides everything they need, they'll be a lot more likely to
start using your application with a good attitude—something I consider crucial to the
success of an application.

Packaging also has a lot to do with an application's ease of use. Applications
without good help files lack part of the packaging they need to make life easy for
the user. You may as well just tell the user to guess about how to use the application,
because they'll never think to look at the README or other file you placed on the
disk with a just a modicum of instructions.

NOTE

*I cover the requirements for creating a good help file in Chapter 17. If you haven't yet created
one for your application, you may want to consider doing so before you read this chapter.*

Not everyone has to deal with every packaging concern. For example, an in-house
programmer wouldn't worry about graphics—unlike someone distributing an application
commercially or as shareware. However, aesthetically pleasing applications affect
the user's attitude toward the application, and anything you can do to improve that
attitude benefits you by reducing service calls and complaints. Even your installation
program has to have a great interface; after all, it's the first part of your program that
the user will see.

This chapter looks at the two most important factors in the first impression a user
develops for the application you write—the various package types and the installation
program. I'll also look at some of the special factors that programmers should consider
in various environments. For example, an in-house programmer will probably have
a few concerns not shared by someone developing shareware. This chapter contains
procedures for using both InstallShield and the newer Microsoft Windows Installer.

Understanding Various Packaging Types

You have to consider many issues when creating an application package. The most
important consideration for developers is the application environment. An in-house
developer won't have the same concerns as someone who plans to deliver an application
for use by someone else. For one thing, the in-house developer probably won't have

much time to get an installation program together—time becomes a factor in most in-house situations.

This section looks at the three most common types of installation environments: corporate, shareware, and shrink-wrap. You'll likely fall into one of the three categories, but you may want to look at the other two because they provide additional helpful tips and hints.

Corporate

Corporate programmers have the least to do to beautify their packaging and the most to do to customize it. Let's face it, the corporate programmer doesn't have to impress anyone with fancy graphics or impressive sound effects. A user-friendly and functional interface is enough.

The corporate programmer is often engaged in creating a custom application. It's common for custom applications, especially database applications, to require specialized files. You'll likely need custom registry entries and a wealth of other custom settings as well. Creating a custom installation program that works on all the workstations in a corporate environment with little help from the programmer is quite an undertaking. Plan to spend a lot of time hand-tuning the installation program you create.

Media is another place where most corporate installation programs differ from the other two categories. You still see shareware or shrink-wrap applications that come on floppies (albeit, not very often). Unless the company you're working for is living in the dark ages, you'll probably use a LAN for distribution purposes. Use the LAN to your benefit to create the application package. Select the most efficient storage method possible—a CD. You can create and test your installation program faster if you rely on a CD version of the package.

Once you've packaged your application on the LAN, add an instruction to the main logon batch file for your server to install the program. The next time the user logs on, your logon batch file will check for the installed application. If it doesn't find the application, the batch file will call the installation program that you've placed on the LAN. Note that this technique works whether you use InstallShield or the Windows Installer.

TIP

The corporate setting is one place where using Universal Naming Convention (UNC) paths in place of standard drive identifiers comes in handy. Using a UNC path for the source directory ensures that everyone can access the required source files for your application without too much effort.

The following list has some other packaging-related suggestions to consider. Just follow those that fit your programming style and organizational needs.

- ▶ **Centralized common file storage**   The standard procedure for distributing shareware or shrink-wrap applications is to place all of the files on the user's machine. As a corporate programmer, you can choose to keep common files like DLLs on the file server instead of the user's machine. There are two benefits to this approach. First, you reduce the space the application requires on the user machine. Second, you reduce the time required to update custom DLLs should the user find an error in one. There are also two downsides to this approach. First, the user has to have a network connection. Second, you could end up increasing network traffic substantially during frequent DLL loading and unloading.

- ▶ **Absolute preferences**   A shareware or shrink-wrap application author can't assume anything about the application environment. You don't have that problem. All you need to worry about is the differences between the machines on your network. If you set all the machines up the same way, you can assume a default destination. Using UNC paths means you can assume an absolute source since the server path name won't change. You can assume a certain amount about the workstation if your network is small and all the machines have similar capabilities. In sum, all this means that you don't have to present the user with as many installation choices and can substantially reduce the complexity of the installation program.

- ▶ **No configuration choices needed**   Just about every shrink-wrap program offers you a choice between three installation configurations: Custom, Typical, and Compact. The Custom choice allows you to choose specific program elements; the Typical configuration is designed for desktop users; the Compact configuration is intended for people who use laptops. In most cases, you can limit your configuration options to two choices: Laptop and Desktop. In fact, you may want to use those terms to keep user confusion to a minimum.

Shareware

Shareware programmers probably have the most challenging job when it comes to packaging their application. One of the main problems is installation size. Unlike the developer who has a high-speed network connection to use or can distribute an application on CD, the shareware developer usually has to make do with a low-speed modem connection to a BBS, online service, or the Internet. It's hard to convince someone to download a 1 MB file.

NOTE

The file sizes in this section are guidelines only. The disk space or time that a potential user will invest in your product depends on many factors, including perceived value and the current level of product exposure. For example, my favorite shareware graphics package takes up a whopping 7MB of hard disk space and is well over 1MB in size when compressed. I still download it because this program is well worth the investment.

OK, so you're a little limited on space. How do you get around this problem? The key is in how you market your product. Most of the successful shareware products use the same graphics and sounds repeatedly. Instead of using one graphic for the installation program and a totally different graphic for the application itself, the shareware programmer is content to use the same graphic for both the installation program and the application. Using subtle programming techniques could allow you to use the application's icon (see Chapter 2) in several places.

Can a shareware developer create installation programs without graphics or sound? Not likely. If you want someone to pay for the application you've created, you'll need to add a little polish. Few (if any) people will pay for a drab application, even if it provides good functionality. Obviously, trying to weigh the space needed by a feature and the amount of pizzazz it provides is difficult.

Another problem that a shareware developer runs into concerns resources. Many shareware developers start out as one-person shops. The developer takes on consulting jobs and other ventures. Time isn't on your side, and it's unlikely you'll have an artist or sound person at your disposal to create the multimedia presentations provided by companies who create shrink-wrap applications. Most people are satisfied if they see a shareware product that's well designed, space conscious (consumes 5MB or less of hard disk space), and provides at least a modicum of polish.

We haven't yet discussed the biggest problem for shareware developers—hardware requirements—and the installation program is the first place you have to deal with it. Corporate developers can get by with a minimum of machine checks and configuration options. Shrink-wrap developers come next—they can print a set of requirements on the box to ensure no one will use their application without sufficient hardware. The shareware developer has no such guarantees. A user of your program could have just about any kind of machine ever made—including an old 8088 PC.

What does this lack of control mean? First, you'll have to build extra detection routines in your installation program to ensure the client meets minimum hardware requirements. Users will rarely read the README file you provide (the one stating the minimum requirements for using the application) and are unlikely to pay attention to them if they do. When the installation fails, the user is going to blame you, not his or her lack of attention. Therefore, you have to build in some type of hardware detection. You'll also need to include application configuration flexibility. For example, you may decide to let the user configure the application for text mode only on an older-technology machine and forego those fancy graphics or sounds.

TIP

The installation program is a good place to sell your shareware product if you have the time and resources to design it properly. Make sure users understand what they'll get in return for buying your product.

The shareware developer does have a few tricks for making the installation program easier to use. While the following list isn't inclusive of everything you could try, it does provide some ideas on what could work. You'll need to try a variety of packaging techniques with your application before you come up with something that works all the time.

▶ **Granular packaging**   One way to get around limited hard disk space and download-time problems is to package the application in several pieces. For example, you could place the main program in one package, the graphics in another, and the sounds in a third package. The users can choose what level of support they're willing to pay for in download time and hard disk space. This concept doesn't come without a price, though. You have to write your application to work without graphics and sounds—or whatever elements you decide to place in a separate package. Your installation program has to provide similar flexibility. It has to know what to do if a user decides to download one packaging element but not another.

▶ **Amplified help**   We discussed the idea of creating separate packages for help files in Chapter 17. One of the ways you can do this is to make a main and an amplifying help file. The main help file would contain explanations for basic commands, while the amplifying help file could contain user tutorials, macro language descriptions, and detailed command descriptions. Again, the user could decide what level of help to pay for in the form of download time and disk space.

TIP

More than a few shareware companies have used modularized programs to enhance sales. For example, ButtonWare usually provided a simple help file and most of the features for a shareware application when a user downloaded it. Buying the application entitled the user to download the full-featured program and complete program documentation.

Shrink Wrap

This section concentrates on what you can learn from shrink-wrap vendors. One of the factors that set a shrink-wrap product apart from shareware is the size of the company producing the application. Larger software companies usually concentrate on one or more products, and they have a large professional group of people to help put the packaging together. However, the average programmer can learn a few things by looking at these shrink-wrap packages.

I've taken notes whenever I installed a shrink-wrap or shareware product over the last few years. Recently, I decided to look over my notes. The results were surprising. For example, the previous section mentions using the installation program as a means to sell your product if you're a shareware vendor, since you have a captive audience and fewer sales resources that are otherwise at your disposal. It may surprise you to find that shrink-wrap software commonly uses the installation program for this purpose but in a different way than a shareware vendor would use it. The user has already purchased the product he or she is installing, but how about add-on products? Shrink-wrap vendors commonly use the installation program to sell add-on products that relate to the application the user is installing.

Shrink-wrap software commonly tells the user what's new about the program during the installation process. The companies figured out long ago that most users don't read the README file, and the installation program is usually the last part of the product to get finished. The shrink-wrap vendor has a captive audience, so it uses the installation program to give users an overview of what they'd learn if they'd actually read the README file.

Vendors pack shrink-wrap installation programs with lots of multimedia presentation materials. Even if you don't have the resources to duplicate the presentation provided by a shrink-wrap vendor, you can study such products to determine what works and what doesn't. Providing a smaller version of the same type of presentation in your installation program is one way to make it look more polished. Creating a nice looking installation program won't make your application work better, but it'll affect the user's perception of your application, which is a very important part of getting the user up and running with a minimum of support.

There are some negative lessons you can learn from shrink-wrap vendors as well. For example, you can make your installation program too complex to test thoroughly. I recently tried installing one product and found that the help screens for the program were for the previous version. The vendor had forgotten to update the screens for the new version of its product. The result? Since the product didn't come with any printed documentation, I didn't have a clue as to whether I should install certain product features. If the vendor had tested the program fully, I would have had the information needed to make an informed feature-oriented installation decision.

Gathering the Files

Never get the idea that you can put an installation program together in a few seconds without research. Any program that runs in the Windows environment is more complicated than even the programmer realizes in most cases. For example, all of the examples in this book rely on C runtime files. Yet I never mention adding these files to your application code, nor do I reference them in any of the source code. Visual C++ automatically adds these files to your SYSTEM folder during installation. You don't need to know about them while you design your application because their inclusion is automatic.

However, now you're trying to put everything needed to run your application into a package for the user. You no longer have the luxury of ignoring those other files—they're part of your application and must be included with the package you send to the user. The problem is figuring out which files to include with your program.

Figuring out which DLLs to ship with your application can be a time-consuming task, especially if you resort to trial and error. Try using these three methods to take some of the trial and error out of the process.

▶ **Method 1**   Use the Windows QuickView utility to view the Import Table entries for your application. The Import Table list tells you which DLLs your application relies on.

▶ **Method 2**   The DumpBin utility can give you a command line view of the requirements of your application. DumpBin is a little more trouble to use, but it finds information hidden from the QuickView utility. You'll also find that it offers more information options. Type **DUMPBIN /IMPORTS** *<Application Name>* at the command line to use this program.

 TIP

You may get a missing-file message when using DumpBin. Both the MSDIS100.DLL and MSPDB50.DLL files are located in the Program Files/DevStudio/SharedIDE/bin directory (assuming you've used the default settings during installation). You need these files along with LINK.EXE found in the VC/bin directory to make DumpBin work.

▶ **Method 3**   Use the Depends utility. It displays a hierarchical list of DLLs called by your application.

Getting a list of files that your executable uses directly isn't the end of the process. You need to check the DLLs it uses for any dependencies. You can ignore files such as USER.EXE since the user will have them installed as part of Windows, but you'll need to watch for files that aren't part of the Windows installation. Manually check each file for its dependencies and then include those files with your application.

TIP

Check a clean machine for a list of default Windows files. You may want to maintain a list of these files for later reference if you plan to create more than one installation program.

Once you have a complete list of the application files, gather them in one place. Copy this set of files to a newly installed copy of Windows (whichever version your application targets). Test your application to make sure it works. You'll get messages if either a file is missing or it needs to go into the SYSTEM folder. Make sure you keep track of the files you place in the SYSTEM folder because you'll have to place them there on the user's machine.

NOTE

Always keep application DLLs in the application folder instead of automatically placing them in the SYSTEM folder. Keeping everything in one place will help you uninstall the program later should the user want to remove it from his or her machine. You'll also have fewer problems with corruption from other programs.

Using InstallShield

This section shows how to package the Sngl_Doc application created in Chapter 2 to send to someone else—well, at least for example purposes. We'll also include the help file from Chapter 17 as part of the package. The following procedure shows how to put a typical installation program together using InstallShield. If you were to pick a specific packaging model for this example, it's very close to the corporate packaging technique that we talked about earlier.

BROWSER ALERT

*Find an InstallShield decompiler at **http://www.tardis.ed.ac.uk/~adq/projects/isdcc/**. This program recreates the script used to create an installation program package. It allows you to see how other developers work with installation programs so you can hone your own skills. You can find out about InstallShield and many other useful packaging products at **http://www.installshield.com/**.*

1. Start InstallShield. You'll see a window containing any projects you have defined and the Project Wizard. Notice the InstallShield link in the lower-right

corner. Clicking it will open your browser and take you to the InstallShield online help site on the Internet.

2. Double-click on the Project Wizard icon in the Projects window. You'll see a Project Wizard - Welcome dialog similar to the one shown here.

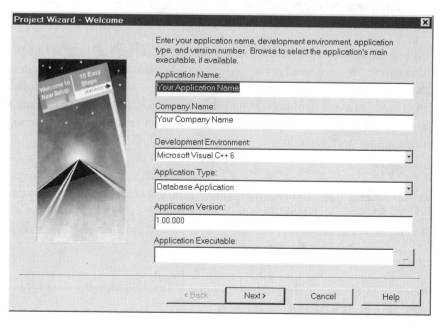

3. Type the name of your application. The example program uses Single Document Application Example.

4. Type your company name. The example program uses A Sample Company.

5. Choose one of the entries in the Application Type field. The example program uses Software Development Application—there isn't a standard utility program type, and the Software Development Application type does allow for utility programs.

6. Type the application version number in Application Version field. Our example program uses 1.0, but you can use any numbering scheme consistent with your company policies.

7. Click the ... (ellipsis) button next to the Application Executable field. You'll see a standard Open dialog that you can use to find the application you want to package on your hard drive. The sample application uses SNGL_DOC.EXE.

8. Click Next. You'll see a Project Wizard - Choose Dialogs dialog. Since we're using the corporate model for our installation program, I unchecked the

Software License Agreement, Setup Type, and Custom Setup dialogs. You'd choose some or all of these dialogs for the other packaging models we discussed earlier in this chapter. Look in the lower-left corner as you move from one dialog entry to the next. You'll see that the Project Wizard gives you a thumbnail view of the dialog. Highlighting a dialog and clicking Preview displays a dialog that looks exactly like the one the user will see. You can modify this dialog later, but it helps to know where you're starting.

9. Choose the dialogs you want to add to the installation program and click Next. You'll see a Project Wizard - Choose Target Platforms dialog. Since we want install our program on any of the supported platforms, we won't have to make any changes. You should be more selective in some situations. Reducing the number of supported platforms reduces the size of the installation program you create and the chance that someone will try to use your program under the wrong version of Windows.

10. Select one or more platforms as needed (but at least one). Click Next. You'll see a Project Wizard - Specify Languages dialog. As with other selections you've had to make so far, more isn't necessarily better. Adding languages will increase the size of the installation program and could add to user confusion as well—choose only the languages you need.

11. Highlight one or more languages (but at least one). Click Next. You'll see a Project Wizard - Specify Setup Types dialog. Since we're using the corporate packaging model, I've chosen the Network setup type. Other packaging models will require you to make other selections, including the most common of all: Custom, Typical, and Compact.

12. Choose one or more setup types. Click Next. You'll see Project Wizard - Specify Components dialog. The example program uses Program Files, Shared DLLs, and Help Files. You'll need to choose each of these options in turn to define the files that go under each component type. A component type is a definition of a major program area. For example, the user may want to include all of the sample files but none of the help files. If you're following the example, highlight Example Files and click Delete. Project Wizard will remove this component type from the installation program.

TIP

You can add new component types as needed to your installation program. For example, you might need to add a Database File component if you've written a database application. All you have to do is click the Add button, and the Project Wizard will add the new entry for you. Type the name of the component, and press ENTER *to complete the addition process.*

13. Add or delete component types as needed. Click Next. You'll see a Project Wizard - Specify File Groups dialog. The example program uses Program Executable Files, Help Files, and Shared DLLs. Normally, you'll create file groups so that all of the files needed for a specific task are copied at one time. File groups can cross component-type boundaries. For example, say the spell checker and the grammar checker both rely on the same set of DLLs but require different rule files. You could define a common file group for the DLLs and two other file groups for the rule files. If the user selected the spell checker but not the grammar checker, InstallShield would copy the spell checker file group and the common DLL file group but not the grammar checker file group. If you're following along with the example, highlight Program DLLs and click Delete. Then highlight Example Files and click Delete.

14. Add or delete file groups as needed. Click Next. You'll see a Project Wizard - Summary dialog like the one that follows. Check the list of options to make sure everything is correct before you ask the Project Wizard to build the installation program for you.

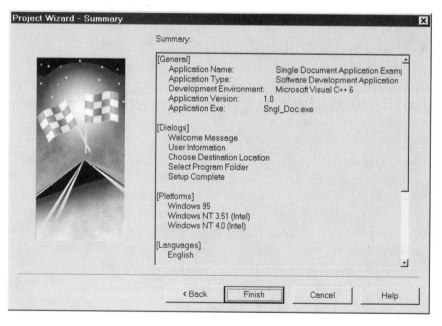

15. Click Finish. InstallShield will create the installation program using the parameters you've just specified. The InstallShield interface will change, as shown in Figure 18-1. You can see the C++ code used to create the program and modify it as you would any other project.

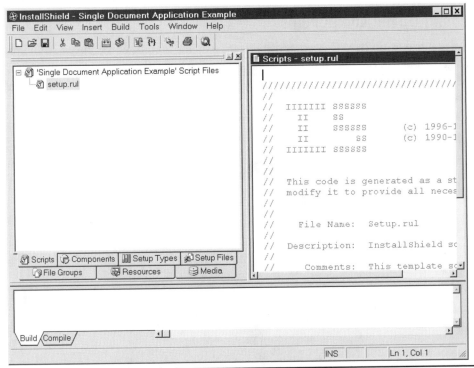

Figure 18-1   *Once you've created a project, InstallShield will generate it for you and then display the resulting source code.*

NOTE

InstallShield doesn't generate source files that are precisely like the ones used in a general project. There are ancillary files like the setup rule (SETUP.RUL) file in Figure 18-1.

The wizard creates a barely usable installation program shell. There's still quite a bit of configuration to do, though, and we'll look at it in the sections that follow. Fortunately, InstallShield will do most of the work for you as you define the various program elements.

BROWSER ALERT

*If you still have InstallShield usage questions after reading this section, there are other sources of information. Look in the product README file because it contains links to many places you need to know about on the Internet. For example, you'll find a link to the newsgroups site at **http://support.installshield.com/newsgroups/default.asp**. This site contains links to several InstallShield-specific newsgroups. You'll find links for newsgroups covering topics like the IDE, scripting, and the use of multimedia.*

Setting Up the Components

The first task we'll need to accomplish is setting up the various components. Remember that a component is a selection that appears during the installation. If you've ever used the custom install feature of an installation program, then you know what a component is. It's the check boxes you use to choose individual program features such as help files.

Configuring the components for your installation program is easy. Click Components and you'll see a Components - Program Files dialog like the one shown next.

Field	Value
Description	
Status Text	
Display Name	
Visible	Yes
Overwrite	ALWAYSOVERWR
Destination	<TARGETDIR>
File Need	STANDARD
Include in Build	Yes
Password	
Encryption	No
CD-ROM Folder	
FTP Location	
HTTP Location	
Miscellaneous	
Comment	
Required Components	None Selected
Included File Groups	None Selected

The components dialog contains a complete list of all the values for the selected component. Remember that we have three components in this case: Program Files, Help Files, and Shared DLLs. Set up all three before you go to the next section. Double-click the Description property and you'll see a Properties dialog.

All of the properties will show similar dialogs. Each Properties dialog will describe what you're supposed to do with this particular property. It allows you to type a value for the property. Type **All the files required to run the application**. Click OK. The Description property will contain the text you just typed.

You don't need to change all of the component properties—what you do need to change depends on the kind of application package you're creating. For example, in our corporate model installation, we don't ever allow the user to choose the installed components, so providing a component description is pointless. The user won't ever see it. You should change some properties regardless of the packaging model. The following list looks at each one.

▶ **Status Text**   The text the user sees while the program copies files from the source to the destination. The Progress dialog will say something like "Copying program files…".

▶ **Installation**   If you've ever been annoyed by a program that copied over the new DLLs you just installed with old ones that don't work, then you'll know why this property is important. It tells InstallShield whether you want to look at the time and date stamp on the component files before you overwrite them. I always choose NEWERVERSION/NEWERDATE or SAMEORNEWERVERSION/SAMEORNEWERDATE instead of the default.

▶ **Destination**   The standard destination for all application files is the target directory. In some circumstances, using the target directory won't work or will waste space on the user's machine. For example, all Visual C++ applications use the C runtime and MFC files. In most cases, you'll copy Shared DLLs component files to the Windows SYSTEM folder.

▶ **Required Components**   A list of dependencies between components. For example, if the user installs the Program Files component, he or she must also install the Shared DLLs component.

TIP

Pay special attention to the FTP Location and HTTP Location properties if you plan to install your application from an Internet or intranet site. These properties allow a user to start the installation from a Web site link and copy the files from your Web server. You normally choose the FTP Location property if the files are on an FTP server.

There's one last item that you must take care of to configure the components. Double-click the Included File Groups property and you'll see a Properties dialog that contains a list of the file groups assigned to a component. I previously talked about an example where you might want to make the spell checker and grammar checker optional components of your installation. They both use the same DLLs but require different rule files. You need to set up three file groups: one with the spelling rule file, another with the grammar rule file, and a third with the common DLLs needed by both. This is the property where you set up that relationship. Click Add and you'll see an Add File Group dialog that contains the three file groups we defined using the Project Wizard.

You need to make assignments between components and file groups before going on in the chapter. Table 18-1 shows the settings I used for the example program.

Component	Property	Value
Program Files	Description	All the files required to run the application
	Status Text	Copying Program Files...
	Overwrite	SAMEORNEWERVERSION/ SAMEORNEWERDATE
	Required Components	Shared DLLs
	Included File Groups	Program Executable Files
Help Files	Description	Files that show you how to use the program
	Status Text	Copying Help Files...
	Overwrite	SAMEORNEWERDATE
	Included File Groups	Help Files
Shared DLLs	Description	Common files used by the program
	Status Text	Copying Shared DLLs...
	Overwrite	SAMEORNEWERVERSION/ SAMEORNEWERDATE
	Destination	<WINSYSDIR>
	Included File Groups	Shared DLLs

Table 18-1 *Component Settings for the Sngl_Doc Installation Program*

Setting Up File Groups

Creating a set of components is a first step. You've defined which components to copy to the hard drive, but you haven't defined which files to use. This is the step where you define a set of files for each of the file groups we defined previously.

1. Click File Groups. You'll see a list of the file groups and the File Groups dialog. To choose a file group, click its entry in the File Groups window on the left side of the display.

2. Click the plus sign (+) next to the Help Files folder in the File Groups window. Click the Links entry under the Help Files folder and you'll see the File Groups - Help Files\Links dialog. This is where you'll define a list of one or more files to include for this file group.

3. Right-click the File Groups - Help Files\Links dialog. Choose Insert Files from the context menu. You'll see a File Open-type dialog. Find the Sngl_Doc.HLP file. Click Open to add this file to the Help Files file group. Add the

Sngl_Doc.EXE file to the Program Executable Files file group. Add the following files from the Windows SYSTEM folder to the Shared DLLs group: MFC70.DLL, MSVCRT.DLL, and MSVCR70.DLL.

Defining Resources

You need to provide identification information for the users. After all, they'll want to know a little something about the program they're installing. Click Resources and you'll see the Resources window. Most changes appear in the Resources - String Table\English dialog shown here:

Identifier	String Value	C...
COMPANY_NAME	A Sample Company	
COMPANY_NAME16	Company	
ERROR_COMPONENT	Component:	
ERROR_FILE	File:	
ERROR_FILEGROUP	File Group:	
ERROR_MOVEDATA	An error occurred during the move ...	
ERROR_UNINSTSETUP	unInstaller setup failed to initialize. ...	
ERROR_VGARESOLUTION	This program requires VGA or bette...	
FOLDER_NAME	Single Document Application Example	
PRODUCT_KEY	Sngl_Doc.exe	
PRODUCT_NAME	Single Document Application Example	
PRODUCT_NAME16	Product	
PRODUCT_VERSION	1.0	
TITLE_CAPTIONBAR	Single Document Application Examp...	
TITLE_MAIN	Single Document Application Example	
UNINST_DISPLAY_NAME	Single Document Application Example	
UNINST_KEY	Single Document Application Example	

Most of the changes we'll make in the Resources - String Table\English dialog won't affect the program at all. The changes identify the vendor or provide help to the user. To change a string, double-click on the Identifier you want to change, and InstallShield will display a dialog that allows you to make the required change. I changed the COMPANY_NAME16 value to "A Sample Company" and the UNINST_KEY value to "Sngl_Doc.EXE."

Determining a Media Type

The last step is to tell InstallShield what type of media you want to use for distributing your application. You'll use CD as the main distribution method in most cases. If your only distribution method is going to be CD, you're done. Otherwise, choose the Media tab and you'll see a Media dialog and window. The following procedure will take you through the steps required to add a floppy media type.

1. Click Media Build Wizard and you'll see a Media Build Wizard - Media Name dialog.

2. Type **Floppy**. Click Next. You'll see the Media Build Wizard - Disk Type dialog. Notice that InstallShield supports a variety of media types, including 2.88MB floppies.

3. Highlight the 3.5" Diskette - 1.44 MBytes option. Click Next. You'll see the Media Build Wizard - Build Type dialog. A full build compresses all the files for your application, creates the required CAB files, and the installation program. The Quick Build option allows you to see if your installation program works as anticipated.

4. Choose the Full Build option. Click Next. You'll see the Media Build Wizard - Tag File dialog. All this dialog does is allow you to enter your company name and associated application information.

5. Type all the required information into the dialog. The example program uses A Simple Company in the Company Name field, Single Document Application Example in the Application Name field, Word Processor in the Product Category field, and Utility Style Text Editor in the Misc. field.

6. Click Next. You'll see a Media Build Wizard - Platforms dialog.

7. Click Next. You'll see a Media Build Wizard Summary dialog like the one shown here. This is your last chance to verify the settings you've used.

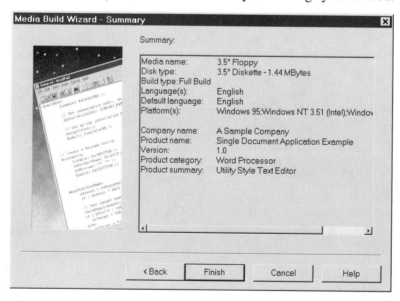

8. Verify your settings. Click Finish. InstallShield will create the new build that you requested.

9. You'll see a Building Media dialog. InstallShield is creating the installation program. When the process is complete, your Building Media dialog should say, "Build completed successfully." Click Finish.

Using Windows Installer

This section will help you learn about Microsoft's latest installation program technology, the Microsoft Windows Installer (MSI). Microsoft changed the Windows 2000/XP installation process for several reasons, most notably the older Setup file process is unreliable at best and doesn't provide an easy method for uninstalling applications. Setup programs also require a lot of work on the part of the user, and a poorly designed Setup program can cause difficulties when situations that the developer didn't consider arise. The problems with using Setup programs are so severe that Microsoft has also made this new technology available on the other Windows platforms (Windows NT and Windows 9x) so that you can use MSI there as well.

There are good reasons for developers to switch to MSI. Creating a Setup program ranks as one of the worst tasks for developers (right above creating help files), because writing a Setup program is a difficult and thankless task. The new MSI file format promises easier installation and uninstallation for both users and developers.

BROWSER ALERT

You can obtain the latest version of the Microsoft Installer SDK at **http://msdn.microsoft.com/ msdn-files/027/001/455/instmsia.exe.** *You can also see the Microsoft Installer SDK Web page (and associated installer SDKs) at* **http://msdn.microsoft.com/downloads/ sample.asp?url=/msdn-files/027/001/455/msdncompositedoc.xml.** *The first step if you're not running Windows 2000/XP is to install the MSI redistributable files. There are separate versions for Windows NT and Windows 9x, so make sure you get the support you need. In addition to the Microsoft Windows Installer SDK, you'll need to download the Visual Studio Installer from* **http://msdn.microsoft.com/vstudio/downloads/vsi/default.asp.** *This product uses MSI technology and makes the process of creating MSI files easier. It's a better version of the Package and Deployment Wizard.*

About the Microsoft Windows Installer

MSI is a new technology that's supposed to provide a faster, easier, and cleaner way to install applications on any machine. That's the main reason that you'll want to begin using this technology right away. It represents the best method of making installation programs easier to build and easier to use, which means you'll spend less time dealing with support calls and more time working on new code. The following sections are going to introduce you to MSI, then tell you about the two tools you'll need to know about in order to use it.

Why Is this Technology Important?

When a developer creates a standard installation program that relies on Setup.EXE, the Setup application contains everything the installation program is capable of doing. A network administrator or other skilled person can't come back later and make changes to the installation package. When you create an MSI file, you end up with two files. The first contains the MSI package, while the second contains the configuration and installation files in an archive with a CAB (cabinet) extension.

Each archive contains an msicab file that's an editable text file you can look into for installation information. This file doesn't differ much from any INF file that you may have worked with in the past. You could conceivably edit this file to add steps, change the destination directory, or perform any other number of tasks. The point is that while this installation program isn't fully configurable, it does provide configuration options.

Older versions of Visual Studio used a kludge setup that had a different installation program tool for each language. I'm glad to see that Visual Studio .NET contains a single installation tool. However, Visual Studio Installer is still a free upgrade for Visual Studio users. This is an especially useful tool because it provides an easy to use and fully integrated solution for building installation programs. Of course, it doesn't hurt to have Visual Studio Installer if you still plan on working with older versions of Visual Studio after the upgrade to Visual Studio .NET.

Understanding the Microsoft Installer SDK

Microsoft designed the Microsoft Windows Installer SDK to help developers write code that uses MSI technology. In other words, if you want to create an installation program the old-fashioned way, you can do it with this product. However, the Microsoft Windows Installer SDK is useful for more than installation programs. You can use it to add install-on-demand capability to your applications. The following sections will answer three major questions about the Microsoft Windows Installer SDK for you.

Why MSI-Enable Your Applications?

Install-on-demand is an incredibly powerful new feature you can add to applications. It allows an application to install new features that it needs, when the user needs them. There will be less cause for hard drive bloat because the hard drive will contain only core features of an application. Using install-on-demand means that the installation program installs only the application pieces that are in use.

Another problem that many developers have is that they create a very rich application, only to find out later that many users are completely unaware of all of the application's gizmos. In some cases, users ask for product updates for features that already exist in the application. Using the Microsoft Windows Installer SDK allows you to add "feature advertising" to your application. When an application detects that a user could benefit from a feature, it can ask whether the user would like to try the feature and if so, will perform the installation automatically.

Finally, MSI provides a self-repair feature. When application damage occurs, the user normally needs to uninstall, then reinstall the application to get it working again. Unfortunately, this also means the user loses time resetting the application configuration. The MSI repair feature allows a user to choose the repair option from a Support Info dialog box to repair an application, rather than reinstall it. Windows automatically presents this dialog when the user selects the support information link in the Add/Remove Programs applet for that application.

An Overview of the MSI Installer SDK Contents

Now that I've piqued your curiosity a bit, let's look at what the Microsoft Windows Installer SDK has to offer. The package includes the usual documentation. You'll also find sample code and a sample application you can use to learn more about this product. There are development tools, including a database validation tool that you can use to check the integrity of any installation database you create. The development tools also include a database authoring tool and some VBScript tools. Finally, you'll find a directory containing the redistributable files that you can use to make a user's machine MSI friendly.

An Overview of a Few Tools

Let's look at some of the practical applications of this SDK (even if you don't want to create an MSI enabled application today). The following list provides a quick overview of some of the more important tools.

▶   **MSIInfo**   You may wonder how to determine whether a problem with an MSI installation is the fault of the MSI file, the files contained in the CAB, or something like a version change. Considering that MSI is new technology, the version question is especially important, because you may find that your installation program works one day and not the next. The MSIInfo utility provided with the Microsoft Windows Installer SDK is the answer to this problem. It prints out information that you won't normally see about an MSI package, including the author of that package and the version number of MSI used to create it.

▶ **MSIDB**   Another interesting tool, MSIDB, allows you to export and import MSI database elements. Everything MSI does to install your application is part of a database, so this is an important utility to know about if you want to create a canned installation program and then replace only small pieces with custom elements. This tool allows you to export and import information such as the summary that identifies the vendor.

> **NOTE**
>
> *MSIDB opens the database file for exclusive use, which makes sense when you consider the work you're performing with it. Make sure you close MSIDB before you attempt to access the database with any other utility. Nothing bad will happen if you don't follow this rule, but the new utility won't be able to access the database and will report an error instead of opening it for you. In other words, don't assume a change you've made to the MSI database for an installation program has gone wrong until you check for the presence of MSIDB.*

▶ **MSIZap**   One of the problems that developers face when working on a new application is finding an uncontaminated machine to test their applications on. I set aside a machine with just the operating system installed for testing purposes. If this machine gets "dirty," I reformat the hard drive and start with a fresh copy of the operating system. MSIZap will zap almost every trace of MSI data from your machine. You can completely clean off every application, or you can concentrate on just one or two applications with specific attributes.

▶ **Orca**   Microsoft doesn't force you to hand-edit the database with a text editor if you don't want to. If you install the Orca utility (it doesn't install as part of the initial Microsoft Windows Installer SDK installation), you'll be able to use this editor to read and modify the contents of a database. The left pane displays all of the tables within the database. The right pane displays the rows and columns of the selected table. Right-click any of these rows and you'll see options for adding or dropping a row. You can also edit the currently selected field by clicking it a second time. (The field will change to all bold characters when it's ready to edit.) The Microsoft Windows Installer SDK Help file contains information about all of the standard tables within a database and how you can use them to create an installation application.

TIP

Text fields within a database are one of the items that a network administrator will want to modify. These fields allow a network administrator to provide company-specific information instead of the generic information provided by the developer. For example, you could include a text field that provides the name and telephone number of the person to contact in case of an installation failure.

This is a brief overview of some of the Microsoft Windows Installer SDK tools— a feature-rich product designed to change the way you write installation programs. Instead of creating full-fledged inflexible applications, you can now create databases of installation steps that you can modify as needed to meet specific requirements. Add to that features like on-demand installation, and you can see why this is a must-have tool for any type of Windows 2000/XP development and a good add-on for development on other Windows platforms.

Understanding the Visual Studio Installer

The Visual Studio Installer represents the easy method for creating installation programs that use the MSI file format. This is a companion product to the Microsoft Windows Installer SDK, which allows you to add MSI features to applications and modify MSI databases. In addition, unlike the Microsoft Windows Installer SDK, this isn't a stand-alone product. It's designed to integrate with Visual Studio.

Before you install this product, you must have a copy of any of the Visual Studio products installed on your machine including Visual Basic and Visual C++. When you finish the installation, you'll see a new Visual Studio Installer entry in the Visual Studio.NET Enterprise Features menu. This product uses the same IDE as the Visual Studio Analyzer, so if you've used that product you'll have a good idea of how to use this one as well.

Creating an MSI File for an Application

Creating a MSI file for a Visual Basic application is relatively easy. This section of the chapter shows you how to create an installation package for a simple application. The Visual Studio Installer is designed to create very complex installation routines containing a number of merge packages as well as standard MSI packages. You'll also find that every aspect of the MSI file is configurable.

NOTE

A merge package has an MSM extension. It contains only the files required to install a single application element, but doesn't contain the installation instructions. You'll use a merge package to incorporate separate application elements. Once you build a merge package, you add it to an MSI file using Visual Studio Installer to create a single package with two elements.

The following procedure shows you how to create a simple MSI package for a Visual C++ application. I'll assume you've already installed Visual Studio Installer.

1. Start Visual Studio Installer. You'll see a New Project dialog box.

2. Select Empty Installer. Type a name (the example uses Simple Install). Click Open. You'll see a new project like the one in Figure 18-2 (this figure shows the file system as well). The various elements of this window should look familiar—it's arranged much like Visual Studio and works in the same way.

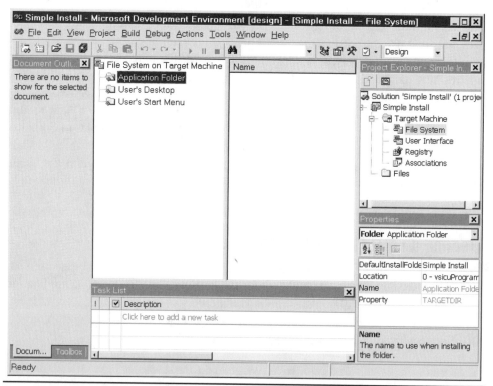

Figure 18-2 *Visual Studio Installer looks and acts like the Visual Studio IDE.*

3. Double-click File System in Project Explorer. You'll see a new window similar to the one shown in Figure 18-2. We'll use the same folders for this installation program as we used for the InstallShield example in the previous section, so we'll need to add some folders.

4. Highlight User's Desktop and press DELETE. Right-click File System on Target Machine and choose Add Special Folder | Windows System Folder from the context menu. Notice that the context menu lists many of the common Windows application folders. You can also create custom folders as needed. Let's add some files to the install program.

5. Select Application Folder in the left pane. Right-click in the right pane. Choose Add Files from the context menu. Add Sngl_Doc.HLP and Sngl_Doc.EXE to the list. Select Windows System Folder in the left pane. Add the following files from the Windows SYSTEM folder to the list in the right pane: MFC70.DLL, MSVCRT.DLL, and MSVCR70.DLL. We've selected all of the applications files. The user will want some shortcuts in the Start Menu to access the application and help file.

6. Select User's Start Menu in the left pane. Right-click in the right pane. Choose Create Shortcut from the context menu. You'll see a Shortcut Properties dialog like the one shown here.

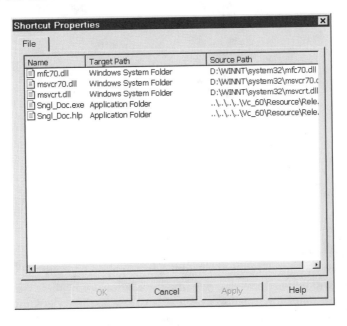

7. Highlight Sngl_Doc.EXE. Click OK. Change the Name property for this entry to Single Document Example.

8. Right-click in the right pane. Choose Create Shortcut from the context menu. You'll see a Shortcut Properties dialog. Highlight Sngl_Doc.HLP. Click OK. Change the Name property for this entry to Single Document Help. Now we need a user interface.

9. Double-click User Interface in Project Explorer. You'll see a list of interface dialogs like the one shown here. The display shows the dialogs the user will see in the order the user will see them. One way to look at this display is as a script of the installation process. Unlike with InstallShield, you don't see what the actual dialog looks like until you create the application. Customization options normally include elements like the background image. I won't add a background image to the sample, but you could use something like the corporate logo for an installation program for this environment. We'll want to make this installation look similar to the one we created in InstallShield, so you'll need to add a new dialog.

10. Right-click Start and choose Add Dialog from the context menu. You'll see an Add Dialog dialog. Highlight Customer Information and click OK. Visual Studio Installer will add the new dialog to the installation application. Since this is a corporate application, we don't need a serial number. Set the ShowSerialNumber property to False. It's time to perform the final customization of the installation

program. Visual Studio Installer provides the same customization options as InstallShield, but you access them in a different way.

11. Select Project | <Project Name> Properties. You'll see a <Project Name> Properties dialog like the one shown next. This dialog allows you to customize various installation program elements—everything from the method used to compile the installation program to company information the user will see. I configured the company options in this dialog the same way that I did for the InstallShield example. Normally, you can accept the other parameters as defaults, unless you company has a special need.

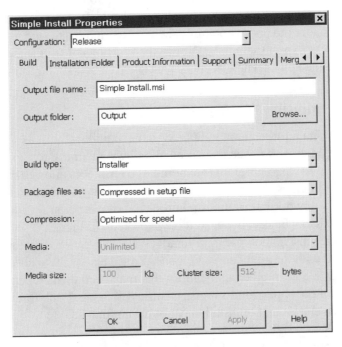

You should have noticed by now that we haven't written any code, and you'll find that you don't need to. There are situations when the most you'll need to do is perform a lot of configuration. Once you finish with the setup process, you'll want to build the installation program.

Use the Build | Build command to build your installation program. The building process occurs in two phases. First, Visual Studio Installer will gather all of the required files, create a database containing all of the required steps, and perform any customization you requested. Second, Visual Studio Installer will compress the files so they take the least amount of space possible. At this point, your installation program is ready to test.

Testing the Install Process

The first step for testing an installation program is to attempt to install the application in question. Move to a clean machine so that you can eliminate sources of outside interference and the contaminated environment of your development machine. It's important that you test the application in a clean environment to make it easier to verify the setup.

Once you install the program, see if it runs. If it does, you're at least half way to ensuring the application will run as anticipated on a user's machine. You'll also want to check for potential problems like file associations.

After you run the application for a while and check all of the user elements, it's time to check under the hood. Look into the registry and make sure all of the registry entries are as you expect them to be. Verify the locations of files and ensure that every file is in the appropriate place.

Testing the Uninstall Process

Applications written for Windows 2000/XP have to uninstall just as well as they install. In fact, Microsoft raised the bar on Windows XP uninstall capability as part of the Windows XP logo program (no more left over pieces allowed). So, the next testing phase is to uninstall the application. In most cases, you won't see any problems with the application during the uninstall process; however, you'll sometimes find that appearances can be deceiving, so it pays to check further.

Make sure the installation program removes the application directory and that all files associated with the application are gone. You'll also want to check that shared files are still available to other applications that may need them. Open RegEdit and verify that all of the application's registry entries are gone. Look for little problems like Start menu entries that uninstall may not have removed.

Problems with the Microsoft Windows Installer

MSI is a new product, which means there's a good chance that all of the bugs aren't worked out yet. Microsoft recognizes this fact and has included a list of bugs they know about in the Visual Studio Installer README file that accompanies the SDK. Make sure you read this file before you begin the installation process, because there are some significant limitations to this product. You may find, in rare cases at least, that one or more of these limitations will prevent you from using the MSI in its current state. However, the MSI file format is the wave of the future, and you should begin making the change sooner rather than later.

Non-Windows 2000 Support

Just how much this problem affects you as a developer depends, in most cases, on what type of installation package you need to create. Windows 2000/XP ships with MSI support. Microsoft has stated that MSI is the preferred installation method for this new platform. You can also get MSI support for Windows 9x and Windows NT machines, since Microsoft would prefer that you use this new technology for these older machines as well. However, since this support is unlikely to appear on older machines any time soon, you'll always have to include the MSI redistributable files with any shrink wrap software package you create. (MSI should become part of Windows Update eventually, which will ensure that most users get it installed on their machines.)

This situation creates two problems. First, any installation program you create will have to check for MSI support on the host machine and either fail gracefully if the support isn't present or offer to install the required support. Part of the reason for using MSI is to reduce installation program complexity, yet the fact that MSI is new means that you may actually increase application complexity in the short term.

The second problem is one of support. Users already complain that installation programs are too difficult to understand and use. Microsoft is very aware of this problem. They've done everything possible to decrease installation program complexity during the last few years. Yet, there always seems to be a glitch in installation that keeps the user from getting the application installed on his or her computer. Using MSI means adding complexity to the setup if the user doesn't have MSI installed. You can be sure that some users will find this confusing, and support costs will increase.

Database and INF Corruption

MSI isn't an application per se; it's actually a database of instructions. You're not creating an application; it's more like a script that the MSI Service interprets. As we've seen throughout the chapter, the instructions used by MSI to install your product are very accessible and open. Anyone can look at them, and it doesn't take very much knowledge at all to modify those instructions. In general, MSI is superior for these very reasons to any installation package you may have used in the past.

Unfortunately, the MSI characteristics can also cause problems. Well-intentioned users or administrators could change vital information in MSI packages or archives, making the installation program perform in ways other than the way you intended. For example, changing a GUID will definitely lead to unanticipated results. Changing one of the lines of instruction in the INF file could make the installation program do a number of things you didn't expect.

You can use policies and lock the CAB file to prevent these problems from happening. For example, the DisableBrowse machine policy will prevent users from locating the source of an application and modifying the files. In short, you need to be proactive about keeping corruption at bay. Hopefully, Microsoft will keep the flexibility and add a little more in the security department for the next release of MSI.

Setup and Deployment Projects

You don't have to rely on using third party products or installing yet another Microsoft SDK to create your next installation program. Visual Studio .NET also comes with several Setup and Deployment Projects, as shown here:

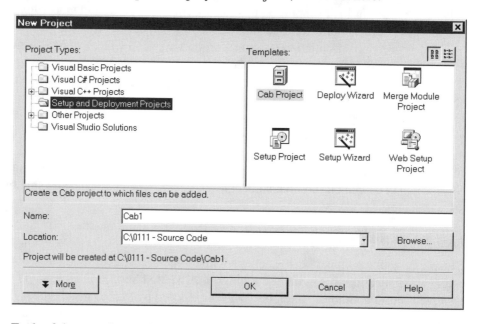

Each of these projects will allow you to package your application. However, not all of these projects will create a setup program that a user can rely on to install your program. For example, the Cab Project is great for compressing application files, but it's more akin to using a ZIP file than creating an installation program. Likewise, the Merge Module Project allows you to create an installation program component, not the entire installation program. The easiest method for creating an installation program is to use the Setup Wizard. The following sections will provide a brief look at each of the Visual Studio .NET deployment and packaging options.

Cab Project

Use the Cab Project when you need to compress files. You can distribute these files as part of an installation program, or simply use this project to put all of the files associated with another project into an easy-to-transfer package. In short, the Cab Project is similar to a ZIP archive.

When you create this project, you'll see the familiar Cab file icon in the Solution Explorer, along with the name of your project. Right-click the project and choose Add | File. You'll see an Add Files dialog. Choose the files you want to add to the Cab, then click Open. Visual Studio will add the files to the project. You can add as many files as needed to complete the package.

You have several options when it comes to building your project. The Build | Build command will create a Cab file for you in one of the output directories of your project. Use the Build | Deploy command if you want to deploy the Cab file to another location. Selecting this second command will start the Deploy Wizard, which we'll explore next.

Deploy Wizard

The Deploy Wizard project provides a step-by-step approach to creating an application package. Other project types call on the Project Deployment Wizard when you choose to deploy, rather than simply build, the project. You can also run this wizard by itself, which is what we'll talk about in this section.

Deploying an application means placing it on a remote machine instead of keeping it on the local machine. For example, you might need to send the current version of your word processor to the server so that everyone will get the upgrade. Contrast this with a setup program that Visual Studio will create locally for later installation on a machine.

You begin this project as you would any other in Visual Studio.NET. Select a project name and directory. Click Install. You'll see a Deployment Project Wizard (1 of 5) dialog box. The following steps will lead you through the process of using this wizard.

1. Click Next. The Deployment Project Wizard will ask you to select a project type, as shown here. You can deploy either Web applications or a rich client

application to a remote machine. The example will use a rich client application.

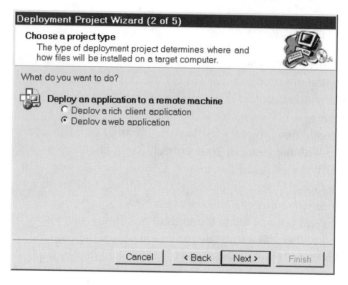

2. Select a project type. Click Next. You'll see a file selection dialog. The example will use the same set of files from Chapter 2 as all of the other installation examples in the chapter. Add Sngl_Doc.HLP and Sngl_Doc.EXE to the list. Add the following files from the Windows SYSTEM folder to the list in the right pane: MFC70.DLL, MSVCRT.DLL, and MSVCR70.DLL.

3. Add your project files to the list. Click Next. The Deployment Project Wizard will ask where you want to deploy the files, as shown here:

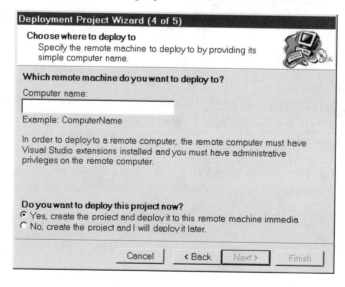

4. Type the name of a location. Click Next. You'll see a Summary dialog, as shown here:

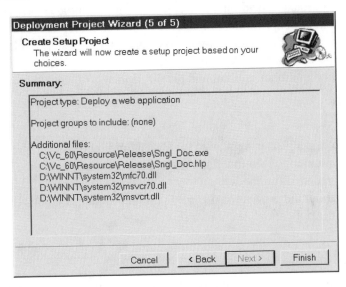

5. Click Finish. If you've set everything up properly, Visual Studio will build the application package and deploy it for you. Otherwise, fix any problems that Visual Studio found, then use the Build | Deploy command to attempt deploying the project again.

Merge Module Project

As previously mentioned, a Merge Module project is actually a piece of a full-fledged installation program. You can create MSI files using more than one component. Each of these components is a merge module. A merge module contains one or more folders, each of which can contain one or more files or other resources. In fact, you can add a folder, file, project output, or component to the list. Here's a sample of what a merge module might look like:

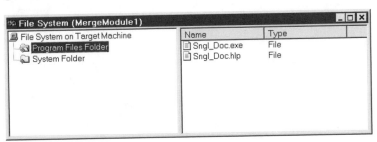

You have full control over the merge module content and settings, just as you do when creating an installation program. For example, you can choose to install a file as a hidden file or make it read-only if necessary. Settings at the folder level determine whether the installation program will always create the folder or if special conditions must exist to create it. For example, you may only want to install a folder if a user selects a specific option. Settings at the merge module level contain information such as the version number, author, and localization.

Setup Project

The Setup Project is a built-in version of the Visual Studio Installer program. However, it might not contain all of the functionality of the separate Visual Studio Installer program (the precise differences are a topic of debate at the time of this writing). You can read about the process of using this project in the previous "Creating an MSI File for an Application" section of this chapter.

Setup Wizard

Using the Setup Wizard allows you to automate many of the tasks required to create a setup program. You still end up with a Setup project, but the wizard helps you through the process of configuring basic project elements. Here's the process you'll go through when using this project type. (I'll assume you've already created a new project and are at the first Setup Project Wizard dialog.)

1. Click Next. The Setup Project Wizard will display a project type dialog that asks what type of project you want to create, as shown next. You have a choice between a rich client and a Web client. You can also choose between a merge module for Windows Installer or a CAB file that someone can download from the Internet. In short, the one wizard will create four different types of installation package. The example will assume a rich client.

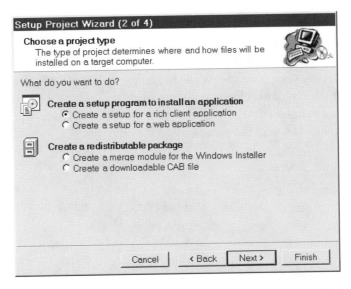

2. Select the project type option. Click Next. The Setup Project Wizard will ask which files to include. We'll use the same Chapter 2 files as before. Add Sngl_Doc.HLP and Sngl_Doc.EXE to the list. Add the following files from the Windows SYSTEM folder to the list in the right pane: MFC70.DLL, MSVCRT.DLL, and MSVCR70.DLL.

3. Select the files you want to add to the project. Click Next. You'll see a summary dialog.

4. Click finish. Visual Studio will configure the project for you.

It's important to understand that the project Visual Studio produces as output is only marginally configured. You still need to add your company information, choose the dialogs that you want the user to see, and generally customize the installation program. This wizard offers a way to start the installation program project faster. It allows you to configure a basic program without forgetting any of the essentials.

Web Setup Project

This project works essentially the same as the deployment project. The difference is that you'll deploy your code to a Web site, rather than to a LAN. You still have access to all of the standard folders, but the project begins with a Web folder setup. In short, this is a template designed to reduce the amount of work required to create a Web deployment. It works the same way as the other projects in this section.

Appendices and Glossary

OBJECTIVES

▶ Learn how to get the best deal on third party components

▶ Obtain an overview of some third party components and control

▶ Discover where you can find more information about Visual C++ .NET

▶ Find a glossary of every technical word and acronym in the book

ActiveX Component Resources

IN THIS CHAPTER:

How to Get the Best Deal

Pitfalls of Buying Components and Tools

Components You May Want for Your Toolbox

This appendix tells you how to find just the right component and looks at some of the third party components available on the market. You'll probably find most of these products in your favorite computer store or programmer's catalog. This appendix isn't complete by any means—it merely shows a selection of ActiveX components from a variety of vendors. This way, if you don't see what you need, you can always contact one of the vendors listed here to see if they can provide the component you need.

BROWSER ALERT

Some of the products in this appendix are from other countries, such as England and Canada. In some cases, developers in the United States may want to try to purchase the products locally instead of relying on an overseas vendor. One of my favorite places to shop is Programmer's Paradise (**http://www.programmersparadise.com/**). You can also find good products at CDW (**http://www.cdw.com/default.asp**) and PC Connection (**http://www.pcconnection.com/**).

How to Get the Best Deal

Choosing a component can be a difficult task. How do you know one component is better than another when the descriptions provided by the vendors that produce them are almost identical? In addition, other features such as royalty rates could make a big difference in the way you view a component. Let's look at some of the criteria you should use when selecting a component. The following list tells what you might want to look for in addition to functionality. This list isn't all-inclusive (some people may have criteria that are unique to their situation), but you'll find that these kinds of considerations will help you make an informed buying decision. The important point is that this list will help you choose between a component that provides a lot of really nice features and one that's best suited to your needs.

BROWSER ALERT

There are many places to look for ActiveX components; some of them allow you to download a demo version of the product. You'll want to check Dave Central (**http://www.davecentral.com**), which provides reviews for many of the software products. This site also provides links to the vendor site so you can learn more about the product. One of the nicer features of this site is 4that it categorizes the software for you. For example, there are separate sections for programming and Web authoring.

▶ **Royalties**   Some companies charge a royalty when you use their product for commercial purposes. If you plan to use their product in a commercial application, you may have to pay the company royalties to maintain the licensing arrangement. Always look for products that don't charge a royalty. That way you don't have to worry about licensing the product. If you don't find one in this category, start looking for an OEM (original equipment manufacturer) licensing arrangement. Sometimes you can find a product with an annual fee or other "one-shot" licensing scheme. Using a product that requires a royalty will also increase the price of your product, so looking around for a royalty-free product is always a good idea.

▶ **Source code**   There's that rare breed of components you can buy with some level of source code support. Some of them require an additional fee to get the source. If you're a consultant or someone who distributes applications commercially, the cost of buying source is minimal compared to what you'll gain by having it. Not only will the source help you learn new programming techniques, but you can also use it to enhance the component you've purchased. Source code is a rarity when buying an ActiveX component, but you do see it offered.

▶ **Recommendations from other programmers**   Buggy software is a common problem today. Unfortunately, companies that produce this kind of software are usually good at marketing and offer just about everything you can imagine without delivering anything of the sort. It doesn't take most programmers long to figure out they should have gotten a few recommendations from other people before buying such products. It's likely that someone has purchased a product that you're thinking about buying. See if you can get a few opinions before you buy.

▶ **Demo or shareware versions**   If you can't get a recommendation from another programmer, finding a demo or shareware version of the product you want to use can save you a lot of grief later. Sure, it won't be full-featured, and some vendors actually make the shareware or demo version hide flaws in the full-featured product, but it's better than buying the product without even viewing it first. If you do try a shareware or demo version, see if other programmers have tried both the demo and final product. The comments they provide will help you understand how the shareware or demo version of the product varies from what you'll actually buy.

▶ **Money-back guarantee**   Vendors are getting smarter as the software industry matures. It's surprising to see how many offer a 30 to 60-day money-back guarantee with their product. What you'll need to find out about first, though, are the money-back guarantee terms. Make sure you can try the product on a small project or two and return it if it doesn't work as advertised. You'll also need to check the return policy of any third party vendors. In a few cases, vendors haven't honored their money-back guarantee when a

programmer bought their product through a third party. Since the third
party seller didn't have a money-back guarantee either, the programmer
ended up eating the cost of the purchase.

▶ **Company stability and support**   Programmers rely on vendors to
provide updates on a regular basis to remain competitive. If the one-man
shop you buy your component from goes out of business tomorrow, how
will you support the product you build with it? The problem doesn't apply
only to practical matters such as new technology; you'll also need support
when a customer calls in with a bug that isn't in your code. You'll find that
interactions between your program and a third party products happen more
often than you'd like. Make sure you buy from a stable vendor who
provides good support.

▶ **Cost per component versus quality**   Some vendors offer a grab bag of
components at a low cost. Be aware that those components may not be the
best quality. Think about your own business. Could you afford to offer a
lot of product for a low cost if it took a lot of time to put the application
together? In most cases, you'll find that a vendor who offers a lot of product
at a low cost must have cut corners somewhere. If someone's willing to offer
you something for close to nothing, make sure you take a hard look at the
product before you buy. You may find that you're getting an extra good buy,
but more often than not you're buying a box of trouble. The component
you get won't be worth the time and effort to install it, much less use in
a project.

▶ **Flexibility**   One of the products discussed in this appendix, Graphics
Server, offers at least six levels of platform support: DLL, VBX, VCL
(Delphi component), OCX, FLL, and C++ class. This range is a real plus
because you never know when you'll need to use a component you bought
for Delphi or Visual C++, for example, on some other platform, such as
Visual Basic. Consultants frequently face this situation, because the job or
the client often dictate which language you'll use for a particular project.
Flexibility takes other forms as well. For example, a communications package
may allow you to use nine or ten different protocols. Products that allow
you to do more than the minimum needed are always a better deal than
those that don't.

▶ **Efficiency**   Some components are less attractive for application building
because they require too many resources. Some vendors try to stick every
bit of functionality known to programmers into one component. Sure, it'll
allow you to write any kind of program in just ten minutes; but it also requires
32 MB of memory to run, which means no one is going to be able to run

the application you build. In addition, even Microsoft is emphasizing the value of small ActiveX component modules. Obviously, components don't require 32 MB of memory to run, but there's an important reason to emphasize this point. You're going to run into situations when you think you have to add one more bell or whistle to a project, only to find users complain that it's slow or won't run well on their machine. Look for the small and efficient components. Get the job done with the least number of resources possible, and the people using your program will be a lot happier.

Pitfalls of Buying Components and Tools

Some people are gadget prone. They need to have every new gadget that appears on the horizon, whether the gadget makes sense or not. Many independent developers are this way because they're looking for anything that will speed the development process and make their company more profitable. However, what happens when you're a manager of a large development company? Having a gadget fetish, in this case, can cost you a job. Most companies frown on purchases that don't affect the bottom line in some positive way.

Many of the large development organizations I've talked with refuse to use any form of third party tool at all, including components. Smaller development houses may have a hard time understanding this policy, because third party components and tools are supposed to make things easier and improve productivity. There's an explanation for these two opposing views of third party products. For large organizations, the reasons not to use third party tools and components are simple.

▶ Components cost quite a bit on a per-seat basis. The cost is much higher for a large organization than for a small one, and even a single gadget buying mistake can cost a lot.

▶ At least some number of third party products are poorly integrated with Visual C++, making it likely that at least some workstations won't be able to use the product. A loss of functionality for one team member incurs problems for the entire team.

▶ Third party products have a learning curve, which increases the complexity of the development environment. Large organizations try to make the programming environment as simple as possible.

Large organizations can still benefit from using third party components and tools. A component library can reduce development time if you get the right components and they work well with your development environment. Likewise, tools in the right hands can make tasks such as debugging complex applications simple. Most large company managers are smart enough to realize there's a potential to increase productivity—they just don't know how to get around the problems of using third party components and tools.

However, large organizations *can* get around some of the problems of using third party tools and components. For example, many third party vendors will send an evaluation copy of a product. Your organization can also buy in bulk, rather than in a piecemeal fashion as many organizations do. After all, a third party component or tool is just like any other piece of software—the only difference is how the individual developers use the software.

Using training tapes or guru techniques reduce the cost of training yet still provide employees with the information needed to use third party packages. It's not necessary to send everyone to a seminar to learn how to use a new product. What you need to do is send someone who's willing to take good notes and provide classes to others on your development staff when back in the office. This person becomes your product guru—the person everyone turns to when there's a question about how to use the product. You should give your guru time to study the ins and outs of the third party product to ensure that the company receives maximum benefit from its use.

NOTE

All prices in this chapter are current list prices as of the time of writing. They may change without notice. Always check with the vendors for product availability and pricing. You may find that they have a new product that works even better than the one listed here.

Components You May Want for Your Toolbox

Finding the right component for your application can save programming time, especially if the component is highly customizable. This section contains a list of some of the more popular components available on the market today. The product list also acquaints you with some of the more popular vendors—many provide a larger array of components than I've provided here. You can always call these vendors to see if they make a component you need before attempting to write one by hand.

Graphics Server
Pinnacle WebWorkz Inc.
Telephone: (800) 231-1293/(206) 625-6900
Fax: (206) 625-9102
Internet: **http://www.graphicsserver.com/**

This is the full-fledged version of the runtime product included with products such as Visual Basic and Delphi. It comes with DLL, VBX, VCL (Delphi component), OCX, FLL, and C++ class support, making it just about the most versatile tool in this appendix. Like the runtime version, the server runs as an independent application outside of your application. However, this product provides a lot more than the runtime version does.

Graphics Server supports primitive commands that draw circles or squares. You can use it to perform complex drawing tasks with many products—even those that provide little in the way of native drawing support. This feature makes Graphics Server more than just an application programming tool; you could potentially use it with a variety of products in a lot of different environments.

If you don't want to work with graphics primitives, and a graph or chart is your goal, you can use the included ChartBuilder product. This is the full-featured version of the Graph control included with Visual Basic. (The latest version of Graphics Server incorporates all of these capabilities into a single product.) Just tell ChartBuilder what data points you want to display and what type of graph or chart to create. It takes care of all the details. There isn't room in this appendix to talk about all of the features of this product, but here are a few more:

▶ You can use Graphics Server SDK with Microsoft Excel and Word for Windows.

▶ Versions 4.5 and above fully support VBA.

▶ It includes support for spline graphs, floating bar graphs, and error bars on all log graphs.

ALLText
TList
MetaDraw
Bennet-Tec Information Systems
50 Jericho Turnpike
Jericho, NY 11753
Voice: (516) 997-5596
Fax: (516) 997-5597
E-mail: controls@bennet-tec.com
Internet: **http://www.bennet-tec.com**

ALLText is essentially a word processor with a little extra oomph. It includes hypertext support, embedded OLE objects for graphics or other document embedding, RTF (rich text format) input and output, and data-aware support. The PEN edition provides support for pen-based computing—a nice feature if you have to provide this kind of support.

RTF is the word processing format used by the Windows help compiler. Many word processors use this format as a means for exchanging data with other word processors. The data-aware support means that ALLText includes the name of the application that created an object as part of the object. You could theoretically provide a small text processor in your application and allow the user to export a file to a full-fledged word processor such as Microsoft Word without too many problems.

TList is an enhanced outlining control. It provides more features than your typical word processor, making it more like the professional outlining tools that you see on the market. One of its special features is the ability to customize items displayed in the outline. For example, you could give an item a special color or use a different icon to display it. This product also supports advanced features such as item hiding, bookmarks, category images, and drag and drop.

MetaDraw is an image object. You can use it to add CAD capability to an application. It also provides a viewer, and you can use it to create hotspots on drawings. These hotspots allow users to select actions. For example, you could use an image on a Web site to provide a link to a destination. The control also allows for hypergraphic events such as mouseover so that you can change the drawing as the user interacts with it.

Communications Library 3.5
Fax Plus
EllTech
2007 Manassas Drive
Woodstock, GA 30189
Fax: (678) 494-2023
Internet: **http://www.elltech.com/**

Communications Library is a general communications library, which means that it provides many generic capabilities that will allow you to build a specific type of communication program. It supports five terminal emulations: ANSI, TTY, VT52, VT100, and VT220. In addition, it provides support for eight file transfer protocols, including Kermit, CompuServe B+, and X, Y, and Z modem. Unlike some packages, the Z modem support also provides auto-recovery support.

Supporting many types of modems is one of the big problems in writing a communications program. Communications Library comes with over 150 initialization strings to support the most common modems. You'll also find a selection of Pascal subprograms and forms. The forms include those required for serial port and parameter selection, phone dialing, and many other functions.

EllTech includes VBXs, DLLs, and 16/32-bit OCXs with Communications Library. It provides OLE 2 support for all of your file transfer needs. The library will support multiple communication ports (eight is the practical limit).

Fax Plus is another communications product from EllTech. You can use it with any class 1, 2, or 2.0 fax modem. Fortunately, the product also includes some components you can use to detect the type of modem—a requirement if you plan to distribute your application commercially.

One of the more interesting features of Fax Plus is that it supports faxes through printed output. In other words, you can build an application in such a way that it can take the printed output from another application and send it as a fax. You can also import BMP, PCX, DCX, or TIFF files to send as faxes. The standard fax format is ASCII text.

Unlike Communications Library, Fax Plus automatically handles the fax modem initialization for you (dependent on modem support). The package also contains sample programs and other documentation to show you how to use the product. Both Fax Plus and Communications Library are royalty free.

MediaSuite
ImageKnife
OLYMPUS Software Europe GmbH
Wendenstraße 14-16
Hamburg, Germany
Voice: +49-40-23773-411
Fax: +49-40-23773-644
Internet: **http://www.olympus-software.com/**

MediaSuite allows you to create all kinds of media presentations using file formats such as AVI. You can use its WinG-based display technology to create transition effects, background buffering of images and sounds, irregular hot spots, and custom cursors. This product also provides animated sprite capabilities. The best part is that you can see all of these capabilities at design time—meaning you won't spend as much time compiling an application or setting up a Web site to test a particular design.

Some of the special MediaSuite capabilities include the ability to decompress Iterated Systems' resolution-independent fractal files. The product includes editors that allow you to perform a variety of tasks, including hot spot definition, batch palette editing, and animated sprite assembly.

ImageKnife is a complex graphics OCX that supports the Microsoft Access Paintbrush Picture OLE Object format. It helps you acquire images using the TWAIN scanner interface. That's the same interface used by CorelDRAW and other similar products. Once you acquire an image, you can change its appearance and store it in a file or database. You could use this library to provide an added level of support for graphics databases using the Access database format. Of course, you aren't limited to Access databases; you can also use this product with other DBMSs that support this graphics format.

Don't get the idea that you can't use ImageKnife for some of the more mundane graphics chores in your application. It also supports other file formats, including BMP, DIB, JPEG, GIF, PCX, TIFF, and Targa. You can display those files as true color (24-bit), Super VGA (8-bit), VGA (8-bit), or monochrome images. This versatility makes ImageKnife a good graphics library for most applications.

Both MediaSuite and ImageKnife come with a 90-day money-back guarantee. You can also include these products in your applications royalty free.

Multi Shape Button, Date Select, Masked Edit, and SysInfo
Aditi Inc.
10940 NE 33rd Place
Suite 204
Bellevue, WA 98004
Voice: (206) 828-9646
Fax: (206) 828-9587
Internet: **http://www.aditi.com/**

NOTE

While you can download these controls (collectively known as Aditi UI Widgets for ActiveX) for free as of this writing, there's no guarantee they'll remain so. In addition, you'll need to contact the vendor regarding licensing and any legal requirements before using these controls on an Internet site.

Multi Shape Button is a button that can adjust its shape in a number of ways, including ellipse, triangle, pentagon, and rhombus. If the control doesn't come with a shape to suit your needs, you can always draw your own shape. Like many other controls of this type, Multi Shape Button allows you to use custom icons and captions for each button state.

Date Select provides a selection box for picking a date. Instead of entering a date by hand, the user clicks a speed button. Highlighting a particular date element (month, day, or year) changes that element when the speed button is clicked. Clicking on another part of the control displays a user configurable calendar.

You can never be certain of what a user will enter at a particular prompt. The results can be disastrous unless you include a lot of error-trapping code. Masked Edit takes all the work out of doing this for you. It restricts user entries to specific, predefined input. Database applications have had this capability for years—it's nice to see it available for the Internet as well. Aditi provides a number of predefined masks for you and also allows you to add any custom masks that you need.

SysInfo allows you to scan a client machine and learn basic parameters about it, such as operating system version and the size of its hard drive. You can also detect processor type. Detecting this kind of information makes it easier for you to provide users with specific feedback messages for errors.

RoboHelp
eHelp
7777 Fay Avenue
Suite 201
La Jolla, CA 92037
Voice: (800) 358-9370
International Voice: (858) 459-6365
Fax: (858) 459-6366
Internet: **http://www.ehelp.com/**

NOTE

This section doesn't even begin to cover all of the tools offered by eHelp—all of which are Internet oriented. Make sure you visit their Web site to learn about other tools that you can use to increase your productivity.

While Microsoft seems bent on moving you away from the Windows Help format, eHelp seems equally determined to move you toward it. RoboHelp allows you to display a Windows help file from the user's browser. You might ask yourself why you need this control. HTML doesn't currently provide the same search capabilities that the Windows Help file format does. In addition, using a help file format that the user is familiar with is one sure way to decrease support calls. Special features of this control include the ability to change the button bitmap (48 come with the product) and the type of help displayed.

Light Lib Business
Light Lib Images
Light Lib Multimedia
Light Lib Magic Menus
Light Lib /400
DFL Software, Inc.
55 Eglinton Avenue East
Suite 208
Toronto, ON M4P 1G8
Voice: (416) 487-2660
Fax: (416) 487-3656
Internet: **http://www.powersoft.com/partners/gallery/download/dfl.htm**

Light Lib Business allows you to create charts and graphs. The actual number of charts and graphs wasn't available as of this writing, but you can be sure it will include the basic 2-D and 3-D chart types: bar, line, pie, gantt complex ribbon, stacked, and percent. The context menu displayed when you right-click the control is special, too. It allows the user either to save the current image as a file or to place it on the desktop as wallpaper. The context menu contains the usual entries such as Copy and Properties as well.

DFL bills Light Lib Images as a complete document and image management library. It provides controls for adjusting an image. For example, you can adjust the image brightness and contrast. The control also provides gamma-correction capabilities. As with most libraries of this type, you can perform image manipulations such as rotating. This control also includes the context menu entries of the Light Lib Business control.

The Light Lib Multimedia controls make your animated presentations better. DFL used to sell the sound and video controls as separate packages, but found that most customers ended up getting both packages anyway. The sound-related controls provide a complete set of adjustments for a typical soundboard that looks very much like the Volume Control dialog provided by Windows 9x/2000. In addition to the volume controls, you'll find a media player and set of file controls. The video-related controls look much like the AVI player provided by Windows 9x/2000. The difference is that the Light Lib player also provides volume controls. This control provides a speed setting as well that allows you to control the rate at which the video plays back.

Are you tired of looking at the same old gray Windows menus? Even if you add icons to them, there isn't a lot you can do to make using a menu fun. The Light Lib Magic Menu control can change all that. Now you can have menus that use an image as a background. You can also add some interesting-looking bitmaps for menu entries, instead of relying on simple icons to get the job done. Best of all, programming is minimal.

Bridging the gap between today's modern LAN and that old mainframe is a concern for more than a few programmers. DFL designed Light Lib /400 to make bridging that gap easier than ever before. For the most part, you'll use this product for client/server application support.

Acrobat ActiveX
Adobe Systems Inc.
345 Park Avenue
San Jose, CA 95110-2704
Voice: (800) 833-6687/(408) 536-6000
Fax: (408) 537-6000
Internet: **http://www.adobe.com/support/downloads/44ae.htm**

Adobe's Acrobat reader has already appeared in several places. If you're a programmer, you've probably used it to read help files in book form on your machine at one time or another. Acrobat uses PDF (Portable Document Format) to display information in a way that makes allowances for the display device. This ActiveX version lets you view PDF files using your browser instead of downloading the file and loading the entire Acrobat reader. You can also add support for this component to applications to provide polished support information or other printable materials.

Online Resource Guide

A s a programmer, you know the value of getting help when you need it rather than trying to solve a problem on your own. After all, it's very likely that someone else has already seen the problem you're working on and has just the solution you need. On the other hand, if you're anything like me, you also know about information overload. Just think of that pile of unread technical journals sitting on your desk. Getting a solution to your problem can involve wading through many "solutions" that won't work. In other words, you may have to fight through an excess of information to find the answer to your question. The problem isn't so much not knowing what information you need or where to find it, but how to track down the right source.

NOTE

I've provided quite a few figures and illustrations in this appendix that are typical of what you'll see on the Internet. However, by the time you actually read this appendix, those Web pages will have changed at least a little. Since the Internet is such a fluid resource, you need to consider most of the figures as examples only; your display will likely look different from how mine looked as I wrote this.

Unless you're hiding in a dark corner somewhere, you'll know that the Internet has become the number one source of information for most people. Most programmers I know have had at least a little experience with the Internet (many are Internet commandos and spend excessive time on the Internet). The type of information that each Web site provides varies, but in the long run you'll find that most of the developer sites provide some level of help you can use to solve a problem. More important, you'll expose yourself to a wealth of new ideas by tuning into discussions of the latest industry trends or programming techniques. The problem with many programmers is that they stop there. You can get a lot more from the Internet if your want to. The following list should give you a few ideas.

▶ **World view rather than local view** If you talk with your buddy down the hall, you're getting the local view of Visual C++ programming techniques. On the other hand, talking with someone on the Internet might give you the English, Australian, or Japanese view of Visual C++ programming techniques. This international flavor provides you with a better appreciation of features you might not have considered important before. In addition, the cultural differences work together to help you see new ways of using features.

▶ **Access to vendor representatives** This is probably one of the reasons you started visiting the Internet in the first place, but most people don't realize what they're really getting. Aside from the talking you do with other users, the Internet also gives you access to vendor representatives. At times, I've started a conversation with three, or even four, people who work for the company whose product I'm using. You'll find that the expert knowledge that the vendor representative provides often mixes with the real-world view of the other users. The result is that you actually get better information from the online service than you could have gotten from the vendor's technical support line.

▶ **Vendor BBS is alive and well**   If you've been programming for any length of time, you probably remember using a vendor BBS to get the information you needed in the not-too-distant past. The Internet provides many of the features you once got from a vendor BBS. For example, you can go online and download the latest patches for any Microsoft product (**http://www.microsoft.com/downloads/search.asp**). The same holds true for other vendors. I've often found a needed NetWare patch on the Novell's Web site (**http://support.novell.com/products/**). Anyone writing an application that requires access to Novell's NetWare knows the significance of being able to get a required patch quickly.

▶ **Hardware vendor access**   How many times have you started working on a device driver or other low-level code only to find that the driver you have doesn't work or that you need additional information from the vendor? If you think the Internet is all software, think again. Creative, ATI, Compaq, Dell, Hewlett-Packard, IBM, and other hardware vendors provide valuable services here too. I think you'll find the hardware presence useful each time you need to download a new driver or ask a configuration question. You'll find the same level of expertise in these areas that you find in the software areas.

NOTE

Don't get the idea that the Internet is an inexhaustible source of proven answers to your problems. Even though the information on the Internet (or any other online service for that matter) is free, it doesn't come with a guarantee of accuracy—not every person you run into when using an online service will be an expert. Most of them are average users like you. However, I've had the pleasure of running into some truly remarkable people from time to time while browsing through the messages. In fact, some people are constantly looking for ways to improve their Visual C++ programming techniques in their spare time. You'll usually find them in a newsgroup or list server somewhere, just waiting to share the programming techniques they've developed with you. Fortunately, you'll also find more than a few experts on these newsgroups as well. Some people just hang around looking for good ideas or good questions. By asking a question, you're actually providing them some food for thought.

The Internet certainly fulfills the idea of an "information highway." You can use it as an extremely valuable research tool. Exchanging ideas with other people has always been a part of the Internet. Creating a Web site for your employees at remote sites to check into is a possibility, too. However, none of these uses for the Internet really tells you what it's all about and how you can use it to your best advantage. That's what this appendix will tell you. I'm going to spend some time telling you about the foundations of the Internet and the tools you can use to explore it.

What you should come away with is a new appreciation for what the Internet's really all about. Surfing the Net should be an experience that helps you meet specific goals and broadens your horizons. The problem is that with such a large number of items on the menu, you could easily get lost.

Finding What You're Looking For

If you do a lot of research on the Internet as I do, you'll realize the benefit of finding what you need quickly. In most cases, this means finding a search engine like Lycos. There are specialty search engines such as Google Groups (a place to find information contained in newsgroups) as well. Although these different search sites can provide radically different results when you make a request, they use similar mechanisms to allow you to make the request in the first place. The following sections discuss techniques for using online resources effectively.

Performing a Search

Let's talk about keyword searches for a second. All you need to do to perform a keyword search is enter one or more keywords into the blank, select a search engine, and then click the Search button. Internet Explorer or Navigator will take you to the appropriate search Web site and start the search for you.

It's time to try out a search. Select Lycos as your search engine (you'll find it at **http://www.lycos.com**), type **ActiveX** in the blank, and then click Search (this will work with either browser). Depending on the security level you've selected, you may see a security dialog before either browser does anything. Click on Yes to clear it. You'll end up on a Web page like the one shown in Figure B-1. You should notice a few things about this page. The first feature is that you can refine your search. Maybe a single keyword really didn't refine the search enough, and you need to find something more specific. I haven't found a one search Web page that doesn't provide this ability in some form. In fact, many of them do provide detailed search mechanisms.

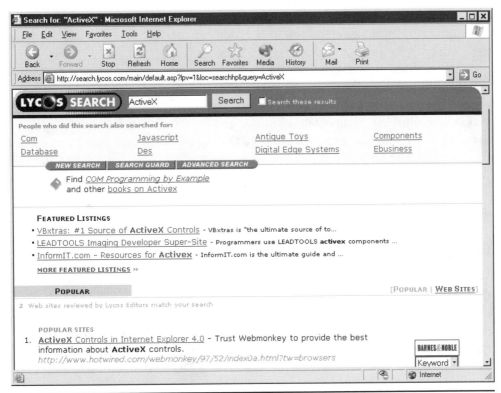

Figure B-1   *A search Web page like Lycos allows you to find specific information on the Internet.*

You should notice something else. Each one of the result entries (also called a "hit") contains a confidence level, expressed numerically (some Web sites provide this feature only as an option, so you may not see it all the time). This tells you how confident the search engine is about the results it found. Normally, the search engine uses a variety of criteria to determine this, like the number of times the keyword appears in an article or other source of information. Obviously, a Boolean search starts to make a confidence calculation more difficult by increasing the number of criteria for which the calculation must account. The method of determining a confidence factor is one of the things that will determine which search engines you use. I use a variety of search engines for different purposes (more on that in a bit).

Some search engines, like Lycos, also provide special features. For example, Figure B-1 shows that Lycos provides a list of related topics (this figure doesn't show confidence levels). You can use this list to find related information quickly. Unfortunately, these specialty features often don't work as well as advertised.

Always take the specialty feature information with a grain of salt, since it doesn't provide a confidence factor and you have no way of knowing what the search engine used as a basis for finding these additional links for you.

Web search pages normally don't list every site that the search engine finds. Notice that Lycos lists only ten of them (other services will allow you to change the number of entries listed as part of the search criteria). You have to click the Next Documents button to see the next group of ten on the list. The order in which you choose to list the various hits determines which sites get listed first. Lycos defaults to listing the sites it finds by confidence level. This makes sense because you want to find the best sites first. You can click the List by Web Sites link if you want an alphabetical listing. Some search engines provide other sorting criteria. For example, the Google Groups site (I'll talk about it shortly) allows you to sort by author as well.

Choosing Search Engines That Work for You

You might think that one search engine would be enough to fulfill your needs, but that simply isn't true. The problem with trying to come up with a "best fit" answer for any of these search engines is that each one works differently. A search engine that works fine for my needs may not work at all for you. I thought it important, therefore, to provide a list of some of the more common search engines and a quick overview of how they work. I'd encourage you to try them all to see what works best for you and in what situations. Table B-1 discusses the search engines I use.

Search Engine	Location on Internet	Description
AltaVista	**http://www.altavista.com/**	A benefit of using this search engine is a lack of information overload. It returns only the amount of information you want about each hit. The service tends to focus on Web pages containing articles, which means you'll get some narrow hits when using it. AltaVista's descriptions use excerpts from articles or other sources of information that's accessed. This service uses a somewhat esoteric Boolean search engine, making it difficult to narrow your search criteria.

Table B-1   *A List of Common Search Web Sites*

Search Engine	Location on Internet	Description
Excite	**http://www.excite.com/**	This service focuses on Web sites rather than pages within a particular site. In other words, you can get to a general area of interest, but then Excite leaves it to you to find the specific information you're looking for. This can be an advantage when you're not really sure about the specifics of a search. A wide view can help you see everything available, then you can make some refinements. Excite also provides a summary of what you'll find at a particular site. It tends to concentrate on discussion groups and vendor-specific information.
FTP Search	**http://archie.is.co.za/ftpsearch**	You might not need to search for files very often, but when you do it's usually an emergency. FTP Search is the best engine around for finding files because you can specify so many specifics about the file you want. You can even specify when you want to perform a case sensitive or case insensitive search for the filename. If you ever need an array of FTP search engines to find what you need, try FTP Search Engines (**http://www.ftpsearchengines. com/**).
Google Advanced Search	**http://www.google.com/advanced_ search**	Google Advanced Search is one of the most complete search engines today on the Internet, but it's also one of the most complex. I've found many items of interest using this search engine when they were completely unavailable on any other search engine. For example, this is one of the best ways to search for information on Microsoft's Web sites because you can check everything at once. I'll often find Knowledge Base articles here that Microsoft's own search engine won't reveal. This site is also adding new search features, such as the ability to look for images.

Table B-1 *A List of Common Search Web Sites* (continued)

Search Engine	Location on Internet	Description
Google Groups	**http://groups.google.com/**	For those of you who remember Deja News, this is the new version of that search engine. You can use this search engine when you need to find information in news and chat groups (among others). The only problem with this particular engine is you might find yourself doing a search more than once to get everything it provides. The engine enables you to search by a specific group or subgroup, or of all the newsgroups on the Internet. In fact, this is the most complete engine you'll ever find for newsgroup work, a real must for some types of research.
HotBot	**http://www.hotbot.com/**	This service provides a fairly broad range of site search options and a very clean interface. Consider this site a halfway point between complexity and the ability to search for what you need without delving through several levels of menus. The search results normally contain links organized by the number of words that matched. You'll see one or two sentences that describe the Web site, making it easier to determine if the site contains what you want.
Infoseek	**http://www.go.com/**	The strength of this particular service is that it provides just the facts. It uses excerpts from articles or other sources of information it finds. The hits are much narrower than some search engines provide because Infoseek concentrates on specific Web pages rather than general sites. The only problem with this particular service is that it severely limits your capability to narrow search criteria.

Table B-1   *A List of Common Search Web Sites* (continued)

Search Engine	Location on Internet	Description
Lycos	**http://www.lycos.com/**	Of the common search engines, Lycos tends to provide the most diverse information. It catalogs both Web sites and pages, but it concentrates on pages whenever possible. Lycos provides a combination of summaries and excerpts to describe the content of a particular hit. Its capability to narrow a search is superior to most search engines available right now. The downside is that there's almost too much detail. If you aren't sure what you're looking for, you'll quickly find yourself searching false leads and ending up with totally unusable information.
Yahoo	**http://www.yahoo.com/**	This search engine provides the best organization of all the engines listed here. It categorizes every hit in a variety of ways, which increases your chances of finding information. This service, however, doesn't provide the broad range of information that you'll find with other search engines. It also relies on very short summaries to explain the contents of a particular hit. Yahoo works well as a first-look type of search engine— something that gives you the broad perspective of a single keyword.
Web Crawler	**http://www.Webcrawler.com/**	This search engine requires a bit more work than most to use because it doesn't provide much in the way of excerpts or summaries. On the other hand, it provides a full Boolean search engine and an extremely broad base of information. The only search engine in this list that provides a broader base is Lycos.

Table B-1   *A List of Common Search Web Sites* (continued)

Microsoft's Presence on the Internet

Microsoft was late to the Internet party, but they've more than made up for it in recent years. If you really want to know what's going on with anything Microsoft, the Internet is the way to go. Microsoft's main URL on the Internet is **http://www.microsoft.com** (its home page is actually located at **http://www.msn.com/**). The number one place that developers want to visit is the Microsoft Developer Network (MSDN) pages (**http://msdn.microsoft.com**). This site contains many white papers, SDK documentation, coding examples, downloads, and other development materials.

You'll also want to visit the Microsoft newsgroups. Many ISPs don't provide full coverage of every Microsoft newsgroup, so you'll want to visit the Microsoft news server at **news.microsoft.com**. You'll find the peer support on the Microsoft newsgroups is very good. In addition, Microsoft employees often participate in the discussions, so you get the best possible answer to your questions. Obviously, that's only the tip of the iceberg, but it's a good place to start. You'll also want to visit the non-Microsoft developer sites that your local ISP does support.

Getting a Good Start

It would be difficult at best to come up with a definitive hierarchy of URLs for all the sites that Microsoft supports. One of the reasons that the Internet is such a good place to provide information is that it's totally free form. In addition, the means for changing the structure of your site resides on your own server. Since Microsoft controls the format and presentation of its Web site, it can, and usually does, change it quite often. Figure B-2 shows how the main MSDN page looked at the time of this writing (note that I've customized this page to my tastes; your page may look slightly different).

BROWSER ALERT

You can search the Microsoft Web site quickly and easily by using its special search engine at **http://search.microsoft.com/us/default.asp**. *This search engine provides special features that allow you to look at a specific kind of Microsoft product or at the entire site. You can also choose the type of search (including the traditional Boolean search) to perform.*

So, the question you need to answer is how you're going to find anything without resorting to the search techniques we discuss earlier in this appendix. Microsoft usually follows the same pattern in creating its Web pages, so coming up with a search method is easy.

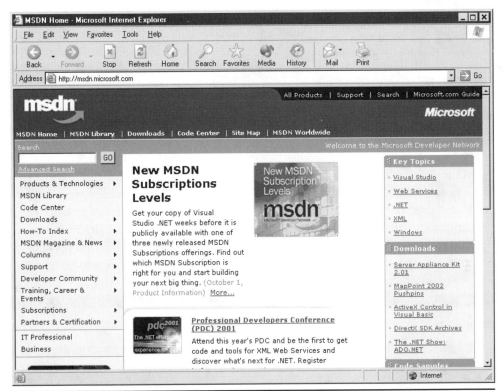

Figure B-2   *The main MSDN Web page gives you some clues for finding information quickly.*

Look at the left side of the page and you'll see a bar. This bar usually contains a list of related topics. Clicking on these links will take you to other sections of the Microsoft Web site—general areas in this case.

You'll also find a method of obtaining specific information on most of Microsoft's Web pages. In this case, you'll need to type a search phrase in the Search field, and then click on Go. You could also select a location from the bar across the top of the page. The sites you can select from on this page take you to areas that cater to other MSDN related needs. Other Microsoft Web pages will take you to places where you can find specifics about the language you're using or other topics of interest.

Finding a Newsgroup

Getting information isn't the only reason to use the Internet; it's important to provide information to other people as well. Newsgroups enable you to exchange information with other people. They also help you obtain additional information or learn how to perform a task by asking detailed questions. Newsgroups provides a cooperative environment for sharing information with peers.

TIP

Make sure you check out all the Web links in this book for newsgroup ideas. Just about every chapter in the book contains a Web link that can help you find Web sites or newsgroups (in some cases, both).

Microsoft provides more than a few newsgroups, and finding the right one might have been a little difficult if it hadn't furnished some kind of menu system. Finding what you need in the way of newsgroups is a three-step process. First, go to **http:// communities.microsoft.com/newsgroups/default.asp?icp=GSS&slcid=us** and you'll find a page like the one shown in Figure B-3. If you're looking for product information, then choose one of the menu entries on the left side. However, many

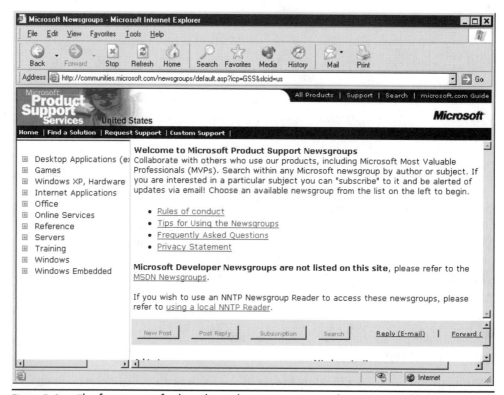

Figure B-3   *The first step in finding the right newsgroup is selecting a product type.*

of you will want to view the MSDN newsgroups, so you'll need to click the MSDN Newsgroups link.

Figure B-4 shows a typical view of the MSDN newsgroups. As you can see, they're in a hierarchical format. Select any category and a subcategory (such as Component Development and COM+). Click the plus sign next to COM+ and you'll see a list of the newsgroups associated with that topic.

Select a newsgroup and you'll see a list of message headings for that newsgroup. The controls on the Web page shown in Figure B-4 enable you to send and receive messages on the newsgroup, even if you don't set up a standard newsreader. You can also type the name of the newsgroup into your newsreader. This enables you to find the newsgroup in the list of newsgroups your newsreader has downloaded. You can then subscribe to the newsgroup and view it normally.

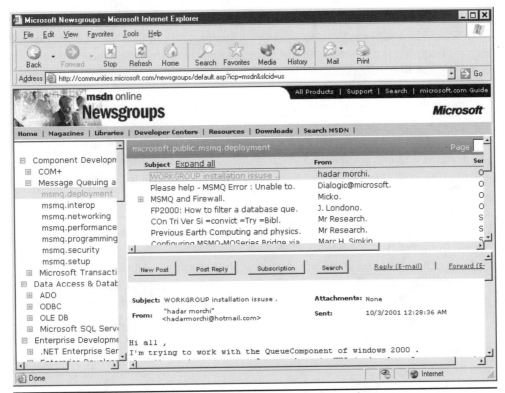

Figure B-4 *Once you select a product type, you can find out what newsgroups are available.*

Microsoft Knowledge Base

Before I get into a full-fledged, detailed look at the Microsoft offerings on the Internet, I'd like to explore one special Microsoft URL called the Microsoft Knowledge Base. The Microsoft Knowledge Base isn't a standard Web site like the others you'll find on the Internet. Rather, it's a library of articles, white papers, and other sources of information that you'll need in order to use specific Microsoft products. We'll see later how this special forum fits into the overall scheme of things.

Right now, I'd like to cover why it's important and show how you use it. I often look at the Microsoft Knowledge Base for information about the future direction of Microsoft products. For example, I was able to find several white papers about Visual C++ .NET, even during the beta process (these white papers have a "Beta" moniker on them to keep them separate from white papers for released products). You can also find out a lot about problems people are having—people just like you—and Microsoft's suggested solutions. Finally, you can find the technical details of a product. It's not too difficult to figure out that the Knowledge Base is more like a fax support line than anything else. However, the method you use to interact with it is a lot different.

The problem with using automated support, in most cases, is that unless you really know what you're looking for, you're not very likely to find it. I've been through some fax support lines that are so unfriendly you won't get any information at all unless you know a specific article name or its number. Microsoft Knowledge Base is different. It provides a search engine that you can use to find the information you're looking for.

So, how do you use this nifty Microsoft offering? Go to **http://search.support. microsoft.com/kb/c.asp**. When you get there, you'll see a search page like the one shown in Figure B-5.

Notice that you need to answer three essential questions. The first asks *what product you're using*. If you don't see your product in the drop-down list, then it's likely that the Microsoft Knowledge Base doesn't provide the information you need. The second question asks *how you want to conduct your search*. In most cases, you'll want to perform a keyword search because you really don't know what to look for. However, there are situations when a Microsoft support person may ask you to look at a specific article number. You can do this by selecting the Specific Article ID Number option. In other cases, you may want to download a driver or other file that a Knowledge Base article refers to instead of the article itself. You can do this using the Specific Driver or Downloadable File option. The third question asks *what you want to find*. You'll enter the keywords, article ID number, or

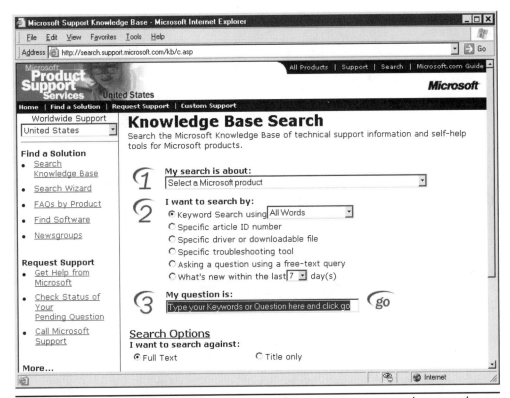

Figure B-5   *The Microsoft Knowledge Base provides an easy to use search engine that helps you find exactly what you need.*

filename that you want to find. Once you've answered these three questions, you can click Find to search the Knowledge Base.

This page does provide two enhancements you can make to the search results. (The first option is just barely visible at the bottom of Figure B-5; make sure you spend some time with the search page online to get familiar with these options.) The first option allows you to choose between performing a full text search (takes longer, but provides more complete information) or a title search only. The second option allows you to add excerpts of the various articles to the article titles displayed on the search result page. The excerpts help you find the information you need without actually going to the article to read it. Often, the first few lines of an article will tell you whether the article is the one that you're looking for.

Glossary

This book includes a glossary so that you can find terms and acronyms easily. It has several important features of which you need to be aware. First, every acronym in the entire book is listed here—even if there's a better than even chance you already know what the acronym means. This way there isn't any doubt that you'll always find everything you need to use the book properly.

Second, these definitions are specific to the book. In other words, when you look through this glossary, you're seeing the words defined in the context in which the book uses them. This might or might not always coincide with current industry usage since the computer industry changes the meaning of words so often.

Finally, the definitions here use a conversational tone in most cases. This means they might sacrifice a bit of puritanical accuracy for the sake of better understanding. The purpose of this glossary is to define the terms in such a way that there's less room for misunderstanding the intent of the book as a whole.

While this glossary is a complete view of the words and acronyms in the book, you'll run into situations where you need to know more. No matter how closely I look at terms throughout the book, there's always a chance I'll miss the one acronym or term that you really need to know. In addition, I've directed your attention to numerous online sources of information, and few of the terms the Web site owners use will appear here unless I also chose to use them in the book. Fortunately, many sites on the Internet provide partial or complete glossaries to fill in the gaps:

- ► Acronym Finder (**http://www.acronymfinder.com/**)
- ► Microsoft Encarta (**http://encarta.msn.com/**)
- ► CKNOW.COM (**http://www.cknow.com/ckinfo/index.htm**)
- ► Webopedia (**http://webopedia.internet.com/**)
- ► yourDictionary.com (formerly A Web of Online Dictionaries) (**http://www.yourdictionary.com/**)

Let's talk about these Web sites a little more. Web sites normally provide acronyms or glossary entries—not both. An acronym site provides only the definition for the acronym that you want to learn about; it doesn't provide an explanation of what the acronym means in everyday computer use. The two extremes in this list are Acronym Finder (acronyms only) and Webopedia (full-fledged glossary entries).

Most of the Web sites that you'll find for computer terms are free. In some cases, such as Microsoft's Encarta, you have to pay for the support provided. However, these locations are still worth the cost because they ensure you understand the terms used in the jargon-filled world of computing.

Webopedia has become one of my favorite places to visit because it provides encyclopedic coverage of many computer terms and includes links to other Web sites. I like the fact that if I don't find a word I need, I can submit it to the Webopedia staff for addition to their dictionary, making Webopedia a community supported dictionary of the highest quality.

One of the interesting features of the yourDictionary.com Web site is that it provides access to more than one dictionary and in more than one language. If English isn't your native tongue, then this is the Web site of choice.

128-bit/40-bit encryption key   See Encryption level

Access control entry   See ACE.

Access control list   See ACL.

Access Token   A definition of the rights that a service or resource requestor has to the operating system. This is the data structure that tells the security system what rights a user has to access a particular object. The object's access requirements are contained in a security descriptor. In short, the security descriptor is the lock and the access token is the key.

ACE (access control entry)   A Windows NT/2000/XP-specific security component. Each object (which could include anything from a file to a piece of memory) contains two access control lists (ACLs). These lists determine what type of access a user, system element, or other type of object will have to the object. Within each ACL are one or more access control entries (ACEs). There's one entry for each user, group, or other object that has access to the object. This entry defines what type of access to grant. For example, a file object can grant read and write rights.

ACL (access control list)   A Windows NT/2000/XP-specific security component. There are two ACLs: the security access control list (SACL), which controls Windows' auditing feature, and the discretionary access control list (DACL), which controls who can actually use the object. The ACLs contain one or more access control entries (ACEs), which determine the actual rights for each user or object for which the ACL grants access.

Active Server Page (ASP)   A special type of scripting environment used by Windows servers equipped with Internet Information Server (IIS). This specialized scripting environment allows the programmer to create flexible Web pages that include server scripts written in a number of languages, such as VBScript, JScript, and PerlScript. The use of variables and other features, such as access to server variables, allows a programmer to create scripts that can compensate for user and environmental needs as well as security concerns. ASP uses HTML to display content to the user.

Active Template Library (ATL)   A special set of header, source, object, and executable files created by Microsoft. The main purpose of ATL is to reduce the size and dependence of COM objects created for use in environments where memory and network bandwidth are a potential problem. For example, an ATL object won't rely on the Microsoft Foundation Classes (MFC). In many cases, the ATL executable is self-contained and doesn't rely on anything other than standard Windows core files. While ATL executable files are smaller than their MFC counterparts, their development is also more complex and they often require the developer to write more code in order to obtain a similar result.

ActiveX control   See OCX.

ActiveX Data Object (ADO)   A local and remote database access technology that relies on OLE-DB to create the connection. ADO is a set of "wrapper" functions that make using OLE-DB and the underlying OLE-DB provider easier. ADO is designed as a replacement for DAO and as an adjunct to ODBC.

ActiveX Data Object Data Control (ADODC)   An unmanaged control used to create a connection to a database. The control doesn't display data, it only makes the dataset available to another control. A developer normally used an ADODC with a grid or other display control.

ActiveX Document   One of several COM-based enabling technologies used on the Internet to display documents in formats that the Internet doesn't support natively, such as the Word for Windows DOC file format. Using ActiveX Document allows the OLE server to take over the browser's frame (menu and other features such as scroll bars) and present the document within the browser window. ActiveX Document is also referred to as ActiveDocument.

ActiveX Movie   One of several COM-based enabling technologies used on the Internet to display real-time video and audio through the use of special file formats such as AVI files. ActiveX Movie may eventually allow companies to provide online presentations that don't require a person's presence at a particular site for participation.

ADO   See ActiveX Data Object.

ADODC   See ActiveX Data Object Data Control.

American Standard Code for Information Interchange (ASCII)   A standard method of equating the numeric representations available in a computer to human-readable form. The number 32 represents a space, for example. The standard ASCII code contains 128 characters (7 bits). The extended ASCII code uses 8 bits for 256 characters. Display adapters from the same machine type usually use the same upper 128 characters. Printers, however, might reserve these upper 128 characters for nonstandard characters. Many Epson printers use them for the italic representations of the lower 128 characters.

Animated GIF   See GIF

API (application programming interface)   A method of defining a standard set of function calls and other interface elements. It usually defines the interface between a high-level language and the lower-level elements used by a device driver or operating system. The ultimate goal is to provide some type of service to an application that requires access to the operating system or device feature set.

Application   The complete program or group of programs. An application is a complete environment for performing one or more related tasks.

Application programming interface   See API.

ASCII   See American Standard Code for Information Interchange.

ASP   See Active Server Page.

ATL   See Active Template Library

AVI (audiovisual interface) file format   A special file format that contains both audio and video in digital format. AVI is currently the most popular method for transmitting multimedia files across the Internet.

Bandwidth   A measure of the amount of data a device can transfer in a given time.

Binary values   Refers to a base 2 data representation in the Windows registry. Normally, used to hold status flags or other information that lends itself to a binary format.

BLOB (binary large object)   A special field in a database table that accepts objects such as bitmaps, sounds, or text as input. This field is normally associated with the OLE capabilities of a DBMS, but some third party products make it possible to add BLOB support to older database file formats, such as the Xbase DBF file format. BLOB fields always imply OLE client support by the DBMS.

BMP files   Windows standard bitmap graphics data format. This is a raster graphic data format that doesn't include any form of compression. It's normally used by Windows, but OS/2 (and various other operating systems) can also use this data format to hold graphics of various types.

Browse   A special application interface element designed to show the user an overview of a database or other storage media (for example, the thumbnail sketches presented by some graphics applications). Think of a browse as the table of contents for the rest of the storage area. A browse normally contains partial views of several data storage elements (records or picture thumbnails in most cases) that a user can then zoom on to see them in their entirety. A browse form normally contains scroll bars or other high-speed interface elements to make it easier for the user to move from one section of the overall storage media to the next.

Browser   A special application normally used to display data downloaded from the Internet. The most common form of Internet data is the HTML (Hypertext Markup

Language) page. However, modern browsers can also display various types of graphics and even standard desktop application files, such as Word for Windows documents, directly. The actual capabilities provided by a browser vary widely and depend on the software vendor and platform.

CAB (cabinet) file A compressed format file similar to the ZIP files used to transfer code and data from one location to another. The CAB format is normally used only by developers.

CAD See Computer-Aided Drafting.

Cascading Style Sheets (CSS) A method for defining a standard Web page template. CSS may include headings, standard icons, backgrounds, and other features that would tend to give each page at a particular Web site the same appearance. The reasons for using CSS include speed of creating a Web site (it takes less time if you don't have to create an overall design for each page) and consistency. Changing the overall appearance of a Web site also becomes as easy as changing the style sheet instead of each page individually.

CCITT (Consultative Committee for International Telegraph and Telephony) This group is now the ITU. Please see ITU for details.

CGI (common gateway interface) One of the more common methods of transferring data from a client machine to a Web server on the Internet. CGI relies on scripts to define how the data should be interpreted. There are two basic data transfer types. The user can send new information to the server or can query data already existing on the server. For example, a data entry form asking for the user's name and address would be an example of the first type of transaction. A search engine page on the Internet (a page that helps the user find information on other sites) is an example of the second type of transaction. The Web server normally provides some type of feedback for the user by transmitting a new page of information once the CGI script is complete. This could be as simple as an acknowledgment for data entry or a list of Internet sites for a data query.

Class ID See CLSID.

Client The recipient of data, services, or resources from a file server or other server type. This term can refer to a workstation or an application. The server can be another PC or an application.

CLR See Common Language Runtime.

CLSID (class ID or identifier) A method of assigning a unique identifier to each object in the registry. Also refers to various high-level language constructs. Every object must provide a unique CLSID. The identifier is generated locally on the machine where the object is created, using some type of special software. (For example, the Microsoft OLE 2 SDK provides a utility for generating CLSIDs.)

High-level languages such as Visual Basic and most C compilers normally perform the CLSID generation sequence automatically for the programmer.

COM (component object model)   A Microsoft specification for an object-oriented code and data encapsulation method and transference technique. It's the basis for technologies such as OLE (object linking and embedding) and ActiveX (the replacement name for OCXs, an object-oriented code library technology). COM is limited to local connections. DCOM (Distributed Component Object Model) is the technology used to allow data transfers and the use of OCXs within the Internet environment. The latest COM technology in Microsoft's bag of tricks is COM+. This technology first appeared in Windows 2000. Its main purpose is to extend the current functionality provided by COM into new areas like remote execution of code.

Common gateway interface   See CGI.

Common Language Runtime (CLR)   The engine used to interpret managed applications within the .NET Framework. All Visual Studio .NET languages that produce managed applications can use the same runtime engine. The major advantages of this approach include extensibility (you can add other languages) and reduced code size (you don't need a separate runtime for each language).

Component object model   See COM.

Computer-Aided Drafting (CAD)   A special type of graphics program used for creating, printing, storing, and editing architectural, electrical, mechanical, or other forms of engineering drawings. CAD programs normally provide precise measuring capabilities and libraries of predefined objects, such as sinks, desks, resistors, and gears.

Console   The generic term for a workstation used to monitor server status information. In most cases, the workstation and server are the same device. Most people associate consoles with a character mode interface, but this connection isn't a requirement.

Container   Part of the object-oriented terminology that's become part of OLE. A container is a drive, file, or other resource used to hold objects. The container is normally referenced as an object itself.

Cookie   One or more special files used by an Internet browser to store site-specific settings or other information specific to Web pages. The purpose of this file is to store the value of one or more variables so that the Web page can restore them the next time the user visits a site. A webmaster always saves and restores the cookie as part of some Web page programming task using a programming language such as JavaScript, Java, VBScript, or CGI. In most cases, this is the only file that a webmaster can access on the client site's hard drive. The cookie could appear in one or more files anywhere on the hard drive, depending on the browser currently in use. Microsoft Internet Explorer uses one file for each site storing a cookie and places them in the

Cookies folder that normally appears under the main Windows directory. Netscape Navigator uses a single file named COOKIE.TXT to store all of the cookies from all sites. This file normally appears in the main Navigator folder.

Cracker   A hacker (computer expert) who uses their skills for misdeeds on computer systems where they have little or no authorized access. A cracker normally possesses specialty software that allows easier access to the target network. In most cases, crackers require extensive amounts of time to break the security for a system before they can enter it.

CryptoAPI   See Cryptographic Application Programming Interface.

Cryptographic Application Programming Interface (CryptoAPI)   The specification provided by Microsoft that enables software developers to add encryption technology to their applications. It uses a 128-bit encryption technology, which means that the developer can't export such applications outside the United States or Canada.

Cryptographic Service Provider   See CSP.

CSP (Cryptographic Service Provider)   A specialty company that deals in certifying the identity of companies, developers, or individuals on the Internet. This identification check allows the company to issue an electronic certificate, which can then be used to conduct transactions securely. Several levels of certification are normally provided within a specific group. For example, there are three levels of individual certification. The lowest merely verifies the individual's identity through an Internet mail address; the highest requires the individual to provide written proof along with a notarized statement. When you access a certified site or try to download a certified document such as an ActiveX control, the browser will display the electronic certificate on screen, allowing you to make a security determination based on fact.

CSS   See Cascading Style Sheets.

DACL (discretionary access control list)   A Windows NT/2000/XP–specific security component. The DACL controls who can actually use the object. You can assign both groups and individual users to a specific object.

DAO   See Data Access Object.

DASS   See Distributed Authentication Security Service

Data Access Object (DAO)   An older data access technology introduced by Microsoft that relies on the Microsoft Access JET engine for local data access. DAO doesn't provide remote access features, although some programmers have been able to establish unreliable connections with it. ADO and OLE-DB have largely replaced this technology.

Data Source Name (DSN)   A name assigned to an Open Database Connectivity (ODBC) connection. Applications use the DSN to make the connection to the database and gain access to specific database resources like tables. The DSN always contains the name of the database server, the database, and (optionally) a resource like a query or table. OLE-DB connections may also use a DSN.

Database management system   See DBMS.

Databinding   The act of creating a connection between an object and a data source element. Binding the data enables the user to interact with the object and manipulate the database.

DBCS   See Double-Byte Character Set.

DBMS (database management system)   A collection of tables, forms, queries, reports, and other data elements. It acts as a central processing point for data accessed by one or more users. Most DBMSs (except those that are free form or text-based) rely on a system of tables for storing information. Each table contains records (rows) consisting of separate data fields (columns). Common DBMSs include Access, Paradox, dBASE, and FileMaker Pro.

DCOM (distributed component object model)   The advanced form of the Component Object Model (COM) used by the Internet. This particular format enables data transfers across the Internet or other nonlocal sources. It adds the capability to perform asynchronous, as well as synchronous, data transfers—which prevents the client application from becoming blocked as it waits for the server to respond. See COM for more details.

DDE (dynamic data exchange)   The ability to cut data from one application and paste it into another application. For example, you could cut a graphic image created with a paint program and paste it into a word processing document. Once pasted, the data doesn't reflect the changes made to it by the originating application. DDE also provides a method for communicating with an application that supports it and for requesting data. For example, you could use an Excel macro to call Microsoft Word and request the contents of a document file. Some applications also use DDE to implement file association strategies. For example, Microsoft Word uses DDE in place of command line switches to gain added flexibility when a user needs to open or print a file.

DDF (Diamond Directive File)   Similar to an INF (information) or a BAT (batch) file, the DDF provides instructions to a CAB (cabinet) creation utility such as DIANTZ for compressing one or more files into a single storage file. CAB files are normally used to distribute data locally, using a CD-ROM or other similar type of media, or remotely, through an Internet or other server connection. The DDF can also list files needed for a complete installation but are stored in other locations. Normally, these missing files will already appear on the user's computer, so downloading them again would waste time. The DDF makes it possible to download them only as needed.

DDK   See Driver Development Kit.

Device-Independent Bitmap (DIB)   A method of representing graphics information that doesn't reflect a particular device's requirements. This has the advantage of allowing the same graphic to appear on any device in precisely the same way, despite differences in resolution or other factors that normally change the graphic's appearance.

Diamond Directive File   See DDF.

DIB   See Device-Independent Bitmap.

Digital Signatures Initiative   See DSI.

Discretionary access control list   See DACL.

Disk Operating System (DOS)   The underlying software used by many PCs to provide basic system services and to allow the user to run application software. The operating system performs many low-level tasks through the basic input/output system (BIOS). The revision number determines the specifics of the services that DOS offers; check your user manual for details.

Distributed Authentication Security Service (DASS)   Defines an experimental method for providing authentication services on the Internet. The goal of authentication, in this case, is to verify who sent a message or request. Current password schemes have a number of problems that DASS tries to solve. For example, there's no way to verify that the sender of a password isn't impersonating someone else. DASS provides authentication services in a distributed environment. Distributed environments present special challenges because users don't log on to just one machine; they could conceivably log on to every machine on the network.

Distributed component object model   See DCOM.

Distributed interNetwork Architecture (DNA)   A term used to describe Microsoft's vision of a three-tier development architecture. The three tiers include the user's desktop, business logic processing on a middle-tier server, and database processing on a back end server. DNA is used to help emphasize various features of Microsoft products like Visual Studio and to help the developer modularize large-scale applications.

Distributed Password Authentication (DPA)   A shared secret authentication method originally started by some of the larger online services like CompuServe and MSN. It allows a user to use the same membership password to access a number of Internet sites when those sites are linked together as a membership organization. In essence, this methodology replicates some of the same features that users can get when using the same password to access multiple servers on a local network. DPA relies on the Microsoft Membership Service for membership authentication and server-specific access information.

DLL (dynamic link library)   A specific form of application code loaded into memory by request. It's not executable by itself. A DLL does contain one or more discrete routines that an application may use to provide specific features. For example, a DLL could provide a common set of file dialogs used to access information on the hard drive. More than one application can use the functions provided by a DLL, reducing overall memory requirements when more than one application is running.

DNA   See Distributed interNetwork Architecture

Domain Controller   One or more special servers that are used to store user, machine, server, and resource configurations. The domain controller maintains a database of information. It's also used to verify the identity of users or other entities that want to log onto the system and use resources under domain control. Windows installations normally have one Primary Domain Controller (PDC) that's in charge of the domain. Backup Domain Controllers (BDC) provide reliability in case the PDC becomes non-functional.

DOS   See Disk Operating System.

Double-Byte Character Set (DBCS)   A non-ASCII method of formatting characters that requires two bytes for each character instead of one. The DBCS allows an application to display words using character sets from non-English speaking countries.

DPA   See Distributed Password Authentication.

Drag and drop   A technique used in object-oriented operating systems to access data without actually opening the file using conventional methods. For example, this system allows the user to pick up a document file, drag it to the printer, and drop it. The printer will print the document using its default settings.

Driver Development Kit (DDK)   A special set of libraries, include files, source code, and utility programs designed to augment the native capabilities of a programming language product. A programmer normally writes driver software to allow applications or the operating system to communicate with the underlying hardware in some way. A DDK is designed to make the development of such software easier. You'll find that most drivers are written to run at the operating system level, so the associated DDK provides utility programs that also operate at that level.

DSI (Digital Signatures Initiative)   A standard originated by the W3C (World Wide Web Consortium) to overcome some limitations of channel-level security. For example, channel-level security can't deal with documents and application semantics. A channel also doesn't use the Internet's bandwidth very efficiently because all the processing takes place on the Internet rather than the client or server. This standard defines a mathematical method for transferring signatures—essentially a unique representation of a specific individual or company. DSI also provides a new method for labeling security properties (PICS2) and a new format for assertions (PEP). This standard is also built on the PKCS #7 and X509.v3 standards.

DSN   See Data Source Name.

Dynamic data exchange   See DDE.

Dynamic link library   See DLL.

EIT SHTTP   See Extended Internet Tag Secure Hypertext Transfer Protocol.

Embedding   Placing a copy of an object within the compound document. Contrast this with linking, in which the object remains outside the container.

Encryption   See Cryptographic Application Programming Interface.

Encryption level   The amount of encryption a file receives. Normally, the size of the encryption key is the determining factor in the strength and level of encryption. Most Internet browsers and local applications use two sizes: 40-bit and 128-bit. A 40-bit key can provide up to 240 key combinations and is considered moderately difficult to break. A 128-bit key can provide up to 2,128 key combinations and is considered very difficult to break. Only the 40-bit key technology is currently approved by the United States government for transport outside the United States or Canada. See Cryptographic Application Programming Interface for additional information.

Extended Internet Tag Secure Hypertext Transfer Protocol (EIT SHTTP) See Secure Hypertext Transfer Protocol (SHTTP).

File Transfer Management System   See FTMS.

File transfer protocol   See FTP.

FTMS (File Transfer Management System)   The Proginet Corporation introduced this ActiveX technology, which brings mainframe data to the desktop. Its Fusion FTMS will work with any development language that supports OLE containers such as Delphi, Visual C++, and PowerBuilder. Essentially, you place an ActiveX control on a form, define where to find the data, and then rely on the control to make the connection. Using this control reduces the amount of labor required to implement and maintain a mainframe connection. A special transfer server on the mainframe completes the package by automating all transfer requests. No longer does an operator have to manually download a needed file to the company's Web site before a client can access it. Users can directly access the data on the mainframe and download it to their local hard drive.

FTP (file transfer protocol)   One of several common data transfer protocols for the Internet. This particular protocol specializes in data transfer in the form of a file download. The user is presented with a list of available files in a directory list format. An FTP site may choose DOS or UNIX formatting for the file listing, although the DOS format is extremely rare. Unlike HTTP sites, an FTP site provides a definite information hierarchy through the use of directories and subdirectories, much like the file directory structure used on most workstation hard drives.

GAC   See Global Assembly Cache.

GDI   See Graphics Device Interface.

GIF (graphics interchange format)   The standard file format used to transfer data over the Internet. There are several different standards for this file format—the latest of which is the GIF89, a standard you'll find used on most Internet sites. The GIF standard was originally introduced by CompuServe as a method for reducing the time required to download a graphic and the impact of any single-bit errors that might occur. A secondary form of the GIF is the animated GIF. It allows the developer to store several images within one file. Between each file are one or more control blocks that determine block boundaries, the display location of the next image in relation to the display area, and other display features. A browser or other specially designed application will display the graphic images one at a time in the order in which they appear within the file to create animation effects.

Global Assembly Cache (GAC)   A central repository for storing public managed components. The GAC contains only components with strong names, ensuring the integrity of the cache.

Globally Unique Identifier (GUID)   A 128-bit number used to identify a component object model (COM) object within the Windows registry. The GUID is used to find the object definition and allow applications to create instances of that object. GUIDs can include any kind of object, even nonvisual elements. In addition, some types of complex objects are actually aggregates of simple objects. For example, an object that implements a property page will normally have a minimum of two GUIDs: one for the property page and another for the object itself.

Gopher   One of several common Internet data transfer protocols. Like FTP, Gopher specializes in file transfers. However, the two protocols differ in that Gopher always uses the UNIX filenaming convention, and it provides a friendlier (graphical) interface than does FTP. Although Gopher transfers tend to be more reliable than those provided by FTP, FTP sites are far more common.

Graphics Device Interface (GDI)   One of the main root components. It controls the way that artistic graphic elements are presented on screen. Every application must use the API provided by this component to draw or perform other graphics-related tasks.

Graphics interchange format   See GIF.

GSS-API (Generic Security Service Application Program Interface)

GUID   See Globally Unique Identifier.

Hacker   An individual who works with computers at a low level (hardware or software), especially in the area of security. A hacker normally possesses specialty software or other tools that allow easier access to the target hardware or software application or network. The media defines two types of hackers that include those that break into systems for ethical purposes and those that do it to damage the system in some way. The proper term for the second group is *crackers* (see cracker for details). Some people have started to call the first group "ethical hackers" to prevent confusion. Ethical hackers normally work for security firms that specialize in finding holes in a company's security. However, hackers work in a wide range of computer arenas. For example, a person who writes low-level code (like that found in a device driver) after reverse engineering an existing driver is technically a hacker. The main emphasis of a hacker is to work for the benefit of others in the computer industry.

Hierarchical   A chart or graph in which the elements are arranged in ranks. The ranks usually follow an order of simple to complex or higher to lower.

HTML (hypertext markup language)   A scripting (markup) language for the Internet that depends on the use of tags (keywords within angle brackets <>) to display formatted information on screen in a non-platform–specific manner. The non-platform–specific nature of this scripting language makes it difficult to perform some basic tasks such as placement of a screen element at a specific location. However, the language does provide for the use of fonts, color, and various other enhancements on screen. There are also tags for displaying graphic images. Scripting tags for using more complex scripting languages, such as VBScript and JavaScript, were recently added, although not all browsers support this addition. The latest tag addition allows the use of ActiveX controls.

HTTP (hypertext transfer protocol)   One of several common data transfer protocols for the Internet. This particular protocol specializes in the display of onscreen information such as data entry forms or informational displays. HTTP relies on HTML as a scripting language for describing special screen display elements, although you can also use HTTP to display nonformatted text.

Hypertext markup language   See HTML.

Hypertext transfer protocol   See HTTP.

IDAPI (Independent Database Application Programming Interface)   A set of Windows function calls and other interface elements (introduced by companies under the lead of Borland). IDAPI is designed to improve access to information contained in database files through the use of a common interface and data-independent access methods.

IDL   See Interface Definition Language.

IETF (Internet Engineering Task Force)   The standards group tasked with finding solutions to pressing technology problems on the Internet. This group can approve standards created both within the organization itself and outside the organization as part of other group efforts. For example, Microsoft has requested the approval of several new Internet technologies through this group. If approved, the technologies would become an Internet-wide standard for performing data transfer and other specific kinds of tasks.

IIS   See Internet Information Server.

ILS   See Internet Locator Service.

IMTF (Internet Management Task Force)   The standards group responsible for implementing new technologies on the Internet. The problem is that it's composed mainly of volunteers. The wheels of progress grind slowly for the IMTF, just as with any other standards organization. It's so slow, in fact, that many companies have come up with their own solutions for making the Internet a friendlier place to work. For example, Microsoft has developed ActiveX in response to specific Internet-related problems, while Netscape has developed Netscape ONE (Open Network Environment).

Independent Database Application Programming Interface   See IDAPI.

INF (information) file   A special form of device or application configuration. It contains all the parameters that Windows requires to install or configure the device or application. For example, an application INF file might contain the location of data files and the interdependencies of DLLs. Both application and device INF files contain the registry and INF file entries required to make Windows recognize the application or device.

Interface Definition Language (IDL)   A programming language construct used to define the interfaces, methods, and parameters of a class. The IDL may use attributes to describe some elements fully using a common methodology. In addition, the IDL normally includes binary elements, such as interface identifiers. For example, COM relies on globally unique identifiers (GUIDs) for identification purposes.

International Telephony Union   See ITU.

Internet Engineering Task Force   See IETF.

Internet Information Server (IIS)   Microsoft's full-fledged Web server that normally runs under the Windows NT/2000 Server operating system. IIS includes all the features that you'd normally expect with a Web server: FTP, HTTP, and Gopher protocols along with both mail and news services. Windows NT Workstation, Windows 9x, and Windows XP can run Personal Web Server (PWS), which is a scaled down version of IIS.

Internet Locator Service (ILS)   A phonebook of people who are currently using NetMeeting. You can use this feature to see who is currently using the product and optionally to join their conversation (if it's open).

Internet Management Task Force   See IMTF.

Internet protocol   See IP.

Internet Protocol Security Protocol (IPSec)   IETF created the IP Security Protocol Working Group to look at the problems of IP security, such as the inability to encrypt data at the protocol level. It's currently working on a wide range of specifications that will ultimately result in more secure IP transactions. For example,

IPSec is used in a variety of object-based group policy schemes. Windows currently uses IPSec for network-level authentication, data integrity checking, and encryption.

Internet Server Application Programming Interface   See ISAPI.

IP (Internet protocol)   The information exchange portion of the TCP/IP protocol used by the Internet. IP is an actual data transfer protocol that defines how the information is placed into packets and sent from one place to another. TCP (transmission control protocol) is the protocol that defines how the actual data transfer takes place. One of the problems with IP that standards groups are addressing right now is that it doesn't encrypt the data packets—anyone can read a packet traveling on the Internet. Future versions of IP will address this issue by using some form of encryption technology. In the meantime, some companies have coupled TCP with other technologies to provide encryption technology for the short term.

IPSec   See Internet Protocol Security Protocol.

ISA   See ISAPI Server Addition.

ISAPI (Internet Server Application Programming Interface)   A set of function calls and interface elements designed to make using Microsoft's Internet Information Server (IIS) and associated products such as Peer Web Server easier. Essentially, this set of API calls provides the programmer with access to the server itself. Such access makes it easier to provide full server access to the Internet server through a series of ActiveX controls without the use of a scripting language.

ISAPI Server Addition (ISA)   A special form of ActiveX control in DLL form that's placed on a Web server. The DLL gets called in one of several ways, such as a request from a client or upon a particular event taking place. There are two forms of ISA: filter and extension. A filter allows you to keep something out or in by monitoring events on your server. For example, you could create an ISA filter that keeps people out of your Web site unless they enter the right password. Another type of filter could prevent files larger than a certain size from getting uploaded to the FTP server on your Web site. Extensions are more like applications or background processes. For example, you could create an extension that allows the user to interact with a database without resorting to using scripts. The same extension could dynamically create Web pages based on the user input and the contents of the database on your server.

ITU (International Telephony Union)   Formerly the CCITT. This group is most famous for its standards concerning modem communications. However, in recent years, it's also begun work with both fax and Internet standards (among other concerns). All of the older ITU standards still use the CCITT moniker. Newer standards use the ITU moniker. Unlike many other standards groups, the ITU is multinational and is staffed by representatives from many different countries.

JEPI   Joint Electronic Payment Initiative.

Joint Pictures Entertainment Group file format   See JPEG file format

JPEG (Joint Pictures Entertainment Group) file format   One of two graphics file formats used on the Internet. This is a vector file format normally used to render high-resolution images or pictures.

JPEG file   See JPEG file format.

KDC   Key Distribution Center.

LAN (local area network)   A combination of hardware and software used to connect a group of PCs to each other and/or to a mini or mainframe computer. Two main networking models are in use: peer-to-peer and client/server. The peer-to-peer model doesn't require a dedicated server. In addition, all the workstations in the group can share resources. The client/server model uses a central server for resource sharing, but some special methods are provided for using local resources in a limited way.

Local area network   See LAN.

Locally unique identifier   See LUID.

LUID (locally unique identifier)   Essentially a pointer to an object, the LUID identifies each process and resource for security purposes. In other words, even if a user has two copies of precisely the same resource option (like a document), both copies would have a unique LUID. This method of identification prevents some types of security access violation under Windows NT/2000/XP.

Macro   A form of programming that records keystrokes and other programming-related tasks to a file on disk or within the current document. Most applications provide a macro recorder that records the keystrokes and mouse clicks you make. This means that you don't even have to write them, in most cases. Macros are especially popular in spreadsheets. Most macros use some form of DDE to complete OLE-related tasks.

Mail Handling Service   See MHS.

Mail Transfer System   See MTS.

MCI   See Media Control Interface.

MDI   See Multiple Document Interface.

Media Control Interface (MCI)   The set of low-level commands to access media devices like CD-ROM drives and soundboards. Each media driver adds its set of commands to the interface. Since each driver uses a similar command set, the programmer can access any device with a minimal amount of code changes.

MFC (Microsoft Foundation Class) files   The set of DLLs required to make many Microsoft applications work. These files contain the shared classes used as a basis for creating the application. For example, a pushbutton is a separate class within these files. Normally, you'll find the MFC files in the Windows SYSTEM folder—they use "MFC" as the starting letters of the filename.

Message Transfer Agent (MTA)   This is an X.400 standard term that refers to the part of a message transfer system (MTS) responsible for interacting with the client. For example, in an e-mail system, the MTA delivers e-mail to the individual users of that system.

MHS (Mail Handling Service)   A method for encrypting and decrypting user mail and performing other mail management services. Most NOSs provide some type of MHS as part of the base system. Several standards are available on the Internet for providing MHS as part of a Web site. The two most notable specifications are IETF RFC1421 from the IETF and X.400 from the ITU (formerly CCITT).

Microsoft Foundation Class files   See MFC files.

Microsoft Management Console (MMC)   A special application that acts as an object container for Windows management objects like Component Services and Computer Management. The management objects are actually special components that provide interfaces that allow the user to access them within MMC to maintain and control the operation of Windows. A developer can create special versions of these objects for application management or other tasks. Using a single application like MMC helps maintain the same user interface across all management applications.

MIME   See Multipurpose Internet Mail Extensions.

MMC   See Microsoft Management Console.

MPR   See Multiple Provider Router.

MSDN   Microsoft Developer Network.

MSMQ   Microsoft Management Queue.

MTA   See Message Transfer Agent.

MTS (Mail Transfer System)   A method of transferring mail from one location to another. In most cases, this requires some form of encryption along with other transport-specific details. Most NOSs provide some type of MTS as part of their base services. However, the Internet requires special transport mechanisms. Several standards are available on the Internet for providing MTS as part of a Web site. The two most notable specifications are IETF RFC1421 from the IETF and X.400 from the ITU (formerly CCITT).

MTS   Microsoft Transaction Server

Multiple Document Interface (MDI)   A method for displaying more than one document at a time within a parent window. The Program Manager interface is an example of MDI. You see multiple groups within the Program Manager window.

Multiple Provider Router (MPR)   A method of using more than one protocol. It allows you to mix and match protected-mode drivers on the same network. You can mix NetBEUI and IPX/SPX, for example, on the same network. In addition, some protocols automatically load when you request a specific service. Data link control (DLC) falls into this category. It provides connections to mainframes and network printers. All network protocols require a network provider. The whole function of the MPR is to accept network requests from the API and send them to the appropriate network provider (NP).

Multipurpose Internet Mail Extensions (MIME)   The standard method for defining the content of Internet messages. This standard allows computers to exchange objects, character sets, and multimedia using e-mail without regard to the computer's underlying operating system. MIME is defined in the IETF RFC1521 standard.

Nested objects   Two or more objects that are coupled in some way. The objects normally appear within the confines of a container object. Object nesting allows multiple objects to define the properties of a higher-level object. It also allows the user to associate different types of objects with each other.

Netscape ONE (Open Network Environment)   A set of specialized application programming interfaces (APIs) and class libraries based on the Internet Inter-ORB Protocol (IIOP) and Common Object Request Broker Architecture (CORBA) specifications that enable a programmer to create customized Internet applications. One of the benefits of this customization is that the programmer could get by without using CGI or other scripting languages to access data on the server, a requirement using standard HTTP. ONE currently includes five Java-based foundation class libraries: User Interface Controls, User Interface Services, Security, Messaging, and Distributed Objects. Future plans include foundation classes for databases and file server directory library access for Novell's NetWare Directory Services (NDS) and other products. This new technology also requires a JavaScript upgrade that Microsoft may or may not support.

Network interface card   See NIC.

Network operating system   See NOS.

NIC (network interface card)   The device responsible for allowing a workstation to communicate with a file server and other workstations. It provides the physical means of creating the connection. The card plugs into an expansion slot in the computer. A cable that attaches to the back of the card completes the communication path.

Node   A single element in a network. In most cases, the term node refers to a single workstation connected to the network. It can also refer to a bridge, router, or file server. It doesn't refer to cabling or to passive or active elements that don't directly interface with the network at the logical level.

NOS (network operating system)   The operating system that runs on the file server or other centralized file- and print-sharing devices. This operating system normally provides multiuser access capability and user accounting software in addition to other network-specific utilities.

Object   When used in the OLE sense of the word, a representation of all or part of a graphic, text, sound, or other data file within a compound document. An object retains its original format and properties. The client application must call on the server application to change or manipulate the object. When used in the component object model (COM) sense of the word, it refers to the encapsulation of data and code into one file. COM objects don't allow direct manipulation of the data they contain. Data in manipulated through the use of methods that the object contains. In most cases, data manipulation is limited to a list of properties exposed by the object that defines the object's operation and other characteristics. Some objects generate events in response to certain types of stimulus from either the system or user. Objects can also receive event notifications through the use of sinks. See the definition of COM for additional details.

Object conversion   A method of changing the format and properties of an object created by one application to the format and properties used by another. Conversion moves the data from one application to another, usually without a loss in formatting and always without a loss of content.

Object Linking and Embedding-Database (OLE-DB)   A low-level database access technology that relies on COM and a vendor-supplied OLE-DB provider rather than the SQL used by ODBC. OLE-DB is designed to work with both remote and local databases. In addition, it can access database managers that don't rely on SQL, like those found on mainframe computers. OLE-DB and ODBC are cooperative, rather than competing, data access technologies. OLE-DB, when coupled with ADO, is designed to replace older database technologies like RDO and DAO.

Object linking and embedding   See OLE.

OCX (OLE Control eXtension)   A special form of VBX designed to make adding OLE capabilities to an application easier for the programmer. Essentially, an OCX is a DLL with an added programmer and OLE interface.

ODBC (Open Database Connectivity)   A set of Windows function calls and other interface elements introduced by Microsoft. ODBC is designed to improve access to information contained in database files through the use of a common interface and data-independent access methods. Normally, ODBC relies on SQL to translate DBMS-specific commands from the client into a generic language. The ODBC agents on the server translate these SQL requests into server-specific commands.

OLE (object linking and embedding)   The process of packaging a filename and any required parameters into an object and then pasting this object into the file created by another application. For example, you could place a graphic object within a word processing document or spreadsheet. When you look at the object, it appears as if you simply pasted the data from the originating application into the current application (similar to DDE). When linked, the data provided by the object automatically changes as you change the data in the original object. When embedded, the data doesn't change unless you specifically edit it, but the data retains the original format and you still use the original application to edit the data. Often you can start the originating application and automatically load the required data by double-clicking on the object. The newer OLE 2 specification allows for in-place data editing as well as editing in a separate application window.

OLE Control eXtension   See OCX.

OLE-DB   See Object linking and embedding database.

ONE   See Netscape ONE (Open Network Environment).

Open Database Connectivity   See ODBC.

PCT (Private Communication Technology)   A protocol being worked on by the IETF and Microsoft. Like SSL, PCT is designed to provide a secure method of communication between a client and server at the low protocol level. It can work with any high-level protocol such as HTTP, FTP, or TELNET. PCT is designed to prevent hackers from eavesdropping on communications between a client and server through the use of encryption, authentication, and digital signatures. As with SSL, client authentication is optional. PCT also assumes that you have TCP or another reliable transport protocol in place. It corrects some inherent weaknesses in SSL by providing extended cryptographic negotiation and other added features.

PDA   See Personal Digital Assistant.

PDF   Portable Document Format.

PEM (Privacy Enhanced Mail)   A set of four approved IETF specifications (IETF RFC1421 through IETF RFC1424) that define the methods for sending and receiving mail on the Internet. Of prime importance are techniques for encrypting and decrypting mail in such a way that optimal privacy is assured with a minimal amount of user interaction. The specification also covers topics related to mail encryption, including the certification of vendors to perform the service and the use of CSPs.

Personal Digital Assistant (PDA)   A very small PC normally used for personal tasks such as taking notes and maintaining an itinerary during business trips. PDAs normally rely on special operating systems and lack any standard application support.

PKI   See Public Key Infrastructure.

Point-to-Point Tunneling Protocol (PPTP)   A technology jointly created by Microsoft, US Robotics, and other members for the PPTP forum used to create virtual private networks (VPNs). A VPN is a private network of computers that uses the Internet to connect some nodes. PPTP incorporates various forms of security to ensure the data transmitted across the Internet (essentially an open network) remains secure. A VPN would allow a user to dial into the corporate network from home.

PPTP   See Point-to-Point Tunneling Protocol

Privacy Enhanced Mail   See PEM.

Private Communication Technology   See PCT.

Private key file   See PVK.

Protocol   A set of rules used to define a specific behavior. For example, protocols define how networks transfer data. Think of a protocol as an ambassador who negotiates activities between two countries. Without the ambassador, communication is difficult, if not impossible.

Public Key Infrastructure (PKI)   A protocol that allows two sites to exchange data in an encrypted format without any prior arrangement. The default method for initiating the exchange is to create a secure sockets layer (SSL) connection. The main difference between this technology and others on the market is that it relies on a public key system of certificates to ensure secure data transfer. The latest specification for SSL is SSL3, which the IETF is calling transport layer security (TLS) protocol. A newer addition to the mix is Private Communication Technology (PCT). PCT still uses public key encryption. One of the benefits of using PKI is that there's no online authentication server required since well-known certification authorities (like VeriSign) issue the certificate when the sender uses the technology publicly.

PVK (private key file)   A file contained on either the client or server machine that allows full data encryption to take place. When the key in this file is combined with the public key provided with a file, the file becomes accessible. Since the PVK file never gets transmitted from one place to another, the level of data communication security is greatly increased. PVK files are used with all kinds of certificate-based communications. For example, getting a personal certificate from VeriSign or another organization involves creating a PVK on your computer. Developers also create a PVK for use with various types of Internet technologies such as ActiveX. The process of creating the private and public keys and assigning them to the actual component is called *signing*. In the same way, signed mail or other communications can greatly enhance security by making the author of the document known.

PWS   Personal Web Server

Queue   Commonly, a programming construct used to hold data while it awaits processing. A queue uses a FIFO (first in/first out) storage technique. The first data element in is also the first data element that gets processed. Think of a queue as a line at the bank or grocery store and you'll have the right idea. There are also hardware queues, which emulate the processing capability of their software counterparts.

RAD (rapid application development)   A tool that allows you to design your program's interface and then write the commands to make that user interface do something useful. Visual Basic and Delphi are both examples of RAD programs.

RAM   See Random Access Memory.

Random Access Memory (RAM)   The basic term used to describe volatile storage within a computer system. RAM comes in a variety of types, each of which has specialized features. These special features make the RAM more acceptable for some storage tasks than for others.

Rapid application development   See RAD.

RDO   Remote Data Objects

RDS   Remote Data Services

Remote access   The ability to use a remote resource as you would a local resource. In some cases, this also means downloading the remote resource to use as a local resource.

Remote procedure call   See RPC.

Rich Text Format   See RTF.

RPC (remote procedure call)   The ability to use code or data on a machine as if it were local. This is an advanced capability that will eventually pave the way for decentralized applications.

RTF (Rich Text Format)   A file format originally introduced by Microsoft that allows an application to store formatting information in plain ASCII text. All commands begin with a backslash. For example, the \cf command tells an RTF-capable editor which color to use from the color table when displaying a particular section of text.

S/MIME   See Secure/Multipurpose Internet Mail Extensions.

S/WAN   See Secure Wide Area Network.

SACL (security access control list)   The SACL controls Windows' auditing feature. Every time a user or group accesses an object and the auditing feature for that object is turned on, Windows makes an entry in the audit log.

SAS   See Storage Area Network (SAN) Attached Storage.

SDI   See Single Document Interface.

SDK   See Software Development Kit.

Secure Hypertext Transfer Protocol (SHTTP)   A technology designed to encrypt messages sent using the Internet. This technology is similar in purpose to Security Sockets Layer (SSL). However, SSL secures the connection between two computers, while SHTTP secures the individual messages. It's possible to use both technologies together to provide enhanced security.

Secure Sockets Layer   See SSL.

Secure Wide Area Network (S/WAN)   This is an initiative supported by RSA Data Security, Inc. The IETF has a committee working on it as well. RSA intends to incorporate the IETF's IPSec standard into S/WAN. The main goal of S/WAN is to allow companies to mix-and-match the best firewall and TCP/IP stack products to build Internet-based virtual private networks (VPNs). Current solutions usually lock the user into a single source for both products.

Secure/Multipurpose Internet Mail Extensions (S/MIME)   A secure method to transfer attachments and other message elements on the Internet. S/MIME supports RSA's public key encryption technology. See MIME for additional details.

Security access control list   See SACL.

Security identifier   See SID.

Server   An application or workstation that provides services, resources, or data to a client application or workstation. The client usually makes requests in the form of OLE, DDE, or other command formats.

ShellX (Shell extension)   A special application that gives some type of added values to the operating system interface. In most cases, the application must register itself with the registry before the operating system will recognize it.

SHTTP   See Secure Hypertext Transfer Protocol

SID (security identifier)   The part of a user's access token that identifies the user throughout the network—it's like having an account number. The user token that the SID identifies tells what groups the user belongs to and what privileges the user has. Each group also has a SID, so the user's SID contains references to the various group SIDs that he or she belongs to, not a complete set of group access rights. You would normally use the User Manager utility under Windows NT to change the contents of this access token. You'll use the Active Directory Users and Computers console when working with Windows 2000 and Windows XP.

Simple Object Access Protocol (SOAP)   A Microsoft-sponsored protocol that provides the means for exchanging data between COM and foreign component technologies, like Common Object Request Broker Architecture (CORBA), using XML as an intermediary.

Single Document Interface (SDI)   A method of displaying information where each window is independent of the other—there's no main window.

Smart Card   A type of user identification used in place of passwords. The use of a smart card makes it much harder for a third party to break into a computer system using stolen identification. However, a lost or stolen smart card still provides user access. The most secure method of user identification is biometrics.

Snap-ins   Component technologies that allow one application to serve as a container for multiple sub-applications. A snap-in refers to a component that's designed to reside within another application. The snap-in performs one specific task from among all of the tasks that the application as a whole can perform. The Microsoft Management Console (MMC) is an example of a host application. Network administrators perform all Windows 2000/XP management tasks using snap-ins designed to work with MMC.

SOAP   See Simple Object Access Protocol.

Software Development Kit (SDK)   A special add-on to an operating system or an application that describes how to access its internal features. For example, an SDK for Windows would show how to create a File Open dialog box. Programmers use an SDK to learn how to access special Windows components such as OLE.

SQL (Structured Query Language)   Most DBMSs use this language to exchange information. Some also use it as a native language. SQL provides a method for requesting information from the DBMS. It defines which table or tables to use, what information to get from the table, and how to sort that information.

SSL (Secure Sockets Layer)   A W3C standard originally proposed by Netscape for transferring encrypted information from the client to the server at the protocol layer. Sockets allow low-level encryption of transactions in higher-level protocols such as HTTP, NNTP, and FTP. The standard also specifies methods for server and client authentication (although client site authentication is optional).

Sticky Keys   One of several special features provided by Microsoft to help the physically challenged use computers better. All newer versions of Windows (starting with Windows NT 4.0) support this feature as part of the Accessibility applet.

Storage Area Network (SAN) Attached Storage (SAS)   One of several methods used to attach a SAN to the servers that it supplies with disk resources. The SAN is directly attached to all of the servers through a special bus. This bus is totally separate from the Ethernet or other common network bus used by the clients. A SAS consists of three major components: SAN interfaces, SAN interconnects, and SAN fabric. These three components may appear as separate elements, but are normally combined in some way. In all cases, data travels from the interface, to the interconnect, to the fabric, to the interconnect, and, finally, to the interface.

Stream object   An encapsulated data container used to transfer information from one object to another. For example, a stream object could move data from application memory to a file on disk.

Structured Query Language   See SQL.

TCP/IP (transmission control protocol/Internet protocol)   A standard communication line protocol developed by the U.S. Department of Defense. The protocol defines how two devices talk to each other. Think of the protocol as a type of language used by the two devices.

TLS   See Transport Layer Security Protocol.

Token calls   Part of the Windows NT/2000/XP security API that deals with user access to a particular object. To gain access to an object, the requesting object must provide a token. In essence, a token is a ticket to gain entrance to the secured object. The security API compares the rights provided by the requesting object's token with those required to gain entry to the secured object. If the requesting object's rights are equal to or greater than those required to gain entry, then the operating system grants access. Tokens are a universal form of entry under Windows NT/2000/XP and aren't restricted to the user or external applications. Even the operating system must use them.

Transport Layer Security Protocol (TLS)   The transport layer is where error detection and correction occur. It ensures that the data sent by the client is received correctly by the server, and vice versa. TLS ensures that the data transmitted between client and server remains private. This may mean using a combination of digital certificates and data encryption to make it difficult for crackers to gain access to the data.

UNC (universal naming convention)   A method for identifying network resources without using specific locations. In most cases, this convention is used with drives and printers, but it can also be used with other types of resources. A UNC normally uses a device name in place of an identifier. For example, a disk drive on a remote machine might be referred to as "\\AUX\DRIVE-C." The advantage of using a UNC is that the resource name won't change even if the resource location does (as would happen if users changed drive mappings on their machine).

Uniform Resource Identifier (URI)   A generic term for all names and addresses that reference objects on the Internet. A URL is a specific type of URI. See also Uniform Resource Locator (URL).

Uniform resource locator   See URL.

Universal naming convention   See UNC.

Universally Unique Identifier (UUID)   Another name for a Globally Unique Identifier (GUID). The two terms are interchangeable.

URI   See Uniform Resource Identifier.

URL (uniform resource locator)   The basic method of identifying a location on the Internet. A resource could be a file, a Web site, or anything else you can access through this medium. The URL always contains three essential parts. The first part identifies the protocol used to access the resource. For example, the letters "http" at the beginning of an URL always signify that the site uses the Hypertext Transfer Protocol and will present some type of visual information. The second part of the URL is the name of a host. For example, the most popular host name is www, which stands for World Wide Web. The third part of the URL is a domain. This is normally the name of the site machine and the kind of site you plan to access. (For example, MyCompany.com would tell you that the domain is a machine named MyCompany and that it's some kind of commercial site.) After the site information are directories, just like you have on your hard drive. So, an URL like http://www.mycompany .com/mysite.html would point to a Web page that uses HTTP on the World Wide Web at mycompany.com.

UUID   See Universally Unique Identifier.

VBA (Visual Basic for Applications)   A form of Microsoft Visual Basic used by applications. It provides more capabilities than VBScript yet fewer than the full-fledged Visual Basic programming language. The basic tenet of this language is full machine access without a high learning curve. VBA was originally designed to allow users to create script-type macros and provide interapplication communication. It's been extended since that time to provide a higher-level programming language for times when VBScript doesn't provide enough capabilities to perform a specific task.

VBX (Visual Basic eXtension)   A special form of 16-bit DLL that contains functions as well as a programmer interface. The DLL part of VBX accepts requests from an application for specific services, such as opening a file. The programmer interface portion appears on the toolbar of a program, such as Visual Basic, as a button. Clicking the button creates one instance of that particular type of control.

Virtual Private Network (VPN)   A special setup that newer versions of Windows provide for allowing someone on the road to use the server at work. The connection is *virtual* because the user can make or break the connection as needed. The reason that this connection has to be private is to deny access to either the client machine or remote server by outside parties. A user gains initial access to the server through an ISP using Dial-Up Networking. After initiating access to the Internet, the user employs Dial-Up Networking to make a second connection to the server using Point-to-Point Tunneling Protocol (PPTP). The setup is extremely secure because it actually uses two levels of data encryption: digital signing of packets and encrypted passwords.

Virtual reality modeling language   See VRML.

Visual Basic eXtension   See VBX.

Visual Basic for Applications   See VBA.

VPN   See Virtual Private Network.

VRML (virtual reality modeling language)   A special scripting (scene description) language that allows a Web site to transfer vector graphic imaging information with a minimum of overhead. The value of this language is that it uses very little actual data to transfer the coordinate information required. VRML is still very much in the experimental stage—transaction speeds are a major concern due to the relatively narrow bandwidth of current dial-up connections and the multitude of changes that take place during a VRML session. Even using minimized data transfer doesn't make VRML a fast performer with the current state of technology.

W3C (World Wide Web Consortium)   A standards organization essentially devoted to Internet security issues but also involved in other issues, such as the special <OBJECT> tag required by Microsoft to implement ActiveX technology. The W3C also defines a wealth of other HTML and XML standards. The W3C first appeared on the scene in December 1994, when it endorsed SSL (Secure Sockets Layer). In February 1995, it also endorsed application-level security for the Internet. Its current project is the Digital Signatures Initiative. W3C presented it in May 1996 in Paris.

WAN (wide area network)   A grouping of two or more LANs in more than one physical location.

Web Services Description Language (WSDL)   A method for describing a service. The file associated with this description contains the service description, port type, interface description, individual method names, and parameter types. A WSDL relies on namespace support to provide descriptions of common elements such as data types. Most WSDL files include references to two or more resources maintained by standards organizations to ensure compatibility across implementations.

Wide area network   See WAN.

Windows MetaFile (WMF)   A special format of the enhanced metafile (EMF) file format, the WMF is used as an alternative storage format by some graphics applications. It's also used by a broad range of application programming languages. This is a vector graphic format, so it provides a certain level of device independence and other features that a vector graphic normally provides.

Wizard   A specialized application that reduces the complexity of using or configuring your system. For example, the Printer Wizard makes it easier to install a new printer.

WMF   See Windows MetaFile.

World Wide Web Consortium   See W3C.

WSDL   See Web Services Description Language.

Index

INTERNATIONAL CONTACT INFORMATION

AUSTRALIA
McGraw-Hill Book Company Australia Pty. Ltd.
TEL +61-2-9417-9899
FAX +61-2-9417-5687
http://www.mcgraw-hill.com.au
books-it_sydney@mcgraw-hill.com

CANADA
McGraw-Hill Ryerson Ltd.
TEL +905-430-5000
FAX +905-430-5020
http://www.mcgrawhill.ca

GREECE, MIDDLE EAST, NORTHERN AFRICA
McGraw-Hill Hellas
TEL +30-1-656-0990-3-4
FAX +30-1-654-5525

MEXICO (Also serving Latin America)
McGraw-Hill Interamericana Editores S.A. de C.V.
TEL +525-117-1583
FAX +525-117-1589
http://www.mcgraw-hill.com.mx
fernando_castellanos@mcgraw-hill.com

SINGAPORE (Serving Asia)
McGraw-Hill Book Company
TEL +65-863-1580
FAX +65-862-3354
http://www.mcgraw-hill.com.sg
mghasia@mcgraw-hill.com

SOUTH AFRICA
McGraw-Hill South Africa
TEL +27-11-622-7512
FAX +27-11-622-9045
robyn_swanepoel@mcgraw-hill.com

UNITED KINGDOM & EUROPE (Excluding Southern Europe)
McGraw-Hill Education Europe
TEL +44-1-628-502500
FAX +44-1-628-770224
http://www.mcgraw-hill.co.uk
computing_neurope@mcgraw-hill.com

ALL OTHER INQUIRIES Contact:
Osborne/McGraw-Hill
TEL +1-510-549-6600
FAX +1-510-883-7600
http://www.osborne.com
omg_international@mcgraw-hill.com

About the CD-ROM

This book comes with numerous coding examples. The source code CD-ROM contains the source code for each example, plus a compiled debug version of all the examples arranged by chapter. In most cases, you'll find the name of the example within the text. The example name is the name of the folder containing the example code.

All of the examples, with the exception of the ASP.NET example in Chapter 10, will work as is from the source code CD-ROM. (See Chapter 10 for details on how to work with the simpleASP example.) Simply copy the code from the source code CD-ROM to your hard drive. You must clear the read-only bit for the example files before you can modify them. Placing the files on the CD-ROM sets this bit. In some cases, the text will direct you to make changes to the source code so that it matches your system. You must make these changes before you attempt to compile the source code.

Some of the examples, especially the database examples, require the Enterprise Architect version of Visual C++ to run. Make sure you read the information in the "What You'll Need" section of the Introduction about the equipment required for this book. Chapter 1 contains detailed instructions on how to set up your workstation and server for use with the book. The examples are unlikely to run with the educational version of Visual C++ .NET, and definitely won't run with older versions of Visual C++.

I'm always interested to hear about your ideas for new examples in the book. If you don't see something you need or if one of the examples doesn't work as anticipated, feel free to contact me at JMueller@mwt.net. I'd also like to hear about your current projects.